D1603746

Christian Dogmatics

A Handbook of Doctrinal Theology

for

Pastors, Teachers, and Laymen

By

JOHN THEODORE MUELLER, TH. D.

Professor of Systematic Theology
Concordia Seminary, St. Louis, Mo.

Εἴ τις λαλεῖ, ὡς λόγια θεοῦ. — 1 Pet. 4, 11.

ST. LOUIS, MO.
CONCORDIA PUBLISHING HOUSE
1955

PRINTED IN U. S. A.

DEDICATED TO THE MEMORY

OF

DR. FRANCIS PIEPER

(1852–1931)

OF WHOSE DOGMATIC WORK

"CHRISTLICHE DOGMATIK"

THE PRESENT VOLUME IS AN EPITOME

FOREWORD.

For over half a century the outstanding teacher of dogmatics at Concordia Seminary was the late Dr. Francis Pieper, whom the Lord called to his reward in June, 1931. His courses in Christian theology were given in German even to the last, and also his great work on dogmatics, his *Christliche Dogmatik,* was written in that language. It will always remain a standard reference work, which students and pastors who possess an adequate knowledge of German will study with profit and pleasure. Nevertheless, since many students of dogmatics do not understand German, a comprehensive text-book on the subject written in English has been desired for some time. Moved by the requests of many students and encouraged by his esteemed teacher and colleague to undertake the work, the undersigned applied himself to the task of writing this one-volume CHRISTIAN DOGMATICS. His aim was to present the voluminous doctrinal material in Dr. Pieper's *Christliche Dogmatik* as clearly, concisely, and, at the same time, as completely and practically as possible in order that the student of doctrinal theology might have a usable compend to introduce him into this important field of sacred theology and the busy pastor an adequate epitome of the Christian faith to assist him in his review of the subject. The intention was not to render a possible translation of Dr. Pieper's *Christliche Dogmatik* unnecessary, nor was it designed to take the place of a larger original work on systematic theology. It was simply to be a sizable handbook of Christian dogmatics pre senting both to the theological student and to the practical pastor the entire subject of doctrinal theology in a brief, yet complete summary according to Dr. F. Pieper's *Christliche Dogmatik.*

While the writer followed Dr. Pieper's standard work rather closely, he did not bind himself to details in form or content. For this reason the book may be used as an independent text-book, complete in itself. Commonly the footnotes were embodied in the text. The purely polemical matter was greatly condensed; but the writer did not deem it advisable to omit it altogether, since confessional Lutheranism cannot assert itself without directing attention to the opposing tendencies of Romanism, Calvinism, synergism, and rationalism, which have always attacked and endangered the Lutheran doctrine.

Dr. Pieper's method of teaching dogmatics was in many ways ideal; nevertheless each instructor in this branch of sacred theology has certain aims in view which will more or less determine his method of presentation. The writer consistently followed Dr. Pieper's custom of quoting Luther and the Lutheran Confessions on the major points on which they have spoken, since the Lutheran student cannot discard their valuable testimony. In addition, however, he has frequently quoted also our older dogmaticians, using as his source the *Doctrinal Theology of the Ev. Luth. Church* by Heinrich Schmid, translated from the German and Latin by Chas. A. Hay and Hy. E. Jacobs. This popular volume presents to the student many helpful passages from the works of our great dogmaticians in a convenient form and therefore deserves diligent study. The writer indeed does not agree with every statement of either Dr. Schmid or the cited dogmaticians, yet it is both interesting and instructive to consider their doctrinal expositions even in brief excerpts. While a fair knowledge of Latin, Greek, and Hebrew will greatly aid the student in understanding this CHRISTIAN DOGMATICS, it may be profitably studied even without the knowledge of these languages. Commonly the Scripture-passages are only indicated, but the reader is expected to compare them carefully, if possible in Greek and Hebrew, since the original often brings out the proof value of a text more distinctly than does the translation. Dr. A. L. Graebner's *Outlines of Doctrinal Theology* may be used for collateral study. The writer has always employed this book in his lectures, both on account of its excellent definitions of the given doctrines and its well-grouped Scripture-passages. However, the greatest profit will be obtained if this volume is used in connection with the more complete treatment of the various heads in Dr. Pieper's *Christliche Dogmatik.*

The writer wishes to thank his esteemed colleagues Dr. E. Engelder, Dr. W. Arndt, and Dr. P. E. Kretzmann for their careful and conscientious reading of the manuscript and their many helpful suggestions. He acknowledges his indebtedness also to Synod's Literature Board, especially to Rev. L. Buchheimer, Rev. A. Doerffler, and Mr. E. Seuel of Concordia Publishing House, to Prof. W. G. Polack and Dr. W. A. Maier for their hearty support and personal interest in the venture, and to his secretary, Rev. F. T. Gabert, for his services in retyping the manuscript.

In view of the fact that this handbook is largely a restatement of Dr. Pieper's *Christliche Dogmatik* the writer has consoled himself with the thought that even the "prince of the theologians of the Augsburg Confession," Martin Chemnitz, was satisfied with publishing a mere commentary on Melanchthon's *Loci Communes,* his justly famous *Loci Theologici,* and that this work proved so eminently successful in the Lutheran Church; also that the well-known dogmatics of John William Baier, his *Compendium Theologiae Positivae,* was really a compend of the theology of Musaeus and "many other orthodox theologians"; and finally, that also John Andrew Quenstedt's *Theologia Didactico-Polemica* followed most closely the outline of John

Frederick Koenig, whose compend of theology, *Theologia Positiva Acroamatica,* was widely used as a text-book. We live by the light of the faith of our fathers.

Since this handbook of doctrinal theology had to be relatively brief, much valuable dogmatic material was omitted. The student will find much additional dogmatic material in *Pastoral Theology* by Dean J. H. C. Fritz, D. D., and in the new *Popular Symbolics* by Drs. Arndt, Engelder, Graebner, and Prof. F. E. Mayer. These three handbooks, supplementing one another, leave hardly any question unanswered that pertains to Christian doctrine and a pure Scriptural practise. It is the writer's privilege to recommend these two important handbooks in connection with the use of this CHRISTIAN DOGMATICS.

We are sure that the readers will appreciate the excellent *Preface* which our esteemed colleague Dr. P. E. Kretzmann has written upon the author's request. This fine conspectus of dogmatic research may be viewed as compensatory since the limited space of the handbook did not permit any adequate treatment of more recent developments in the field of dogmatics. It may also serve the student who is more deeply interested in the modern phases of dogmatic lore as an outline and canon by which to orient his own studies.

May this CHRISTIAN DOGMATICS, then, go forth on its errand of assisting all students of dogmatics who desire to use it in their study of Christian doctrine! Shortcomings though it may have, it is nevertheless a clear and correct testimony of "God's Word and Luther's doctrine pure"; for it was composed with constant consideration of our Lord's command: "If any man speak, let him speak as the oracles of God," 1 Pet. 4, 11.

St. Louis, Mo. JOHN THEODORE MUELLER.

PREFACE.

In supplying a preface for the handbook of doctrinal theology which is herewith being offered to the theological world, the undersigned is fully aware that he will add nothing to the intrinsic value of the book. Yet in doing so, he is yielding to the repeated requests of the esteemed author, who desired a special introduction presenting a brief survey of doctrinal theology from the time of Schleiermacher to the present day. The supposition is that a foreword of this kind may serve some little purpose as a kind of foil to set off the beauty of a strictly confessional theology as compared with the frequently false, or at least inadequate, presentation found in the great majority of books on dogmatics which have been issued in the century since the death of Schleiermacher, in 1834. It is with this purpose in mind that this short introduction is written.

We must begin, naturally enough, with SCHLEIERMACHER himself (1768—1834), for his influence has dominated the theological thinking of some of the most prominent dogmaticians since his time. The theology of Schleiermacher is largely, if not entirely, subjectivistic, as his chief writings, his *Reden ueber die christliche Religion* (1799) and his *Christlicher Glaube nach den Grundsaetzen der evangelischen Kirche, im Zusammenhang dargestellt* (1821—22), clearly show. There can be no doubt that he was governed by certain points in the system of Spinoza, and there is evidence also of his being influenced by the philosophy of Kant. His early theology was clearly pantheistic, the ideas of God and of the universe converging in his presentation, while Christ was to him the archetype of a pure consciousness of God and the mediator of genuine piety. His idea of religion was not that of a knowledge based upon the objective revelation of God, but the consciousness of a person's "absolute dependence" upon God. The "overworld" of Schleiermacher is one which man "intuits" by faith, and faith to him is practically nothing but the immediate self-consciousness of man's relationship to this "overworld." His concept of sin and guilt is that of mere inadequacy on the part of man. To him Christ is not Himself the object of faith, but merely the archetype of the proper and ideal condition of soul in the case of every believer. According to Schleiermacher the essence of redemption and reconciliation consists in man's becoming conscious of the eternal unity. His "religion" is thoroughly and entirely a religion of feeling. If a person has reached that state of mind in which he feels that he is in fellowship of life with Christ, regardless of the Gospel revelation, he may be sure of his redemption, of his salvation. Schleiermacher did not permit one Christian doctrine to stand unchallenged, but subverted every fundamental truth, from the inspiration of the Bible to the doctrine of the last things.

Yet Schleiermacher found many adherents in his own day as well as many followers after his death, so that we may even speak of a school which was, and to some extent is, governed by his religious philosophy. One of the most prominent theologians among the contemporaries of Schleiermacher was DE WETTE (1780—1849), who entered into friendly relations with the older teacher during his sojourn in Berlin. De Wette really denies revelation in the Scriptural sense. His doctrinal system is based upon the Kantian criticism, and he favored the theory of religion as feeling. He is the predecessor of Wellhausen and of the modern higher criticism. He insisted upon the distinction between intelligent, ideal, and esthetic convictions in religious matters, and his insistence upon this intelligent (or intellectual) appreciation of the doctrine of Christ deprived the Gospel of its Christian content, although he usually clothed his dogmatic presentations in the garb of the old orthodox terms. Another man who was first a pupil and then a friend of Schleiermacher was TWESTEN (1789—1876), who made the principles of his teacher his starting-point, but went beyond the idea of dogma as presentations of pious conditions of mind in an effort to establish objective truth. When Twesten, in 1835, became Schleiermacher's successor in Berlin, he maintained a mediating position between Marheinecke and Hengstenberg, *the former being an exponent of Hegelianism,* which excludes redemption and prayer and has no adequate conception of personality and no consciousness of sin, the latter representing a neo-orthodox legalism, although he did splendid service in opposing higher criticism. Twesten's attitude of mediation became so strongly unionistic that he defended the association of all Christians living in one place at the same time, even without doctrinal agreement. A third man whom we must name as a faithful disciple of Schleiermacher is SCHWEIZER of Zuerich (1808—1888). He became the exponent of the Reformed type of his teacher's ideas and may be called a predecessor of K. Barth. His position showed an eminently speculative spirit, and his subjectivism is seen in his insistence that dogmatics must go to the living consciousness of the Christian for its material instead of to the objective certainty of the Word of God alone.

More dangerous to sound confessionalism in many respects than Schleiermacher was ALBRECHT RITSCHL (1822—1889), a man who gained some of his ideas from Kant, others from Schleiermacher, of whom he states that he was the only one since the Reformation to employ the scientific method of proof in theology. He subverts the very foundation of truth by referring to the "precarious medium of the theory of inspiration," and he sought the facts of theology in religious consciousness. He rejected the deity of Christ, merely conceding that Jesus was a religious genius, a religious hero, who had progressed so far in moral and spiritual attainments that to the Christian He has "the value of God." On the atonement of Christ he wrote a large monograph, in which he defends a doctrine which leaves out the cardinal points of the vicarious sacrifice of the Savior. The immortality of the soul is treated in his theology as an indifferent matter. The most objectionable feature of Ritschlianism is its two-facedness. It uses the old theological terms with new meanings; the negative liberal thought is clothed in the old orthodox expressions. While Ritschl retained a semblance of Christian theology, he either changed the Christian doctrine substantially or rejected it outright. His favorite expression is "the kingdom of God," by which he means a general organization or fellowship of men, whose chief distinguishing mark is mutual activity on the basis of love, but without the objective truth of the Gospel.

Among the university teachers of Germany who were strongly influenced by Ritschl (in some cases also by Schleiermacher) the following exerted considerable influence: WILHELM HERMANN († 1922), who modified his teacher's "reflections" concerning the historical Jesus by emphasizing intuition to such an extent as to make the term *Christ-mysticism* applicable to his teaching, while the Bible was regarded by him as nothing but a form in which the Christian faith expresses itself, thus making his teaching strongly "modernistic"; HERMANN SCHULTZ († 1903), who also advocated an immediate religious contemplation of Christ, whose historicity he regarded as problematical and whose deity he denied; then J. Gottschick, P. Lobstein, Julius Kaftan, — one of the strongest exponents of the Ritschlian school, although he tried to return to the Confessions, — Th. Haering, who held wrong views concerning the guilt of man, H. H. Wendt, who is farther away from the truth, F. Kattenbusch, who is confessional in his attitude, P. Drews, who faces in the other direction, E. W. Mayer, O. Kirn, who denies the vicarious satisfaction and most other fundamental truths of the Bible, K. Thieme, and others. Among the American clergymen who were strongly influenced by Ritschlianism are W. A. Brown, C. F. Clarke, G. B. Smith, Wm. De Witt Hyde, G. W. Gladden, Rauschenbusch, King, Sellars, Ward, Vedder, and others, most of whom became the exponents of the social gospel with its destruction of the fundamental truths of Scripture.

In Germany other forces beside the theology of Schleiermacher were at work during the first half of the nineteenth century. The last exponent of formal rationalism was PAULUS of Heidelberg († 1851); men who were influenced by the pantheistic philosophy of Schelling and Hegel were J. M. DAUB († 1856), who was very active in the field of religio-historical research, and MARHEINICKE († 1846), whose doctrinal theology was influenced throughout by Hegel. About this time there was also a revival of Pietism, with a rather romantic coloring, favored by men like Novalis and Tholuck (who, with all his excellencies, could not understand *confessional* Lutherans), the movement stressing in particular the *feeling* of sin and of grace, also a supranaturalism and "Biblicism (a dead literalism)," which differed widely from the attitude taken by Fr. Strauss. In the midst of this turmoil we find certain trends which resulted in three more or less distinct schools of religious or theological thought.

The first of these schools was that which is now known as the extreme *liberal school,* with LUDW. FEUERBACH (†1872) as one of its first great exponents and FERD. CHR. BAUR (1792—1860) as its chief apostle. The latter is the founder of the so-called *Tuebinger Schule,* which became notorious for its attack on practically every tenet of orthodox Biblical introduction and on every Christian doctrine. In his case the statement came true: "A theology that ceases to be a theology of the heart and to make the historical Christ the center of the Christian life will eventually suffer shipwreck with regard to its faith." Yet the evil and detrimental influence of this movement was very great, not only through the work of men like Schwegler, Planck, and others in Germany, but also through the work of British and American theologians, who felt that the false higher criticism introduced by Bauer and carried on by men like Hilgenfeld must contain some elements of truth. These men practically killed the truth in the circles in which they moved.

The liberal Tuebingen school found strong opposition in the *confessional school* centering in Erlangen, but equally powerful in the faculties at Leipzig and Rostock. The most important exponents of this school deserve more than a passing mention because they were strong defenders of the Bible truth and of the Lutheran Confessions, even if they erred in occasional matters. "The Erlangen theology presumed to be genuinely Lutheran, but frequently gave up the principle that Christian theology must be based on Scripture alone." The fact that most of these men were accused of orthodox traditionalism is decidedly in their favor. VON HOFMANN (1810—1877) is the father of the *Ich-theologie,* a man who denied the verbal inspiration. His most notable doctrinal work is his *Schriftbeweis.* His attempt to prove the authenticity and divine origin of Christianity from its records was a mighty attempt, but this very effort caused him to lose sight of the transcendental presuppositions of history, so that his presentation of the doctrine of the Scriptural kenosis, of the vicarious atonement, and of justification is entirely false. HARLESS (1806 to 1879), who "wanted to be more orthodox than the old Lutheran teachers," but sometimes failed in his attempt, was especially active in the fields of catechetics and of church music. His *Theological*

Encyclopedia gives his views of the Church and of many other doctrines, and his *System of Christian Ethics* marks an epoch in Protestant literature. THEODOSIUS HARNACK (1817—1889), who made a special study of Luther's theology, was opposed to the state church and did some excellent work, but erred, for example, in making the Gospel a modification of the Law. HOEFLING (1802—1853) was especially active in the field of liturgics, in which his *magnum opus* was the monograph *Das Sakrament der Taufe,* but in which he also erred in the doctrine of the ministerial office. VON ZEZSCHWITZ (1825 to 1886) was particularly prominent in the field of catechetics; his confessional standpoint was soundly Lutheran, opposing both Romanism and the Prussian Union. FRANZ DELITZSCH (1813—1890) is notable on account of his monumental work in the field of exegesis. He was broader in his views than von Hofmann, and his theology was not free from theosophic influences, just as he made certain concessions to the liberal position in the field of Biblical criticism, against which a conservative theologian must be on his guard. GOTTFRIED THOMASIUS (1802—1875) was great both as a writer and as a teacher and preacher, his most notable writing being *Christi Person und Werk,* in which unfortunately he teaches an unscriptural kenosis. FRANZ FRANK (1827—1894) wrote the monumental work *Theologie der Konkordienformel,* a veritable storehouse of the history of dogma in the sixteenth century, and that threefold masterpiece of theological learning, *System der christlichen Gewiszheit — der christlichen Wahrheit — der christlichen Sittlichkeit.* It is unfortunate that Frank, with all his amazing learning, clung to a false subjectivism, so that he did not place the Scriptures in the first place as the objective *principium cognoscendi.* LUTHARDT (1823—1902) was active in the field of exegesis as well as in systematic theology (*Kompendium der Dogmatik;* 13th edition by Jelke, 1933), his chief errors being in the doctrines of inspiration, the office of Christ (kenoticism), and regarding synergism. He was for many years editor of the *Allgemeine Ev.-Luth. Kirchenzeitung,* which tried to uphold the sound Lutheran position. KLIEFOTH (1810—1895), an opponent of von Hofmann in many points, is known for his extensive work in the field of liturgics and of church polity, for his opposition to territorialism and unionism, for his ecclesiasticism and hierarchical tendencies. He was one of the founders of the *Allgemeine Ev.-Luth. Konferenz.* KAHNIS (1814—1888) in his earlier career was a subordinationist and even departed radically from the doctrine of the Trinity, but in later years became much more conservative, as his *Lutherische Dogmatik* reveals. Yet he continued to hold false views on inspiration and to dissent in the doctrine of the Trinity and of the Lord's Supper. PHILIPPI (1809—1882) took a very decided stand against modern subjectivism and in his *Kirchliche Glaubenslehre* follows the dogmaticians of the orthodox age more

closely than Thomasius. One of the most important writers is
Wm. Rohnert (†1902), who stands four-square upon Scripture as the
one source and norm of all Christian theology, although he is not
correct in his doctrine of the election. Other men who might here
be mentioned are Hase (*Hutterus Redivivus*), — otherwise rationalistic, — Schmid (*Dogmatik der ev.-luth. Kirche* — Lutheran), Hoppe
(*Dogmatik des deutschen Protestantismus* — Reformed), Schnecken-
burger (*Zur kirchlichen Christologie*), Martensen (*Dogmatik*), who
denied that Christ was inspired, Sartorius (*Die heilige Liebe*), a ke-
noticist, and Oettingen (*Die lutherische Dogmatik*), who wrote in
the spirit of the Erlangen school.

The third group, or school, is that of the *compromise theologians*
(the Halle school), representatives of which were found at practically
all theological schools of Prussia. Kattenbusch says that these theologians may well be called the modern Philippists, whose tendencies
were fashioned as a result of the "awakening," or second surge of
Pietism, as a consequence of which they combined "Biblicism" with
a scientific attitude toward the Bible. In this group we may well place
HENGSTENBERG (1802—1869), who was especially prominent in Old
Testament exegesis and exerted a great influence through his editor-
ship of the *Evangelische Kirchenzeitung*. He was opposed to rationalism, but was himself not always trustworthy in his views, his alle-
gorizing in particular often leading him into the errors of the *Berle-
burger Bibel*. NITZSCH (1787—1868) is another mediating theologian,
whose *System der christlichen Lehre* was strongly influenced by
Schleiermacher's subjectivism, just as he strongly favored the union
of Lutherans and Reformed bodies. THOLUCK (1799—1877), with all
his apparent originality and undoubted brilliancy, was influenced by
Pietism, Moravianism, Schleiermacher, Neander, and even Hegel. He
assumed the possibility of errors in the Bible. JUL. MUELLER (1801
to 1878) is notable in particular for his *Christliche Lehre von der
Suende* with its assumption of an intelligible (intellectual) self-
decision and for his vacillating position concerning the Prussian
union. LANDERER (1810—1878) tried to mediate between Baur and
Beck and constructed Christology along anthropocentric lines.
DORNER (1809—1884) is rightly considered one of the most prominent
theologians of the nineteenth century, his chief monograph being his
Lehre von der Person Christi, in which unfortunately he presented
a false kenosis doctrine. His Christology throughout is influenced by
philosophy. Other men who may be said to belong to this group are
Koestlin (*Luthers Theologie*), Luecke (*Johannes-Kommentar*), Gasz
(*Geschichte der protestantischen Dogmatik*), and especially Rothe
(*Theologische Ethik*), who takes a very critical position over against
the Bible.

The newer form of the Erlangen theology is represented by

Ihmels († 1933), who is not adequate in a number of points in his doctrinal position, particularly because of his denying the sacrificial concept of Christ's obedience unto death; *R. Seeberg,* who champions the "modern-positive" attitude toward theology, following Frank in many respects, so that he, like him, does not, *e. g.,* quite accept the Gospel as an actual means of grace; *J. Kunze* († 1927), who was a faithful disciple of Luthardt; *Theodor Kaftan* († 1932), who denied the verbal inspiration; *Beth,* and others. Among the more recent theologians of the compromise or mediating school is Lemme († 1928), a pupil of Dorner, M. Kaehler († 1912), Cremer († 1903), Zoeckler († 1906), known especially for his *Handbuch der theologischen Wissenschaft,* and Schnedermann. In the more liberal field we have the names of Lipsius († 1892), Pfleiderer († 1908), and Luedemann. German theologians who are at the present time studying the theology of Luther and the Lutheran Confessions with more or less pronounced success are *Elert (Morphologie des Luthertums),* Şommerlath, Doerne, Jelke, K. Schneider, *Koeberle, Holl, Kurtz,* and *K. Stange.*

Meanwhile we also have a *religio-historical school* in Germany and elsewhere, with a fairly strong renascence of the ideas of Schleiermacher and Ritschl. Here we must place De Lagarde († 1891), Overbeck († 1905), Ernst Troeltzsch († 1923), Aulén, and others. Of a more Ritschlian cast are Luettge, Mulert, Stephan, Titius, Wehrung, Wobbermin, and Fabricius, some of whom have also recast some of Schleiermacher's ideas. Girgensohn († 1925) is often called a confessional theologian, but his *Grundriss* is not at all adequate on many questions of Christology and soteriology. — Some of the more prominent writers in Stange's *Zeitschrift fuer systematische Theologie* are P. Althaus, Jr., and E. Hirsch. The influence of A. v. Harnack († 1930), a follower of Ritschl, and of R. Sohm († 1917), is generally acknowledged.

At the present time the following men are most prominent in the field of systematic theology in Germany: R. OTTO, whose great monograph *Das Heilige* passed through twenty-two editions in fifteen years and was translated into seven languages; F. HEILER, who regards himself as a spiritual disciple of W. Loehe and is influencing doctrine through his book *The Spirit of Worship* and his monthly journal *Die Hochkirche;* KARL HEIM, a very prolific writer, who operates strongly with the element of introspection; KARL BARTH, with his "dialectical theology" (a "combatant theology favoring vehement discussion"), or "theology of crisis," which opposes relativism and represents a pessimism which practically denies the certainty of salvation; *Gogarten, Thurneysen,* and *Brunner,* who are closest to Barth, together with *O. Piper.* Among the Ritschlian eclectics of recent years are Martin Rade and Horst Stephan. The Northern countries have the following theologians: Goeransson, Nygren, Lindroth, Scharling,

Madsen, Krarup, Bang, Geismar, Gisle Johnson, Krogh-Touning, and Fredrik Petersen.

In the general field of English theology few outstanding works were produced during the last century. Some of the more prominent writers of England in the field of doctrinal theology were Cobb, Christmas, Stuart, Lyddon, Gore, and Moule, with Sydney Cave as a representative of the extra-Anglican theology in the liberal field. Of American writers in the field the names of the two Hodges (Presb.), father and son, deserve a prominent place; but the writings of Hopkins (Congr.), Hall, F. J. (Episc.), Shedd (Presb.), Clark (Episc.), Strong (Baptist), Sheldon (Meth. Episc.), Mackenzie (Congr.), and Knudson (Boston Univ.) are often quoted, while the field of social theology has strong exponents, such as Rauschenbusch, Sellars, Brown, De Witt, G. B. Smith, Clarke, Vedder, and others. This latter group may also be designated as Modernists, especially Brown, with men like Fosdick, Grant, and Cadman as other exponents. These men are really the new rationalists, except that they profess an adherence to the forms, and use the terms, of orthodox Christianity, which they have emptied of their real contents.

Within the ranks of the Lutheran theologians of America not a few books in the field of doctrinal theology have appeared. In Latin we have WALTHER's edition of Baier's *Compendium*. In the English field we have the names of C. P. KRAUTH (*The Conservative Reformation*), Weidner (various monographs), Valentine (not soundly Lutheran), Voigt, Jacobs, Gerberding, Lindberg, Hove, Stump, Mellenbruch, and Reu (English and German). The works of HOENECKE (*Ev.-Luth. Dogmatik,* thetical) and of F. PIEPER (*Christliche Dogmatik,* discussional) are soundly confessional and orthodox and are written with constant reference to late developments, especially in Germany.

May the book which is herewith presented to the English-speaking theological world serve to arouse and maintain a new interest in the sound doctrine of Jesus Christ, the God-man and Savior of the world!

St. Louis, Mo., during Holy Week, 1934.

P. E. KRETZMANN.

TABLE OF CONTENTS.

	PAGE
NATURE AND CONCEPT OF THEOLOGY	1
Introduction to Sacred Theology (*Prolegomena*)	1
1. The Scriptural Viewpoint of the Christian Theologian	1
2. Of Religion in General	4
3. Of the Number of Religions in the World	6
4. The Two Sources (*Principia Cognoscendi*) of the Existing Religions	14
5. The Cause of Divisions in Christendom	17
6. Christianity the Absolute Religion	25
7. The Christian Religion and Christian Theology	29
8. Christian Theology	30
9. Theology Further Considered as a Habitude	33
10. Theology Considered as Doctrine	37
11. Divisions of Theology Conceived as Doctrine	43
A. Law and Gospel	44
B. Fundamental and Non-Fundamental Doctrines	47
Primary and Secondary Fundamental Doctrines	52
Non-Fundamental Doctrines	56
C. Open Questions, or Theological Problems	58
12. The Church and Its Dogmas	60
13. The Purpose of Christian Theology	64
14. The External Means by which Sacred Theology Accomplishes Its Purpose of Saving Sinners	66
15. Theology and Science	67
16. Theology and Positive Assurance	72
17. Theology and Doctrinal Progress	74
18. Theology and Academic Freedom	76
19. Theological Systems	79
20. Theological Methods	84
21. The Acquisition of the Theological Habitude	86
THE DOCTRINE OF HOLY SCRIPTURE	90
1. Holy Scripture the Only Source and Norm of Faith	90
2. Holy Scripture the Word of God	98
3. The Inspiration of the Bible	101
4. The Relation of the Holy Spirit to the Holy Writers	106
5. Objections to the Doctrine of Inspiration	107
6. The Doctrine of Inspiration and Confessional Lutheranism	115
7. The Denial of the Doctrine of Inspiration — Its Cause and Its Consequences	118
8. The Properties of Holy Scripture	120
A. The Divine Authority of Holy Scripture	120
B. The Divine Efficacy of Holy Scripture	133
C. The Divine Perfection, or Sufficiency, of Holy Scripture	137
D. The Divine Perspicuity of Holy Scripture	138

PAGE

THE DOCTRINE OF GOD 143

1. The Natural Knowledge of God 143
2. The Holy Trinity 147
3. The Doctrine of the Holy Trinity in Controversy 150
4. The Doctrine of the Holy Trinity and the Terminology of the Christian Church 153
5. The Holy Trinity Revealed in the Old Testament 158
6. God's Essence and Attributes 160
   1. The Doctrine in General 160
   2. The Negative Attributes 163
   3. Positive Attributes 167

THE DOCTRINE OF THE DIVINE DECREES 176

THE DOCTRINE OF CREATION 179

1. Definition of Creation 179
2. The Order of Creation 179
3. The Hexaemeron 180
4. The Six Days of Creation Considered in Detail 181
5. The Unity of the Human Race 185
6. Special Questions Regarding the Creation Report 186
7. Creation an External Act of God 187
8. The Ultimate End of Creation 188

THE DOCTRINE OF DIVINE PROVIDENCE 189

1. Definition of Divine Providence 189
2. The Objects of Divine Providence 190
3. The Relation of Divine Providence to Secondary Causes 190
4. Divine Concurrence in Good and Evil Actions 191
5. Divine Providence and Free Will 193

THE DOCTRINE OF THE ANGELS 196

1. The Existence of Angels 196
2. The Name "Angel" 196
3. The Nature of the Angels 197
4. The Number and Ranks of Angels 199
5. Good and Evil Angels 199
6. The Holy Service of the Good Angels 201
7. The Evil Work and Eternal Punishment of the Evil Angels 202

THE DOCTRINE OF MAN 205

A. Man Before the Fall 205
1. Man Created in the Image of God 205
2. Definition of "Image of God" 205
3. The Relation of the Divine Image to the Nature of Man 206
4. Immediate Results of the Divine Image 208
5. The Divine Image and Woman 209
6. The Ultimate End of the Image of God in Man 209

PAGE

B. The State of Corruption 210
    a. Of Sin in General 210
1. Definition of Sin 210
2. The Divine Law and Sin 211
3. How the Divine Law can be Known 213
4. The Causes of Sin 214
5. The Consequences of Sin 215
    b. Original Sin 216
1. Definition of Original Sin 216
2. The Corrupt Mind and Will of Man 219
3. The Negative and Positive Sides of Original Sin 221
4. The Universality of Original Sin 222
5. The Cause of Original Sin 223
6. The Effects of Original Sin 223
    c. Actual Sins 224
1. Definition of Actual Sin 224
2. The Causes of Actual Sin 225
3. The Doctrine of Offense 226
4. The Doctrine of Obduration 227
5. The Scriptural Doctrine of Temptation 228
6. The Classification of Actual Sins 228

THE FREEDOM OF THE WILL 236

THE GRACE OF GOD TOWARD FALLEN MANKIND 242
1. The Necessity of Divine Grace 242
2. Definition of Divine Grace 243
3. Attributes of Justifying Grace 246
4. The Theological Terminology Regarding the Divine Will of
    Grace 251

THE DOCTRINE OF CHRIST 255

A. The Doctrine of the Person of Christ 256
1. Introduction 256
2. The True Deity of Christ 256
3. The True Humanity of Christ 258
4. The Personal Union 263
5. The Communion of Natures 268
6. The Communication of Attributes 272
    The First Genus 273
    The Second Genus 275
    The Third Genus 284

B. The Doctrine of the States of Christ 287
1. Definition of Christ's State of Humiliation 287
2. Erroneous Views Regarding Christ's Humiliation 289
3. The Several Stages of the Humiliation 292
4. The State of Exaltation 295
5. The Several Stages of Christ's Exaltation 296

PAGE

C. The Doctrine of Christ's Office 301
    a. The Prophetic Office of Christ 303
    1. The Execution of This Office in the State of Humiliation .. 303
    2. The Execution of the Prophetic Office in the State of Exaltation 304
    b. The Sacerdotal Office of Christ 305
    1. The Vicarious Atonement 309
    2. Objective and Subjective Reconciliation 310
    3. Rejection of Errors Pertaining to Christ's Vicarious Atonement 311
    4. The Priestly Intercession of Christ 313
    c. The Kingly Office of Christ 314
    Errors Regarding the Kingly Office of Christ 317

THE DOCTRINE OF SOTERIOLOGY 319

THE DOCTRINE OF SAVING FAITH 321
    1. The Necessity of Faith 321
    2. The Nature of Saving Faith 322
    3. Concerning the Terms *Knowledge, Assent,* and *Confidence* .. 325
    4. Why Saving Faith Justifies 326
    5. Faith Viewed as a Passive Act or a Passive Instrument ... 327
    6. Concerning the Expressions *True Faith* and *Living Faith* .. 329
    7. Faith and the Assurance of Salvation ,.................. 329
    8. Can the Believer Be Sure of Possessing Saving Faith? 330
    9. The Faith of Infants 332
    10. The Use of the Term *Faith* in Scripture 333

CONVERSION, OR THE BESTOWAL OF FAITH 336
    1. Scriptural Basis of the Doctrine 336
    2. The Scriptural Definition of Conversion 336
    3. The Starting-point and the Terminus of Conversion 340
    4. The Efficient Cause of Conversion 342
    5. The Means of Conversion 346
    6. The Internal Motions in Conversion 349
    7. Conversion Is Instantaneous 350
    8. The Grace of Conversion Is Resistible 352
    9. Transitive and Intransitive Conversion 352
    10. Continued Conversion 353
    11. Reiterated Conversion 354
    12. Objections against Divine Monergism in Conversion 355
    13. The Pernicious Character of Synergism 360
    14. Synonyms of Conversion 362

JUSTIFICATION BY FAITH 367
    1. Definition of Justification 367
    2. Justification by Faith Alone 369
    3. The Doctrine of Justification the Central Doctrine of the Christian Religion 371

PAGE

4. The Christian Terminology by which the Doctrine of Justification by Faith is Guarded against Error 373
5. Justification on the Basis of Works 379
6. The Effects of Justification 380

THE DOCTRINE OF SANCTIFICATION AND GOOD WORKS 384

1. Definition of Sanctification 384
2. The Efficient Cause of Sanctification 386
3. The Inner Motions of Sanctification 387
4. The Means by which Sanctification is Accomplished 389
5. The Necessity of Sanctification and Good Works 390
6. The Imperfection of Christian Sanctification in This Life .. 396
7. The Doctrine of Good Works 403
   A. Definition of Good Works 403
   B. The Works of the Heathen 408
   C. The Christian's Growth in Good Works 411
8. The Reward of Good Works 415
9. The Great Value of Good Works 417
10. Perversion of the Doctrine of Good Works 420
11. Sanctification and the Christian Life 424
    A. The Christian Life and the Cross 424
    B. The Christian Life and Prayer 428
    C. The Christian Life and the Hope of Eternal Life 434

THE DOCTRINE OF PRESERVATION 436

THE DOCTRINE OF THE MEANS OF GRACE 441

1. Definition of the Term 441
2. The Means of Grace in General 442
3. Erroneous Doctrines Regarding the Means of Grace 448
4. The Importance of the Doctrine of the Means of Grace ... 457
5. The Means of Grace in the Form of Absolution 458
6. The Means of Grace in the Old Testament 465
7. The Means of Grace and Prayer 467

THE LAW AND THE GOSPEL 470

1. Definition of Law and Gospel 470
2. Features that Are Common to Both the Law and the Gospel 471
3. The Law and Gospel Considered as Opposites 473
4. The Close Connection between the Law and the Gospel 477
5. The Art of Distinguishing between the Law and the Gospel 480
6. By whom the Proper Distinction between the Law and the Gospel is Set Aside 484

THE DOCTRINE OF HOLY BAPTISM 486

1. The Divine Institution of Baptism 486
2. What Makes Baptism a Sacrament 488
3. Baptism a True Means of Grace 491

PAGE

4. The Use of Baptism 496
5. Whom the Church should Baptize 497
6. The Administrants of Baptism 499
7. The Necessity of Baptism 499
8. Regarding Baptismal Customs 500
9. The Baptism of John the Baptist 504

THE DOCTRINE OF THE LORD'S SUPPER 506

1. The Divine Institution of the Lord's Supper 506
2. The Relation of the Lord's Supper to the Other Means of
   Grace 507
3. The Scriptural Doctrine of the Lord's Supper 509
4. The Lutheran Doctrine and the Words of Institution 520
5. Different Accounts of the Words of Institution 532
6. The Material Elements in the Lord's Supper 524
7. What Makes the Lord's Supper a Sacrament 528
8. The Purpose of the Lord's Supper 533
9. Who may be Admitted to the Lord's Supper 537
10. The Necessity of the Lord's Supper 540

THE DOCTRINE OF THE CHRISTIAN CHURCH 541

A. The Church Universal 541

1. Definition of the Term 541
2. Erroneous Doctrines Concerning the Church 543
3. The Properties of the Christian Church 547
4. The Glory of the Christian Church 549
5. How the Church is Founded and Preserved 551

B. Concerning Local Churches 553

1. Definition of the Term 553
2. The Divine Institution of Local Churches 555
3. Orthodox and Heterodox Churches 556
4. Heterodox Churches and True Discipleship 558
5. The Inadmissibility of Spiritual Fellowship with Heterodox
   Churches 559
6. Separatists, or Schismatics 560
7. The Representative Church 561

THE DOCTRINE OF THE PUBLIC MINISTRY 563

1. Definition of the Term 563
2. The Public Ministry and the Spiritual Priesthood of All
   Believers 564
3. The Public Ministry is a Divine Appointment or Ordinance 566
4. Is the Public Ministry Necessary? 569
5. The Call into the Ministry 570
6. Of Ordination 574
7. The Christian Ministry does Not Constitute a Spiritual Estate 576
8. The Power of the Public Ministry 578

PAGE

9. The Relation of Christian Ministers to One Another 579
10. The Public Ministry Is the Supreme Office in the Church ... 580
11. Of Antichrist 580

THE DOCTRINE OF ETERNAL ELECTION 585
1. Definition of the Term 585
2. How Believers are to Consider Their Election 589
3. The Objects of Eternal Election 593
4. The Relation of Faith to Eternal Election 598
5. The Purpose of the Doctrine of Eternal Election 602
6. Holy Scripture Teaches No Election to Damnation 606
7. Why Many Reject the Scriptural Doctrine of Eternal Election 610

THE DOCTRINE OF THE LAST THINGS (ESCHATOLOGY) 613
1. Temporal Death 613
2. The Condition of the Soul between Death and the Resurrection 616
3. The Second Advent of Christ 619
4. The Resurrection of the Dead 625
5. The Final Judgment 630
6. The End of the World 631
7. Eternal Damnation 633
8. Eternal Salvation 639

NATURE AND CONCEPT OF THEOLOGY.
(De Natura et Constitutione Theologiae.)

Introduction to Sacred Theology.
(Prolegomena.)

1. THE SCRIPTURAL VIEWPOINT OF THE CHRISTIAN THEOLOGIAN.

Owing to the diverse views and tendencies prevailing among theologians to-day, it is necessary for the Christian theologian, before presenting to his readers his dogmatic treatise, to declare in clear and unmistakable terms from which viewpoint it has been written.

The viewpoint of the present-day *modernistic theologian* is that truth must be determined by human reason in the light of scientific research. The theological Liberalist therefore does not recognize Holy Scripture as the source and norm of faith, but holds that this ancient standard of Christian doctrine has been superseded by the standards of reason and philosophy which he himself has established. From this viewpoint his dogmatic treatise is written, and since this viewpoint is anti-Scriptural and unchristian, it follows that his whole theology is rationalistic, naturalistic, and diametrically opposed to the Word of God.

The viewpoint of the *Roman Catholic theologian* is that truth must be determined by both Holy Scripture and the "infallible" traditions of the Church as these are formally set forth in the papal decretals and decisions. Thus he accepts as a source and norm of faith, in addition to Holy Scripture (to which he falsely adds the Apocrypha), something that is foreign and even opposed to Holy Scripture and ascribes to it the same authority as to the Word of God. This erroneous viewpoint proves the antichristian character of papistical theology; for it, too, is in direct opposition to Holy Scripture.

The viewpoint of the modern rationalizing Protestant theologian is that, while Holy Scripture is indeed a "divine-human record of revealed truths," which contains the doctrines that Christians must believe for their salvation, these saving truths must be determined, not by any authoritative statement of the Scriptures, but rather by the Christian "faith-consciousness" or the "regenerate and sanctified mind" or the "Christian experience" of the theologian *(das christliche Glaubensbewusstsein, das wiedergeborne Ich, das christliche Erlebnis).* In his opinion not the objective statement of Holy Scripture, but rather the "sanctified self-consciousness of the dogmatizing subject" *(das fromme Selbstbewusstsein des dogmatisierenden Subjekts)* is in·the last analysis the norm which decides what is divine truth and what is not. Modern rationalistic theology is therefore a movement away from Holy Scripture *(eine Los-von-der-Schrift-Bewegung)* to a source and norm of faith established by man himself. This movement may differ in degree, but is always the same in kind. It is basically anti-Scriptural and has its source in the unbelief of the corrupt flesh. The viewpoint of the modern rationalistic theologian must therefore likewise be rejected as unchristian and opposed to Holy Scripture.

The viewpoint from which the present dogmatic treatise is written is that *Holy Scripture is the only source and norm of Christian faith and life,* for the simple reason that the Bible is the divinely inspired Word of God, which is absolutely infallible and inerrant, both as a whole and in each individual passage. Hence, whenever it speaks on any point of doctrine or life, the matter is fully decided. *Scriptura locuta, res decisa est.* This viewpoint identifies Holy Scripture with the Word of God; its claim is, not merely that the Bible contains the Word of God, but that it *is,* fully and absolutely, in all its parts, the Word of God.

The fact that *this viewpoint* is *the only correct one* is proved by the statements and the attitude of both Christ and His inspired apostles. Our divine Savior accepted no other norm than Holy Scripture, and He invariably rejected the traditions of the Pharisees and the "reasonings" of the Sadducees. When He declared His divine doctrines and refuted errors, He constantly based His teachings on the immovable foundation of the written Word of God. Thus at the beginning of His ministry He met the temptations of Satan with the emphatic assertion "It is written," Matt. 4, 4, and He adhered to this principle throughout His ministry. Cp. John 5, 39; Matt. 5, 17—19; John 8, 31. 32; etc.

Also the apostles regarded Holy Scripture, including their own inspired teachings, both oral and written, as the sole source and norm of faith. Cf. Gal. 1, 8; 2 Tim. 3, 15—17; Titus 1, 9; 1 Cor. 14, 37; 2 Pet. 1, 19—21; etc. When in the age of the

Reformation the Bible was restored to its rightful place as the sole authority of the Christian faith, Luther once more proclaimed it to be "the fountain of all wisdom." (St. Louis Ed., I, 1289 ff.) The great Reformer declared: "You must believe that God Himself speaks in the Bible, and your attitude must be in accordance with that belief." (III, 21.) Those who, like the scholastic theologians, deviated from the Word of God and based their views and doctrines on the ground of reason or philosophy, were branded "monsters" *(portenta)* by Luther. The claim of modern rationalistic theologians that Luther's attitude with regard to the authority of Holy Scripture was "rather free" *(eine freiere Stellung)* is disproved by his own clear and emphatic statements to the contrary. And like Luther all true Christian theologians have at all times maintained that the Bible is the inspired Word of God and therefore the only source and norm of Christian faith, — a truth which they stoutly upheld against all gainsayers.

Modern rationalistic theologians declare that they cannot identify Holy Scripture with the Word of God or accept it as the sole norm of faith. They aver that their sense of actuality *(Wirklichkeitssinn)* does not permit them to do so, but instead demands another norm outside and beyond Holy Scripture, for example, their "Christian consciousness," their "Christian experience," and the like. In reality, however, this claim only goes to prove how gravely they are deceiving themselves; for the knowledge of divine truth can be gained only from the Word of God. The Christian faith therefore can be based solely upon God's Word. Our divine Lord states emphatically that we shall know the truth only if we continue in His Word as proclaimed by Himself and by His inspired prophets and apostles, John 8, 31. 32; 17, 20; Eph. 2, 20.

How truly Christ has spoken the history of the Christian Church amply shows; for all theologians who at any time have rejected Holy Scripture as the sole norm of faith have invariably denied the specific Christian doctrines, such as the vicarious atonement of Christ, justification by grace through faith, etc. (Cf. Dr. F. Pieper, *Christliche Dogmatik,* Vol. I, 4 ff.) Thus Hofmann, the father of modern subjective theology *(Ichtheologie),* denied Christ's vicarious satisfaction and taught the pagan theology of salvation without the redemptive work of Christ. It is, moreover, proved by the confusion of doctrine *(Lehrverwirrung)* which has resulted whenever the principle that Holy Scripture is the sole authority in religion has been either ignored or surrendered. This confusion in doctrine prevails whenever norms different from Holy Scripture are accepted as the basis of Christian doctrine; for subjective theology can never supply the Christian Church with a true and certain basis of faith. Without Holy Scripture as the sole source and standard of faith the Church is without any foundation whatsoever on which it can rest its faith; it finds itself in a maelstrom of conflicting subjective views, all of which are fatal to the Christian faith.

2. OF RELIGION IN GENERAL.

The etymology of the term *religion* is still a matter of controversy. The Lutheran dogmatician Hollaz writes: "Some suppose the term *religion* to be derived from *religare* (Lactantius), others from *relegere* (Cicero). According to the former derivation, religion signifies the obligation rightly to worship God or something which imposes upon man obligations and duties. According to the latter etymology, religion is diligent attention to those things which pertain to the worship of God. The former derivation is more generally received." (*Doctr. Theol.*, p. 21.)[1] The Lutheran dogmatician Quenstedt cites as synonyms of religion the Greek terms ϑρησκεία, Jas. 1, 26; εὐσέβεια, 1 Tim. 4, 8; λογικὴ λατρεία, Rom. 12, 1. However, none of these terms is really synonymous with religion, although each designates and emphasizes a particular phase of it. True religion is communion with the true God through faith in Jesus Christ; it is nothing more and nothing less. Still the controversy concerning the etymological meaning of religion need not trouble us, since in the final analysis the denotation of a word does not depend on its etymological derivation, but rather on its usage *(usus loquendi)*.

However, from the common usage of the term *religion* we can derive no satisfactory definition of religion if we desire to include both the Christian religion and the non-Christian religions. While both Christians and non-Christians employ the term *religion,* each of these groups connects with it its own specific concepts and meanings, and, as we shall see, these are contradictory. The matter deserves careful attention.

Investigation shows that *all heathen religions stand in direct opposition to the Christian religion.* They are all, without exception, religions of the Law. To the heathen, religion means the earnest endeavor of men to reconcile the deities by their own efforts

1) *The Doctrinal Theology of the Ev. Luth. Church.* By H. Schmid; tr. by Jacobs and Hay.

or works, such as worship, sacrifices, moral conduct, asceticism, etc. In this respect all non-Christian religions agree, no matter how much they may differ in individual details. Nor can we expect anything else; for the heathen by nature do not know the Gospel (1 Cor. 2, 6—10: "We speak . . . the hidden wisdom, . . . which none of the princes of this world knew"), but only the divine Law, namely, so far as this is written in their hearts. Hence all their religious thoughts move within the sphere of the Law, so that from beginning to end their religions are, and indeed must be, *religions of the Law.*

Christians, on the contrary, believe true religion to consist in the very opposite. *To Christians, religion means true faith in the Gospel of Jesus Christ,* or in the gracious message, revealed in Holy Scripture, that a perfect reconciliation has been effected between God and man through the vicarious atonement *(satisfactio vicaria)* of the divine-human Christ, the Redeemer of the world. Hence religion in the true sense of the term may be ascribed only to believers in Christ Jesus. And that is precisely what God's Word teaches on this point. True religion, according to God's Word, is communion with God through faith in Jesus Christ. Thus St. Paul testifies: "Knowing that a man is not justified by the works of the Law, but by the faith of Jesus Christ, even we have believed in Jesus Christ that we might be justified by the faith of Christ and not by the works of the Law," Gal. 2, 16.

Whenever theologians or entire denominations within external Christendom deny the cardinal doctrine of justification by grace, through faith in Christ, either in whole or in part, these individuals or church-bodies surrender the Christian conception of religion and adopt the pagan view. They are apostates from the Christian faith, as St. Paul declares: "Christ is become of no effect unto you whosoever of you are justified by the Law; ye are fallen from grace," Gal. 5, 4. In short, the doctrine of salvation by faith and that of salvation by works are opposites *(opposita),* which necessarily exclude each other, so that, if any one trusts in his works for salvation, he no longer in deed and truth professes the Christian religion.

The basic difference between the Christian religion and all other so-called religions has been aptly pointed out by Prof. Max Mueller of Oxford University, who writes: "In the discharge of my duties for forty years as professor of Sanskrit in the University of Oxford I have devoted as much time as any man living to the

study of the sacred books of the East, and I have found the one
key-note, the one diapason, so to speak, of all these so-called sacred
books, . . . the one refrain through all — salvation by works. They
all say that salvation must be purchased, must be bought with
a price, and that the sole price, the sole purchase-money, must be
our works and deservings. Our own Holy Bible, our sacred Book
of the East, is from beginning to end a protest against this doctrine.
Good works are indeed enjoined upon us in that sacred Book of
the East; but they are only the outcome of a grateful heart; they
are only a thank-offering, the fruits of our faith. They are never
the ransom-money of the true disciples of Christ. Let us not shut
our eyes to what is excellent and true and of good report in these
sacred books; but let us teach Hindus, Buddhists, and Moham-
medans that there is only one sacred Book of the East that can
be their mainstay in that awful hour when they pass all alone into
the unseen world. It is the sacred Book which contains that
faithful saying, worthy to be received of all men, women, and
children, and not merely of us Christians, that Christ Jesus came
into the world to save sinners." (Cf. Pieper, *Christliche Dogmatik,* I, 15 ff.)

3. OF THE NUMBER OF RELIGIONS IN THE WORLD.

The number of religions in the world has been variously
estimated. We commonly speak of four different religions: Christian, Jewish, Mohammedan, and pagan. While such an enumeration may be employed in common speech, it must never be forgotten that in the final analysis *all religions must be reduced to
two classes: religions of the Law,* that is, religions which endeavor
to reconcile the Deity by works of the Law; *and the religion of the
Gospel,* that is, the belief, divinely wrought and engendered by
the Holy Ghost through the means of grace, that God has been
reconciled to the sinner without any works on his part, through
the vicarious atonement of Christ Jesus, and that salvation is
thus God's free gift, appropriated by the sinner through faith in
Christ Jesus.

This division of religions into two distinct and mutually exclusive groups is truly in accordance with Scripture. Holy Writ
acknowledges as true religion only that which teaches that the
sinner is saved through faith in Christ. It distinctly declares it to
be the mission of the Christian Church to displace all man-made
religions and to establish throughout the world the religion of the
saving Gospel of Jesus Christ. Our Lord's Great Commission

reads: "Go ye into all the world and preach the Gospel to every creature. He that believeth and is baptized shall be saved, but he that believeth not shall be damned," Mark 16, 15. 16. To St. Paul the glorified Savior said: I am sending thee to the Gentiles "to open their eyes and to turn them from darkness to light and from the power of Satan unto God that they may receive forgiveness of sins and inheritance among them which are sanctified by faith that is in Me," Acts 26, 17. 18. According to this express statement of Holy Writ all who do not believe the Gospel are kept in darkness and in the power of Satan, from which they can be delivered only through sanctification by faith.

Thus the Word of God recognizes only the Christian religion as true and as capable of bringing salvation to men; it alone deserves the name of religion since it alone reunites sinful man with God. If man-made forms of worship are called religions, this term is applied to them in an improper sense, just as idols are termed "Gods" although in reality they are not Gods. Since this is the case, it is impossible to find a general religious concept or definition by which all religions existing in the world, both the true and the false, may be grouped in a single class. Christianity, by its very origin, does not belong in the category of man-made religions.

All who deny this and maintain that such a general religious concept or definition can be established overlook the essential difference between the religion of Christ and religions of human origin. Religion has been defined as "the personal relation of man to God." This definition, it has been asserted, is broad enough to include both the Christian religion and the pagan religions. However, its inadequacy becomes apparent as we begin to analyze "man's relation to God." Since all men are sinners, their relation to God by nature is that of fear and despair and, consequently, of hatred toward God. This miserable condition is attested both by Scripture and experience. According to the clear teaching of God's Word all men who are not born again through faith in Christ are "without Christ," "have no hope," and are "without God in the world," Eph. 2, 12. In spite of their earnest endeavors to reconcile God by their works they continue in their fear and hopelessness; for they remain under the curse and condemnation of the divine Law. This fact St. Paul asserts when he writes: "As many as are of the works of the Law are under the curse," Gal. 3, 10. The same apostle declares also that "the things which the Gentiles sacrifice they sacrifice to devils and not to God," 1 Cor.

10, 20. In short, as long as a person is without faith in Christ, his personal relation to God is a relation of dread, despair, and hopelessness and therefore also of enmity against God, Rom. 8, 7.

However, the personal relation to God changes as soon as a person becomes a child of God through faith in Christ; then he obtains "a good conscience," 1 Pet. 3, 21, the assurance of divine grace, the conviction that his sins are forgiven, and the inestimable hope of eternal life. "If any man be in Christ, he is a new creature; old things are passed away; behold, all things are become new," 2 Cor. 5, 17. St. Paul describes this blessed relationship in beautiful terms Rom. 5, 1. 2, where he writes: "Therefore, being justified by faith, we have peace with God through our Lord Jesus Christ, by whom also we have access by faith into this grace wherein we stand and rejoice in hope of the glory of God." And again, v. 11: "We also joy in God through our Lord Jesus Christ, by whom we have now received the atonement." The believer's personal relation to God is therefore the very opposite of the personal relation to God which is found in the unbeliever; it is a relation of peace, joy, and happiness.

Again, religion has been defined as "the method of worshiping God." This definition is quite adequate as far as the Christian religion is concerned, but as a definition of religion in general it is woefully inadequate, since all non-Christian religions are certainly not "methods of worshiping God." True worship of God is possible only through faith in Christ, as our Lord emphatically tells us when He declares: "All men should honor the Son even as they honor the Father. He that honoreth not the Son honoreth not the Father, which hath sent Him," John 5, 23. Every "worship of God" without Christ dishonors God; therefore, far from being worship of God, it is in reality blasphemy and opposition to God. Indeed, it is devil-worship, as St. Paul declares: "The things which the Gentiles sacrifice they sacrifice to devils and not to God," 1 Cor. 10, 20. In these words the apostle affirms in no uncertain terms that the heathen cannot worship the true God. Though they be ever so earnest in their endeavor to placate their deities, their worship is a service of devils.

The reason for this is clear. All non-Christian religions err with regard to the object as well as to the method of worship. The heathen worship objects that are not divine and thus give the glory belonging to God to another and His praise to graven images, Is. 42, 8. Such blasphemous worship is an abomination in the sight of God and therefore the very opposite of true worship. But the non-Christian religions are in error also with respect to the method of worship. Since the heathen are ignorant of the divine Savior of men and therefore do not know that they must trust in Him for salvation, they seek to quiet their consciences whenever these are aroused to a consciousness of sin and guilt, and to reconcile the objects of their worship, by good works. But reliance on good works for justification offends God and provokes Him to anger. "As many as are of the works of the Law are under the curse," Gal. 3, 10. That is God's verdict, His own condemnation of a worship offered to Him on the basis of human merit.

In short, religion in general cannot be defined as "the method of worshiping God"; for that definition is applicable only to the Christian religion, not to any other. This fact has been decisively asserted by our Lutheran dogmaticians. Hollaz writes: "Religion, improperly speaking, signifies the false; properly speaking, the true method of worshiping God." (*Doctr. Theol.*, p. 22.) This distinction is as vital as it is correct.

Recently religion has been defined also as "the endeavor of man to secure, supplement, and perfect personal and social life with the aid of a higher, supernatural power." This endeavor, the German theologian Kirn avers, is common to all religions, so that it supplies us with a general concept for the definition of religion. However, this definition applies only to the religions of the Law, or the non-Christian religions, which certainly endeavor to "secure, supplement, and perfect personal life" through human efforts and works. It is the common denominator of all religions outside of Christianity; the erroneous opinion that a man must save himself by good deeds *(opinio legis)* is inherent by nature in all men. The Christian religion, however, differs radically from this false notion. In fact, from beginning to end it is a protest against the false doctrine that a man must "secure, supplement, and perfect life" by his own efforts. It rejects altogether the doctrine of work-righteousness and establishes as its prime and basic principle the fact that a sinner is justified by grace alone, without the deeds of the Law. It is largely because of this vast divergence between the Christian religion and the religions of work-righteousness that the Gospel of Christ is a stumbling-block to the Jew and foolishness to the Greek, 1 Cor. 1, 23; 2, 14. Man, blinded by sin, does not desire a way to salvation that is purely by grace, through faith in a divine Savior.

It is evident from the foregoing that Christianity, since it is the only true religion, dare not be placed in the same class with man-made religions. There is no general religious concept or definition that embraces the distinctive tenets of Christianity and of the man-made religions; Christianity is quite in a class by itself. It alone is the true religion, while all the others are counterfeit; and just as little as counterfeit coin is real money, so little can man-made religions substantiate their claim of being real religions. If the term *religion* is applied to them, it is done in a wholly improper sense. If we do designate them as "religions," we do it in the same sense in which we term counterfeit coins "money" or in which Holy Scripture applies to the heathen idols the term "gods" (אֱלֹהִים). The application of the name in this case never means that the object thus designated is in reality that which the name expresses. The heathen idols are not Gods, nor are the heathen forms of worship religions in the true sense of the term.

Quenstedt accordingly writes (I, 28): "The term *religion* is used either improperly and falsely *(abusive)* or properly. Improperly and falsely it is used for false religion, namely, for the heathen, the Mohammedan, and the Jewish religions, in which sense Calixtus, in the *Theological Apparatus,* treats of the divers religions of the world, in spite of the fact that there is only one true religion, namely, the Christian." In keeping with this doctrine our Lutheran dogmaticians never sought a general religious concept or definition to comprehend both the Christian and the non-Christian religions, but placed the Christian religion in a class by itself as the only religion and classed all others as false and as unworthy of the name. This classification alone is Scriptural.

But here the objection has been raised that the old orthodox dogmaticians were devoid of an adequate psychological, philosophical, and historical understanding of the various non-Christian religions and that for this reason it is clear why they failed to appreciate these forms of worship. This lack of appreciation, it is maintained, has been supplied by modern research work in the psychology of religion, the philosophy of religion, and in comparative religion *(Religionsgeschichte)*. Yet, as we shall see, even the results of these investigations do not disprove the correctness of the old dual division of religions into the true and the false.

Modern religious psychology endeavors to point out "the similarity of the psychological phenomena" *(die Gleichartigkeit der psychologischen Erscheinungen)* found in both the Christian religion and the non-Christian religions. This similarity, it is said, was overlooked by the older theologians, and their inability to find a general concept or definition to cover both the Christian religion and the non-Christian religions is attributable to this fact. However, we may state in reply to this charge that, after all, the psychological phenomena of the Christian religion and of the non-Christian religions are not similar at all; in fact, essentially they are diametrically opposed to each other. In the heart of the non-Christian we commonly find such "psychological phenomena" as the consciousness of guilt, an accusing and condemning conscience, fear of punishment, flight from God, and an inward hatred of Him — and all these coupled with the constant desire to placate the Deity by good works. But since good works cannot reconcile God, we find in addition the "psychological phenomena" of terror of death, hopelessness, and despair. These "psychological phenomena" are clearly attested by Holy Scripture, Eph. 2, 12: "having no hope"; Heb. 2, 15: "who through fear of death were all their lifetime subject to bondage." The candid confessions of honest and earnest heathen thinkers emphatically confirm what Holy Scripture teaches on this point; they all reecho the tragic note of spiritual despair as they contemplate human sinfulness and guilt.

However, in the soul of the believing child of God we find the very opposite "psychological phenomena," such as the consciousness of guilt removed and of sin forgiven, peace with God (Rom. 5, 1—3), filial love of God and implicit trust in His grace, triumph over death, and the sure hope of eternal life. And all these "psychological phenomena" are combined with the consecrated desire to serve God in deed and in truth, out of heartfelt gratitude for His unmerited gift of grace. Gal. 2, 20: "The life which I now live in the flesh I live by the faith of the Son of God, who loved me and gave Himself for me." St. Paul affirms the diversity of the "psychological phenomena" which he experienced before and after his conversion. He writes, 1 Cor. 15, 9. 10: "I persecuted the Church of God; but by the grace of God I am what I am." Furthermore, in order to assure his readers of the blessedness of their Christian calling, he continually directs their attention to the diversity of the "psychological experiences" which they had undergone, first as benighted heathen and afterward as enlightened Christians. Eph. 2, 5: "Even when we were dead in sins, hath [He] quickened us together with Christ." Cf. Eph. 2, 11—22; 1 Cor. 12, 2. 27; etc.

The similarity of the "psychological phenomena" which modern students of religious psychology assert so strongly is only a *formal,* not a *material,* similarity. Thus, both Christians and heathen engage in worship; yet how radically different is their worship in all its essentials! Christians pray, and so do the heathen; yet what a vast difference there is between the Christian and the pagan prayer! Hence religious psychology, too, cannot deny the essential difference between the Christian and the non-Christian religions and must therefore admit that the dual division of religions into the true and the false is correct.

The same holds true of the historical study of religion. Comparative religion *(Religionsgeschichte)* demonstrates the fact that all religions outside the Christian religion are "religions of the Law," or "religions of works," maintaining as their basic principle that man must earn his salvation by worthy deeds. The glad tidings of salvation by grace through faith, on the other hand, is found in the Bible only, not in any other so-called book of religion. Thus the historical study of religion also can establish no other division of religions than that of the Lutheran dogmaticians, who placed in the first group the Christian religion, which teaches salvation by grace, and in the second group all man-made religions, which teach salvation by works. "Work-religions" may differ in non-essential details, which depend on climatic, psychological, and racial factors, but they all agree in the common fundamental principle of salvation by works.

Finally, the philosophical study of religion, or philosophy of religion, also cannot lead us beyond the dual division of religions in two distinct kinds, the one true and the other false. The student of religious philosophy can, of course, operate only with the natural knowledge of God, or the divine Law written in the heart of man. But when he does define religion on purely natural premises, that is, when he views religion wholly apart from divine revelation, his conclusion must necessarily be that religion is essentially man's effort to reconcile God on the basis of meritorious conduct. Thus Socrates, the greatest of Greek philosophers, although he surpassed all the others by the loftiness and sublimity of his philosophico-religious ideas, nevertheless demanded that in the hour of his death a cock be sacrificed to Aesculapius. Socrates conceived the need of a savior far greater than any possible human savior; yet since the true Savior was unknown to him, he was obliged to trust in his works for salvation. Also Immanuel Kant, who is commonly regarded as the foremost religious philosopher and is still the greatest of all modern philosophers, affirmed that from the viewpoint of pure philosophy the essence of religion must be regarded as "morality" and that the Christian doctrine of the atonement can have no place in any speculative system of religion. Religious philosophy must therefore always conceive of religion as the effort of man to win salvation by works. Thus the dual division of religions established by Christian divines of bygone centuries must be retained even to-day.

There is, however, a system of religious philosophy which seeks to build up its rationalistic speculations on the basis of Holy Scripture. The advocates of this type of religious philosophy admit that the revealed truths of Holy Scripture lie beyond the intellectual comprehension of man. For this reason these must be believed and accepted as true *a priori*. Yet the theologian should not remain satisfied with this simple act of believing. Through faith in the divine truths of revelation he must progress to their intellectual apprehension. What the ordinary believer knows by faith the theologian must understand. So Anselm of Canterbury, the father of medieval scholasticism, declared: *"Credo, ut intelligam."* Anselm's purpose, in a way, was laudable. He sought to meet and refute the skeptics of his time, who *a priori* rejected the revealed truths as false because they are unintelligible to human reason. Anselm demanded that the revealed truths should first be believed in order that they might be dialectically demonstrated and rationally understood. His underlying principle was that "a Christian through faith must progress to understanding and not through understanding to faith." *"Christianus per fidem debet ad intellectum proficere, non per intellectum ad fidem accedere."* The disciples of Anselm are the modern advocates of "scientific theology," falsely so called, who, like their medieval teacher, assert that faith must be elevated to knowledge, because only in this way the Christian religion can be perceived and demonstrated as the absolute truth.

This endeavor, however, to harmonize faith with reason is unscriptural. Jesus assures us that we shall know the truth only if we continue in His Word by faith, John 8, 31. 32. In the same spirit, St. Paul asserts that all teachers of the Church who do not adhere to the truth of Christ Jesus by simple faith are "proud, knowing nothing, but doting," 1 Tim. 6, 3. 4. Thus both Christ and St. Paul are opposed to the endeavor of "scientific theologians" to elevate faith to knowledge and the revealed truth to a human science. The reason for this is evident. The Christian religion cannot be brought down to the level of man's intellectual comprehension without losing its supernatural character and content. History shows very plainly how fatal the endeavor to "elevate" faith to knowledge has proved itself. Anselm denied the active obedience of Christ, Abelard denied His vicarious atonement, and in recent times the adherents of "scientific theology" have denied both the divine inspiration of Holy Scripture and the justification of a sinner by grace, through faith in Christ. Thus both the formal and the material principles of Christianity have been denied, and the whole Christian religion has been eviscerated of its divinely revealed content. The ultimate consequence of the application of philosophy to theology is Modernism or agnosticism.

Incidentally, also this last consideration proves the correctness of the dual division of religions into the true and the false; for the content of the Christian religion is of such a nature that it is either completely received by faith or is completely rejected, since the mysteries of revealed truth are not recognized as such by human reason. The perverted reason of man acknowledges as true only the religion of the Law, or of works, while with all its might it contends against the religion of faith. On the other hand, Holy Scripture condemns as false all religions of works, just as it declares unregenerate human reason to be blind, dead, and absolutely unable to perceive the things of the Spirit of God, 1 Cor. 2, 14.

4. THE TWO SOURCES (PRINCIPIA COGNOSCENDI) OF THE EXISTING RELIGIONS.

As we have seen, there are but two essentially different religions, the religion of faith, or of the Gospel, and the religion of works, or of the Law. So also there are but two actual sources (*principia cognoscendi,* principles of knowledge) from which these two divergent religions are taken. The religion of works is of human origin; it is a man-made religion, having its source and origin in the human heart, in which God has inscribed His divine Law, so that also the heathen, who have not the Word of God as set forth in Holy Scripture, Rom. 2, 14, "know the judgment of God" (δικαίωμα, the norm of right, *Rechtssatzung*), Rom. 1, 32, and "show the work of the Law written in their hearts," Rom. 2, 15. On the basis of the divine Law, inscribed in the human heart, conscience accuses and condemns man whenever he does wrong, and so he is burdened with the consciousness of guilt, "they are without excuse," Rom. 1, 20, "their conscience also bearing witness and their thoughts the mean while accusing or else excusing one another," Rom. 2, 15.

Thus condemned by his conscience, man seeks to reconcile the Deity by "good works," such as worship, sacrifices, etc. The *Apology* rightly says: "But works become conspicuous among men. Human reason naturally admires these, and because it sees only works and does not understand or consider faith, it dreams accordingly that these works merit remission of sins and justify. This opinion of the Law *(haec opinio legis)* inheres by nature in men's minds; neither can it be expelled, unless when we are divinely taught. But the mind must be recalled *(revocanda mens est)* from such carnal opinions of the Word of God." (Art. III, 197.)

The "opinion of the Law" of which the *Apology* here speaks, namely, the erroneous view that works merit remission of sins and justify the sinner, St. Paul calls "the religion of the flesh." So he writes to the Galatians, who sought justification on the ground of their merits: "Are ye so foolish? Having begun in the Spirit, are ye now made perfect by the flesh?" Gal. 3, 3. Luther correctly explains this passage as follows: "Here *flesh* is nothing else than the righteousness, the wisdom, of the flesh and the thoughts of reason, which endeavors to be justified by the Law." (St. L. Ed., IX, 288 ff.) That this is indeed the meaning of the word *flesh* in this passage the context clearly proves. The passage thus teaches the truth that every religion which seeks to acquire divine grace and remission of sins through human endeavors is not of God, but of man. Its source is the perverted, unregenerate heart.

The religion of the Gospel, or of faith, on the contrary, is not of man, but of God, who has revealed it by His inspired prophets and apostles in Holy Scripture. 1 Cor. 2, 6—10: "We speak wisdom among them that are perfect; yet not the wisdom of this world; . . . but we speak the wisdom of God in a mystery, even the hidden wisdom, which God ordained before the world unto our glory; which none of the princes of this world knew. . . . But as it is written, Eye hath not seen nor ear heard, neither have entered into the heart of man the things which God hath prepared for them that love Him. But God hath revealed them unto us by His Spirit," etc.

The religion of faith is therefore in the strictest sense of the term "wisdom of God," 1 Cor. 1, 24. It is "God-made," and its only source is God's Book, the inspired Scriptures, John 5, 39; Rom. 16, 25. 26; Eph. 2, 20; 1 John 1, 3. 4. Quenstedt writes

(I, 33): "The sole, proper, adequate, and ordinary source of theology and of the Christian religion is the divine revelation contained in the Holy Scriptures; or, what is the same, the canonical Scriptures alone are the absolute source of theology, so that out of them alone the articles of faith are to be deduced and proved." Again, I, 36: "Divine revelation is the first and last source of sacred theology, beyond which theological discussion among Christians dare not proceed." (*Doctr. Theol.,* p. 27 f.) This Scriptural truth must be maintained against every form of rationalism, by which at all times false teachers have sought to pervert the divine truth. Rationalistic doctrine (Pelagianism, Semi-Pelagianism, synergism, etc.) is not of God, but carnal, anti-Scriptural opposition to God. Essentially it is paganism, which destroys divine truth wherever it is accepted and allowed to hold sway in theology. Quenstedt is right when he writes (I, 38): "Human or natural reason is not the source of theology and supernatural things." (*Doctr. Theol.,* p. 28.)

But neither is *tradition* a source of the Christian faith. Calov is fully in accord with Holy Scripture when he declares: "We contend that over and above the written Word of God there is at present no unwritten Word of God concerning any doctrine necessary to Christian faith and life, not comprehended in the Scriptures, that ever came forth from the apostles, was handed down by tradition, was preserved by the Church, and is to be received with equal reverence." (*Doctr. Theol.,* p. 28.) This is truly Lutheran and Scriptural doctrine. We are to seek God's Word only in God's Book, never anywhere else, as also Quenstedt emphatically states when he writes (I, 44): "The consent of the primitive Church or of the Fathers of the first centuries after Christ is not a source of Christian faith, neither primary nor secondary, nor does it produce a divine, but merely a human or probable belief." (*Doctr. Theol.,* p. 28.)

Lastly we must reject also the so-called *private revelations* as sources of faith; for, as Hollaz rightly points out, "after the completion of the canon of Scripture no new and immediate divine revelation was given to be a fundamental source of doctrine, 1 Cor. 4, 6; Heb. 1, 1. 2." (*Doctr. Theol.,* p. 28.)

The doctrine of a *fixed revelation,* that is, of a divine revelation given us only in the Word of Christ and His prophets and apostles, is plainly the doctrine of Scripture. Eph. 2, 20: "And [ye] are built upon the foundation of the apostles and prophets,

Jesus Christ Himself being the chief Corner-stone." For this reason *Christian theology,* on the basis of Holy Scripture, *can acknowledge only one source and standard of true religion,* namely, the inspired, infallible written Word of God, or *Holy Scripture.*

The religion of faith dates back to the beginning of the Old Testament, since it was revealed to Adam and Eve immediately after the Fall, Gen. 3, 15. It was afterwards proclaimed continually by the holy prophets and was truly believed by all the Old Testament saints. Gen. 15, 6: "And he [Abram] believed in the Lord; and He counted it to him for righteousness." In the New Testament both Christ and His apostles constantly point back to the promises of faith revealed in the Old Testament. Luke 24, 27: "And beginning at Moses and all the prophets, He expounded unto them in all the Scriptures the things concerning Himself." Acts 10, 43: "To Him give all the prophets witness that through His name, whosoever believeth in Him, shall receive remission of sins." Rom. 3, 21: "But now the righteousness of God without the Law is manifested, being witnessed by the Law and the Prophets." Rom. 4, 3: "Abraham believed God, and it was counted unto him for righteousness." All these passages confirm the truth that also in the Old Testament men were saved solely through the true religion of faith in Christ. The divine Law never had the function to save sinners; its chief purpose is to convince sinners of their sin and guilt. Gal. 3, 24: "Wherefore the Law was our schoolmaster to bring us unto Christ that we might be justified by faith." Rom. 3, 20; 7, 7.

5. THE CAUSE OF DIVISIONS IN CHRISTENDOM.

Since all non-Christian religions are man-made, having their source in man's endeavor to earn remission of sins by works, it is not strange that they should appear in many and diverse forms. The *Apology* writes: "And because no works pacify the conscience, new works, in addition to God's commands, were from time to time devised (the hypocrites nevertheless used to invent one work after another, one sacrifice after another, by a blind guess and in reckless wantonness, and all this without the Word and command of God, with wicked conscience, as we have seen in the Papacy)." (Art. III, 87.) This statement the *Apology* applies, first of all, to the papists, but it holds true with respect to all the religions of works. Just because the old works never pacify the guilty conscience, new works must be tried to effect a cure of the sin-troubled conscience; and so in all man-made religions there is an endless multiplication of "good works."

However, while divisions may thus be expected among the adherents of man-made religions, one preferring this good work and another that, so that each pagan sect has its own forms of worship as well as its own gods, there ought not to be any divisions among the adherents of the religion of faith, since this religion has only *one source of doctrine,* namely, Holy Scripture, which by its divine message of grace satisfies the human heart and appeases the human conscience by offering free remission of sins to all who believe in Christ. In other words, Christians having the one Word of God and holding to the one faith in Christ ought not to be split into factions, or parties.

In addition to this, Holy Scripture very sternly condemns all divisions, demanding that all believers should "endeavor to keep the unity of the Spirit in the bond of peace," Eph. 4, 3. St. Paul states the reason for this demand very clearly when he adds (vv. 4—6): "There is one body and one Spirit, even as ye are called in one hope of your calling; one Lord, one faith, one Baptism, one God and Father of all, who is above all and through all, and in you all." The divisions existing at Corinth so horrified Paul that he wrote: "Is Christ divided?" 1 Cor. 1, 13. All believers in Christ are equally members of His body, and so there is no cause whatever for any possible division in the Christian Church.

Yet such divisions exist, and they have existed since the first proclamation of the Christian faith, so that there always have been sects within the visible Church. These divisions have been variously explained by climatic or racial differences, under the plea that the peoples of the various zones are variously affected in their religious emotions. However, all these explanations are inadequate and even false; they are disproved by the simple fact that true believers in Christ who actually do keep the unity of the Spirit in the bond of peace are found the world over, no matter what kind of climatic or racial differences may exist among men.

No indeed! *The origin and the existence of divisions within Christendom* are to be attributed to more serious causes. According to Holy Scripture they *are due to false prophets and apostles,* who, unfaithful to the pure Word of God, in the name of the Christian religion disseminate their own perverse notions and discard the specific beliefs of Christianity, above all the fundamental doctrine of the Gospel that man is justified by grace, through faith, without the deeds of the Law. Such pseudapostles troubled even the churches founded by Paul and his colaborers. Rom. 16, 17: "I beseech you, brethren, mark them which cause divisions and offenses contrary to the doctrine which ye have learned; and avoid them." 1 Cor. 14, 37: "If any man think himself to be a prophet or spiritual, let him acknowledge that the things that I write unto you are the commandments of the Lord." Gal. 1, 6—8: "I marvel that ye are so soon removed from Him that called you into the grace of Christ unto another gospel. . . . But there be some that trouble you and would pervert the Gospel of Christ. But though we or an angel from heaven preach any other gospel unto you than that which we have preached unto you, let him be accursed." Phil. 3, 18: "For many walk of whom I have told you often, and now tell you even weeping, that they are the enemies of the Cross of Christ." The malicious attempts of such pseudapostles to pervert the Gospel of Christ, in particular the central doctrine of Christianity: salvation by grace alone, through faith in the vicarious atonement of the divine Redeemer, explain for all time the existence of divisions within Christendom.

The truth of this assertion becomes obvious when we examine the major divisions existing within the Christian Church: the Romanistic division, the Reformed division, various divisions within the Lutheran Church, and the modern rationalistic schools of theology with their innumerable ramifications.

The Roman Catholic Church, while in principle acknowledging the divine authority of Holy Scripture, nevertheless insists that the Bible must be interpreted according to the decisions of the Church, which, in the final analysis, are those of the Pope, who, as Luther points out in the *Smalcald Articles* (Part III, Art. VIII, 4), claims to have all rights within the shrine of his heart *(in scrinio pectoris)*. The result of such interpretation of Holy Scripture according to the sense of the "holy Mother Church" *(sancta mater ecclesia)* is that the cardinal article of the Christian faith, the doctrine of justification by grace alone, through faith in Christ, is not only rejected, but expressly anathematized, so that all true Christians who base their hope of salvation solely on Christ Jesus and not also on their works and on the merits of the saints are pronounced accursed. (*Council of Trent*, Sess. VI, Cans. 11. 12. 20.) Thus the Romanistic division, or sect, deprives the Christian religion of its specific character and content, and its whole theology is, as St. Paul styles it, "a religion of the flesh."

Romanism is built upon two fundamental errors, which Holy Scripture most stringently condemns: the infallibility of papal authority in religion and the meritoriousness of man's good works. It is above all these two errors that make the Church of Rome an antichristian sect.

The Reformed faction likewise acknowledges the divine authority of Holy Scripture in principle. In fact, over against Lutheranism the Reformed Church makes the claim that it is "more exclusively Scriptural" than the Lutheran Church, which, it says, has always been inclined to be "historical" and "conservative" in accord with the principle that church traditions and customs may be retained whenever they can be reconciled with the Word of God. But this distinction between Reformed and Lutheran theology is not based on facts. Reformed theology is not "more exclusively Scriptural" than Lutheran theology. On the contrary; while Romanistic theology demands the interpretation of Holy Scripture according to the *sancta mater ecclesia,* Reformed theology insists that the Bible must be interpreted according to human reason, or according to rationalistic axioms.

Thus, guided by rationalistic axioms, Reformed theology rejects, first of all, the doctrine of the means of grace, that is, the doctrine that the Word of God and the Sacraments are the divinely ordained means by which the Holy Gnost directly works regeneration, conversion, and sanctification. The doctrine of the means of grace is clearly stated in Holy Scripture, Rom. 1, 16; Titus 3, 5. 6; Acts 2, 38, etc. But in opposition to this Scriptural truth Reformed theology asserts the rationalistic axiom that "efficacious grace acts immediately." In other words, Reformed theology separates the sanctifying operations of the Holy Ghost from the means of grace under the plea that the Holy Spirit needs no vehicle by which to enter the hearts of men. (Zwingli, *Fidei Ratio;* Calvin, *Inst.,* IV, 14. 17; Hodge, *Syst. Theol.,* II, 684; etc.) It was this rationalistic axiom, consistently and strenuously applied, which caused the division between the Lutheran Church and the Reformed sects. Against Romanism, Luther had to defend the truth that the Word of God must not be perverted by the rationalistic views of the "Church"; against Zwinglianism he had to defend the truth that the Word of God must not be perverted by the rationalistic views of individual theologians.

Again, Reformed theology applies a rationalistic principle when it treats the doctrines of the person of Christ and of the

Lord's Supper. It emphatically denies the real presence of Christ's body in the Lord's Supper, maintaining that His presence in the Sacrament is only spiritual, that is, a presence effected by the faith of the believer. In other words, Christ is present in Holy Communion only to the extent that the believing communicant is united with Him by faith. This denial of the Real Presence is manifestly in opposition to the clear words of Christ's institution of the Holy Supper: "Take, eat; this is My body." It rests solely on the rationalistic principle that Christ's body, being a truly human body and having as such only a visible and local mode of presence *(visibilis et localis praesentia),* cannot be truly present in the Lord's Supper because it is locally enclosed in heaven. That is to say, moved by human reason, Reformed theology denies the illocal mode of presence of Christ's body, taught in such passages as John 20, 19: "When the doors were shut, . . . came Jesus and stood in the midst"; Luke 24, 31: "And He vanished out of their sight," etc.

Holy Scripture ascribes this illocal presence of Christ's human nature to Him by virtue of the personal union with its resulting communion of the two natures and the communication of attributes. But on the basis of reason Reformed theology denies the communion of the two natures of Christ and the communication of attributes. It asserts that "the finite is not capable of the infinite." From this rationalistic principle follows another, namely, that Christ's body cannot have an illocal presence and since the Ascension is therefore enclosed in heaven. The split between Zwinglianism and Lutheranism must be attributed to the maintenance and defense of these two rationalistic axioms on the part of the former. Luther was unable to extend to Zwingli the hand of Christian fellowship at Marburg (1529) because the latter showed a "different spirit," namely, the spirit of rationalism, which is diametrically opposed to the Christian faith.

Lastly, Calvinistic theology denies the universality of divine grace *(gratia universalis)* and teaches that the grace of God is particular *(gratia particularis), i. e.,* that it does not embrace all men, but the elect only, while all others are eternally predestinated to perdition. This doctrine is in direct opposition to Holy Scripture, which throughout affirms the universality of God's grace and, besides, asserts that the damnation of a sinner is not due to any failure on the part of God to provide for his salvation, John 1, 29; 3, 16 ff.; 1 John 1, 2; 1 Tim. 2, 4—6; etc. On what grounds,

then, does Reformed theology deny the universality of divine grace?
Here again it employs a rationalistic axiom as a premise on which
to rest its false doctrine. The rationalistic principle is: "We must
assume that the *result* is the interpretation of the purpose of God."
(Hodge, *Syst. Theol.*, II, 323.) Reformed theology reasons thus:
"Since actually not all are saved, we must assume that God did
not intend to save all." In this way Calvinistic theology rejects
Holy Scripture in favor of an argument drawn from reason, or
a rationalistic axiom; and on this departure from the Word of
God and its consequent enthronement of reason the Reformed faction is founded. Just as soon as its theology ceases to be rationalistic, it will also cease to be separatistic.

Within the pale of the Reformed denomination itself the strict
Calvinistic doctrine of the particularity of divine grace has been
emphatically denied by the Arminian party. Arminian theology
denied the Calvinistic error that God from eternity has predetermined a certain number of men to damnation. However, on the
other hand, Arminian theology erred by denying that grace alone
(sola gratia) saves sinners. Over against the doctrine of *sola
gratia,* so clearly taught by Luther, it reasoned that man's conversion and salvation depends, at least to some extent, on his cooperation and the exercise of his free will. Calvinism denies the *gratia
universalis,* while Arminianism denies the *sola gratia.* Thus also
Arminianism is a departure from Holy Scripture, which ascribes
man's conversion exclusively to divine monergism, Eph. 1, 19;
Phil. 1, 29; 1 Cor. 1, 23; 2, 14. Arminianism simply revamped
the error of Erasmus, who, Luther said, "seized him by the
throat" when he taught that man by nature has the ability to apply
himself to divine grace *(facultas se applicandi ad gratiam)* and
thus to cooperate in his conversion.

What has just been said of Arminianism applies also with
regard to synergism (an error taught within the Lutheran Church).
Synergism also denies the *sola gratia* and affirms, in opposition to
Holy Scripture, that man's conversion depends in part on his right
conduct, self-decision, lesser guilt, etc. Synergism was introduced
into Lutheran theology by Melanchthon, who maintained that there
are three causes of salvation: the Holy Ghost, the Word of God,
and man's assenting will. This doctrine is distinctly antichristian
and, if actually believed, will prevent the sinner's conversion, since
saving faith is engendered only in a contrite heart, which trusts
for salvation alone in divine grace. If synergists are actually saved,

it is only because they give up their false doctrine and cling solely to God's grace in Christ Jesus while smarting under the terrors of conscience *(terrores conscientiae)*. It is said of Melanchthon that he personally did not believe his false doctrine; for invariably when imploring God as a penitent sinner, he appealed exclusively to divine grace for salvation. Nevertheless this influential teacher, by promulgating his synergistic errors, caused divisions within the Lutheran Church that did incalculable harm and are still troubling the Church in many ways. Thus also within Lutheran Christendom divisions and offenses have been caused by manifest departures from Holy Scripture.

Finally we may speak of the divisions within Christendom that owe their origin to modern "scientific theology." Modern rationalistic theology, which dates back to Schleiermacher and Ritschl, denies the Christian doctrine that Holy Scripture is God's own, infallible Word and hence discards it as the only source and norm of doctrine. It thus rejects the only principle by which the Christian Church may preserve its inherent and essential unity; for the unity of the Church does not consist in external forms, but in doctrinal agreement, which must necessarily cease if Holy Scripture is rejected as the only norm of faith.

Modern theology suggests as norms of faith the "Christian experience," "Christian consciousness," "the regenerate heart," etc.; but all these "norms" in the final analysis coincide with carnal reason, which by its very nature is in opposition to divine truth. This is conclusively proved by the results, found everywhere where the "norms" just named have been adopted. Thus modern rationalistic theology unanimously denies the cardinal doctrine of justification by grace, through faith, teaching in its place the paganistic doctrine of salvation by work-righteousness. Again, it denies the fundamental Christian doctrine of the divine inspiration of Holy Scripture and consequently also its inerrancy. Thus it rejects the two distinctive articles of the Christian faith and causes divisions and offenses contrary to the teachings of Christ and His apostles. The Christian Church demands of modern theology that it must surrender its opposition to Holy Scripture as the only source and norm of faith and to the vicarious atonement of Christ as the only means of a sinner's justification. And that is Christ's own demand, John 8, 31. 32; 1 Pet. 4, 11.

The point, then, is clear: Divisions within Christendom owe their origin and existence to actual departure from Holy Scripture and its divine doctrines. Wherever they exist, they may be traced to the perversion and rejection of divine truth and must be condemned as the vicious work of Satan and his false prophets.

The confessional Lutheran Church itself has been styled a "sect" within Christendom by non-Lutheran writers. But no charge is more unjust than that. The charge is due to a complete misunderstanding of the Reformation. The Lutheran Reformation was not an effort to found a new sect, or division, within Christendom, but to restore the corrupted Church to its ancient apostolic purity in doctrine and practise. The confessional Lutheran Church is therefore the ancient Church of Christ and His apostles, purified from the corruptions of papistical errors and restored on the basis of Holy Scripture. Its character is truly ecumenical; for its doctrines are not peculiar views and tenets, distinct from those of the Apostolic Church, but the very doctrines around which the ancient ecumenical creeds of Christendom center. Its theology is that of the Holy Bible, and of the Bible alone; its doctrine is the divine truth of God's Word. *The Lutheran Church is therefore the orthodox visible Church of Christ on earth.* This is both its claim and its glory, and it challenges every charge of sectarianism made against it.

We freely admit of course that also within the Lutheran Church divisions have been caused by departures, both in doctrine and in practise, from Holy Scripture and from the Lutheran Confessions. Hence, when we use the term *Lutheran Church,* we do not include those divisions, or parties, but refer exclusively to that Lutheran Church or those Lutheran churches which are thoroughly Scriptural and thoroughly Lutheran both in doctrine and in practise. In other words, the Lutheran Church is that Church which stands four-square on the principles of the Reformation.

With regard to *Christian unity* it must be emphatically stated that this is not the work of man, but of divine grace, John 17, 11—15. 20. 21; Ps. 86, 11; etc. Human influence, wisdom, and ingenuity do not suffice to preserve the unity of faith or doctrine. That precious boon is the gift of the Holy Spirit, who graciously bestows and maintains it through the Word of God. For this reason all Christians must diligently pray for the unity of the Spirit and zealously use the means of grace, by which alone it is preserved. For wherever the Word of God is despised or rejected, no true unity of faith can prevail. Christians remain united in the faith only as long as they stand united upon God's pure Word.

6. CHRISTIANITY THE ABSOLUTE RELIGION.

The Christian religion is the absolute religion, inasmuch as it is absolutely perfect, neither requiring, nor being capable of, improvement or development. It is God-given (θεόσδοτος) and therefore precisely as God would have it to accomplish its beneficent purpose of saving sinners. When we ascribe to the Christian religion perfection or absoluteness, we do not mean to say that it is a "logically complete whole" *(ein logisch vollkommenes Ganzes)* or a logically complete and perfect system, in which there are no missing links of thought. The Christian's knowledge, the apostle says, and he includes his own, is but fragmentary. 1 Cor. 13, 12: "Now I know in part." What Christianity knows of divine wisdom through revelation is only a part of the unsearchable knowledge of God.

Again, the Christian religion is not perfect, or absolute, in the sense of constituting the best system of morality *(die vollkommenste Moral)*, although that, of course, is true. The moral theology of Holy Scripture is indeed perfect, for it centers in, and aims at, perfect love of God and the neighbor, Matt. 22, 37—40. Both its demand and its goal are perfect love, Matt. 5, 48: "Be ye therefore perfect, even as your Father which is in heaven is perfect." But this perfect morality does not constitute the essence of the Christian religion; it is rather the effect, or fruit, of the Christian faith, which the Holy Spirit implants in the human heart through the means of grace, or, as we may say briefly, it is the result of Christianity, not Christianity itself, 1 John 4, 9—21; Rom. 12, 1.

Nevertheless the Christian religion is absolute, that is, altogether perfect and unsurpassable. There are two reasons for this. In the first place, the Christian religion is not a moral code, teaching men how they may reconcile God by good works, but it is divine faith in the amazing fact that God through Christ "reconciled the world unto Himself, not imputing their trespasses unto them," 2 Cor. 5, 19. In that sense the Christian religion is absolute, that is, perfect and unsurpassable; for through the Gospel of Christ it offers to sinful mankind a perfect and incomparable reconciliation, effected through the vicarious atonement of the Son of God, the divine Redeemer of the world, who for us and in our stead satisfied the demands of divine justice *(active obedience)* and paid the penalty of sin *(passive obedience)*, Gal. 4, 4. 5; 3, 13; Is. 53; 2 Cor. 5, 21. Every sinner who believes this reconciliation, or forgiveness of sin, is justified, or declared righteous, by grace, without the deeds of the Law, Acts 26, 18; Luke 24, 46. 47; Rom. 10, 17; 1 Cor. 2, 4. 5; Rom. 3, 28; 5, 1. That is the glorious gift which Christianity freely offers to all sinners. It announces to lost mankind .that God by grace imputes to sinful man, who in himself is ungodly and condemned, the perfect righteousness of Christ through faith or that He covers the unrighteousness of the penitent believer with the perfect righteousness of His divine Son, Jesus Christ. Rom. 4, 5: "To him that worketh not, but believeth on Him that justifieth the ungodly, his faith is counted for righteousness." 1 John 2, 2: "He [Christ] is the Propitiation for our sins, and not for ours only, but also for the sins of the whole world." That is the wonderful absoluteness, or perfection, of the Christian religion: it proffers perfect reconciliation and salvation by grace and puts the believer into perfect and complete possession of God's choicest gifts — His divine grace, His complete pardon, His peace, which passes all understanding, in short, spiritual and eternal life. Thus Christianity fully accomplishes what religion should accomplish — it reunites sinful mankind with the holy God and restores to him all he has lost through sin. Col. 2, 10—14: "And ye are complete" (perfect, $\pi\epsilon\pi\lambda\eta\varrho\omega\mu\acute{\epsilon}\nu\upsilon\iota$), "in Him," etc.

It goes without saying that the Christian religion is absolute, or perfect, only if it is preserved in its purity, that is to say, if its character as a religion of grace and faith is fully maintained, or if its central doctrine of justification by grace, through faith in the vicarious atonement of Christ, is retained unadulterated. If this chief doctrine of the Christian religion is perverted or removed, then Christianity becomes dechristianized, a neopagan religion, unworthy of the name it bears, and incapable of saving sinners. Thus Romanism, which teaches justification through "infused grace" *(gratia infusa)* and consequently by "good works" *(Council of Trent,* Sess. VI, Cans. 11. 12. 20), paganizes Christianity in its central teaching, and the result is that the sinner fails to obtain divine pardon and, besides, is burdened with the curse of uncertainty *(monstrum incertitudinis)* as to his state of grace. Gal. 5, 4: "Christ is become of no effect unto you whosoever of you are justified by the Law; ye are fallen from grace."

Similarly the doctrine of justification by grace, through faith in Christ, is corrupted by the rationalistic Protestant theologians of to-day, who reject the Scriptural doctrine of Christ's vicarious atonement and in its place inculcate their own erroneous "theories of atonement." They, too, deny the central Gospel truth that men are justified by faith alone, and through their man-made theories of atonement they paganize the Christian religion. (*The Moral Example Theory:* Christ's death should induce men to repent, reform and mend their conduct. *The Governmental Theory:* Christ died simply to show erring man that sin is displeasing in God's sight, since God's government of the world necessitates such manifestation of wrath against sin. *The Declaratory Theory:* Christ died to show how much God loves man, etc.) The central article of Christianity is likewise denied and perverted by all Pelagians, Arminians, and synergists, who maintain that man's salvation depends, at least in part, on his good conduct and works. The Christian religion, if so perverted, is deprived of its very essence and is therefore no longer absolute, or perfect, since in its paganized form it is unable to save sinners.

In the second place, the Christian religion is absolute, that is, perfect and unsurpassable, because its source and norm is not the fallible word of erring men, but the infallible Word of the inerrant God, as this is set forth in Holy Scripture, John 10, 35; 2 Tim. 3, 15—17; 1 Pet. 1, 10—12; Eph. 2, 20. Since Holy Scripture is divinely inspired, it is the absolute divine truth, John 17, 17; and the Christian religion, which is drawn from this absolute truth, is the only true religion, whereas all other religions, falsely so called, are in fact not religions at all. This fact must be given great emphasis to-day; for at present unionistic and syncretistic tendencies are very strong even in Christian circles, and norms outside of, and contrary to, Holy Scripture are so readily adopted. *Holy Scripture is the only norm of faith,* and only that is true religion which is true Scripture-teaching.

This truth we stoutly affirm not only against Modernism, which rejects Holy Scripture altogether, but also against modern rationalizing theology, which establishes as norms, besides Holy Scripture, such things as "Christian consciousness," "Christian conviction," "Christian experience," etc., and no less against Romanism, which declares tradition to be a source and rule of faith. In short, all who desire to maintain the Christian religion as the absolute religion must adhere to both the doctrine of justification by grace, through faith in the vicarious atonement of Christ, and to the doctrine that Holy Scripture, as the inspired, inerrant Word of God, is the only source and standard of faith. The Christian religion is absolute only if it is presented and taught as God Himself has given it to us in His Word.

The Christian religion was given to sinful mankind immediately after the Fall and was then, as it is now, the only absolute
religion because it alone offered to, and bestowed upon, men salvation from sin through faith in the divinely appointed Redeemer
of the world, Gen. 3, 15; Acts 10, 43. Throughout the Old Testament the Gospel of Christ was proclaimed no less than in the
New Testament, John 5, 39; 8, 56; Acts 10, 43, although in the
New Testament the preaching of the Gospel is clearer and more
complete than in the Old Testament. When Holy Scripture speaks
of the abrogation of the Old and the institution of the New Testament, this does not refer to the preaching of the Gospel, which
is the essence of Christianity, but to the Mosaic covenant of the
Law, which has been abolished by the coming of Christ, Jer. 31,
31—34; Heb. 8, 6—13; Gal. 3, 17 ff.; Col. 2, 16. Thus, while in
the Old Testament divine revelation was progressive in the sense
that the message of Christ's coming and redemption was announced
ever more clearly and fully, the religion which God gave to
Adam and Eve after the Fall was from the very beginning absolute, that is, perfect and complete, because it was adequate to accomplish the salvation of sinners. The claim that the Old Testament presents to us essentially different religions, such as the
patriarchal, the Mosaic, the prophetic, etc., is unfounded and contradicts the incontestable statements of Holy Scripture, Acts
15, 10. 11; Rom. 4, 3—6; Heb. 11. Christ was always the only
Savior of all sinners, and no one has ever been saved except
through faith in Him. Acts 4, 12: "Neither is there salvation in
any other; for there is none other name under heaven given
among men whereby we must be saved."

In view of the fact that the Christian religion is the only true
religion, it is incorrect to speak of it as "the highest religion" or
"the most perfect religion" or "the climax of all religions," etc.
Such superlatives express only a difference in degree, whereas the
difference between Christianity and all other religions so called is
one of kind. Christianity is a God-made religion; all others are
man-made. For this reason it is objectionable also to say that
Christianity offers to man "the highest satisfaction." As a matter
of fact, Christianity alone offers satisfaction to sinful men, since it
alone conveys and seals to them the grace of God, forgiveness of
sins, and life eternal. The character of absoluteness belongs only
to the religion of Jesus Christ.

When the question is considered as to what constitutes the

essential difference between the Old and the New Testament, we must seek the difference not in the religion itself, but in the accidental feature of greater clearness and fulness. Essentially the two are the same. The doctrinal content does not differ; for in both we find the same Moral Law, and the same Gospel-message, that sinners are saved alone by God's grace in His Son, our Savior. This is attested by Christ Himself, who not only declared the Old Testament to be the divine truth, John 5, 45—47; 10, 35; 5, 39, but also affirmed that He is the Christ of the Old Testament, Luke 24, 25—27. Our divine Lord became incarnate not to teach a new religion, but to fulfil the Old Testament prophecies concerning Himself and by His holy suffering and death to secure the salvation promised by the prophets, Matt. 5, 17—19; Rom. 3, 28—31; Col. 2, 10—14. As Christ, so also the apostles, especially St. Paul, declared the Old Testament Scriptures to be able to make believers wise unto salvation through faith which is in Christ Jesus, 2 Tim. 3, 15—17. Likewise St. Paul expressly teaches that the doctrine of justification by grace, through faith, is not a new doctrine, but the doctrine proclaimed by the prophets in the Old Testament and believed by all Old Testament believers, Rom. 3, 21. 22; chap. 4. From all this it is obvious that the religion of the Old Testament is essentially the Christian religion, which by its very nature is perfect and unsurpassable, or the absolute religion of God.

7. THE CHRISTIAN RELIGION AND CHRISTIAN THEOLOGY.

There are theologians who suggest the following distinction between Christian religion and Christian theology. They say that the Christian religion in its subjective sense is the knowledge of God which is possessed by every Christian believer, while Christian theology in its subjective sense is the knowledge of God which is possessed by the official teachers of the Church. Rightly understood, this distinction may be accepted; for Holy Scripture, while teaching that all believers possess knowledge of God, emphasizes the fact that the official teachers of the Church must possess knowledge of God in a higher degree, John 6, 45; 1 Cor. 12, 29; 1 Tim. 3, 2; 2 Tim. 2, 2. In these passages it is taught that, while believers are "all taught of God," yet they are not "all teachers" and that bishops, or ministers, must be "apt to teach" and must therefore have the doctrines of God's Word committed unto them in such a way that they "shall be able to teach others." — Nevertheless it must be maintained that there is no essential difference

between religion and theology. Both have the same principle
(principium cognoscendi), or source, namely, Holy Scripture, and
both are received in one and the same manner, namely, through
faith in the Word of God. John 8, 31. 32: "If ye continue in My
Word, then are ye My disciples indeed; and ye shall know the
truth."

We hold, then, that both the *religious* and the *theological*
knowledge are fundamentally the same and are obtained by the
same method, namely, through the believing study of, and prayerful
meditation upon, God's Word. Whatever is not taken from, or
whatever goes beyond, Holy Scripture is neither religion nor
theology, but human speculation. *Quod non est biblicum, non
est theologicum.* This truth must be held over against all rationalistic theologians, who assert that Christian theology is something
that lies beyond the Christian religion as basically different from it,
and in particular, that the Christian theologian intellectually comprehends the mysteries of faith, whereas the ordinary Christian
believer merely accepts them by faith. That such views are
disastrous both to religion and theology requires no further proof.
As a matter of fact, Christian theology is not a speculative system
of philosophy, the substance of which lies within human intellectual comprehension; but it is "the wisdom of God in a mystery,"
1 Cor. 2, 7. (The meaning of Paul's statement is evidently: "In
speaking the wisdom of God, we proclaim a mystery.") For this
reason a childlike faith in God's Word is essential no less to the
Christian theologian than to the ordinary Christian believer.
A theologian is a Christian theologian only inasmuch as he implicitly believes in Christ and unconditionally accepts His Word.

8. CHRISTIAN THEOLOGY.

Etymologically considered, the term *theology* may be defined
as "the Word concerning God" (λόγος περὶ ϑεοῦ). In the subjective sense the term denotes the knowledge of God *(Gottesgelahrt-
heit)* as it inheres in the theologian; in its objective sense it designates the doctrine concerning God as it is presented in a book or
treatise. (Cp. the meaning of psychology, physiology, biology,
geology, etc.) Thomas Aquinas summarizes the meaning and
function of theology as follows: *"Theologia a Deo docetur, Deum
docet et ad Deum ducit."* The name *God* in connection with λόγος,
however, always denotes the object, so that theology in its objective sense is properly the doctrine which teaches God *(Deum docet).*

The term *theology* in its common significance *(usus loquendi)* does not occur in Holy Scripture. It is therefore a *"vox non ἔγγραφος, sed ἄγραφος, quamvis non ἀντίγραφος,"* that is to say, a term used not in, but outside Scripture, yet one that is not against Scripture. The heading of St. John's *Revelation*, Ἀποκάλυψις Ἰωάννου τοῦ θεολόγου, as Gerhard correctly points out, was not selected by the author of that book, but was added by later copyists. This fact proves that the term *theology* was widely used already by the earliest Christian writers and was quite generally understood also in its specific meaning. However, the term *theology* was used also by non-Christian authors, and this fact must not surprise us, since man by nature has a certain knowledge of God, the divine Law being inscribed in his heart, Rom. 1 and 2. Pagan writers applied the term *theology* to the doctrine of God as this was taught by their poets and philosophers, whom some styled *theologians*. Thus Aristotle says of Thales and of the philosophers before Thales, who speculated on the origin of things, that they *theologized* (θεολογήσαντες). Cicero declares expressly: *"Principio Ioves tres numerant, qui* THEOLOGI *nominantur."* (Cp. Aristotle, *Metaph.,* I, 3; Cicero, *De Natura Deorum,* III, 21.)

Nevertheless the term *theology* has not always been used in the same sense. This varying use of the term need not give us any concern since the word itself does not occur in Holy Scripture and may therefore be employed in sacred theology in different significations, as long as it is not made to represent something that in itself is condemned by God's Word. The concepts which it is made to express should themselves be Scriptural. The term is used correctly and in accordance with Holy Scripture if it denotes —

1. The particular knowledge of God which those possess who are called to administer the public ministry, in other words, the special knowledge of pastors and teachers of the Church, 1 Tim. 3, 2;

2. The particular knowledge of God which is demanded of those who are called to prepare Christian ministers and teachers for their high calling, or the special knowledge of theological professors, 2 Tim. 2, 2;

3. The general knowledge of God which all true believers possess, especially the experienced Christians, whose knowledge of spiritual matters has been deepened by much prayerful meditation and practical experience in their profession of Christ, so that they

themselves, in their limited sphere, are competent to teach others, 1 Pet. 3, 15; Col. 3, 16;

4. The special knowledge of certain parts of the Christian doctrine, in particular, the doctrine of the deity of Christ and of the Trinity. Thus Gregory Nazianzen (died ca. 390) was called ὁ θεόλογος because he defended the deity of Christ with special distinction. And Basilius applied the term *theology* to the doctrine of the Holy Trinity. (Cp. Pieper, *Christliche Dogmatik,* Vol. I, p. 47.)

As the term is applied generally, it denotes in its abstract sense, or objectively, either the entire Christian doctrine *(usus generalis)* or the particular doctrine concerning God *(usus specialis).*

If the term *theology* is employed in the above significations, it is used in conformity with Holy Scripture and therefore correctly. But if it is applied to any doctrine that goes beyond Scripture or to a system of doctrine that is not exclusively based on Scripture, but rather on "Christian consciousness," "Christian experience," "Christian tradition," etc., it is misapplied. For whatever is not drawn from Scripture is not theology at all, but human speculation, and that after all is nothing else than error and delusion, 1 Tim. 6, 3. 4: "knowing nothing."

In this treatise we use the term *theology* both subjectively, or concretely, to denote the spiritual ability (ἱκανότης, *habitus*) to teach and defend the Word of God, in short, to administer the functions of the Christian ministry in the true Scriptural manner (2 Cor. 3, 5. 6), and objectively, or abstractly, for the Christian doctrine, either in whole or in part, presented either orally or in writing, 2 Tim. 1, 13. Both uses are Scriptural. Subjective, or concrete, theology is the spiritual habitude of the Christian teacher; objective, or abstract, theology is the product, or result, of this ability. Also, we hold that the first meaning of the term is the primary, since theology must first be found in the soul of a person before that person can teach and present it either by word or in writing. If we call the product of the inherent ability *theology,* this is done by way of metonymy, the effect being named after the cause. For the Christian theologian this distinction is of paramount importance because it constantly reminds him that studying theology means not simply the intellectual apprehension of a number of facts, but the true regeneration, conversion, and sanctification of his own heart, from which his whole ministerial service must flow.

Dr. A. L. Graebner, in his *Outlines of Doctrinal Theology* (p. 1), defines theology in its subjective, or concrete, sense as follows: "Theology is a practical habitude of the mind, comprising the knowledge and acceptance of divine truth, together with an aptitude to instruct others toward such knowledge and acceptance and to defend such truth against its adversaries." Theology in its objective, or abstract, sense he defines (p. 2) as "an oral or written exhibition of the truths, doctrines, principles, etc., by virtue of the knowledge, acceptance, maintenance, and practical application of which a theologian is a theologian."

9. THEOLOGY FURTHER CONSIDERED AS A HABITUDE.

Theology as a habitude, or ability, is described in all those Scripture-passages which depict the character and qualifications of the true Christian minister, who, in the sense of Holy Scripture, is a true theologian, possessing the ability (*ἱκανότης,* sufficiency) to administer the functions of the ministry in the divinely appointed manner. On the basis of Holy Scripture we may therefore describe the theological habitude as follows: —

a. The theological habitude is a *spiritual* habitude *(habitus spiritualis, supernaturalis),* that is to say, an ability which is implanted in the soul not by natural gifts, but by the Holy Ghost. It presupposes personal faith in Christ's vicarious atonement and consequently the regeneration, or conversion, of the theologian. Unbelieving ministers or teachers do not deserve the name of theologian; and in the sense of Holy Scripture they are not theologians, though they may have apprehended the doctrines of the Word of God intellectually and be able to present them clearly and correctly. In other words, there is no *theologia irregenitorum,* or theology of the unregenerate, since the souls of the unconverted and unbelieving are not inhabited and actuated by the Holy Ghost, but by the "prince of this world," that is, Satan. Eph. 2, 2: "Wherein in time past ye walked according to the course of this world, according to the prince of the power of the air, the spirit that now worketh in the children of disobedience." Holy Scripture always describes a true minister of Christ as a penitent, believing child of God, who ascribes to divine grace both his sufficiency and his call into the ministry. 2 Cor. 3, 5: "Not that we are sufficient of ourselves to think anything as of ourselves; but our sufficiency is of God, who also hath made us able ministers of the New Testament." 2 Tim. 2, 1 ff.: "Be strong in the grace that is in Christ

Jesus," etc. A true minister of Christ, or theologian, is therefore a sanctified believer. 1 Tim. 3, 2 ff.: "A bishop must be blameless, . . . of good behavior, . . . apt to teach," etc.

Unbelieving and unregenerate ministers hold their sacred office not by God's will, but only by His permission. Although their personal unbelief does not render inefficacious the Word they preach and the Sacraments they administer, provided they preach the Word of God in truth and purity and administer the Sacraments according to Christ's institution, yet the incumbency and administration of the sacred office by hypocrites greatly dishonors the Lord and is an offense to the Church and a perpetual menace to the faith and piety of their hearers. Jer. 14, 14—16: "The prophets prophesy lies in My name. I sent them not, neither have I commanded them. . . . By sword and famine shall those prophets be consumed. And the people to whom they prophesy shall be cast out in the streets." Cp. also Jer. 23, 11—32; Ezek. 13, 3—9; etc.

It was this important truth, namely, that a true theologian is a sincere believer, that prompted our dogmaticians to describe theology, first of all, as a *habitus spiritualis vel supernaturalis* (θεόσδοτος), conferred by the Holy Spirit through the Word of God. Baier thus writes (I, 69): "Theology is by its very nature a supernatural habitude, acquired not by any powers of our own, but by the powers of grace through the operation of the Holy Ghost." He adds that all theology which is not wrought by the Holy Ghost is so called only in an improper sense. *(Ita nonnisi* AEQUIVOCE *dicta theologia est.)* So also Luther writes: "A doctor of Holy Scripture no one can make for you except the Holy Spirit from heaven, as Christ says, John 6, 45: 'And they shall be all taught of God.'" (St. L., X, 339.) The spiritual habitude of theology implies also faith in Holy Scripture as the divinely inspired, infallible Word of God; and this faith, too, is the work and gift of the Holy Ghost.

b. The theological habitude further includes the ability to refrain from all human opinions and thoughts on God and divine things, to draw all doctrines from Holy Scripture, and thus to teach nothing but God's Word. John 8, 31. 32: "If ye continue in My Word, then are ye My disciples indeed." St. Paul writes to Timothy, 1 Tim. 6, 3. 4: "If any man teach otherwise and consent not to wholesome words, even the words of our Lord Jesus Christ, and to the doctrine which is according to godliness, he is proud, knowing nothing, but doting about questions and strifes of words."

That the "words of our Lord Jesus Christ" are not merely the words which our Savior Himself spoke during His sojourn on earth, but all the inspired writings of the prophets and the apostles, is proved by various passages, John 17, 20; 1 Pet. 1, 10—12; Eph. 2, 20; etc. These passages disqualify and bar all teachers of the Church who, while rejecting Holy Scripture as the sole source and norm of faith, draw their doctrines from false sources, such as "Christian traditions," the "regenerate heart," "Christian consciousness," "private revelations," "Christian experience," etc. Luther, in his exposition of Jer. 23, 16, correctly remarks: "Behold, all prophets who do not preach out of the mouth of God deceive, and God forbid that we should hear them." (St. L., XIX, 821.)

c. The theological habitude includes, moreover, the ability to teach the whole Word of God as it is set forth in Holy Scripture. In order to attest his ministerial faithfulness, St. Paul said to the elders of Ephesus, Acts 20, 27: "I have not shunned to declare unto you all the counsel of God." Christian ministers must proclaim the whole Word of God in its truth and purity to be "pure from the blood of all men," as St. Paul witnesses concerning himself, Acts 20, 26: "Wherefore I take you to record this day that I am pure from the blood of all men." It is for this very reason that the apostle so earnestly admonishes Timothy, 1 Tim. 4, 16: "Take heed unto thyself and unto the doctrine; continue in them; for in doing this, thou shalt both save thyself and them that hear thee." A Christian teacher should therefore "take heed unto the doctrine," study it with great zeal and diligence, preach it fully and without admixture of human opinion, and thus prove himself faithful by presenting to his hearers all the doctrines of God's Word. Matt. 28, 20: "Teaching them to observe all things whatsoever I have commanded you." 1 Cor. 4, 2: "Moreover, it is required in stewards that a man be found faithful." Jer. 48, 10: "Cursed be he that doeth the work of the Lord deceitfully" (marginal note: "negligently"). Such ability, however, is not of man's own power, but of God.

d. The theological habitude implies also the ability to convince the gainsayers. Titus 1, 9: "Holding fast the faithful Word as he hath been taught that he may be able by sound doctrine both to exhort and to convince the gainsayers." Holy Scripture never prohibits polemics, but rather commands it, since controversy, if carried on in the commendable spirit of Christian charity, is never destructive, but highly profitable to the Church. Every kind of polemics that is prompted by, and exhibits, a carnal, factious spirit is, of course, an abuse of Christian controversy and is therefore forbidden. Titus 3, 9: "But avoid foolish questions and genealogies and contentions and strivings about the Law; for they are unprofitable and vain." 2 Cor. 10, 3: "For though we walk in the flesh, we do not war after the flesh." Again, true polemics requires not only the refutation of false doctrine, but also the clear and Scriptural presentation of the true doctrine in order that the opponent may be won over to the divine truth; for this, after all, is the final purpose of all true polemics, that falsehood may be eliminated and divine truth be received. Toleration of false doctrine within the Church is unfaithfulness to God's Word and therefore unfaithfulness to God Himself, who has entrusted His truth to the care of His Church, Matt. 28, 19. 20.

For this reason also the ministry of Christ and His apostles was largely spent in polemics; for while they were teaching the truth, they always testified against error. Matt. 7, 15: "Beware of false prophets, which come to you in sheep's clothing; but inwardly they are ravening wolves." Rom. 16, 17: "I beseech you, brethren, mark them which cause divisions and offenses contrary to the doctrine which ye have learned; and avoid them." False doctrine is so pernicious and so displeasing to God that He demands not only the refutation of all error, but also the excommunication of the errorist in case he proves himself a heretic. Rom. 16, 17: "And avoid them." 2 John 10: "If there come any unto you and bring not this doctrine, receive him not into your house, neither bid him Godspeed." Clearly and emphatically Holy Scripture rejects every form of syncretism, or unionism.

No matter what the motives may be that induce men to depart from Holy Scripture and to cause divisions and offenses contrary to the truth of God's Word, they must all be condemned as carnal and sinful. There are no "noble" motives for causing divisions within the Church; they are all equally reprehensible and ungodly. Holy Scripture describes them as follows: belly service, Rom. 16, 18; pride, 1 Tim. 6, 4; the inordinate desire for honor, John 5, 44; unwillingness to suffer for Christ's sake, Gal. 6, 12; envy, Matt. 27, 18; perversity, 1 Tim. 6, 4; John 16, 3; 1 Tim. 1, 13; the personal vanity and viciousness of theologians, 2 Tim. 3, 1—9; etc. "Many heresies have arisen in the Church only from the *hatred of the teachers*." (*Apology,* III, 121.) . Divisions within the Church are therefore not pleasing to God, nor do they exist by the will of God, but they are God's just punishment-upon those who do not love the truth. 2 Thess. 2, 10—12 : "Because they received not the love of the truth that they might be saved, for this cause God shall send them strong delusion that they should believe a lie, that they all might be damned who believed not the truth, but had pleasure in unrighteousness."

e. The theological habitude lastly embraces the ability to suffer for the sake of Christ and His Word. 2 Tim. 2, 3 : "Thou therefore endure hardness as a good soldier of Jesus Christ"; v. 9 : "Wherein I suffer trouble as an evil-doer, even unto bonds. But the Word of God is not bound." The suffering of Christians in general and of Christian ministers in particular is caused by the world's hatred of, and contempt for, God's Word. 1 Cor. 1, 23 : "We preach Christ Crucified, unto the Jews a stumbling-block and unto the Greeks foolishness." The result of the world's antagonism to the Gospel of Christ is described by our Savior as follows: "Ye shall be hated of all nations for My name's sake," Matt. 24, 9. Unwillingness to suffer for the Gospel's sake leads to compromises with error, to the denial of divine truth, and in the end to apostasy from divine grace. 2 Tim. 2, 12 : "If we suffer, we shall also reign with Him; if we deny Him, He also will deny us." Unless the Christian, and above all the Christian theologian, is ready for Christ's sake to renounce ease and friendship, to take upon himself loss of honor and property, and even to lay down his life for the sake of divine truth, he cannot serve his Master as this is required of him.

The theological habitude (*habitus practicus* ϑεόσδοτος), then, is the ability, divinely bestowed, to teach the pure and unadulterated Word of God, to declare the whole counsel of God unto salvation, to oppose and refute false doctrine, and to suffer for Christ's sake all the consequences which the proclamation of the Word of God entails.

10. THEOLOGY CONSIDERED AS DOCTRINE.

As theology in its subjective sense is the habitude, or ability, to teach the Word of God as set forth in Holy Scripture in all its truth and purity, so Christian theology in its objective sense, or conceived as doctrine, is nothing more and nothing less than the true and pure presentation of the doctrine of Holy Scripture. 1 Pet. 4, 11 : "If any man speak, let him speak as the oracles of God." Titus 2, 7—10 : "In doctrine showing uncorruptness, gravity, sincerity, sound speech, that cannot be condemned, . . .

showing all good fidelity, that they may adorn the doctrine of God, our Savior, in all things." The claim of being a Christian theologian may be properly made only by him who teaches nothing but Scripture doctrine.

This doctrine, however, is not drawn or developed from human reason, but is taken in all its parts solely from Holy Scripture. The function of the Christian theologian therefore consists merely in grouping in distinct paragraphs and chapters and under proper heads the various teachings which Holy Scripture inculcates in its several passages on one given subject. If he applies synthesis and analysis, it is merely in the formal arrangement of the various Scripture doctrines. So far as the doctrines themselves are concerned, he allows them to stand, neither adding thereto nor taking away from them, no matter whether they appear consistent with reason and experience or not. In this way the Christian theologian secures his "system of doctrine" or his "dogmatic theology."

In accord with this principle the Lutheran theologian Pfeiffer writes (*Thes. Herm.,* p. 5): "Positive theology [dogmatic theology], rightly estimated, is nothing else than Holy Scripture itself, arranged under proper heads in clear order; wherefore no member whatsoever, not even the least, must be found in that body of doctrine which cannot be supported from Holy Scripture, rightly understood." (Baier, I, 43. 76.) Luther very aptly calls all true theologians "catechumens and disciples of the prophets, because they repeat and preach only what they have heard and learned from the prophets and apostles." (St. L., III, 1890.) This faithful repetition *(Nachsagen)* of the teachings of the prophets and apostles by the Christian theologian is to Luther a matter of such grave concern that he writes: "In the Church no other doctrine should be taught or heard than the pure Word of God, that is, Holy Scripture; otherwise both teachers and hearers shall be damned." (Cp. Pieper, *Christl. Dogmatik,* I, p. 56.) The same truth is expressed in the axiom *Quod non est biblicum, non est theologicum.*

The Christian theologian must therefore exclude from his system of doctrine all opinions and speculations of men, and he must teach nothing but God's own immutable truth and doctrine *(doctrina divina)* as it is exhibited in Holy Scripture *(doctrina e Scriptura Sacra hausta).* This demand is made by God Himself. Col. 2, 8: "Beware lest any man spoil you through philosophy and vain deceit, after the tradition of men, after the rudiments of the world, and not after Christ." And this divine demand pertains not merely to the chief doctrines, on which man's salvation depends directly, but to all teachings of Holy Scripture, Matt. 28, 20: "Teaching them to observe all things whatsoever I have commanded you." In whatever matter Holy Scripture has definitely spoken the Christian theologian must suppress his own views, opinions, and speculations and adhere unwaveringly to the divine truths revealed in Holy Scripture. In no case is he permitted to inject into the body of divine truth his own figments and fabrications, and at no time must he allow his reason the prerogative of doubt, criticism, or denial, but every thought must everywhere be brought into captivity to the obedience of Christ, 2 Cor. 10, 5. That is the demand which God Himself makes on all who would serve Him as theologians; in every instance they are to attest and proclaim His Word and not their own.

All teachers of the Church who refuse to do this are not Christian theologians, but false prophets, against whose pernicious work God warns His saints. Jer. 23, 16: "Hearken not unto the words of the prophets that prophesy unto you. . . . They speak a vision of their own heart and not out of the mouth of the Lord." And in the New Testament this warning is reiterated with no less emphasis, 1 Tim. 6, 4; 2 John 8—11; Rom. 16, 17; etc. Luther's insistence on faithfulness in teaching God's Word is well known. He writes: "If any one wishes to preach, let him keep silence with respect to his own words." "Here in the Church he should not speak anything but the Word of this generous Host; otherwise it is not the true Church. Therefore he must say, 'God speaks.'"

Emphasizing the great truth that all doctrine taught in the Church must be *divine* doctrine, our Lutheran dogmaticians asserted that all theology proclaimed by the Christian theologian must be *ectypal theology,* or *derived theology* (*theologia* ἔκτυπος), that is, a reprint, or reproduction, of *archetypal theology* (*theologia* ἀρχέτυπος), or *original theology,* as it is originally in God Himself. Hollaz explains these terms as follows: "Archetypal theology is the knowledge which God has of Himself and which in Him is the model of that other theology which is communicated to intelligent creatures. Ectypal theology is the knowledge of God and divine things communicated to intelligent creatures by God after the pattern of His own theology." (*Doctr. Theol.,* p. 16.)

Modern rationalistic theology has rejected this distinction as useless and misleading; in reality, however, it is most profitable, since it expresses the Scriptural truth that God's ministers must speak only what He Himself teaches in His Word. Moreover, the distinction is Scriptural; for it declares very clearly that all true knowledge of God inheres originally and essentially in Him and that it is by divine grace that the knowledge which is necessary for man's salvation has been revealed by Him to His prophets and apostles. Matt. 11, 27: "No man knoweth the Son but the Father, neither knoweth any man the Father save the Son and he to whomsoever the Son will reveal Him." To ectypal theology belongs also the natural knowledge of God, which man derives either from the Law written in his heart or from the works of God, Rom. 1, 19 ff.; 2, 14. 15. Also this natural knowledge of God man owes to God's revelation of Himself, Acts 14, 17; 17, 26. 27. Nevertheless this natural knowledge of God, while true and useful in its place, is not sufficient to save sinners, since it does not include the Gospel of God's grace in Christ Jesus. For this reason the only ectypal theology which may constitute the source of the Christian religion is that of Holy Scripture, or the written Word of God. Whatever is beyond, and contrary to, Holy Scripture does not correspond to archetypal theology and is condemned by Scripture as vain talking (ματαιολογία). 1 Tim. 1, 6: "From which some, having swerved, have turned aside unto vain jangling."

The paramount truth that all doctrine taught in the Church must be Scripture doctrine has been all but universally discarded by modern rationalistic theologians. The present-day "scientific theology" no longer recognizes Holy Scripture as the only source and norm of the Christian faith; on the contrary, it regards the identification of Christian theology with the doctrine of Scripture as an "abnormality" and a "repristination of a discarded theological viewpoint." Nitzsch-Stephan writes: "No one bases his dogmatics any longer in the old Protestant way on the norma normans, i. e., Holy Scripture." (Cp. Pieper, Christl. Dogmatik, I, 65.) In place of Holy Scripture modern rationalistic theology accepts as the norm and standard of faith the dictates of human reason, more or less disguised under the terms "Christian consciousness," "Christian experience," "Christian self-assurance," etc., while it denounces true loyalty to the Word of God as "Biblicism," "Intellectualism," etc., which can produce only a "mere intellectual Christianity," "a dead orthodoxy without inner warmth," and the like.

However, in demanding for itself these unscriptural norms,

modern rationalistic theology only deceives itself, as even a cursory examination of the matter will show. Thus, for example, Christian experience can in no way serve as a source or norm of faith, since the true Christian experience is never prior to Holy Scripture, but depends upon, and follows, its acceptance; that is to say, only he who believes the Word of God as set forth in Holy Scripture experiences in his heart both the terror of guilt and the comfort of grace. As a person studies and accepts the divine Law, he becomes convinced that he is a sinner; as he studies and accepts the Gospel, he becomes convinced that his sin is forgiven through faith in Christ. In short, there is no true Christian experience of sin and grace without the means of grace, or the Word of God. This is the true reason for Christ's emphatic command that repentance and remission of sins should be preached in His name among all nations, Luke 24, 47. Cp. also Acts 26, 20.

Thus the Christian experience becomes actual only through the preaching and acceptance of the Word of God; or we may say, the Word of God is the only means by which the Holy Ghost works the Christian experience of repentance and faith, Rom. 7, 7; 1, 16. 17. On the other hand, where the Word of God is not preached, there is no true Christian experience. The proof for this truth is furnished by the very advocates of Christian experience as a norm of faith. Schleiermacher, for example, who insisted upon Christian experience as a norm of faith, rejected the central doctrine of Christianity by denying the vicarious atonement of Christ and consequently also the doctrine of justification by grace, through faith. Schleiermacher's experience moved him ultimately to rely upon his good works for salvation. But such an experience, as is evident, is not Christian, but carnal, rationalistic, and pagan, in short, the very opposite of Christianity.

So also the "Christian faith" or "Christian consciousness" can in no way serve as a source and standard of Christian theology; for as the "Christian experience," so also the "Christian faith" or "Christian consciousness" results from faithful acceptance of Holy Scripture. Now, since the "Christian faith" is the fruit of Holy Scripture, it can never be the source and norm of Christian theology, as little as the apple growing on a tree can be its own cause or source. But just as the apple is produced by the tree, so the Christian faith is produced by Holy Scripture; it is found only where Holy Scripture is adhered to and believed. Rom. 10, 17: "Faith cometh by hearing." John 17, 20: "Who believe through their Word." Hence every "Christian faith" or every "Christian consciousness" which is not rooted in the Word of God, but presumes to judge the Word of God, is not Christian, but carnal and antichristian, 1 Tim. 6, 3—5.

What Luther writes on this point is certainly true and deserves conscientious consideration. He says: "Faith teaches, and holds to, the truth; for it clings to Scripture, which neither lies nor deceives. Whatsoever does not have its origin in Scripture most assuredly comes from the devil." All who wish to make the "Christian faith" or "Christian consciousness" a norm of faith would do well to heed this severe, but correct condemnatory verdict. Our Savior declares: "If ye continue in My Word, then are ye My disciples indeed." Such statements as these settle the question so far as the *Christian* theologian is concerned; his discipleship as well as his theology is grounded only on God's Word and on nothing else. All theology that is not drawn from God's Word opposes the Gospel and subverts the Christian faith, as the rationalistic theology of all subjective or "I theologians" proves, from Aquinas, Scotus, and Schleiermacher down to the present-day Modernists. Wherever the Word of God is not accepted in its truth and purity, there can be no genuine Christian theology.

Nor can the "regenerate heart," or the "regenerate I," serve as a source or norm of the Christian faith, since a person is truly regenerate only as long as he, in simple faith, believes Holy Scripture. Mark 16, 16 b: "He that believeth not shall be damned." The "regenerate heart" which modern rationalistic theologians would set up as a standard of faith is, in the final analysis, the carnal and unbelieving mind of an unregenerate person, rising in rebellion against the mysteries of the faith. This is proved by the fact that practically all who accept their "regenerate heart" as a norm of faith deny both the inspiration and the infallibility of Holy Scripture. Such an outrage, however, no truly regenerate heart will perpetrate.

From this it is clear that all theologians who reject Holy Scripture as the only source and standard of faith have fallen into the error of a most pernicious self-delusion. Their very insistence upon another source and norm outside Holy Scripture proves the spirit of unbelief which either consciously or unconsciously governs their minds. Rationalistic theology demands other norms than the Word of God for the very reason that it is rationalistic and unchristian. The believing child of God says with Samuel: "Speak, Lord; for Thy servant heareth,"

1 Sam. 3, 9. Only blind unbelief and wicked rebellion against God presume to judge His Word by establishing norms of faith in opposition to the revealed divine truth.

Modern rationalistic theology prides itself on its true evaluation of the "historical character" of the Christian religion. But orthodox theology has never denied this "historical character"; in fact, the historicity of Christianity has always been asserted by believing theologians, on account of their firm faith in Holy Scripture. Indeed, just because of their faith in the "historical character" of the Christian religion they are opposed to all norms that are put forth in opposition to Holy Scripture. For "historical Christianity" can be learned only from the Bible, not from any other source. Tradition cannot reveal it to us, nor can it originate with human reason. Only what Christ and His holy apostles tell us of the Christian religion in the Bible is "historical Christianity." The "historical Christ" whom modern rationalistic theologians wish to construct outside Holy Scripture and the "historical Christianity" which they desire to build up apart from Holy Scripture are alike unhistorical and false, for they are figments of unbelieving minds. For the true "historical Christian religion" we must rely solely on the Bible, Matt. 28, 19. 20; John 8, 31. 32; 17, 20; Eph. 2, 20.

In short, rationalistic theology is a product of unbelief and as such is intrinsically false, ungodly, and unscriptural. Our divine Lord invariably affirmed, "It is written"; modern rationalistic theologians contemptuously reject that formula and substitute for it their own subjective opinion, "I believe" and "I think." Thus they teach their own word, not the Word of God. Modern rationalistic theology can be cured of its ingrained falsity only by returning to Holy Scripture and adopting Luther's fundamental principle: "All trust is in vain which is not founded upon the Word of God. God wished to present to us His will and counsels through His Word alone, not by means of our fancies and imaginations." (St. L., VI, 70; III, 1417.)

11. DIVISIONS OF THEOLOGY CONCEIVED AS DOCTRINE.

Theology, considered objectively, is Christian doctrine, or Bible doctrine, which, as we have seen before, is inspired in all its parts, so that in the whole Bible there is not a single teaching which is not divinely given and profitable for salvation. Nevertheless, while it is the scope and purpose of the entire Bible to save

sinners from eternal perdition, distinctions must be made between
the various Bible doctrines regarding their special function and
importance. We thus speak of 1) Law and Gospel; 2) fundamental and non-fundamental doctrines; 3) theological problems,
or open questions.

A. LAW AND GOSPEL.

The distinction between Law and Gospel is one that is made
by Holy Scripture itself. For while at times the term *Law* is used
for the entire Word of God or every revealed truth in Holy Scripture (Ps. 1, 2; 19, 7; 119, 97), nevertheless this term, in its
proper and narrow sense, has a distinct meaning, which properly
does not apply to the whole revealed Word of God. So, too, the
term *Gospel* is sometimes applied to the entire doctrine of the
Bible (Mark 1, 1—15; Phil. 4, 15). Yet in its strict sense each
of these terms denotes a definite message, which must not be identified with the entire Scripture content. Therefore, properly or
strictly speaking, the Law is not Gospel, nor is the Gospel Law, but
the two are opposites. Accurate definitions of them will readily
prove this. The *Formula of Concord* defines the Law thus: "The
Law is properly a divine doctrine which teaches what is right and
pleasing to God and reproves everything that is sin and contrary
to God's will." The same confession defines the Gospel in its
narrow sense as follows: "The Gospel is properly such a doctrine
as teaches what man who has not observed the Law and therefore
is condemned by it is to believe, namely, that Christ has expiated,
and made satisfaction for, all sins and has obtained and acquired
for him, without any merit of his, forgiveness of sins, righteousness
that avails before God, and eternal life." (Epitome, V, 2. 4.)
These definitions are Scriptural and nicely show the fundamental
difference between the Law and the Gospel. How essential this
difference is, is obvious from the fact that Holy Scripture expressly
excludes the Law from the province of salvation. Its pronouncement is: "By grace are ye saved, . . . not of works," Eph. 2, 8. 9.
"Therefore by the deeds of the Law there shall no flesh be justified," Rom. 3, 20. "Therefore we conclude that a man is justified
by faith, without the deeds of the Law," v. 28.

This distinction between the Law and the Gospel, which is so
clearly taught in Holy Scripture, the Christian theologian must
conscientiously observe and neither weaken the condemning force
of the Law nor diminish the saving comfort of the Gospel. He
must declare without qualification the whole guilt and condemna-

tion of sin which the Law reveals. Ezek. 3, 18: "When I say unto the wicked, Thou shalt surely die and thou give him not warning nor speakest to warn the wicked from his wicked way to save his life, the same wicked man shall die in his iniquity; but his blood will I require at thine hand." So also the Christian theologian must proclaim fully and without any qualification the whole consolation of the Gospel with its matchless offer of divine grace, pardon, and eternal life. Matt. 11, 28: "Come unto Me, all ye that labor and are heavy laden, and I will give you rest." 1 Cor. 2, 2: "For I determined not to know anything among you save Jesus Christ and Him crucified."

Unless the Law and the Gospel are thus preached as two distinct and contradictory doctrines (Luther: *plus quam contradictoria*), the Christian religion is deprived of its distinct content, is paganized by the introduction of work-righteousness as a cause of salvation, and is therefore rendered incapable of saving sinners. The sinner indeed needs the Law in order that he may know his sin and the condemnation of God which rests upon him because of his sin; but he needs the Gospel in order that he may know divine grace, which through Christ Jesus has fully removed his sin and offers full forgiveness to him. Gal. 3, 10: "Cursed is every one that continueth not in all things which are written in the Book of the Law to do them"; v. 13: "Christ hath redeemed us from the curse of the Law, being made a curse for us." Whenever the Law with its condemnation is weakened and sinners are taught to rely for salvation on the works of the Law, though only in part, then the Gospel, too, is corrupted, since a weakened Law means a weakened Gospel. The final result is that the sinner is robbed of the salvation which is offered in the Gospel; for this offer is received only by those who implicitly trust in its divine promises and cast themselves upon God's mercy, in short, by those who absolutely repudiate the error of salvation by works. Gal. 5, 4: "Christ is become of no effect unto you whosoever of you are justified by the Law; ye are fallen from grace." Gal. 3, 10: "As many as are of the works of the Law are under the curse." As the Law must forever remain the "ministry of condemnation," so the Gospel must forever remain the "ministration of righteousness," 2 Cor. 3, 9. For a person is a Christian only in so far as he comforts himself against the terrors of conscience with the free and full promise of forgiveness, "without the deeds of the Law."

This fundamental truth requires special emphasis to-day in

view of the fact that both Romanism and modern Protestant sectarianism have discarded the Scriptural distinction between Law and Gospel and have mingled the two into each other. (Cp. Pieper, *Christliche Dogmatik,* I, 84 ff.)   The reason for this is obvious. Both Romanism and modern sectarianism are basically pagan; for both insist upon work-righteousness as a condition of salvation. Now, where work-righteousness is consistently taught, the distinction between Law and Gospel necessarily is eliminated, and each is deprived of its distinctive character.   Salvation by works has room only in that type of theology which affirms that sin is not as hideous as Holy Scripture pictures it and that divine grace is not as glorious as the Gospel proclaims it.   In other words, the paganistic error of salvation by work-righteousness is possible only if neither the Law nor the Gospel is taught in its truth and purity. Against this pernicious corruption of God's holy Word let every true theologian be warned.   Our divine Lord says: "Whosoever therefore shall break one of these least commandments and shall teach men so, he shall be called the least in the kingdom of heaven," Matt. 5, 19; and St. Paul writes: "But though we or an angel from heaven preach any other gospel unto you than that which we have preached unto you, let him be accursed," Gal. 1, 8. — With regard to the use of Law and Gospel the following distinctions must be conscientiously observed: —

a. *Knowledge of sin must be taught from the Law; forgiveness of sin must be taught from the Gospel.*   Rom. 3, 20: "Therefore by the deeds of the Law there shall no flesh be justified." Rom. 1, 16. 17: "I am not ashamed of the Gospel of Christ; for it is the power of God unto salvation to every one that believeth. . . . For therein is the righteousness of God revealed from faith to faith, as it is written, The just shall live by faith." All who teach forgiveness of sin from the Law or on the basis of work-righteousness are not Christian theologians, but false prophets, Gal. 5, 4.   "I would they were even cut off which trouble you," Gal. 5, 12.   Since by the Law there is the knowledge of sin, it must be preached to secure sinners, who, filled with carnal pride, refuse to admit their guilt. Rom. 3, 19: "That every mouth may be stopped and all the world may become guilty before God."   On the other hand, the Gospel must be proclaimed to contrite hearts, that is, to penitent sinners, who have been humbled by the Law, make no assertion of having any merit whatsoever of their own, and gladly accept salvation as a free gift.   Luke 4, 18: "He hath anointed Me to preach the

Gospel to the poor; He hath sent Me to heal the broken-hearted."
It is needless to say that the right apportionment of Law- and
Gospel-preaching must remain a matter of pastoral wisdom. Never-
theless the true minister of Christ is above all a preacher of the
Gospel and will therefore not deny his hearers a full and abundant
measure of Gospel comfort.

b. By means of the *Law* the Christian theologian teaches *what
good works are;* but by means of the *Gospel* he *produces true joy
and zeal to do good works,* Matt. 15, 1—6; 22, 35—40; 19, 16—22;
Rom. 12, 1; Gal. 5, 24—26; Eph. 6, 5—10; 2 Cor. 8, 8. 9; etc.
These diverse functions of the Law and the Gospel have been fittingly expressed by the axiom: *Lex praescribit; evangelium inscribit.* Luther writes: "A legalistic preacher compels by threats
and punishments; a preacher of grace calls forth and moves by
showing divine goodness and mercy." (St. L., XII, 318.)

c. *The Law checks sin only outwardly,* while it *increases sin
inwardly;* but *the Gospel,* by converting the sinner, *destroys sin
both inwardly and outwardly.* Rom. 7, 5: "For when we were in
the flesh, the motions of sins, which were by the Law, did work in
our members to bring forth fruit unto death." V. 6: "But now
are we delivered from the Law, that being dead wherein we were
held, that we should serve in newness of spirit and not in the old-
ness of the letter." Rom. 6, 14: "Sin shall not have dominion
over you; for ye are not under the Law, but under grace." This
important truth is stated in the axiom: *"Lex necat peccatorem,
non peccatum; evangelium necat peccatum, non peccatorem."*
Luther writes: "Hence, whoever knows well this art of distinguishing between Law and Gospel, him place at the head and call him
a doctor of Holy Scripture." (St. L., IX, 802.)

B. FUNDAMENTAL AND NON-FUNDAMENTAL DOCTRINES.

The doctrines of Holy Scripture have been fittingly divided
into fundamental and non-fundamental doctrines. The purpose of
this division is not to discard certain teachings of the Word of
God as practically unimportant or unnecessary. Such a procedure
would be in direct opposition to Scripture itself. Matt. 28, 20:
"Teaching them to observe *all things* whatsoever I have commanded you." Rom. 15, 4: "For *whatsoever things* were written
aforetime were written for our learning that we through patience
and comfort of the Scriptures might have hope." According to
these words, God demands of the Christian theologian that he
teach the entire Scriptural content, adding nothing and taking

away nothing. Nevertheless the distinction of which we speak is fully Scriptural and serves an excellent purpose. It helps the Christian theologian to recognize and distinguish those doctrines of God's Word which "are so necessary to be known that, when they are not known, the *foundation* of faith is not savingly apprehended or retained." (Hollaz.) In other words, the fundamental doctrines are those "which cannot be denied consistently with faith and salvation, being the very foundation of the Christian faith." (Quenstedt.)

In order that we may understand this, we must remember that not everything that Holy Scripture teaches is the object or foundation of justifying and saving faith. For instance, we are not saved by believing that David was king or that the Pope in Rome is the great Antichrist. However, the Christian theologian does not for that reason deny these facts, for they are taught in God's infallible Word. But these truths, which the theologian accepts as such, are non-fundamental as far as saving faith is concerned. Saving faith is faith in the forgiveness of sins through the vicarious atonement of Jesus Christ, or trust in the statement of Scripture that God justifies a sinner without the works of the Law, for Christ's sake. That is the essence of the Christian religion, the foundation on which the entire Christian hope is built. Of this essence and foundation nothing can be removed without destroying the whole Christian religion. Any one who denies even a particle of this fundamental doctrine is outside the pale of the Christian Church. Luther says very correctly: "This doctrine [of justification by faith] is the head and corner-stone, which alone begets, nourishes, builds up, preserves, and protects the Church, and without this doctrine the Church of God cannot exist one hour." (St. L., XIV, 168.) Again: "As many in the world as deny it [justification by faith] are either Jews, or Turks, or papists, or heretics." (IX, 24.) Because of its paramount importance our Lutheran dogmaticians have called the doctrine of justification by grace through faith in Christ's vicarious atonement "the most fundamental of all doctrines" *(articulus omnium fundamentalissimus).*

The doctrine of justification by grace, through faith in Christ's atonement, however, presupposes and includes other fundamental doctrines. These are —

a. *The doctrine of sin and its consequences.* All who deny the Scriptural doctrine of sin cannot have saving faith; for saving faith is implicit trust in God's gracious forgiveness of sins. The true Christian believes that all his sins, both original and actual, are fully pardoned for Jesus' sake. In other words, he believes both the divine Law, which condemns sin, and the divine Gospel, which pardons sin. Both doctrines, the doctrine of sin and that of forgiveness of sins, are fundamental. This truth our Savior affirms when He says that "repentance and forgiveness of sins should be preached in His name among all nations," Luke 24, 47. According to Christ's direction the preaching of repentance for sin, or of contrition, must precede the preaching of forgiveness. Our divine Lord further illustrates this great truth by the Parable of the Pharisee and the Publican. The Pharisee, who did not believe the Scriptural doctrine of sin and therefore did not regard himself as a sinner, could not be justified; in his opinion he had no need of justification and forgiveness. The publican, on the other hand, believed the fundamental doctrine of sin, declared himself guilty and lost, and, trusting in divine grace, received forgiveness through faith. In short, saving faith can exist only in a contrite heart, that is, in a heart which is terrified and sorry because of its sin. Is. 66, 2: "To this man will I look, even to him that is poor and of a contrite spirit and trembleth at My Word." Is. 57, 15: "I dwell with him that is of a contrite and humble spirit." Ps. 34, 18: "The Lord is nigh unto them that are of a broken heart and saveth such as be of a contrite spirit." Cp. Ps. 51, 16. 17; Luke 4, 18; Matt. 11, 28. Hence we rightly classify the doctrine of sin among the fundamental doctrines of Holy Scripture.

b. *The doctrine of the person of Christ.* The doctrine of the person of Christ is fundamental because saving faith is trust in the divine-human Redeemer, who died for the sins of the world. For this reason the denial both of Christ's true deity and of His true humanity makes saving faith impossible. Our divine Lord very severely discountenanced the opinions of those who regarded Him as John the Baptist, Elias, Jeremiah, or as one of the prophets and required of His disciples that they believe in Him as "the Christ, the Son of the living God," Matt. 16, 13—17; cp. also 1 John 1, 1—4. Modern rationalistic theologians, who deny the true deity of Christ and ascribe deity to Him only *honoris causa* (cp. Ritschl's declaration: "In our judgment we ascribe to Him the value of a God"), are not Christians, but Unitarians and therefore *extra ecclesiam;* that is to say, the doctrine of God which modern rationalistic theology inculcates is essentially paganistic, since it rejects the true God of the Bible. It is self-evident that true faith in the divine Christ must include also faith in the Triune God. In other words, the true Christian, who believes in the deity of Christ, believes also that the true God is none other than the *unus Deus,* Father, Son, and Holy Ghost; for without faith in the Father no one can believe in the Son, Matt. 16, 17; 11, 27; and again, without the Holy Ghost no one can call Jesus Lord, 1 Cor. 12, 3; Rom. 8, 15; John 16, 13—15. The Scriptural doctrine of the Holy Trinity is therefore as fundamental as is that of the deity of Christ. — However, also the doctrine of Christ's true humanity is fundamental; for the denial of the substantial humanity of Christ (cp. the error of the Docetae) implies the denial of His actual suffering and death. Saving faith is trust in the vicarious atonement of the theanthropic Christ ($\vartheta\varepsilon\acute{a}\nu\vartheta\rho\omega\pi\sigma\varsigma$), John 1, 14—17: "The Word was made flesh; . . . and of His fulness have all we received, and grace for grace. . . . Grace and truth came by Jesus Christ." Hence we rightly classify among the fundamental doctrines of the Christian religion the doctrines of the Holy Trinity, of Christ's true deity, and of His true humanity.

c. *The doctrine of Christ's vicarious atonement.* Saving faith is faith in Christ not merely as a Teacher of the divine Law or as an Ensample of Virtue or as the "Ideal Man," as modernistic theology maintains, but faith in Christ as "the Mediator between God and men," who has given His life as a ransom for many, and as "the Lamb of God, which taketh away the sin of the world," 1 Tim. 2, 5. 6; Matt. 20, 28; Eph. 1, 7; John 1, 29. All who decline to put their trust in the vicarious satisfaction of Christ (Is. 53, 1—6) are obliged to trust for reconciliation and pardon in their own good works and thus exclude themselves from the grace of God secured by Christ's substitutionary death, Gal. 5, 4. That is true of all who depart from the Scriptural doctrine of justification by grace, through faith, and reject the *sola gratia* and the *sola fide.* The Semi-Pelagianist, the Arminian, and the synergist, if they consistently hold to their error, are as much *extra ecclesiam* as the Unitarian and the Modernist. The warning of the *Apology* is well in place: "Most of those errors which our adversaries defend, overthrow faith, as their condemnation of the article concerning the remission of sins, in which we say that the remission of sins is received by faith. Likewise it is a manifest and pernicious error when the adversaries teach that men merit the remission of sins by love to God prior to grace. In the place of Christ they set up their works, orders, masses, just as the Jews, the heathen, and the Turks intend to be saved by their works." (Art. IV, 22.) If within those churches which teach the pagan doctrine of work-righteousness individual persons still remain Christians, this is due to the surpassing grace of God, as the *Apology* rightly reminds us: "Therefore, even though Popes or some theologians and monks in the Church have taught us to seek remission of sins, grace, and righteousness through our own works and to invent new forms of worship, which have obscured the office of Christ and have made out of Christ not a Propitiator and Justifier, but only a Legislator, *nevertheless the knowledge of Christ has always remained with some godly persons."* (Art. III, 271.)

d. *The doctrine of the Word of God.* The Word of God, that is, the external Word of the holy Gospel, which Christ commanded His blessed apostles to preach and teach to all nations (Matt. 28, 19. 20; Mark 16, 15. 16) and which is set forth in Holy Scripture, is both the *object* and the *means* of saving faith. It is the object of saving faith because saving faith believes the Gospel, Mark 1, 15; Rom. 1, 1. 2; it is the means of saving faith since saving faith is engendered only through the Gospel, Rom. 10, 17; 1, 16; John 17, 20; Jas. 1, 18. Every "faith" that is not produced by the Word of God is not faith, but a figment of the mind, or fancy. Such faith Luther rightly styles "faith in the air." True, saving faith is always God-made, never man-made, 1 Tim. 6, 3. 1 Cor. 2, 1—5: "That your faith should not stand in the wisdom of men, but in the power of God." For this reason the doctrine of the Word of God is likewise a fundamental doctrine. The penalty of the rejection of the Gospel is damnation, Mark 16, 15. 16.

e. *The doctrine of the resurrection.* Modern rationalistic theology discards the Scriptural doctrine of the resurrection, denying both Christ's glorious resurrection and the resurrection of all the dead on Judgment Day. In place of the resurrection it teaches the immortality of the soul. Holy Scripture, however, affirms that the denial of the resurrection involves the denial of the entire Gospel of Christ, 1 Cor. 15, 12—19. It unqualifiedly condemns those who deny the resurrection as having made shipwreck of their faith and erred concerning the truth, 1 Tim. 1, 19. 20; 2 Tim. 2, 17. 18. Hymenaeus and Alexander, who denied the doctrine of the resurrection, were delivered by St. Paul "unto Satan that they may

learn not to blaspheme." The denial of the resurrection is therefore tantamount to blasphemy of Christ. It is for this reason that
we classify the doctrine of the resurrection among the fundamentals
of the Christian religion.

When we speak of the fundamental doctrines of the Christian
religion, we of course mean these doctrines as they are presented
in Holy Scripture, not the dogmatic formulation of these teachings,
or the dogmas of the Church. Dogmas may be faulty; the teachings of Holy Scripture are infallible. Nevertheless it must be
borne in mind that, whenever the doctrines of Holy Scripture have
been formulated correctly, the rejection of such dogmas, or creeds,
is nothing less than the rejection of Holy Scripture itself. Thus
Modernists, who reject the Apostles' Creed or the Nicene Creed or
the Athanasian Creed, reject the very Word of God; for the doctrines expounded and defended in these confessions are the teachings of Holy Scripture.

Primary and Secondary Fundamental Doctrines.

The fundamental doctrines of the Christian religion may be
divided into *primary* and *secondary* fundamental doctrines. This
distinction is not only Scriptural, but also practical and useful, for
it helps the Christian theologian to discriminate rightly between the
fundamental doctrines themselves. As we have learned, fundamental doctrines are such as constitute the foundation of the Christian faith; yet not all fundamental doctrines constitute this
foundation in the same manner. Hollaz rightly observes: "All
the fundamental articles of faith must necessarily be known, but
the grades of this necessity are different." (*Doctr. Theol.*, p. 99.)
Thus the *primary fundamental articles* are of such absolute importance that, if they are denied, there is no foundation whatever
on which saving faith may rest. All the doctrines enumerated before under the heading "Fundamental Articles of Faith" are to be
classified as primary fundamental articles; for if these are cast
aside, Christianity cannot exist.

Secondary fundamental doctrines, on the other hand, while
also serving as a foundation of faith, do not do so primarily and
absolutely. Examples of secondary fundamental doctrines are
those of Holy Baptism and the Lord's Supper. These two Sacraments, instituted by Christ have been given to us as a foundation of faith besides the Gospel; for the same grace and forgiveness proffered and conveyed to us in the Word of God are proffered

NATURE AND CONCEPT OF THEOLOGY.

and conveyed to us also in them. Acts 2, 38: "Repent and be baptized, every one of you, for the remission of sins." Matt. 26, 28 (Luke 22, 19 f.) : "This is My blood of the new testament, which is shed for many for the remission of sins." On this gracious offer of pardon, sealed by Christ in the Sacraments, the Christian faith rests, and in the same manner and to the same degree as it rests on our Lord's offer of pardon in the Word. For this reason the doctrines of Holy Baptism and Holy Communion are fundamental; they are the foundation of the Christian's faith. Nevertheless a person may be ignorant of these doctrines, or he may even err with regard to them and yet be saved, provided he clings to the promise of forgiveness offered in the Gospel. The reason for this is obvious. The entire forgiveness which Christ has secured for sinners by His death on the cross is offered and conveyed to the believer in the Gospel, so that, if he trusts in the Gospel promise, he possesses by faith all the merits of Christ, together with spiritual life and eternal salvation. This does not mean that the sacramental promise is superfluous. The Christian Church can never dispense with the Sacraments, since they convey the spiritual blessings of the Savior in a particularly close and comforting manner. The Sacraments are the *visible Word (Verbum visibile)* and the individual application *(applicatio individualis)* of divine grace. But the Christian believer who trusts in the divine promise of pardon which is offered in the Gospel to all men is already in possession of salvation. The Sacraments offer nothing new; they only seal and confirm the same grace and the same absolution which the Gospel announces, gives, and confers. In this sense the Sacraments are not absolutely necessary; and for this reason we call the doctrines of Holy Baptism and Holy Communion secondary fundamental doctrines. Nor should we reject this distinction; for it points out to us where we must draw the line between Christians and non-Christians. Thus the believing children of God in the Reformed churches err with regard to the *essence* and *purpose* of the Sacraments, and this error we must regard as one which is both dangerous and pernicious. Still they trust in the grace which is offered to them in the Gospel, and as long as they do that, we cannot deny that they have the saving faith. In other words, we must still regard them as Christians, though as weak and erring Christians and such as constantly endanger their state of grace by not accepting the whole Word of Christ. What has just been said of the children of God in the

Reformed churches pertains also to the believers in other sects and in the Roman Catholic Church. As long as a believer trusts in the grace of Christ offered in the Word, as did the thief on the cross, he is saved, even though he has never received the blessings of the Sacraments. Hollaz is quite right in saying of the secondary fundamental articles as such: "A simple want of acquaintance with them does not prevent salvation, but the pertinacious denial of, and hostility to, them overturns the foundation of faith." (*Doctr. Theol.,* p. 98 f.)

In his remark concerning the secondary fundamental doctrines, Hollaz directs our attention to a very important truth. The distinction between primary and secondary fundamental doctrines must never be abused in the interest of tolerating false doctrine. A pertinacious denial of, and manifest hostility to, the secondary fundamental doctrines, the same as to all doctrines of Holy Scripture, must in the end overturn the foundation of the faith; for this implies resistance offered to the Holy Spirit. Of this we must continually remind all errorists, even if we cannot deny their state of grace. Let every Christian theologian remember: —

a. That he is commanded by Christ to teach all the doctrines of God's Word and not to ignore or deny a single one. Matt. 28, 20: "Teach them to observe all things whatsoever I have commanded you."

b. That every departure from the Word of God, according to God's express statement, is a scandal (σκάνδαλον), or offense. Rom. 16, 17: "Mark them which cause offenses contrary to the doctrine which ye have learned." No theologian can teach errors without giving offense to others; and this is a most serious matter. Matt. 18, 7: "Woe to that man by whom the offense cometh!" Cp. also Luke 17, 1. Rom. 14, 13: "That no man put a stumbling-block, or an occasion to fall, in his brother's way." 2 Cor. 6, 3: "Giving no offense in anything that the ministry be not blamed."

c. That every one who sets aside the clear testimony of God's Word in a single point rejects the entire Word of God as the only source and standard of faith; for Holy Scripture must be believed and taught not merely in its general application, but all its parts, indeed all its words, must be accepted as divine truth. Luther rightly says: "The Holy Spirit [speaking in Holy Scripture] cannot be separated or divided, so that He should teach and have us believe one doctrine as true and another as false." (St. L., XX, 1781.) All the teachings of God's Word are so intimately interwoven with one another that, if one is denied, all the rest are likewise affected by such denial; that is to say, "one error produces another," as the history of dogma proves. If there are exceptions to this rule, they must be attributed to the wonderful sustaining grace of God alone. Due to God's grace an erring theologian sometimes, by a strange "fortunate inconsistency," does not personally believe what he officially teaches; or again, he does not, in his own life of faith, draw the deadly inferences which his rationalistic rejection of divine truth suggests. Thus many a synergist who officially affirmed man's cooperation in conversion in his own personal dealings with God as a penitent sinner disavowed this pernicious error and trusted for salvation in God's grace alone. Again, erring theologians who publicly and officially denied the universality of divine grace nevertheless proclaimed and asserted the universal character of God's grace and of Christ's redemption when they preached the Gospel to the common people. This fortunate difference between theory and practise they owed to the unspeakable mercy of God, who earnestly desires the salvation of sinners.

However, also this truth must not be abused to promote indifference in doctrine. While we admit that there is a "fortunate inconsistency," we must remember that there is an "unfortunate consistency," by which theologians who offend in one point are led to offend in many points and even in all. In other words, the proclamation of one error consistently leads to the proclamation of others and in the end to the denial of the entire Scriptural truth. Against this fatal consequence of denying God's Word and indulging in error Luther earnestly warns all Christian theologians when he writes: "You must not say, I purpose to err as a Christian. Christian erring occurs only from ignorance." (St. L., XIX, 1132.) Luther admits that there is such an anomaly as "Christian erring"; that is to say, even a true Christian at times errs due to weakness or to ignorance. But this "Christian erring" becomes an "unchristian erring" as soon as a person deliberately and knowingly yields to error. Such "unchristian erring" must needs overturn the foundation of faith and endanger salvation. Let the Christian theologian, then, be warned. Indifferentism with respect to the doctrines of Holy Scripture and spiritual unionism resulting therefrom are diametrically opposed to God's Word, which declares: "A man that is an heretic, after the first and second admonition reject, knowing that he that is such is subverted and sinneth, being condemned of himself," Titus 3, 10. 11. Holy Scripture never justifies the teaching of error, but always and most vehemently condemns it as an *offense, σκάνδαλον.*

d. That the whole Church, in order to preserve unadulterated the purity of doctrine, must continually guard against every error by which Satan would cause divisions and offenses. To this end it must rebuke even the slightest error and departure from the truth that is in Christ Jesus. Gal. 5, 9: "A little leaven leaveneth the whole lump." It is the "little leaven" of false doctrine with which the whole corruption of the entire Christian theology usually begins. Modernism, with its crass rejection of all the Scriptural truths that are necessary to salvation, is but the result of the indifferentism of such theologians and churches as allowed the "little leaven" a place in their system of dogmas. Let errorists deny the doctrine of verbal inspiration, and the whole doctrine of inspiration will fall. Let the *sola gratia* be removed from the *corpus doctrinae,* and the rejection of Christ's vicarious atonement will follow. The Christian theologian cannot err in "little things" without sooner or later erring also in the "great things" of salvation. That is the "unfortunate consistency" of tolerating error. How deadly it is all earnest Christians know who have studied the history of the Christian Church in the light of Holy Scripture.

Non-Fundamental Doctrines.

Non-fundamental doctrines of Holy Scripture are such as do not constitute the foundation of faith, inasmuch as they do not offer and convey to sinners forgiveness of sins and thus make them children of God through faith in Christ. They do not form the foundation of saving faith, but rather *strengthen* the faith which already exists. Hollaz describes non-fundamental doctrines as "parts of the Christian doctrine which one may be ignorant of or omit and yet be saved" (*Doctr. Theol.,* p. 92). Such doctrines are, for example, those of the angels, of Antichrist, etc. As we see, these doctrines do not create saving faith in Christ, but they are given for the comfort or warning of those who already believe in Christ. This does not mean that the non-fundamental doctrines are useless; in many respects their importance is indeed very great, and so they may not be dispensed with. Thus the doctrine concerning the holy angels glorifies divine grace and strengthens our faith in God's merciful providence. Both quantitatively and qualitatively this doctrine constitutes a weighty part of Christian theology. This fact the Christian theologian must never overlook.

Again, the doctrine concerning Antichrist instructs with regard to, and warns us against, the greatest fraud ever perpetrated within Christendom, and evangelical theology would suffer a most serious loss if this doctrine were eliminated. Accordingly also the non-fundamental doctrines are necessary and must be inculcated with becoming earnestness and emphasis. 2 Tim. 3, 16: "All Scripture is given by inspiration of God and is profitable for doctrine, for reproof, for correction, for instruction in righteousness." Nevertheless the non-fundamental doctrines are not properly the object of saving faith; for faith relies on the gracious Gospel-promise of pardon through faith in the redemption of Jesus Christ; in this sense alone they are non-fundamental. Whoever declares them to be non-fundamental in the sense that they can be dispensed with denies both the divine authority and the perfection of Holy Scripture and thus denies a fundamental doctrine. Baier's warning with regard to this matter should be heeded here. He writes: "At the same time [while we admit that there are *non-fundamental* doctrines] we are to be careful in regard to this point lest by embracing or professing error we rashly sin against divine revelation and God Himself; especially, lest through the persuasion of others something be maintained, contrary to conscience, through which the foundation and the truth of one or more of the fundamental articles of the faith are overturned. For thus, as by a mortal sin, faith and the Holy Spirit may be, and are, entirely driven away." (*Doctr. Theol.,* p. 97.) This warning applies also to the historical, archeological, and scientific facts and statements contained in Holy Scripture. While these are not fundamental, we wickedly reject the divine authority of Holy Scripture if we presume to deny them to be absolutely true; for an erring Scripture is not authoritative. Indeed, an errant Bible cannot be believed at all; for if it is false in non-fundamental points, how can it be true in its fundamental teachings? If we cannot rely on it when it teaches us earthly things, how much less can we do so when it speaks of heavenly things. Hence, while the Christian theologian acknowledges non-fundamental doctrines in Holy Scripture, he believes and declares the entire Holy Scripture, in all its parts and in all its statements, to be the divine truth which must be proclaimed to men. The distinction between fundamental and non-fundamental doctrines is made by him merely to distinguish clearly between those teachings of God which are the foundation of justifying faith and those which are not.

C. OPEN QUESTIONS, OR THEOLOGICAL PROBLEMS.

Open questions must not be defined as points of doctrine "on which men cannot agree" or "which the Church has left undecided in its Confessions," but as questions which Holy Scripture itself has left open, or unanswered, or has not answered clearly. This definition of open questions is very important; for not human, but only Scriptural authority determines what must be taught in the Christian Church, namely, the entire content of Holy Scripture, Matt. 28, 20; not a definite doctrinal platform which certain theologians or churches have drawn up. In other words, Holy Scripture alone is the spiritual teacher of men, not the Church or the theologian in the Church. The spirit of indifferentism and unionism has always set up false standards regarding the issue of open questions. Guided by a vicious principle of religious toleration, theologians again and again have erred on this point by exalting their limited human reason above the inspired Word of God and "opening" or "closing" questions at their own will. Over against this unscriptural practise it must be maintained that open questions owe their existence alone to the silence of Scripture and not to any fixation of doctrine by the Church or to any policy of expediency advocated by parties in controversy. Since the doctrine of Holy Scripture is God's Word, men have no right whatever to decide what to teach and what not to teach or to determine which should be closed and which should be open questions. That is a matter outside their jurisdiction.

As we study Holy Scripture, we find that, in agreement with its scope and purpose, it does not answer every question which men may desire to have answered. For instance, it does not explain how sin originated or could originate since all creatures were originally created "very good." Nor does Holy Scripture answer the question whether the soul of a child comes into being either by creation or traduction (creationism; traducianism). Questions on which the Word of God is silent we call theological problems, or open questions. To these questions we may add also the *crux theologorum,* which has always puzzled the minds of inquisitive theologians: Why are some converted and others not, though by nature all men are in the same guilt *(eadem culpa)* and are saved by grace alone *(sola gratia)? (Cur alii, alii non? Cur non omnes? Cur alii prae aliis?)* Since God's Word does not answer these questions, the theologian should not endeavor to do so. All attempts to do so are both *anti-Scriptural,* because the theologian is to speak only as the oracles of God, 1 Pet. 4, 11, and *unscientific,* since he who takes it upon himself to answer such questions presumes to know what he cannot know. Divine truth is apprehended only through faith, or by simply believing what Holy Scripture teaches. John 8, 31. 32. Hence, whatever doctrine is drawn from any other source than Christ's Word is not theology, but mere speculation or downright ignorance, 1 Tim. 6, 4.

The proper attitude of the Christian theologian toward open questions, or theological problems, is therefore that of confessing that he is incapable of solving them since the source of his faith, Holy Scripture, furnishes him no data. Reusch very pertinently says: *"Inutilis est eorum cognitio, et vanae sunt de eisdem disputationes."* (*Annotationes in Baieri Comp.,* 1757, p. 52.) However, such disputations are not only useless, but directly dangerous. Of this Luther reminds us when he says that the Gospel is hindered mainly by two things, namely, first, if sinners are taught to trust in their good works, and secondly, if useless questions are propounded the answering of which causes the chief parts of the Christian doctrine to be neglected. (St. L., IX, 863 ff.) Open questions are certainly not "open" in the sense that the Christian theologian may allow his imagination to run wild on matters which God has wisely refused to reveal. If he indulges in speculations, these must always be kept within the bounds of the analogy of faith, or the clear revelation of God's Word. But it is safer and better for a theologian not to speculate at all, since his own views may easily lodge in his theological system and be taught as a part of divinely revealed truth. Let the Christian theologian learn to say *nescio* wherever Holy Scripture does not speak with clearness and definiteness, remembering that both in revealing truths and in withholding facts which we should like to know God had in mind our salvation, 2 Tim. 3, 15—17.

In this connection we may discuss also the important question, "What are articles of faith?" Articles of faith, as our dogmaticians have always affirmed, have their origin solely in Holy Scripture. That means that the Christian Church accepts and believes only such doctrines as are unmistakably taught in Holy Scripture. Hollaz describes an article of faith as "a part of the doctrine revealed in the written Word of God concerning God and divine things and proposed to the sinner to be believed for his salvation." However, since it is true that some articles of faith contain truths which man's natural knowledge of God and

the contemplation of God's works in nature disclose to him, for
example, those concerning the existence of God, the articles of
faith have been divided into *mixed articles,* that is, such as are
manifest also from the light of nature, and *pure articles,* or such
as are known only from the study of Holy Scripture. (Baier.)
But also the former, the mixed articles, are articles of faith only
inasmuch as they are directly taught in God's Word. The true
Christian theologian recognizes no source of divine truth other
than the Bible.

12. THE CHURCH AND ITS DOGMAS.

Since the Christian theologian is to teach only what Holy
Scripture teaches and nothing else, the question has been raised
whether creeds, dogmas, or confessions are rightfully given a place
in the Christian Church. The question has been denied by both
conservative and modernistic theologians. Modernistic theology
favors a creedless, or undogmatic, Christianity. Its plea is that the
real function of the Church is to spread the "social gospel" and
not the supernatural Gospel of Christ, with which our present
advanced age is no longer in sympathy. Modernistic theology is
therefore absolutely present-worldly, not otherworldly. It proposes
a theology for this life, not one for the life to come *(eine Dies-
seitigkeits-, nicht eine Jenseitstheologie).* This theology, so it is
claimed, is one of good works, to be done now, and not one of
comforting words with respect to a possible future existence.
Because modernistic theology is so constituted, it regards creeds,
dogmas, and confessions not only as unnecessary, but also as injurious. Creeds are said to impede the free progress and development of the Church and its activity. Thus modernistic theology
must needs be opposed to dogmas. Modern theologians of a more
conservative type oppose creeds for a somewhat different reason.
Their claim is that dogmas and confessions prevent the necessary
"progress in theology" *(Lehrfortbildung),* which must take place
if the Church is to remain a living organism. In fact, this type
of theologian holds that the doctrines of the Church are ever-
living and expanding factors, forever subject to change as newer,
fuller, and deeper revelations are given to men. Therefore the
Church must not be fettered by the chains of definite creeds, since
these prevent the progress, or development, of doctrine. As we see,
in the final analysis the difference between the two types of theologians is not so very great. It is a difference in degree, not in

kind. Both reject Holy Scripture as the sole rule and norm of faith and in its place enthrone reason or science.

From the objections just now considered it is obvious that the animosity of modern liberalistic and rationalistic theology is primarily directed not against the creeds, or dogmas, themselves, but against Holy Scripture. These rationalists object to creeds because they object to divinely revealed truths. Their creedless theology is tantamount to a theology without the Holy Bible. They wish to follow their own words, not the Word of God.

This hatred against Holy Scripture is, however, found also in churches that favor creeds. Roman Catholic theology, for example, is built up entirely on definite creeds. Because the Church of Rome accepts the ancient confessions of the unadulterated Christian Church, we still consider it as being within the pale of Christendom. But it has hedged in these ancient creeds by later creeds whose tenor is antichristian and which actually make void what the ancient Christian confessions declare. Moreover, these specifically papistical creeds are in direct opposition to Holy Scripture, for they reject Scripture as the only rule of faith and flatly contradict its central doctrines. They affirm that the Pope as the head of the Church is the infallible norm of faith, that a sinner is justified by works, that the doctrine of justification by grace, through faith in Christ, is anathema, that the merits and intercessions of the saints avail for salvation, and so forth. Such creeds quite obviously do not deserve a place in the Christian Church; for they are not Christian, but antichristian. But also in the Calvinistic churches we find creeds that stand in opposition to the pure Word of God. The specifically Calvinistic creeds deny the universality of God's grace and of Christ's redemption, the efficacy of the means of grace, the true presence of our Lord's body in the Holy Supper, the communion of natures in the person of Christ, and the resulting communication of attributes, etc. Such creeds must not be tolerated in the Christian Church because they are unscriptural and rationalistic.

The Christian Church, which has for its source of faith only the infallible Word of God (Eph. 2, 20), must under no condition acknowledge as right and legitimate any dogma, or doctrine, which is not a clear teaching of Holy Scripture. Or we may say: The dogma of the Christian Church is the doctrine of the Holy Bible. Whatever the written Word of God declares and teaches is *eo ipso* a church dogma, no matter whether it is especially formulated or not. The question is not: Is this or that doctrine clearly stated in the Confessions? but: Is this or that doctrine set forth in God's Word? If it is set forth in Holy Writ, it is for this reason a church dogma, even though not a word is said about it in the Confessions of the Church. The reason for this is not difficult to perceive. The Christian Church is not the lord of God's doctrine, but only its servant. Its paramount purpose is not to create new doctrines, but to preach the doctrines which its divine Lord has revealed. Matt. 28, 20: "Teaching them to observe all things whatsoever I have commanded you." Luther's dictum applies here with full force: "The Church of God has no authority to establish any article of faith, just as it never has established any nor ever will establish any." So also Quenstedt rightly says (1, 36): "Divine revelation is the first and last source of sacred theology, beyond which theological discussion among Christians dare not proceed." (*Doctr. Theol.*, p. 28.) This does not mean that the Church should not have any articles of faith or any confessions, but it does mean that all its articles of faith must be in deed and truth "declarations" of the faith that has been delivered to it by God in His holy Word. Thus Christians universally accept the ancient confessions of the Christian Church because these profess and defend nothing but Scripture doctrine. This is true even though the technical theological terms which they employ to express the doctrine of God's Word, such as "Trinity," "consubstantial," etc., are not found in Holy Scripture. So also the specifically Lutheran Confessions, which were added at the time of the Reformation and after Luther's death to defend the doctrine of the Word of God against Romanism, sectarianism, and enthusiasm, profess only Scripture doctrine. We say this not in a spirit of carnal pride, but in the holy conviction of that loyalty to Christ and His Word which He demands of His disciples. Dogmas (creeds, confessions) have a rightful place in the Christian Church provided they teach the doctrines of God and not doctrines of men. If, however, they set forth doctrines in opposition to God's Word, they must be renounced and rejected; for the Christian Church must teach the Word of its divine Lord, nothing else.

What has just been said of dogmas and creeds in general applies with equal force to the theological treatises of individual teachers of the Church. No theologian should be listened to in the Church, and no dogmatic treatise should be regarded as worthy of consideration, unless they profess and defend the truth which is in Christ Jesus. The dogmatician who draws his teachings from any other source than Holy Scripture perpetrates an inexcusable fraud upon the Church and deserves excommunication from the Church as a false prophet, Rom. 16, 17; 2 John 10. 11; 1 Tim. 4, 16. God's earnest and persistent demand is: "If any man speak, let him speak as the oracles of God," 1 Pet. 4, 11. This applies to all ministers and teachers who have been called to instruct the Christian people in general. Christian ministers, teachers, and missionaries must proclaim to their hearers God's Word, not their own, so that in the whole Christian Church, in its schools and colleges, in its churches and homes, not one doctrine is taught that is not in agreement with Holy Scripture.

If the dogmas and creeds of the Church are truly and absolutely Scriptural, they are of great value also for preserving the inner connection of the various theological disciplines and securing their truly theological character. Commonly we speak of theology as dogmatic, historic, exegetic, and practical. This division is both practical and useful. It assists the theological student in distinguishing one subject from the other and so prevents confusion as he takes up the study of sacred theology. Nevertheless, in the final analysis the purpose of the various theological disciplines is the same; each is to teach God's Word together with its specific applications. The dogmatic theologian inculcates with special emphasis the several doctrines of Holy Scripture; the exegetic theologian sets forth the same doctrines while he expounds to his hearers the meaning of the words of the sacred text; the historic theologian exhibits the same doctrines as they react upon men in history; and the practical theologian applies the same doctrines to the special needs of the Christian congregation. While, therefore, the four theological disciplines may be distinguished from one another by their particular scope, they all center in the one paramount purpose of proclaiming, expounding, and defending the Word of God; and this one purpose, the teaching of God's Word, preserves their inner connection, unifying the whole course of theology. At the same time this one purpose of inculcating God's Word preserves also the truly theological character of each discipline. It is this factor that makes historic theology, or exegetic theology, or practical theology, *theology* in the true sense of the term. If historic theology goes beyond the Word of God, it is no longer theological; and the same is true of dogmatic, exegetic, and practical theology. In short, these branches are theology only in as far as they teach and expound the Word of God set forth in Holy Scripture. As soon as theologians present their own views, they are teaching philosophy or speculation, not theology; for this is as much the Word *of* God as it is the word *about* God.

In view of the general apostasy among theologians to-day the truth just stated certainly requires constant emphasis. The crisis that troubles the Christian Church to day calls for renewed loyalty to the Word of God. If the Church is to be healed from its manifold ills, it must apply the age-old precious remedy which God has ordained for the salvation of men, the unadulterated Word of God. Christ's command is: "Preach the Gospel," Mark 16, 15. That divine injunction binds all Christians, and in particular all Christian teachers, to the Word of God for all time. *"Quod non est biblicum, non est theologicum."* This is an axiom which the Christian Church must ever respect and heed; if it fails to do this, it is an apostate Church and dishonors our Lord, who built His Church on the foundation of the prophets and apostles, He Himself being the chief Corner-stone.

13. THE PURPOSE OF CHRISTIAN THEOLOGY.

In the performance of his sacred functions the Christian theologian must at all times conscientiously keep in mind the true objective of his theological activity. The purpose of sacred theology, so far as it regards lost and perishing mankind, is not the spread of culture, nor the establishment of civic righteousness on earth, nor the satisfaction of the intellectual craving of the human mind, nor the enrichment of human knowledge, but the eternal salvation (σωτηρία, *salus aeterna*) of sinners. In other words, the purpose of sacred theology is not academic or speculative, but intensely and absolutely practical *(habitus practicus)*; it is to lead perishing souls to Christ and through Him to communion with the true God, here in time inchoatively and hereafter in eternity perfectly. This exalted purpose of Christian theology Holy Scripture expressly states in indisputable terms. 1 Tim. 4, 16: "Take heed unto thyself and unto the doctrine . . . ; for in doing this, thou shalt both save thyself and them that hear thee." Mark 16, 15. 16: "Preach the Gospel. . . . He that believeth . . . shall be saved." If modern rationalistic theology rejects eternal salvation as the primary and preeminent purpose of sacred theology, it is because this obnoxious type of pseudotheology is not Biblical, but carnal; not the divine theology of Christ's Gospel, but the man-made theology of a social gospel. The Lutheran dogmatician Meisner is right when he declares: "Whoever does not continually pursue, and keep in mind in his entire study *(Theorie),* this purpose [the salvation of men] does not deserve the name of a true theologian." (*Lehre und Wehre,* 14, 76.)

In accordance with the principle just stated the Lutheran divines have defined the purpose of sacred theology as follows: "Sacred theology occupies itself with man inasmuch as he is a sinner and must be restored to eternal salvation." This definition is truly Scriptural. The object of sacred theology is not man in general, but *homo peccator,* or sinful man, for whose salvation God has sent His only-begotten Son into the world "that whosoever believeth in Him should not perish, but have everlasting life," John 3, 16. True, also the state, or the civil government, deals with men as sinners *(homines peccatores),* but its purpose is not the eternal salvation of men, but only their earthly, or temporal, welfare, in particular the protection of human life and property. Its interest therefore attaches only to this present life, not to the life that is to be after death. The state has therefore no jurisdiction in the sphere of a man's spiritual and eternal life; its functions cease where this begins. However, to offer to, and bestow upon, sinful men eternal happiness in the life to come, and this through faith in Christ Jesus, engendered by the divinely instituted means of grace, that is the special and proper function of sacred theology. Its message to fallen mankind reads: "He that believeth on the Son hath everlasting life; and he that believeth not the Son shall not see life, but the wrath of God abideth on him," John 3, 36.

The final purpose of sacred theology *(finis ultimus)* is therefore the eternal salvation of men. The intermediate purpose *(finis intermedius)* may be defined as the generation and preservation of saving faith in Christ Jesus unto life eternal. Rom. 1, 5: "By whom we have received grace and apostleship for obedience to the faith among all nations, for His name" (that men of all nations might be led to obey Christ in true faith). The Christian theologian therefore performs his holy office, first of all, in order that sinners may believe in Christ and obtain salvation through Him. But sacred theology effects not only conversion, but also sanctification and good works. This objective the Christian theologian must constantly bear in mind, urging with holy zeal those entrusted to his care to be zealous of good works. Titus 3, 8: "These things

I will that thou affirm constantly that they which have believed in God might be careful to maintain good works." However, good works are not the means by which eternal salvation is obtained, but rather the effects and fruits of faith. Good works, in the Scriptural sense of the term, are such works as are done by those who already have obtained salvation through faith in Christ. Rom. 3, 28: "A man is justified by faith, without the deeds of the Law"; 6, 22: "But now, being made free from sin and become servants to God, ye have your fruit unto holiness." Eph. 2, 10: "For we are His workmanship, created in Christ Jesus unto good works, which God hath before ordained that we should walk in them." From this it follows that all who preach good works as a condition or means of salvation are under the curse, Gal. 3, 10. On the other hand, the Christian minister who in accordance with Holy Scripture proclaims salvation by God's grace alone, through the very preaching of the Gospel truly produces good works that please God and glorify Him. Titus 2, 14: "Who gave Himself for us that He might redeem us from all iniquity and purify unto Himself a peculiar people, zealous of good works." 1 Tim. 6, 18: "That they be rich in good works." This does not mean that the Christian theologian neglects the divine Law, for the divine Law is the Word of God just as truly as the Gospel. But he employs the Law in its rightful place, to show what good works are and what God demands of the believer with regard to them. The willingness and power to do good works, however, he produces alone through the preaching of the Gospel. The Christian theologian must therefore be able rightly to apply both the Law and the Gospel.

14. THE EXTERNAL MEANS BY WHICH SACRED THEOLOGY ACCOMPLISHES ITS PURPOSE OF SAVING SINNERS.

The external means which the Christian theologian employs to accomplish the salvation of sinners are not the carnal weapons suggested by man's wisdom, such as external coercion, the sword of the civil government, legal enactments, social service, the perfecting of church organization, etc. On such things theologians are prone to rely if they are guided by principles of reason, as the history of the Christian Church proves. Erring theologians within the Christian Church have always advocated carnal means to maintain and spread church power. Holy Scripture, however, condemns these means, not only as unprofitable, but as even downright injurious. For all of them are based upon the Law; and while the Law can check the gross outbursts of sin and improve the sinner outwardly, it cannot change his heart by producing in it true faith in Christ. But where there is no true faith in Christ, there is also no salvation. Hence the only means by which the Christian theologian can accomplish his preeminent, divinely prescribed purpose of saving sinners unto eternal life is the Gospel of Christ. Matt. 28, 19. 20: "Go ye therefore and make disciples of all nations by baptizing them . . . , teaching them to observe all things whatsoever I have commanded you." Mark 16, 15: "Preach the Gospel to every creature." Acts 20, 32: "I commend you . . . to the Word of His grace, which is able to build you up." 2 Tim. 3, 15: "Thou hast known the Holy Scriptures, which are able to make thee wise unto salvation." Rom. 10, 17: "Faith cometh by hearing and hearing by the Word of God." These divine injunctions of Holy Scripture the Christian theologian must constantly bear in mind in order that he may not be misled toward relying on any means suggested and advanced by his carnal heart, but may exclusively employ the powerful, living Word of God, by which alone sinners are transformed into children of God and governed and kept through faith unto salvation. In the Christian Church, as in the entire activity of the Christian theologian, the Word of God must rule alone. It is the only efficacious means of grace because it alone is prescribed by God. Luther very correctly declares: "Christians cannot be ruled by any other means than by the Word of God; for Christians must be ruled by faith, not by external measures. Faith, however, can come only through God's Word, not through any word of man, as St. Paul teaches, Rom. 10, 17: 'Faith cometh by hearing and hearing by the Word of God.'" (St. L., X, 406.) Let the Christian theologian, then, rely alone on God's Word for the successful execution of the work of the holy ministry; for it alone is the imperishable foundation of Christ's holy Church. Cp. 1 Cor. 3, 10—14.

15. THEOLOGY AND SCIENCE.

The question whether the term *science* may be applied to sacred theology has caused no little debate among theologians. Some with great vehemence have affirmed it; others with the same vehemence have denied it. The question itself is not difficult to answer, provided the term *science* is used and understood precisely in the same meaning. It is quite obvious that the term *science* as employed in its common meaning cannot be applied to sacred theology. Christian theology is not a science in the same sense as, for instance, geology, psychology, biology, etc., are sciences. It differs from these sciences not only in subject-matter, but also in source, method, and purpose. Its subject-matter is the divine truth, set forth in Holy Scripture; its source, the Holy Bible; its method *(medium cognoscendi),* faith; its purpose, the salvation of sinners. Sacred theology therefore does not deal with human knowledge, or man's wisdom, obtained by human study, contemplation, or research, as do the common sciences established by philosophers and scientists. The Christian theologian gains his wisdom directly from the Bible, whose truths he receives by faith. The heart of sacred theology is the message of Christ's vicarious atonement, which was revealed to men from heaven; for by nature man could not know or ascertain it, 1 Cor. 2, 6—10. By nature man can know only the divine Law, which God has written into his heart, Rom. 1, 18 ff.; 2, 14. 15. He has a natural knowledge of God, and this innate knowledge of divine things can be developed through reason and experience; both intensively and extensively it may be increased by contemplation and study. But the Gospel of Christ's redemption does not lie within the natural knowledge of fallen man. It is a "mystery," whose gracious revelation he owes entirely to God and which he knows alone through faith in Holy Scripture. From all this it is obvious that sacred theology cannot be called a science in the ordinary sense of the term.

Again, sacred theology is not a science in the sense that it represents a higher Christian knowledge, which is above the simple religion of faith professed by the common Christian and which like the human sciences is capable of intellectual apprehension and logical demonstration. Sacred theology is not an advanced type of Christianity; it is not a philosophy of religion, but deals exclusively with the revealed truths of Holy Writ, which the theologian both accepts and apprehends by faith, John 8, 31. 32; Rom. 1, 5; 1 Cor. 13, 12. What the Christian theologian knows of divine, spiritual things he knows only from the Word of God. If he knows more concerning the divine truths revealed by God than the ordinary believer, his knowledge exceeds that of the latter merely extensively, not intensively; that is to say, he is conversant with the inspired truths of Holy Scripture to a greater extent simply because he devotes more time to the study of the Holy Bible than the average Christian does. Hence the difference between the

NATURE AND CONCEPT OF THEOLOGY.

knowledge of the theologian and that of the ordinary Christian is one of degree, not one of kind. By this we mean to say that the theologian does not *understand* the divine mysteries of faith whereas the Christian church-member only *believes* them; for also the theologian knows only so much as he believes. To say it in other words, also with the Christian theologian, faith is knowledge, and knowledge is faith. The philosophical, philological, and historical facts which the theologian knows and operates with in contradistinction to the ordinary believer do not belong to the essence of Christian theology, but constitute merely the external scientific apparatus, or outward means, by which he approaches and studies Holy Scripture. They are merely his tools, or instruments, never a source of spiritual knowledge from which he is to draw opinions or doctrines beyond and contrary to the Word of God. The attempt of modern rationalistic theology to elevate the Christian faith to a science is nothing else than self-deception, and in the final analysis it is tantamount to the rejection of Holy Scripture as the only principle of Christian knowledge, or the only source of faith (*principium cognoscendi*).

Nevertheless Christian theology may be rightly called a science if by that term we understand a *definite* knowledge, or *accurate* and *reliable* information, in opposition to mere views, opinions, and hypotheses. Understood in this sense, Christian theology is the science of sciences, or the science *par excellence,* the perfect science. This claim we make and sustain for Christian theology because it is God's own infallible wisdom and not the fallible wisdom of man. To err is human (*errare humanum est),* but it is impossible for God to err (*errare in Deum non cadit).* John 17, 17: "Thy Word is truth." John 10, 35: "The Scripture cannot be broken." Holy Scripture is in every part inerrant, and therefore Christian theology, which is drawn from Holy Scripture, is the most definite, most accurate, and most reliable, in fact, the only definite, the only accurate, and the only reliable science in the world. It is the *divine* science, which cannot err.

This is the Christian conviction which every true Christian theologian must hold. If he does not have it, if he doubts the truth of what he declares and proclaims to his hearers, he is not a truly Christian theologian, but a reed shaken with the wind, and he has no business at all to teach or preach in the Christian Church. A Christian theologian must be so deeply convinced of the truth of his message that he is able to say with Paul: "But though we or an angel from heaven preach any other gospel unto you than that which we have preached unto you, let him be accursed," Gal. 1, 8. This truth must be emphasized over against modern agnostic theology, which denies the possibility of knowing the truth and claims that it is impossible for a theologian to be subjectively assured of his possessing the truth. This agnostic denial sets aside Christ's definite promise: "If ye continue in My Word, . . . ye shall know the truth," John 8, 31. 32. These words are Christ's own guarantee that, if in true faith we accept His Word as it is set forth in Holy Writ and as we also possess and confess it in our Christian dogmas, creeds, and confessions, we shall become convinced of its absolute truth. Faith is always assurance of the truth as it is revealed in the Bible and presented in Christian theology, or doctrine. Nor is such assurance a mere personal or human conviction *(fides humana),* produced by evidence of reason, but it is a divine assurance *(fides divina),* produced directly by the Holy Ghost through the Word of God. 1 Cor. 2, 5: "That your faith should not stand in the wisdom of men, but in the power of God." John 16, 13: "When He, the Spirit of Truth, is come, He will guide you into all truth." By the Holy Spirit, through the external Word of Holy Scripture, the Christian theologian is so guided into all truth that he can know and teach with absolute certainty the truth which is in Christ Jesus. 1 Cor. 2, 12: "We have received . . . the Spirit, which is of God, that we might know the things that are freely given to us of God." True Christian theology is therefore no less certain than is Holy Scripture, and the Christian theologian must be no less assured of the truth of the doctrine which he teaches than He is of the objective truth of Holy Scripture. Luther very aptly remarks: "The Holy Spirit is no skeptic and has not written doubts or opinions in our hearts, but statements of fact, which are more certain and firm than life itself with all its experiences." (St. L., XVIII, 1680.) — Christian theology is therefore justly called a science, because it is a knowledge that is absolutely true and certain.

In spite of this fact, however, it is preferable not to define Christian theology primarily as a science, because the term *science* is subject to so much misunderstanding and downright abuse. Modern rationalistic theology invariably employs the term to denote by it the scientific demonstration of divine truth in accord with the principles of human reason. Fundamentally it regards theology as only a more exalted form of philosophy, and hence it applies to it the same principles and methods which are ordinarily employed to demonstrate philosophical truths. Against this mode of procedure the Christian theologian must needs object; for Christian theology with its revealed mysteries is incapable of rational proof or intellectual demonstration. 1 Cor. 2, 14: "The natural man receiveth not the things of the Spirit of God, . . . neither can he know them." As long as a person is unconverted, no amount of reasoning will render the divine truths of revelation acceptable to him; in fact, the more he allows his reason to mull over them, the more foolish and unreasonable they will seem to him. Hence philosophy can never lead to faith; invariably it leads away from true faith, as the "theology" of modern rationalistic theologians proves. Since, then, human reason is incapable of apprehending the divine mysteries of faith intellectually, Christ simply charged His apostles to preach the Gospel and not to demonstrate it rationally to men, Mark 16, 15. 16. They were to go out and proclaim the truth, but not to turn their divinely given message into a philosophical system acceptable to natural man. In accordance with this command, St. Paul testifies of his ministry at Corinth: "My speech and my preaching was not with enticing words of man's wisdom, but in demonstration of the Spirit and of power," 1 Cor. 2, 4.

On the basis of the truth just stated our dogmaticians defined sacred theology as a *habitus exhibitivus,* not as a *habitus demonstrativus*. By this they meant to say that Christian theology is the ability to exhibit, or preach, the Gospel, but not to prove it true by human arguments of reason or philosophy. As the Christian theologian proclaims the truth, he wins souls for Christ, but not as he endeavors to prove true the mysteries of faith by principles of human reason. This also is the meaning of the axiom: "The best apology of the Christian religion is its proclamation." Let the Gospel be made known, and it will of itself prove its divine character. Christian apologetics has therefore only one function: it is to show the unreasonableness of unbelief. Never can it demonstrate the truth with "enticing words of man's wisdom." The reason for this is evident. Unbelief is as unreasonable as it is untrue; it projects the plea of intelligence, while at the bottom of it lies the vicious tendency to do that which is evil. John 3, 20: "For every one that doeth evil hateth the light, neither cometh he to the light, lest his deeds should be reproved." To expose this malice of the carnal heart and to demonstrate the folly of infidelity in upholding its vicious claims is all that can be expected of Christian apologetics. Never can Christian apologetics take the place of the simple preaching of the Word of God. — In this connection it may also be stated that there are no scientific reasons against the Christian faith. Wherever the Christian faith is opposed, the opposition has its source not in true science, but in vicious infidelity. The rejection of revealed divine truth can in no case be justified on reasonable grounds; it is the perverted reason of man only that disavows the truth which is in Christ Jesus.

16. THEOLOGY AND POSITIVE ASSURANCE.

In the preceding chapter we pointed out the truism that the Christian theologian must be personally sure of the truth which he teaches. The question how this positive subjective assurance may be secured *(erkenntnis-theoretische Frage)* is being discussed with much vigor within both the conservative and the liberalistic camps. Quite commonly it is thought to be a problem involving most serious difficulties. These difficulties, however, appear only if the theologian surrenders the objective truth of Holy Scripture. As long as he accepts Scripture as the only source and norm of faith, the question is indeed a most simple one. Our divine Lord teaches emphatically both that personal Christian assurance exists and that it is obtained through faith in His Word. John 8, 31. 32: "If ye continue in My Word, . . . ye shall know the truth." This faith, which in itself is perfect assurance, is effected through the Word of God by the Holy Ghost. 1 Cor. 2, 5: "That your faith should not stand in the wisdom of men, but in the power of God." Luther rightly says: "Man is certain passively, just as the Word of God is certain actively." *(Homo est certus passive, sicut Verbum Dei est certum active.)* That means according to Luther's own explanation: "Where this [God's] Word enters the heart with a true faith, it makes the heart as firm, sure, and certain as it is itself, so that it [the heart] becomes so absolutely firm and hard against every temptation, the devil, death, or whatever it may be that it boldly and proudly despises, and mocks at, everything that would doubt, tremble, be evil, or angry, for it knows that the Word of God cannot lie." (St. L., III, 1887.) This statement is truly Scriptural. Personal, or subjective, assurance is most certainly obtained through the Word of God, and only through the Word of God, as Holy Scripture testifies. On the other hand, every kind of subjective assurance which does not flow from God's Word through faith is self-made and hence nothing but ignorance and self-deception, 1 Tim. 6, 3. 4.

This is the Christian theologian's reply to the false claim of modern rationalistic theology, which asserts that the real personal, or subjective, assurance is "self-assurance" *(Selbstgewissheit)*, or assurance which the theologian owes to his own regenerate self. This error, which was first proposed by Schleiermacher, has been quite generally adopted, even by theologians of the positive wing. This erroneous view rejects Holy Scripture as the only source and norm of faith; and so its advocates rely on their "Christian consciousness" or their "Christian experience" as the norm of their faith. Accordingly their "Christian theology" is built not exclusively on Holy Scripture, but on their "regenerate heart" or their own "sanctified ego"; and it is from this that they propose to derive their positive personal assurance of divine truth. But every assurance thus obtained must be rejected as false, since it is neither Christian nor scientific nor assurance at all. It is not Christian because it discards the specifically Christian foundation of faith; it is not scientific because it makes the human mind an authority in matters of which natural man is totally ignorant; it is, lastly, not assurance, but imagination, because the Christian theologian can know the divine truth only in so far as he continues in the Word of God. The unchristian character of modern rationalistic theology proves conclusively that it is impossible to draw the Christian faith from any other source than Holy Scripture; for this brand of theology does not only reject the specific doctrines of the Christian religion, but it also sets up contradictory teachings in opposition to Holy Scripture and the Christian faith. Thus modern rationalistic theology denies the Scriptural doctrine of justification by grace, through faith, and teaches in its place salvation by work-righteousness. Such "assurance" therefore rests upon grounds which God's Word positively condemns.

In short, divine truth can be known by men, or what is the same thing, the human mind is capable of personal assurance of the divine truth. But this assurance is actual only if the theologian clings to Holy Scripture and in simple faith believes what God has spoken in His written Word. It is the unique characteristic of the Word of God both that it is absolute truth and that it renders the believer absolutely certain of its being such. If this is denied, the possibility and actuality of faith must likewise be denied; for personal assurance is nothing else than personal faith.

17. THEOLOGY AND DOCTRINAL PROGRESS.

Modern rationalistic theology of both wings, the conservative no less than the liberalistic, demands theological progress, or doctrinal development, in accord with the advanced and ever-advancing religious vogues of the age *(Lehrfortbildung)*. Its claim is that Christian theology cannot be stagnant, but must adjust itself to the varying views of the times. So insistent it is with regard to this matter that it brands all Christian theologians who oppose doctrinal development as unfaithful to their high commission. In modern rationalistic circles loyal theologians, who cling to Holy Scripture as the only norm of faith, are styled "repristinating theologians" *(Repristinationstheologen),* a term that implies both censure and contempt.

However, as a matter of fact theological progress, or doctrinal development, is impossible and must be condemned as apostasy from the Christian faith. The reason for this is obvious. According to Holy Scripture Christian theology constitutes a unit, which is complete and perfect in itself and hence incapable of either addition or subtraction. Matt. 28, 20: "Teaching them to observe all things whatsoever I have commanded you." 2 Thess. 2, 15: "Stand fast and hold the traditions [the doctrines] which ye have been taught." Rev. 22, 18: "If any man shall add unto these things, God shall add unto him the plagues that are written in this book." Christian theology, or Christian doctrine, is therefore, according to the express teachings of Holy Scripture, a fixed body of divine truths, which must never be altered, neither increased by human additions nor diminished by omissions of any kind. The Christian theologian must acknowledge and proclaim "all the counsel of God." Cp. Acts 20, 20. 21. 27: "I kept back nothing that was profitable unto you, but have showed you and have taught you publicly and from house to house, testifying both to the Jews and also to the Greeks, repentance toward God and faith toward our Lord Jesus Christ. For I have not shunned to declare unto you all the counsel of God." In addition to this Holy Scripture very emphatically affirms that the Church of Christ is built "upon the foundation of the apostles and prophets, Jesus Christ Himself being the chief Corner-stone," Eph. 2, 20. The "foundation of the apostles and prophets" is the fixed doctrine which these holy men have written in Holy Writ by inspiration of the Holy Ghost. So also our Lord declares that those who are saved shall be saved through the Word of the apostles, John 17, 20. Moreover, the Word of God warns all believers most impressively against all errorists that pervert this fixed and definite Word either through addition or subtraction. Acts 20, 29: "After my departing shall grievous wolves enter in among you, not sparing the flock." 1 Tim. 4, 1: "In the latter times some shall depart from the faith, giving heed to seducing spirits and doctrines of devils." Hence both Christ and His apostles declare that the Christian doctrine is a perfect and complete body of inspired truths, which must be preserved pure and unadulterated. Every possibility of doctrinal progress, or development, is therefore excluded. Evolution in the realm of doctrine or theology is as preposterous and unscriptural as it is in the realm of nature, or creation. Holy Scripture affirms positively that the same God who made man also gave to him the divine doctrine by which he must be saved. Over this divine doctrine man has no jurisdiction; it is God's sanctuary, which sinful man must not defile either by addition or subtraction, or, to use the modern euphemism, by doctrinal development.

To this the objection has been raised that the Christian Church has at all times actually developed the Christian doctrine by establishing creeds and confessions. But this objection involves an intolerable fallacy. In its creeds the Christian Church has never developed the Christian doctrine, but only declared the express doctrine of Holy Scripture in its full truth and purity against the errors of heretics and schismatics. Thus the Apostles' Creed, the Nicene Creed, the Athanasian Creed, and the like, are not declarations of new, man-made teachings, but the very doctrines of Christ and His apostles set forth in Holy Scripture. Whenever the formulation of creeds necessitated the coining of terms not found in Holy Scripture (ὁμοούσιος, θεοτόκος, mere passive, etc.), this was done only to present the Scriptural doctrine in clearer light, but never to foist man-devised and unscriptural teachings upon the Christian Church. So also the particular Lutheran Confessions are only specific declarations of the Scriptural doctrine against the errors of Romanism, Calvinism, and enthusiasm. Luther writes very truthfully: "We fabricate nothing new, but retain, and hold to, the old Word of God as the ancient Church confessed it; hence we are, just like it, the true ancient Church, teaching and believing the same Word of God. For this reason the papists blaspheme Christ Himself, the apostles, and the whole Christian Church when they call us innovationists and heretics. For they find nothing with us but the old [doctrine] of the ancient Church." (St. L., XVII, 1324.)

That theological progress, or doctrinal development, is intrinsically impossible is proved experimentally by the fact that all attempts to develop the Christian doctrine have invariably led to the perversion of divine truth. Modern rationalistic theology, which champions doctrinal development as a prerequisite for the continued existence of the Church, has completely surrendered the very doctrines with which Christianity stands or falls, such as the doctrines of inspiration, of the vicarious atonement of Christ, of justification by grace alone, through faith, etc. Its doctrinal development has proved so fatal that it has virtually destroyed Christian theology and enthroned in its place a paganistic body of principles and teachings. And the reason for this is not hard to find. At the foundation of all doctrinal development lies the blind, perverse, and satanic rationalism of the carnal heart, which cannot bear the sound doctrine of God's holy Word and consequently is determined to teach what is opposed to the saving truth which is in Christ Jesus. Our divine Lord condemned this rationalistic spirit of unbelief when He told the Pharisees: "Ye are of your father the devil, and the lusts of your father ye will do. He abode not in the truth because there is no truth in him. When he speaketh a lie, he speaketh of his own; for he is a liar and the father of it," John 8, 44. Let the Christian theologian remember that the Christian religion is the absolute religion, which is so complete and perfect in itself that St. Paul could write: "But though we or an angel from heaven preach any other gospel unto you than that which we have preached unto you, let him be accursed," Gal. 1, 8. If sound Biblical theology must go by the name of "repristination theology," then let the Christian theologian glory in that term. For that is the only kind of theology which deserves a place in the Christian Church, since it is the only kind of theology which Jesus Christ, the Head and King of the Church, recognizes as true and divine. May God in His mercy retain in His Church "repristinating theologians"! For they are theologians after His heart, whom He will honor and glorify throughout eternity as the true builders of His Zion.

18. THEOLOGY AND ACADEMIC FREEDOM.

Modern rationalistic theology demands that the official teachers of the Church, both in the pulpit and in the lecture chair, should be invested with full academic freedom. That is to say, they should be allowed to assert their subjective opinions, without any restrictions whatsoever; even Holy Scripture must not be forced upon

NATURE AND CONCEPT OF THEOLOGY.

them as the only source and standard of the faith which they are to inculcate. The ancient Christian rule that in the Christian Church the Word of God alone must be taught is rejected as "servitude of the letter," "unworthy academic coercion," "legalism," etc. (*Buchstabenknechtschaft, unwuerdiger Lehrzwang, gesetzlicher Geist usw.*). However, this demand for academic freedom is in direct opposition to Holy Scripture; it is a freedom that is carnal and ungodly, since it involves full scope to criticize, condemn, and reject the Word of God. The academic freedom which modern rationalistic theology seeks for itself must therefore be repudiated as antichristian and atheistic; for it insists upon freedom from God and Christ.

As a matter of fact the true freedom of a Christian consists in this, that he has been liberated from his own sin-bound will and has become a servant of Jesus Christ. Rom. 6, 22: "But now being made free from sin and become servants of God." The essence of true Christian liberty is therefore loyalty, obedience, and subjection to the Word of the Lord. John 8, 31. 32: "If ye continue in My Word, then are ye My disciples indeed; and ye shall know the truth, and the truth shall make you free." As soon as the theologian relinquishes the Word of God as his only source and norm, he ceases to be a δοῦλος Χριστοῦ and becomes a slave of men. Then he has not obtained freedom at all, but has exchanged the holy service of Christ for the unholy thraldom of human opinions, views, and judgments; in place of the divine Master he now serves a human taskmaster, even if this taskmaster is only his own carnal heart. How wrong it is for a theologian to demand freedom to teach his subjective views in place of the infallible Word of God becomes clear as we carefully consider what Holy Scripture teaches with respect to this.

a. The Word of God affirms that the Christian Church till the end of time has only one Teacher, Christ Jesus, the Son of God. Matt. 23, 8: "But be not ye called Rabbi; for one is your Master, even Christ; and all ye are brethren." As the one Master, or Teacher, Christ commanded His apostles to teach all nations all things whatsoever He has commanded, Matt. 28, 20. Christ's own divine Word as set forth by the holy prophets and apostles in the Scriptures is the only saving truth, which the Christian Church should believe and proclaim. Gal. 1, 8: "But though we or an angel from heaven preach any other gospel unto you than that which we have preached unto you, let him be accursed." Eph. 2, 20: "And [ye] are built upon the foundation of the apostles and prophets." In this manner Holy Scripture positively asserts that all teaching in the Christian Church should be nothing else than the teaching of God's Word. Negatively, Holy Scripture condemns the inculcation of human opinion in place of the Word of God by calling all those who insist upon teaching doctrine other than Christ teaches in Holy Scripture, *antichrists*. 1 John 2, 18: "As ye have heard that antichrist shall come, even now are there many antichrists"; v. 22: "Who is a liar but he that denieth that Jesus is the Christ? He is antichrist, that denieth the Father and the Son." The demand of modern rationalistic theology that the theologian must be given free scope to present his own theology is therefore thoroughly anti-Scriptural.

b. All Christians are commanded in clear and unmistakable terms to hear such teachers only as proclaim the Word of God in its complete truth and purity. All theologians who are disloyal to the "words of our Lord Jesus Christ" should be rejected as deceivers, ignoramuses, and enemies of the faith and must be avoided. 2 John 10: "If there come any unto you and bring not this doctrine, receive him not into your house, neither bid him Godspeed." 1 Tim. 6, 3. 4: "If any man teach otherwise and consent not to wholesome words, even the words of our Lord Jesus Christ, . . . he is proud, knowing nothing, but doting." Rom. 16, 17: "Mark them which cause divisions and offenses contrary to the doctrine which ye have learned and avoid them." These warnings apply not only to ministers of the Gospel, but also to theological professors, who have been called to instruct the future teachers and preachers of the Christian Church. Also their Christian call and profession requires of them that they be absolutely true to the Word of God in their whole ministry of teaching, John 8, 31. 32.

The disastrous consequences of academic freedom granted to ministers and theological professors are apparent in all churches where such freedom has been in vogue. As a result of this ungodly freedom we find in these denominations: 1) hopeless confusion in doctrine and endless wrangling concerning theological problems, by which these churches have been made to suffer complete disruption (*e. g.,* the denominations in which Modernists and Fundamentalists are engaged in interminable controversy); 2) the absolute denial of the basic Christian truths taught in Holy Scripture, such as the divine inspiration of the Bible, the vicarious atonement of Christ, the justification of a sinner by grace, through faith, the resurrection of the dead, etc. Academic freedom resulted at once in "progressive theology," that is, in the liberalizing of theology according to the standards of human reason and modern science, until it has become thoroughly anti-Biblical. Present-day Modernism, which is the direct consequence of academic freedom, is a complete revolt against the sacred theology of God's Word and is in itself the rejection of Biblical Christianity.

The true Christian theologian rejoices in the possession of divine truth as offered in Holy Scripture, by which he has become free from every delusion and error. His constant endeavor is to make known to men bound and perishing in sin the saving and liberating truths of Christ, the divine Liberator of sin-lost men. Loyalty, obedience, and subjection to the Word of God constitute for him the supreme, glorious, and perfect liberty, which he must hold, guard, and protect against all odds. John 8, 36: "If the Son therefore shall make you free, ye shall be free indeed." It is for this reason that he so strenuously repudiates the academic freedom which unbelieving and unfaithful theologians now demand for themselves.

19. THEOLOGICAL SYSTEMS.

The peculiar nature of Christian theology has given rise to the question whether it is proper in the field of theology to speak of theological systems. The answer to the question depends of course on the meaning in which the term *system* is used. Christian theology, or doctrine, is indeed a system inasmuch as it presents to the student a complete unit *(ein abgeschlossenes Ganzes)*. It is a system inasmuch as it is "an orderly arrangement of parts or elements into a whole" or "an organized body of truth." The one author of Christian theology is the one, true, and living God, who proclaims the divine truth in the Old as well as in the New Testament, by Moses no less than by Paul, so that Holy Scripture sets forth, not the subjective views of Moses, or Isaiah, or Peter, or Paul, or John, etc., but the sacred doctrine of God Himself. Scripture doctrine is everywhere and in the same degree divine doctrine *(doctrina divina)*.

Again, in this divine doctrine, clearly and infallibly stated in Holy Scripture, the article of justification by grace, through faith in Christ, is the central teaching, to which the other articles of faith either lead up *(articuli antecedentes)* or point back *(articuli consequentes)*. 1 Cor. 2, 2: "I determined not to know anything among you save Jesus Christ and Him crucified." Acts 20, 27:

"I have not shunned to declare unto you all the counsel of God."
In all of St. Paul's preaching, which, according to his own testimony, embraced "all the counsel of God" unto salvation, the doctrine of Christ Crucified for the sins of the world was basic and
pivotal.

In view of this close connection of the various Christian doctrines with its central teaching and with one another, a connection
which is so intimate that errors in one point must inevitably produce errors also in the others, Christian theology may certainly be
called a system. And we apply the term especially to point out
not only the absolute unity of the whole body of truth, but also
the perfect coherency of its elemental parts. Luther is right in
saying: "In philosophy a small error in the beginning is a very
serious error in the end. So also in theology a slight error will
destroy the whole doctrine. For the doctrine is like a mathematical
point; it cannot be divided, that is, it cannot brook either subtraction or addition. Hence the doctrine must be one certain,
perpetual, and round golden ring, in which there is no break.
If even the least break occurs, the ring is no longer perfect."
(St. L., IX, 644 f.) Whoever, for instance, errs with respect to the
Holy Trinity must err also with regard to the deity of Christ;
or whoever teaches synergism cannot teach in its unadulterated
form the doctrine of divine grace. Just because Christian theology
is a system, it does not permit any perversion or denial of a single
one of its doctrines; for every perversion of its constituent parts
must necessarily destroy the entire system.

Nevertheless Christian theology may not be called a system
in the sense in which human systems of knowledge are so called.
In science and philosophy a system is "an orderly collection of
logically related principles and facts, arranged so as to express the
whole range of truth in any department." In that sense sacred
theology is not a system; for it is not constructed by human reason
on the basis of a given fundamental principle. Its author is not
man, but God. In it reason has only an instrumental, not a magisterial, function *(usus instrumentalis, non usus magisterialis)*. Nor
does it deduce and demonstrate its truths from a given premise or
principle, but it merely inculcates the truths set forth in Holy
Scripture, with the proper emphasis on the cardinal doctrine of
justification by grace. In other words, the analysis and synthesis
which the theologian applies never go beyond the Word of God.
Wherever Holy Scripture contains *lacunae,* or omissions, the system
of the Christian theologian likewise contains *lacunae,* or omissions.

The true theologian teaches only what Holy Scripture teaches, not more and not less. His system is only a declaration and statement of Scriptural doctrine.

This is a point of the greatest importance, and only as the theologian continually and conscientiously observes it, will he be kept from the fatal mistake of adding to the Word of God human opinions and doctrines, a perversion of Christian doctrine against which Holy Scripture most earnestly warns. Let the Christian theologian therefore bear in mind the basic truth that in the system of Christian doctrine, while it is complete so far as its scope is concerned, that is, so far as it pertains to the salvation of sinners, we may nevertheless speak of "missing links"; that is, there remain questions which Scripture does not answer. For example, Holy Scripture sets forth most emphatically the *sola gratia* and the *universalis gratia;* that is to say, sinners are saved solely by grace, and divine grace desires the salvation of all sinners. This being true, the question arises: "Why, then, are not all men saved?" The proposed explanation that the difference lies in men *(aliquid discrimen in homine),* since some are better than others, is most strenuously denied by God's Word, which declares that all men by nature are in the same guilt *(in eadem culpa).* Rom. 3, 22—24: "For there is no difference; for all have sinned and come short of the glory of God, being justified freely by His grace, through the redemption that is in Christ Jesus."

With the same emphasis Holy Scripture denies also the Calvinistic explanation that God has eternally predetermined some to damnation. Hence it is clear that Holy Scripture does not answer the question *Cur alii, alii non?* This does not mean that Holy Scripture does not give us any information with regard to the question of salvation and damnation. It tells us clearly that, if sinners are saved, they are saved solely by grace and that, if they are lost, they are lost through their own fault. Nevertheless, when we compare two individual sinners, as David and Saul, or Peter and Judas, and ask, "Why was the one saved and the other not?" *(Cur alii prae aliis?),* this question remains unanswered. Nor is it proper for the Christian theologian to endeavor to answer the question; for in that case he must draw on human reason to decide what is properly a matter of divine revelation. Attempts to solve the particular point in question have resulted either in Calvinism, the denial of universal grace, or in synergism, the denial of grace alone. But the Christian theologian must affirm both the *univer-*

salis gratia and the *sola gratia.* In the system of Christian doctrine therefore *lacunae,* or doctrinal "missing links," must be admitted, as St. Paul himself declares when he writes: "We know in part, and we prophesy in part," 1 Cor. 13, 9. The Christian theologian must know and teach in part only, that is, only as the divine truths which he is to inculcate are clearly set forth in Holy Scripture. In connection with this point we may note also the following truths: —

a. Holy Scripture, in all its parts, is the divinely inspired, infallible Word of God, in which He teaches man the only way to salvation. To this way of salvation, which is both complete and perfect, the Christian theologian must add nothing, neither must he take away from it even the least particle, John 10, 35; 2 Tim. 3, 16; 2 Pet. 1, 21; John 8, 31. 32; Rev. 22, 18—20. Any change or perversion of the divine Word is a scandal, which offends God and ultimately renders impossible the salvation of sinners, which God has purposed by giving His Word to men.

b. Modern rationalistic theology, which denies the fundamentals of the Christian doctrine for the very reason that it rejects the divinely inspired Word of God as the only source and norm of faith, seeks to construct its own unified system of teachings *(ein einheitliches Ganzes)* on the basis of "Christian consciousness," "Christian experience," "regenerate reason," etc. In other words, it substitutes for the true *principium cognoscendi* a false standard of doctrine and dethrones Holy Scripture from its exalted eminence of being the only authority in religion. To the modern rationalistic theologian Holy Scripture is only an "authentic record" of divine revelation, in which divine and human elements are incongruously blended and from which his "enlightened mind" must glean the truths that are to constitute his "system of theology." Or to state it in different terms, modern rationalistic theology refuses to identify the Word of God with Holy Scripture; for it regards Holy Scripture as only containing the Word of God. These theologians hold that the subjective judgment of the individual must decide just what is the Word of God, or divine truth, in Holy Scripture. This procedure must be condemned as a *crimen laesae maiestatis* against the divine Lord, as a revolt against His divinely established authority, and as a downright rejection of His holy Word, which must result in unspeakable confusion and perversion. This is evident from the fact that the pantheistic system of Schleiermacher and the modernistic system of Ritschl, both of which are built up on the subjective authority of human reason, equally reject the Gospel of Christ and inculcate doctrines in direct opposition to it. The appeal of rationalistic theologians to "Christian consciousness," "Christian experience," and the like, as foundations of systems of faith are a mere pretense to conceal their unholy endeavor of casting aside Holy Scripture and its divine doctrines and teaching their own word.

c. The Christian theologian, in performing his functions as a teacher of the Church, must always remember that all the statements of Holy Scripture are infallible truths, which nothing can overthrow, and that it is therefore his sacred duty to present these truths just as they are set forth in Holy Scripture, without addition or subtraction. Systems of philosophy or of science are constructed by human reasoning on the basis of facts or theories gathered by the originator himself; but sacred theology is a science which God Himself, its divine Author, presents to men complete and perfect and altogether adequate for its divinely designed purpose. Hence men are to preach the Word of God and not to philosophize about it; they are to be preachers, not demonstrators, of the truth. The Christian theologian has completely accomplished his task if he has set forth clearly and unmistakably the sacred truths taught by God in Holy Scripture. Nothing more is asked of him, but also nothing less.

d. The Christian theologian's work of systematizing therefore consists only in presenting the several divine truths given in Holy Scripture under their proper heads. These truths are derived from the proof-passages *(sedes doctrinae),* that is, from the clear and unmistakable passages in which the particular doctrines are set forth, and not from the "entirety of Scripture" or the "scope of Scripture" *(vom Schriftganzen).* The purpose of this systematizing is to present "all the counsel of God," or to teach each and every doctrine which God's Word teaches. If the theologian goes beyond this, if he presents his own personal views as the teaching of God's Word, he is no longer a Christian theologian, but a false prophet.

e. The charge so frequently made that Luther himself developed his doctrines, in particular the doctrine of justification by grace, is refuted by his own statements on this point. According to his own confession the great Reformer never operated with "the scope of Scripture," but with Scripture-passages so clear and unmistakable that upon these his doctrines rested as upon an impregnable rock. It is for this reason that Luther's theology is so thoroughly Scriptural. He constructed no system of doctrine outside and beyond the written Word of God, but received and taught in simple faith the sacred truths positively set forth in the *sedes doctrinae* of Holy Scripture. He was a systematician whose whole system of doctrine was rooted in, and governed by, God's Word. He writes: "It is certain that whosoever does not rightly believe or desire one single article ... certainly does not believe any at all with true earnestness and right faith. And whosoever is so presumptuous as to deny God or call Him a liar in one word [of Scripture], and does this deliberately, ... will also deny God in all His words and in all of them call Him a liar. Therefore it is necessary to believe all and everything truly and fully or else believe nothing. The Holy Spirit does not allow Himself to be separated or divided, so that He should teach or have us believe one doctrine as true and another as false." ·(St. L., XX, 1781.)

f. In conclusion it may be said that the rationalistic systems of theology, which pride themselves so smugly on their inner harmony and perfection, are after all decidedly imperfect and incomplete. They cannot be otherwise, since human reason is unable to answer in a satisfactory manner the paramount questions which properly belong to the sphere of divine revelation. In other words, unless God answers for us the questions pertaining to the great verities of spiritual knowledge, they never will be answered. Consequently, wherever the Holy Spirit, the infallible Revealer of divine truth, saw fit to be silent with respect to doctrinal issues, human reason must likewise be silent. Theologians who propose to construct complete systems of truth on the basis of their reason or their subjective theology perpetrate a piece of fraud which is unpardonable and which leads to downright apostasy from the Word of God, to uncertainty in spiritual matters, and to endless confusion and contradiction. For all who err from Scripture err from truth in general; and the systems of doctrine that are not Scriptural are likewise not rational. For this the history of dogma furnishes abundant proof.

20. THEOLOGICAL METHODS.

In the presentation of the dogmatic material Lutheran divines have employed, in the main, two methods, the *synthetic* and the *analytic*. The synthetic method proceeds from cause to effect, while the analytic method pursues the opposite course, from effect to cause. Synthetically arranged, the dogmatic grouping presents, first, God as the Cause and Principle of all things created; next, the means by which sinful and apostate mankind is brought back to communion with God; and lastly, the glorious salvation itself to which the believer attains. Analytically, the dogmatic material would be grouped as follows: Salvation, as the final objective of man; next, the means by which salvation is attained; and lastly, God as the divine Giver and Author of salvation.

The analytical method has been preferred by the later theologians of the Lutheran Church for the avowed reason that theology, being a practical subject, should first present man's final goal as the vital idea in Christian doctrine. After all, however, the grouping of the doctrinal material is of little consequence as long as Holy Scripture is recognized as the only source and standard of faith, from which alone the theologian must draw his teachings. If the doctrine is taken from any other source than Holy Scripture, either method is equally unsatisfactory; if the theologian remains loyal to God's Word, both methods may be employed with equal success. In the final analysis, not the method of presenting the theological material, but faithfulness to Scripture, is the prime requisite of a good dogmatic treatise.

The synthetic method was commonly used within the Lutheran Church by the early dogmaticians, such as Melanchthon, Chemnitz, Hutter, Gerhard. The analytic method was followed by Dannhauer, Koenig, Calov, Quenstedt, Baier, Hollaz, and others. Occasionally we find a combination of the two methods. The time is past when a dogmatic treatise is judged by its method, though a modified form of the synthetic method perhaps is now given the preference. But what the Christian Church must demand of all dogmatic treatises or books is a clear, thorough, and practical presentation of the Scriptural truths. The only theology which deserves a place in Christ's Church is the sacred theology which God Himself has given in Holy Scripture. From this surpassing treasure of divine truth the Christian theologian dare not deviate in the slightest; if he does, he is disloyal to the charge entrusted to him. In his system of theology the two distinctive principles of the Christian faith, the *sola Scriptura* and the *sola gratia,* must stand preeminent; otherwise his entire theology becomes rationalistic, paganistic, and destructive, a disgrace to the name of Christ and a menace to His Church. *Quod non est biblicum, non est theologicum.* All dogma that is not founded upon this axiom does not deserve the name of Christian theology.

21. THE ACQUISITION OF THE THEOLOGICAL HABITUDE.

Our Lutheran dogmaticians have rightly emphasized the great truth that "the theologian is not born, but made." *(Theologus non nascitur, sed fit.)* By this axiom they wished to say that no man by nature is a theologian nor can become a theologian by his own reason or strength. Theology is a God-given habitude. *(Theologia est habitus practicus θεόσδοτος.)* Hence the Holy Spirit Himself must make a person a theologian. How the Holy Spirit accomplishes this is excellently described by Luther in the famous dictum: *Oratio, meditatio, tentatio faciunt theologum.* This is the best description of theological methodology which has ever been attempted; for it names, briefly, yet fully, all the elements that cooperate in the making of a true theologian.

It recognizes first of all the necessity of *prayer*. With regard to prayer as a means by which to acquire the theological habitude, Luther writes: "For this reason you should despair of your wisdom and reason; for with these you will acquire nothing, but by your arrogance cast yourself and others into the pit of hell, as did Lucifer. Kneel down in your chamber and ask God in true humility and seriousness to grant you His Holy Spirit through His beloved Son in order that He may enlighten you, guide you, and grant you a true wisdom." (St. L., XIV, 434 ff.) That sincere and constant prayer is an indispensable factor in the acquisition of the theological habitude is attested not only by all true theologians who have served the Christian Church in the spirit of its divine Lord, but also by Holy Scripture itself. John 15, 7. 8: "If ye abide in Me and My words abide in you, ye shall ask what ye will, and it shall be done unto you. Herein is My Father glorified that ye bear much fruit; so shall ye be My disciples"; 16, 24: "Ask, and ye shall receive, that your joy may be full." Jas. 1, 5: "If any of you lack wisdom, let him ask of God, that giveth to all men liberally and upbraideth not; and it shall be given him."

The second requisite in Luther's methodology is *meditation,* or study. Of this Luther writes: "In the second place, you should meditate, and not only in your heart, but also outwardly, the oral Word and the express words that are written in the Book, which you must always consider and reconsider and read and read over with diligent attention and reflection to see what the Holy Ghost means thereby. And take care that you do not become weary of it, thinking that you have read it sufficiently if you have read, heard, or said it once or twice and understand it perfectly. For in this way no great theologian is made, but they [who do not study] are like immature fruit, which falls down before it is half ripe. For this reason you see in this psalm [Ps. 119] that David is always boasting that he would speak, meditate, declare, sing, hear, read, day and night and forever, yet nothing else than alone the Word and the commandments of God. For God does not purpose to give you His Spirit without the external Word. Be guided by that. For He did not command in vain to write, preach, read, hear, sing, and declare His external Word." By meditation, Luther, then, understands the constant study of Holy Scripture as the pure and infallible Word of God, by which the Holy Ghost not only converts and sanctifies sinners, but also renders the theologian capable of doing the work of a truly Christian teacher in the fear of God, in other words, by which He bestows the theological habitude. It is clear that such constant study of God's Word is commanded also in Holy Scripture. 1 Tim. 4, 13: "Till I come, give attendance to reading"; v. 15: "Meditate upon these things; give thyself wholly to them, that thy profiting may appear to all"; 6, 20: "O Timothy, keep that which is committed to thy trust, avoiding profane and vain babblings and oppositions of science falsely so called."

Concerning *temptation* as a means by which the Holy Spirit creates or enhances the theological habitude, Luther writes: "In the third place, there is *tentatio,* that is, trial. That is the true touchstone, which teaches you not only to know and understand, but also to experience, how true, sincere, sweet, lovely, powerful, comforting, the Word of God is, so that it is the wisdom above all wisdom. Thus you see how David, in the psalm just mentioned, complains about all manner of enemies, wicked princes and tyrants, false prophets and factions, which he must endure because he always meditates, that is, deals with God's Word in every possible way, as stated. For as soon as the Word of God bears fruit through you, the devil will trouble you, make you a real teacher, and teach you through tribulation to seek and to love the Word of God. For I myself — if I am permitted to voice my humble opinion — must thank my papists very much for so buffeting, distressing, and terrifying me by the devil's fury that they made me a fairly good theologian, which otherwise I should never have become."

As Luther here says, his whole theology grew out of his trials and troubles, which forced him to seek strength and comfort in Holy Scripture. And Luther experienced trials both from within and from without. First he was troubled by *tentationes* within his heart. Before he became a Christian theologian, he was plagued with the agony of a troubled conscience, produced by his insistence on work-righteousness as the means of obtaining pardon. From this state of dread and anguish he was at last rescued by the knowledge and understanding of the blessed Gospel, from which he indeed learned how "true, sincere, sweet, lovely, and powerful the Word of God is." Afterwards, when he began to proclaim the Gospel of Christ in its purity and truth, trials came to him from without. He was stigmatized as a heretic and schismatic, not only by the Romanists, but also by the enthusiasts of his time, so that again he was forced "to seek and love the Word"; and thus he became so established in, and convinced of, the divine truth that he could say: "Here I stand, I cannot do otherwise." Trials, or *tentationes,* therefore, made Luther a "fairly good theologian," because they compelled him to anchor his hope only in the Word of God. And so every Christian who aspires to become a true theologian must seek, study, and cling to, Holy Scripture until he regards it as the "wisdom above all wisdom."

Luther concludes his remarks on his famous axiom with the words: "Then [namely, if you follow the rule of David exhibited in Ps. 119] you will find how shallow and unworthy will appear to you the writings of the Fathers, and you will contemn not only the books of the opponents, but also be ever less pleased with your own writing and teaching. If you have arrived at this stage, you may surely hope that you have just *begun* to be a real theologian, one who is able to teach not only the young and unlearned, but also the advanced and well-instructed Christians. For Christ's Church includes all manner of Christians — young, old, weak, sick, healthy, strong, aggressive, indolent, simple, wise, etc. But if you consider yourself learned and imagine that you have attained the goal and feel proud of your booklets, teaching and writing, as though you had done marvelously and preached wondrously, and if you are much pleased because people praise you before others and you must be praised or otherwise you are disappointed and feel like giving up, — if you are minded like that, my friend, just grab yourself by the ears, and if you grab rightly, you will find a fine pair of big, long, rough donkey ears. Then go to a little more expense and adorn yourself with golden bells, so that, wherever you go, people can hear you, admiringly point at you with their fingers, and say, 'Lo and behold, there is that wonderful man who can write such excellent books and preach so remarkably!' Then certainly you will be blessed, yes, more than blessed, in the kingdom of heaven — indeed, in that kingdom in which the fire of hell has been prepared for the devil and his angels! In fine, let us seek honor and be haughty wherever we may. In this Book, God's glory alone is set forth, and it says: *'Deus superbis resistit, humilibus autem dat gratiam. . . . Cui est gloria in secula seculorum. Amen.'*"

Luther's emphasis upon true humility as a requisite of a true theologian is certainly in place, since the Holy Spirit with His sanctifying and sustaining gifts is present only in a contrite, humble heart. To the humble alone God gives the grace of true theology.

THE DOCTRINE OF HOLY SCRIPTURE.
(De Scriptura Sacra.)

1. HOLY SCRIPTURE THE ONLY SOURCE AND NORM OF FAITH.

The Christian Church is much older than Holy Scripture, that is, it existed long before God gave His written Word to men; for until the time of Moses God called and preserved His Church by oral teaching *(viva voce)*. The Christian Church began immediately after the Fall, when God proclaimed to fallen mankind salvation through faith in the Seed of the Woman, who was to destroy the works of the devil; and Adam and Eve penitently believed the *Protevangelium* (Gen. 3, 15). This method of orally promulgating His Word was retained by God until the time when He called Israel out of Egypt and made it His chosen people, or His Church, Gen. 4, 26; 13, 4; 20, 4; Acts 10, 43; Ex. 17, 14; 24, 4. 7; etc.

However, after God had commanded His prophets to put His Word in writing, His Church was rigidly bound to the written Word, and it was not permitted either to add to the Scriptures or to take anything away from them, Deut. 4, 2; 12, 32; Josh. 1, 7; 23, 6. For the Church of the Old Testament the prophetic Scriptures constituted a fixed canon, to which only God Himself could make additions, John 5, 39; Luke 16, 29. In the time of the New Testament, God added to the existing and acknowledged Scriptures of the prophets the holy writings of the apostles, to form, together with the Scriptures of the Old Testament, the inerrant foundation upon which His Church is built, Eph. 2, 20; 1 Pet. 1, 10—12.

With the revelations of Christ and His holy apostles the Scriptural canon is now complete, and the Christian Church is to look for no more revelations from God, John 17, 20; Eph. 2, 20; Heb. 1, 1—3. Luther writes very aptly: "That we may do: If we, too, are holy and have the Holy Spirit, we may boast of being catechumens and pupils of the prophets, inasmuch as we repeat and preach what we have heard and learned from the prophets and apostles and are sure that the prophets have taught it. In the Old Testament those are called 'the children of the prophets' who did not teach anything of their own or anything new, as did the prophets, but taught what they had received from the prophets." (St. L., III, 1890.)

If the question is asked where the New Testament Church may unerringly find the word of the apostles, they themselves point us to their holy writings and tell us that what they proclaimed orally is the same as that which they recorded in their sacred Scriptures, 1 John 1, 3. 4; 2 Thess. 2, 15. Though the apostles did not put into writing *everything* that they taught orally, nevertheless everything that is required for salvation is found in abundance in their writings, since they record with great diligence God's counsel of salvation through faith in Christ Jesus, John 21, 25; Phil. 3, 1. In addition, the holy apostles insisted upon their written word as the only source and norm of faith against all errorists of their time, demanding that all who regarded themselves as prophets must follow the Lord's commands as these are laid down in their writings, 1 Cor. 14, 37. 38; 2 Thess. 2, 2. St. Paul especially put his own signature to his epistles in order that these might be distinguished from spurious apostolic epistles, 2 Thess. 3, 17. Both the prophets and the apostles thus attest that Holy Scripture, or the written Word of God, is the only source and norm of faith and life, or the true *principium cognoscendi (Schriftprinzip)*.

This fundamental truth has been denied in various ways. The principle of Scripture, or the fact that Holy Scripture is the only source and norm of faith, has been abrogated by the substitution of something else for God's Word.

a. *Human reason* has been substituted for Scripture. By human reason we mean everything that man knows of God and divine things outside of Holy Scripture, or simply man's natural knowledge of God. This natural knowledge of God, however, cannot be the source of man's faith, since it is limited to the Law and its demands, Rom. 1, 20. 21. 32; 2, 15, and does not include the precious Gospel of Christ, or the message of reconciliation through the vicarious satisfaction of the incarnate Son of God, by which alone sinners can be saved, 1 Cor. 2, 6 ff.; Rom. 1, 16. Any one who makes human reason the norm of faith commits the logical fallacy of μετάβασις εἰς ἄλλο γένος and excludes himself from the Christian Church, since he substitutes for divine truth his own fallible wisdom, which rejects God's free salvation offered in the Gospel as foolishness, 1 Cor. 1, 21—25. The Christian Church therefore repudiates all forms of rationalism, Unitarianism, and Modernism, which regard human reason, or human science, as the source of faith, and condemns its proponents as being outside the pale of the Church *(extra ecclesiam)*.

By human reason, however, we denote also the *means* by which man perceives and thinks. This is the so-called ministerial use of reason *(usus rationis ministerialis, organicus)* and is quite distinct from its magisterial use *(usus rationis magisterialis)*. Reason in this sense has a legitimate and necessary place in theology, since the Holy Spirit implants and preserves saving faith through the Word of God which is received into the human mind, Rom. 10, 14. 17; John 5, 39; Matt. 24, 15; Luke 2, 19. To the ministerial use of reason belongs also the study of the languages in which Holy Scripture was originally written, and in particular that of logic and grammar, because the Holy Spirit, in giving to man God's Word, was pleased to accommodate Himself to the laws of human thought and speech. Luther makes the remark that God is incarnate in Holy Scripture *(Scriptura Sacra est Deus incarnatus).* In the same sense our Lutheran dogmaticians say that "theology must be grammatical" *(theologia debet esse grammatica),* which means that, if the theologian desires to understand Scripture, he must observe the fixed laws by which human speech and expression is governed. Luther urged this truth so vigorously as to maintain that any one who errs in grammar cannot but err also in his theology.

By distinguishing between the ministerial and the magisterial use of reason, our Lutheran dogmaticians also decided the question whether sacred theology and human reason, or Christian truth and human philosophy, really contradict each other. Their contention was that, since truth is always the same, such a contradiction could occur only if perverted reason presumed to be an arbiter in matters lying beyond its specific domain. With regard to the articles of faith they averred that these are not *contrary* to reason, but only *above* reason and that, if seemingly they did contradict reason, they were contrary only to *corrupt* reason or to the *perversion* of reason in the interest of falsehood and enmity against God.

However, the Christian theologian must expect the warfare between theology and perverted reason, or science falsely so called, to continue because ever since the Fall man by nature has been at enmity with God, Rom. 8, 7, and regards the very essence of the Christian religion, or the Gospel of Jesus Christ, as foolishness, 1 Cor. 2, 14. In consequence of his innate hatred against God and divine things, which always reveals itself in proud and arrogant rejection of His Word, natural man will never cease to oppose divine truth on the ground of his own supposed knowledge, so that unbelieving philosophers and atheistic scientists will always charge

Scripture with teaching falsehood (atheistic evolution). Gerhard is quite right when he says (II, 371): "We must distinguish between reason before and after the Fall. The former, as such, was never opposed to divine revelation; the latter has frequently been thus opposed through the influence of corruption."

b. *The enlightened reason,* which is also known as "Christian consciousness," "Christian experience," "Christian conviction," "Christian assurance," etc., has been substituted for the Word of God. It is true, every believer in Christ has an enlightened mind, but as far as he is a Christian, he never insists upon his enlightened reason as a source or norm of faith, since he owes his illumination entirely to the living power of the Word of God, Rom. 1, 16; and he knows that his reason will at once sink back into spiritual ignorance as soon as he departs from Christ's enlightening Gospel. Hence all who set up the enlightened mind of the Christian as a *principium cognoscendi* apart from Scripture deceive themselves, since their very desire to enthrone their enlightened reason as a judge of faith proceeds from their unenlightened reason, or their proud carnal mind, 1 Tim. 6, 3—5. Reason, inasmuch as it is illuminated by the Holy Ghost through the Word, never presumes to judge Scripture, but faithfully adheres to God's Word in all things and glories in its sacred teachings, John 8, 31. 32; 2 Cor. 10, 4. 5; 1 Cor. 1, 18. 24. Luther writes very correctly: "The Holy Spirit never operates without or before the Word, but He comes with and through the Word and never goes beyond the Word." (St. L., XI, 1073.)

c. *The general scope of Scripture ("das Schriftganze," "the whole of Scripture").* The advocates of this theory claim that the Christian articles of faith must not be drawn from Scripture-passages treating of the individual doctrines *(sedes doctrinae, dicta probantia),* but from the general scope or tenor of the Bible, which Schleiermacher, who first propounded this false view, called *"das Schriftganze,"* or the "whole of Scripture." Modern rationalizing theologians have readily assented to Schleiermacher's proposition; but we must reject it as utterly unadoptable, since the whole of a thing necessarily involves all its component parts, and as absolutely unscriptural, since Christ and His apostles invariably refuted error by referring to distinct Scripture-passages, Matt. 4, 4. 7. 10; Rom. 1, 17; 1 Cor. 10, 7—10; Gal. 4, 22 f. Schleiermacher's contention that "it is a most precarious procedure to quote Scripture-passages in a dogmatic treatise and, besides, in itself quite inadequate" (*Glaubenslehre,* I, § 30) was only a pretext to justify his unscriptural method of deriving the theological truths from his reason, or the "pious self-consciousness." Scripture declares of every theologian who repudiates the sacred doctrines set forth in God's Word: "If any man consent not to wholesome words, even the words of our Lord Jesus Christ, he is proud, knowing nothing, but doting about questions and strifes of words," 1 Tim. 6, 3. 4.

d. *The Church, in particular the decisions of church councils, synods, Popes,* etc., is substituted for Scripture by many. According to Holy Scripture, however, the Christian Church has no authority whatever to teach any doctrine besides and beyond the Word of its divine Master Jesus Christ, laid down in the writings of His prophets and apostles, Matt. 23, 8. 10; 28, 20; John 17, 20; Eph. 2, 20; 1 Pet. 1, 10—12. Hence the Church cannot be regarded as a judge of faith, but according to the will of its Lord it is to function till the end of time merely as a herald, or messenger, of God's Word, John 8, 31. 32. Whenever a Church puts forth doctrines of its own fabrication, it disowns the principle of Scripture and falls under the condemnation of Christ: "In vain they do worship Me, teaching for doctrines the commandments of men," Matt. 15, 9. The "consensus of the Church" *(consensus ecclesiae)* is not what Christian teachers have opined on this or that point of doctrine, but what they have declared as divine truth on the basis of Scripture, that is to say, in agreement with the witness of the holy prophets and apostles. According to Holy Scripture all those who reject the teachings of God's Word are antichrists, 1 John 2, 22, among whom the most perverse is the great Antichrist, "who opposeth and exalteth himself above all that is called God or that is worshiped, so that he as God sitteth in the temple of God, showing himself that he is God," 2 Thess. 2, 3. 4. The declaration of papal infallibility (1870) must be regarded as intolerable blasphemy and antichristian rebellion against God. In vain do papistic theologians quote Matt. 16, 18 as a proof that the Church, in particular the Pope, cannot err; for Christ promises to His Church His sustaining presence only under the condition that it faithfully teaches "unto the end of the world" "all things whatsoever I have commanded you," Matt. 28, 20. As long as the Church adheres to the Word of Christ, it cannot err; but as soon as it departs from the divine Word, it cannot but err, since in that case it has no other source to draw from than proud, perverted reason.

With respect to the witness of the Christian Church two extremes must be avoided; on the one hand, it must not be underestimated or rejected as worthless; on the other hand, it must not be overestimated, as if the testimony of the Church were in itself a *principium cognoscendi.* The *Formula of Concord* states the matter very correctly: "We believe, teach, and confess that the sole rule and standard according to which all dogmas together with all teachers should be estimated and judged are the prophetic and apostolic Scriptures of the Old and of the New Testament alone. . . . Other writings, however, of ancient or modern teachers, whatever name they bear, must not be regarded as equal to the Holy Scriptures, but all of them together be subjected to them and should not be received otherwise or further than as witnesses, in what manner after the time of the apostles and at what places this [pure] doctrine of the prophets and apostles was preserved." (Epitome, *Triglot,* p. 777. Cf. the distinction between *norma normans, sc.,* Scripture, and the *norma normata, sc.,* the Confessions of the Church.) With regard to the so-called "consensus of the fathers" (*consensus patrum, i. e.,* the agreement of the Church Fathers) Quenstedt shows that this does not exist; for many writings of the teachers of the ancient Church have been lost, and "the consensus of a few fathers cannot be accepted as the consensus of the whole Church." (Cf. the definition of the *consensus patrum* by Vincentius of Lerinum: *"Quod ubique, quod semper, quod ab omnibus creditum est,"* which is practically worthless.)

e. *Private revelations (revelationes immediatae, revelationes novae).* Private revelations are supposedly new doctrines which God gives to individuals to explain, correct, and supplement Holy Scripture. Fanatics, asserting that they had received private revelations, arose even in the time of the apostles, 1 Cor. 14, 37; 2 Thess. 2, 2; and in their wake there followed in the second and fourth centuries the Montanists and Donatists. At the time of Luther's Reformation, the "heavenly prophets," the Anabaptists and Schwenkfeldians, rejected the "external Word" and in its place stressed the "inner word," stigmatizing obedience to Scripture as "letter service" *(Buchstabendienst);* while in modern times the Christian Church must cope with the enthusiasm of such religious organizations as the Quakers, Swedenborgians, Irvingites, and others. In addition to these visionaries it must oppose also those who separate the operation of the Holy Ghost from the Word of Scripture and rely on private revelations as the norm of their faith, *e. g.:* —

a. The *Romanists,* who ascribe to their Popes the charisma of infallible teaching outside and beyond Scripture. With regard to the Papacy, Luther writes in the *Smalcald Articles:* "The Papacy also is nothing but sheer enthusiasm, by which the Pope boasts that all rights exist in the shrine of his heart, and whatever he decides and commands with [in] his Church is spirit and right, even though it is above and contrary to Scripture and the spoken Word." (Part III, Art. VIII, 4.)

b. The *Calvinists,* who teach that the saving work of the Holy Spirit occurs *immediately, i. e.,* outside and apart from the Word. (Hodge: "Efficacious grace acts immediately.")

c. All modern *rationalistic theologians,* who deny that Holy Scripture is the inerrant Word of God and therefore propose to draw the Christian doctrine from their "pious self-consciousness," their "Christian experience," and the like, while they stigmatize loyalty to Scripture as "letter theology," "intellectualism," "Biblicism," etc. The result of enthusiasm in religion is always the same, no matter whether it is practised by papists, Calvinists, or modern rationalists, as Luther well points out in the *Smalcald Articles,* in which he writes: "Enthusiasm adheres in Adam and his children from the beginning (from the first fall) to the end of the world, (its poison) having been implanted and infused into them by the old dragon, and is the origin, power (life), and strength of all heresy, especially of that of the Papacy and Mahomet." (Part III, Art. VIII, 9.) Luther says with regard to the pious pretenses of the enthusiasts: "They say these things only in order that they may lead us away from the Bible and make themselves masters over us, so that we should believe their dream sermons." (St. L., V, 334 f.)

The question of whether God deigns to reveal new doctrines outside, and apart from, the Bible is definitely decided in His Word, which binds all Christian believers to Holy Scripture as the sole source and norm of faith, John 17, 20; Eph. 2, 20. In Christ Jesus, the Light and Savior of the world, all divine revelations culminate, the prophets in the Old Testament pointing forward to His coming and the apostles witnessing to His incarnation, Passion, resurrection, ascension, and session at the right hand of God. Since Christ's prophetic and sacerdotal ministry has been accomplished (John 1, 18), men require no further revelations for their salvation because every doctrine needed for both faith and life of the Christian is amply supplied in the writings of the prophets and apostles,

Rom. 16, 17; 1 Tim. 6, 3 ff.; Luke 16, 29—31. Lutheran dogmaticians have aptly remarked with reference to the "new revelations" of the enthusiasts: "Either they contain what Scripture already teaches, and in that case they are superfluous; or they propound teachings contrary to the Bible, and in that case they are injurious and must be rejected."

f. *Historical investigation.* Modernists, rejecting the historical character of the New Testament, assert that they must go beyond Scripture to ascertain who the "historical Christ" really was and what He actually taught. To accomplish this purpose, they subject the records of the evangelists to a critical scrutiny in the light of comparative religion. The "historical Christ" whom they obtain by this procedure is divested of all supernatural properties and His doctrine of all supernatural elements. They make of Him a mere human teacher, whose doctrines are little more than an ethical code. In opposition to this preposterous method the true followers of Christ declare that the "historical revelation of the way of salvation is found only in the Bible" and that, as Luther correctly asserts, "we know nothing of Christ apart from and without His Word and much less of His teaching; for any 'Christ' who proposes an opinion outside the Word of Christ is the abominable devil, who applies to himself the holy name of Christ in order that he may thus sell to us his infernal venom." (St. L., XVII, 2015.) The truth of this statement is proved by the actual results of the modern historico-critical school of theology; for while it violently rejects all the sacred truths set forth in the Bible, it is unable to construct a satisfactory system of doctrines which may comfort the sinner in his spiritual distress. Its influences have proved only destructive, never edifying or helpful.

The reason for this is clear. After all, there can be only two sources of doctrine: Scripture and human reason. Any one who repudiates Holy Scripture as the true *principium cognoscendi* is obliged to draw his doctrine from his perverted mind or carnal heart, which at best retains only an imperfect knowledge of the divine Law originally inscribed in the human consciousness, so that natural man, knowing nothing at all of the true God and His glorious salvation through faith in Christ, is compelled to hold the *opinio legis,* or salvation by good works, to be the supreme religious precept. Ultimately every rejection of God's Word terminates in agnosticism or atheism. He who is without the divine Word is *eo ipso* also without God and without hope, Eph. 2, 12.

2. HOLY SCRIPTURE THE WORD OF GOD.

In contradistinction to all other books in the world Holy Scripture is the Word of God. As the writings of Plato are the word of Plato and those of Cicero are the word of Cicero, just so the Scriptures of the Old and New Testaments, which the prophets and apostles wrote by divine inspiration, are throughout, from beginning to end, the words of God Himself. This is not a "dogmatic construction," as rationalistic theologians have contended, but it is God's own testimony, given in Scripture. Hence Christian believers affirm not merely that the Bible *contains* God's Word, but that it *is* God's Word, that is to say, "Holy Scripture and the Word of God are interchangeable terms."

Holy Scripture is therefore a unique book; for it is neither a human nor a divine-human record of "revealed salvation facts," but God's own inspired and inerrant Word. The books of Christian authors contain God's Word as far as these pious writers have drawn from the Bible what they have written. But Scripture does not belong to this class of writings, but is in a class by itself. That was Luther's attitude toward the Holy Bible, and it is that of every true Christian believer, who readily subscribes to what Luther writes on this point: "You must deal with Scripture in such a way that you think just as God Himself has spoken." (St. L., III, 21.) The same truth Luther affirms when he says: "Holy Scripture did not grow upon the earth." (St. L., VII, 2095.)

Even sincere Christians at times forget this paramount truth because in Holy Scripture God speaks to us not only in simple, every-day terms, but also of very ordinary matters, things pertaining to the affairs of our earthly life. As a matter of fact, as Christ Himself during His sojourn on earth "was made in the likeness of man and found in fashion as a man," Phil. 2, 7. 8, so that some believed Him to be "John the Baptist, Elias, Jeremias, or one of the prophets," Matt. 16, 14, so also God's Word is set forth in Holy Scripture in the common speech of men and accommodated to our common earthly needs. Luther warns all believers: "I beg and warn most faithfully every pious Christian not to be offended at the simple speech and narrative which he will frequently meet with; let him not doubt, no matter how simple it may appear, that these are nothing but words, works, judgments, and narratives of the divine majesty, omnipotence, and wisdom. For this is the Scripture, which makes fools of all the wise and prudent and is open alone to the lowly and simple, as Christ Himself says in Matt. 11, 25. Therefore give up your pride and haughty spirit and regard Scripture as the greatest and most precious sanctuary and the richest mine, which can never be fully exhausted, in order that you may find the divine wisdom, which God here presents so plainly and simply that He may quench our pride." (St. L., XIV, 3 f.) In spite of its simplicity we therefore identify Holy Scripture with God's Word and declare that it is God's Word from beginning to end and in every part. In this we follow God's own directions given in Holy Scripture; for as we study that holy Book, we find:

a. That in the New Testament the Scriptures of the Old Testament are directly and absolutely quoted as *God's Word*. We thus read, Matt. 1, 22. 23: "All this was done that it might be fulfilled which *was spoken of the Lord by the prophet* [Is. 7, 14], saying, Behold, a virgin shall be with child," etc. In Matt. 2, 15 we read: "That it might be fulfilled which *was spoken of the Lord by the prophet* [Hos. 11, 1], saying, Out of Egypt have I called My Son." In Acts 4, 25. 26 the words of Ps. 2, 1. 2 are quoted as having been *"spoken of God* by the mouth of His servant David." Acts 28; 25 f. quotes the words in Is. 6, 9. 10 as words "which *the Holy Ghost spake* by Esaias the prophet." In Heb. 3, 7 ff. we find a quotation from Ps. 95, 7 f., with the express remark, *"as the Holy Ghost saith."* Finally, in Rom. 3, 2 the Holy Scriptures, which were entrusted to the Church of God of the Old Testament, are directly called "the words of God" (τὰ λόγια τοῦ θεοῦ). In fact, according to the unmistakable testimony of Christ the Old Testament Scriptures are so absolutely the Word of God that He says of them: "The Scripture cannot be broken," John 10, 35. The reference in this instance, sc., to Ps. 82, 6, is of great importance; for there magistrates are called "gods" (אֱלֹהִים, θεοί). This appellation, according to our Savior, was not a mistake and could not be a mistake because "the Scripture cannot be broken." From this passage therefore as well as from many others we learn that the Bible is verbally inspired, so that every word in Scripture is God's own infallible Word.

The series of passages in which the Old Testament Scriptures are called "God's Word" is supported by another group of texts, in which the Scriptures are presented as so absolutely divine that all things foretold in them must be literally fulfilled, indeed, that all events that occur in this world are directed by God's will, as revealed in Scripture. This takes Holy Scripture out of the class of human writings and places it in a class by itself, as God's own holy Book. Thus in John 17, 12 our Savior speaks of the apostasy of Judas and the loss of his soul and adds that this came about "that the Scripture might be fulfilled." Christ's own betrayal and capture in Gethsemane had to take place in order that "the Scripture might be fulfilled," Matt. 26, 54. Similarly we read in Luke 24, 44 ff. that Christ had to suffer, die, and rise again "because all things must be fulfilled which were written in the Law of Moses and in the Prophets and in the Psalms [*viz.*, in the entire Old Testament] concerning Me." Olshausen is right in arguing that in the New Testament the quotations from the Old Testament are referred to not as proofs from human writings, but as incontrovertible testimonies of their being *divine* writings. But the fact that the Old Testament Scriptures are God's own Word was stated by Christ Himself when He gave the command: "Search the Scriptures; for in them ye think ye have eternal life, and they are they which testify of Me," John 5, 39.

b. The fact that the Scriptures of the New Testament occupy the same canonical position as those of the Old Testament and are therefore in the same manner and to the same degree the Word of God is proved by a number of clear passages. In 1 Pet. 1, 10—12, the apostle first establishes the fact that the prophets of the Old Testament testified beforehand the sufferings of Christ and the glory that should follow through "the Spirit of Christ which was in them," but then adds: "Which [the sufferings of Christ and His glory] are now reported unto you by them that have preached the Gospel unto you with the Holy Ghost (ἐν πνεύματι ἁγίῳ, *by* the Holy Ghost) sent down from heaven." According to this passage the apostles in the New Testament proclaimed the Gospel *by the same Spirit of Christ* which was in the prophets of the Old Testament, so that their writings are the Word of God in the same sense and to the same degree as were those of the prophets. If the objection is raised that this passage refers to the oral word of the apostles, we may quote passages in which the apostles place their written word on the same level with their spoken word and demand for it the same reverence and obedience, 1 John 1, 3. 4; 2 Thess. 2, 15; 1 Cor. 14, 37; 2 Cor. 13, 3. As in 1 Pet. 1, 10—12, so also in Eph. 2, 20 the word of the apostles in the New Testament is accorded the same divine dignity and authority as the word of the prophets in the Old Testament; for both are declared to be the foundation upon which the Church is built. In addition to this, Christ states expressly that Christians would believe in Him and hence obtain salvation "through their [the apostles'] word," John 17, 20, which proves that their word is God's own Word; for this alone is able to save souls, Rom. 1, 16; Jas. 1, 21.

3. THE INSPIRATION OF THE BIBLE.

Holy Scripture does not merely attest the fact that it is God's Word: it also explains the peculiar manner in which God gave His Word to men. It clearly teaches that the Word of God was inspired, or inbreathed into certain holy men, whom God called to be the official writers of His holy Book, so that "all Scripture is given by inspiration of God" (πᾶσα γραφὴ θεόπνευστος), 2 Tim. 3, 16. Scripture emphatically declares with regard to the sacred writers of God's Book: "The prophecy came not in old time by the will of man, but holy men of God spake as they were moved (φερόμενοι) by the Holy Ghost," 2 Pet. 1, 21. Since the holy men of God spake as they were moved by the Holy Ghost, they evidently wrote not their own words, but those which God Himself put into their minds. This truth is unmistakably taught by St. Paul; for he writes: *"Which things also we speak, not in the words which man's wisdom teacheth, but which the Holy Ghost teacheth,* comparing spiritual things with spiritual," 1 Cor. 2, 13. The same apostle also declares that Christ was speaking in him, 2 Cor. 13, 3; and of his writings he states that they are "the commandments of the Lord," 1 Cor. 14, 37. The writings of the prophets and apostles are therefore the Word of God; they were divinely inspired to write the books embodied in our Bible.

In the Scripture-passages which set forth the doctrine of inspiration the following truths are distinctly expressed: —

a. The inspiration was not simply *"inspiration of thoughts" (suggestio realis)* nor *"inspiration of persons" (inspiratio personalis),* but *verbal inspiration (suggestio verbalis, Verbalinspiration), i. e.,* an inspiration by which the Holy Ghost inbreathed the very words which the holy penmen were to write. In 2 Tim. 3, 16 Scripture is said to be "God-breathed" (θεόπνευστος), which means that it owes its origin to God notwithstanding the fact that it was written by men. In 2 Pet. 1, 21 the apostle distincly declares that the holy men, borne along (φερόμενοι) by the Holy Ghost, spoke, *i. e.,* brought forth words (ἐλάλησαν). Similarly St. Paul says in 1 Cor. 2, 13: "Which things we speak in words taught by the Spirit" (λαλοῦμεν διδακτοῖς [λόγοις] πνεύματος). In all these passages the verbal inspiration of the Bible is clearly affirmed; for since words are the necessary means for conveying thoughts, it lies in the very nature of inspiration that the very *words* were supplied to the holy writers.

All those who deny the verbal inspiration of the Bible and

substitute for it "personal inspiration" or "thought inspiration" deny the Scriptural doctrine of inspiration altogether and are compelled to teach in its place a mere "illumination," which is common to all believers. Consequently they annul the distinction which Scripture itself makes between the *norma normans* of the prophetic and apostolic writings and the *norma normata* of the uninspired books of illuminated dogmaticians and other teachers of the Church. In other words, with the denial of the verbal inspiration the Bible becomes a human book, which has no greater authority than any other Christian book. But just this very thing the Bible stamps as false by proclaiming itself to be the divine source and norm of faith, to which all believers owe their salvation, Eph. 2, 20; John 17, 20; Luke 16, 29; John 8, 31. 32. For this reason we reject the statement of Hastings: "Inspiration applies to *men,* not to written words" (*Encycl. of Rel. and Eth.,* II, 589) and profess with R. W. Hiley: *"This miraculous operation of the Holy Ghost* [divine inspiration] *had not the writers themselves for its object,— these were only His instruments and were soon to pass away; — its objects were the holy books themselves."* (*The Inspiration of Scripture,* 1885, p. 50.) Baier's definition of inspiration is in full agreement with what Scripture itself teaches on the subject: "Divine inspiration was that agency by which God supernaturally communicated to the intellect of those who wrote not only the correct conception of all that was to be written, but also the conception of *the words themselves* and of everything by which they were to be expressed and by which He also instigated their will to the act of writing." (*Doctr. Theol.,* p. 39.)

b. The inspiration was not a mere *divine assistance* or *direction (assistentia, directio, gubernatio divina),* but the actual impartation of all the words *(suggestio verborum)* of which Holy Scripture consists. Just as on Pentecost the Holy Spirit graciously "gave utterance" to the apostles, Acts 2, 4, so He "gave them utterance" when He impelled them to write down God's Word and perpetuate it in Holy Scripture. This truth is clearly expressed in the term "God-breathed" (θεόπνευστος), which declares that Scripture has not merely been *directed* by God, but *inspired* by Him. Of course, the Holy Ghost also guided, directed, and governed the holy prophets and apostles, so that they actually wrote down the words which He suggested to them; but it is contrary to Scripture to identify this divine assistance with the divine act of inspiration. Through mere divine guidance or preservation from error Scripture would have become an errorless human book, but mere divine guidance could not have made it an inerrant Book of God, or God's own Word. Such it became only through divine inspiration, or the divine *suggestio verborum.*

Together with the divine words also their concepts were suggested to the holy writers *(suggestio realis),* so that on their part the act of writing was not merely a mechanical effort, but rather a "conscious, volitional, and intelligent act." The Bible written by them was at the same time *God's Book (causa principalis)* and *their own book (causae instrumentales).* Gerhard correctly says (II, 26) : "The instrumental causes of Holy Scripture were holy men of God, 2 Pet. 1, 21; that is, men peculiarly and immediately elected and called by God for the purpose of committing to writing the divine revelations. Such were the prophets of the Old Testament and the evangelists and apostles of the New Testament, whom we therefore properly call the amanuenses of God, the hand of Christ, and the scribes, or notaries, of the Holy Spirit, since they neither spoke nor wrote by their own will, but, borne along by the Holy Spirit *(φερόμενοι ὑπὸ τοῦ πνεύματος ἁγίου),* were acted upon, led, moved, inspired, and governed by the Holy Ghost. They wrote not as men, but as *'men of God,'* that is, as servants of God and peculiar organs of the Holy Ghost. Therefore, when a canonical book is called a 'book of Moses,' the 'Psalms of David,' an 'epistle of Paul,' etc., this is merely a reference to the agent and not to the principal cause." Concerning the efficient, or principal, cause of Scripture, Quenstedt says (I, 55) : "The efficient, or principal, cause of Scripture is the Triune God, 2 Tim. 3, 16 (the Father, Heb. 1, 1 f.; the Son, John 1, 18; the Holy Ghost, 2 Sam. 23, 2; 1 Pet. 1, 11; 2 Pet. 1, 21) : a) by an original decree; b) by subsequent inspiration, or by ordering that holy men of God should write, and by inspiring what was to be written." *(Doctr. Theol.,* p. 42.)

With regard to the manner in which the holy penmen wrote by divine inspiration, Quenstedt writes (I, 55) : "God therefore alone, if we wish to speak accurately, is to be called the Author of the Sacred Scriptures; the prophets and apostles cannot be called the authors except by a kind of *catachresis."* Again (I, 52) : "Not as though these divine amanuenses wrote *ignorantly* and *unwillingly,* beyond the reach of, and contrary to, their own will; for they wrote *cheerfully, willingly,* and *intelligently.* They are said to be *φερόμενοι,* driven, moved, urged on, by the Holy Ghost, not as though they were in a state of unconsciousness, as the enthusiasts pretended to be, or in a certain ἐνθουσιασμός, as the heathen claimed with regard to their soothsayers; nor, again, . . . as though the prophets themselves did not understand their own prophecies or the things which they wrote, . . . but [they are properly called amanuenses] because they wrote nothing of their own accord, but everything at the dictation of the Holy Ghost." (*Doctr. Theol.*, p. 43.)

c. Inspiration extends not merely to a part of Scripture, for example, to its important doctrines, or such matters as before were unknown to the holy writers, but the entire Bible *(plenary inspiration)*. This fact is proved by the passage *"All Scripture* is given by inspiration of God," 2 Tim. 3, 16. From this statement we derive the axiom: "Whatever is a part of Holy Scripture is given by divine inspiration." Hence the inspiration includes the whole of Scripture, no matter whether it was specially revealed to the holy writers or whether they knew it before or whether it was ascertained through study and research. For this reason the historical, geographical, archeological, and scientific matters contained in Scripture are as truly inspired as are its foremost doctrines. Those who deny this and assume degrees of inspiration destroy the very concept of inspiration.

Hollaz thus writes on this point: "There are contained in Scripture historical, chronological, genealogical, astronomical, scientific, and political matters, which, although the knowledge of them is not actually necessary to salvation, are nevertheless divinely revealed, because an acquaintance with them assists not a little in the interpretation of the Holy Scriptures and in illustrating their doctrines and moral precepts. If only the mysteries of the faith which are contained in the Holy Scriptures depend on divine inspiration and all the rest, which may be known by the light of nature, depends merely on divine direction, then not all of Scripture is inspired. But Paul declares that *the whole of Scripture* is divinely inspired. Therefore not only the mysteries of the faith, but also the remaining truths revealed in Scripture, which may be known also from the light of nature, are divinely suggested and inspired." (*Doctr. Theol.*, p. 46.)

In the Lutheran Church, George Calixtus († 1656) taught that only the chief articles of faith were inspired, while the less important matters or those which were known to the holy writers before they were inspired to write were put down by mere divine direction or guidance so as to preserve them from error. But this doctrine was rejected by the Lutheran dogmaticians as militating against the theopneusty of the whole of Scripture (πᾶσα γραφή). The error of Calixtus has been championed also by Romanistic, Calvinistic, and modern rationalistic Lutheran dogmaticians.

d. Since Holy Scripture is the divinely inspired Word of God, its perfect inerrancy in every part and every statement is *a priori* certain because of the infallibility of its divine Author. However, Christ directly affirms the absolute inerrancy of Scripture when He declares: "Scripture cannot be broken," John 10, 35. His reference in this instance was to a single word (ϑεοί, אֱלֹהִים, Ps. 82, 6), and if Scripture cannot be broken in the case of a single term, then the whole of it must be absolutely true. Similarly the apostles frequently refer to *single words* in the Old Testament as divinely inspired and as able to prove truths which they wished to impress upon their readers. Cf. Gal. 3, 16 with Gen. 17, 7: "He saith not, And to seeds, as of many; but as of one, And to thy Seed, which is Christ"; also Matt. 22, 43. 44 with Ps. 110, 1: "The Lord said unto my Lord"; also John 10, 35 with Ps. 82, 6. Such references prove that not only the very words *(suggestio verbalis),* but even the very forms in which they occur *(suggestio literalis)* have been inspired. In accord with this is God's prohibition not to add to His Word nor to take away from it even the least particle, Deut. 4, 2; 12, 32; Prov. 30, 5. 6; Rev. 22, 18. 19, as also Christ's warning that "whosoever shall break one of these least commandments shall be called the least in the kingdom of heaven," Matt. 5, 19, since "it is easier for heaven and earth to pass than *one tittle* of the Law to fail," Luke 16, 17; Matt. 5, 18. Hence, as St. Paul professed: "I believe *all things* which are written in the Law and in the Prophets," Acts 24, 14, so also every believing Christian must regard Holy Scripture in its entirety as divinely inspired and therefore absolutely infallible. Luther writes: "Scripture has never erred" (St. L., XV, 1481), and Calov: "No error, even in unimportant matters, no defect of memory, not to say untruth, can have any place in all the Scriptures" *(Doctr. Theol.,* p. 49). Similarly Hollaz declares: "Divine inspiration, by which *the subject-matter* and *the words,* those to be spoken as well as those to be written, were immediately suggested to the prophets and apostles by the Holy Spirit, preserved them free from all error in the preaching as well as in the writing of the divine Word." *(Ibid.)*

e. The inspiration of Holy Scripture includes lastly also the *divine impulse and command to write (impulsus et mandatum scribendi).* The *impulsus scribendi* is proved by the fact that the holy writers are said to have been *moved* (φερόμενοι, 2 Pet. 1, 21)

to write, and for this reason the apostle adds the statement:
"Prophecy came *not by the will of man.*" In other words, the Holy
Scriptures were written, not because men, but because God willed
this. Hollaz is therefore right when he says: "Inspiration denotes the antecedent *divine instigation* or *peculiar impulse* of the
will to engage in writing as well as the immediate illumination by
which the mind of the sacred writer was fully enlightened."
(*Doctr. Theol.,* p. 43.) And Quenstedt writes: "All the canonical books of the Old and the New Testament were written by God,
who *peculiarly incited and impelled* the sacred writers to engage
in the work." (*Doctr. Theol.,* p. 44.) Answering the objection of
papistic theologians that it is impossible to trace a special divine
command in every instance, Gerhard declares (II, 30): "In the
holy men of God the *external command* and the *internal impulse*
coincide; for what else is that divine impulse than an internal and
secret command of precisely the same authority and weight as one
that is external and manifest?" *(Ibid.)* The Roman Catholic doctrine, according to which the inspiration of the Bible is admitted,
the *impulsus scribendi,* however, denied, is self-contradictory; for if
God gave Scripture by divine inspiration, then He surely also
moved the holy writers to record His Word. Roman Catholic
theology denies the *mandatum divinum* in the interest of exalting
the unwritten traditions above the written Word of God, just as
modern rationalistic Protestant theologians deny the *impulsus
scribendi* in the interest of elevating their reason (their "Christian consciousness" or "Christian experience") above the Bible.
In both cases the denial is prompted by insubordination over
against the divine Author of the Bible.

4. THE RELATION OF THE HOLY SPIRIT TO THE HOLY WRITERS.

The relation of the inspiring Holy Spirit to the inspired holy
writers is clearly described in all those passages of Holy Scripture
which tell us that the Lord — or the Holy Ghost — spoke *"by the
prophets"* (Matt. 1, 22; 2, 15) or *"by the mouth of the prophets"*
(Acts 1, 16; 4, 25), and this in such a manner that the word of
the prophets and the apostles was by this very act the Word of God
(Heb. 3, 7; Rom. 3, 2). All these expressions declare that the Holy
Spirit employed the holy writers as His organs, or instruments, or
that they were "His mouth" in revealing His holy Word, both
orally and in writing. To describe this instrumental character of

the holy writers, our dogmaticians as well as the ancient Church Fathers called them "penmen," "amanuenses," "the hand of Christ," "scribes and notaries of the Holy Ghost," etc. These expressions are perfectly correct as long as the *tertium comparationis* in these figures of speech is strictly kept in view. What these terms express is the simple fact that the holy writers were agents of God in handing down His Word, either orally or in writing. It is self-evident that the holy writers were not mechanical, but *conscious* and *intelligent* instruments, so that they wrote *"cheerfully, willingly,* and *intelligently"* (Quenstedt). Modern rationalistic theologians therefore ought to accept these expressions as truly Scriptural and not heap mockery upon those who use them. In the final analysis their contempt for these terms is prompted by contempt for the Holy Bible itself and its divine doctrine of inspiration.

The Scriptural phrase "by the prophets" accounts also for the variety of style which is found in Holy Scripture. If the various books of the Bible evince different styles of writing, this is because the Holy Ghost engaged different men (kings, peasants, fishermen, scholars, etc.) to compose His holy Book. Quenstedt remarks on this point (I, 76) : "There is a great diversity among the sacred writers in regard to style and mode of speaking, which evidently arose from the fact that the Holy Spirit accommodated Himself to the ordinary mode of speaking, leaving to each one his own manner ; yet we do not thereby deny that the Holy Spirit suggested the particular words to these individuals." (*Doctr. Theol.,* p. 47 f.) Questions such as the following : "Was the Old Testament written originally with vowel-points or not?" "May the language of the Bible be called classic?" and many others which have been raised in connection with the doctrine of inspiration, are purely historical and have nothing to do with the doctrine of inspiration. For this reason no controversies ought to be waged about them. Let it suffice to say that in all external matters the Holy Spirit accommodated Himself to the peculiar conditions that prevailed at the time when He gave His Word to the world.

5. OBJECTIONS TO THE DOCTRINE OF INSPIRATION.

As early as the sixteenth and seventeenth centuries, papists, Socinians, Arminians, and enthusiasts assumed that Holy Scripture contains certain errors. Even Calvin occasionally imputed to the evangelists general inaccuracies and incorrect quotations from the Old Testament. Within the Lutheran Church, as already stated, George Calixtus, in the seventeenth century, departed from the Scriptural doctrine of inspiration by teaching that in all matters that are not essential or that were known to the holy writers they were not inspired, but merely directed or preserved from error. At the close of the eighteenth and at the beginning of the nineteenth century the prevailing rationalism resulted in the complete surrender of the entire Christian doctrine, including that of the divine inspiration of the Bible. Present-day Modernism is a direct excrescence of this crass rationalism. Modern "positive" or "conservative" theology, which rejected the bland and stupid rationalism of the preceding era, failed to return to the Scriptural doctrine of inspiration, and even modern "Lutheran" theologians in Germany reject the verbal inspiration of the Bible, or the doctrine that Holy Scripture is *a priori* God's Word, maintaining that the character of Scripture must be determined historically, or *a posteriori*, by way of human investigation.

The result of their "investigation" therefore is that the Holy Scripture is *not* the Word of God, but rather a human account of divine revelations *("Offenbarungsurkunde")*, which, though more or less influenced by the Holy Spirit, is not without error and must therefore be subjected to the critical judgment of Bible scholars. These theologians still speak of "inspiration"; yet-they do not mean that true inspiration by which Holy Scripture has become the unique source and norm of faith until the end of time (John 17, 20; Eph. 2, 20), but merely an intensified illumination, which is found more or less in all Christian authors.

The same may be said of most American theologians, although among them Charles Hodge, William Shedd, and Benjamin Warfield have defended the Scriptural doctrine of verbal and plenary inspiration. In Germany there is at the present time hardly a single outstanding university professor who still upholds the doctrine of verbal and plenary inspiration. This all but universal denial of inspiration is one of the saddest chapters in the history of the Christian Church; for every one who repudiates the inspiration of the Bible subverts the foundation upon which the Christian faith rests and falls under the condemnation of God, Matt. 11, 25. In the last analysis all objections to the inspiration of the Bible flow from the carnal, unbelieving heart, Rom. 8, 7; 1 Cor. 2, 14.

Among the objections raised against the Biblical doctrine of inspiration the following may be noted: —

a. *The different style in the various books of the Bible,* or more exactly, the claim that God's peculiar style would be found throughout the Bible were He really its divine Author. Our reply to this criticism is that in general God's unique style is indeed noticeable throughout Holy Scripture, which bears the ineffaceable imprint of its divine Author on every page. The simplicity, majesty, and sublimity of the Biblical style are found in no book written by men; in fact, the style of the Bible is so unique that there is only *one Holy Bible* in the world. We may apply to Scripture the words that were spoken with regard to our Savior: "Never man spake like this man," John 7, 46. If within this general scope the various books of the Bible differ from one another somewhat in style and diction, we must remember that the Holy Spirit, in giving His holy Word to men, always accommodated Himself to the holy writers whom He employed in His holy service. Calov says very fittingly: "There may be recognized in it [the Bible] a condescension of the Holy Spirit; for He sometimes accommodated Himself to the ordinary method of speaking, allowing the writers their own style of speech." This, correctly understood, is the "human side" of Scripture. This expression, however, must not be taken in the sense of modern rationalistic theologians, who apply it to certain portions of Holy Writ, which they reject as "erroneous" and therefore as "uninspired."

In opposition to modern rationalistic theology the Christian believer stands firm upon the vital truth that Holy Scripture has no "uninspired parts" whatsoever, but that it is in all its parts the inerrant Word of God, given by divine inspiration. Instead of criticizing the different styles of Scripture, men ought to recognize in this fact God's gracious condescension and wonderful love; for by giving us His heavenly doctrines through so many different writers, who address us in so many different ways, He rendered His sublime Word all the more intelligible and acceptable to mankind. Had God spoken to us in the language which is used in heaven, not a single person in this world could have understood His Word and learned from it the way of salvation, 2 Cor. 12, 4.

b. *The variant readings in the copies of Scripture.* Variant readings *(variae lectiones)* are indeed found in the copies of the holy writings of the prophets and apostles that have been preserved to us. However, since the variant readings occur only in the copies, they furnish no argument whatsoever against the divine inspiration of the Bible, since the variants owe their origin to lapses in transcription. In spite of the variant readings, however, the texts which we have to-day contain the Word of God both in its original purity and its original entirety. This we know *a priori* from Christ's direct promise (John 17, 20; 8, 31. 32; Matt. 28, 20; John 10, 35; Matt. 24, 35; Luke 21, 33; 16, 17) and *a posteriori* from the fact, ascertained by scientific investigation, that in spite of the numerous *variae lectiones* not a single doctrine of God's Word has been rendered doubtful or uncertain. God, who has given us His Word, has also graciously preserved it to the present day and will preserve it to the end of time *(gubernatio divina).* We recognize God's providence also in the many repetitions of His doctrines throughout the Bible. As a result of this, even if entire books *(Antilegomena)* or entire passages (Mark 16, 9—20) are called into question, we may still prove the divine doctrines from other books and passages in the Bible, which are universally acknowledged as authentic and canonical *(Homologumena).*

c. *The study and research of the holy writers.* Independent study and historical research were indeed carried on at times by the holy writers; for they themselves tell us that they were prompted to write not only new revelations, but also such things as they knew in consequence of their general study and their special experience, Gal. 1, 17—24; Luke 1, 1ff. However, this fact does not disprove the doctrine of inspiration, since the Holy Spirit utilized for His beneficent purpose of giving to fallen man the Word of God also the general knowledge of the sacred penmen, just as He utilized their natural gifts and talents (experience, style, culture, etc.). Inspiration is not mere revelation, but the divine prompting *(impulsus scribendi)* to record the truths which God desired that men should know in words He Himself supplied, 2 Sam. 23, 2ff. Some of these truths were given the holy writers by direct revelation, 1 Cor. 11, 23; 14, 37; 2, 7—13; others were known to them by experience, Acts 17, 28; Gal. 2, 11—14; others, again, by direct investigation and special research, Luke 1, 1ff.

In the treatment of the doctrine of divine inspiration the question is not: "How did the holy writers obtain the truths which they wrote?" but rather: "Did the Holy Ghost prompt the sacred writers to write down certain words and thoughts which God wanted men to know?" The fact that this was actually the case is clearly taught in Holy Scripture, 2 Tim. 3, 16; 2 Pet. 1, 21, so that the doctrine of inspiration is beyond dispute. When on Pentecost the apostles proclaimed to the multitude salvation by the risen

Savior, who had suffered and died for the sins of the world, they announced facts which to a large extent were known to them by experience, John 20, 20 f.; 21, 12; yet of all the words which they proclaimed Scripture says: "They began to speak . . . *as the Spirit gave them utterance,*" Acts 2, 4. Not only in that Pentecostal preaching, but in the composition of all their writings the Holy Spirit "gave utterance" to the apostles.

d. *Alleged contradictions in the Bible.* In connection with this point we distinguish between *external* and *internal* contradictions. By external contradictions we mean the seeming historical discrepancies in the Bible. Internal contradictions pertain to doctrines. With regard to *real* contradictions in doctrine, we know *a priori* that none can occur, — though to human reason this often appears to be the case, — since the whole Bible is the Word of the infallible God, 2 Tim. 3, 16; 2 Pet. 1, 21. Even if two doctrines of Scripture *seem* to contradict each other *(e. g., gratia universalis, electio particularis),* the Christian theologian never admits a real contradiction, 2 Cor. 1, 18—20, but only a partial revelation, 1 Cor. 13, 9, which will be perfected in glory, 1 Cor. 13, 10. 12. For this reason the Christian believer teaches both doctrines side by side in their given purity, without any attempt on his part to bridge over the gap or to solve the apparent discrepancy, Rev. 22, 18. 19.

Seeming historical discrepancies (external contradictions) occur in Scripture especially in quotations from the Old Testament, 1 Cor. 10, 8 and Num. 25, 9. The variants in the manuscripts, owing to faulty transcription, add to the number of these seeming contradictions. The wonder, however, is not that such seeming contradictions do occur in the Bible, — for we must not forget that the copyists were fallible men, who were subject to error in transcribing the sacred text, — but rather that, relatively speaking, there are so few of them and that in most cases they can be satisfactorily adjusted. (Cf. Dr. W. Arndt's *Does the Bible Contradict Itself?*)

But even if the Christian theologian cannot adjust an apparent historical discrepancy to his full satisfaction, he does not charge Scripture with error, but leaves the matter undecided, mindful of Christ's declaration that "the Scripture cannot be broken," John 10, 35. Particulars with regard to this subject belong to the domain of Christian isagogics, where they receive detailed consideration; but the dogmatician is concerned with the matter in so far as it is his duty to point out the correct principles which must guide the Bible student in his estimation of Scripture as God's inspired Word. Foremost among these is the basic truth that it is unworthy of a Christian theologian to criticize the inerrant Word of God; for it is his function to teach the Gospel, Mark 16, 15. 16; Matt. 28, 20, and not to oppose the infallible Word by his own fallible views and judgments, 1 Tim. 6, 3—5. (Cf. Luther on the historical reliability of Scripture, St. L., XIV, 490 ff.) In passing, we may add that the seeming historical discrepancies in the Bible never affect the doctrines which Scripture teaches for our salvation.

e. *Inaccurate quotations in the New Testament.* It is asserted that the Bible cannot be the inspired Word of God because the New Testament so frequently quotes the Old Testament "inaccurately" and even "wrongly." The argument is that, if the Bible were the infallible Word of God, the citations from the Old Testament that are given in the New Testament would always be exact, or literal. This, however, is not the case. Sometimes the apostles quote the Old Testament literally; sometimes they quote the reading of the Septuagint; at other times they quote the Septuagint, but correct it according to the Hebrew original; finally, sometimes they reproduce neither the Hebrew text nor the Septuagint, but state the general scope of the text in their own words. This divergent manner of quoting the Old Testament, however, does not disprove the fact of divine inspiration of the Bible; on the contrary, it rather proves it, since evidently the divine Author of the whole Bible quoted His holy words as it pleased Him. Had the New Testament writers been impostors, they would have been obliged to quote the Old Testament literally in every instance; for it would have been in their interest to prove to their readers their extensive acquaintance and perfect agreement with the Old Testament. As it was, the Holy Spirit, who spoke through them, directed them to cite and apply the Word of God as the occasion required and as His holy purposes were best served, Gal. 4, 21—31. It is always the privilege of an author to quote his writings as he sees fit, and this prerogative must not be denied to the Holy Spirit.

f. *Trivial matters in Scripture.* The inspiration of the Bible has further been denied on the ground that it contains "trivial things" *(levicula)* and, besides, bad grammar, poor rhetoric, barbarisms, solecisms, and the like. Examples of trivial matters, it is asserted, are the minutely reported domestic affairs of the patriarchs; their manifold sins and failings, the dietetic prescription for

Timothy that he should use a little wine for his stomach's sake, 1 Tim. 5, 23, Paul's request for his cloak, books, and parchments, 2 Tim. 4, 13, and others. These *levicula,* it is said, are unworthy of the Holy Spirit and would not have been mentioned by Him if He really were the Author of Scripture.

However, this argument does not apply; for if God made the vine, should He not prescribe its correct use? If He deigned to establish the home, should He not picture in Scripture a few home scenes for our instruction, warning, and comfort, 2 Tim. 3, 16? If the very hairs on our heads are all numbered, Matt. 10, 30, must not the "trivial things" in the lives of God's saints be regarded as of the greatest concern to Him? Some of the most weighty lessons of faith and piety attach to the "trivial things" which Holy Scripture inculcates (the right use of the divinely prescribed means; the apostle's devotion to the Gospel in spite of his poverty; the apostle's studiousness, which prompted him to demand books even when he was in prison). It is not the business of any theologian to prescribe to God what kind of Bible He should write or to find fault with the Bible which He did write, but to teach with holy reverence and devout submission the entire Word of salvation which God in His infinite grace was pleased to bequeath to lost mankind as the source of faith and the norm of life, Acts 20, 17—28.

The argument against the inspiration of Scripture which is based upon the so-called barbarisms, solecisms, grammatical errors, etc., must be rejected as ignoring the well-known fact that the New Testament was written in the κοινή, or the universal popular speech of that time, which differed greatly from classical Greek, but was understood by practically all peoples and tribes in the Roman Empire. The Holy Spirit chose this language because He wished the writings of His holy penmen to be understood by the common people, Col. 4, 16; 1 Thess. 5, 27, from whose ranks the first Christian churches were largely organized, Rom. 16, 3—15. The Greek of the New Testament is not "vulgar" or "bad" Greek; it was the vernacular of the people *(Volkssprache)* in the period when Christianity was spread in the heathen world and the Holy Bible was written. The Hebraisms in the New Testament are not anomalies, but are found in all writings where Jewish influence exerted itself upon the common Greek.

g. *Special Scripture-passages are said to deny inspiration.* Those who deny the divine inspiration of the Bible also point out certain Scripture-passages which allegedly contradict the fact of inspiration. Of these the foremost is 1 Cor. 7, 12: "To the rest speak I, not the Lord," contrasted with 1 Cor. 7, 10: "Unto the married I command, yet not I, but the Lord." Luther explains this passage by saying that here the apostle does not inculcate a divine commandment, but merely gives counsel in a matter which concerned the life of the Corinthian Christians. "He distinguishes his words from those of the Lord in such a way that the Word of the Lord should be a commandment, but his word should be a counsel." (St. L., VIII, 1058.) This explanation is supported by 1 Cor. 7, 25. Both statements are certainly inspired; but while v. 2 of this chapter gives the principle, v. 12 ff. the apostolic counsel for the contingency. It must not be overlooked that St. Paul wrote this entire epistle as "an apostle of Jesus Christ through the will of God," 1 Cor. 1, 1, so that "the things that he wrote" were "the commandments of the Lord," 1 Cor. 14, 37. It has been suggested, moreover, that, since Paul was accustomed to support his statements by quotations from the Old Testament or from the teachings of Jesus, he merely wished to indicate that in this instance he had no definite commandment from the Lord to which he might refer his readers, but was uttering a hitherto unexplained truth as an inspired apostle. This explanation is quite plausible, since manifestly in 1 Cor. 7, 10 he alludes to Matt. 19, 6. 9. Certainly this one passage gives us no right whatever to deny the divine inspiration of Scripture, which is attested in so many clear passages, especially since the apostle himself deprecates this conclusion, 1 Cor. 14, 37.

h. *The alleged evil consequences of the doctrine of inspiration.* This argument is preferred quite commonly by the exponents of modern theology. Asserting that the "Christian consciousness" or "Christian experience" or human reason must be recognized as a *principium cognoscendi* and chafing under the divine restraint, 1 Pet. 4, 11, they allege that belief in the divine inspiration of Holy Scripture would result in "intellectualism," "Biblicism," "letter service," "the constraint of the free spirit of investigation," "the failure to find new religious truths," "the inability of the theologian to accommodate himself to present-day religious thought," "sectarianism," and the like.

All these objections may be traced back to the same source, namely, to the averseness of rationalistic and naturalistic theologians to being bound to divine truth definitely fixed in a Scriptural canon. As a matter of fact, if the Bible is God's holy Book, given to men as the only source and norm of faith and life until the end of time, then any doctrine which is contrary to Scripture is *eo ipso* condemned and rejected. Rationalism repudiates the doctrine of divine inspiration in order that it may spread its own false teachings and pernicious errors. But just for that very reason the Word of God is so emphatic in condemning every departure from God's holy truth revealed in Scripture, Rom. 16, 17; 2 John 9—11; 1 Tim. 1, 3; 6, 3 ff., and in inculcating the most steadfast adherence to the Bible, Matt. 5, 18—19; Rev. 22, 18. 19. In the last analysis there is only one reason why men reject the doctrine of the divine inspiration of the Bible, namely, unbelief, or revolt against God and His established Word.

6. THE DOCTRINE OF INSPIRATION AND CONFESSIONAL LUTHERANISM.

In answer to the claim that the doctrine of inspiration is a "dogmatic construction," which owes its origin to the later dogmaticians of the Lutheran Church, we point to the fact that already in its Confessions the Lutheran Church upheld the plenary inspiration of the Bible, although at that time the doctrine was not in controversy, so that there was no pressing need for presenting it in detail. A few quotations from our Confessions show in what way the writers regarded the Holy Bible. We read: "Whence have the bishops the right to lay these traditions upon the Church . . . when *Peter,* Acts 15, 10, *forbids to put a yoke* upon the neck of the disciples *and Paul says,* 2 Cor. 13, 10, that the power given him was to edification? *Did the Holy Ghost in vain forewarn of these things?*" (*Augsburg Conf.,* Art. XXVIII.) Again: "You have now therefore, reader, our *Apology,* from which you will understand not only what the adversaries have judged, . . . but also that they have condemned several articles contrary to *the manifest Scripture of the Holy Ghost.*" (*Apol.,* § 9. *Triglot,* p. 101.) Again: "In this way the distinction between the Holy Scriptures of the Old and the New Testament and all other writings is preserved, and *the Holy Scriptures alone remain the only judge, rule, and standard according to which, as the only touchstone, all dogmas shall and must be discerned and judged* as to whether they are good or evil, right or wrong." (*Formula of Concord,* Epitome, § 7; *Triglot,* p. 779.)

From these and many other statements in our Confessions it is obvious that their writers regarded the Holy Bible as the inspired and infallible Word of God; hence the claim that the doctrine of verbal and plenary inspiration is "an artificial theory of the later dogmaticians" *("eine kuenstliche Theorie der spaeteren Dogma-tiker")* is unfounded. The later Lutheran dogmaticians taught no other doctrine concerning Holy Scripture than that which was maintained and defended in the Lutheran Confessions.

Closely related to the claim just stated is another, namely, that Luther himself did not regard the Bible as verbally and plenarily inspired, but that he assumed a "free attitude" on this point. However, Luther's position, or attitude, toward the Bible was the very opposite of "free"; for time and again he professed himself to be bound to God's Word, set forth in Scripture, as the following statements of his plainly show: "Holy Scripture was spoken through the Holy Ghost." (St. L., III, 1895.) Again: "The Bible is 'God's Letter' to men." (I, 1055.) Again: "The Bible did not grow upon earth." (VII, 2095.) Etc. While Luther's chief opponents, the papists, asserted the traditions, the decisions of the church councils, and the decrees of the Popes to be sources of faith, Luther recognized but one standard of faith — God's Book, the Bible. In it "the Holy Spirit so speaks to us" that even "the trivial things" in it are the teachings of the "high divine Majesty." (St. L., XIV, 2 ff.) In it "the absolutely pure mouth of the Holy Spirit" revealed even the "atrocious, indecent tale" of Judah and Tamar (Gen. 38) for our comfort. (St. L., II, 1200 ff.) Even as to historical and scientific matters recorded in Scripture we must "do the Holy Spirit the honor of admitting that He is more learned than we are." (St. L., III, 21; XV, 1481.) The Holy Spirit did not commit any mistakes even in the chronology of Scripture. (St. L., I, 713 ff.) Modern rationalistic theologians hold that there are "degrees of inspiration," a view which practically denies the entire inspiration of Scripture. Luther, on the contrary, "assigned the whole Bible to the Holy Ghost." (St. L., III, 1890.) *Ad* Ps. 127, 3 he says that not only the words *(vocabula),* but the very mode of expression *(phrasis)* is divine *(divina).* (St. L., IV, 1960.)

In view of these express declarations of Luther the alleged proofs from his writings on behalf of his "free position" sink into insignificance from the very outset. Luther is supposed to have taught that the Bible contains "hay, straw, and stubble," in other words, truth and error. But this quotation is incorrect; for when using those words, Luther did not refer to the Biblical writers, but to the interpreters of the Bible. (Kawerau, *Theol. Lit.-Ztg.,* 1895, p. 216; cf. also *Christliche Dogmatik,* Vol. I, p. 346 ff.) What

Luther here says of the interpreters of the Bible in olden times (St. L., XIV, 150) is true of all Bible interpreters to this day; for sometimes they err in explaining the sacred text.

Again, Luther is said to have taught that certain passages in Scripture are "inadequate." The reference in this case is especially to Gal. 4, 21ff., on which passage he remarked that in a controversy with Jews *(contra Iudaeos),* who did not accept Paul's apostolic authority, it is less valid in controversy *(in acie minus valet)* than others; or according to some German translations, it is *"zum Stich zu schwach,"* that is to say, it does not convince. By this expression, however, Luther did not mean to deny the doctrine of inspiration, but merely wished to indicate that Paul's allegory, as used in this passage, would not convince an unbelieving Jew, who did not accept the apostle's authority. This certainly is true, especially since Paul in his interpretation departs from the literal sense of the words and shows its allegorical meaning, as Luther rightly points out. (Cf. St. L., I, 1150.)

Moreover, Luther's "free position" with respect to Scripture is supposed to appear from his sharp distinction between the *Homologumena* and the *Antilegomena* in the New Testament canon. We admit the fact that Luther did make distinctions *(e. g.,* the epistle of James he calls a "strawy epistle" as compared with Paul's epistles, St. L., XIV, 91); but at the same time he regarded *all the prophetic and apostolic Scriptures* as God's divinely inspired Word, just as we do to-day, though we, too, acknowledge the distinction between *Homologumena* and *Antilegomena.* Furthermore it is said that Luther accepted a "canon within the canon," since he limited the divine authority of the Bible to those books which *"urge Christ" ("Christum treiben").* The passages on which this contention is based are found in the St. Louis Ed. (XIV, 129, and XIX, 1441) and read: "Whatever does not urge Christ is not yet apostolic, even if St. Peter or St. Paul should teach it. On the other hand, whatever teaches Christ, that is apostolic, even if Judas, Annas, Pilate, or Herod should do it." And: "If our adversaries insist upon Scripture, we insist upon Christ against Scripture." As strange as these statements may sound when they are removed from their context, they become perfectly clear when they are considered in their connection. By *Scripture* Luther here does not mean the Bible *per se,* but as it was falsely interpreted by the papists. This fully explains the second quotation. The first is explained by the fact that

Luther here assumes a case which in reality can never occur, since neither St. Paul nor St. Peter could teach anything without "urging Christ," nor would Annas, Pilate, or Herod "urge Christ," no matter what they presumed to teach. Luther's insistence here was upon the authority of the divine Christ whom the Bible teaches from beginning to end as the Church's only Lord, Luke 24, 25—27; Acts 10, 43.

Whatever other arguments have been advanced to prove Luther's "free position" with regard to Holy Scripture come under the same category as those cited above. In the interest of their pernicious designs modern theologians either misquote Luther or misapply his statements. In spite of this, however, they cannot disprove the clear words in which Luther emphatically professes his devoted loyalty to Scripture as God's own inspired Book.

7. THE DENIAL OF THE DOCTRINE OF INSPIRATION — ITS CAUSE AND ITS CONSEQUENCES.

The amazing apostasy of modern Protestant theologians from the Biblical doctrine of inspiration is strikingly depicted in Hastings's *Encyclopedia,* where we read: "Protestant scholars of the present day, imbued with the scientific spirit, have no *a-priori* theory of the inspiration of the Bible. . . . They do not open any book of the Old or New Testament with the feeling that they are bound to regard its teaching as sacred and authoritative. They yield to nothing but what they regard as the irresistible logic of facts. . . . And if in the end they formulate a doctrine of the divine influence under which the Scriptures were written, this is an inference from the characteristics which, after free and fair investigation, they are constrained to recognize." And again: "To sum up, the old doctrine of the equal and infallible inspiration of every part of the Old Testament . . . is now rapidly disappearing among Protestants. There is in reality no clean dividing-line between what is and what is not worthy of a place in the Scriptures." (VII, 346, *et al.*) In a similar vein the late Theodor Kaftan wrote: "We are realists" *(Wirklichkeitsmenschen),* which he explains to mean: "We do not regard as authoritative what Scripture teaches of itself, but only what we profess as divine truth according to the impression which Scripture makes upon us." (*Moderne Theologie des alten Glaubens,* 2, pp. 108. 113.)

This express denial of the divine inspiration of Holy Scripture in spite of its own clear and unmistakable testimony is prompted, in the last analysis, only by unbelief, or the sheer refusal of human reason to accept the truth of God's Word. It was so in Christ's time, when our Lord reproved the unbelieving Jews: "Because I tell you the truth, ye believe Me not. . . . If I say the truth, why do ye not believe Me? He that is of God heareth God's words; ye therefore hear them not because ye are not of God," John 8, 45—47, and so it is to-day. In His criticism of the unbelief of the Pharisees, Christ became very severe and rebuked them thus: "Ye are of your father the devil, and the lusts of your father ye will do. He was a murderer from the beginning and abode not in the truth, because there is no truth in him. When he speaketh a lie, he speaketh of his own; for he is a liar and the father of it," John 8, 44. This criticism of the carnal heart, which rejects God's Word, applies with the same force and emphasis to-day. Rationalistic theologians to-day accuse the "later Lutheran dogmaticians" of having invented "an artificial theory" ("eine kuenstliche Theorie") when they taught the verbal and plenary inspiration of the Bible; they thus became guilty of a historical falsehood. In addition, they resort to logical fallacies to bolster up their rejection of God's Word, claiming that the doctrine of inspiration is disproved by the different style of the various writers, their private study and research, the variae lectiones in the copies, and the like. However, the real source of every denial of the doctrine of inspiration is unbelief.

The consequences of the denial of Biblical inspiration are indeed far-reaching. As a matter of fact, Christianity stands and falls with this doctrine; for if there is no inspired Scripture, there can be no divine doctrine. In particular, all who deny the divine inspiration of the Bible, and as long as they do so, have no possibility of ever knowing the divine truth; for this is possible only in case men "continue in Christ's Word," John 8, 31. 32; 1 Tim. 6, 3. 4. Moreover they give up faith in the Christian sense, since faith comes alone by hearing God's Word, Rom. 10, 17; Jas. 1, 18; 1 Pet. 1, 23. So, too, they give up Christian prayer with all its temporal and eternal blessings; for this presupposes faithful adherence to the words of Christ, as He Himself teaches: "If ye abide in Me and My words abide in you, ye shall ask what ye will, and it shall be done unto you," John 15, 7. Again, they give up the possibility of triumphing over death; for only he "shall never see death" who keeps Christ's saying, John 8, 51. They also give up the only means by which the Christian Church is built upon earth, namely, the precious Gospel of Christ, Mark 16, 15. 16;

Matt. 28, 19. 20; 2 John 9. 10. They likewise give up the only means by which the Christian Church may be preserved in its true unity of faith, Eph. 4, 3—6, as Luther rightly says: "The Word and the doctrine must make Christian unity and communion." (St. L., IX, 831.) In addition, they give up all *communion with God,* since we can find our precious Lord only in His Word, John 6, 67—69; 17, 17; Luke 11, 28; John 5, 24. Lastly they pervert the "wisdom that is from above," or "the wisdom of God in a mystery, which God ordained before the world unto our glory," but which "has never entered into the heart of man," Jas. 3, 17; 1 Cor. 2, 7—9, into a doctrine of men, or into a "wisdom which descendeth not from above, but is earthly, sensual, devilish," Jas. 3, 15; for the denial of the divine inspiration of the Bible is invariably joined with the denial of the saving Gospel of Christ and with the teaching of the pagan doctrine of work-righteousness. Rationalism begins with the disavowal of the doctrine of inspiration and ends with the repudiation of all the divine doctrines of Holy Scripture, unless by God's grace this destructive process is checked by a "fortunate inconsistency," by which in practise the conclusions are *not drawn* from the premises that are theoretically maintained. If Paul's earnest warning "Be not deceived; God is not mocked; for whatsoever a man soweth, that shall he also reap," Gal. 6, 7, applies anywhere, it applies especially to man's attitude toward the Scriptural doctrine of divine inspiration.

8. THE PROPERTIES OF HOLY SCRIPTURE.

Because the Bible is the Word of God, it possesses distinct divine properties, or attributes *(affectiones divinae).* These are: divine authority *(auctoritas divina),* divine efficacy *(efficacia divina),* divine perfection *(perfectio divina),* and divine perspicuity *(perspicuitas divina).* It is self-evident that these divine properties must be denied to Scripture if its divine inspiration is rejected, for they follow from the fact that the Bible is God's own inspired and infallible Word.

A. THE DIVINE AUTHORITY OF HOLY SCRIPTURE.

By the divine authority of Holy Scripture we mean the peculiar quality of the whole Bible according to which as the true Word of God it demands faith and obedience of all men and is and remains the only source and norm of faith and life. Our Savior Himself acknowledged and asserted the divine authority of the Bible by quoting it in all cases of controversy as the only standard of truth,

John 10, 35; Matt. 4, 4—10; 26, 54; Luke 24, 25—27; etc. And the holy apostles claimed divine authority not only for the Scriptures of the Old Testament, but also for their own inspired writings, 1 Cor. 14, 37. 38; 2 Cor. 13, 3; Gal. 1, 8; 2 Thess. 3, 6. 14; 2, 15. Whoever therefore rejects Scripture or subjects it to human censorship and criticism becomes guilty of high treason against God; for Scripture possesses its divine authority not because of the holy men who wrote it nor because of the Christian Church, which reveres and teaches it, but from the living God, who has inspired holy men to write it. In other words, the Bible has divine authority because it is in every part the inerrant Word of the living God. Just because it is a God-breathed Scripture (γραφὴ θεόπνευστος), it is authoritative (αὐτόπιστος) and must therefore be both believed and obeyed. Because of its authority we believe the Bible on its own account, since it is the unique Book of God in which the sovereign Lord speaks to us. This fact we express dogmatically by saying that the divine authority of Holy Scripture is *absolute*, or free from dependence upon anything else for its existence and its certainty *(auctoritas absoluta)*.

The divine authority of Holy Scripture is divided into causative authority *(auctoritas causativa)* and normative authority *(auctoritas normativa)*. The causative authority of Holy Scripture is that by which it engenders and preserves faith in its own teachings through its very word, Rom. 10, 17. The normative, or canonical, authority of Holy Scripture is that by which it is the only norm and rule of faith, or the divinely instituted arbiter between truth and falsehood, John 5, 39; Luke 16, 29; Gal. 1, 8.

If the question is asked how Scripture exercises its causative authority, or how we may become sure of its divine truth, we must distinguish between divine assurance *(fides divina)* and human assurance *(fides humana)*. The *fides divina* (faith assurance, spiritual assurance, Christian assurance) is wrought directly by the Holy Ghost through the Word *(testimonium Spiritus Sancti)*. In other words, Scripture attests itself as the divine truth, John· 8, 31. 32. Of this Quenstedt (I, 97) writes: "The ultimate reason by and through which we are led to believe with a divine and unshaken faith that God's Word is God's Word is the intrinsic power and efficacy of that Word itself, or the testimony and seal of the Holy Spirit, who speaks in and through Scripture, because the bestowment of faith . . . is a work that emanates from the Holy Spirit." *(Doctr. Theol.,* p. 55.) Of the internal witness of the Holy Ghost, by which divine faith in Scripture is engendered, Hollaz writes thus: "By the internal testimony of the Holy Spirit is here understood the supernatural act of the Holy Spirit, through the Word of God, attentively read or heard, . . . by which He moves, opens, and illuminates the heart of man and incites it to faithful obedience." *(Ibid.)*

That the Word of God, which the Holy Spirit has given to us through the prophets and apostles, really possesses causative authority, or the power of attesting itself as the divine truth, independently of any external proof *(fides humana),* is clearly taught in Holy Scripture. To the Corinthians St. Paul writes that his "speech and preaching was in demonstration of the Spirit and power," 1 Cor. 2, 4. 5, which means that the preaching of the apostle was spiritually effective in working faith and obedience in his hearers. To the Thessalonians the same apostle writes that they received the Word of God which they heard of him not as the word of men, but, as it is in truth, the Word of God, and this because the divine Word "effectually worketh in you that believe," 1 Thess. 2, 13. 14. Again to the Corinthians, St. Paul writes that his Gospel came unto them not only in word, but also in power and in the Holy Ghost and in much assurance, so that they became followers of the Lord, 1 Cor. 1, 5. 6. The same causative authority as St. Paul ascribes to the divine Word in these passages Christ asserts, when He says: "If any man will do His will, he shall know of the doctrine whether it be of God or whether I speak of myself," John 7, 17. From John 6, 40 we learn that "to do His will" means to hear and believe the divine Word, so that He ascribes the working of divine assurance to the divine Word itself. In this way, then, and only in this way. do we receive divine assurance of the truth of God's Word: Scripture attests itself as the true Word of God through the power of the Holy Ghost, who operates through the divine Word. This truth is of great practical importance; for whenever doubts arise in the heart of the Christian regarding the divine Word, the only way in which to dispel them is to "search the Scriptures," John 5, 39, since they are the divine means by which the Holy Spirit enlightens and confirms him in the divine truth, 1 John 5, 9. 10; John 3, 33; 2 Cor. 1, 20—22; Eph. 1, 13.

Against the charge of Roman Catholic theologians that Lutheran theology here argues in a circle *(argumentum in circulo, idem per idem)* we reply that, if Scripture cannot be relied upon in its testimony concerning itself, it cannot be relied upon in any other of its teachings. Moreover, the Lutheran argument regarding the causative authority of Scripture is not an *argumentum in circulo,* but rather one from effect to cause *(ab effectu ad causam),* and whoever denies the validity of this reasoning has no other choice than agnosticism and atheism. Quenstedt says very rightly (I, 101): "The papists therefore wrongly accuse us of reasoning in a circle when we prove the Holy Scriptures from the testimony of the Holy Spirit and the testimony of the Holy Spirit from the Holy Scriptures. Else it would also be reasoning in a circle when Moses and the prophets testify concerning Christ and Christ concerning Moses and the prophets." *(Doctr. Theol.,* p. 56.)

While the *fides divina,* or spiritual assurance, is the gift of the Holy Spirit through the Word (faith engendered through the Word by the Holy Ghost), the *fides humana,* or human assurance, is based upon arguments or processes of reason. These arguments are either *internal* or *external.* The *internal* proofs for the divine authority of Holy Scripture relate to its marvelous style, the unique harmony of its parts, the sublime majesty of its subjects, its amazing predictions of future events and their remarkable fulfilment, the sublimity of its miracles, and the like. The *external* proofs relate to the astounding effects which the Bible has wrought wherever it was spread, such as the conversion of men steeped in spiritual ignorance and vice, the heroic faith of the martyrs, the moral and social improvements which the Gospel has effected, etc. As the rational study of the book of nature points to its divine Creator, so the rational study of the book of revelation suggests that it is the work of a divine Author and that therefore it is more reasonable to believe than to disbelieve its claims (the scientific proof for the divine authority of Scripture).

All these arguments are utilized in Christian apologetics to demonstrate the futility of infidelity and its atheistic claims. But all arguments of reason do not beget "a divine, but merely a human faith; not an unshaken certainty, but merely a credibility or a very probable opinion" (Quenstedt). Hence the value of these arguments must not be overestimated, for they can never make any person a believing child of God. But neither must they be underestimated, since they are of great value in refuting the flippant charges of infidels and in strengthening Christians against the very doubts which from time to time arise in their own hearts. Cf. 1 Cor. 15, 12—19; Acts 17, 28. Nevertheless, no matter how reasonable these arguments may be, they never produce repentance and faith, since the conversion of a sinner is effected alone through the preaching of the Word of God, the Law bringing about contrition (*terrores conscientiae,* Rom. 3, 19. 20) and the Gospel, faith in Christ, Matt. 28, 19. 20; Acts 2, 37—39; Mark 16, 15. 16.

In his ministry the Christian theologian employs arguments of reason chiefly to induce unconverted persons to read or hear God's Word, or we may say he uses them just as church-bells, which invite men to listen to the proclamation of the divine truth. In no case, however, may he employ them as substitutes for the Law and the Gospel, or the Word of God, Luke 16, 29—31; 24, 47. 48.

If the question is asked how a person may be sure whether his assurance is *fides divina* or *fides humana,* the following points must be considered. The testimony of the Holy Spirit never occurs: a. *outside, or in opposition to, Holy Scripture* (enthusiasm), so that the "Christian assurance" or the "Christian experience" of all who reject the Bible as the Word of God is mere self-deception; b. *by means of mere arguments of reason* or *on the ground of human authority* ("I believe the Bible because the Church teaches it"); c. *together with the repudiation of Christ's vicarious satisfaction,* so that the assurance of divine grace which Modernists claim (Ritschl, Harnack) is pure fiction. On the other hand, the testimony of the Holy Spirit occurs in all true believers who accept Holy Scripture as the Word of God, and that upon its own witness, for this very faith in Scripture is the *testimonium Spiritus Sancti.* To this truth all true believers must hold, especially in hours of trial, when they do not feel the gladdening effects of the Spirit's witness in them, 1 John 5, 9. 10. The very fact that they are believers proves the effective presence of the Holy Ghost in their hearts, for without the Holy Spirit it is impossible to have saving faith, 1 Cor. 12, 3; Acts 16, 14.

With regard to the effects of the testimony of the Holy Spirit in the believer the *Formula of Concord* rightly argues that these must not be judged *ex sensu,* or by feeling, since the Holy Ghost is always operative in his heart as long as he adheres to God's Word, no matter whether he feels His operation or not. The feeling of the Spirit's operating grace belongs to the fruits of faith in the truth of the Gospel and thus to the external witness of the Holy Ghost *(testimonium Spiritus Sancti externum),* while His internal witness *(testimonium Spiritus Sancti internum)* is identical with saving faith, or true confidence in the divine promises of the Word. In the same vein Luther writes: "We do not distinguish the Holy

Spirit from faith, nor is He contrary to faith; for He is Himself the assurance in the Word, who makes us certain of the Word, so that we do not doubt, but believe most certainly and beyond all doubt that it is just so and in no respect whatever different from that which God in His Word declares and tells us." (Erl. Ed., 58, 153 f.)

By virtue of its normative or canonical authority, Holy Scripture is the only norm of faith and life and therefore also the only judge in all theological controversies. As the only rule of faith, Scripture performs both a directive and a corrective function; for, on the one hand, it directs the thoughts of the human mind in such a way that they abide within the bounds of truth; and, on the other, it corrects errors, inasmuch as it is the only standard of right and wrong (Hollaz). Calov says very correctly (I, 474): "The Holy Scriptures are a rule according to which all controversies in regard to faith or life in the Church should, and can be, decided, Ps. 19, 7; Gal. 6, 16; Phil. 3, 16; and as a norm they are not partial, but complete and adequate, because besides the Scriptures no other infallible rule in matters of faith and life can be given. All other rules besides the Word of God are fallible; and on this account we are referred to the Holy Scriptures as the only rule, Deut. 4, 2; 12, 28; Josh. 23, 6; Is. 8, 20; Luke 16, 29; 2 Pet. 1, 19, to which alone Christ and the apostles referred as a rule, Matt. 4, 4 ff.; 22, 29. 31; Mark 9, 12; John 5, 45; Acts 3, 20; 18, 28; 26, 22." (*Doctr. Theol.*, p. 61.)

With regard to the *use* of Scripture as the norm of faith (*norma doctrinae, iudex controversiarum*), it must be held that not only theologians (2 Tim. 2, 2), but also all Christians in general should so employ the Word of God (Acts 17, 11), since it is their duty to supervise the ministry of their teachers (Col. 4, 17), to avoid all false prophets (Rom. 16, 17; Matt. 7, 15), and to spread the pure Gospel of Jesus Christ by personal evangelism (Col. 3, 16; 1 Pet. 2, 9). The spiritual ability to judge all matters of faith and doctrine Holy Scripture ascribes to all believers in express words, John 6, 45; 10, 4. 5. 27. Hence whoever denies the ability and authority of all Christians to judge questions of Christian doctrine or life opposes Christ and reveals himself as an antichrist. Luther writes very earnestly on this point: "To know and to judge matters of doctrine is a privilege which belongs to every believer, and every one is anathema who infringes upon this right even but a little. For in many incontestable passages of Scripture,

Christ has granted this privilege to His Christians, for instance, in Matt. 7, 15: 'Beware of false prophets,' etc. This warning He addressed to the people in contrast to their teachers, commanding them to avoid all false prophets. But how can they avoid them if they do not know them? And how can they know them if they have no right to judge [their doctrine]? Yet Christ gave to the people not only the right, but also the command to judge, so that this one passage suffices against the verdicts of all Popes, fathers, church councils, and schools that ascribed the authority to judge and pass sentence [upon the teachers of the Church] only to bishops and priests, and robbed the people, or the Church, the queen, in a most ungodly and sacrilegious manner." (St. L., XIX, 341.)

On the other hand, however, it must be affirmed that Christians must judge doctrinal matters not according to their own thoughts, but solely according to Scripture, 1 Pet. 4, 11, since in all matters of doctrine it alone is the *iudex controversiarum.* The objection of the papists that Scripture as a "dumb book" is unable to decide any matter is in opposition not only to Holy Scripture itself, which claims for itself this very authority, Matt. 4, 4ff.; Rom. 3, 19; John 7, 51, but also to reason, by which men are prompted to use authoritative records to decide issues in controversy (cf. the decisions of the Supreme Court). Every sensible person clearly understands what is meant by such phrases as "The Law decides," or "The Bible decides." Holy Scripture certainly is more capable of deciding questions of controversy than are the papal decretals, to which the papists have recourse in determining what to teach. Our Lutheran dogmaticians were quite right when they declared: "Scripture is never mute except where under the Papacy it is prevented from speaking." *(Scriptura Sacra non est muta nisi in papatu, ubi prohibetur loqui.)*

In what manner controversial questions should be decided by the use of Holy Scripture may be stated briefly thus: First determine the controversial point *(status controversiae)* and then place it in the light of all clear Scripture-passages that treat of the particular point in question *(sedes doctrinae; dicta probantia).* In this manner Holy Scripture is given an opportunity to exercise its judicial function, not indeed by external compulsion *(vi externa),* but by internal persuasion *(vi interna).* Just so Christ employed the Scriptures as a judge in controversy when He said to the Pharisees: "There is one that accuseth you, even Moses, in whom ye trust," John 5, 45; for here He referred to Moses inasmuch as he is speaking in Holy Scripture.

By adhering to Holy Scripture as the sole source and norm of faith, the true visible Church of Christ on earth proves its orthodox character; in other words, the orthodox Church of Christ on earth is found only where Holy Scripture is obeyed and followed in all questions of faith and life. It was for this reason that Luther so earnestly emphasized the doctrine of *sola Scriptura* as the formal principle of the Reformation and that to-day the confessional Lutheran Church insists upon this doctrine with the same determination. As soon as a Church, either in theory or in practise, rejects the authority of Scripture *(Schriftprinzip),* it ceases to be orthodox and becomes heterodox, that is to say, an erring Church, or a sect.

In connection with the normative authority of Holy Scripture it must be emphasized that human reason in its magisterial use *(usus magisterialis)* must never be allowed a place beside the Bible. In other words, man's natural knowledge of God, even so far as it is correctly retained in his perverted intellect, must never be co-ordinated with, but always be subordinated to, God's Word. Unless this is done, Scripture is not allowed to stand as the only judge of faith. But human reason in its ministerial, or instrumental, sense or reason as "the receiving subject or apprehending instrument" (Hollaz) must certainly be employed whenever Scripture is used as the norm of faith; for "as we see nothing without eyes and hear nothing without ears, so we understand nothing without reason" (Hollaz). This so-called instrumental use of reason *(usus organicus; usus instrumentalis)* implies both the correct use of the laws of human speech (grammar) and of the laws of human reasoning (logic), because God, in giving His Word to men, accommodated Himself both to the canons of human speech and thought. This truth we considered already when we referred to Melanchthon's dictum: *Theologia debet esse grammatica,* and to Luther's statement that whoever errs in grammar is bound to err also in doctrine.

However, just as human reason in general, so also human logic in particular serves the theologian only as a formal discipline (the science of correct and accurate thinking) and not as a philosophy or a metaphysical system, in which sense the term is sometimes used. In addition, even when logic is employed as a formal discipline (the science of reasoning), it must always be kept within its legitimate bounds. In other words, the theologian must always

128 THE DOCTRINE OF HOLY SCRIPTURE.

be on his guard against fallacies, or against untruths derived from the misuse of logic. For example, from the general truth of Scripture "God so loved the world" every person in this world may argue: "God so loved me," since the concept "world" includes every human being. In other words, the conclusion attained must always be a truth already contained in the premises, or in the Scriptural statements, according to the axiom: "Whatever inferences *(consequentiae legitimae)* are drawn from the declarations of Scripture must be proved as being directly expressed in the clear words of Scripture." *("Was man aus den Schriftwahrheiten erschliesst, muss als in den Schriftworten ausgedrueckt nachgewiesen werden.")*

On the other hand, when logic is used to propose new doctrines not *set forth* in Scripture, the authority of Scripture *(Schriftprinzip)* is annulled, and logic is made to serve as a teacher of false doctrine. Examples of misapplied logic are the following: "Since God has not elected all men, He does not desire to *save* all men." Or: "Since Peter was saved and Judas was lost, there must have been in Peter some cause why he was saved." Or: "Since every body is in space locally, Christ's body cannot be truly present in the Lord's Supper." Or: "Since the finite is incapable of the infinite, there can be no communication of attributes in the person of the God-man." Or: "As many persons as there are, so many essences; hence there must be three essences in the Godhead." Misdirected logic has proved the source of so many errors in theology that Gerhard's warning is well taken (II, 371): "Not human reason, but divine revelation is the source of faith; nor are we to judge concerning the articles of faith according to the dictates of reason; otherwise we should have no articles of faith, but only decisions of reason. The cogitations and utterances of reason should be restricted and restrained within the sphere of those things which are subject to the decisions of reason and not be extended to the sphere of such matters as are placed entirely beyond the reach of reason." *(Doctr. Theol.,* p. 32 f.)

With respect to the use of Holy Scripture as the only source and norm of faith our Lutheran dogmaticians rightly said that it is God's Book designed for all men, Luke 16, 29—31; John 5, 39; Acts 17, 11; even for children, 2 Tim. 3, 15; 1 John 2, 13. *(Finis cui Scripturae sunt omnes homines.)* For this reason the papal injunction against universal Bible-reading is antichristian. However, it is equally true that all men should use Holy Scripture for obtaining salvation, 2 Tim. 3, 15, and not merely for the purpose of enriching their knowledge in general or of improving their style. *(Finis cuius Scripturae Sacrae fides in Christum et salus aeterna est.)* From this it is clear that it is also the will of God that the Bible should be translated into the various languages used in the world. *(Versiones Scripturae Sacrae non solum utiles, sed etiam necessariae sunt.)* The duty of translating the Bible into foreign languages is included in Christ's command to teach all nations, Matt. 28, 20.

While Holy Scripture is the absolute norm of faith *(norma normans, norma absoluta, norma primaria, norma decisionis),* the Lutheran Church recognizes its officially received Confessions, or Symbols, as secondary norms *(norma normata, norma secundum quid, norma secundaria, norma discretionis),* or as true declarations of the doctrines of Holy Scripture, which all Lutheran theologians must confess and teach. For this reason the confessional Lutheran Church demands of all its public teachers and ministers a *bona-fide* subscription to all its Confessions as the pure and unadulterated declarations of God's Word *(quia,* not *quatenus). In other words, no public minister is permitted to administer his sacred office unless he declares himself convinced that the Lutheran Confessions set forth the pure Word of God.*

However, while Holy Scripture as the deciding norm *(norma decisionis)* is absolutely necessary, the Confessions as the distinguishing norm of the Church *(norma discretionis)* are only relatively necessary. The former decides which doctrines are true or false; the latter, whether a person has clearly understood the true doctrines of Scripture. *(Norma discretionis discernit orthodoxos ab heterodoxis.)*

Although Scripture sufficiently attests itself as the divine truth in the believer's heart, God in His infinite wisdom has provided that it should be attested also historically. That is to say, by proper historical investigation we fully know which books were composed by the sacred writers (prophets and apostles), through whom God wished to give His Word to the world. This historical evidence is of great value, on the one hand, against the papists, who by their antichristian decrees elevate human books to the dignity of the divine Scriptures, and, on the other, against unbelieving higher critics, who seek to degrade the Holy Scriptures to the level of human compositions. In addition, the historical evidence on behalf of the authenticity and integrity of the Bible is of value also for believing Christians, since at times the testimony of the Holy Spirit in their hearts may be weakened or suppressed entirely by doubts.

For the divine authority of the Old Testament we have the express testimony not only of the Jewish Church, but also of our omniscient Savior, who without qualification acknowledged the Bible that was in use at His time as canonical, Luke 16, 29; 24, 44; John 5, 39; 10, 35; Matt. 5, 17. Had the Jewish Church erred regarding its canon, our divine Lord could not have declared it to be "the Scriptures," John 5, 39. The Old Testament *Apocrypha* were received as canonical neither by the Jewish Church nor by Christ. The fact that the Roman Catholic Church nevertheless elevated them to canonical rank proves its antichristian character. For the Scriptures of the New Testament we have Christ's direct statement and promise that both His own and the apostles' Word shall be preserved and acknowledged as the infallible norm of faith to the end of time, Matt. 24, 35; John 17, 20; Eph. 2, 20. If the divine Word is not recognized as such, the fault rests not with Scripture, but with the blindness and perverseness of those who decline to believe God's Word.

The historical testimony of the canonical books of the New Testament has been adequately supplied by the ancient Christian Church *(ecclesia primitiva)*. Its acknowledgment of the four gospels, the Acts, the thirteen epistles of Paul, the First Epistle of John, and the First Epistle of Peter was unanimous *(Homologumena)*. With regard to the Epistle to the Hebrews, the Second Epistle of Peter, the Second and the Third Epistle of John, the Epistle of James, the Epistle of Jude, and Revelation, doubts were expressed, so that they were classified as *Antilegomena*. (Cf. Eusebius, *Church History,* Bk. III.) Nevertheless, though the canonical character of the *Antilegomena* was questioned by some, each received sufficient testimony to entitle it to a place in the canon, from which all spurious apostolic writings (pseudepigraphs) were rigidly ruled out. In case, however, the authority of the *Antilegomena* as a source and norm of faith should be denied to-day (cf. Luther's verdict on the Epistle of St. James), the same doctrines which are set forth in them may be sufficiently proved from the *Homologumena,* since the *Antilegomena* do not contain a single doctrine that is not taught in the *Homologumena.*

The question whether also the later Christian Church has the authority to declare certain books to be canonical must be denied most emphatically. When the ancient Church differentiated between *Homologumena* and *Antilegomena,* this was a purely historical procedure, involving nothing more than the question whether certain books were written by such and such an apostle of Christ or not; but when in the sixteenth century the Council of Trent, contrary to the historical judgment of the early Church, declared that also the Apocrypha should rank as canonical, it arbitrarily added to the fixed canon writings which neither Christ nor His holy apostles accepted as such. The later Christian Church cannot change or supplement the established canon, because it is not in a position to furnish the historical evidence which is required to pronounce a certain book canonical or not. The Lutheran dogmatician Chemnitz very correctly called it an antichristian undertaking to eliminate the distinction between the *Homologumena* and the *Antilegomena* which the ancient Christian Church has established.

With regard to the manner in which the primitive Church proceeded in fixing the Biblical canon, Chemnitz writes (*Ex. Trid.,* I, 87): "The testimony of the primitive Church in the times of the apostles concerning the genuine writings of the apostles the immediately succeeding generations constantly and faithfully retained and preserved, so that, when many others [writings] afterwards were brought forward, claiming to have been written by the apostles, they were tested and rejected as supposititious and false, first, for this reason, that it could not be shown and proved by the testimony of the original Church either that they were written by the apostles or approved by the living apostles and transmitted and entrusted by them to the Church in the beginning; secondly, because they proposed strange doctrine not accordant with that which the Church received from the apostles and which was at that time still preserved in the memory of all." (*Doctr. Theol.,* p. 85.)

With regard to the gospels of Mark and Luke and the Acts of the Apostles it may be said that the ancient Church placed these unanimously and without any qualification among the *Homologumena,* though they were not written by apostles. This was done on the ground that the two gospels were composed under the supervision of St. Peter and St. Paul, respectively, while the Book of Acts was accepted as a canonical Scripture fully approved by St. Paul. Since the ancient Christian Church has placed these writings among the *Homologumena,* the question concerning their place in the canon ought not to cause any difficulties to-day; at best it is only of academic interest.

The integrity of the New Testament may be assumed *a priori,* since Christ assures us that His Word, as this is set forth in the writings of the holy apostles, or in Holy Scripture, John 17, 20; Eph. 2, 20; John 8, 31. 32, shall never pass away, Matt. 24, 35. The integrity of the Old Testament is guaranteed by Christ's direct and express testimony, John 5, 39.

With respect to the various versions of the Bible we rightly hold that not only the original Hebrew and Greek texts, but also the translations of these texts are really and truly God's Word, provided they fully agree with the original reading. On the other hand, where translations deviate from the original texts and teach anything contrary to them, they must be rejected as not being the Word of God. Since translators never write by inspiration of the Holy Ghost, but are subject to the common failings of men, all Bible versions must be diligently compared with the original text to ascertain whether they are correct or not, and for this reason the theologian ought to possess an adequate knowledge of Hebrew and Greek.

However, the gap between the original text and its translations must not be widened unduly, so as to create doubts regarding their authority; for the language of Scripture is in most instances so direct and simple that any translator who performs his work conscientiously is compelled by the clear and direct language of Scripture to reproduce the sense of the original. Even the Vulgate sets forth the chief truths of the Christian faith with sufficient clearness though it is fraught with errors from beginning to end. However, the arbitrary promulgation of the Vulgate as the only authoritative text by the Roman Catholic Church was an act so altogether contrary to the spirit of Christ and His apostles that it furnishes additional proof that the papal Church is the Church of Antichrist.

Luther's methodological advice that the minister, when teaching the Catechism, "should above all things avoid the use of different texts and forms, but adopt one form and adhere to it, since the young and ignorant people will easily become confused if we teach thus to-day and otherwise next year, as if we thought of making improvements," applies also to the use of Bible translations in the pulpit or wherever else Christian ministers may instruct the common people.

B. THE DIVINE EFFICACY OF HOLY SCRIPTURE.
(Divina Efficacia.)

Because Holy Scripture is the inspired Word of God, it possesses not only divine authority, but also divine efficacy, that is to say, the creative power to work in man, who by nature is spiritually dead, both saving faith and true sanctification, Rom. 10, 17: faith; 1 Pet. 1, 23: regeneration; John 17, 20: faith and sanctification. The Word of God does not merely teach man the way of salvation and show him the means by which he may attain it; but by its truly divine power (*vis vere divina*) it actually converts, regenerates, and renews him. This unique efficacy is possessed by no other book in the world nor by any discourse of man unless these repeat God's Word as set forth in the Bible; for the divine efficacy of Scripture is nothing else than God's power in the Word, Rom. 1, 16. Luther is certainly right when he writes (*Smalcald Art.,* VIII, 3: "We must firmly hold that God grants His Spirit or grace to no one except through or with the preceding outward Word." And again (*Large Cat.,* 101): "Such is the efficacy of the Word, whenever it is seriously contemplated, heard, and used, that it is bound never to be without fruit, but always awakens new understanding, pleasure, and devoutness and produces a pure heart and pure thoughts. For these words are not inoperative or dead, but creative, living words."

In opposition to all erroneous doctrine on this point, which either denies the divine efficacy of Scripture altogether and ascribes to it only a moral direction and instruction (Unitarianism, Pelagianism) or separates the divine power from the Word (enthusiasm, Calvinism), we further describe the divine efficacy as follows: —

a. The Word of God set forth in Scripture does not operate in a natural way, *i. e.,* neither through logical demonstration, appealing to reason, nor through rhetorical eloquence, appealing to the emotions, but in a supernatural manner (*efficientia vere divina),* inasmuch as the Holy Spirit, who is inseparably combined with the Word, persuades the human mind of the divine truth through the very Word which it contemplates. This is clearly attested by St. Paul, who writes: "My speech and my preaching was . . . in demonstration of the Spirit and of power," 1 Cor. 2, 4. Quenstedt says correctly: "It is the *innate* power and tendency of God's Word always to convince men of its truth." (*Verbum Dei virtutem exerce per contactum hyperphysicum.)*

b. The divine Word of Holy Scripture has infinite, almighty

power (*vis infinita, potentia Dei, omnipotentia*), for the same almighty power which is *essentially* in God is by way of communication (*communicative*) in His Word. This truth is propounded in the following Scripture-passages: Rom. 1, 16. 17: "It is the power of God unto salvation"; Eph. 1, 19. 20: "Who believe according to the working of His mighty power"; 2 Cor. 4, 6: "God, who commanded the light to shine out of darkness, hath shined in our hearts [*sc.*, through the Gospel], to give the light of the knowledge of the glory of God in the face of Jesus Christ." Baier writes, in full agreement with all these passages: "The same infinite virtue which is essentially *per se* and independently in God and by which He enlightens and converts men is communicated to the Word." (*Doctr. Theol.*, p. 505.)

c. The divine power which inheres in the Word is not irresistible, but resistible (*efficacia resistibilis*); that is to say, the saving effects of the Word may be withstood though in itself the Word is omnipotent, Matt. 23, 37; 2 Cor. 4, 3. 4. This resistible character of the divine Word Quenstedt describes as follows: "Accidentally it may be inefficacious, not from any deficiency of power, but by the exercise of perverseness, which hinders its operation, so that its effect is not attained." This fact is asserted in Acts 7, 51, where the apostle addresses the hardened Jews thus: "Ye stiff-necked and uncircumcised in heart and ears, ye do always resist the Holy Ghost; as your fathers did, so do ye." How the omnipotent Word of God may be resisted by impotent man is indeed unintelligible to human reason; yet for this we have an analog in the realm of nature, where natural life, though it owes its origin and existence to God's omnipotent power, may be destroyed by man's feeble hand. Luther's canon of judgment in this matter is correct: "When God works through means, He can be resisted; but when He works without means, in His revealed glory (*in nuda maiestate*), He cannot be resisted." Thus the spiritual resurrection, which is effected through the means of grace, Luke 2, 34; Eph. 2, 1; Col. 2, 12, may be resisted, 1 Cor. 1, 23; 2 Cor. 2, 16, while the bodily resurrection, which will be effected by God's sovereign command, cannot be resisted, Matt. 25, 31. 32; John 11, 24.

d. The divine power must never be separated from the Word of Scripture; that is to say, the Holy Ghost does not operate beside or outside the Word (enthusiasm, Calvinism, Rathmannism in the Lutheran Church), but always in and through the Word,

Rom. 10, 17; 1 Pet. 1, 23; John 6, 63. This important Scriptural truth our Lutheran theologians have always maintained against the Reformed (Zwingli: "The Holy Spirit requires no leader or vehicle" [*dux vel vehiculum*]; Hodge: "Efficacious grace acts immediately"). The practical result of the separation of the divine power from the divine Word of Scripture is the rejection of the Bible as the only source and norm of faith *(norma normans)*. This is proved by the very fact that the enthusiasts have invariably placed the "inner word" *(verbum internum),* or the "spirit," above Holy Scripture *(verbum externum),* assigning to the latter an inferior place in the realm of divine revelation. To the enthusiasts the Bible is only a *norma normata,* or a rule of faith subject to the "inner word," that is, to their own notions and figments of reason. On the other hand, the practical result of the acceptance of the Scriptural doctrine that the Holy Spirit is inseparably united with the Word is the absolute subjection of every thought to the Word of God, as this is set forth in the Bible, 2 Cor. 10, 5. In this case every doctrine which is opposed to Scripture is rejected as false, no matter to what source it may be attributed, whether it be the "spirit," the "inner word," the "inner light," "reason," "science," "the Church," "the Pope," and the like. Unless we fully accept the Scriptural doctrine that the Holy Spirit is indissolubly united with the Word of Scripture, we cannot regard this precious Book of God as the only source and standard of faith. It was for this reason that our Lutheran theologians so strenuously defended the inseparable unity of the Word and the Spirit. Hollaz writes, for example: "The efficacy of the divine Word is not only objective or significative, like the statue of Mercury, for instance, which points out the path, but does not give the power or strength to the traveler to walk in it; but it is effective, because it not only shows the way of salvation, but saves souls." (*Doctr. Theol.,* p. 504.)

Whenever in our Christian prayers we ask God "to give His Spirit and power to the Word," we do not imply that at times the Spirit is absent from the Word with His divine and effective power, but we rather confess by these words that our own human effort or skill in applying the Word of God is of no avail whatever, 1 Cor. 3, 6. Luther in his exposition of Ps. 8, 3, writes on this point: "We must put off the foolish confidence that we ourselves can effect anything through the Word in the hearts of our hearers; rather should we diligently continue in the prayer that God alone,

without us, would render mighty and active in the hearers the
Word which He proclaims through preachers and teachers." (St. L.,
IV, 626.)

In their controversy with the enthusiasts (Reformed) the Lutheran theologians averred that Holy Scripture is efficacious also
extra usum. By this phrase they meant to say that the Holy Spirit
is perpetually connected with the Word, so that it retains its power
even when not in use. This truth had to be maintained also against
the Lutheran theologian Rathmann, who contended that the "divine
efficacy is external to the Word." Against this error the efficacy of
the Word even when not in use *(extra usum)* was maintained in
order that the Word of God might not be reduced to the level of
human words (cf. *Doctr. Theol.,* p. 507). The statement regarding the efficacy of the Word of God *extra usum* was thus used to
emphasize the Scriptural truth that God's Word is always in itself
a "power of God unto salvation," Rom. 1, 16.

Although the Holy Ghost is always active through the Word,
we must not judge His activity from feeling *(ex sensu).* The
Formula of Concord comments on this point: "Concerning the
presence, operation, and gift of the Holy Ghost we should not and
cannot always judge *ex sensu,* as to how and when they are experienced in the heart; but because they are often covered and occur
in great weakness, we should be certain from, and according to,
the promise that the Word of God preached and heard is [truly]
an office and work of the Holy Ghost, by which He is certainly
efficacious and works in our hearts, 2 Cor. 2, 14 ff.; 3, 5 ff." (Thor.
Decl., II, 56.)

While we ascribe divine efficacy to the entire Word of God as
set forth in Holy Scripture, we, nevertheless, rightly distinguish
between the efficacy which is proper to the Law and that which is
proper to the Gospel. The divine Law has the power to make
men "guilty before God," Rom. 3, 19, since "by the Law is the
knowledge of sin," Rom. 3, 20. More than this the Law cannot do;
its sphere is the working of contrition *(contritio, terrores conscientiae).* The Gospel, on the other hand, works faith and so
regeneration and conversion, Rom. 10, 17; 5, 1. However, by this
very operation it inscribes the divine Law into the heart, Jer.
31, 31 ff.; that is to say, it makes man willing to obey the Law
with a cheerful and ready mind, Ps. 110, 3; Rom. 12, 1; Gal. 2, 20.
(Lex praescribit, evangelium inscribit.) Moreover, by this very
operation it also relieves man from the fear of death and gives him

power to triumph over this last foe, 1 Cor. 15, 55. Through the power of the Gospel the sinner, who by nature is subject to death, Heb. 2, 15, and without hope in the world, Eph. 2, 12, is received into Christ's Kingdom of Grace, John 3, 16—18, and finally into His Kingdom of Glory, Phil. 1, 3—6; Eph. 1, 16—19; 1 Pet. 1, 3—5.

C. THE DIVINE PERFECTION, OR SUFFICIENCY, OF HOLY SCRIPTURE.
(Perfectio Scripturae Sacrae.)

The divine perfection, or sufficiency, of Holy Scripture is that property by which it teaches everything that is necessary for salvation. Gerhard defines this property of Scripture as follows (II, 286) : "The Scriptures fully and perfectly instruct us concerning all things necessary to salvation." The Scripture proof for this doctrine is clearly set forth in 2 Tim. 3, 15—17; John 17, 20; 1 John 1, 3. 4. Since Holy Scripture is sufficient, or perfect, it requires no supplementation either through traditions (papists) or new revelations (enthusiasts) or doctrinal progress or development (modern rationalistic theologians). The way of salvation taught in the Bible is absolutely complete, Matt. 28, 20; Mark 16, 15. 16. Gerhard, arguing against the Romanists, rightly says: "Laying aside tradition, we adhere to Scripture alone."

When considering the divine sufficiency of Holy Scripture, we must carefully observe the following points: —

a. Holy Scripture does not contain everything which men may know; for with regard to matters of earthly concern it offers very little instruction (the Bible is not a "text-book of science"). Earthly affairs are treated in Scripture only in so far as they pertain to the divine counsel of salvation (the creation of the world, etc.).

b. Holy Scripture does not reveal all divine things which man might desire to know; for also in the spiritual sphere its proper scope is the saving of sinners, 2 Tim. 3, 16—18; 1 Cor. 13, 12; Rom. 11, 33.

c. Nevertheless, Holy Scripture contains all things "necessary to be known for the Christian faith and life and, therefore, for the attainment of eternal salvation" (Quenstedt). All those who deny this truth reject the *Schriftprinzip,* or the basic Christian doctrine that Holy Scripture is the only source and norm of faith. The papists make of Scripture a restricted norm *(norma remissiva)* and teach a *perfectio implicita Scripturae Sacrae;* that is to say,.

they regard Scripture as sufficient only when its teachings are supplemented by those of the Church, or the Pope. The papists thus degrade Scripture to a *norma normata*.

Its holy doctrines, Scripture sets forth either in direct words (κατὰ ῥητόν) or according to the sense (κατὰ διάνοιαν). For the first we may cite the express teaching of salvation by grace, through faith in Christ, John 3, 16; Rom. 3, 24. 28; for the latter, the doctrine of the Holy Trinity, Matt. 28, 20. However, Holy Scripture never states mere "general principles" from which the Christian theologian or the Christian Church must "develop" the doctrines; for it is not a book of "general principles," but of doctrines. In order that the theologian may be kept from teaching false doctrine, he must constantly bear in mind that he is to teach nothing but what Scripture itself teaches in clear words. That is what Luther means when he writes: "In the Christian doctrine we must not assert anything which Holy Scripture does not teach." (St. L., XIX, 592.) Again: "All Christian articles must be of such a nature that they are not only certain to the Christians themselves, but also are so confirmed by manifest and clear Scripture-passages that they can stop the mouths of all [adversaries], so that they can say nothing against them." (St. L., XVIII, 1747.)

D. THE DIVINE PERSPICUITY OF HOLY SCRIPTURE.
(Perspicuitas, Claritas Scripturae Sacrae.)

When we say that Holy Scripture is perspicuous, or clear, we mean that it sets forth all doctrines of salvation in words so simple and plain that they can be understood by all persons of average intelligence. The Lutheran dogmatician Baier expresses this thought as follows: "Any man acquainted with the language, possessed of a common judgment, and paying due attention to the words may learn the true sense of the words . . . and embrace the fundamental doctrines." The perspicuity of Scripture is definitely taught in clear passages: Ps. 119, 105. 130; 19, 7. 8; 2 Pet. 1, 19; 2 Tim. 3, 15. In addition to this, it is presupposed in all those passages in which all men are exhorted to search the Scriptures for salvation, John 5, 39; Luke 16, 29; Acts 17, 11; 2 Thess. 2, 15; Is. 34, 16; 1 John 2, 13. 14. Whoever, therefore, rejects the perspicuity of the Bible (papists, enthusiasts, modern rationalistic theologians) must also reject the basic truth that Scripture is the only *principium cognoscendi,* thus compelling the Christian believer to base his faith upon the human expositions either of the Church or of individual Bible scholars.

Keeping in mind that Holy Scripture is a clear book, the Christian exegete must scrupulously refrain from foisting upon its sacred text his own subjective views *(eisegesis)* and regard it as his sole function to exhibit the true meaning of God's clear Word (*exegesis:* the leading forth of the sense of Scripture) ; in other words, he must allow Scripture to interpret itself. *(Scriptura Scripturam interpretatur; Scriptura sua luce radiat.)* Negatively the function of the Christian exegete may be described as the removal of all textual difficulties by proper grammatical instruction and of all misinterpretations by erring expositors; positively, as the exhibition of the true sense of the text *(manuductio ad nudam Scripturam)* in the light of its context and parallel passages.

Hence a true Christian exegete must possess the following qualifications: a) He must regard the whole Bible as the inerrant Word of God; b) he must treat Holy Scripture as a book which is clear in itself; c) he must conscientiously point out the real sense of the text; and d) he must be able to refute the erroneous human opinions which false teachers or misguided orthodox theologians have foisted upon the text.

With regard to the perspicuity of Holy Scripture we may yet observe the following points: —

a. Holy Scripture is preeminently clear with respect to those things that are necessary for salvation. We readily admit that Scripture contains passages which are more or less obscure not only to the average Christian, but also the Christian theologian. But this fact does not disprove the doctrine of the perspicuity of the Bible. The passages which in themselves are obscure do not set forth fundamental articles of the Christian faith, but pertain, as our dogmaticians have said, commonly to "onomastic, chronological, topographical, allegorical, typical, or prophetical matters" (Quenstedt). Of the passages which propound doctrines some are less clear than others or, as Gerhard remarks: "What is obscurely expressed in one passage is more clearly explained in others," and in all such cases the more obscure must be interpreted in the light of the clear *(sedes doctrinae; analogia fidei)*. But also this fact does not disprove the doctrine of Biblical perspicuity. In his exposition on Ps. 37 Luther comments very aptly: "But if any one of them (the papists) should trouble you and say: 'You must have the interpretation of the Fathers, since Scripture is obscure,' then you must reply: 'It is not true. There is no clearer book upon earth than is Holy Writ, which in comparison with all other books is like the sun in its relation to all other lights.' They say such things only because they want to lead us away from Scripture and elevate themselves to the position of masters over us in order that we might believe their dream sermons. . . . For that is indeed true: Some passages in Scripture are obscure, but in these you find nothing but what is found in other places and in clear and plain passages. Then came the heretics and explained the obscure passages according to their own reasonings, and with these they combated the clear passages and foundation of faith. So the Fathers fought them with the clear passages, and with them they shed light upon the obscure, proving in this way that what is said obscurely in some passages is set forth clearly in others. Do not permit yourselves to be led out of, and away from, Scripture, no matter how hard they [the papists] may try. For if you step out of Scripture, you are lost; then they will lead you just as they wish. But if you remain in Scripture, you have won the victory and you will regard their raging in no other way than when the crag of the sea smiles at the waves and billows. All their writings are nothing else than waves that rock to and fro. Be assured and certain that there is nothing clearer than the sun, I mean, Holy Scripture. If a cloud drifts before it, nothing else than the same clear sun is nevertheless behind it. If then you find an obscure passage in Scripture, do not be alarmed, for surely the same truth is set forth in it which in another place is taught plainly. So if you cannot understand the obscure, then cling to the clear." (St. L., V, 334ff.) These defiant statements of Luther reecho the clear truths which Holy Scripture itself teaches concerning its perspicuity, Ps. 119, 105; 2 Pet. 1, 19f. (Cf. also Luther's defense of the perspicuity of Scripture in his famous work *De Servo Arbitrio.* St. L., XVIII, 1681 ff.)

b. The perspicuity of Scripture must not be identified with comprehensibility of its mysteries of faith *(perspicuitas rerum).* The very doctrines which we must believe for our salvation, for instance, the incarnation of Christ, the Holy Trinity, the personal union of the two natures in Christ, the atonement through Christ's vicarious suffering and death, etc., will always remain unintelligible to human reason *(res inevidentes).* But these incomprehensible mysteries of our faith are set forth in words so intelligible *(perspicuitas verborum)* that every person of ordinary intelligence who understands human speech can receive them into his mind *(apprehensio simplex)* and through the supernatural operation of the Holy Ghost can apprehend them also spiritually (*apprehensio spiritualis sive practica*). For this reason our Lutheran dogmaticians have called the perspicuity of Scripture a *claritas verborum,* or *claritas externa,* or *claritas grammatica,* etc. On this point Gerhard quotes Luther (I, 26), who writes: "If you speak of the *internal clearness,* no man understands a single iota in the Scriptures by the natural powers of his mind unless he has the Spirit of God; for all men [by nature] have obscure hearts. The Holy Spirit is required for the understanding of the whole of Scripture and of all its parts. If you refer to the *external* clearness of Scripture, there is nothing that is left obscure or ambiguous, but all things brought to light in the Word are perfectly clear." (*Doctr. Theol.,* p. 73.) The whole doctrine of the clearness of Scripture may be summed up as follows: Scripture is clear *externally (claritas verborum)* to all men of sound minds, *internally (claritas spiritualis)* only to believers, and *essentially* (*claritas rerum,* the understanding of the mysteries of the faith) only to the saints in heaven, 1 Cor. 13, 12.

From all this it is obvious to whom Holy Scripture must remain an obscure book, namely, to all —

a. Who understand neither human speech in general nor Scriptural speech in particular;

b. Who are so filled with prejudice that they refuse to give the words of Scripture honest consideration;

c. Who foolishly endeavor to comprehend the divine mysteries by means of their blind reason;

d. Who are filled with enmity against the divine truths which Scripture teaches, Ps. 18, 26; John 8, 43—47; 2 Cor. 4, 3. 4. This explains why so many errorists arrogantly reject Holy Scripture as an obscure book. "Blind unbelief is sure to err and scan His work in vain." (Cowper.)

"Blind unbelief" has also suggested the objections which have been preferred against the perspicuity of Holy Scripture. Among these we may note the following: —

a. *The institution of the holy ministry. Answer:* Christ did indeed institute the public ministry, not, however, to render the Bible clear, but to preach the Gospel, which the Bible propounds so clearly, Mark 16, 15. 16; Matt. 28, 19. 20, and by this means to guide men to heaven, Heb. 13, 17; Ezek. 3, 18.

b. *The dissensions and factions within the visible Christian*

Church. *Answer:* These, alas! exist, but only because men insist on rejecting the clear doctrines of Scripture, John 8, 31. 32; 1 Tim. 6, 3 f.

c. *Obscure passages occur in Scripture.* *Answer:* Such passages do not disprove the perspicuity of Scripture since the doctrines of salvation are taught with great clarity. St. Augustine rightly says: "In the clear passages of Scripture everything is found that is necessary for faith and life."

d. *The unintelligible mysteries of the faith.* *Answer:* These mysteries are indeed beyond the grasp of human reason, but they are taught in language so plain that it is intelligible even to a normal child.

e. *Special passages of Scripture allegedly admit its obscurity.* Passages such as 2 Pet. 3, 16 and 1 Cor. 13, 12 have been pointed out by those who deny the perspicuity of Scripture. *Answer:* St. Peter declares that among the things which St. Paul writes in his epistles (ἐν αἶς) there are *some* that are hard to be understood (δυσνόητα). Holy Scripture indeed contains many things which admittedly are "hard to be understood." However, this does not disprove its perspicuity; for wherever it teaches the way of salvation, it is perfectly clear.

In 1 Cor. 13, 12 St. Paul does not speak of Holy Scripture, but of our knowledge of God and divine truth, which now is mediate and imperfect, but which in heaven will be immediate and perfect. Hence also this passage does not disprove the perspicuity of Scripture.

The perspicuity of Scripture is denied both by the papists ("The Scriptures are not of themselves clear and intelligible even in matters of the highest importance." Cardinal Gibbons, *The Faith of Our Fathers,* p. 111) and the enthusiasts. The papists claim that the Scriptures must be interpreted by the Church, or the Pope, while the enthusiasts assert that they must be expounded by means of the "inner light." In the last analysis both papists and enthusiasts resort to human reason to expound Scripture, just as modern rationalists do, who aver that the Bible must be interpreted in the light of modern intelligence. In all three cases the charge against God's holy and clear Book of salvation is prompted by deliberate opposition to the blessed Gospel of Christ, 1 Cor. 1, 22. 23.

THE DOCTRINE OF GOD.
(De Deo.)

1. THE NATURAL KNOWLEDGE OF GOD.
(Notitia Dei Naturalis.)

Whatever man knows of God he knows through God's own revelation of Himself either in the realm of nature or in the realm of grace, that is to say, either through God's work of creation and providence or through His holy Book, the Bible. Hence we rightly speak of a natural knowledge of God and of a supernatural or revealed (Christian) knowledge of God. Had God not revealed Himself, man never would have known Him, since God is the absolute, perfect Personality, who dwells "in the light which no man can approach unto," 1 Tim. 6, 16.

By means of his natural knowledge of God, man knows that there is a personal, eternal, omnipotent Divine Being, who has created this world and still preserves and rules all things and who is holy and just, demanding what is good and punishing what is evil. This natural knowledge of God is mediated to man —

a. *By God's created works* (ποιήματα θεοῦ, *creaturae Dei*), which in themselves bear witness to their omnipotent Creator. In Rom. 1, 20 St. Paul attests that, though God Himself is invisible, man nevertheless knows of Him and, in particular, of His personality, eternity, omnipotence, and sovereignty "by the things that are made." That this is true is proved by the testimony of many heathen philosophers, as, for example, by Aristotle and Cicero. Cicero writes (*Tuscul. Disput.*, I, 28): *"Deum non vides; tamen Deum agnoscis ex operibus eius."* This natural knowledge of God is so certain that the apostle says of all agnostics and atheists, who deny His divine existence and commands, that "they are without excuse." (The cosmological proof of God's existence.)

b. *By God's continued operation in the realm of nature and of human history.* In Acts 14, 15—17 St. Paul asserts that God "left not Himself without witness, in that He did good and gave rain from heaven and fruitful seasons, filling our hearts with food and gladness." The knowledge which man gains from God's continued self-manifestation in human history is described by the apostle in Acts 17, 26—28, where he declares that God has made and governs all men in such a manner "that they should seek the Lord" and that "in Him we live and move and have our being" in such a way that even the heathen poets have professed: "We are also His offspring." (The historical proof of God's existence.)

c. *By the divine Law written in the heart of man.* By means of this Law, men "know the judgment of God," Rom. 1, 32, and without the revealed Law "do by nature the things contained in the Law," "their conscience also bearing witness and their thoughts the mean while accusing or else excusing one another," Rom. 2, 14. 15. (The moral proof of God's existence.)

In view of these facts the antitheistic theories held by men are not the results of sound reasoning, but rather the effects of man's perverse, wilful suppression of the natural knowledge of God, which He has implanted into the human heart, Rom. 1, 18. They do not represent progress in human religious thought, but rather spiritual and moral decadence.

Atheism denies God's existence, although by nature man has a distinct knowledge of God, Rom. 1, 19; Ps. 14, 1. *Polytheism* divides God into many divine entities, although the knowledge which man by nature has of God is monotheistic (Rom. 1, 20: "His eternal power"). *Hylozoism* endues matter with life and denies that God is the extramundane and supramundane Ruler and Judge of men, though by nature man knows "the judgment of God," Rom. 1, 32. *Materialism* denies the reality of spirit and ignores the distinction between matter and mind, so that there is in materialism no God and no human soul and no immortality, but only persistence of matter and force. *Pantheism* is the doctrine that God is all and all is God, so that nothing exists outside of God. *Deism* admits that there is a personal God, who has created the world and has impressed upon it the laws that govern it, but it teaches that after this, God withdrew from the world and left it to the reign of natural laws. *Pessimism* regards the world and life as essentially evil and holds that the world, if not the worst that it can be, is at least sufficiently evil to be worse than none at all. *Atheistic evolution* denies the existence of God, asserts the eternity of matter and force, and attributes the development of the cosmos to purely natural forces (Keyser). *Theistic evolution* holds that God created the primordial material and that evolution has since been His *modus operandi* in developing it to its present status. *Agnosticism* maintains that we cannot know whether there is a God or not. *Positivism* teaches that we can know only *phenomena,* but not *noumena,* or the essence of things. Hence it is agnostic in regard to God, the soul, and the substance of things.

All these anti-Biblical theories are in opposition to the natural knowledge of God which Holy Scripture very clearly and emphatically ascribes to man, Rom. 1, 19. 20. 32; 2, 14. 15.

The natural knowledge of God is true as far as it goes, Rom. 1, 18, for what it teaches of God's personality, eternity, omnipotence, sovereignty, holiness, and righteousness agrees with revealed religion. Innate *(notitia innata)* though it is (Rom. 2, 14. 15: "A law unto themselves"; "the work of the Law written in their hearts"), it can nevertheless be expanded and further confirmed *(notitia acquisita)* by the contemplation of the works and ways of God in nature and history, Acts 17, 27. 28, though it may also be corrupted and changed into error (antitheistic theories) through the moral depravity existing in man, Rom. 1, 18.

The natural knowledge of God is of great benefit to man because it is the foundation of the civil righteousness *(iustitia civilis),* Rom. 2, 14; Acts 17, 27, of natural man, and the starting-point for the proclamation of the revealed Law by Christian missionaries. Luther rightly declares that, had God not written the Law into man's heart, we would have to preach a long time before man's conscience would be smitten. (St. L., III, 1053.) When St. Paul preached the Word of God to the Athenian philosophers, he began by appealing to their natural knowledge of God, Acts 17, 23—29.

The natural knowledge of God is of great value also because upon the basis of it man constructs the so-called rational proofs for God's existence to combat unbelief. Thus the *ontological proof* argues from the existence of the idea of God in man to the actuality of His existence. The *cosmological proof* concludes that the world must have a First Cause back of all the secondary causes that are operative in nature. The *teleological proof* argues from the design and purpose which are everywhere evident in nature. The *moral proof* argues from the existence of our moral constitution to the existence of a Supreme Moral Being. The *historical proof* draws from the history of man the conclusion that there is a divine Ruler who guides all affairs of the world to an end which He has in view. The *theological proof* argues God's existence from the fact that the idea of God need never be explained to men, since all men in the world know who is meant by that term. Hence the natural knowledge of God must not be underestimated, since God has bestowed it upon man to govern him in His Kingdom of Power *(in regno potentiae),* holds him accountable for his attitude toward it, Rom. 1, 18—32, and rewards his respecting and obeying it with temporal blessings, Ex. 1, 20. 21.

In spite of all this, however, the natural knowledge of God is not sufficient to secure man's salvation. Quenstedt writes on this point (I, 261) : "The natural knowledge of God is not adequate to secure everlasting life, nor has any mortal ever been redeemed, nor can any one ever be redeemed, by it alone," Acts 4, 12; Rom. 10, 17; Mark 16, 15. 16; Gal. 3, 11; Eph. 4, 18; 2, 12; Gal. 4, 8. (*Doctr. Theol.,* p. 110.)   Since the natural knowledge of God does not embrace the Gospel, 1 Cor. 2, 7—10, but only the Law, Rom. 2, 14. 15, its practical result is nothing more than a guilty conscience, Rom. 1, 20; 2, 15, fear of death, Heb. 2, 15, the state of condemnation, Gal. 3, 10, and utter hopelessness, Eph. 2, 12.   Man by nature knows that there is a just and holy God, Rom. 1, 21, but not that the eternal demands of His perfect justice have been satisfied by the vicarious satisfaction of Christ, 1 Cor. 1, 21.   In addition, while man by nature knows that there is a God, he does not know who this true God is, 1 Cor. 1, 21; Acts 17, 24. 25; Matt. 28, 19. 20.

While man's natural knowledge of God coincides in some points with the supernatural, or revealed, knowledge of God *(articuli mixti),* the Christian theologian bases all that he teaches of God alone on Holy Scripture, because this is the only divinely appointed source and norm of faith *(principium cognoscendi).* It alone teaches the precious Gospel-truths of God, by which man is saved *(articuli puri).*   The Lutheran dogmatician Chemnitz writes of this *(Loci Theol.,* I, 22) : "The *saving* knowledge of God, through which we obtain eternal life, is that revealed through the Word, in which God makes known Himself and His will.   To this revelation God has bound His Church, which knows, worships, and glorifies God only as He has revealed Himself in this Word, so that in this way the true and only Church of God may be distinguished from all heathen religions." *(Doctr. Theol.,* p. 111.)

The *Christian knowledge* of God, which we obtain from Holy Scripture, and from no other source, is not only theistic, but also Trinitarian ;. that is, the Christian believer knows and worships God only as the Holy Trinity, Father, Son, and Holy Ghost, three distinct persons in one inseparable essence.   This Christian knowledge of God is not a mere supplement to man's natural knowledge of God, but an entirely new revelation, by which man is enabled to know God truly and fully, Matt. 28, 19. 20; 1 Cor. 8, 4—6, and to worship Him by true faith as his Savior, Is. 41, 14; 42, 5—8; 43, 1—3. 10—12; 44, 1—8; 45, 20—25.

For this reason every Christian description of God must incorporate also the Holy Trinity; that is to say, whenever a Christian theologian describes God, he must describe Him as the one God who is Father, Son, and Holy Ghost. Calov is right when he says (II, 282): "Those who do not include a statement of the three Persons in the description of God do not present that doctrine in a form at all genuine or complete, since without these it does not yet appear who the true God is." (*Doctr. Theol.*, p. 117.)

2. THE HOLY TRINITY.

According to Holy Scripture, God is one in essence, but in this one essence there are three distinct Persons, Father, Son, and Holy Ghost. This is the Christian doctrine of God. (Luther: *Scriptura Sancta docet esse Deum simplicissime unum et tres, ut vocant, personas verissime distinctas.*" (St. L., X, 176 f.) This doctrine of Scripture the Christian Church expresses by the term "Trinity."

That God is one in essence, though three in person, Holy Scripture teaches distinctly; its doctrine of God in both the Old and the New Testament is exclusively monotheistic. According to Scripture, God is one, and besides this one God there is no God. (Deut. 6, 4: "Hear, O Israel: the Lord, our God, is one Lord"; 1 Cor. 8, 4: "There is none other God but one.") All idols of the heathen Holy Scripture designates as "non-gods," Jer. 2, 11; "vanities," אֱלִילִם, Lev. 19, 4, or as things which are wholly without real existence. Cp. the descriptions of idols in Is. 44, 6—20; Jer. 2, 26—28; Ps. 115, 1—9; 135, 15—17. In the New Testament St. Paul writes with equal emphasis: "An idol is nothing in the world," 1 Cor. 8, 4, and from this he draws the basic Christian doctrine: "But to us there is but one God," 1 Cor. 8, 6.

With the paramount truth of God's existence Holy Scripture immediately connects the demand of divine adoration. The one true God, who has revealed Himself in His Word, must be adored and served by all men. (Ex. 20, 3: "Thou shalt have no other gods before me"; Mark 12, 29. 30: "And Jesus answered him, The first of all the commandments is, Hear, O Israel: The Lord, our God, is one Lord. And thou shalt love the Lord, thy God, with all thy heart, and with all thy soul, and with all thy mind, and with all thy strength.") As polytheism eliminates the very concept of God, so also it destroys true worship. Hence, if the heathen would worship God, they must turn from their idols to the true God.

(Acts 14, 15: "Ye should turn from these vanities, ἀπὸ τούτων τῶν ματαίων, unto the living God.")

However, while Holy Scripture most earnestly inculcates the doctrine of God's unity, it teaches at the same time that the one God is the Holy Trinity. When Christ sent forth His disciples to teach all nations, He expressly commanded them to baptize "in the name of the Father and of the Son and of the Holy Ghost," Matt. 28, 19. However, "Father, Son, and Holy Ghost" are designations of three persons; hence the Christian Church teaches, on the basis of Scripture: "God is one, and yet in the one divine essence are three distinct persons." ("Father, Son, and Holy Ghost, three distinct persons in one divine essence and nature, are one God, who has created heaven and earth," *Smalcald Art.,* First Part.) As Holy Scripture connects with the doctrine of the unity of God the demand that this one God must be worshiped, so also it demands that the one true God should be adored as the Holy Trinity. In other words, not one Person of the Godhead should be worshiped, but all three. (1 John 2, 23: "Whosoever denieth the Son, the same hath not the Father"; 5, 12: "He that hath not the Son hath not life"; John 5, 23: "All men should honor the Son even as they honor the Father. He that honoreth not the Son honoreth not the Father which hath sent Him.") On the basis of this clear doctrine of Scripture the *Apology of the Augsburg Confession* affirms (Art. I): "We declare that we believe and teach that there is one divine essence, undivided, etc., and yet, that there are three distinct persons, of the same divine essence and coeternal, Father, Son, and Holy Ghost. This article we have always taught and defended, and we believe that it has, in Holy Scripture, sure and firm testimonies that cannot be overthrown. And we constantly affirm that those thinking otherwise are outside the Church of Christ and are idolaters and insult God."

In order that we may hold to the pure Scriptural doctrine concerning the Holy Trinity, we must maintain, on the basis of Scripture, that each Person in the Godhead is the entire God *(totus Deus),* or that each Person has the whole divine essence without division or multiplication *(sine divisione et multiplicatione).* "Of these Persons each one is the whole God, besides whom there is no other God." Luther. By the expression *sine divisione* we mean to say that the divine essence with its attributes is not divided among the three Persons, so that the Father has one-third, the Son one-third, and the Holy Ghost one-third, but that each Person has the whole divine essence entire and undivided. This is not a "dog-matical construction," but Scriptural doctrine. Col. 2, 3: "In whom are hid all the treasures of wisdom and knowledge"; 2, 9: "In Him [Christ] dwelleth all the fulness of the Godhead bodily." By the expression *sine multiplicatione* we declare that there are not three distinct sets, or series, of divine attributes, so that the Father has one set, the Son another, and the Holy Ghost a third, but that the one and same essence with all its divine attributes belongs to the Father, the Son, and the Holy Ghost, according to number *(numero, secundum numerum)*, not merely according to kind *(specie)*. Of men it must be said that there are as many essences as there are persons *(quot personae, tot essentiae)*, but of God, Holy Scripture testifies that the three Persons of the Godhead have one and the same essence with all its attributes numerically. *Tres personae, una essentia divina, individua, unus Deus.* This sublime truth Holy Scripture teaches in the following passages: John 10, 30: "I and My Father are one (ἕν)"; John 5, 17: "My Father worketh hitherto, and I work"; 5, 19: "The Son can do nothing of Himself but what He seeth the Father do; for what things soever He doeth, these also doeth the Son likewise"; 10, 37: "If I do not the works of My Father, believe Me not." This truth the Creed of Athanasius professes as follows: "We worship one God in Trinity, and Trinity in Unity; neither confounding the Persons nor dividing the Substance. For there is one Person of the Father; another of the Son, and another of the Holy Ghost. But the Godhead of the Father, of the Son, and of the Holy Ghost is all one: the glory equal, the majesty coeternal. Such as the Father is, such is the Son, and such is the Holy Ghost. . . . So like-wise the Father is almighty, the Son almighty, and the Holy Ghost almighty. And yet they are not three Almighties, but one Al-mighty. So the Father is God, the Son is God, and the Holy Ghost is God. And yet they are not three Gods, but one God. . . . And in this Trinity none is before or after other; none is greater or less than another; but the whole three Persons are coeternal together and coequal: so that in all things, as is afore-said, the Unity in Trinity and the Trinity in Unity is to be wor-shiped." *(Triglot,* p. 33.)

The Scriptural doctrine of the Holy Trinity is absolutely in-comprehensible to the human mind; for on the basis of Scripture we profess one undivided and indivisible God, so that each Person is the entire God *(totus Deus);* and yet three really distinct Persons, so that, when the Son became incarnate, He alone became man and not the Father or the Holy Ghost, and when the Son suffered and died, He alone suffered and died and not the Father or the Holy Ghost. This truth is beyond reason, for according to reason the Unity annuls the Trinity and the Trinity the Unity. In other words, human reason must assume either one God or three Gods. It cannot reconcile Unity with Trinity nor Trinity with Unity. Consequently all errorists on this point have denied either the Unity or the Trinity.

3. THE DOCTRINE OF THE HOLY TRINITY IN CONTROVERSY.

The Christian doctrine of the Holy Trinity has been strenuously controverted, on the one hand, by errorists who denied the three Persons (Monarchians, Unitarians, Antitrinitarians) and, on the other, by errorists who denied the one essence (Tritheites). The Monarchians may be divided into two classes: the *Modalistic Monarchians,* or *Patripassians,* known in the East as *Sabellians,* who held that the three Persons of the Trinity are but three different energies or modes of the same divine person, so that the Son and the Holy Ghost are but different manifestations (πρόσωπα) of the Father; and the *Dynamic Monarchians,* or *Adoptionists,* who held that the Son was a mere man and the Holy Ghost the Father's divine energy in the creatures (Paul of Samosata, Photinians, Arians, Socinians, Unitarians, Modernists). In opposition to Monarchianism, which denies the three distinct Persons, the Christian Church holds that Father, Son, and Holy Ghost are not three modes or energies of one person, but three distinct persons, or individuals. This truth is proved a) by the very terms Father, Son, and Holy Ghost, which never designate qualities or energies inhering in a person, but always Persons subsisting of themselves. (*Augsb. Conf.,* Art. I: "And the term *person* they use as the Fathers have used it, to signify not a part or quality in another, but that which subsists of itself.") This truth is also proved b) by the personal works of the individual Persons, such as speaking, willing, reproving, etc., which Scripture ascribes not only to the Father, but also to the Son and to the Holy Ghost. *(Actiones semper sunt suppositorum intelligentium, . . . opera sunt personis propria.)* To the Son Scripture ascribes the acts of knowing, Matt. 11, 27, of declaring, John 1, 18, of willing, John 17, 24, etc.; to the Holy Ghost it ascribes the acts of speaking, Acts 28, 25, of teaching,

John 14, 26, of reproving, John 16, 8, etc. This truth is furthermore proved c) by express passages of Scripture in which the Father is called another (ἄλλος) than the Son, John 5, 32. 37, or in which the Holy Ghost is called another (ἄλλος) than the Son, John 14, 16.

As the Monarchians deny the three Persons of the Godhead, so other errorists deny the unity of God and teach three distinct divine essences in place of the one undivided and indivisible divine essence. Of these errorists the *Tritheites* coordinate the three essences, while the Subordinationists subordinate them, ascribing to the Father priority of essence. All Subordinationists deny the one true God and teach polytheism; for since they affirm that the Son and the Holy Ghost are "God in a lesser degree" than is the Father, they assume three distinct divine essences, or three gods, of whom one is the supreme Lord, while the others are inferior deities. In opposition to this error the Christian Church teaches that the three Persons in the one Godhead are fully coordinate, that is, that they are God in the same manner and the same degree, because the divine essence, which is numerically one *(una numero divina essentia),* belongs to each Person entire and undivided. This doctrine rests upon clear and decisive Scripture-passages. In Matt. 28, 19 three distinct and entirely coordinate Persons are described as having the same name (ὄνομα). Again, to the Son and to the Holy Ghost are ascribed a) the same divine names as to the Father, including the *nomen essentiale et incommunicabile* יְהֹוָה (the Son: Jer. 23, 6; John 1, 1; the Holy Ghost: 2 Sam. 23, 2; Acts 5, 3. 4); b) the same divine attributes, such as eternity, omnipotence, omniscience, omnipresence, goodness, mercy, etc. (the Son: Col. 1, 17; John 10, 28; John 21, 19; Matt. 28, 20; 2 Cor. 13, 14; the Holy Ghost: Heb. 9, 14; Is. 11, 2; 1 Cor. 2, 10—12; Ps. 139, 7); c) the same divine works, such as creation, preservation, miracles, etc. (the Son: John 1, 1—3; Col. 1, 16; John 5, 17; 6, 39; the Holy Ghost: Ps. 33, 6; Job 33, 4; Acts 10, 38); d) divine adoration and worship (the Son: John 5, 23; Phil. 2, 10; the Holy Ghost: Is. 6, 3; 2 Cor. 13, 14; Num. 6, 26). Thus the true deity of the Son and of the Holy Ghost is strenuously affirmed in Scripture.

Hence whenever the Father is called the First, the Son the Second, and the Holy Ghost the Third Person of the Godhead, this does not denote any subordination or any inequality in respect to time *(tempore)* or dignity *(natura vel dignitate),* but merely indicates the Scriptural truth that the Son is from the Father, John 1, 14, and the Holy Ghost from the Father and Son, Matt. 10, 20; Gal. 4, 6. Or we may say this order of enumeration shows the divine mode in which the Three Persons subsist in the Godhead *(modus subsistendi)*. But that the Son was generated from the Father does not render Him inferior to the Father, nor does the spiration of the Holy Ghost render the Spirit inferior to the Father and the Son, because the divine generation and spiration are eternal acts, or timeless processes, by which the Son and the Holy Ghost, together with the Father, possess the same divine essence and majesty. The Creed of Athanasius declares: "In this Trinity none is before or after other; none is greater or less than another; but the whole three Persons are coeternal together, and coequal: so that in all things, as is aforesaid, the Unity in Trinity, and the Trinity in Unity is to be worshiped." When Christ says of Himself: "The Father is greater than I," John 14, 28, He speaks of Himself according to His human nature in His state of humiliation. Athanasius: *Aequalis Patri secundum divinitatem, minor Patre secundum humanitatem.* The fact that the Father was "greater" than the Son in the latter's state of humiliation ceased when Christ was exalted, John 14, 28; Eph. 1, 20—23; Phil. 2, 9—11.

Again, when Scripture says that God created the world *by the Son,* Heb. 1, 2; John 1, 3, it teaches by no means any subordination of the Son to the Father, but rather the divine mode of operation *(modus operandi) ad extra.* For as the Son is of the Father, so also His operation is from the Father, while that of the Holy Ghost is from the Father and the Son. Nevertheless, the divine operation remains one according to number *(una numero potentia)* and belongs to each Person entire, so that it is not distributed among the Three Persons. For this reason Holy Scripture sometimes ascribes the whole work of creation to one single Person without naming the others. (Creation ascribed to the Son John 1, 1—3; Heb. 1, 10.) Gerhard writes (IV, 4): "But that one true God is Father, Son, and Holy Ghost; therefore in Scripture the work of creation is ascribed to the Father and to the Son and to the Holy Ghost. Of the Father it is affirmed 1 Cor. 8, 6; of the Son, John 1, 3; Col. 1, 16; of the Holy Ghost, Job 26, 13; 33, 4; Ps. 104, 30. We conclude therefore that creation is an undivided action of the one and true God alone, namely, of the Father, Son, and Holy Ghost." *(Doctr. Theol.,* p. 162.) And

Hollaz writes: "In Holy Scripture and the Apostles' Creed the work of creation is ascribed in a peculiar manner to God the Father a) because of the order of working: for this reason that what the Father has of Himself to do and to create the Son of God and the Holy Ghost have of the Father; b) because in the work of creation God the Father by His most efficacious word of command manifested His own omnipotence, Gen. 1, 3; c) because creation is the first work *ad extra* and therefore, by appropriation, is affirmed of the First Person of the Godhead." *(Ibid.)*

4. THE DOCTRINE OF THE HOLY TRINITY AND THE TERMINOLOGY OF THE CHRISTIAN CHURCH.

The question has been debated whether such terms as are not found in Scripture may be used when a doctrine of the Christian religion is presented or taught, *e. g.,* the doctrine of the Holy Trinity. In reply to this question we say that all terms which express the clear doctrine of God as revealed in Scripture should be used without fear, especially those in which the Christian Church defends the divine truth against error. Furthermore, it must be affirmed that all who believe as the Church does should also speak as the Church. Those who needlessly or frivolously invent new terms not only confuse the Church by new and unaccustomed expressions, but also expose themselves to the suspicion that they seek their own glory and endeavor to introduce new and erroneous doctrines. Hence the use of new terms in the doctrine of the Holy Trinity must be discouraged.

Against Monarchianism, on the one hand, and Tritheism, on the other, the Christian Church teaches that there are three Persons in one essence *(tres personae in una essentia, τρεῖς ὑποστάσεις καὶ μια οὐσία)*. Against Arianism, in particular, which affirmed that the λόγος is a creature of God (κτίσις, ποίημα), the Nicene Council declared that the Son is "of one substance" with the Father *(ὁμοούσιος, coessentialis, consubstantialis)*. The meaning of these terms is not that the Son is of *like* essence with the Father *(ὁμοιούσιος, unius essentiae specie)*, but that the one and same essence, which exists but once in God, is alike that of the Father and of the Son *(unius essentiae numero)*, so that the Son is "God of God" and "very God of very God." This doctrine is truly Scriptural, John 10, 30.

The word *essence (οὐσία, essentia)*, used of God, signifies the divine nature with all its attributes, which exists but once *(singu-*

laris) in the Three Persons *(una numero essentia)*. "By the term *essence,* or *οὐσία,* is meant the divine nature as it is in itself, all of which, with its attributes, is most simply one and singular, and thus also of the Three Persons the essence is only one." (Baier.) The term *essence* is therefore applied to God in a unique sense. When we apply it to men, namely, to denote something which is common to all men, the word is used as a generic term *(nomen universale)* or as an abstract noun *(nomen abstractum),* which denotes something that does not exist concretely, but is merely abstracted from the concretely existing human beings. (Ex.: It is the essence of man to think or to will.) However, when we speak of the divine essence which is common to the Father, Son, and Holy Ghost, the term *essence* is neither generic nor abstract, but concrete *(nomen concretum),* denoting something that exists actually and concretely and belongs to the three divine Persons as one in number *(numero).* In other words, the term *essence* denotes God Himself as He divinely exists as One in Three. "The essence of God is God's spiritual and independent nature, common to the three divine Persons." (Hollaz.)

By the term *person (persona, ὑπόστασις)* we understand in the realm of human thought an individual and rational being existing by itself *(suppositum intelligens).* Thus all men and angels are persons. But also this term, when used of God, is applied in a unique sense; for when we say that the Father, Son, and Holy Ghost are three persons *(personae, ὑποστάσεις, πρόσωπα),* we, on the one hand, reject the erroneous opinion that there are three qualities or energies *(Potenzen)* and affirm that they are three rational individuals; yet, on the other hand, we deny that the Three Persons are three distinct essences, or three distinct Gods, and affirm that, while they are three rational individuals, so that the Father is not the Son nor the Son the Holy Ghost, nevertheless, the Three Persons have only one and the same divine essence in number *(una numero essentia)* and exert only one and the same power *ad extra (una numero potentia).* Hence, while the Three Persons are distinguished from one another not merely notionally *(notionaliter),* but really *(realiter),* they are in essence numerically one. When we speak of men, the axiom applies: As many persons, so many essences *(Quot personae, tot essentiae);* but when we speak of God this axiom does not apply, since there are three distinct divine Persons, and yet there is only one divine Essence, or God.

With respect to the term *Trinity,* Luther admitted that it does not "sound well so to call God"; but he adds that, since the article of the Holy Trinity is so far beyond our human mind and language, God must pardon us if we stammer and prattle about it as well as we can, provided only that our faith is pure and right; for the term *Trinity* merely expresses the truth that God is three in person and one in divine essence. From this it is clear that the term *Trinity,* just as the other terms used in explaining the doctrine of God, has not been coined to satisfy reason, but only to express the doctrine of Scripture concerning the true God. Human reason, when judging the Christian doctrine of God, must choose either between Unitarianism or Tritheism; in other words, it must either deny the three divine Persons (Monarchianism) or the one divine essence (Tritheism; Subordinationism). For this reason the Christian theologian must *a priori* desist from presenting the doctrine of the Holy Trinity in such a way as to make it comprehensible to reason. Every attempt of this kind involves either a self-deception, *i. e.,* the supposition that things have been explained which cannot be explained, or a surrender of the Christian doctrine of God. Nevertheless, though the doctrine of the Holy Trinity is beyond reason, it is not against reason or self-contradictory, since Unity is not predicated of God in the same relation as Trinity. A real contradiction would exist only if the Christian doctrine would affirm: "There is one essence, and there are three essences; there is one person, and there are three persons." However, the Christian doctrine of God is: "There is one divine essence, and there are three divine Persons."

With respect to the relation of the Three Persons to one another the Christian Church teaches as follows: The real distinction of the Persons *(realis distinctio, non tantum notionalis)* is based upon the facts that the Father from eternity has generated the Son, John 1, 14, while the Father and the Son have spirated the Holy Spirit, John 14, 26; 15, 26.

These divine acts of generation and spiration are called personal acts *(actus personales)* because they are not common to the Three Persons, but belong to, and distinguish, the individual Persons in the Godhead. To the Father, Holy Scripture ascribes the act of generation, John 1, 14, by which He communicated to the Son the fulness of the Godhead, or the entire divine essence, Col. 2, 3. 9. Hence the Father possesses the divine essence unbegotten (ἀγεννηθῶς), while the Son possesses it begotten (γεννηθῶς).

Scripture, moreover, affirms that the Father and the Son have spirated the Holy Ghost, Matt. 10, 20; Gal. 4, 6; for just as the Second Person is called the Son of the Father, so the Third Person is called the Spirit of the Father and of the Son. Through the spiration the Holy Ghost received the entire divine essence, Matt. 28, 19; Acts 5, 3. 4, so that He is from eternity true God with the Father and the Son.

On the basis of the *personal acts,* or the *opera ad intra* (generation and spiration), we distinguish the *notiones personales* of the Three Persons: the ἀγεννησία *(innascibilitas)* of the Father, the γεννησία *(nascibilitas)* of the Son, and the ἐκπόρευσις *(processio, spiratio passiva)* of the Holy Ghost, and also the *proprietates personales*: the paternity *(paternitas)* of the Father, the sonship *(filiatio)* of the Son, and the procession *(processio)* of the Holy Ghost. By *personal properties* we mean those peculiarities which one Person of the Godhead possesses in relation to one of the other Persons or to both, and by *personal notations* we mean the marks by which in general one Person can be recognized as distinct from another. These terms must not be regarded as superfluous; they are necessary to distinguish the divine Persons, as Scripture itself does.

In connection with the spiration of the Holy Ghost we must consider also the question of the *Filioque,* or whether the Holy Ghost was spirated also by the Son. The Eastern Church denied the *Filioque,* while the Western Church, on the basis of Scripture, affirmed it; for Holy Scripture ascribes the same relation of the Holy Ghost to the Son as it does to the Father. As He is called the Spirit of the Father, Matt. 10, 20, so He is also called the Spirit of the Son, Gal. 4, 6; and as He is sent of the Father, John 14, 26, so He is said to be sent also of the Son, John 15, 26. Because the Holy Spirit proceeds also from the Son, Christ could breathe and bestow Him upon His disciples, John 20, 22.

The *actus personales* are also called *inward operations (opera ad intra)* because they occur within the Godhead and extend from one Person to another (generation and spiration). From the inward operations we distinguish the *outward operations (opera ad extra),* or the works in which the three Persons of the Godhead cooperate, or concur (creation, redemption, sanctification, etc.). Of the inward operations the axiom holds: "The inward operations are divided." *(Opera ad intra divisa sunt.)* Of the outward operations the axiom obtains: "The outward operations are undivided."

(Opera ad extra sunt indivisa.) These axioms express the Scriptural truth that the inward operations are performed by individual Persons, while the outward operations are performed by the Three Persons in common, or together. If at times Scripture ascribes creation to the Father, redemption to the Son, and sanctification to the Holy Ghost, this is done by *appropriation,* which, however, does not exclude the divine operation of the other Persons. The only *opus ad extra* in which the Father and the Holy Ghost did not directly concur, was the work of redemption (the incarnation, suffering, death, resurrection, and exaltation of Christ) ; for while it is true that the Son was sent by the Father and sustained by Him in His redemptive work, and while it is equally true that He was anointed with the Holy Ghost (Ps. 45, 7 ; Heb. 1, 9 ; Acts 10, 38) for His work, Scripture ascribes the work of redemption to Christ alone, Eph. 2, 13 ; Col. 1, 20 ; 1 John 1, 7. To express this unique character of Christ's redemptive work, the dogmaticians have called it an *opus mixtum,* or a work which Christ accomplished alone, but in the performance of which He was not without the Father and the Holy Ghost. (For the *actus personales* compare Luther's exposition of the Three Symbols, St. L., X, 993 ff.)

The name *Father* is sometimes used *essentially* (οὐσιωδῶς), referring to the divine Persons equally (Jas. 1, 17 ; 2 Cor. 6, 17. 18 ; Luke 12, 32), and sometimes *personally* (ὑποστατικῶς), referring alone to the First Person of the Godhead, John 10, 30 ; 14, 9 ; 1 John 2, 23. So also the name *Spirit* is used *essentially,* John 4, 24, and *personally,* Matt. 12, 31 ; Mark 1, 10.

By the term περιχώρησις *(immanentia, immeatio, circumincessio)* is understood the mutual and most intimate inherence *(inexistentia mutua et singularissima),* by which one Person on account of the unity of the divine essence is within another, John 14, 11 ; 17, 21. By this term the Christian Church precludes the error of regarding the Three Persons as subsisting separately alongside one another. By the term *equality* Christian theology expresses the fact that one divine Person is in itself not greater than another, and by the term *sameness,* that the Three Persons have the same nature and consequently also cooperate in the same *opera ad extra,* John 5, 19. 17.

On the basis of Holy Scripture, Hollaz defines the Three Persons as follows : "a) God the Father is the First Person of the Godhead, neither begotten nor proceeding, but from eternity begetting the Son, the substantial image of Himself, and with the

Son from eternity breathing forth the Holy Spirit, creating, preserving, and governing all things, sending His Son as the Redeemer and the Holy Ghost as the Sanctifier of the human race. b) The Son of God is the Second Person of the Godhead, begotten of the Father from eternity, of the same essence and majesty with the Father, who with the Father from eternity breathes forth the Holy Spirit and in the fulness of time assumed human nature in His own Person that He might redeem and save the human race. c) The Holy Spirit is the Third Person of the Godhead, of the same essence with the Father and the Son, who from eternity proceeds from the Father and the Son and in time is sent forth by both to sanctify the hearts of those who are to be saved." (*Doctr. Theol.*, p. 134.)

In connection with the terminology of the Church regarding the doctrine of God we may consider the debated question whether God may be logically defined or not. In replying to the question, our dogmaticians distinguish between "a perfect definition, which exactly conforms to accurate logical rules, and a general description, drawn from Scripture." (Gerhard.) The inadmissibility of a definition of God in the strict sense is argued, in the main, a) from the want of a genus, since God has no true and logical genus, and b) from the divine perfection of God, He being the Supreme Being, so that nothing is beyond Him. (Gerhard.) Nevertheless, though God cannot be logically defined as creatures are defined since He belongs in a class by Himself, a general description of God, drawn from Scripture, is sufficient for such a knowledge of God as is needed for salvation. Accordingly God has been described as "the first Being, who is of Himself and the Cause of all other things," or more completely, by Melanchthon (*Loci Theol.*, I, 13): "God is a spiritual essence, intelligent, eternal, true, good, pure, just, merciful, most free, of vast power and wisdom — the eternal Father, who begat the Son, His own image, from eternity, and the Son, the coeternal image of the Father, and the Holy Spirit, proceeding from the Father and the Son."

5. THE HOLY TRINITY REVEALED IN THE OLD TESTAMENT.

That the doctrine of the Holy Trinity is clearly taught in the New Testament is a fact readily admitted by all Christians. The Unitarians, who deny even the New Testament proof for the Trinity, are outside the pale of the Christian Church. The Holy

Trinity is revealed: a) in the solemn formula of Baptism given by Christ, Matt. 28, 19, in which the three Persons of the Godhead are represented as equal in authority, dignity, and essence; b) in the wonderful theophany at the baptism of Christ, Matt. 3, 16. 17, where the three Persons of the Godhead were distinctly manifested; c) in the inspired benediction of St. Paul, 2 Cor. 13, 14, where the spiritual blessings of the Three Persons are expressly named. The passage 1 John 5, 7 is too doubtful to be used as a proof for the Holy Trinity. It is said that Cyprian († 258) quotes it in his work *De Unitate Ecclesiae: "Et iterum de Patre et Filio et Spiritu Sancto scriptum est: 'Et tres unum est.'"* Nevertheless it is best to disregard this passage altogether as a proof-text for the doctrine of the Holy Trinity.

However, while all Christians admit the proofs for the Trinity as given in the New Testament, it has been claimed that the Old Testament, while containing indications and traces *(indicia et vestigia)* of the Holy Trinity, does not exhibit the doctrine so clearly that it could be believed or taught on the basis of the Old Testament passages (Calixtus; modern theologians). To this charge our dogmaticians replied (Gerhard, III, 218): "We do not say that in the Old Testament there is the same clearness and evidence of the testimonies concerning the Trinity as in the New Testament; but we assert that from the Old Testament some testimonies, in exhibiting the doctrine of the Trinity, both can and ought to be cited, since God always from the beginning revealed Himself thus in order that the Church at all times might acknowledge, worship, and praise Him . . . as three distinct Persons in one essence." *(Doctr. Theol.,* p. 157.) As a matter of fact the Old Testament contains not only mere "indications" of the Holy Trinity, but clear passages, in which the doctrine is unmistakably set forth. Such passages are those: a) in which God speaks of Himself in the plural number, Gen. 1, 26; b) in which the Lord speaks of the Lord, Gen. 19, 24; c) in which the Son of God is expressly named, Ps. 2, 7; d) in which three Persons of the Godhead are distinctly enumerated, Gen. 1, 1. 2; 2 Sam. 23, 2; Ps. 33, 6; Is. 42, 1; 48, 16. 17; 61, 1; e) in which the name Jehovah or God is thrice repeated in the same relation, Num. 6, 24—26; Ps. 42, 1. 2; Is. 33, 22; Jer. 33, 2; Dan. 9, 19; f) from the trisagion of the angels, Is. 6, 3; g) from the passages in which the Angel of the Lord (מַלְאַךְ יְהֹוָה) is identified with God, Gen. 48, 15. 16; Ex. 3, 1—7; h) from the reference of Christ to the Old

Testament when He proved the true deity and divine personality of the Son of God, Matt. 22, 41—46 compared with Ps. 110, 1. Certainly no one has ever been saved who did not believe in the true God (the Triune God) and the true Savior of the world (the Second Person of the Godhead), since this truth is stated so clearly in Scripture, Acts 4, 12; John 5, 23; 1 John 2, 23. Nor is the plan of salvation which is taught in the New Testament different from that which was taught in the Old Testament, Rom. 3, 21—24; 4, 1—3. We rightly hold therefore that the doctrine of the Holy Trinity is so clearly set forth in the Old Testament that the believers in the Old Testament most assuredly had a true knowledge of God and of the promised Savior, His beloved Son.

6. GOD'S ESSENCE AND ATTRIBUTES.
(De Essentia et Attributis Dei.)
1. THE DOCTRINE IN GENERAL.

Holy Scripture describes God as the Supreme Being (ens omnium excellentissimum) or as the absolutely Perfect Essence (Deut. 10, 17: "God of gods and Lord of lords"; 1 Tim. 6, 15. 16: "the blessed and only Potentate," μόνος δυνάστης), or simply as the Absolute Being (ens primum), who "is before all things" and by whom "all things consist," Col. 1, 17. At times Scripture applies the name god or gods to creatures (dii nuncupativi, λεγόμενοι θεοί), either because they perform real (John 10, 35; Ps. 82, 6) or supposed (Deut. 4, 28) divine functions, and are therefore vested either rightly or wrongly with divine authority (1 Cor. 8, 5, propter analogiam quandam, vel veram, vel fictam). Nevertheless Scripture distinguishes clearly between the so-called gods (dii nuncu pativi) and the one, true, and living God, 1 Cor. 8, 5. 6; Matt. 19, 17. Magistrates (Ps. 82, 6) and idols (Deut. 4, 28) are indeed called gods (אֱלֹהִים, θεοί), but God alone is Jehovah (יְהֹוָה, nomen Dei essentiale et incommunicabile).

The names which Holy Scripture applies to the true God are not empty titles, but describe God according to His divine essence, attributes, and works. This is true especially of the essential and incommunicable name of God "Jehovah," which He Himself explains as "I Am That I Am" (Ex. 3, 14. 15) or as the eternal, unchangeable divine Being (Luther: "lauter Ist," that is, pure Being). This explains why that name is never applied to creatures. (Is. 42, 8: "I, Jehovah; that is My name.") The real pronunciation of the tetragrammaton is perhaps Yahweh (יְהֶוָה), but since the pronunciation "Jehovah" has become current in the Church, it would be intolerable pedantry to insist upon the supposed "original pronunciation."

When we describe human beings, we ascribe to them both a nature and attributes. Just so Holy Scripture, accommodating itself to the laws of human thought and speech, ordinarily speaks of God as possessing both a divine essence and divine attributes. In other words, it speaks of God's attributes, such as omnipotence, grace, love, etc., as inhering in the divine essence. Nevertheless the attributes of God are not accidents *(accidentia),* but His very divine essence, since God is absolutely simple in His divine Being, Ex. 3, 14. 15. "The properties, or attributes, of God are His very essence. No accidents may be predicated of God." Or we may say: Since we cannot conceive of an absolutely simple being *(ens simplex),* God has graciously revealed Himself to us according to attributes.

In this way we gain of God an adequate conception, which, though incomplete, is essentially correct, 1 Cor. 13, 9—12. Of the divine attributes Gerhard writes (III, 84): "The attributes exist inseparably in God; for as it is impossible that the essence of an object may be separated from the object itself, so also the attributes cannot be separated from God, since they are the very essence of God." *(Doctr. Theol.,* p. 122.) And Calov (II, 222): "If the attributes really differed from the essence after the manner of accidents, a composition in God would be predicated." *(Ibid.)* Our dogmaticians are therefore right in saying that "the divine attributes are distinguished from the divine essence, not really, but only according to our mode of conceiving." *"Essentia et attributa in Deo non realiter, sed nostro concipiendi modo differunt; distinguuntur autem et ab essentia divina et inter se propter intellectus nostri imperfectionem. Attributa divina, quamvis in Deo non distincta, in nostris tamen conceptibus distinguenda sunt."* Since, however, Scripture carefully distinguishes between the various attributes of God, the Christian theologian, too, must distinguish between them, as, for example, between divine justice and grace, divine wrath and love, etc. Where this distinction is not observed, the entire theology becomes false. (Cp. the denial of the Law on account of the Gospel.)

When treating the doctrine of the divine essence and attributes, the question has been debated: "In what sense are essence and attributes ascribed to God and to creatures?" The answer is:

Not a) univocally *(univoce)*, so that they belong to God and the creatures in precisely the same meaning, nor b) equivocally *(aequivoce)*, so that the attributes when used of God have an entirely different meaning than when they are used of creatures, but c) analogically *(analogice)*, so that the attributes ascribed to creatures bear an analogy, or resemblance, to the attributes of God; that is to say, the attributes belong rightly both to God and men, but not in the same manner nor in the same degree. When we say, "God lives, and man lives," or, "God loves, and man loves," we ascribe to God perfect, absolute, and independent life and love, but to man imperfect, relative, and dependent life and love. The same attributes which God has in Himself as His most perfect, divine essence man has from God as His free gifts, and not indeed as his essence, but as accidents, which may be lost. Col. 1, 17: "He is before all things, and by Him all things consist"; Acts 17, 28: "In Him we live and move and have our being." The basic difference between the Creator and the creatures determines also the difference in the possession of attributes. The importance of properly deciding the question is patent from the following: If we ascribe the essence and attributes to God and creatures univocally (Duns Scotus, † 1308), the essential difference between God and the creatures is denied, and the creatures are coordinated with God and made divine (pantheism). On the other hand, if we ascribe the essence and attributes to God and creatures equivocally (Peter Aureolus, † 1321; the Franciscans), it is impossible for us to know God (agnosticism), since then we cannot tell what really the attributes in God mean. (What does it mean when God is said to be Love? 1 John 4, 16.) However, if we ascribe the essence and attributes to God by way of analogy, or resemblance, then in our contemplation of God we rise from the imperfection of the human attributes to the absolute perfection of the divine, Is. 49, 15. Augustine says: *"Condescendit nobis Deus, ut nos consurgamus."*

The divine attributes have been divided into negative and positive, or quiescent and operative, or absolute and relative, or immanent and transient, etc. But no matter how we may classify the divine attributes, we must in every case acquire our knowledge of them only from Holy Scripture, never from reason or speculation. In other words, God Himself must inform us what we are to understand by divine omnipotence, divine love, divine grace, etc. Many pernicious errors have arisen from the fact that theologians endeavored to determine the divine attributes *a priori,* or from reason. For instance, on the basis of divine love errorists have denied divine justice (the necessity of Christ's vicarious atonement, Modernism, Unitarianism) and the possibility of eternal punishment (Russellism, Universalism). As the doctrine of the Holy Trinity, so also that of the divine essence and attributes is beyond reason, since God is absolutely incomprehensible; we know of God's attributes only so much as He Himself has revealed to us.

In more recent times, dogmaticians have classified the divine attributes according to God's relation *(Bezogenheit zur Welt)* or non-relation *(Abgezogenheit zur Welt)* to the world, or according to God's absolute essence (eternity, etc.), His absolute sovereignty (omnipotence, etc.), and His absolute goodness (love, etc.), or according to God's divine existence, knowledge, and will, etc. While some of these are quite helpful and commendable, the modern classifications in general improve very little on those of our older dogmaticians so far as their *practical* value is concerned. All the classifications of the divine attributes are more or less inadequate.

2. THE NEGATIVE ATTRIBUTES.
(Attributa Negativa.)

The negative attributes are those by which all imperfections which we observe in creatures are removed from God, since nothing in any way imperfect can be ascribed to Him. They are also called *quiescent* (ἀνενέργητα), since they have no specific reference to the actions of God, or *immanent (absoluta)* attributes, since they describe the divine essence absolutely and in itself. These attributes are: divine unity, simplicity, immutability, infinity, immensity, eternity, omnipresence.

a. *Divine unity (unitas)* is the attribute of God by virtue of which the divine essence is absolutely single; not only undivided, but also indivisible. Unity is ascribed to God a) *absolutely,* that is, the divine essence is neither divided nor divisible, John 4, 24; Ex. 3, 14. 15, and b) *exclusively,* since besides God there is no God, Deut. 6, 4; 4, 35. (Cp. *Doctr. Theol.,* p. 118 ff.)

b. *Divine simplicity (simplicitas)* is the divine attribute of God according to which He is truly and really uncompounded (not compounded of matter and form, of integral parts, of substance and accident, of nature and subsistence). Hollaz writes: "God is said to be one, not in kind *(specie),* but in number *(numero),* since He is a being entirely alone, not only in Himself undivided, but also indivisible because of the entire simplicity of the divine essence,

as there is no composition in God." (Ex. 3, 14. 15: "I Am That
I Am.") The attribute of spirituality, John 4, 24, is comprised in
that of simplicity.

c. *Divine immutability (immutabilitas)* is the attribute of God
according to which He is liable to no change whatever, neither as
to existence (Rom. 1, 23; 1 Tim. 1, 17; 6, 16) nor as to accidents
(Jas. 1, 17) nor as to will or purpose (Num. 23, 19; Prov. 19, 21;
Mal. 3, 6). If Holy Scripture ascribes to God change of mind
(Gen. 6, 6; 1 Sam. 15, 11) or change of place (Gen. 11, 5), it does
this in accommodation to our mode of perceiving. These passages
do not assert that God is subject to change as men are (1 Sam.
15, 29), but must be understood in a manner becoming God
($\vartheta\epsilon o\pi\rho\epsilon\pi\tilde{\omega}\varsigma$). Gerhard writes (I, 110): "The affections which
Scripture ascribes to God do not prove any mutability of the
divine essence; for those things which are spoken of anthropo-
pathically ($\dot{\alpha}\nu\vartheta\rho\omega\pi o\pi\alpha\vartheta\tilde{\omega}\varsigma$) must be understood in a sense becoming God ($\vartheta\epsilon o\pi\rho\epsilon\pi\tilde{\omega}\varsigma$)." Scripture thus speaks of God in a
twofold manner: a) as He is in Himself, immutable and incor-
ruptible, forever exalted over space and time, 1 Sam. 15, 29;
Ps. 90, 4; and b) as He accommodates Himself to our conception
of space and time, 1 Sam. 15, 11; Gen. 11, 5. Nevertheless, wherever Scripture pictures God anthropomorphically or anthropo-
pathically, this is not a mere *modus loquendi*, but a true description of God, though after our human mode of perceiving. In other
words, when the immutable God is said to be angry or jealous
(1 Pet. 5, 5) toward the wicked or gracious (Luke 1, 52. 53) to
penitent sinners, we must regard Him precisely as these expressions describe Him, though in a manner conforming with His
divine perfection. *In Deum nulla cadit mutatio.*

The question whether the work of creation or of incarnation
changed the immutable God, Gerhard answers as follows (I, 124):
"By no means; for in time He did that which from eternity He
had decreed in His immutable will." The reason for this is evident.
The creation was not something occurring in God (pantheism), but
rather something outside God (Christian dualism), namely, the
calling into being of things that did not exist before, but had been
determined by God from eternity (decree of creation). Neither was
the incarnation any change in the divine essence, but the assump-
tion of the human nature into the person of the $\lambda\acute{o}\gamma o\varsigma$, as determined
by God from eternity (decree of redemption).

d. *Divine infinity (infinitas)* is that attribute of God according to which He is contained within no bounds either of time (eternity) or of space (immensity). Scripture ascribes to God infinity a) as to His essence, Ps. 145, 3, and b) as to His attributes, Ps. 147, 5. Hence we say correctly that not only God in Himself (divine essence) is infinite, but that also His knowledge, power, wisdom, grace, love, etc., are infinite.

e. *Divine immensity (immensitas)* is that attribute of God according to which He cannot be measured by, or included in, any local confines, Jer. 23, 24; 1 Kings 8, 27. Quenstedt defines the divine immensity as "the interminable ubiety, by virtue of which God cannot but be everywhere in His own essence," or as "the absolute interminability of the divine essence." Since God cannot be measured by, or included in, anything finite, Is. 40, 15—17, we should not judge Him by our reason (Unitarians), but regard Him precisely as Scripture pictures Him, 1 Tim. 6, 16, *i. e.,* as the divine Being who is exalted over all creatures.

f. *Divine eternity (aeternitas),* absolutely so called (in opposition to "long time"), is that attribute according to which the divine essence is without beginning or end, without succession or change, Ps. 102, 27; 90, 2; Gen. 21, 33; Is. 40, 28; 1 Tim. 1, 17; Rev. 1, 4; etc. Scripture uses the doctrine of the divine attributes both for our warning and for our consolation. For when we oppose God, we oppose the one, immutable, infinite, immense, eternal divine Being whose wrath and punishment are endless, 2 Thess. 1, 9; and on the other hand, when we entrust ourselves to God, we are putting our confidence in the one, immutable, infinite, immense, eternal divine Being, whose love and mercy are equally endless, 1 Thess. 4, 17; 2 Cor. 5, 1.

In connection with God's divine eternity we may consider also His divine aseity *(aseitas),* according to which God is absolutely of Himself and independent of anything outside Himself, Rom. 11, 33—36. *(Aseitas est attributum, quo Deus liberrima ipsius causa est et nemini quidquam debet, sed ipse solus est rerum omnium Auctor.)*

g. *Divine omnipresence (omnipraesentia)* is the attribute of God according to which He is illocally, but essentially, everywhere. Quenstedt: "God is actually present to all His creatures." With respect to God's omnipresence we must note the following: —

1. God is omnipresent with regard to His essence, not only with regard to His divine operation, Jer. 23, 24; in other words, God never operates *in absentia* (Calvinists), for wherever He

works, there He is, Ps. 139, 7—10. Gerhard writes (III, 122):
"God is present to all things, not only by virtue and efficacy, nor
only by sight and knowledge, but also in His entire and individual
essence; for He is immense and infinite, not only in power and
knowledge, but also in essence." (*Doctr. Theol.*, p. 125.)

To Christ, according to His human nature, Scripture ascribes
a local presence (*praesentia localis,* Luke 2, 12), an illocal presence
(*praesentia illocalis,* John 20, 19), and a repletive presence *(praesentia repletiva,* Eph. 1, 23; 4, 10).

2. God is present in all creatures, yet He is never a part of
them, but always remains the transmundane, transcendent God.
Deus nunquam in compositionem creaturarum venit. The omnipresence of God must therefore not be understood in the sense of
pantheistic immanence. While it is true that God is so intimately
joined to all creatures that in Him they live and move and have
their being, Acts 17, 28; Col. 1, 17, nevertheless the difference
between God and His creatures always remains as great as that
between the infinite and the finite, Num. 23, 19; 1 Sam. 15, 29.
Gerhard writes (III, 122): "God is everywhere present, not
συνεκτῶς, so as to be comprehended, but συνεκτικῶς, so as to comprehend and contain all things." (*Doctr. Theol.*, p. 125.) Again:
"The Scholastics say that God is everywhere, not locally or by way
of circumscription . . . nor definitely . . . , but repletively; yet
this must not be understood in a gross and corporeal manner . . . ,
but in a divine manner, so that God, though He is confined to no
place because of the immensity of His essence, yet contains all
places." *(Ibid.)* Against the objection that God cannot be present
in "impure places" (Erasmus) we must hold that "God is everywhere and fills all things," *Deum esse ubique et replere omnia*
(Luther). That God is thus everywhere both *enter et potenter* is
a clear Scriptural doctrine, Eph. 1, 20—23; 4, 10.

3. God is omnipresent, yet a) without multiplication *(multi-
plicatio)* of His essence (polytheism), b) without extension *(extensio),* c) without contraction *(rarefactio),* d) without division
(divisio), and e) without commingling *(commixtio).* In other
words, we must not think of God's omnipresence in a corporeal
way, as if He, when present, occupied space or were subject to
space (1 Kings 8, 27; Is. 66, 1); for "God's presence is a) illocal,
b) indivisible, c) incomprehensible to our reason, d) effective and
operative, and e) containing within itself all things" (Gerhard).

The true doctrine of God's omnipresence is of special importance for the right understanding of the Lord's Supper *(Real Presence)*.

In connection with the doctrine of the divine omnipresence a number of questions may be considered. The first is: "Is the universe infinite?" or: "Is there any space outside this universe?" On the basis of Scripture this question must be denied, since space belongs to creation and all creatures are in God, Col. 1, 17; Acts 17, 28. To predicate infinity of space would be tantamount to deifying the universe, which as a creature is finite. *Deus dat loco et rebus, quae sunt in loco, suum esse.* The second question is: "Is there in the divine manifestations of wrath or grace any special approach of the divine essence *(specialis approximatio essentiae divinae)?*" In view of God's immensity this question must be answered in the negative, since the divine essence is never separated from the creatures, but is always present; yet as anthropopathic expressions such Scripture statements as John 14, 23; Gen. 11, 5 are to be considered not as a mere mode of speaking *(modus loquendi)*, but as an assertion of truth which, properly (ϑεοπρεπῶς) understood, is designed for either our comfort or warning. The last question: "Was God essentially operative before Creation?" must be classified among the foolish questions, which are unprofitable and vain, Titus 3, 9. Since God has not revealed anything with respect to any creative work before this world was made, human speculation on this point is useless. Nevertheless, on the one hand, we must not regard God as ever having been essentially inoperative; on the other, we have no Scriptural ground to assume that God ever created a universe before this present world. The warning which applies from God's omnipresence is clear from Jer. 23, 24; Ps. 139, 7 ff., the comfort from Ps. 23, 4; Matt. 28, 20.

3. POSITIVE ATTRIBUTES.

The positive attributes *(attributa ἐνεργητικά, positiva, operativa, transeuntia, relativa)* are those by which we ascribe to God, in a specific and singular sense, all the perfections which we find in His creatures. These are: life, knowledge, wisdom, will, holiness, justice, veracity, power, goodness (grace, mercy, love, longsuffering, etc.).

a. *Divine life (vita)* is the attribute of God by which He always is and shows Himself active. In particular, God is life 1) *essentially,* since He is αὐτόζωος, having life ἐν ἑαυτῷ, John 5, 26, that is, He is life in Himself and of Himself, by His own

nature and essence; 2) *effectively,* since He is the cause and origin
of all life outside Himself, Acts 17, 28; Deut. 32, 39. Negatively
this attribute is expressed by *immortality,* 1 Tim. 6, 16, and *incorruptibility,* Rom. 1, 23; 1 Tim. 1, 17. In contradistinction to the
idols of the heathen, God is the "living God," Acts 14, 15, to whom
all creatures owe their existence, Acts 17, 25. The warning connected with this attribute may be deduced from Heb. 10, 31; the
consolation from 1 Tim. 3, 15; 4, 10.

b. *Divine knowledge (scientia)* is the attribute of God by
which He through one simple and eternal act of His mind knows
all things which have been, are, and shall be, or even in any way
can be, that is, all things which are conditionally future or possible,
1 Sam. 2, 3; 1 John 3, 20; 1 Kings 8, 39; Ps. 7, 9; 34, 15; 139, 1;
Prov. 15, 3. God's knowledge is distinguished from human knowledge: a) by its extent, since God knows all things (John 21, 17:
omniscientia), the future things (Is. 41, 22. 23: *praescientia*), all
possible and conditionally future or possible things (1 Sam. 23, 12;
Matt. 11, 23: *scientia de futuro conditionata, scientia media*);
b) by His manner of knowing, since God knows all things whatsoever through one simple and eternal act of the mind *(Deus res non
per species intelligibiles, sed in se sive in esse proprio cognoscit.
Homo res adspicit, Deus perspicit.)* Thus God knows the very
thoughts of men. 1 Kings 8, 39; Acts 15, 8; John 2, 25. The revelation of God's perfect knowledge should serve for our warning,
Is. 41, 22. 23; Ps. 139, 12, and for our consolation, Is. 66, 2; Matt.
6, 32. To describe God's perfect knowledge, our dogmaticians have
divided it also into: 1) *natural knowledge (scientia naturalis,
essentialis),* according to which God fully knows Himself; 2) *free
knowledge (scientia libera),* according to which He knows all things
outside Himself; and 3) *mediate knowledge (scientia media),* according to which He knows all possible and conditionally future
or possible things.

In this connection we may consider the important question:
"How does God's infallible foreknowledge agree with the freedom
of man's will and human responsibility?" The question is important, since, on the basis of God's infallible foreknowledge, men
have denied either the freedom of the will and human responsibility
(Stoicism) or, on the basis of the human responsibility, the infallible foreknowledge, or omniscience, of God (Atheism, Agnosticism). While the question involves mysteries which we cannot
solve in this life, Scripture nevertheless teaches the following:

a) The foreknowledge of God embraces all things and is infallible, Ps. 139, 1—4; Rev. 3, 15. b) God's foreknowledge is not the efficient cause of the evil which He foresees. The *Formula of Concord* teaches correctly: "The foreknowledge of God is nothing else than that God knows all things before they happen, as it is written Dan. 2, 28. This foreknowledge extends alike over the godly and the wicked, but it is not the cause of evil, neither of sin, namely, of doing what is wrong (which originally arises from the devil and the wicked, perverse will of man), nor of their ruin [that men should perish], for which they themselves are responsible; but it only regulates it, and fixes a limit to it how long it should last, and all this to the end that it should serve His elect for their salvation, notwithstanding that it is evil in itself." (Epitome, XI, 3. 4.)

Our confession thus distinguishes correctly a) between the divine foreknowledge and the origin of evil and b) between the divine foreknowledge in general and the special divine foreknowledge (Amos 3, 2; Gal. 4, 9: *nosse cum affectu et effectu*), to which the saints of God owe their election and salvation. Rom. 8, 29. 30: "Whom He did foreknow, He also did predestinate." With regard to the mysteries which remain in spite of these revelations the *Formula of Concord* rightly exhorts all believers "not to reason in their thoughts, draw conclusions, nor inquire curiously into these matters, but adhere to His revealed Word, to which He points us." (Thor. Decl., XI, 54—57.)

When the question is asked: "Do all things happen as God foreknows them?" then indeed the answer must be in the affirmative. When the question is asked: "Do men act under coercion?" the answer must be in the negative. Judas's betrayal of Christ was a voluntary performance of evil, John 14, 26—30, just as Peter's confession of Christ was a voluntary performance of good, John 6, 65—71. Neither acted under coercion, though the one was under sin, the other under grace. Holy Scripture rigorously rules out all fatalistic or deterministic speculations.

While there is neither a *prius* nor a *posterius* in God, but all things are ever present before Him, Heb. 4, 13, Holy Scripture nevertheless in accommodation to our feeble understanding speaks of God's foreknowledge *(praescientia)*, since we have no conception at all of the perpetual "to-day" or "present," Ps. 2, 7. Just so the Christian theologian must therefore speak when he describes the divine knowledge with respect to future events. The question whether prescience may be ascribed also to men, angels, and departed spirits must be answered in the negative, Matt. 24, 36; Mark 13, 32.

c. *Divine wisdom (sapientia)* is that attribute of God by which He disposes and ordains all things in a most admirable manner for the attainment of His end, Job 12, 13; 28, 20; Rom. 11, 33. God's wisdom stands in close connection with His knowledge, so that the two often appear together (Rom. 11, 33: σοφίας καὶ γνώσεως; 1 Cor. 12, 8: λόγος σοφίας, λόγος γνώσεως). While the exact distinction between the two attributes is not clearly stated in Scripture, we may for all practical purposes distinguish between them as we do between intelligence and wisdom, so that σοφία denotes the practical application of γνῶσις. Scripture ascribes to God wisdom especially a) in the realm of nature (Ps. 104, 24: creation and preservation) and b) in the realm of grace (1 Cor. 2, 6 ff.). Hence we should not criticize the wisdom of the only-wise God, 1 Tim. 1, 17; Rom. 16, 27, as Modernists and atheists do when they reject Scripture as the only source of truth and blaspheme the divine method of creation (Mosaic creation report) and redemption *(satisfactio vicaria),* but we should rather admire and adore it, Rom. 11, 33, with holy reverence and fear.

d. *Divine will (voluntas)* has been treated by our dogmaticians sometimes as a separate attribute and sometimes as supplementary to the divine attribute of wisdom. In that case they deduce from the will of God the attributes of holiness, justice, truth, goodness, etc. (Baier). The manner of treating the subject is immaterial as long as the doctrine that is presented is Scriptural.

As Scripture ascribes to God an intelligent mind (Rom. 11, 34: νοῦς), so it ascribes to Him also will, 1 Tim. 2, 4; John 6, 40; 1 Thess. 4, 3. The will of God is the divine essence itself, seeking that which is good and opposing that which is evil. As to the causes of the divine will *(causae voluntatis divinae),* Scripture describes God a) in His supreme majesty, as independent of anything outside Himself, or as absolutely sovereign in Himself, Rom. 11, 36. Viewed in this manner, God is not moved by anything but by Himself; or we may say, in Him cause and effect coincide. *Non sunt in Deo causae formaliter causantes.* But Scripture speaks of God also b) from the viewpoint of human understanding; that is to say, since God in His divine essence is unintelligible to us, it leads us to distinguish in Him between cause and effect and to regard Him as provoked to wrath by sin, Jer. 2, 19, and as moved to grace by Christ's redemption, Rom. 3, 24. *In Deo sunt causae virtualiter causantes.* It is only when we speak of God in this Scriptural way that we can properly distinguish between Law and Gospel.

Although there is but one will in God, which is identical with His divine essence (no contradictory wills), yet, on the basis of Scripture, we may distinguish between: —

1. *The first and the second divine will (voluntas prima, voluntas secunda; voluntas antecedens, voluntas consequens).* The first will of God *(voluntas antecedens)* is that by which He earnestly desires the salvation of all sinners, John 3, 16. 17; the second will *(voluntas consequens)* is that by which He judges and condemns all those who reject His grace in Christ Jesus, John 3, 18. This distinction we hold against the double election of Calvinism, according to which God from eternity elected some to salvation and others to damnation.

2. *The irresistible and the resistible divine will (voluntas irresistibilis, voluntas resistibilis).* God's will is irresistible whenever it exerts itself absolutely, or whenever God acts in His absolute majesty and sovereignty (Creation, Final Judgment, 2 Cor. 5, 10; Matt. 25, 31 ff.); it is resistible whenever it exerts itself through means (rejection of divine grace offered in the Gospel, Matt. 23, 37). However, neither this nor the first distinction must be abused in the interest of synergism.

3. *The absolute and the ordinate divine will (voluntas absoluta, voluntas ordinata).* God's absolute will exerts itself without means, John 2, 1—11; Luke 1, 15; the ordinate will exerts itself through means (conversion through the means of grace, Rom. 10, 17; Titus 3, 5; 1 Pet. 1, 23 ff.; Mark 16, 15; Matt. 28, 19. 20). To reject the divinely ordained means of grace means to espouse the error of enthusiasm.

4. *The gracious will and the conditional divine will (voluntas gratiae, voluntas conditionata).* The gracious will of God exerts itself in the salvation of men, for He desires that all men should be saved by grace, through faith, without the deeds of the Law, or good works, Rom. 3, 28; Eph. 2, 8. 9; Rom. 11, 6; Gal. 3, 10 f.; the conditional will of God is that by which He demands perfect obedience of all who would be saved by the Law, Gal. 3, 10. 12. Since the Fall no man can be saved by the deeds of the Law; the conditional will of God after the Fall is therefore a stern reproof of the folly of attempting salvation by works, Luke 10, 28.

5. *The revealed and the hidden divine will (voluntas revelata, signi; voluntas abscondita, beneplaciti).* The revealed will of God embraces the entire revelation of Scripture, 1 Cor. 2, 12—16; the hidden will of God includes all things which He has left unrevealed in His Word, Rom. 11, 33. 34. While we should diligently study the revealed will of God in Holy Scripture, the attempt to explore His hidden will must be condemned as both foolish and arrogant.

e. *Divine holiness (sanctitas)* is that attribute of God by which He, conformably to His own Law, desires all things that are right and good, Deut. 32, 4; Ps. 92, 15; Lev. 11, 44; 1 Pet. 1, 15. In particular, God is holy a) essentially, inasmuch as He is by His divine essence most supremely exalted over all creatures, in which sense *holiness* denotes God's supreme majesty and comprises all His other attributes, Is. 6, 3; John 12, 41; b) efficiently, inasmuch as He is the Author of all holiness and stands in direct opposition to sin, 1 Pet. 1, 16; Lev. 11, 44. 45. The holiness of God should move us to appear before Him with great reverence, Gen. 18, 27; Ex. 3, 5, and, at the same time, with great boldness and confidence, since Christ by His vicarious atonement has made peace between the Holy God and sinful man, Rom. 5, 1; 5, 10; Eph. 3, 11. 12.

f. *Divine justice (iustitia)* is that attribute of God by which He is perfectly just and righteous in His divine essence, Ps. 92, 15, and by which He, in conformity with His own perfect, righteous essence, demands of men that which is just, Hos. 14, 9; Ps. 1, 5. 6. Hollaz fitly defines the justice of God as follows: "Justice is a divine attribute by virtue of which God wishes and does all those things which are conformed to His eternal Law, Ps. 92, 15, prescribes suitable laws to creatures, Ps. 19, 7, fulfils His promises made to men, Is. 45, 23, rewards the good, Rom. 2, 5—7; 2 Thess. 1, 6. 7, and punishes the wicked, Ps. 119, 137; Rom. 1, 32; Acts 17, 31; 2 Thess. 1, 6; Rom. 3, 8. 19." Since God is God, He is *exlex,* that is, He is not under the Law, but is Himself the perfect norm of justice. *Deus iustus est, quia omnia suae legi conformiter vult aut facit.*

The justice of God, applied to men, is a) *iustitia legalis,* or the divine righteousness revealed in the Law, and b) *iustitia evangelica,* or the divine righteousness revealed in the Gospel, which has been secured for sinners through Christ's vicarious atonement. The *iustitia legalis* may again be described as a) *legislatoria,* inasmuch as it is the norm of human righteousness, Matt. 22, 37 ff.;

b) *remuneratoria,* inasmuch as it rewards the good, 2 Tim. 4, 8; and c) *vindicativa (punitiva, ultrix),* inasmuch as it punishes the evil, 2 Thess. 1, 4—10. The *iustitia evangelica* is the essence of the Christian religion, since upon it the salvation of man rests. The question whether God, according to His *iustitia vindicativa,* punishes sin adequately must be answered in the affirmative.

g. *Divine veracity (veracitas)* is that attribute of God by which He is unfailing in speaking the truth and keeping His promises, Num. 23, 19; Heb. 6, 18; Deut. 32, 4. The revelation of this attribute implies a peculiar condescension on the part of God, since man through unbelief doubts both the threats of the Law and the promises of the Gospel, Ps. 90, 11; Is. 53, 1; John 12, 38. Just because of human unbelief, God has graciously revealed to us that, while all men are liars, Ps. 116, 11; Rom. 3, 4, He Himself is Truth, Titus 1, 2; John 3, 33; Heb. 6, 18; Matt. 24, 35; John 10, 35. In view of God's veracity we should fear His wrath, Gal. 6, 7, and trust in His promises, Rom. 10, 11; Titus 1, 2.

h. *Divine power (potentia)* is that attribute of God by which He can accomplish everything that can possibly be done without implying any contradiction in His divine essence. Quenstedt defines the power of God (I, 293) thus: "Power is that by which God independently, through the eternal activity of His own essence, can do absolutely everything that does not involve a contradiction." (*Doctr. Theol.,* p. 120.) God's perfect power is distinguished from the imperfect and relative power of man both with regard to manner and extent; for, with regard to the first, God's power is His will, Gen. 1, 3; Ps. 115, 3 (*Deus producit volendo),* while, with regard to the second, His power embraces all things that are in conformity with His perfect essence, Matt. 19, 26; Luke 1, 37. Because God has infinite power, we must not speak of Him as if He had exhausted Himself when creating this universe (pantheism). Nor must we conclude from God's power what in our estimation He ought to do. Thus the conclusion of rationalistic theologians that, since God is almighty, He ought to forgive sin without Christ's vicarious suffering and death is a blasphemy.

God exerts His power in two ways, namely: a) by means (*causae secundae)* and b) without means. The first is God's ordinate power (*potentia ordinata); the second is His absolute power (*potentia absoluta, immediata).* In both instances the same almighty power is brought into action, Ps. 33, 6—9. Whenever God works *absolutely* what ordinarily He accomplishes by means, we are confronted with miracles (John 2, 11: σημεῖα; Acts 2, 43: τέρατα καὶ σημεῖα). With respect to miracles we must hold, on the basis of Scripture, a) that God can perform miracles whenever He pleases, since He is the sovereign Lord and the laws of nature, which in themselves are never invariable (evolutionists), are nothing else than His own divine will applied to the things created; but b) that we should use the divinely ordained means, both in the realm of nature and of grace, and not presumptuously demand miracles on our behalf, Luke 11, 16; Matt. 12, 39. The *fides heroica,* which with extraordinary confidence in God performs miracles, is not judged by this rule; but let the person who endeavors to perform miracles be sure that his "faith" is really *fides heroica* and not presumption.

The denial of God's omnipotence on the ground that He cannot lie, steal, die, etc., must be condemned as blasphemous sophistry. *Sunt sophismata, quibus definitio rei tollitur.*

i. *Divine goodness (bonitas)* in its objective sense is that attribute of God by which His divine essence is perfectly conformed to His divine will, or His absolute perfection, Matt. 19, 17. Relatively also the creatures of God are good, Gen. 1, 31, even after the Fall, namely, inasmuch as they are creatures of God, 1 Tim. 4, 4. However, creatures possess no essential goodness, or perfection, but are good only as God's handiwork. In contradistinction to all creatures, God alone is good, or good in and of Himself (τὸ αὐτοαγαθόν). Gerhard writes of God's goodness in this sense: *"Deus est vere bonus et solus bonus et omnis bonitatis causa."* The Scriptural truth that God alone is absolutely and in Himself good (essential Goodness) and that men are only relatively, or dependently, good should preserve us from pride and envy and move us to humility and gratitude, 1 Cor. 4, 7; 1 Pet. 2, 1. Gerhard writes: "All good things come down upon us and our neighbor from God; who is envious of his neighbor opposes God Himself, the Giver of all gifts, and is truly a θεόμαχος (a God-fighter)."

While divine goodness in its objective sense denotes the absolute divine perfection, or the divine essential goodness, in its subjective sense it denotes His gracious disposition and conduct toward His creatures, Ps. 145, 9; 36, 6. 7. According to Scripture, God is good a) in general, to all creatures, Ps. 136; b) in particular, to all men, Matt. 5, 45; c) more especially, to men as sinners, John 3, 16; and d) in a most special sense, to His believing saints, Rom.

8, 28; 1 Cor. 2, 9; Deut. 33, 3; John 16, 27. God's goodness toward us should always move us to grateful love to Him, 1 John 4, 19.

Under the attribute of divine goodness *(bonitas relativa),* we may group a) divine grace, as goodness unmerited by men, Titus 3, 5; Rom. 3, 24; b) divine mercy, as goodness toward men in need, Luke 1, 78. 79; c) divine love, as goodness desiring communion with men, John 3, 16; d) divine patience and long-suffering, as goodness waiting for man's repentance, 1 Pet. 3, 20; 2 Pet. 3, 9. These attributes deserve consideration above all others, for they are the true scope of Scripture and the great theme in which Christian preaching centers, 1 Cor. 2, 2. The entire Gospel-message may be summed up in the divine attribute of goodness, for what it proclaims is nothing else than the manifestation of divine grace, love, mercy, long-suffering, friendliness, etc., in Christ Jesus, our Lord, 1 John 4, 9. The revelation of all other divine attributes would be dreadful indeed were it not for God's goodness in Christ. But as God is good, so those who through faith in Christ have become His dear children should likewise be good, gracious, merciful, Luke 6, 36; Matt. 5, 44. 45; Eph. 4, 32; Col. 3, 12.

God's goodness has been objected to on the ground that His punishments are frequently severe and destructive. While Scripture does not deny this fact, Matt. 24, 21. 22, it points out the great truth that even God's dire punishments are motivated by His saving love; for by them He calls sinners to repentance, Luke 13, 1—3. However, all who deny the Bible as the only source of faith, the Triune God as the only true God, and Christ as the only Savior from sin can never hope to share in the eternal blessings of God's goodness, grace, and love.

THE DOCTRINE OF THE DIVINE DECREES.

(De Decretis Divinis.)

The acts of God are divided into two kinds, internal *(opera ad intra),* and external *(opera ad extra),* the latter being either immediate (performed without instrumental causes) or mediate (performed through intermediate causes).

The internal acts, or operations, of God are again of two kinds, personal and essential. The personal internal acts of God terminate within the Godhead and pertain to the divine Persons by whom they are performed as peculiar to such Persons (generation and spiration). The essential internal acts of God also terminate within the Godhead, but in them the three Persons of the Trinity concur. These essential internal operations of God are called the eternal decrees of God. Of these there are three: a) the decree of creation, b) the decree of redemption, and c) the decree of predestination.

a. The decree of creation is that essential internal act of the Triune God "by which He purposed to create in the beginning of time heaven and earth and all creatures, for the manifestation of His wisdom, goodness, and power" (A. L. Graebner). The decree of creation is taught in Job 28, 26. 27; Acts 15, 18; Gen. 1, 26; Acts 17, 26; Ps. 136, 5—9.

b. The decree of redemption is that essential internal act of the Triune God by which He most graciously and wisely purposed to redeem fallen and lost mankind through the vicarious atonement of the incarnate Son of God, Jesus Christ, and thus to prepare a way of salvation for the whole world, whose fall He had foreseen, but not decreed. The decree of redemption is taught in Acts 2, 23: "Delivered by the determinate counsel and foreknowledge of God"; Acts 4, 28: "To do whatsoever Thy counsel determined before to be done"; Eph. 1, 7—10: "In whom we have redemption through His blood, . . . according to the riches of His grace; wherein He hath abounded toward us in all wisdom and prudence . . . according to His good pleasure which He hath purposed in Himself"; 1 Pet. 1, 20: "Who [the incarnate Son of God, our Redeemer] verily was foreordained before the foundation of the world"; Gal. 4, 4. 5: "When the fulness of time was come, God sent forth His Son, made of a woman, made under the Law, to redeem them that were under the Law"; John 3, 16: "God so loved the world that He gave His only-begotten Son," etc.

c. The decree of predestination is that essential internal act of the Triune God by which He from eternity, moved only by His grace and the redemption of Jesus Christ, purposed to sanctify and save by faith, through the means of grace, all saints who finally enter into life eternal. The decree of predestination is taught in Eph. 1, 4: "He has chosen us in Him [Christ] before the foundation of the world"; 2 Thess. 2, 13: "God hath from the beginning chosen you to salvation"; Eph. 3, 11: "According to the eternal purpose which He purposed in Christ Jesus, our Lord"; 2 Tim. 1, 9: "Who hath saved us . . . according to His own purpose and grace, which was given us in Christ Jesus before the world began"; Rom. 11, 5: "There is a remnant according to the election of grace"; Acts 13, 48: "As many as were ordained to eternal life believed"; Rom. 8, 29. 30: "Whom He did foreknow He also did predestinate to be conformed to the image of His Son. . . . Whom He did predestinate, them He also called; and whom He called, them He also justified; and whom He justified, them He also glorified"; 1 Pet. 1, 2: "Elect according to the foreknowledge of God the Father, through sanctification of the Spirit, unto obedience and sprinkling of the blood of Jesus Christ"; Matt. 22, 14: "Many are called, but few are chosen"; Mark 13, 20. 22: "For the elect's sake, whom He hath chosen, He hath shortened the days . . . to seduce, if it were possible, even the elect."

The doctrine of election will be treated at greater length under its proper head. Here we refer to it only inasmuch as it belongs to the eternal decrees of God. But in passing, we may say that from the eternal decree of predestination there must be excluded every form of synergism (denial of the *sola gratia*) and every form of Calvinism (denial of the *gratia universalis*). For this reason we affirm a) God did not choose the elect in view of their faith *(intuitu fidei),* and b) God did not predestinate any one to damnation, but earnestly desires all men to be saved *(vocatio seria).* The apparent discrepancy between particular election *(electio particularis)* and universal grace *(gratia universalis)* we acknowledge as a mystery, which is indeed beyond reason, but which we should neither criticize nor try to explain. All attempts to harmonize the two doctrines have resulted either in synergism (the elect were chosen in view of their better conduct, which is opposed to Rom. 3, 22. 23) or in Calvinism (God does not desire to save all, which is opposed to John 3, 16; 2 Cor. 5, 19. 20; 2 Pet. 3, 9; Acts 17, 30; 1 Tim. 4, 2). The *Formula of Concord* rightly says:

"However, since God has reserved this mystery for His wisdom and has revealed nothing to us concerning it in His Word, much less commanded us to investigate it with our thoughts, but has earnestly discouraged us therefrom, Rom. 11, 33 ff., we should not reason in our thoughts, draw conclusions, nor inquire curiously into these matters, but should adhere to His revealed Word, to which He points us." (Thor. Decl., XI, 55.)

Dr. A. L. Graebner summarizes the decree of predestination as follows: "The decree of predestination is an *eternal* act of God (Eph. 1, 4; 3, 11; 2 Tim. 1, 9; 2 Thess. 2, 13), who *for His goodness' sake* (2 Tim. 1, 9; Rom. 9, 11; 11, 5) and because of *the merit of the* foreordained *Redeemer* of all mankind (Eph. 1, 4; 3, 11) purposed to lead into everlasting life (Acts 13, 48; 2 Tim. 2, 10; Rom. 8, 28. 29), by the way and means of salvation designated for *all mankind* (Eph. 1, 4. 5; 1 Pet. 1, 2), a certain number (Acts 13, 48; Matt. 20, 16; 22, 14) of certain persons (2 Tim. 2, 19; John 13, 18) and to procure, work, and promote what would pertain to their final salvation (Rom. 8, 30; Eph. 1, 11; 3, 10. 11; Mark 13, 20. 22)." (*Outlines of Doctrinal Theology,* § 51.)

THE DOCTRINE OF CREATION.
(De Creatione.)

1. DEFINITION OF CREATION.

In contradistinction to pagan pantheism, which regards the universe as an emanation from, or a manifestation of, God, so that God and the universe are identical, and to pagan dualism, which assumes the eternal existence of matter (ὕλη ἄμορφος, τὸ μὴ ὄν), fashioned by a deity (νοῦς, τὸ ὄν) into this present world, Holy Scripture teaches that the Triune God created all things that exist outside Himself, *i. e.,* the universe, out of nothing. By "nothing" we do not mean any already existing matter *(nihil positivum),* but a state of non-existence *(nihil negativum).* From Gen. 1, 1, Heb. 11, 3, and Rom. 4, 17 we learn that before the creation of the world nothing existed but God Himself. Calov writes (III, 899): "Creation does not consist in emanation from the essence of God, nor in generation, nor in motion, or natural change, . . . but in outward action, by which through infinite power things are produced from nothing." (*Doctr. Theol.,* p. 164 f.) Gerhard says (IV, 7): "Away with the dreams of the Stoics, who devised two eternal principles, νοῦς and ὕλη, mind, or God, and matter, which, they imagined, during the ages of eternity was a confused chaos and at a certain time was at length brought into form by 'mind.'" *(Ibid.)* Against pantheism, both ancient and modern, Hollaz writes thus: "Creation is a free divine action, because God framed the universe, not induced thereto by necessity, as though He needed the services of creatures, . . . but freely, as He was able to create or not, to create and to frame sooner or later, in this or in another matter." *(Ibid.)* The question why God did not create the world sooner Hafenreffer describes as a "question of madmen curiously inquiring into such things as are of no profit." *(Ibid.)*

2. THE ORDER OF CREATION.

According to Holy Scripture, God did not create all things "at once, but gradually, observing an admirable order" *(ordo creationis).* As the first chapter of Genesis affirms, God, in creating all things, proceeded from the lower to the higher, until He finally made man as the crown of His creative work. In general, the work of creation comprises three steps: a) the production, on the first day, of the crude material, "which was the germinal source, as it were, of the entire universe" (Quenstedt); Luther: *moles coeli et terrae;* b) the separation and disposition of simple creatures during the first three days (light on the first day; the firmament on the second; the separation of the earth from the waters on the third); c) the furnishing and completion of the world, which was brought to perfection in three more days (the celestial bodies on the fourth day; the fish and fowl on the fifth; the creation of land animals and of man on the sixth).

We thus distinguish between immediate and mediate creation, the former being the creation of the *moles coeli et terrae* out of nothing and the latter the arrangement of the previously created material.

This order of creation must, however, not be interpreted as an evolutionary process; for according to Scripture the world was not developed by forces resident in matter itself, but by the creative power of God. (Gen. 1, 1: "God created"; v. 3: "God said.") The creatures thus came into existence through the omnipotent command of the personal, transmundane Creator. This truth our dogmaticians have expressed by the statement: "The efficient cause of creation is God, and He alone" (Calov). Nor can experimental science gainsay it, since it can prove neither a development of organic things from inorganic *(generatio aequivoca)* nor a development of higher forms from the lower *(Deszendenztheorie; Transmutationshypothese)*.

Evolution must be rejected as untenable even on rational grounds, a) since it does not account for the existence of primeval matter and b) since it rests upon a principle disproved by nature, namely, on the supposed transmutation of the homogeneous into the heterogeneous (transmutation of species). Scripture, on the other hand, accords with reason in the following points: a) the creation of all things by an omnipotent God; b) the orderly procedure in the work of creation; c) the propagation of creatures after their kind, Gen. 1, 21. As all creatures came into existence through the creative command of God, so they are preserved and propagated through the divine omnipotent will, Acts 17, 28. The existence of the universe to-day with all its manifold creatures is due to the blessing which God pronounced upon the whole creation after the completion of His creative work, Gen. 1, 22; Col. 1, 17.

3. THE HEXAEMERON.

Holy Scripture teaches distinctly that the whole universe was created within six days of twenty-four hours each (hexaemeron). To change the six days into a mere moment (Athanasius, Augustine, Hilary.) or to expand them into periods of millions of years is equally contrary to Scripture. (Gen. 1, 31; 2, 2; Ex. 20, 9. 11: "Six days shalt thou labor. . . . For in six days the Lord made heaven and earth.") Since the Mosaic creation record is the only authentic report which we have of the miracle of creation (no man was present at the creation, and no one can show from the now existing world how it once sprang into existence), we must regard every attempt to correct or supplement the record of Genesis as unscientific pretense. Evolution proper is atheistic and immoral, while theistic evolution is neither in accord with Scripture nor with the basic principles of evolution proper. To deny the inspired character of the Book of Genesis means to contradict the testimony of the divine, omniscient Christ, who accepted also this book as canonical, Matt. 19, 4—6; John 5, 39.

4. THE SIX DAYS OF CREATION CONSIDERED IN DETAIL.

The First Day. — The expression "In the beginning" (בְּרֵאשִׁית) means as much as "when this world began to be." "There was no material of creation *(materia ex qua)* with respect to the things created on the first day" (Quenstedt). Only since things outside God have begun to exist, there is a beginning. Before that there was no "beginning," because God has no beginning, Ps. 90, 1. 2, and outside Him there was nothing. Time and space must therefore be traced to God's omnipotent fiat of creation; they are creatures of the infinite God. The words "In the beginning," Gen. 1, 1, correspond to the same words (ἐν ἀρχῇ) in John 1, 1; only the Book of Genesis records what God then did, while the Gospel of John informs us who existed in the beginning (the Father and the Son).

The expression "heaven and earth" is a Scriptural designation of the universe *(das Weltall),* or the "all" (τὰ πάντα), of which St. Paul speaks in Col. 1, 17 and Acts 17, 24: "the world and all things therein." However, since the divine record in Genesis describes in detail the creation of the various creatures out of the original substance *(mediate creation),* we rightly understand the expression to denote the *rudis moles coeli et terrae,* or the crude material, which was the "germinal source of the entire universe." Together with the earth, God created the water, since this surrounded the earth, Gen. 1, 2.

The term *heaven* must not be taken in the sense of a "highest heaven" (empyrean, *coelum empyrium*), a supposed region of pure fire, in which God dwells with the angels and saints (papists, Calvinists). Quenstedt rightly calls this supposed empyrean a *merum figmentum*. The expression *heaven and earth* in Gen. 1, 1 (אֵת הַשָּׁמַיִם וְאֵת הָאָרֶץ), as just stated, simply denotes the *Weltstoff*, to borrow a term of modern dogmatics.

The term *tohuvabohu* (תֹהוּ וָבֹהוּ), which our Authorized Version translates "without form and void," in Jer. 4, 23 denotes a desolate country. In Gen. 1, 2, however, it denotes the chaotic condition of all created things before God's creative hand had separated and arranged them in order. The theory that Gen. 1, 1 reports the restitution of a world previously created, but destroyed at the fall of the evil angels (Kurtz), has no Scriptural foundation whatever and must be rejected as a figment of human speculation.

The "light," which God created on the first day, was the elemental light, to which He on the fourth day added the "two great lights in the firmament" to govern day and night, summer and winter, seed-time and harvest, Gen. 1, 14. According to Scripture, light existed before the celestial bodies. "By the word of His power God created light, elemental light, brought it into being in the midst of the darkness, and commanded it to shine out of darkness, 2 Cor. 4, 6. Ever since the first day of the world the regular recurrence of darkness and light marks the period of one day, as we now divide it into twenty-four hours." (Kretzmann, *Pop. Com.*, I, 2.)

The Second Day. — On the second day, God created the expansion, or the "firmament" (רָקִיעַ), by which is meant not the stratum of atmosphere above the earth, but rather the visible vault of the sky (Luther). According to Gen. 1, 6—8 the "firmament" divides the waters above and those below it, so that we must conceive of waters beyond the visible vault of the sky. The creation report everywhere exhibits God's omnipotent power and majesty, but does not answer all questions which the ever-curious mind of man is inclined to put.

The Third Day. — On the third day, God gathered the waters under the heaven together unto one place, so that the dry land appeared. "God here finished His creative work on inanimate matter, when His almighty command bade the waters from below the heavens, below the firmament which He had constructed, be gathered together into a single place, by themselves. In chaos the mixture of solids and liquids had been so complete as to preclude the designation 'dry land.' But now the solids and liquids were to be separated, so that dry land as we know it was visible." (Kretzmann, *Pop. Com.,* I, 2.) As soon as God caused the dry land to appear, He adorned it "with grass and herb yielding seed after his kind and the tree yielding fruit, whose seed was in itself, after his kind," Gen. 1, 12 (the law of propagation). According to Scripture the plants were before the seed, since God created mature plants, "yielding seed."

The Fourth Day. — On the fourth day, God created the sun, moon, and stars, Gen. 1, 14 ff. The "matter out of which" *(materia ex qua)* God made the celestial bodies is not stated; but the holy writer describes their purpose *(finis cuius)* and the recipients *(finis cui)* of their *blessings,* Gen. 1, 14—18. While Holy Scripture does not teach an astronomical system, nevertheless it stresses the following truths: a) The earth was before the sun, just as also the light was before the sun. b) The earth does not serve the sun, but, *vice versa,* the sun serves the earth, and both the sun and the earth serve man, who has been created for the purpose of serving God. Within the bounds of these basic truths all astronomical ideas of the Christian theologian must be confined. All so-called astronomical systems suggested by men rest upon hypotheses, which are beyond positive proof. Over against the astronomical systems of scientists the Christian theologian must therefore maintain: a) Scripture never errs, not even in matters of science, John 10, 35; 2 Tim. 3, 16. b) Scripture accommodates itself to human conceptions, but never to human errors, since it is always truth, John 17, 17. c) We know so little concerning astronomical data that it is both foolish and unscientific to supplement, correct, or criticize Scripture on the basis of human speculative systems. d) It is unworthy of our Christian calling to discard the inerrant Word of Scripture in favor of the "assured results" of science falsely so called. Hence in a controversy on this point a Christian must always maintain the divine authority of Scripture. But he must not believe that by convincing an unbeliever of the truth of the Mosaic narrative he may convert him, since conversion is accomplished only through the preaching of the Law and the Gospel.

The Fifth Day. — On the fifth day, God created "the moving creature that hath life" in the water and the "fowl that may fly above the earth," Gen. 1, 20. 21. While the *materia ex qua* of the first was water, that of the second is not stated directly. Nevertheless the matter out of which these and other creatures were made was in no wise self-creative (evolution). *Materia est principium passivum; non concurrit cum Deo ad aliquid creandum.*

The Sixth Day. — On the last day, God created both "the beasts of the earth" and, as the crown of His creative work, man, Gen. 1, 24. 27. The question whether animals and plants which after the Fall have become injurious to man were created at this time may be answered as follows: They were indeed created within the six creation days, but their functions were in complete accord with man's well-being. Even to-day the "harmful things" (poisonous plants and minerals) may be used by man for his benefit. However, since before the Fall nature was not yet under the curse and corruption of sin, even these creatures yielded to man their willing service.

The supreme glory of man, as the crown of creation, appears from the following facts: a) Man's creation was preceded by a divine consultation in which the three Persons of the Godhead concurred, Gen. 1, 26. b) While all creatures came into existence through the almighty divine word, God formed the body of man out of the dust of the ground, Gen. 2, 7, and breathed into his nostrils the breath of life, so that he became a living soul, Gen. 2, 7b. c) God made man an intelligent and rational being to rule in His stead over the world, which was created for him by the beneficent Creator, Gen. 2, 7b; 1, 28. d) God made man in His own image, so that he was like God in holiness, righteousness, and wisdom, Eph. 4, 24; Col. 3, 10. e) God supplied Adam with a helpmeet, who was made in the divine image and endowed with intelligence and an immortal soul, Gen. 2, 22—24.

The question of dichotomy or trichotomy must be decided on the basis of such passages as describe man according to his essential parts, Matt. 10, 28; 16, 26; Gen. 2, 7. On the basis of these passages most Lutheran dogmaticians have declared themselves in favor of dichotomy. Passages quoted by trichotomists are Luke 1, 46. 47; 1 Thess. 5, 23, etc.; but none of these furnishes incontrovertible evidence in proof of trichotomy. That Scripture uses the terms *spirit* (πνεῦμα) and *soul* (ψυχή) interchangeably is clear from the fact that those who have departed this life are called either spirits (1 Pet. 3, 19), or souls (Rev. 6, 9). Dichotomy certainly offers less difficulty in explaining the phenomena of human existence in general.

The Mosaic narrative of the creation of the world must not be regarded as an allegory or myth, but must be taken as a true historical account of actual happenings. Only a literal interpretation is fair to the text.

According to Holy Scripture, creation was that free act of the Triune God by which "in the beginning, for His own glory, He made, without the use of preexisting materials, the whole visible and invisible universe" (Strong). This doctrine stands in close relation to God's holiness and benevolence, Rom. 8, 20—23; 2 Cor. 4, 15—17, as well as to His wisdom and free will, Ps. 104, 24; 136, 5. Those who deny the doctrine of creation as taught in Scripture may as well deny also the Scriptural doctrine of redemption, since the account of the former is no less inspired than is the account of the latter. "*All* Scripture is given by inspiration of God," 2 Tim. 3, 16, and Christ's command is to accept as divine truth the *whole Bible,* John 5, 39; 10, 35.

5. THE UNITY OF THE HUMAN RACE.

On the basis of Scripture we maintain that Adam, created by God on the sixth day of the hexaemeron, was the first of all men and the parent of the entire human race throughout the whole world, 1 Cor. 15, 45. 47; Gen. 2, 5; Acts 17, 26; Rom. 5, 12. Hence we reject the error of Isaac Peyrere (1655), who taught that, while the Jews descended from Adam, Gen. 2, 7 ff., the Gentiles came from preadamites, Gen. 1, 26 ff., so that they date back to ages before the creation of the ancestor of the Jews. But the Mosaic narrative allows the assumption neither of preadamites nor of coadamites, since it teaches most emphatically that Adam is the parent of all men, Acts 17, 26. With this doctrine agree also the conclusions of outstanding anthropologists, who, on grounds apart from divine revelation, have affirmed the unity of the human race (Alexander von Humboldt).

While Adam was created first and independently, Gen. 2, 18, Eve was created dependently from Adam, a complete rational individual, taken from man according to soul and body, Gen. 2, 21—24. The rib from which God built (בָּנָה) Eve, must not be understood as a mere rib, but as a living, vital substance, including everything of which she consisted essentially, Gen. 2, 23; Acts 17, 26. (Cp. Luther's explanation, St. L., I, 157.) While Eve was Adam's equal in the enjoyment of the divine blessings, both temporal and spiritual, her social status was one of subordination to Adam, for whose sake she was created, Gen. 2, 18; 1 Cor. 14, 34—36; 1 Tim. 2, 11—15.

6. SPECIAL QUESTIONS REGARDING THE CREATION REPORT.

a. While Holy Scripture informs us exactly how and when man was created, it gives us no account whatever concerning the creation of the angels. Nevertheless they, too, were made within the hexaemeron, Gen. 2, 1. 2. Since Scripture reveals to us everything that is necessary for salvation, we should not try to supplement the divine record by human speculation.

b. Whether Moses received the facts recorded in his narrative by immediate revelation or through oral tradition is immaterial. Since the Book of Genesis is canonical, it is divinely inspired, 2 Tim. 3, 16; John 10, 35, and therefore contains God's own account concerning the beginning of the world and the human race.

c. The two creation narratives of Genesis (chaps. 1 and 2) are not contradictory records (Jean Astruc, † 1766), but chap. 2 rather supplements the account of chap. 1. In Gen. 1 we have a general description of the work of creation, while Gen. 2 brings the fact of creation in relation to the history of God's Church in the Old Testament. For this reason Gen. 2 is both supplementary and explanatory. (Cp. אֱלֹהִים in Gen. 1; and יְהֹוָה אֱלֹהִים in Gen. 2.) The history of the Church of God, the Creator (אֱלֹהִים), which is begun in Gen. 2, is therefore narrated as that of the Church of Jehovah (יְהֹוָה), the eternal Lord of His people.

d. As the soul of Eve was produced by propagation from Adam, so, it is generally held among Lutheran dogmaticians, the souls of children are produced by propagation rather than by direct creation (traducianism, not creationism). "The soul of the first man was immediately created by God; but the soul of Eve was produced by propagation, and the souls of the rest of men are created not daily, . . . but by virtue of the divine blessing are propagated, *per traducem,* by their parents." (Quenstedt.) Traducianism is inferred: a) from the primeval blessing of God, Gen. 1, 28; 9, 1; b) from God's rest and cessation from all work on the seventh day, Gen. 2, 2; c) from the production of the soul of Eve, Gen. 2, 21. 22; d) from the general description of generation, Gen. 5, 3; e) from Ps. 51, 5, etc.

e. The act of creation must be regarded as a free act of God *(actio libera),* so that God was not compelled to create the world by any inner necessity of His divine essence, Ps. 115, 3. To say that the act of creation was a necessary divine act *(actio necessaria)* would be tantamount to pantheism and nullify the very concept of a personal, sovereign God.

f. While Holy Scripture assures us that the universe as it came
forth from the creative hand of God was "very good" (Gen. 1, 31:
טוֹב מְאֹד), it would be folly to affirm that the world as created by
God was the very best that God could have made (the "optimism"
of Leibniz). We must judge this world by God's own standards,
as these are presented to us in His Word. For this reason we say
that the world was very good in the sense that it accorded perfectly
with the divine will or that it was just as God desired it to be.

7. CREATION AN EXTERNAL ACT OF GOD (OPUS AD EXTRA).

Creation, as an *opus ad extra,* is the work of the Triune God.
Hence it is ascribed to the Father (1 Cor. 8, 6), to the Son (Heb.
1, 10; John 1, 3; Col. 1, 16), and to the Holy Ghost (Gen. 1, 2;
Ps. 33, 6). Yet, though the Three Persons of the Trinity concurred in this work, the creative power, or omnipotence, to which
the universe owes its existence, is numerically one *(una numero
potentia),* so that we must not speak of three creators, but only of
one, John 5, 17. "Creation is an action of the one God. . . . It is
likewise an action of God alone, which neither ought to be, nor
can be, ascribed to any creature." (Chemnitz.) Nor must we speak
of a distribution of the one divine power among the Three Persons,
as if the Father performed a third, the Son a third, and the Holy
Ghost a third of the creative work. Holy Scripture never distrib-
utes the divine creative act among the Three Persons, though at
times it appropriates it to a distinct divine person (cf. passages
above).

Again, when Scripture occasionally declares that all things
were made by the Father through the Son or the Holy Ghost,
Ps. 33, 6, this "must not be construed into any inequality of persons, as the Arians blasphemously asserted that the Son was God's
instrument in creation, just as the workman uses an ax" (Chemnitz); but this mode of speaking rather indicates the mystery of
the Holy Trinity, according to which the Son has His divine essence and divine power eternally from the Father and the Holy
Ghost has His divine essence and divine power eternally from the
Father and Son.

Chemnitz rightly remarks respecting this point (*Loci Theol.,*
1, 115): "The prepositions (ἀπό, διά, ἐν) do not divide the nature,
but express the properties of a nature that is one and uncon-
founded." Likewise Hollaz says: "The three Persons of the
Godhead are not three associated causes, not three Authors of

creation, but one Cause, one Author of creation, one Creator."
Flacius: "*Vox autem* PER *non significat hic* INSTRUMENTUM, SED
PRIMARIAM CAUSAM." Luther: "It is the way of Scripture to say:
The world was made through Christ by the Father and in the
Holy Ghost. . . . It employs this manner of speaking to indicate
that the Father has His divine essence not from the Son, but,
vice versa, that the Son has it from the Father, He being the first
and original Person in the Godhead. Hence it does not say that
Christ has made the world through the Father, but that the Father
made it through the Son, so that the Father remains the First
Person, and from Him, yet through the Son, all things appear.
So John says (John 1, 3): 'All things were made by Him'; and
in Col. 1, 16 we read: 'All things were created by Him and for
Him'; and Rom. 11, 36: 'For of Him and through Him and to
Him are all things.'" (St. L., XII, 157 ff.) Chemnitz adds this
warning (*Loci Theol.,* I, 115): "We must not dispute too curiously concerning the distinction of Persons in the work of creation,
but let us be content with the revelation that all things were created
by the eternal Father, through the Son, while the Holy Ghost
hovered over them. (Rom. 11, 36.)" (*Doctr. Theol.,* p. 162 ff.)

8. THE ULTIMATE END OF CREATION.

According to Holy Scripture the ultimate end of creation is
the glory of God; in other words, the world was created ultimately
for God's own sake, Prov. 16, 4, or for His glory, Ps. 104, 1 ff. For
this reason not only men, but all creatures are exhorted to praise
God, Ps. 148. By His creation God manifested in particular:
a) His goodness, Ps. 136; b) His power, Ps. 115; c) His wisdom,
Ps. 19, 1 ff.; 104, 24; 136, 5. The objection offered here that it is
an unworthy conception of God to regard Him as having made all
things for His own glory is a) anti-Scriptural, since Holy Scripture teaches this very truth, Rom. 11, 36; b) unreasonable, since it
measures God by human standards; c) atheistic, since it dethrones
God and puts man in His place; for if the world was not made
primarily for God's sake, then man himself must be the ultimate
end of creation. However, while the ultimate end of creation is
the glory of God, the intermediate end of creation is the benefit
of man, Ps. 115, 15. 16. Quenstedt writes (I, 418): "God made
all things for the sake of man, but man He made for His own
sake, Ps. 115, 16; 60, 7. 8." *Finis cuius creationis mundi gloria
Dei; finis cui homo. Macrocosmus in gratiam microcosmi con-
ditus est.*

THE DOCTRINE OF DIVINE PROVIDENCE.
(De Providentia Dei.)

1. DEFINITION OF DIVINE PROVIDENCE.

As God has created the world, so He also sustains it and continually cares for all His creatures, particularly man. Just that is what we mean when we speak of God's providence (*providentia, πρόνοια, διοίκησις*). Augustine says: "God is not a workman who, when he has completed his work, leaves it to itself and goes his way." Gerhard: "God, the Creator of all, did not desert the work which He framed; but by His omnipotence up to the present time preserves it, and by His wisdom He rules and controls all things in it."

While the fact of divine providence may be known by men from the contemplation of nature, Rom. 1, 19. 20; Acts 14, 17, and of history, Acts 17, 26—28, Holy Scripture, because of the blindness and perverseness of the human mind, Is. 1, 2. 3, teaches it with great emphasis and much detail, Matt. 6, 25—32. Gerhard (IV, 52) writes: "The knowledge of divine providence sought from the book of nature is weak and imperfect, not from the fault of nature itself, but from that of our mind; but more certain and perfect is the knowledge of divine providence which is obtained from Scripture." (*Doctr. Theol.*, p. 174.) The Christian theologian regards Scripture as the only source (*principium cognoscendi*) of also this doctrine.

The providence of God manifests itself in particular: a) in His gracious preservation of all creatures (*conservatio*); b) in His gracious cooperation with all that occurs (*concursus*); c) in His gracious direction and government of the whole universe (*gubernatio*). We therefore distinguish as special acts of divine providence: God's preservation, Ps. 36, 6; God's concurrence, Acts 17, 28; and God's government, Jer. 10, 23; Prov. 20, 24. A complete definition of divine providence therefore reads: "Divine providence is the external act of the entire Trinity (*opus ad extra*) whereby God a) most efficaciously upholds the things created, both as an entirety and singly, both in species and in individuals; b) concurs in their actions and effects; and c) freely and wisely governs all things to His own glory and the welfare and safety of the universe, especially of the godly."

The act of divine providence includes the preservation of all creatures not only in their being, Acts 17, 28; Col. 1, 17, but also in their activities, Matt. 5, 45; Acts 14, 17; Ps. 104, 10—30. In other words, the creatures have not only their being in God, but also perform their functions through Him. For this reason our dogmaticians have called the preservation of the world *(conservatio mundi)* a continuous creation *(creatio continuata)*. Rightly understood, this expression is Scriptural. While divine providence is the work of the Triune God, it is of special comfort to all believers that Holy Scripture ascribes the preservation and government of the world especially to our Lord and Savior Jesus Christ, whom God has made the Head of His Church, Heb. 1, 3; Col. 1, 17; Eph. 1, 20—23.

2. THE OBJECTS OF DIVINE PROVIDENCE.

According to Holy Scripture divine providence embraces not only the universe in general, Col. 1, 17, but also all creatures individually: a) plants, Matt. 6, 28—30; b) animals, Matt. 6, 26; c) men, Acts 17, 26; Ps. 33, 12—15. The special object of divine providence according to Scripture is the Christian Church, for whose sake all things exist and whose welfare all must serve, Rom. 8, 28; Heb. 1, 14; Matt. 16, 18. All objections raised against the Scriptural truth that divine providence embraces all things, even the least, Matt. 10, 30; Luke 21, 18; 12, 6, for example, that God would be too heavily burdened by caring for all things or that the small affairs of life in that case would receive undue emphasis in comparison with the important matters, must be rejected as perverse notions of the carnal and unbelieving heart, which destroy the very concept of God; for just because God is God, does He care for all things, Acts 17, 28.

3. THE RELATION OF DIVINE PROVIDENCE TO SECONDARY CAUSES (CAUSAE SECUNDAE).

In His cooperating providence, God employs secondary causes *(causae secundae),* or means by which He preserves and directs the things which He has made. This is what we mean when we speak of divine concurrence. The relation of divine providence to such secondary means must be carefully noted; for in the divine act of concurrence both God works and the means *(causae secundae)* work. However, the operation of the means is not coordinate with that of God, but rather subordinate to it, so that the secondary causes work only so far and so long as God works through them,

Ps. 127, 1. To emphasize this truth, our dogmaticians have said that the divine concurrence is not previous (actio praevia), but the operation of God and that of the means is numerically one (una numero actio). In other words, God concurs, but He does not precur; He cooperates, but does not "preoperate." "Concurrence is not antecedent, but occurs when the action itself is produced." (Hollaz.) Thus bread nourishes, medicine cures, water quenches thirst, etc., only because of God's continuous influence upon His creatures (Dei continuus in creaturas influxus). It is for this reason that God is called the First Cause (causa prima) and the creature the second cause (causa secunda), though the action of God and that of the creature is simultaneous. This is the Scriptural doctrine of divine concurrence, which is as much opposed to deism as it is to pantheism.

With respect to the laws of nature, Scripture teaches that they are not detached from the divine will, but are simply God's will exerted in the being and action of the creatures in order that they may be preserved both in their existence and operation. Scripture acknowledges no immutable laws of nature apart from the divine will; for while they may be immutable to feeble man, they are not immutable to the omnipresent God, who by His almighty power governs all things according to His will, Ps. 115, 3; 135, 6.

4. DIVINE CONCURRENCE IN GOOD AND EVIL ACTIONS.

With respect to the divine concurrence in the actions of moral agencies (men, angels) a distinction must be made between good and evil acts. With regard to evil acts (sins) Scripture teaches a) that God in His perfect holiness is so unalterably opposed to every evil work that He absolutely forbids and condemns it (Decalog); b) that God frequently prevents evil acts from occurring, Gen. 20, 6; and c) that, whenever He permits them to happen, He so controls them that they must serve His wise and holy purposes, Gen. 50, 20; Rom. 8, 28. Nevertheless the question remains: "How does God cooperate in evil actions that actually do occur?" On the one hand, we cannot say that these acts are done without God, for this would deny His divine concurrence (atheism); on the other hand, however, we must not ascribe to God these acts in so far as they are evil (pantheism). In other words, the divine concurrence makes God neither the author of, nor an accomplice in, evil acts.

The difficulty is satisfactorily removed if we bear in mind the dividing-line which Scripture here suggests; for while it is true that God concurs in evil acts, He concurs in them only in so far as they are acts *(quoad materiale),* not in so far as they are evil *(quoad formale).* "God concurs in producing the 'effect,' but not the 'defect.'" The proof for the first *(quoad materiale)* is given in Acts 17, 25—28; for men live, move, and have their being in God, and receive life, breath, and all things from Him, not only when they do good, but also when they do evil. The second *(quoad formale)* is proved from Deut. 32, 4; Ps. 92, 15, etc.; for there it is stated that the "Lord is upright" and that "there is no unrighteousness in Him." God's work is perfect; for He is "a God of truth and without iniquity; just and right is He."

Of course, this does not explain the whole mystery in divine concurrence, but it shows us within what confines we must restrict our thoughts on this matter. Speculations that go beyond this either result in self-deception, or they deny the truths of Scripture (Acts 17, 28: God's providence; Deut. 32, 4: His righteousness). The doctrine that man alone is responsible for his evil deeds though God concurs in them must be strenuously maintained on grounds of both Scripture and conscience. The pantheistic error that God must be held accountable for human transgression is repudiated not only by Scripture, but also by man's own conscience (Rom. 2, 15: "their thoughts accusing").

Holy Scripture describes God's concurrence in evil actions also as permission (permissive providence). We therefore speak Scripturally when we say: "God permits evil, or suffers it to occur," Ps. 81, 12; Acts 14, 16; Rom. 1, 28, etc. As Hollaz rightly points out, such permission is a) not kind indulgence, as though it did not offend God when men commit sin; b) nor a mitigation of the Law, as though God granted men license to sin under certain circumstances; c) nor a weakness in God or a defect of knowledge or power on His part, as though He were ignorant of it or could not check it; d) nor indifference to sin, as though God were an unconcerned witness of it; but e) a negative act, inasmuch as God does not place insuperable difficulties in the way of the sinner, but allows him to rush into iniquity, Matt. 26, 23. "God indeed permits, but does not will that which He permits." (Quenstedt.) Frequently also God, in His most righteous judgment *(iustitia vindicativa),* punishes sin with sin, Rom. 1, 24—28. But even in these cases He neither wills the original evil act, nor has He pleasure in the superadded sin. God is never the cause or abetter of sin, Ps. 5, 4—6; Rom. 1, 18 f.

With respect to God's concurrence in good acts we must distinguish between acts that are done a) in His Kingdom of Power *(regnum potentiae)* and b) in His Kingdom of Grace *(regnum gratiae)*. The first are civilly good works *(iustitia civilis)* and the second spiritually good works *(iustitia spiritualis)*. The *iustitia civilis* God works in the unregenerate by His almighty government of all things *(regnum potentiae)* and rewards it with earthly and temporal blessings, Ex. 1, 20. 21. The *iustitia spiritualis* God works in the regenerate by the gracious operation of the Holy Ghost, who bestows not only the ability to do good *(potentia agendi),* but also works the good act itself *(ipsum agendi actum),* as Scripture clearly testifies, Phil. 2, 13; 2 Cor. 3, 5; Phil. 1, 29.

5. DIVINE PROVIDENCE AND FREE WILL (LIBERTAS A COACTIONE).

Although men live, move, and have their being in God, they remain free, or self-determining, beings, who are personally responsible to God for whatever they do *(libertas a coactione,* freedom from coercion). This truth is taught in Scripture, Acts 17, 30, and is supported by experience. (Rom. 1, 32: "Who, knowing the judgment of God, that they which commit such things are worthy of death.")

In this connection we may consider also the question: "Must things happen just as they do happen *(necessitas immutabilitatis),* or could they happen otherwise *(contingentia rerum)?* On the basis of Scripture we maintain both the *necessitas immutabilitatis* and the *contingentia rerum;* the first, from the viewpoint of divine providence; the second, from the viewpoint of human responsibility. Thus the betrayal, condemnation, and death of Christ had to occur since God by His gracious plan of salvation had decreed all this to happen from eternity, Acts 4, 27. 28; Matt. 26, 54. Yet neither Judas nor Pilate was coerced by God to perpetrate the crimes by which the Savior was delivered into death, Luke 22, 21—23; Matt. 26, 24; John 19, 12. For this reason our dogmaticians have said: *Ratione providentiae Dei, quae omnia regit, necessario omnia fieri recte dicuntur; respectu hominis libere et contingenter res fiunt et aguntur omnia in rebus humanis.* If the *necessitas* is denied, the alternative is atheism or epicureanism

("Things happen without God") ; if the *contingentia* is denied, the alternative is fatalism or Stoicism ("Man is coerced to sin").

In view of the fact that "with respect to man all things happen freely and contingently" *(respectu hominis libere et contingenter res fiunt),* man is bound, both in the realm of nature and of grace, to the means which God has appointed for his welfare. In bodily sickness he must apply medicine; for the sickness of his soul he must apply the means of grace (the Word and the Sacraments), through which God works and preserves faith, Rom. 10, 17. It is both foolish and sinful to try to ascertain divine providence *a priori,* by setting aside the divinely prescribed means; for in that case we arrogantly endeavor to explore God in His sovereign majesty (Luther: *in nuda maiestate*) and thus tempt Him, Matt. 4, 6. 7.

Similar to the truth just discussed is the question concerning the end of human life *(terminus vitae).* Also here we must maintain both the necessity and the contingency. For Scripture teaches, on the one hand, that the days of a man are so determined that he cannot pass the appointed bounds, Job 14, 5; this is said with respect to divine providence *(ratione providentiae Dei).* On the other hand, Scripture teaches that God often changes the natural limit of human life with respect both to the godly and the wicked. He prolongs the life of the godly either as a reward for their obedience, Ex. 20, 12; Prov. 3, 1. 2; 4, 10, or for the common good of His Church, 2 Cor. 1, 10. 11; Phil. 1, 23. 24; or He shortens their life to preserve them from distress and evil, Is. 57, 1. 2. Whenever God shortens the life of the wicked, this is to be regarded as a just punishment for their wickedness, Gen. 38, 7. 10. All this, however, is said *respectu hominis,* or from the viewpoint of contingency.

From the viewpoint of contingency *(respectu hominis)* we must therefore say that the limit of human life is not absolutely and immutably decreed, Is. 38, 5. For the sake of clearness our dogmaticians have also said that men die either by the dispensing or by the permissive providence of God; that is to say, if men use the prescribed means (Acts 27, 33 ff.: food; 1 Tim. 5, 23: medicine; Eph. 6, 2. 3: piety; 2 Kings 20, 1—6: prayer; Acts 9, 25: avoidance of danger, etc.), they will by the grace of God attain to that limit of life which His dispensing providence has fixed; but if they reject the prescribed means, transgress His divine laws, and live wickedly, their life will be shortened by His permissive providence, 2 Sam. 18, 14; 17, 23; Gen. 9, 6; Ex. 21, 12, etc. All Scripture-passages that describe the *terminus vitae*

in terms of contingency must be regarded as a gracious condescension on the part of God to our feeble understanding in order
that we may use for our admonition or consolation the divine
truths which He has graciously revealed for our temporal and
eternal good. But even in cases where life is shortened or length-
ened, God must not be regarded as mutable in His essence or
decrees, since what appears to us as either shortening or length-
ening of life has been decreed by Him from eternity. In other
words, man dies exactly when God has willed that he should die,
Luke 12, 20; 2, 26; Phil. 1, 23. 24; Judg. 6, 23; Ps. 90, 3—10.
Beyond this our thoughts dare not go since Scripture itself sets
this limit.

THE DOCTRINE OF THE ANGELS.
(De Angelis.)

---

1. THE EXISTENCE OF ANGELS.

The doctrine of the holy angels must be drawn not from reason, according to which their existence is at best only probable, but alone from Scripture, which from Genesis to Revelation teaches their existence, Gen. 3, 24; 32, 1. 2; Ps. 104, 4; Rev. 12, 7. In other words, also of this doctrine Scripture is the only *principium cognoscendi.* Modern rationalistic theology rejects the doctrine of the angels ("There is no personal devil. Even the existence of good angels cannot be proved"), just because it has discarded Scripture as the only source of faith.

However, while Holy Scripture clearly teaches the existence of angels, it does not state definitely the time of their creation, though this was within the hexaemeron. Certainly the angels were not created before the world, since prior to the creation no creature existed, John 1, 1—3; Col. 1, 16. Nor were they created after the sixth day of creation, since God on that day ceased to create, Gen. 2, 2. 3. Scripture informs us definitely that on the sixth day "the heavens and the earth were finished and all the host of them," Gen. 2, 1, which certainly includes the angels.

2. THE NAME "ANGEL."

The term *angel* (מַלְאָךְ, ἄγγελος), by which Holy Scripture designates this class of creatures, does not describe their essence, but their office *(nomen officii)* and signifies "one sent," or a messenger. The nature of the angels is described by the term *spirit* (πνεῦμα). That the name *angel* is a designation of office is clear from the fact that Scripture ascribes it a) to ministers of the divine Word, Mal. 2, 7; Matt. 11, 10, and b) to the Son of God, the "uncreated Angel," as the supreme and unique Messenger of God, Mal. 3, 1; John 3, 17. 34; Is. 63, 9; Gen. 48, 16, etc. The important question, "When does the Scriptural expression *Angel of the Lord* (מַלְאַךְ יְהֹוָה) denote the *Angelus increatus,* or Christ?" our dogmaticians answer as follows: "Whenever the name Jehovah or divine works and worship are ascribed to the Angel in Scripture, then this Angel must be understood to be the Son of God."

3. THE NATURE OF THE ANGELS.

The angels are spirits (*πνεύματα*), that is, spiritual beings, who are without any bodily form whatsoever. To ascribe to them even an ethereal corporeity, as has been done in ancient and modern times, is opposed to Luke 24, 39 and Eph. 6, 12, where corporealness is absolutely denied to spirits. The bodies in which angels from time to time appeared to men, Gen. 18, 2; 19, 1, were only assumed *(unio accidentalis)*. The consumption of food by angels, Gen. 18, 8; 19, 3, must be regarded neither as a natural eating nor as a mere form, but as an act which is as incomprehensible to us as is their temporary assumption of an accidental body. *"Homines edunt et bibunt ob egestatem, angeli autem instar flammae consumunt cibum ob potentiam,"* says J. A. Osiander. The temporary consumption of food like the temporary assumption of a body served to convince the persons to whom they appeared of their true presence. While the angels are *πνεύματα,* Heb. 1, 14, and God is *πνεῦμα,* John 4, 24, yet the difference between the angels and God is as vast as is that between the finite creature and the infinite Creator. In contradistinction to the human soul, which is an incomplete spirit *(spiritus incompletus),* because it has been created as an essential part of man in union with the body, the angels are complete spirits *(spiritus completi),* because they exist properly as spirits In contradistinction to God, the infinite Creator, the angels are finite creatures. Like men in this respect they are real persons (*ὑποστάσεις*), endowed with intelligence and will, Eph. 3, 10; Heb 1, 14. Intelligence and will may be predicated also of the fallen angels, Gen. 3; Matt. 4, though their mind is perverse and their will depraved. According to Scripture the angels, though being immaterial beings, can nevertheless react upon the bodies of men, Gen. 19, 16; Matt. 4, 5, much in the same manner as the human soul reacts upon the body. Since the angels are intelligent beings, they are capable of becoming acquainted both with one another and with men, Luke 1, 13. 19. Yet they know only as creatures, not as God, so that omniscience and prescience must be denied to them. Whatever knowledge they have they possess a) by virtue of their peculiar nature (2 Sam. 14, 20: natural knowledge); b) by divine revelation (1 Pet. 1, 12; Luke 2, 9—12: revealed knowledge); c) by the beatific vision which they enjoy (Matt. 18, 10: beatific knowledge).

Since the angels are spiritual beings, we ascribe to them the

following attributes: a) indivisibility, which is due to their in-
corporeity, or immateriality; b) invisibility, which is a consequence of their spirituality; c) immutability, inasmuch as they
are not subject to physical changes: they do not beget, nor are
they begotten, Matt. 22, 30; they are neither increased nor diminished; they neither grow old, nor do they decay; and yet they are
not absolutely immutable, as God is, but only relatively, or in
relation to men; d) immortality, inasmuch as they do not die,
though God could annihilate them if He so willed; e) endless
duration, inasmuch as they have a beginning, but not an end, Matt.
18, 10; Jude 6; f) illocality, because as incorporeal beings they
occupy no space, but are present at a certain place *definitely (in ubi
definitivo),* though not omnipresently like God, who is everywhere
present *repletively;* g) agility or velocity, inasmuch as they are
able to change the "where" of their presence with extreme celerity,
though without local motion, such as must be predicated of material bodies.

As intelligent beings the angels moreover possess freedom of
will and, in view of the service for which they are designed, great
power. The will of angels is free with respect both to a) immanent acts, such as choosing or rejecting, Jude 6, and b) external
acts, such as moving about, speaking, praising God, etc., Luke 2,
9—15. Though the evil angels, being declared enemies of God,
cannot but oppose Him, yet they do so of their own free will,
John 8, 44. The power of the angels is very great, Ps. 103, 20;
2 Thess. 1, 7; 2 Kings 19, 35; yet it is a finite power, completely
under the control of God, Job 1, 12. While their power is super-
human, Ps. 91, 11. 12, or greater than that of man, Luke 11, 21. 22,
they are not omnipotent, but subject to God, who rules over them,
Dan. 7, 10. While, strictly speaking, only God performs miracles
(Ps. 72, 18), nevertheless Holy Scripture teaches that the good
angels (2 Kings 19, 35) and the prophets (2 Kings 6, 5. 6) and
apostles (Acts 3, 6—12) performed miracles in His name and
by His divine power (Ex. 15, 23—25). Whenever the devil
performs deeds that to men seem to be miracles *(mirabilia seu
mira),* these are in reality "lying wonders" and "strong delusions,"
with which God permits him to deceive such as "believe not the
truth, but have pleasure in unrighteousness," 2 Thess. 2, 9—12.

The claim that angels once mingled with men by marriage,
Gen. 6, 2, is as foolish as it is anti-Scriptural, Matt. 22, 30.

4. THE NUMBER AND RANKS OF ANGELS.

According to Holy Scripture the number of angels is very large (Dan. 7, 10: "thousand thousands and ten thousand times ten thousand"; Luke 2, 13: "a multitude of the heavenly host"; Ps. 68, 17: "twenty thousand, even thousands of angels"). All these expressions are symbolical numbers, standing for uncounted thousands. How great is the goodness of God, who created so many holy ministers for the benefit of man!

That there are ranks, or orders, among the angels is clear from the special names given them in Scripture (Gen. 3, 24: cherubim; Is. 6, 2: seraphim; Col. 1, 16: thrones, dominions, principalities, powers; 1 Thess. 4, 16: archangel). Also among the evil angels there are greater and lesser spirits (Matt. 25, 41: "the devil and his angels"; Luke 11, 15. 18. 19: "Beelzebub, the chief of the devils"). However, we can neither determine the number of the angels, nor can we describe the ranks, or orders, among them since Holy Scripture does not give us adequate information on this subject, nor does it always enumerate the angelic ranks in the same order (cp. Col. 1, 16 with Eph. 1, 21), so that we cannot tell which is the higher and which the lower. Gregory Nazianzen: *"Ordo angelorum notus est ei, qui ipsos ordinavit."* Baier aptly remarks that, while the angels differ from one another with respect to rank, they do not differ from one another with respect to kind and nature *(specie et essentia)*. In the appointment of ranks, or orders, among the angels we witness the wisdom of God, who is not "the author of confusion," 1 Cor. 14, 33.

5. GOOD AND EVIL ANGELS.

As to their first estate *(status originalis)* all angels were originally created equally righteous, good, and holy; for they were to glorify God and render Him holy service *(status gratiae)*. That means that in the beginning all angels were positively good, not morally indifferent, nor tainted by a proclivity to evil. This is clear from the divine verdict "very good," Gen. 1, 31. That there are now two classes of angels, the good and the evil, is due to the fact that some angels did not remain in the original state, but of their own accord fell away from God into sin. From the state of grace *(status gratiae)* they thus passed into the state of misery *(status miseriae)*.

The good angels are those who persevered in the goodness, righteousness, and holiness in which they were first created. They have been confirmed by God in that which is good *(in bono con-firmati)* as a gracious reward for their obedience, so that they can no longer lose their goodness and become evil *(non posse peccare)*. Thus the good angels reached the goal for which they were orig-inally created; for they forever behold God in holy service, having passed from the state of grace into the state of glory *(status gloriae)*. This truth is taught in Matt. 18, 10; 6, 10; 1 Tim. 5, 21; Luke 20, 36; Gal. 1, 8.

Since Scripture identifies the good angels with the "elect angels" (1 Tim. 5, 21), they persevered in their concreated right-eousness and holiness in accord with God's eternal election. How-ever, Scripture nowhere teaches that the evil angels fell into sin because from eternity they were predetermined to damnation; on the contrary, the evil angels left their own habitation, Jude 6, or sinned, of their own accord.

By evil angels we, then, mean those angels who did not per-severe in their concreated wisdom and righteousness, but of their own free will turned away from God, became perpetual enemies of God and man, and have been divinely doomed to be plagued with eternal torments *(in malo confirmati)*. The eternal punishment of the evil angels is taught in Matt. 25, 41; Rev. 20, 10; 2 Pet. 2, 4; Jude 6. By what special motive the disobedience of the evil angels was prompted Scripture does not teach with certainty; but it is probable *(ratio probabilis)* that it was their impious pride which moved them to apostatize from God. The time when the evil angels first sinned cannot be determined with certainty; but their rebellion occurred before the fall of man, since man's fall into sin was instigated by the devil, Gen. 3, 1—14; John 8, 44. That the evil angels can never be restored to holiness and happiness is a fact known also to them, Matt. 8, 29 and should not be gainsaid by men (Universalism), since Scripture emphatically describes the fire which has been prepared for the devil and his angels as an everlasting fire, Matt. 25, 41. While the good angels were con-firmed in bliss when they entered into the state of glory, Matt. 18, 10; 25, 31, the evil angels, when entering into the state of misery, became hardened in evil, so that they incessantly think perversely of God and divine things. Hollaz: "The evil angels know God, but they dreadfully shudder at the divine knowledge," Jas. 2, 19.

To the question "Why may not the wicked angels be restored to favor?" Gerhard replies: "It is better to proclaim the wonderful philanthropy and mercy of the Son of God towards the fallen race of man . . . than to scrutinize beyond due limits the causes of that most just judgment by which God delivered the angels who had fallen away from Him to be cast in chains of darkness into hell, reserved for judgment." (*Doctr. Theol.*, p. 215.)

6. THE HOLY SERVICE OF THE GOOD ANGELS.

The good angels are so confirmed in holiness that they always behold God and perpetually enjoy His goodness, Matt. 18, 10. With this beatific vision there is joined indissolubly the purest love of God; for in the state of glory they neither can sin (impeccability) nor desire to sin (2 Cor. 11, 14: "an angel of light"). The objection that the good angels in the state of glory are no longer morally free since they are impeccable is based upon a false conception of moral freedom. The angels are free moral agencies, and yet their will is directed only to that which is holy (Rev. 14, 10: "in the presence of the holy angels"). In this respect the saints in heaven will be equal to the holy angels, Luke 20, 36. With regard to the election of the angels (1 Tim. 5, 21), we must hold on the basis of Scripture: a) that the angels were not elected in view of Christ's redemption since they never became sinners, Heb. 2, 16; b) that the evil angels were not rejected by an absolute eternal decree (papists, Calvinists), but were reserved unto eternal judgment because of their apostasy, 2 Pet. 2, 4.

In accord with their beatific vision and perfect love of God the good angels render perpetual service to God, Is. 6, 3; Luke 2, 13, and to His saints on earth, Ps. 104, 4; 103, 20. 21; Heb. 1, 14. So far as God is concerned, He is not in *need* of the service of the holy angels since He does not require it for His own bliss *(non ex quadam Dei indigentia)*; however, He has willed it *(ex voluntate Dei libera)*. In particular, the holy angels serve children, Matt. 18, 10; but also all believers in their work and calling, Ps. 91, 11. 12, and at their death, Luke 16, 22. The question whether each believer and especially each Christian child has a special guardian angel, Scripture does not answer with sufficient clearness, Matt. 18, 10; Acts 12, 15.

While the holy angels, according to Scripture, also serve the political estate, Dan. 10, 13; Is. 37, 36, and the domestic estate, Ps. 34, 7; Matt. 18, 10, the object of their special ministry is the Christian Church; for they a) reverence and promote the message of salvation, Luke 2, 13; 1 Pet. 1, 12; Eph. 3, 10; b) rejoice at the repentance of sinners, Luke 15, 10; c) minister God's Word to men, Deut. 33, 2; Gal. 3, 19; Luke 2, 10—12; d) protect the saints of God, Jude 9; e) are present at public worship, 1 Cor. 11, 10; 1 Tim. 5, 21f.; f) will announce the final Judgment, Matt. 25, 31; 1 Thess. 4, 16; g) and assist in its execution, Matt. 24, 31; 13, 41; 25, 31; 13, 42.50; Mark 13, 27.

On account of this holy service we should highly esteem God's blessed angels (modern rationalistic theology regards the doctrine of the angels as superfluous), rejoice in their ministry, and think of them with pious awe, 1 Tim. 5, 21, though we should not honor them by divine worship *(cultus religiosus)*, since they are only creatures, to whom no worship is due, Rev. 22, 8. 9. Baier writes thus: "On account of these perfections which we discover the angels to possess and because they favor and assist us very greatly, it is also becoming that we praise and love them and take heed lest we offend them by evil deeds. But it is not becoming to us to direct our prayers to the angels. For that is impious and idolatrous." *(Doctr. Theol.,* p. 213.)

7. THE EVIL WORK AND ETERNAL PUNISHMENT OF THE EVIL ANGELS.

The wicked angels are evil not because they were so created, but because they willingly fell away from God *(non ortu, sed lapsu)*. We are not in a position to say why God did not provide a Redeemer for the fallen angels as He did for fallen man; but Quenstedt suggests as a probable reason *(probabilis ratio)* that the devils sinned without any temptation (Jude 6), while Eve was deceived by Satan (Gen. 3, 1—7) and Adam was tempted by his wife. But in no case must this explanation be used to limit the free compassion of the gracious God upon men. The fall of the evil angels affected their intelligence *(vis intelligendi, intellectus)*. Scripture describes them, on the one hand, as exceedingly cunning, Gen. 3, 1ff.; 2 Cor. 11, 3; Eph. 6, 11, on the other hand, however, as indescribably stupid, because they defeat their own purposes. Thus Christ's death, which Satan promoted, Luke 22, 53, was his own undoing, John 12, 31.

The evil angels constantly exhibit and exert their enmity toward God, Rev. 12, 7, and attempt the temporal and eternal ruin of man, Gen. 3, 1ff.; 1 Pet. 5, 8. In their endeavor to injure man they harm him a) in his body, Luke 13, 11. 16; b) in his earthly possessions, Job 1, 12 ff.; Matt. 8, 31. 32; c) in his soul, John

13, 27; Acts 5, 3; Eph. 2, 2. 3. Unbelief *(status incredulitatis)*, with its dreadful punishment of eternal damnation, Mark 16, 16, is the result of Satan's pernicious work in men, Eph. 2, 1. 2; 2 Cor. 4, 4; Matt. 13, 25. All who refuse to believe the Gospel do as Satan prompts them; for he holds them in his power, Acts 26, 18; Col. 1, 13. The very denial of the personal existence of a devil is the result of the devil's operation in the human heart, 2 Cor. 11, 14.

On the basis of Holy Scripture we distinguish between spiritual obsession *(obsessio spiritualis)* and physical obsession *(obsessio corporalis)*. The first applies in a wider sense to all unbelievers, who are held captive by Satan in spiritual darkness, Col. 1, 13, and in a narrower sense to those wicked persons whose minds are possessed, filled, and actuated by Satan in an intensified way (Judas, the Pharisees). Passages dealing with spiritual obsession in this sense are: Luke 22, 3; John 13, 2; Acts 5, 3; 2 Thess. 2, 9—11; 2 Cor. 4, 4. Spiritual obsession does not remove human responsibility, Matt. 25, 41, since the person so obsessed sins of his own free will, John 8, 43—45. Bodily obsession occurs when the devil immediately and locally inhabits and governs the body, controlling it according to his will, Mark 5, 1—19; Luke 8, 26—39. Bodily obsession is an affliction which may befall even true, believing Christians, as the passages just quoted show. In all cases of bodily obsession a person has no intellectual, emotional, and volitional functions of his own, but as long as the obsession endures, Satan, who is personally ($\varkappa \alpha \tau' \ o \dot{v} \sigma \acute{\iota} \alpha \nu$) present in him, acts in and through him, so that in all cases of bodily obsession human responsibility ceases. (Cp. cases in which persons who are bodily obsessed deplore in moments of recovery the blasphemies which they uttered.)

The fury of the evil angels is directed especially against the Church of Christ; for they a) constantly seek to destroy it by their onslaughts in general, Matt. 16, 18; b) try to prevent hearers from accepting the Word of God, Luke 8, 12; c) spread false doctrine, Matt. 13, 25; 1 Tim. 4, 1ff.; and d) incite persecutions against the kingdom of Christ, Rev. 12, 7. In particular, Satan has wrought unspeakable harm in the Church by inflicting upon it the tyranny and doctrinal perversions of Antichrist, 2 Thess. 2. For the purpose of ruining the Church, the devil also troubles the political estate (1 Chron. 21, 1; 1 Kings 22, 21. 22) and the domestic estate (1 Tim. 4, 1—3; 1 Cor. 7, 5; Job 1, 11—19). Scripture teaches also that God employs the evil angels to punish the wicked for their rejection of truth (2 Thess. 2, 11. 12) and to try the faithful (Job 1, 7 ff.; 2 Cor. 12, 7).

The punishment of the evil angels is eternal torment in hell, Matt. 25, 41. The question whether the fire of hell is material (real fire) or immaterial (torment) we may leave undecided; for, on the one hand, Scripture speaks of the fire of hell in terms of real fire, Mark 9, 43; Rev. 14, 10. 11; 21, 8; on the other, it teaches that all material things in their present form shall cease with Judgment Day, 2 Pet. 3, 10—12. In either case the torment will be unspeakably great, Luke 16, 24; Matt. 25, 46; 2 Thess. 1, 9; Jude 6. 7. All who deny that the damnation of the devil and his angels is everlasting must also deny the *eternal* salvation of the believers, Matt. 25, 46, since the term (αἰώνιος) is used to describe the endless duration of both heaven and hell.

In conclusion, let us remember that all things that Holy Scripture reveals concerning the fall, the works, and the punishment of the evil angels are written for our warning in order that we may escape the just judgment of God by believing in Him who destroyed the works of the devil, 1 John 3, 8.

THE DOCTRINE OF MAN.
(De Anthropologia.)

The doctrine of man falls into two divisions: a) the state of integrity *(status integritatis)* and b) the state of corruption *(status corruptionis).*

A. Man Before the Fall.
(De Statu Hominis ante Lapsum.)

1. MAN CREATED IN THE IMAGE OF GOD.

The state of integrity is the original condition of man. Man was created after the image of God, in wisdom, holiness, and righteousness. The state of integrity is proved in Scripture a) by God's general verdict "very good," Gen. 1, 31, and b) by the special statement that God made man in His image, Gen. 1, 26. 27. For all practical purposes the designations image, צֶלֶם, and likeness, דְּמוּת, may be treated as synonyms. Luther: *"ein Bild, das uns gleich sei";* Baier: *"imago simillima."*

In his original state man bore a resemblance to God because He Himself was the pattern, or archetype, after which man was made. According to Scripture, Adam was created after the likeness of the Triune God, Gen. 1, 26, and not after that of Christ alone (the error of Osiander).

2. DEFINITION OF "IMAGE OF GOD."

The divine image consisted not simply in man's original endowment with intelligence and will, so that he, in contradistinction to all animals, was a rational being, but above all in the right disposition of his intellect and will, so that by means of his undepraved intellect he knew God and divine things and by means of his uncorrupt will desired only that which God wills. Also his appetition *(appetitus sensitivus)* was in complete accord with the divine norm of holiness, so that in the state of integrity man was entirely upright and uncorrupt in all his endowments, powers, and attributes. Calov writes (IV, 389): "It is called a state of integrity because man in it was upright and uncorrupt (Eccl. 7, 29) in intellect, will, the corporeal affections, and endowments and in all things was perfect. It is also called the state of innocence because man was innocent and holy, free from sin and pollution." *(Doctr. Theol.,* p. 220.) Man's state of integrity is proved also by the fact that Adam and Eve were in perfect agreement with God's commandments, Gen. 2, 19 ff.; 3, 2. 3. In the New Testament the image of God is described in Col. 3, 10 ("knowledge") and Eph. 4, 24 ("righteousness and true holiness").

The evolutionistic view, according to which man was originally a brute, without the faculty of speech and without moral endowments, is therefore anti-Scriptural. According to Scripture, man was not created as a beast, but as the lord of all the other creatures of God, Gen. 1, 26—31; 2, 16—23. In addition to perfect moral endowments man was blessed also with great intellectual endowments, so that he possessed an undimmed and blissful knowledge of God, as also an intuitive knowledge of God's creatures (science), such as no scientist after the Fall has ever attained, Gen. 2, 19—20. 23. 24. Luther very aptly comments that Adam was an *insignis philosophus*.

As we reject the evolutionistic delusion, so also the papistical error that man was originally in a state of moral indifference *(in statu purorum naturalium)*, in which he was neither positively good nor positively evil, but morally "neutral," or indifferent. In opposition to this erroneous opinion, Scripture teaches that originally man's will was in perfect conformity with the holy will of God *(sanctae Dei voluntati conformis et amore et fiducia Dei praeditus)*. Not merely was he inclined toward all that is good and God-pleasing, but he himself was positively good and holy. The spiritual and moral excellences of man in his state of integrity are summed up in the expression *original, concreate righteousness (iustitia originalis concreata)*, which describes his absolute conformity with divine holiness and the absolute purity of his desires and appetites.

3. THE RELATION OF THE DIVINE IMAGE TO THE NATURE OF MAN.

The original wisdom, righteousness, and holiness of man in his first estate were not a "supernatural" gift of God, superadded to him to render his original estate complete and perfect (papists: *donum supernaturale, donum superadditum*), but a concreate gift *(donum concreatum, iustitia originalis, iustitia concreata)*, since he received the image of God at the very moment of his creation, Gen. 1, 26. 31. For this reason man's nature after the Fall is no longer in an uncorrupt state *(natura integra, in puris naturalibus)* as the papists teach, but in a state of corruption *(natura corrupta,*

natura sauciata). Though the image of God does not constitute
the nature of man, since even after the Fall he is still a true man,
yet the divine image belonged to the nature of the uncorrupt man
or to the uncorrupt human nature. It is certainly a proof of total
corruption that man, though he was created for the glory of God
and still knows of His existence and rule (Rom. 1, 19), should
neither love nor adore the Creator, but worship the creature.
Therefore we declare on the basis of Scripture that man through
the Fall has entirely lost the image of God in its proper sense,
that is, his concreate wisdom, righteousness, and holiness, so that
his intellect now is veiled in spiritual darkness, 1 Cor. 2, 14, and
his will is opposed to God, Rom. 8, 7.

In view of this fact the question arises, How are we to understand such passages as Gen. 9, 6 and Jas. 3, 9? Luther and other
dogmaticians (Philippi, Hofmann) explain them as describing
man as he was originally and as he should again become through
faith in Christ Jesus (restoration of the divine image through
regeneration). Melanchthon, Baier, Quenstedt, and others regard
them as teaching a divine image in a wider sense, namely, inasmuch as man, even after the Fall, is still an intelligent, self-
determining rational being, who even now, though feebly, rules
over the creatures of God. But also those theologians who speak
of an image of God in the wider sense admit that the divine image
in its proper sense was lost through the Fall, Col. 3, 10; Eph.
4, 24. For the sake of clearness and accuracy it is preferable to
adopt Luther's explanation of the passages quoted. The unregenerate are so far from possessing the divine image that they are said
to have no hope and to be without God in the world, Eph. 2, 12,
as also, that what they sacrifice they sacrifice to the devils and
not to God, 1 Cor. 10, 20.

The seat of the divine image was not the body, but the soul
of man; for the knowledge of God together with holiness and
righteousness inheres properly in the soul. Nevertheless also the
body shared in the divine image, since it is the organ of the soul.
For this reason bodily immortality *(immortalitas corporis)* was an
immediate result of man's possession of the divine image. Death
entered into the world through the Fall, Gen. 2, 17; Rom. 5, 12;
6, 23. The claim that death is caused by the matter of which the
body consists must be regarded as a pagan view. Since man originally was without sin, he was free also from painful and destructive sufferings, Gen. 3, 16 ff. The original condition of man was

therefore one of supreme happiness; for a) his soul was wise and holy; b) his body was free from suffering and death; c) his condition of life was most blessed; and d) his condition of habitation was most pleasant, since God placed him into a garden of pleasure, called Paradise, to dwell there and enjoy His goodness forever, Gen. 2, 8—15 (גַּן־בְּעֵדֶן; פַּרְדֵּס; παράδεισος).

The intimate communion and blissful association of uncorrupt man with the holy God, Scripture itself cites as a proof of the *status integritatis,* Gen. 2, 19 ff.; so also the fact that our first parents were naked, yet not ashamed, Gen. 2, 25. Cf. Luther, St. L., I, 170.)

4. IMMEDIATE RESULTS OF THE DIVINE IMAGE.

According to Scripture the immediate results of the divine image in man were a) immortality, b) dominion.

That Adam and Eve were created immortal is clear from Gen. 2, 17; Rom. 5, 12; 6, 23. Had they not sinned, they never would have died. Death was threatened them if they would become disobedient to their Creator. Whether they would have dwelled endlessly in Paradise, or whether God would have received them into heaven in His own time Scripture does not say. With respect to immortality we rightly distinguish between absolute and relative, or conditional, immortality. The former denotes absolute freedom from death and its destructive power, in which sense God, the angels, the human souls, and the bodies of the saints in heaven and of the damned in hell are immortal. The latter denotes freedom from the natural tendency to die, yet so that death could happen under a certain eventuality, in which sense man in the state of integrity was immortal. It is one thing *not to be able to die,* another *to be able not to die,* and still another *not to be able not to die.* The first is said of the saints in heaven; the second, of Adam and Eve in their state of integrity; the third of all sinners after the Fall (Quenstedt).

Man's dominion over the creatures, according to Scripture, was an immediate result of his possession of the divine image *(iustitia originalis concreata).* The dominion of man must be regarded as real sovereignty, so that all the other creatures willingly rendered him service. After the Fall man possesses only a faint vestige of this absolute dominion *(species dominii, nudus titulus dominii),* since now he must apply force and cunning to control the creatures over which he endeavors to rule. The rebellion of the creatures against man is the direct consequence of his own rebellion against God, or of the loss of his concreated wisdom, holiness, and righteousness, and should continually remind him of the heinousness of sin and of the dreadfulness of its effects, Ps. 39, 4—6.

5. THE DIVINE IMAGE AND WOMAN.

Not only Adam, but also Eve possessed the divine image. This is clear a) from Gen. 1, 27; b) from Col. 3, 10; Eph. 4, 24, compared with Gal. 3, 28; for with regard to the renewal after the image of God there is no difference between male and female; and c) from Gen. 1, 28, where dominion is ascribed to the woman as well as to the man. Nevertheless the woman in her relation to the man occupied a position of subjection even before the Fall; for not only was she taken from man, but she was also created as his helpmeet, Gen. 2, 18—22; 1 Cor. 11, 7—9; 1 Tim. 2, 11—13.

This divine order must not be subverted; for it is the will of God that the woman should not usurp authority over the man by ruling over him. But, on the other hand, the woman should not be tyrannized or made a slave; for though she was not taken from the head of Adam to govern him, yet neither was she taken from his feet to be trodden under by him. Luther says: "Woman should be regarded with reverence; for she is God's handiwork. She was created that she might be a helpmeet for her husband, bring up children, and rear them in faith and piety." Both the man and the woman serve best in that relation or sphere in which God has created each, Eph. 5, 21—33; Titus 2, 3—5; 1 Cor. 7, 20, whereas the abrogation of the divine order will result in confusion and injury for human society, Prov. 1, 24—33. (Cp. Luther, St. L., V, 1517; II, 540; II, 687; XVI, 2280.)

6. THE ULTIMATE END OF THE IMAGE OF GOD IN MAN.

In His infinite grace, God bestowed His divine image upon man in order a) that he might know and serve Him and experience perfect enjoyment in communion with Him, and b) that he might be His representative ruler upon earth, Gen. 1, 27. 28. As after the Fall the redemption of man was motivated by divine love, John 3, 16, so also the creation of man in God's image before the Fall, Ps. 104, 23. 24; 136, 1—9. Although man in the state of integrity intimately knew God, he did not know the eternal decree of redemption; for this was especially revealed to him after the Fall, Gen. 3, 15. Hence our first parents knew God as gracious in Himself, but not as gracious on account of Christ's vicarious atonement. After the Fall and the promulgation of the protevangelium the divine object of man's knowledge and adoration has therefore become different; for now he trusts and adores God as gracious only through the priceless redemption of the Savior, Luke 1, 77. The Biblical concept of salvation (σωτηρία, salus) cannot be applied to man's state of integrity, since it presupposes both sin and the redemption from sin, Luke 19, 10.

B. The State of Corruption.
(De Statu Peccati.)

Through the Fall *(peccatum originans)* man has lost his concreate righteousness and holiness *(iustitia originalis concreata),* so that he is now in a state of corruption *(in statu corruptionis).* This state is defined by Quenstedt as follows (II, 48): "The state of corruption is that condition into which man voluntarily precipitated himself by his own departure from the chief Good, thus becoming both wicked and miserable." *(Doctr. Theol.,* p. 231.) The fall of man was therefore neither his exaltation (Gnosticism), nor the most fortunate event in human history (Schiller), nor a critical stage in his evolutionistic development (modern evolutionism), nor a necessary step in his moral and intellectual progress (pantheism). The fall of man was apostasy from God, Gen. 3, 14—19, and therefore evil both in its nature and in its effects, Gen. 3, 22—24; Rom. 5, 12. Hence it is as a sinner *(homo peccator)* that fallen man is the subject of sacred theology *(subiectum operationis theologiae),* whose purpose it is to restore in him the image of God through faith in Christ Jesus, 2 Cor. 3, 5. 6. 18. For this reason the doctrine of sin constitutes an essential part in Christian theology, Rom. 1, 18—32; 2, 1—12. — Commonly the doctrine of sin is treated under three heads: a) Sin in General *(De peccato in genere);* b) Original Sin *(De peccato originali);* c) Actual Sins *(De peccatis actualibus).*

A. OF SIN IN GENERAL.
(De Peccato in Genere.)

1. DEFINITION OF SIN.

According to Scripture, man should be in complete conformity with the divine will *(conformitas cum voluntate Dei),* as this is revealed in the divine Law (νόμος). Every departure from the norm of the divine Law is sin (ἀνομία), no matter whether it consists in a state or condition *(status, habitus)* or in actual deeds *(actiones internae et externae)*. Considered etymologically, sin is, in the first place, a negative concept (*ἀνομία*), and as such it denotes man's lack of conformity with the divine Law *(carentia conformitatis cum lege)*. So Scripture defines sin (1 John 3, 4: "Sin is lawlessness," *ἀνομία*). But sin is also a positive concept, and as such it denotes opposition to, or transgression of, the Law, so that positively sin is a violation of the Law. So, too, Scripture defines sin (1 John 3, 4: "He does lawlessness, *τὴν ἀνομίαν ποιεῖ;* Matt. 7, 23: "Ye that work lawlessness," *ἐργαζόμενοι τὴν ἀνομίαν*). The reason for this is obvious. Man, destitute of righteousness, is at the same time in constant, active rebellion against the divine Law. In other words, after the Fall man wilfully refuses to recognize the obligation he has toward God (Rom. 1, 18. 32) and constantly breaks the divine Law, since his carnal mind is enmity against God, Rom. 8, 7. On the basis of Holy Scripture we therefore describe sin, a) negatively, as a lack of righteousness or of conformity with the divine will *(carentia conformitatis cum lege);* b) positively, as actual opposition to the divine will *(carnalis concupiscentia sive inclinatio ad malum)*.

When defining sin, we must beware of the error of the papists and rationalists, who condemn as sinful only those evil acts which are done consciously and deliberately. Against this pernicious error the *Apology* testifies: "But in the schools they [the papists] transferred hither from philosophy notions entirely different, that because of passions we are neither good nor evil, we are neither deserving of praise nor blame. Likewise, that nothing is sin unless it be voluntary (inner desires and thoughts are not sins if I do not altogether consent thereto). These notions were expressed among philosophers with respect to civil righteousness and not with respect to God's judgment." (Art. II (I), § 43.) According to Scripture both the evil deeds, 2 Sam. 12, 13, and the evil thoughts and desires, Jas. 1, 15; Rom. 7, 17; Matt. 5, 28, are sins, even if they are done unknowingly and without deliberation, Rom. 7, 19; 1 Tim. 1, 13. Indeed, according to Scripture even the inherited corruption, which yet cleaves to the Christian and which he earnestly deplores, is sin in an absolute sense, Eph. 2, 3; John 3, 5. 6; Rom. 7, 19. 24.

2. THE DIVINE LAW AND SIN.

Since sin is "lawlessness" (*ἀνομία*), it is necessary to know what law Scripture means when it describes sin as a "transgression of the Law." If the doctrine of the divine Law is perverted by

man's adding to or subtracting from it, then also the doctrine of
sin must needs be perverted. It is therefore necessary that we
define that Law the transgression of which makes a thought or
deed sinful. The *Formula of Concord* describes the Law in the
sense in which it is here used as a "divine doctrine in which the
righteous, immutable will of God is revealed, what is to be the
quality of man in his nature, thoughts, words, and works in order
that he may be pleasing and acceptable to God." (Thor. Decl.,
Art. V, 17.) This definition is Scriptural; for only God can decree
laws for men, since this is His divine prerogative, Jas. 4, 12. Laws
enacted by men are binding only if God Himself has given men
authority to make them and so has given the human laws divine
sanction. This is the case with all laws of civil government and
with all parental commandments, Rom. 13, 1; Col. 3, 20, provided
they do not contradict the divine Law, Acts 5, 29. But this is not
the case with the so-called "laws of the Church," since God has
expressly withheld from the Church legislative authority, Matt.
23, 10. Hence in the Church only those laws are to be acknowledged as binding which have been enacted by God Himself.

In all matters where no special divine laws obtain, decisions
should be reached by Christians through mutual agreement on
the basis of Christian love, 1 Cor. 16, 14. Of the Pope, Luther
rightly says that he has filled the whole world with a satanic obedience, since he has taught men to obey, not the Law of God, but
his own pernicious laws (St. L., I, 765). While it is true that only
God's immutable will constitutes the divine Law which binds all
men, it is equally true that the whole divine Law, with all its
demands and prohibitions, must be taught by the Church. For
as little as the Church has authority to make laws of its own, just
so little has it authority to discard any laws which God has made,
Matt. 5, 17—19; Mark 7, 6—13.

Since the Old Testament ceremonial laws have been abolished
through the coming of Christ, Gal. 4, 9—11; 5, 1—4, they are no
longer in force in the New Testament, Col. 2, 16, so that the immutable will of God which now obligates all men must be identified
with the Moral Law, Matt. 22, 37—40; 1 Tim. 1, 5. For this
reason we define sin in general as a deviation from the divine
Moral Law, no matter whether that Law has been written in the
human heart or communicated to man by positive precept. For the
Jews in the Old Testament also every deviation from the ceremonial or political laws constituted a sin; but since in the New

Testament these laws have been abolished by God's express will, Col. 2, 16, it would be a sin to reinstitute them as necessary and binding upon the consciences of New Testament believers, Matt, 15, 9; Gal. 5, 1—4. The laws which God enacted as temporary man must not declare to be permanent.

3. HOW THE DIVINE LAW CAN BE KNOWN.

Through the Fall the absolute knowledge of the divine will which God at creation had planted into the human soul was greatly weakened or obscured. For this reason man after the Fall no longer knows the divine will, or Law, with certainty, though his conscience (συνείδησις, conscientia) in a measure still functions, Rom. 2, 14. 15. Moreover, after the Fall, conscience may err (conscientia erronea), so that man often regards as forbidden what God allows (eating of certain foods at certain times, drinking of spirituous liquors, etc.), or, vice versa, regards as allowed what He has forbidden (worshiping idols, trusting in one's works for salvation). So also conscience may entertain doubts (conscientia dubia) with regard to the propriety of certain acts, or it may suggest no more than a mere probability (conscientia probabilis) of right or wrong, so that man remains uncertain with regard to the course which he must follow. Conscience, after the Fall, is therefore no longer a safe standard of what God wills or forbids. The only inerrant norm by which God's immutable will may be known with certainty is Holy Scripture, which contains a complete revelation of the divine Law, Matt. 5, 18. 19; Gal. 3, 23. 24, though properly this was given to men for the sake of the Gospel, Rom. 3, 19—22.

From Holy Scripture we know with certainty which laws were meant to be temporary and which, on the other hand, all men at all times must obey, Col. 2, 16. 17; Gal. 5, 1. 2. The immutable will of God is the *Moral Law,* which binds all men and obligates them to obedience, Matt. 22, 37—40; Rom. 13, 8—10. While the Moral Law is summarily comprehended in the Decalog, the Ten Commandments, in the form in which they were given to the Jews, Ex. 20, 1—17, must not be identified with the Moral Law, since they contain ceremonial features, Ex. 20, 8—11; Deut. 5, 12—15. Only in its New Testament version may the Decalog be identified with the Moral Law, or the immutable will of God, Rom. 13, 8—10; Jas. 2, 8; 1 Tim. 1, 5. (Cp. Luther, St. L., XX, 146 ff.)

It is self-evident that commandments given to individual believers *(mandata specialia)*, Gen. 22, must not be interpreted as applying to men in general. That the Mosaic laws regarding the prohibited degrees of consanguinity and affinity, Lev. 18, pertained not only to the Jews, but to men in general is indicated by the text itself, Lev. 18, 24—30, though the levirate command was temporary, obligating only the children of Israel (Deut. 25, 5—10; cp. v. 10: "His name shall be called in Israel," etc.)

4. THE CAUSES OF SIN.

While fallen man in his state of depravity is always inclined to shift the responsibility for his sin on God or on other creatures, Gen. 3, 12. 13, Holy Scripture teaches expressly that God is in no way whatever the cause of man's sin. Hence God must be charged with sin neither directly ("God created man with the evil tendency to sin") nor indirectly ("God is a cause of sin in so far as He concurs in evil actions," *quoad materiale*).

Questions such as "Why did God create man subject to temptation?" or "Why does He still allow men to be tempted by sin?" belong to the "unsearchable judgments and ways" of God, which are past finding out, Rom. 11, 33—36. We neither can answer them, nor should we try to answer them, Job 40, 1—5; 42, 1—6. Perverted reason will either charge God with being the cause of sin (pantheistic determinism) or deny the reality of sin (atheism). According to Scripture, however, God was the cause of sin neither in the devil, John 8, 44, nor in man, Gen. 1, 31; nor does He approve or abet sin in any person, Gen. 2, 17; 3, 8; 4, 6. 7; Ps. 5, 4. 5. Not even in evil actions, in which He concurs *quoad materiale,* does God will the sinfulness of such actions (John 19, 11 compared with Luke 22, 52. 53). Also the fact that God permits sin (Acts 14, 16) or punishes sin with sin (Rom. 1, 26; 2 Thess. 2, 11) must not be construed as if He were in any way the cause of evil; for in all these cases He manifests His punitive justice *(iustitia vindicativa)*. According to Scripture the external, or remote, yet principal, *cause of sin is Satan,* who sinned first and then seduced man into sin, John 8, 44; 2 Cor. 11, 3; Rev. 12, 9, while the internal and *directly efficient cause of sin is man's corrupt will,* which permits itself to be enticed into sin by Satan (Gen. 3, 6. 17; John 8, 44: "The lusts of your father ye will do"). The *Augsburg Confession* says (Art. 19): "Although God does create and preserve nature, yet the cause of sin is the will of the wicked, that is, of the devil and ungodly men." Hence man is responsible for his sin, or a sinner *(subiectum quod peccati),* in spite of the fact that he is misled into sin and held captive in it by the devil, Eph. 2, 2. The *subiectum quo,* or the proper seat of sin, is the soul (intellect and will) of man, though the body shares in his sin, since it is the organ of the soul. To regard the soul as pure and the body as polluted is a pagan error (Gnosticism). Since Holy Scripture condemns all men as sinners, Rom. 3, 4—23, the papistical doctrine of the immaculate conception of Mary must be rejected as antichristian, 2 Thess. 2, 9. 10.

5. THE CONSEQUENCES OF SIN.

Because sin is lawlessness (ἀνομία), which God has expressly forbidden, man through sin becomes guilty before God, Rom. 3, 19 *(reatus culpae)* and subject to His most just punishments, Gal. 3, 10 *(reatus poenae).* How sin should be punished (the manner and extent of punishment) is not for guilty man to decide, but has been determined and decreed by God Himself, Deut. 9, 5; Rom. 6, 23; Matt. 25, 41.

The transgression of our first parents was immediately followed by death (Gen. 2, 17; Rom. 5, 12) in its threefold aspects as a) spiritual death, inasmuch as they lost the divine image and became alienated from God and entirely corrupt in their whole nature, Gen. 5, 3; John 3, 5. 6; b) temporal death, inasmuch as they were now subject to bodily dissolution with all its incidental diseases and miseries, Gen. 3, 16—19; and c) eternal death, inasmuch as they were now under the curse of eternal damnation, 2 Thess. 1, 9; Matt. 25, 41. However, the sentence of death was stayed by the promise of the divine Redeemer of the sinful human race, Gen. 3, 15. Since all descendants of Adam share in his guilt and corruption, Rom. 5, 12; Ps. 51, 5, all without exception are under the curse and condemnation of the Law, Rom. 3, 19—23. But as they share in Adam's sin, so they share also in the redemption of the Savior who was promised to our first parents, Rom. 5, 15—21.

The guilt and punishment of sin must be constantly emphasized by the Christian theologian, since man in his depravity refuses to believe what the divine Law teaches with regard to sin and its consequences. He denies the temporal punishments of sin (disease, death), explaining them as natural events; and he denies the eternal punishment of sin, Matt. 25, 41; 2 Thess. 1, 9, though his conscience accuses and condemns him, Rom. 1, 32; 2, 15.

Even believers, in so far as they are flesh, refuse to believe the severity of God's threats, Ps. 90, 11. 12, and therefore Christ Himself so earnestly proclaimed the truth that the divine punishment of sin is eternal, Mark 9, 43—48.

While the effusions of divine wrath upon the wicked must be regarded as a real punishment for sin *(poena vindicativa),* the sufferings of believers in this life (1 Cor. 11, 32) are in reality fatherly chastisements *(castigationes paternae),* which flow not from wrath, but from love (Ps. 94, 12; Heb. 12, 6; Rev. 3, 19), though in form and appearance they do not differ from the punishments of the wicked. Luther rightly calls the chastisement of God's saints a "gracious and joyous punishment."

B. ORIGINAL SIN.
(De Peccato Originali.)

1. DEFINITION OF ORIGINAL SIN.

Original sin *(peccatum originale),* or the state of depravity, which followed Adam's transgression and which now inheres in all his posterity, embraces a) hereditary guilt *(culpa hereditaria)* and b) hereditary corruption *(corruptio hereditaria).* That the guilt of Adam is imputed to all his descendants is taught in Rom. 5, 18: "By the offense of one, judgment came upon all men to condemnation"; v. 19: "By one man's disobedience many were made sinners." The hereditary corruption of all descendants of Adam is clearly taught in Ps. 51, 5: "I was shapen in iniquity, and in sin did my mother conceive me"; John 3, 6: "That which is born of the flesh is flesh." That the word *flesh* ($\sigma\acute{\alpha}\varrho\xi$) here denotes corruption (corrupt flesh) is proved by v. 5: "Except a man be born of water and of the Spirit, he cannot enter into the kingdom of God." Therefore the term is here used precisely as in Rom. 8, 7: "the carnal mind" ($\tau\grave{o}$ $\varphi\varrho\acute{o}\nu\eta\mu\alpha$ $\tau\tilde{\eta}\varsigma$ $\sigma\alpha\varrho\varkappa\acute{o}\varsigma$). According to Scripture, God, then, imputes (חָשַׁב, $\lambda o\gamma\acute{\iota}\zeta\epsilon\tau\alpha\iota$) the guilt of Adam to all his descendants (Rom. 5, 12: "for that, $\grave{\epsilon}\varphi'$ $\tilde{\phi}$, all have sinned").

Hence, while the expression "original sin" is not a Scripture-term ($\nu o\xi$ $\check{\alpha}\gamma\varrho\alpha\varphi o\varsigma$), but one coined by the Church, the matter which it denotes is truly Scriptural. Original sin is so called a) because it is derived from Adam, the root and beginning of the human race; b) because it is connected with the origin of the descendants of Adam; and c) because it is the origin and fountain of all actual transgressions (Hollaz.) In Scripture it is described

a) as indwelling sin, Rom. 7, 17; b) as a law in the members, Rom. 7, 23; and c) as lust (ἐπιθυμία), Jas. 1, 14. 15. All these expressions depict original sin with respect to its nature or its effects.

Hollaz defines original sin thus: "Original sin is the thorough corruption of human nature, which by the fall of our first parents is deprived of original righteousness and is prone to every evil." The *Formula of Concord* declares: "Original sin is not a slight, but so deep a corruption of human nature that nothing healthy or uncorrupt has remained in man's body or soul, in his inner or outward powers." (Epit., Art. I, 8.) A more extended definition is given by Quenstedt (II, 52): "Original sin is a want of original righteousness, derived from the sin of Adam and transmitted to all men who are begotten in the ordinary mode of generation, including the dreadful corruption and depravity of human nature and all its powers, excluding all from the grace of God and eternal life and subjecting them to temporal and eternal punishments, unless they be born again of water and the Spirit or obtain the remission of their sins through Christ." (*Doctr. Theol.,* p. 242.)

In opposition to the Scriptural doctrine of original sin, all Pelagians and modern rationalistic theologians deny that a foreign sin *(peccatum alienum)* can rightly be imputed to Adam's descendants. They claim that men can be charged only with the evil deeds which they themselves have committed. However, Scripture teaches the imputation of Adam's guilt to his descendants in such a way that, if the imputation of guilt is denied, also the imputation of Christ's righteousness to Adam's descendants must be denied. Rom. 5, 18. 19: "As by the offense of one, judgment came upon all men to condemnation, even so by the righteousness of One the free gift came upon all men unto justification. As by one man's disobedience many were made sinners, so by the obedience of One shall many be made righteous." The imputation of original guilt belongs to the stubborn facts which Scripture teaches as undeniable truth. The objection that the guilt of Adam cannot be charged to his descendants because "the son shall not bear the iniquity of the father," Ezek. 18, 19. 20, ignores the fact that "God as Judge, in agreement with His supreme judicial authority, punishes man's crime of violating His majesty also in his descendants" (Quenstedt). — God *does* impute Adam's guilt to his descendants, and He is just in doing so. But that same God in love imputes to sinners also Christ's righteousness so that they may be saved.

Original corruption *(corruptio hereditaria)* is transmitted to all men through the ordinary mode of generation, Ps. 51, 5; John 3, 6. Since Christ was conceived by the Holy Ghost in the womb of the Virgin Mary, Luke 1, 35, His nature was not corrupted by sin (immaculate conception). However, for Mary, His mother, no immaculate conception can be claimed, since she was born according to the ordinary mode of generation, Luke 1, 27, and was therefore in need of a Savior herself, Luke 1, 47. In reply to the objection that godly parents cannot transmit sin to their children since their sins have been forgiven, Gerhard says: "Carnal generation is not according to grace, but according to nature"; and Augustine: "In begetting, he [the parent] does not give that whence one is regenerated, but whence one is generated." (*Doctr. Theol.,* p. 243.)

While original corruption may be known to some extent from reason (Horace: *"Nam vitiis nemo sine nascitur";* Cicero: *"In omni continuo pravitate et in summa opiniorum perversitate versamur, ut paene cum lacte nutricis errorem suxisse videamur"*), the *Smalcald Articles* rightly declare: "This hereditary sin is so deep and horrible a corruption of nature that no reason can understand it, but it must be learned and believed *from the revelation of Scripture.*" (Part III, Art. I, 3.) And the *Formula of Concord:* "But if it is further asked what kind of an *accidens* original sin is, that is another question, of which no philosopher, no papist, no sophist, yea, no human reason, however acute it may be, can give the right explanation, but all understanding and every explanation of it must be derived solely from the Holy Scriptures, which testify that original sin is an unspeakable evil and such an entire corruption of human nature that in it and all its internal and external powers nothing pure or good remains, but everything is entirely corrupt, so that on account of original sin man is in God's sight truly spiritually dead, or with all his powers dead to that which is good." (Thor. Decl., I, 60.)

With respect to original corruption all those err a) who deny it altogether, asserting that children are corrupted not by propagation *(generatione),* but by the bad example of others *(exemplo);* b) who admit the corruption of human nature, but deny that it is sin, since only *voluntary* transgression is sin *(peccatum voluntarium);* and c) who minimize original corruption (Semi-Pelagians, synergists). However, wherever the doctrine of original corruption is minimized, there also the doctrine of salvation by grace alone *(sola gratia)* is perverted; for the *sola gratia* always presupposes the total corruption of human nature *(intima corruptio naturae humanae)*.

2. THE CORRUPT MIND AND WILL OF MAN.

Holy Scripture is very explicit in describing the effects of original corruption on the intellect and will of man. With respect to the *intellect,* original sin implies a total want of spiritual light, so that man by nature cannot know or understand the truths of God's Word which pertain to his conversion and salvation. Indeed, he is so blinded that he regards the Gospel as foolishness, 1 Cor. 2, 14, while he looks upon the very Law which condemns him, Gal. 3, 10—12, as the true way to salvation, Gal. 3, 1—3; Eph. 4, 17. 18. This dense spiritual darkness is not removed by education or culture, 1 Cor. 2, 6—9; Col. 2, 8, but solely by the Holy Ghost through the Gospel, Acts 16, 14; 2 Cor. 4, 6. While the intellect of corrupt man is unable to know the Gospel and is thus at fault negatively, it positively is prone to pass rash and false judgments concerning spiritual things, Acts 2, 13; 17, 18. 32, and to harden itself against the divine truth, Acts 7, 51.

The *Formula of Concord* describes this deplorable state of natural man as follows: "By the fall of our first parents man was so corrupted that in divine things pertaining to our conversion and the salvation of our souls he is by nature blind, so that, when the Word of God is preached, he neither does nor can understand it, but regards it as foolishness; also, that he does not of himself draw nigh to God, but is and remains an enemy of God until he is converted, becomes a believer (is endowed with faith), is regenerated and renewed, by the power of the Holy Ghost through the Word when preached and heard, out of pure grace, without any cooperation of his own." (Thor. Decl., II, 5.)

Again: "Although man's reason or natural intellect indeed has still a dim spark of the knowledge that there is a God, as also of the doctrine of the Law, Rom. 1, 19 ff., yet it is so ignorant, blind, and perverted that, when even the most ingenious and learned men upon earth read or hear the Gospel of the Son of God and the promise of eternal salvation, they cannot from their own powers perceive, apprehend, understand, or believe and regard it as true, but the more diligence and earnestness they employ, wishing to comprehend these spiritual things with their reason, the less they

understand or believe, and before they become enlightened and are
taught by the Holy Ghost, they regard all this only as foolishness
or fictions, 1 Cor. 2, 14; 1, 21; Eph. 4, 17 ff.; Matt. 13, 11 ff.; Luke
8, 18; Rom. 3, 11. 12. Accordingly the Scriptures flatly call natural man in spiritual and divine things darkness, Eph. 5, 8; Acts
26, 18; John 1, 5. Likewise the Scriptures teach that man in sins
is not only weak and sick, but defunct and entirely dead, Eph.
2, 1. 5; Col. 2, 13." (Thor. Decl., II, 9. 10.)

With respect to the *will* of fallen man Holy Scripture teaches
a) that it actually and constantly opposes the divine Law, Eph.
2, 3; 1 Pet. 4, 3. 4, and b) that on account of its total corruption
it cannot but oppose God's will. Rom. 8, 7: "It is not subject to
the Law of God, neither indeed can be." The will of natural man
is therefore both in constant opposition to God and in constant
agreement with Satan and his evil will, Rom. 8, 7; Eph. 2, 1;
John 8, 44; Rom. 6, 17. 20; Heb. 2, 15. Even the externally good
deeds of natural man *(iustitia civilis)* do not flow from true love
of God, Eph. 2, 12, but at best from natural sympathy or compassion and similar causes, though generally such "good works"
have their source in vainglory and work-righteousness, Matt. 23,
25—28.

The *Augsburg Confession* rightly declares (Art. II): "Since
the fall of Adam all men begotten in the natural way are born
with sin, that is, without the fear of God, without trust in God,
and with concupiscence." And the *Formula of Concord* says: "In
spiritual and divine things the intellect, heart, and will of the
unregenerate man are utterly unable by their own natural powers
to understand, believe, accept, think, will, begin, effect, do, work,
or concur in working, anything; but they are entirely dead to
what is good, and corrupt, so that in man's nature since the Fall,
before regeneration, there is not the least spark of spiritual power
remaining nor present by which of himself he can prepare himself for God's grace, or accept the offered grace, nor be capable of
it for and of himself, or apply or accommodate himself thereto,
or by his own powers be able of himself, as of himself, to aid, do,
work, or concur in working, anything towards his conversion either
wholly or half or in any, even the least or most inconsiderable, part,
but that he is the servant (and slave) of sin, John 8, 34, and a captive of the devil, by whom he is moved, Eph. 2, 2; 2 Tim. 2, 26.
Hence the natural free will according to its perverted disposition
and nature is strong and active only with respect to what is *displeasing and contrary to God*." (Thor. Decl., II, 7.)

As the will of natural man is opposed to God, so also his *appetition (appetitus sensitivus),* which, prompted by inordinate desires, impels him to rush into all manner of vices that seem agreeable to his perverted senses, although these are prohibited by the divine Law, Rom. 1, 32; 1, 26 ff.; 13, 13. Original sin is therefore "the root and fountainhead of all actual sins," as the *Formula of Concord* rightly states (Thor. Decl., I, 5).

It is this constant opposition to the divine will and habitual inclination to evil *(habitualis inclinatio ad malum)* that makes original sin a positive evil, or sin in the full sense of the term, indeed, the "chief sin" *(principium et caput omnium peccatorum).* The *Augsburg Confession* declares (Art. II) : "This disease, or vice of origin, is truly sin, even now condemning, and bringing eternal death upon, those not born again through Baptism and the Holy Ghost. They condemn the Pelagians and others [Semi-Pelagianism, Scholasticism] who deny that original depravity is sin and who, to obscure the glory of Christ's merit and benefits, argue that man can be justified before God by his own strength and reason."

3. THE NEGATIVE AND POSITIVE SIDES OF ORIGINAL SIN.

As already pointed out, Holy Scripture describes original sin both a) as a defect, or lack of concreated righteousness *(carentia iustitiae concreatae),* and b) as concupiscence, that is, as a constant, vicious disposition to evil *(habitualis inclinatio ad malum).* This is taught in Rom. 7, 23 : "I see another law in my members, warring against the law of my mind"; Gal. 5, 17 : "The flesh lusteth against the Spirit"; etc. It is as concupiscence that original sin is something positive *(positivum quid).* However, sin is not positive in the sense that it is a material substance, which subsists of itself *(substantia materialis, quae proprie subsistit).* Original sin is not a *substantia,* that is, a self-existent essence, but an *accidens,* that is, an accidental matter, which does not exist by itself essentially, but inheres in a self-existent essence. Hence we must distinguish between human nature, which also after the Fall is the work of God, and the corruption of human nature, or original sin, which is the work of the devil.

This truth the *Formula of Concord* strenuously maintains against every form of Manicheism (Flacianism), which assumes two existent substances, of which one is essentially good and the other essentially evil. (*Formula of Concord,* Art. I. Augustine: "Original sin is not the nature itself, but an *accidens vitium in natura,* that is, an accidental defect and damage in nature." Thor. Decl., I, 55.)

On the other hand, our confession contends against Pelagianism and synergism with equal emphasis that original sin as an *accidens* is not "a slight, insignificant spot sprinkled or a stain dashed upon the nature of man or a corruption only in some accidental things, along with and beneath which the nature nevertheless possesses and retains its integrity and power even in spiritual things" (Thor. Decl., I, 21), but "such an unspeakable evil and such an entire corruption of human nature that in it and all its internal and external powers nothing pure or good remains, but everything is entirely corrupt, so that on account of original sin man is in God's sight truly dead" (Thor. Decl., I, 60). Thus our Lutheran confession avoids both the Scylla of Manicheism and the Charybdis of Pelagianism.

4. THE UNIVERSALITY OF ORIGINAL SIN.

Holy Scripture teaches very emphatically that *all* descendants of Adam are corrupted by original sin, so that not a single human being after the Fall is uncorrupt or without the taint and pollution of sin, Rom. 5, 12; 3, 23; John 3, 5. 6. For this reason our dogmaticians say that the *subiectum quod* of original sin are all men born in the course of nature *(naturaliter nati)*. Christ was not subject to original sin because He was conceived through the miraculous operation of the Holy Ghost, Matt. 1, 20; Luke 1, 35. The anti-Scriptural decree of Pope Pius IX (1854), which in the interest of Mariolatry ascribed to the mother of Christ an immaculate conception, proves the antichristian character of the Papacy.

The doctrine of the universality of original sin is of the greatest importance for the right understanding of the doctrine of the means of grace. In particular, it is the foundation of the doctrine of Baptism; for since all children are "flesh born of the flesh," John 3, 6, and Baptism is the divinely ordained washing of regeneration, Titus 3, 5, regarding which Christ commanded that "all nations" should be baptized, Matt. 28, 19, it is obvious that children, whom God desires to be saved through the means of grace, Matt. 19, 14. 15, should receive Holy Baptism. The opinion that children born of Christian parents are unspotted by sin is opposed to the clear teaching of Scripture, Ps. 51, 5; John 3, 6.

5. THE CAUSE OF ORIGINAL SIN.

The cause of original sin *(peccatum originale)* is not God, who in His just wrath condemns and punishes this sin, Eph. 2, 3, but a) the devil *(causa remota),* who seduced our first parents, Gen. 3, 1 ff.; John 8, 44; 2 Cor. 11, 3; and b) our first parents themselves *(causa propinqua),* who allowed themselves to be misled, Rom. 5, 12; 1 Tim. 2, 14. Hollaz writes: "Our first parents are the proximate cause of the original blemish, from whose impure nature the original stain has flowed into our hearts. Everything follows the seeds of its own nature. No black crow ever produces a white dove, nor does a ferocious lion beget a gentle lamb; and no man polluted with inborn sin ever begets a holy child." *(Doctr. Theol.,* p. 239.)

6. THE EFFECTS OF ORIGINAL SIN.

The effects of original sin in man are a) death with all its temporal and eternal punishments and b) the manifold actual sins, of which each human being, being born in sin, is guilty.

Original sin entails, first of all, spiritual death, or the alienation of sinful man from the holy God, Eph. 2, 1. 5. 12. Unless spiritual death is removed through conversion, temporal death, Ps. 90, 7—9, which is a direct punishment of the first transgression, Gen. 2, 17, is followed by eternal death, or endless damnation, Matt. 25, 41; 2 Thess. 1, 9. The divine injunction "In the day that thou eatest thereof thou shalt surely die," Gen. 2, 17, was literally fulfilled, since spiritual death followed immediately upon the transgression, and our first parents were at once subject to temporal and eternal death.

The answer to the question how the eating of the fruit of the forbidden tree could produce results so dreadful is given by Scripture itself. The disastrous consequences of the first transgression were due not to any poisonous substance in the fruit itself nor to the fact that the devil had taken possession of the tree, but devolved upon Adam and Eve because in eating of the forbidden fruit, they transgressed the divine commandment, Gen. 2, 17. If it is further asked why God did not make another commandment the test of man's obedience, the Lutheran theologian Brenz replies: "Since the Moral Law was already written in man's heart, it pleased God to try his [man's] faith by a commandment not already made known to him." However, it must not be forgotten that all these questions in the last analysis belong to the unsearchable judgments of God, which lie beyond the grasp of human reason.

Original sin is the source of all actual transgressions, so that all actual sin comes from within man, Mark 7, 21—23; Ps. 51, 3—5; for since the fountain has been polluted, the waters flowing from it are likewise unclean. Because God is not the author of sin, but hates and condemns it, Ps. 11, 5; 5, 4. 5, His wrath and just punishments rest upon guilty man, Rom. 3, 19, both on account of his original sin and his actual sins, Eph. 2, 3; Rom. 5, 18.

C. ACTUAL SINS.
(De Peccatis Actualibus.)

1. DEFINITION OF ACTUAL SIN.

By actual sin *(peccatum actuale)* we understand all lawlessness (ἀνομία) which is done, or committed. It thus stands in contradistinction to that ἀνομία which all men inherit from their parents through their sinful birth *(quae in omnes homines per carnalem generationem derivatur)* and on account of which they are condemned as sinners *(imputatio peccati Adamitici; corruptio hereditaria),* even when they have not yet broken the divine Law through transgression of individual commandments, Rom. 5, 19. Or, more briefly described: "Actual transgression is every act, whether external or internal, which conflicts with the Law of God." (Hutter.) Luther very fittingly calls original sin "person sin," "nature sin," or "essential sin," because it is "not a sin which is committed," but one which "inheres in the nature, substance, and essence of man, so that, though no wicked thought ever should arise in the heart of corrupt man, no idle word were spoken, no wicked deed were done, yet the nature is nevertheless corrupted through original sin." *(Formula of Concord,* Epit., I, 21.) Actual sins are divided into sins of commission and omission, that is, sins which occur by doing *(agendo)* what the divine Law prohibits or by omitting *(omittendo)* what the divine Law commands. For this reason Hollaz defines actual sin thus: "Actual sin is a turning away, by a human act either of commission or omission, from the rule of the divine Law, incurring responsibility for guilt *(reatus culpae)* and liability to punishment *(reatus poenae)*." *(Doctr. Theol.,* p. 252.)

The omission of the good which the Law demands is an actual sin, because it is prompted by hatred against God, love of evil, and wilful neglect of duty in opposition to conscience, Rom. 1, 32;

Luke 12, 47. 48. To actual sins belong also all evil thoughts and desires with regard to both doctrine and life, Matt. 5, 28; Gen. 20, 9; Matt. 15, 19; Rom. 7, 7. In Holy Scripture actual sins are called "works of the flesh," Gal. 5, 19; "unfruitful works of darkness," Eph. 5, 11; "deeds of the old man," Col. 3, 9; "dead works," Heb. 6, 1; 9, 14; "unlawful deeds," 2 Pet. 2, 8, all of which expressions characterize these sins with respect to their nature and source. — Our Lutheran Catechism aptly defines actual sin as "every transgression of the divine Law in desires, thoughts, words, and deeds." We recommend this definition as one that is clear, simple, and eminently practical.

2. THE CAUSES OF ACTUAL SIN.

Actual sins are prompted by causes within man (causae peccati actualis intra hominem) and causes outside man (causae peccati actualis extra hominem).

The real cause of actual sins within man is his corrupt nature (corruptio hereditaria), as Scripture declares. Rom. 7, 17: "It is no more I that do it, but sin that dwelleth in me." In particular, Scripture mentions as causes of actual sins: a) the spiritual ignorance which results from hereditary corruption, 1 Tim. 1, 13; Matt. 26, 65. 66, cp. with Acts 3, 17; b) sinful emotions and passions, such as fear (Matt. 14, 30; Mark 14, 66 ff.; Gal. 2, 12), wrath (Luke 9, 54. 55; 4, 28. 29), and the like; however, neither man's ignorance nor his sinful passions excuse the evil deeds which are committed because of them, nor do they remove the sinfulness of such acts, 1 Tim. 1, 15; Luke 22, 62; c) the habitual evil inclination (habitus vitiosus) which is produced and confirmed by repeated sinful acts, Jer. 13, 23; for though the inclination to evil is innate in man, there is also an acquired evil inclination, or a vicious disposition, which has its source in his sinful practises (inclinatio ad malum acquisita; peccatum habituale acquisitum; habitus vitiosus acquisitus). It is self-evident that man is responsible also for the sins that have their source in his vicious habits and practises, Rom. 1, 24—27, and which in moments of sober reflection he may earnestly deplore (e. g., a confirmed drunkard).

As causes of actual sins outside man, Scripture mentions a) the devil, who not only actuates the unregenerate, Eph. 2, 2; 1 Cor. 10, 20, but also seeks to seduce the regenerate into sin, 1 Chron. 21, 1; Luke 22, 31; Matt. 16, 23. How Satan tempts believers to commit actual sins is well illustrated by his temptation of Christ, though he could not prevail against Him, Matt. 4, 1ff. b) Men who mislead persons to sin by their false teachings, Rom. 16, 17. 18; 2 Tim. 2, 17, by ungodly or immoral words and writings, 1 Cor. 15, 33, and by wicked deeds, 2 Pet. 2, 1—3, are also causes of actual sins.

Though God is in no way the cause of actual sin, or of evil deeds, yet He is the author of evil in the sense of tribulation or affliction, Is. 45, 7. This truth Holy Scripture sets forth for the comfort of all believers who endure trials and chastisements in this life, Acts 14, 22, to the glory of God, 2 Cor. 12, 9, and their own good, Rom. 8, 28.

3. THE DOCTRINE OF OFFENSE.

The sin of tempting any one to evil, Scripture describes as giving offense, Rom. 16, 17. For one to give offense means to teach or do anything by which another is occasioned either not to believe or to believe error or to lead a wicked life, so that his faith is either endangered or even destroyed. For this reason Scripture warns us most solemnly against the crime of giving offense, Matt. 18, 6ff.; Mark 9, 42ff.; Luke 17, 1. 2.

However, according to Scripture, offense is given not only by doing that which is evil (false doctrine, wicked life), but also through the unwise use of adiaphora (Rom. 14: eating meat, drinking wine); for in this way weak brethren may be occasioned to do something which their erring consciences regard as wrong. Rom. 14, 20: "It is evil for that man who eateth with offense"; 14, 23: "He that doubteth is damned if he eat because he eateth not of faith." A Christian should not entertain erroneous views concerning adiaphora, Rom. 14, 14. 22; nevertheless, if, being a weak Christian, he has not the right knowledge, 1 Cor. 8, 7, he must under no circumstances do what he regards as wrong, Rom. 14, 15. 21. 23.

From this follows the general rule of Christian conduct that believers must at all times be willing to yield their Christian liberty unless the truth of the Gospel is at stake, Gal. 5, 1. 12. But if a person who claims to be weak in Christian knowledge demands that his error should be acknowledged as truth and insists upon promulgating it as such, he is no longer a "weak brother," whose "weakness" can be tolerated, but a false prophet, who judges and condemns true believers for using their right knowledge, Col. 2, 16; Gal. 5, 1—3. If a person takes offense because a confessing Christian is compelled to use his Christian liberty on account of the confession involved, no guilt attaches to such a Christian for using his liberty for the Gospel's sake. The guilt rather attaches to those who compel the true Christian to insist upon his liberty, Gal. 2, 4. 5; cp. with Acts 16, 3.

On the basis of Scripture we rightly distinguish between an offense which is given and one which is taken. An offense is taken when a person who is spiritually blind and corrupt takes occasion to sin from words or acts which in themselves are right. Thus the Jews were offended at Christ and His Gospel because of their self-righteousness, Rom. 9, 32, while the Gentiles were offended at Christ Crucified because of their carnal pride, 1 Cor. 1, 22. 23. This type of offense will continue till the end of time, Luke 2, 34; Rom. 9, 33; 1 Pet. 2, 8. Christians are offended at Christ when they renounce Him because of the suffering which His confession entails, Matt. 24, 10; 13, 21. It is for this reason that Christ so earnestly warns His followers: "Blessed is he whosoever shall not be offended in Me," Matt. 11, 6.

4. THE DOCTRINE OF OBDURATION.

Whenever ungodly men take offense at the preaching of the divine Word in such a manner that the more they hear, the more they resist the Holy Spirit, they are said to harden their hearts against the divine truth, Ex. 8, 15; Ps. 95, 8; John 12, 40. In the process of hardening degrees may be recognized, so that not every case of obduracy is beyond recovery, Acts 3, 14—17. As God is not the cause of the offense which is taken at His Word, so He is not the cause of the hardening of those who refuse to believe, Acts 7, 51—54, though Scripture speaks also of obduration as an act of God, Ex. 7, 3; Rom. 1, 24—26. The direct cause of obduration is a) the devil, who blinds the human mind and fills the heart with wickedness, 2 Cor. 4, 4; Acts 5, 3; Eph. 2, 2; and b) man himself, who of his own will rejects divine grace, Matt. 13, 15; 23, 37, while God hardens man not causally, but judicially and permissively, Rom. 1, 24. 26; Acts 7, 42. Hence the divine act of obduration may be described as a judicial act of God by which, on account of antecedent, voluntary, and persistent wickedness, He justly permits the obstinate sinner to harden himself by withdrawing from him His Holy Spirit and delivering him into the power of Satan, Luke 22, 3.

5. THE SCRIPTURAL DOCTRINE OF TEMPTATION.

According to Scripture there is a) a temptation for good *(tentatio probationis)* and b) a temptation for evil *(tentatio seductionis).* The first comes from God and is designed for the trial and strengthening of faith, Gen. 22, 1—18; Deut. 13, 1ff.; Ps. 66, 10f. By sending *tentationes probationis* upon His children, God does not become the author of sin; for a) He proportions all trials to the strength of His saints, 1 Cor. 10, 13, and b) sustains His beloved most graciously in their faith whenever they are tempted, Luke 22, 31. 32; 1 Cor. 10, 13. For this reason those who resist and overcome temptation do so not by their own strength or worthiness, but solely by the grace of God, Rom. 11, 20—22; 2 Cor. 12, 9.

Temptations for evil *(tentationes seductionis)* come a) from the devil, Matt. 4, 1ff.; 1 Pet. 5, 8; b) from the world, 1 John 2, 15—17; and c) from the flesh, Jas. 1, 14; cf. 1 Thess. 3, 5; 1 Cor. 7, 5; 1 Tim. 6, 9; Mark 14, 38. It is of great comfort to all believers that Christ, who Himself was tempted, has promised to sustain His followers in their temptations, Heb. 2, 18; 4, 15; 2 Pet. 2, 9.

6. THE CLASSIFICATION OF ACTUAL SINS.

The purpose of classifying actual sins is to point out more definitely and to describe more clearly the numerous transgressions to which the believer is subject, Job 9, 2. 3. Our interest in the classification is therefore entirely practical. It urges us to consider the manifold temptations by which Satan, the world, and our own flesh are bent on seducing us into vice and shame, Matt. 26, 41; 1 Cor. 10, 12, to cleanse ourselves from all filthiness of the flesh and spirit by daily repentance, and to perfect holiness in the fear of God, 2 Cor. 7, 1; Heb. 12, 1. 2. Hence the classification of actual sins must not be regarded as unnecessary or useless, but rather as highly profitable, especially since Holy Scripture itself distinguishes between sins, 1 John 5, 16; Jas. 4, 17; John 19, 11. Just because "all Scripture is profitable for . . . correction and instruction in righteousness," 2 Tim. 3, 16, it vividly depicts either by express word, 1 Cor. 5, 9—11, or by example, 2 Sam. 11, 4. 24; Matt. 26, 48f., the uncountable transgressions which threaten the Christian in his life on earth, Ps. 19, 12. 13.

a. *Voluntary and involuntary sins.* On the basis of clear Scripture statements we distinguish between voluntary and in-

voluntary sins. The former (peccata voluntaria, malitiae, pro-
aeretica) are such sinful acts in which man transgresses the divine
Law by a deliberate volition, contrary to the dictates of conscience,
John 13, 26. 27. 30. The latter (peccata involuntaria) are such
sinful acts as are committed without sure knowledge (peccata
ignorantiae, 1 Tim. 1, 13) or without a deliberate purpose of
the will (peccata infirmitatis, peccata praecipitantiae, Luke 22,
55—62). Involuntary sins are accordingly divided into sins of
ignorance and of infirmity. However, only in the case of Christians do we speak of sins of infirmity, since all unbelievers, being
dead in trespasses and sins, Eph. 2, 1, and captive in the power of
Satan, Eph. 2, 2; 2 Tim. 2, 26, desire the very sins into which
they are misled by the devil, Eph. 2, 3; John 8, 44. But the believer, as a new creature in Christ, 2 Cor. 5, 17, detests the sins
which he commits, Rom. 7, 15, and earnestly wills that which is
good, Rom. 7, 19. 22—24. As sins of infirmity, or involuntary sins,
we must regard also the sinful emotions, that is, the inordinate
thoughts and desires (motus inordinati subitanei), which suddenly
arise in Christians out of their carnal heart (σάρξ) without and
against their will, Gal. 5, 17. 24. (Cp. Luther, St. L., IX, 1032.)
Infants cannot be said to be guilty of deliberate sins (peccata pro-
aeretica; Deut. 1, 39; Jonah 4, 11); but they may not be declared
free from actual sins, because they are flesh born of the flesh, John
3, 6, and as such always in opposition to the divine will, Gal. 5, 17;
Gen. 8, 21; Ps. 51, 5. On the other hand, also in infants the Holy
Spirit, through the means of grace (Baptism, Titus 3, 5) works
faith, Matt. 18, 6, and the works of faith, Ps. 8, 2, so that they,
as new creatures in Christ, resist the evil emotions of the flesh,
Matt. 18, 3. 4.

Voluntary sins must be considered not only with respect to
the will, but also with respect to conscience. For this reason we
regard as voluntary sins also those committed against conscience.
These are fourfold, inasmuch as a person may sin a) against a correct conscience (conscientia recta), which is in agreement with the
divine Law, Rom. 1, 32; or b) against an erring conscience (conscientia erronea), in which case he sins both when he disregards
(Rom. 14, 14; 1 Cor. 8, 7. 10—12) and when he follows his misguided conscience, which is at variance with the divine Word. An
erring conscience therefore leads to sin both when it is obeyed
and when it is disobeyed (cp. the case of a person who is bound by
his conscience to worship saints); or c) against a probable con-

science *(conscientia probabilis)*, as in that case he either neglects the duty of ascertaining the right course of action, Ps. 119, 9. 11, or acts in doubt, Rom. 14, 23; or d) against a doubting conscience *(conscientia dubia)*, since in such cases he should not act at all, Rom. 14, 23.

b. *Sins of commission and of omission.* Sins of commission *(peccata commissionis)* are positive acts, by which negative precepts of God are violated. Sins of omission *(peccata omissionis)* consist in the neglect of acts prescribed by affirmative precepts of God (Hollaz). In sins of commission accordingly that is done which God has forbidden, Ex. 20, 13—17; in sins of omission that is omitted which God demands, Jas. 4, 17. Although sins of omission are not always done intentionally or by an express purpose of the perverted will, yet every omission of that which is good is a sin in the true sense of the term, since man has been created for the very purpose of serving God by always doing that which is good, *i. e.*, commanded by Him. *Ipsum non facere, quod praeceptum, peccatum est*, Matt. 28, 20; Ezek. 37, 24.

c. *Sins against God, against the neighbor, and against oneself.* Sins against God are those which are directed against the First Table of the Decalog, Matt. 22, 37. 38; Gen. 39, 9. Sins against the neighbor are directed specifically against the Second Table, Matt. 22, 39; Lev. 19, 17. Sins against oneself are those which, like fornication and impurity in general, defile the body, 1 Cor. 6, 18. Nevertheless we must remember that every sin against the neighbor or against oneself is a sin only because it is primarily committed against God, Ps. 51, 4; Gen. 39, 9. *Omne peccatum in Deum committitur.*

d. *Grievous and less grievous sins.* Every transgression of the divine Law is rebellion against God (ἀνομία, lawlessness, פֶּשַׁע) and therefore damnable, Gal. 3, 10. From the viewpoint of damnability therefore we cannot speak of "smaller" and "greater" sins. Still Scripture itself distinguishes degrees in sinning (John 19, 11, μείζονα ἁμαρτίαν). Children before the years of discretion *(anni discretionis)* are less culpable than are adults, Deut. 1, 39. Servants who know the will of the Lord and yet refuse to do it shall be beaten with many stripes, Luke 12, 47, while such as sin against Him in ignorance shall receive only few stripes, v. 48. From this it is clear that as there are degrees in sinning, there are degrees also in the eternal punishment which the damned will suffer. The most grievous of all sins is unbelief, John 3, 18. 19; 16, 9.—The classification of sins into sins of the heart, of the mouth, and of the actual deed *(peccata cordis, oris, operis)* does not always indicate degree, since a sin of the heart (unbelief, implacability, etc.) may be more grievous than a sin of the mouth or of the actual deed (cf. an angry word spoken in haste; an evil deed done without malice, on the spur of the moment). When judging whether one sin is more grievous than another, we must consider a) the person sinning; b) the impelling cause; c) the object involved; d) the Law violated; and e) the consequence of the sin. Nevertheless every sin renders man guilty before God, Rom. 3, 19.

e. *Mortal and venial sins.* Mortal sins *(peccata mortalia)* are all sins which actually precipitate the transgressor into a state of wrath, death, and condemnation, so that, if he should die without repentance, his punishment would be eternal death, John 8, 21. 24; Rom. 8, 13. All sins of unbelievers are mortal sins since unbelievers reject Christ, for whose sake alone God pardons sin, Rom. 3, 24; Eph. 1, 7; Acts 4, 12. When we speak of mortal sins of "believers," we mean such sins as grieve the Holy Spirit, Eph. 4, 30, and destroy faith (David's murder and adultery, Ps. 32, 3. 4). "A mortal sin is that by which the regenerate, overcome by the flesh and not remaining in a regenerate state, transgress the divine Law by a deliberate purpose of the will, contrary to the dictates of conscience, and thereby lose saving faith, reject the gracious influence of the Holy Spirit, and cast themselves into a state of wrath, death, and condemnation." (Hollaz.) — Venial sins *(peccata venialia)* are the involuntary sins of believers, which, though in themselves deserving eternal death, are forgiven for Christ's sake, in whom the believer trusts and in whose strength he continually repents of his sins, Ps. 19, 12. 13; 51, 9—12.

On this point the papists err, who teach that certain sins are in themselves mortal *(superbia, avaritia, luxuria, ira, gula, invidia, acedia)*, while others in themselves are venial and so deserve only temporal punishments. The Calvinists err in this matter by teaching that the elect never lose faith or fall from grace, even when they commit enormous sins *(peccata enormia)*.

With mortal sins may be identified the so-called dominant and with venial sins the so-called non-dominant sins. In unbelievers all sins are dominant, since they are dead in trespasses and sins and are in the power of Satan, Eph. 2, 1—3. The blessed state in which sin is no longer dominant in man is found in believers only, Rom. 6, 12. 14. If believers give up the struggle

against sin, Gal. 5, 16. 17, so that it again reigns over them, they
have fallen from grace and lost faith, Gal. 5, 4; 1 Cor. 5, 11.

f. *Crying sins.* Crying sins *(peccata clamantia)* are such as
invoke God's punishments in a special degree.   Examples of crying
sins mentioned in Scripture are the following: a) the fratricide
committed by Cain, Gen. 4, 10; b) the sins of the Sodomites, Gen.
18, 20; c) the oppression of the Israelites by the Egyptians,
Ex. 3, 9; d) the oppression of widows and orphans, Ex. 22, 22. 23;
e) the withholding of wages from hired laborers, Jas. 5, 4; f) the
persecution of Christians, Rev. 6, 9. 10.   In general, we may describe as crying sins all crimes committed against the helpless
(widows, orphans, the poor, the oppressed, etc.), whose cause God
Himself must champion and defend, Ex. 3, 7—9; 22, 21—24;
Is. 3, 13—15.

> *Clamitat ad coelum vox sanguinis et Sodomorum,*
> *Vox oppressorum, viduae, pretium famulorum.*

g. *Pardonable sins and the unpardonable sin.*   A pardonable
sin *(peccatum remissibile)* is a sin of which it is possible to repent,
while the "unpardonable sin" *(peccatum irremissibile)* excludes the
possibility of repentance.   Since all sins are pardonable except the
sin against the Holy Ghost, Matt. 12, 31. 32; Mark 3, 22—30;
Luke 12, 10, which is the only irremissible sin that Scripture records, this sin requires special consideration.   However, the classification just given must not be abused in the interest of carnal
security and indifference toward sin.   Every sin is pardonable
only if the sinner in true repentance trusts in the vicarious satisfaction of Christ.   It is only from the viewpoint of divine grace
that sins are pardonable, not from that of human merit, Rom.
4, 5—8.   There is no "guiltless sin" before God, Rom. 3, 19;
Gal. 3, 10.

h. *The sin against the Holy Ghost.*   The sin against the Holy
Ghost is described in Scripture as "blasphemy against the Holy
Ghost," Mark 3, 28. 29.   This blasphemy is distinguished from that
directed against Christ, Matt. 12, 32, which, as our Savior expressly
teaches, is pardonable.   As Scripture references to the sin against
the Holy Ghost our dogmaticians consider also 1 John 5, 16 and
Heb. 6, 4—6; 10, 26. 27.

The sin against the Holy Ghost is unpardonable because it is
directed, not against the divine person of the Holy Ghost, but
against His divine office or His gracious operation upon the human
heart.   *Peccatum in Spiritum Sanctum non in personam, sed in*

officium Spiritus Sancti committitur. That is the nature, or essence, of this sin. However, not every resistance against the work of the Holy Ghost comes under the head of this sin; otherwise every person in the world would commit this unpardonable sin, since by nature all men resist the Holy Spirit, 1 Cor. 2, 14; Rom. 8, 7.

The sin against the Holy Ghost is committed only when the Holy Spirit has clearly revealed the divine truth to the sinner and the sinner nevertheless utters blasphemies against it. Hence this sin must not be identified a) with that of final impenitence *(impoenitentia finalis)* nor b) with blasphemy of the divine truth flowing from spiritual blindness, 1 Tim. 1, 13, nor c) with the denial of the divine truth through fear, Luke 22, 61. 62. The sin against the Holy Ghost consists in the perverse, persistent denial and rejection of the divine truth after the latter has been sufficiently acknowledged and accepted as such, joined with voluntary and atrocious blasphemy. In other words, it is the malicious and blasphemous rejection of the Gospel by a hardened sinner, who through the gracious illumination of the Holy Ghost has been fully convinced of its divine truth. Hollaz writes: *"Peccatum in Spiritum Sanctum est veritatis divinae evidenter agnitae et in conscientia approbatae malitiosa abnegatio, hostilis impugnatio, horrenda blasphematio et omnium mediorum salutis obstinata et finaliter perseverans reiectio."*

Most dogmaticians teach that the sin against the Holy Ghost can be committed only by those who were regenerated, though others, and among these Baier, maintain that it occurs also in the unregenerate, namely, in the very moment when the Holy Ghost is about to convert them and to this end convicts them of the divine truth. The reason why the sin against the Holy Ghost is unpardonable is because it is malicious and persistent resistance against the converting and sanctifying work of the Holy Ghost, through which alone sinners are saved.

The Calvinists err in teaching that the sin against the Holy Ghost is unpardonable for the reason that God from eternity has predetermined to damnation those who maliciously resist the divine truth. Over against this error it may be shown that Christ earnestly desired to save the very Pharisees who rejected His Word and committed the sin against the Holy Ghost, Matt. 12, 22—32; 23, 37.

The question whether the sin against the Holy Ghost still occurs must be answered in the affirmative, since Matt. 12, 31. 32 and its parallel passages are general statements and so apply at all times. From 1 John 5, 16 we conclude that in certain cases those who commit the sin against the Holy Ghost may be known; for in this passage believers are asked not to intercede for such ("I do not say that he," etc.). At the same time we must not be hasty in charging with this sin a person who may appear to us to be guilty of it, but rather continue in the testimony of the truth as we have opportunity, warning the wrong-doer against the dreadful offense which our Lord so strongly condemns, just as He Himself earnestly warned the Pharisees against it, Matt. 12, 22—32.

Whether Heb. 6, 4—6 and 10, 26. 27 treat of the sin against the Holy Ghost is an exegetical question, though many scholars believe that these two passages speak of this sin. In Heb. 12, 17 the word "repentance" refers to Isaac rather than to Esau, the meaning of the text being that Esau with all his tears could not prevail on his father to change his mind and turn Jacob's blessing to his advantage, Gen. 27, 34—38.

Only divine grace can preserve us from the sin against the Holy Ghost. If they were left to themselves, all who have come under the gracious operation of the Spirit of God would commit this heinous sin. Those who are in great distress of mind because they fear that they have committed it should take comfort from the fact that this unforgivable sin is committed only by such as maliciously spurn and blasphemously reject the grace of God in Christ Jesus, not, however, by any one who repents of his sins and longs for the forgiveness which the Gospel offers. To him apply such passages as Matt. 11, 28; 9, 13; John 6, 37.

i. *Other classifications.* 1. *Secret sins and manifest sins.* Secret sins are those which are known either to the transgressor alone (Ps. 32, 3—5) or besides to him only to a few others who either rightly (Matt. 18, 15. 16) or wrongly (Lev. 5, 1; Prov. 29, 24) desire them to remain hidden. Open sins are such as have become known to many, 1 Tim. 5, 20; 1 Cor. 5, 1. This division is of great importance for the proper treatment of disciplinary cases.

2. *Personal sins and foreign sins whose guilt we share.* Personal sins are those which the sinner himself commits, 2 Sam. 12, 13, while foreign sins whose guilt we share are transgressions committed by others with our knowledge, sanction, concurrence,

or aid. We participate in the sins of others if we command, counsel, consent to, or connive at, their evil deeds, or do not oppose them nor give information concerning them, so that we become morally responsible for such sins, 2 Sam. 11, 15—21.

Holy Scripture warns us most emphatically against participating in the sins of others, Eph. 5, 7. 11; 1 Tim. 5, 22; 2 John 11; Rev. 18, 4. In particular, believers should avoid false teachers lest they share in their offense of publishing false doctrine, 2 John 11; 2 Cor. 6, 14—18; Rom. 16, 17. 18. But we offend in this point also by taking pleasure in the sins of others, Rom. 1, 32. Such pleasure in the sins of others is awakened especially by listening to immoral or blasphemous conversation, 1 Cor. 15, 33; Eph. 4, 29; 1 Tim. 6, 20; 2 Tim. 2, 16, or by associating with wrong-doers in general (unionism, Ps. 1, 1; Eph. 5, 11; Ps. 26, 4. 5).

THE FREEDOM OF THE WILL.
(De Libero Arbitrio.)

Among the effects of original sin we must enumerate also the loss of the freedom of the will in spiritual matters. The term "free will" *(liberum arbitrium)* is used in a twofold meaning. In the first place it denotes the faculty to will *(facultas volendi),* by which man is distinguished from all irrational creatures. Free will in this sense is called also formal freedom, or freedom from coercion *(libertas a coactione).*

When we use the term in this sense, we say that man through the Fall has not lost his free will; for although corrupt man is so perverted that he cannot do otherwise than sin *(non potest non peccare),* he nevertheless sins not against his will, but of his own free will. In other words, he is never coerced to sin, but commits sin of his own choice, John 8, 44. Hutter writes: "Sometimes the term *will,* or *choice,* is used to designate the faculty of the soul, indeed the very substance of the will itself, whose function is simply that of willing. Thus regarded, scarcely any one will deny free will to man." And Gerhard: "The question is not whether the essence of the will has survived the Fall; for this we emphatically maintain, namely, that man has not lost his will, but the soundness of it." *(Doctr. Theol.,* p. 260.)

However, the term "free will" has been used also in the sense of "spiritual power" by which corrupt man can desire that which is spiritually good, prepare himself for divine grace, fulfil the divine Law out of true love for God, accept and believe the Gospel, and thus either convert himself entirely or at least cooperate in his conversion. To distinguish "free will" in this sense from the mere faculty of willing, dogmaticians have called it spiritual freedom *(libertas spiritualis)* or material freedom.

When the term "free will" is used in this sense, we, on the basis of Scripture, emphatically deny that man after the Fall has a "free will." 1 Cor. 2, 14: "The natural man receiveth not the things of the Spirit of God; for they are foolishness unto him; neither can he know them because they are spiritually discerned"; John 6, 44: "No man can come to Me except the Father which hath sent Me draw him"; Rom. 8, 7: "The carnal mind is enmity against God; for it is not subject to the Law of God, neither indeed can be"; Eph. 2, 1: "You hath He quickened who were dead in trespasses and sins."

If, then, the natural man does not receive the spiritual things, but regards them as foolishness; indeed, if he is dead in trespasses and sins and is enmity against God, then certainly he is without the power to will that which is spiritually good, to apply himself to divine grace, and to prepare himself for, or to cooperate in, his conversion. Gerhard writes: "Understanding the term *liberty* as describing the free power and faculty of choosing the good and rejecting the evil that was possessed by Adam, we maintain that Luther was perfectly correct in saying: 'Free will is a title without the thing itself, or a thing with nothing but a title.'"

Similarly the *Formula of Concord* says: "In spiritual and divine things, which pertain to the salvation of the soul, man is like a pillar of salt, like Lot's wife, yea, like a log and a stone, like a lifeless statue, which uses neither eyes nor mouth, neither sense nor heart. For man neither sees nor perceives the terrible and fierce wrath of God on account of sin and death, but ever continues in his security, even knowingly and willingly. . . . All teaching and preaching is lost upon him until he is enlightened, converted, and regenerated by the Holy Ghost." (Thor. Decl., II, 20. 21). And again: "Therefore the Scriptures deny to the intellect, heart, and will of the natural man all aptness, skill, capacity, and ability to think, to understand, to be able to do, to begin, to will, to undertake, to act, to work, or to concur in working, anything good and right in spiritual things as of himself, 2 Cor. 3, 5; Rom. 3, 12; John 8, 37; 1, 5; 1 Cor. 2, 14; Rom. 8, 7; John 15, 5; Phil. 2, 13." (Thor. Decl., II, 12—14.)

But while our Confessions thus teach that man in spiritual matters has no free will, it admits on the basis of Scripture that the will of natural man is free in worldly affairs and even to some extent in the exercise of civil righteousness (*iustitia civilis, carnalis, operum*). The *Apology of the Augsburg Confession* affirms: "The human will has liberty in the choice of works and things which reason comprehends by itself. It can to a certain extent (*aliquo modo*) render civil righteousness, or the righteousness of works; it can speak of God, offer to God a certain service by an outward work, obey magistrates, parents; in the choice of an outward work it can restrain the hands from murder, from adultery, from theft. Since there is left in human nature reason and judgment concerning objects subjected to the senses, choice between these things, and the liberty and power to render civil righteousness, are also left." (Art. XVIII, 70.)

The qualification which is here made, namely, that man in the things enumerated has a free will only "to a certain extent" *(aliquo modo),* is very important, since by nature he is so dead in trespasses and sins and captive in Satan's power, Eph. 2, 2; Col. 1, 13; 2 Tim. 2, 26; Acts 26, 18, that his civil righteousness leaves much to be desired. The *Apology* therefore rightly adds: "The power of concupiscence is such that men more frequently obey evil dispositions than sound judgment. And the devil, who is efficacious in the godless, as Paul says Eph. 2, 2, does not cease to incite this feeble nature to various offenses. These are the reasons why civil righteousness is rare among men, as we see that not even the philosophers themselves, who seem to have aspired after this righteousness, attained it." (Art. XVIII, 71.)

The Scriptural doctrine that man in spiritual matters has no free will at all, but is completely blind, dead, and inimical to God, has always been absolutely denied by synergists and Semi-Pelagians. The *Formula of Concord* describes the synergistic error as follows: "Man is not absolutely dead to good in spiritual things, but is badly wounded and half dead. Therefore, although the free will is too weak to make a beginning and to convert itself to God by its own powers and to be obedient to God's Law from the heart, nevertheless, when the Holy Ghost makes a beginning and calls us through the Gospel and offers us His grace, the forgiveness of sins, and eternal salvation, then the free will, from its own natural powers, can meet God and to a certain extent, although feebly, do something towards it, help, and cooperate thereto, can qualify itself for, and apply itself to, grace, and apprehend, accept it, and believe the Gospel, and can also cooperate by its own powers with the Holy Ghost in the continuation and maintenance of this work." (Thor. Decl., II, 77.)

In opposition to this error the *Formula of Concord* declares: "In spiritual and divine things the intellect, heart, and will of the unregenerate man are utterly unable by their own natural powers to understand, believe, accept, think, will, begin, effect, do, work, or concur in working, anything, but they are entirely dead to what is good, and corrupt, so that in man's nature since the Fall, before regeneration, there is not the least spark of spiritual power remaining nor present, by which of himself he can prepare himself for God's grace or accept the offered grace, nor be capable of it for and of himself, or apply or accommodate himself thereto, or by his own powers be able of himself, as of himself, to aid, do, work, or concur in working, anything towards his conversion, either wholly or half or in any, even the least or most inconsiderable, part; but he is the servant of sin, John 8, 34, and a captive of the devil, by whom he is moved, Eph. 2, 2; 2 Tim. 2, 26. Hence the natural free will according to its perverted disposition and nature is strong and active only with respect to what is displeasing and contrary to God." (Thor. Decl., II, 7.)

Among the arguments that have been used to oppose the Scripture-doctrine of man's total loss of free will in spiritual matters the following may be considered as the most important: —

1. It must be true that natural man has a free will in spiritual matters since St. Paul declares that the "Gentiles do by nature the things contained in the Law," Rom. 2, 14. — *Reply:* St. Paul here describes only the external obedience *(quoad materiale)* of the heathen and not the true obedience, which flows from faith and love toward God *(quoad formale);* for the same apostle who declares that the heathen do the things contained in the Law also declares that they are without God and without hope in the world, Eph. 2, 12, alienated from God, Col. 1, 21, and His enemies, Rom. 8, 7. While to a certain extent the heathen may exercise themselves in civil righteousness *(iustitia civilis),* they are incapable of spiritual righteousness *(iustitia spiritualis). Homo reiicit evangelium naturā, credit gratiā.*

2. Natural man must have a free will in spiritual matters, since God commands him to obey the Law and to believe the Gospel, Matt. 22, 37—39; Acts 16, 31. — *Reply:* From the divine command we must not infer the human ability to comply with the divine command. *(A praecepto divino ad posse humanum non valet consequentia.)* The same Word of God which demands obedience to the Law, Gal. 3, 10, and faith in the Gospel, Mark 1, 15; Acts 16, 31, teaches also that natural man cannot obey the Law, Eccl. 7, 20; Ps. 143, 2; Is. 64, 6, nor believe in Christ by his own strength, John 6, 44; 2 Cor. 3, 5. Yet neither are the commands of the Law *(adhortationes legales)* useless, Luke 10, 28, nor are the Gospel exhortations *(adhortationes evangelicae)* in vain, Matt. 11, 28; for by the former the Holy Spirit works knowledge of sin, Rom. 3, 20, while by the latter He works faith, Rom. 10, 17; 1 Cor. 12, 3, so that the good and gracious will of God is actually accomplished in the sinner, who is called to repentance, by the preaching of the divine Word.

3. Natural man must have a free will in spiritual matters since

his conversion without his cooperation would imply coercion on God's part. — *Reply:* The conversion of a sinner is indeed the work of God's almighty power, Eph. 1, 19; but it is not an irresistible or coercive power since it may be resisted, Matt. 23, 37. However, the very nature of conversion excludes the idea of coercion; for it consists essentially in the gracious drawing of the sinner by God Himself, John 6, 44, which is accomplished through the means of grace, Rom. 10, 17. The *Formula of Concord* says: "[We reject] also when the following expressions are employed, . . . namely, that . . . the Holy Ghost is given to those who resist Him intentionally and persistently; for, as Augustine says, in conversion God makes willing persons out of the unwilling and dwells in the willing." (Epit., II, 15.)

4. Natural man must have a free will in spiritual matters since God works only the power to believe, but not faith itself. — *Reply:* This argument is based upon a false premise; for God "worketh in you both to *will* and to *do* of His good pleasure," Phil. 2, 13. (Cp. also Eph. 1, 19; Phil. 1, 29.) In other words, the very faith by which we are saved is God's gracious gift and work in us.

5. Natural man must have a free will in spiritual matters; for without his cooperation in conversion not he, but the Holy Spirit would believe. — *Reply:* The fallacy involved in this argument becomes clear when we consider that, though temporal life is the gift of God, bestowed upon man without his cooperation, yet the person so endowed with life himself lives, so that God does not do the living for him. It is the same with faith, which indeed is God's gift, but at the same time a gift that the believer himself possesses. 2 Tim. 1, 12: "I know whom *I* have believed."

6. Natural man must have a free will in spiritual matters since he can read the Bible, hear the Word of God, exercise himself in civil righteousness, etc. — *Reply:* All these works are external only, and not the fruits of true faith in Christ and of true love to God. The self-righteous Pharisee remained unconverted though he did all this and more, Luke 18, 10—14.

7. Natural man must have a free will in spiritual matters; for if he can damn himself by refusing to believe, it follows with irresistible logic that he can also save himself by desiring and endeavoring to believe. — *Reply:* Scripture teaches very emphatically that the one does not follow from the other, Hos. 13, 9.

All these and other objections to divine monergism in conversion flow from the carnal heart, which is as proud as it is self-righteous. Those who have advanced these arguments might be divided into three classes: —

a) Pelagians, "who taught that man by his own powers, without the grace of the Holy Ghost, can turn Himself to God, believe the Gospel, be obedient from the heart to God's Law, and thus merit the forgiveness of sins and eternal life." (*Formula of Concord,* Epit., II, 9 ff.)

b) Semi-Pelagians (Arminians), "who teach that man by his own powers can make a beginning of his conversion, but without the grace of God cannot complete it." *(Ibid.)*

c) Synergists, who teach "that, . . . if the Holy Ghost by the preaching of the Word has made a beginning and therein offered His grace, then the will of man from its own natural powers can add something, though little and feebly, to this end, can help and cooperate, qualify, and prepare itself for grace, and embrace and accept it, and believe the Gospel." *(Ibid.)*

From the gross synergism of Melanchthon, who taught that man can cooperate in his conversion by his natural powers, we distinguish the subtle synergism of the later dogmaticians (Latermann), which claims that man can cooperate in his conversion with spiritual powers bestowed on him by the Holy Ghost. Both types place the cause of conversion and salvation in man himself. But man cooperates towards his conversion neither by natural nor by spiritual powers; not by natural powers, since by nature he is an enemy of God; and not by spiritual powers bestowed upon him, since he is already converted as soon as he is in possession of spiritual powers.

Regarding this point the *Formula of Concord* teaches: "Through this means, namely, the preaching and hearing of His Word, God works and breaks our hearts and draws man, so that through the preaching of the Law he comes to know his sins and God's wrath and experiences in his heart true terrors, contrition, and sorrow, and through the preaching and consideration of the holy Gospel concerning the gracious forgiveness of sins in Christ a spark of faith is kindled in him, which accepts the forgiveness of sins for Christ's sake and comforts itself with the promise of the Gospel; and thus the Holy Ghost (who works all this) is sent into the heart, Gal. 4, 6." (Thor. Decl., II, 54.)

THE GRACE OF GOD TOWARD FALLEN MANKIND.

(Dei Gratia erga Homines Lapsos.)

---

1. THE NECESSITY OF DIVINE GRACE.

According to the express teaching of Holy Scripture no man after the Fall can be justified and saved by the deeds of the Law, or through good works. Rom. 3, 20: "By the deeds of the Law there shall no flesh be justified in His sight." All who endeavor to acquire salvation by the works of the Law shall not be justified, but damned. Gal. 3, 10: "As many as are of the works of the Law are under the curse." The reason for this is that no man after the Fall can fulfil the divine Law or satisfy the claims of divine justice. Rom. 3, 10: "There is none righteous, no, not one"; 3, 23: "All have sinned and come short of the glory of God." Hence, so far as the divine Law is concerned, all men after the Fall are forever lost and condemned, Matt. 19, 26; Rom. 8, 3. 4.

Yet, as Scripture clearly teaches, it is the gracious will of God that not a single sinner in the world be lost, 2 Pet. 3, 9; 1 Tim. 2, 4. For this reason God has most mercifully provided a way of salvation by which every sinner can be saved, John 3, 16; Matt. 18, 11, namely, the way of grace, through faith in Christ, without the works of the Law. Rom. 3, 24: "Being justified freely by His grace, δωρεὰν τῇ αὐτοῦ χάριτι, through the redemption, διὰ τῆς ἀπολυτρώσεως, the ransom, that is in Christ Jesus"; Eph. 2, 8. 9; "By grace are ye saved, through faith; and that not of yourselves, it is the gift of God; not of works, lest any man should boast." This gracious way of salvation is revealed in the Gospel, for which reason this is called "the Gospel of the grace of God," Acts 20, 24. The doctrine of salvation by grace through faith is both the basic and the distinctive article of Christianity, by which it is distinguished from all man-made religions as the only true and divine religion, Mark 16, 15. 16; Acts 4, 12; for whereas all man-made religions teach salvation by works, Christianity proclaims as its central and fundamental message the gracious remission of sin through faith in Christ Jesus, Acts 10, 43; 26, 18.

Since sinful man is saved alone by grace, the Scriptural statements that sinners are saved by the Gospel, Rom. 1, 16, or by Baptism, 1 Pet. 3, 21, or by faith, Luke 7, 50, must all be understood in relation to saving grace. In particular, they are descriptive of the means by which saving grace is conferred and appropriated without any merit, or work, on the part of the sinner. To be saved by the Gospel, by Baptism, by faith, etc., means to be saved by grace, without the deeds of the Law, through the divinely appointed means, by which alone the merits of Christ can be received.

From the viewpoint of fallen man we speak of the *necessity* of divine grace, since without grace it is impossible for the sinner to be saved. However, from the viewpoint of God divine grace must be viewed, not as necessary, but as free, because God was not moved by any necessity inherent in His essence to save guilty mankind, but alone by His mercy and compassion, John 3, 16; Luke 1, 78. *Deus est causa libera beatitudinis nostrae.* The view that the redemption of the world was a necessary unfolding of the divine essence must be rejected as a pantheistic delusion.

2. DEFINITION OF DIVINE GRACE.

Saving grace (*gratia salvifica*, χάρις σωτήριος), by which God is moved to forgive sin and to bestow salvation upon fallen mankind, is His gracious disposition *(gratuitus Dei favor),* or benevolent inclination, mediated through Christ's vicarious atonement, revealed in the Gospel, and witnessed to the world in order that it may be believed by all men, Rom. 3, 24. 25; John 20, 31. Luther: "God's love or favor, which He cherishes toward us in Himself"; "*Gottes Huld oder Gunst, die er zu uns traegt bei sich selbst.*" *Gratia Dei aliquid in Deo, sc. affectus Dei benevolus, est non qualitas animi in hominibus.* Synonyms of grace, in this sense, are love (John 3, 16), mercy (Titus 3, 5), kindness (Titus 3, 4), etc., all of which describe more fully God's benevolent disposition by which He is moved not to condemn, but to save, fallen mankind by faith in His beloved Son.

Although the term *grace* properly denotes God's unmerited favor in Christ Jesus, Scripture uses it also to describe the spiritual gifts or excellences which God, as the gracious Lord, works in all believers and by virtue of which they begin to fulfil the Law (willing and faithful service, 1 Pet. 4, 10; patience in suffering, 1 Pet. 2, 19; conscientious administration of the office of the ministry, Rom. 15, 15. 16; etc.). In this case the effect, by way of metonymy, is named after the cause, or the gifts of grace are named after their divine Source. *Nomen gratiae per metonymiam [effectus pro causa] pro donis ex benevolentia Dei in nos collatis sumitur.*

Grace in this sense must be definitely excluded as a cause of forgiveness of sin and salvation, since Scripture teaches expressly that the sinner is justified and saved without the deeds of the Law, Rom. 3, 28; Eph. 2, 8. 9. The believer owes his salvation not to inherent or infused grace, or the grace which is in him, but alone to the benevolent disposition in God, or the *gratuitus Dei favor*. In other words, when we say that we are saved by grace, we do not refer to divine grace as it exerts itself in us, but as it is found outside of us, in God. So also faith does not justify and save either as a good quality *(nova qualitas),* or as a good work *(opus per se dignum),* or as a gift of God *(donum Spiritus Sancti),* or as a source of good works in us, but alone as the receiving means (ὄργανον ληπτικόν), by which man, who in himself is ungodly, appropriates to himself the grace of God and the merits of Christ through implicit trust in the promises of the Gospel.

In short, faith justifies solely by virtue of its object, which is Jesus Christ, the Crucified, Gal. 2, 16; 1 Cor. 2, 2. Luther: *Non per se aut virtute aliqua intrinseca fides iustificat, sed simpliciter quatenus habet se correlative ad Christum.* This truth Scripture teaches clearly by placing faith in opposition to works whenever it describes the way in which the sinner is justified. Rom. 4, 5: "To him that worketh not, but believeth on Him that justifieth the ungodly, his faith is counted for righteousness"; Eph. 2, 8. 9: "By grace are ye saved, through faith, . . . not of works."

This sharp distinction between grace as God's unmerited favor and grace as a gift of God *(donum gratiae)* in the article of justification is of the greatest importance; for all who teach that grace in the sense of infused grace *(gratia infusa)* is either the sole or a concomitant cause of justification inculcate salvation by works and have fallen from grace, Gal. 5, 4. In reality, while retaining the Christian terminology, they are teaching the paganistic doctrine of work-righteousness.

This pernicious mingling of grace and the gifts of grace is the basic error of the Roman Catholic Church, which in the *Decisions of the Council of Trent* (Sess. VI, Can. XI) has anathematized the definition of justifying grace as *gratuitus Dei favor,* from which infused grace must be rigidly excluded. But also the Reformed are obliged to rely on infused grace for justification since they deny that God's grace *(gratia universalis)* is seriously offered to all sinners in the Gospel and the Sacraments. They are therefore compelled to rely for the personal assurance of their justification on something within themselves or upon their renewal, or their good works, in short, upon infused grace. The same is true of all enthusiasts who assume a revealing and sanctifying operation of the Holy Ghost outside the divinely appointed means of grace (the Word and the Sacraments), no matter by what names they may be known. Zwingli, in *Fidei Ratio: "Dux autem vel vehiculum Spiritui non est necessarium."* Since in this case the believer cannot rely for justification and salvation on the objective promises of God, he must rely on the feeling of grace *(sensus gratiae)* within his heart, or upon divine grace as it exerts itself in him.

It is true, wherever the grace of God in Christ Jesus is accepted in true faith, there good works must needs follow, and at times there will also be the comforting feeling of divine grace. But if the believer puts his trust in his spiritual renewal or in the presence of grace in his heart, Christ's perfect work of redemption, or the objective reconciliation effected by Him, 2 Cor. 5, 19, is denied. But then also the essence of justifying faith, which is trust in the objective divine promises of grace, Rom. 4, 18. 25, is denied. In the final analysis, then, also the certainty of salvation must be denied; for if salvation is based upon good works, such a person's hope of heaven is absolutely futile.

By reaffirming the true definition of justifying grace as *gratuitus Dei favor* and excluding from it the false conception of infused grace, correcting in this respect even St. Augustine, the Church of the Reformation returned to the apostolic purity of the Christian faith. The confessional Lutheran Church of America follows in the footsteps of the great Reformer and in the article of justification sharply distinguishes between grace and the gifts of grace, or between God's unmerited favor and its benefactions in the believer's heart. For this reason it constantly bears witness not only against Catholicism, Zwinglianism, and enthusiasm, but also against synergism (Arminianism), which denies the *sola gratia* and places the cause of man's justification to some extent in him *(aliquid in homine),* thus inducing him to trust for salvation both in divine grace and in human goodness.

While the synergists include man's moral conduct, or his self-decision, or his right attitude toward grace, in justifying faith, the Arminians insist that justifying faith embraces also the good works of believers. According to their teaching the believer, seeking assurance of his salvation, must trust in the divine grace *within himself (gratia infusa),* or in his sanctification.

From the above it is obvious how important it is for the Christian theologian to maintain the Scriptural definition of justifying grace; for without it he can neither teach the true doctrine of justification as revealed in the Gospel nor exclude from justification the doctrine of salvation by good works, nor can he rightly comfort any sinner who seeks assurance of salvation. Hence, wherever the Scriptural doctrine of justifying grace is perverted, the entire Christian doctrine becomes corrupted and paganized. It is for this reason that Luther and all orthodox Lutheran theologians so earnestly insisted upon having this Bible doctrine taught in the Church, that justifying grace is God's unmerited favor in Christ Jesus. The *Apology* declares: "It is necessary that in the Church of Christ the Gospel be retained, *i. e.,* the promise that for Christ's sake sins are freely remitted. Those who teach nothing of this faith . . . altogether abolish the Gospel. (Art. IV (II), 120. *Triglotta,* p. 155.) Chemnitz says: "*Gratia in articulo iustificationis intelligenda est de sola gratuita misericordia Dei.*" With this definition of justifying grace the Christian Church stands or falls *(articulus stantis et cadentis ecclesiae).*

3. ATTRIBUTES OF JUSTIFYING GRACE.

The attributes, or adjuncts, of justifying grace are as follows:

a. *Justifying grace is grace in Christ.* Justifying grace is not absolute grace, or grace bestowed upon the sinner by a fiat of the divine sovereign will, but grace mediated through Christ, or grace in or for the sake of Christ. In other words, according to Scripture, God is gracious to sinful and condemned mankind only in view of the fact that the incarnate Son of God through His vicarious atonement *(satisfactio vicaria)* has ransomed all sinners from the curse and condemnation of the Law. Rom. 3, 24: "Being justified freely by His grace, through the redemption that is in Christ Jesus." The price which Christ paid for the redemption of guilty mankind was that He of His own free will placed Himself both under the obligation (Gal. 4, 4. 5, *obedientia activa*) and the curse and punishment (Gal. 3, 13, *obedientia passiva*) of the divine Law which man had violated.

Divine grace therefore does not exclude divine justice *(iustitia Dei vindicativa),* but rather presupposes or implies the satisfaction of its demands through Christ's vicarious death, Rom. 8, 3. 4. For this reason the Gospel, which offers divine grace to all men, Titus 2, 11, is not a message of grace apart from Christ's death (Modernists, rationalists, Harnack: "The Son of God does not belong into the Gospel"), but "the Word of Reconciliation," λόγος τῆς καταλλαγῆς, 2 Cor. 5, 19, that is, the unique message that God "hath reconciled us to Himself by Jesus Christ," or that "God was in Christ, reconciling the world unto Himself."

Scripture thus leaves no room for grace without the payment of the penalty of man's sin. God neither forgives sin by ignoring His justice, nor does He accept the worthless ransom-price (good works), which men offer Him to satisfy the eternal claims of His justice. Divine grace for sinners could be secured only through the unspeakable sacrifice of Christ's vicarious obedience, Heb. 7, 26. 27; Eph. 2, 13—16; Col. 1, 20—22. Hence the axiom: "Divine grace and human merit exclude each other; but divine grace includes the divine merits of Christ."

Luther very aptly writes on this subject: "I have often said before that faith in God alone is not sufficient, for also the *costs* must be paid. The Turks and the Jews also believe in God, but without the means and the costs. And what is the cost? That the Gospel shows. . . . Christ here teaches that we are not lost, but have eternal life, that is, that God so loved us that He was willing to pay the cost, the putting of His only, beloved Child into our misery, into hell and death, which He made Him drink to the dregs." (St. L., XI, 1085 ff.) Again: "Though grace is given to us for nothing, so that it does not cost us anything, yet it cost some one else on our behalf very much; for it has been secured through an uncountable, infinite treasure, namely, through God's Son Himself." *(Ibid.)*

Such questions as, "Could not God be gracious to men because of His sovereign power as supreme Judge, without Christ's atonement?" or, "Is it not a thought unworthy of God that His grace toward sinners had first to be purchased by the perfect obedience of His Son?" are both useless and foolish; for the fact that God is gracious to sinners only for Christ's sake is emphatically stated in His Word and must be believed by all men if they desire to obtain divine grace and eternal life, 2 Cor. 5, 18—20. All who teach that God is gracious to sinners without the death of Christ (Unitarians, Modernists, Ritschl, Harnack, etc.) reject the Christian faith, champion pagan doctrine, and are outside the pale of the Christian Church; for the Christian Church is the communion of believers who trust in the gracious remission of their sins through the blood of Christ, Gal. 3, 26; Eph. 1, 7. So Chemnitz writes:

Extra Christum nulla gratia et misericordia Dei erga peccatores nec debet nec potest recte cogitari. (*Harm. Ev.,* c. 28, p. 152.) Hence those who deny Christ's vicarious atonement likewise deny the grace of God.

However, divine grace is denied also by those who claim that Christ's atonement was in itself not adequate as a ransom, but was declared and accepted as such for the acquittal of the sinner by God's own mere volition (the theory of acceptilation; Scotists, Arminians). This theory, in the final analysis, ascribes the forgiveness of sins to God's sovereign will and thus reduces the value of Christ's vicarious. suffering and death. But Scripture bases divine grace not merely in part, but *wholly* on Christ's atoning work, so that there is no grace for sinners but that which is in Christ Jesus, Rom. 3, 24; Acts 4, 12. According to Scripture the expression "the Gospel of the grace of God" (Acts 20, 24) and "Jesus Christ and Him crucified" (1 Cor. 2, 2) are synonymous, so that he who preaches the one must preach also the other.

The *Augsburg Confession* emphasizes this truth when it says: "Also they teach that men cannot be justified before God by their own strength, merits, or works, but are freely justified for Christ's sake, through faith, when they believe that they are received into favor and that their sins are forgiven for Christ's sake, who by His death has made satisfaction for our sins. This faith God imputes for righteousness in His sight, Rom. 3 and 4." (Art. IV. Cp. also Luther, St. L., XII, 261 ff.)

b. *Justifying grace is universal (gratia universalis).* The unmerited favor and love of God in Christ Jesus extends not merely to some (the elect), but to all men without exception. *Gratia Dei salvifica erga homines lapsos non particularis, sed universalis est.* This paramount truth Scripture teaches in all passages in which it declares a) that Christ is the Savior of the whole world, of all men, John 3, 16; 1, 29; 1 John 2, 2; 1 Tim. 2, 4; Titus 2, 11; b) that God earnestly desires that each individual person be saved, 2 Pet. 3, 9; Ezek. 33, 11; 18, 23. 32; c) that salvation has been secured even for those who reject the grace of God and are thus lost on account of their unbelief, Matt. 23, 37; Acts 7, 51; 1 Cor. 8, 11; 2 Pet. 2, 1. The universality of divine grace is denied by all who limit the purpose and efficacy of divine grace to the elect (particularism, *gratia particularis*).

These errorists may be divided into three groups: a) Supralapsarians: God decreed to create some to damnation; b) Infralapsarians: God decreed to leave some in the state of damnation into which they had fallen through their own fault *(praeteritio);* c) Amyraldists: God indeed offers grace to all, but bestows faith only upon the elect.

Every form of particularism is anti-Scriptural, being based upon the fallacy that, since not all men are actually saved, God does not desire the salvation of all. Misled by their error, all particularists claim that the term *world* (John 3, 16; 1, 29) signifies "the elect," and they substitute for God's universal counsel of grace (1 Tim. 2, 4) a *voluntas signi,* in opposition to which stands His *voluntas beneplaciti.* That is to say, God indeed wishes to save all men according to that will which He has revealed in Scripture (*voluntas signi,* the revealed will); but by His secret will *(voluntas beneplaciti,* the will of His purpose), which is not revealed in Scripture, He wishes to save only the elect.

According to Calvinistic doctrine, God, in the final analysis, is the cause why some are not saved, while Scripture expressly teaches that those who are not saved perish through their unbelief, or rejection of divine grace, Luke 7, 30; Acts 13, 46; 7, 51; Matt. 23, 37. Charles Hodge writes: "It cannot be supposed that God intends what is never accomplished; that He purposes what He does not intend to effect. . . . If all men are not saved, God never purposed their salvation and never devised, and put into operation, means designed to accomplish that end. We must assume that *the result is the interpretation of the purposes of God."* (*Systematic Theol.,* II, 323.)

In order to support the doctrine of particularism, the Synod of Dort (1618—19) declared that God can never be resisted whenever He earnestly offers His grace to men *(irresistible grace).* But also this doctrine is anti-Scriptural; for Scripture affirms that the operation of the Holy Spirit through the Gospel can be resisted, Acts 7, 51; Matt. 23, 37, though the operation is itself one of divine power, Eph. 1, 19. 20. As in the realm of grace God can be resisted when He works through means, so also in the realm of nature; for life, which is originated and sustained alone by divine omnipotence, Acts 17, 28, can nevertheless be destroyed by feeble man. God indeed cannot be resisted when He deals with man in His sovereign majesty (Luther: *in nuda maiestate,* Matt. 25, 31 ff.); but when He approaches man through means, resistance on his part is always possible.

If the objection is raised that God becomes the cause of a

sinner's damnation at least in cases where He hardens his heart (cf. the divine judgment of obduration), we reply that according to Scripture God very earnestly offers His grace even to those who harden their hearts, Rom. 10, 21; Ex. 5, 1 ff. The divine judgment of obduration is never absolute or arbitrary; God hardens only those who first have hardened themselves by resisting His Word and will, Rom. 11, 7. 20.

c. *Justifying grace is serious and efficacious (gratia seria et efficax).* In spite of the fact that divine grace can be resisted *(gratia resistibilis),* we must not regard it as a "fruitless wish" or an "indifferent complacency by which God does not desire to effect or obtain the things which please Him" *(otiosa complacentia, nuda velleitas),* but as both serious and efficacious. That is to say, God seriously purposes, by sufficient and efficacious means, to effect the salvation of all men, Rom. 2, 4; 1, 16.

This truth is proved from a) the divine command to preach the Gospel to *every creature,* Mark 16, 15. 16, and make disciples *of all nations,* Matt. 28, 19. 20, which certainly must not be construed as mockery on the part of God; b) His divine promise to grant His Holy Spirit to all who hear His Word in order that He may work in them saving faith, Zech. 12, 10; Acts 2, 17. 18; Ezek. 11, 19. 20; 36, 26. 27; Acts 2, 38; 7, 51; c) His comforting assurance that He will not only begin, but also perform, finish, the good work in all believers, Phil. 1, 6; and d) His most serious endeavor to work faith in those who resist the Holy Spirit, Matt. 23, 37; Acts 7, 51, so that, if the wicked perish, they do so solely through their unbelief, 2 Cor. 4, 3. 4.

In opposition to Scripture the efficaciousness of divine grace is denied a) by all particularists (Calvinists), who limit God's efficacious desire to effect salvation in men to the elect; b) by all synergists, who teach that God works in man only the ability to believe, not faith itself, since the latter, they say, depends on man's own decision or good conduct or his omission of malicious opposition. However, according to Scripture, God bestows not only the power to believe, but also faith itself, Phil. 1, 29. In opposition to Pelagianism and synergism, Scripture teaches that all who believe in Christ believe solely by virtue of divine grace and not through their own power or effort *(sola gratia),* while over against Calvinism it affirms that those who remain in unbelief do so not because divine grace is inefficacious in their case, but because they maliciously resist the Holy Spirit.

It is true, when we maintain universal and serious grace *(gratia universalis, gratia seria et efficax),* on the one hand, and the *sola gratia,* on the other, the question arises: "Why, then, are some saved and others not *(cur alii, alii non?),* though all men by nature are in the same guilt and corruption *(in eadem culpa)?*" The particularists (Calvinists) answer the question by denying the *gratia universalis;* the synergists, by denying the *sola gratia.* Both solutions are alike unscriptural, since Holy Writ most emphatically teaches both, *gratia universalis* and *sola gratia.* The true Lutheran Church does not attempt any solution of the question at all, but regards it as an unsolvable mystery, which human reason should not try to explore. The two truths regarding man's salvation which Holy Scripture clearly reveals are: a) Those who are saved are saved by grace alone, without any merit on their part; b) those who are lost are lost through their own fault. Beyond these two revealed facts no Christian theologian dare go. (Cp. *Formula of Concord,* XI, 54—59.)

Also with respect to the heathen we must maintain the *gratia universalis* because Holy Scripture includes all men in the gracious counsel of salvation. To deny the clear Scripture-teaching of universal grace because many heathen have never received the Gospel of salvation is an offense against the very divine grace which has enriched the world with the saving truth, Mark 16, 15. 16; Matt. 28, 19. On the basis of Scripture we therefore believe that God's gracious will extends to the heathen also, though actually thousands of them perish without the Gospel. Nor are we to assume that the heathen are saved without the divinely appointed means of grace, Eph. 2, 12, since Holy Scripture teaches that the means of grace (the Word and the Sacraments) are appointed for the salvation of all sinners, Mark 16, 15. 16; Matt. 28, 19. 20. The opinion that the heathen may be converted after death is anti-Scriptural, Heb. 9, 27. The passage 1 Pet. 3, 18 ff. does not treat of salvation possible after death, but of the condemnation of those who during their life on earth refused to accept the saving Word of God.

4. THE THEOLOGICAL TERMINOLOGY REGARDING THE DIVINE WILL OF GRACE.

The unmerited favor and love of God which He cherishes toward all sinners in Christ Jesus is called also God's good and gracious will. 1 Tim. 2, 4: ϑεὸς ϑέλει. On the basis of clear Scripture-passages depicting God's disposition toward mankind we speak of the divine will as being ordinate, conditional, antecedent and consequent, revealed and hidden, etc. Care must be taken that these terms are rightly understood and properly used.

a. The divine will by which God earnestly desires the salvation of all men *(voluntas gratiae)* is not absolute *(voluntas absoluta),* but ordinate *(voluntas ordinata),* inasmuch as it is based upon Christ's vicarious obedience *(satisfactio vicaria)* and on God's part embraces the conferring means (the Word and the Sacraments, *media δοτικά)* and on the part of man the receiving means (faith, *medium ληπτικόν).* In other words, God earnestly desires to save all men, but only for Christ's sake and by faith, which He Himself works in man through the means of grace, Mark 16, 15. 16; Rom. 10, 17. The divine will of grace may be called absolute only in the sense of its being entirely independent of human merit or worthiness; it is not absolute in the sense of being independent of the merit of Christ.

b. The expression *conditional will (voluntas conditionata)* is ambiguous and may be used both correctly and wrongly. It is used correctly when it is employed in the sense of ordinate will *(voluntas ordinata),* that is to say, when it expresses the paramount truth that God desires to save sinners only through Christ, through the means of grace and faith kindled by these. It is used wrongly when it is employed in the synergistic sense, that man's salvation depends, in part at least, on his cooperation in conversion or that man's salvation is conditioned by his good conduct.

If the objection is raised that Scripture itself conditions man's salvation upon his obedience, we distinguish between God's will as revealed in the Law and His will as revealed in the Gospel *(Gesetzeswille, Evangeliumswille).* The divine Law indeed demands perfect obedience of all men, Matt. 22, 37—40, and to this demand is attached the promise: "This do, and thou shalt live," Luke 10, 28. Such legal promises always presuppose a real condition; for if a person keeps the Law perfectly, he merits eternal life.

However, because sinful man, corrupted by the Fall, cannot keep the divine Law perfectly, God in His infinite grace has given lost mankind the wonderful Gospel promise that every sinner should be saved by grace, through faith, without the deeds of the Law, Rom. 3, 28; Gal. 2, 16. This is the gracious will of God revealed in the Gospel, which offers and conveys salvation to all men as a free gift, Eph. 2, 8. 9. Hence in all Scripture-passages which say that, if sinners believe, they shall live, John 6, 47; 20, 29; Acts 13, 39; 16, 31, the protasis must not be regarded as a real condition, but merely as showing the *way* or *manner* in which a sinner is saved. The statement of Christ "He that believeth on Me hath everlasting life," John 6, 47, does not mean: "Provided you fulfil the condition of believing, you have eternal life," but: "You have eternal life by faith," faith being the receiving means of salvation, not its meritorious cause, Rom. 3, 28. Heerbrand: *Fides non est conditio, neque ut conditio requiritur, . . . sed est modus quidam, oblatum beneficium et donatum per et propter Christum accipiens. Manus non conditio dicitur, sed medium et instrumentum, quo eleemosyna accipitur.*

c. The distinction between *voluntas antecedens (prima)* and *voluntas consequens (secunda)* is Scriptural if it is understood in the sense of John 3, 16—18. It is indeed the gracious will of God that all men should believe in Christ and be saved by faith in Him *(voluntas antecedens)*. However, if sinners reject the grace of God and maliciously refuse to believe in Christ, then it is God's will that they should be damned, Mark 16, 15. 16. Thus the *voluntas antecedens* applies to all men, while the *voluntas consequens* applies to all who perish through their unbelief.

Nevertheless, as Gerhard rightly remarks, this division distinguishes not the will by itself, which in God is one and undivided, just as also His essence is one, but its twofold relation. According to the first, God, as Gerhard comments, acts as a most gracious father *(benignissimus pater)*; according to the second, as a most just judge *(iustissimus iudex)*. The expressions *antecedent will* and *consequent will* have not always been used in the same sense, so that much confusion has resulted from their use. Hollaz thus uses the term *voluntas consequens* in an unscriptural sense when he says: "The consequent will is that by which God . . . elects those to eternal life who, He foresees, will use the ordinary means and will persevere in faith to the end of life." (*Doctr. Theol.*, p. 282.)

The will of God is said to be antecedent and consequent a) neither with regard to time, as though the antecedent will preceded the consequent in time, since God is free from any limitations of time; b) nor with regard to the divine will itself, as though there were two actually distinct wills in God; but c) according to our mode of conception, so that we may clearly know that God desires to save all believers and to damn all unbelievers. Hence the antecedent will of God is rightly defined as His will of mercy *(voluntas misericordiae)* and His consequent will as His will of justice *(voluntas iustitiae).* Luther: "God does not deal with us according to His majesty, but puts on a human form and speaks to us throughout Scripture as man to man." (St. L., I, 1442.)

d. The distinction between the revealed will *(voluntas revelata, voluntas signi)* and the hidden will *(voluntas abscondita, voluntas beneplaciti)* of God is used correctly if the former is referred to the divine will revealed in Scripture, 1 Cor. 2, 10. 16, and the second to the divine will which man neither knows nor can know, Rom. 11, 34. The revealed will of God includes both the Law, by which He demands of all men perfect obedience and threatens to damn all who transgress His commandments, and the Gospel, according to which God is willing to save all sinners by grace, through faith in Christ, without the deeds of the Law. This revealed will is fittingly called the "will of the sign" *(voluntas signi)* because God has manifested it to us by the sign of His Word. The hidden will *(voluntas abscondita, voluntas beneplaciti)* embraces the "unsearchable judgments" of God and "His ways which are past finding out," Rom. 11, 33—35, as these are shown in the lives of both nations and individuals (Esau and Jacob, Jews and Gentiles, Rom. 9—11).

These unsearchable judgments the Christian theologian must not try to explore; much less should he endeavor to explain them *(Cur non omnes?)* by denying either the *gratia universalis* (Calvinism: "God does not desire to save all men") or the *sola gratia* (synergism, Arminianism, Semi-Pelaganiasm: "Man is not saved by grace alone"). The folly of both Calvinism and synergism consists in the futile endeavor to change the hidden will of God into a revealed will or to ascertain that which God has not revealed in His Word, an attempt which needs must be futile since the "revelations" thus supplied do not come from God, but from the ignorant, blinded human mind.

THE DOCTRINE OF CHRIST.
(Christologia.)

Since the grace of God toward sinful mankind is not absolute, or arbitrary, but mediate (in Christ Jesus, Rom. 3, 24), the redemption of our Savior constitutes its indispensable foundation, 1 Cor. 3, 11.

The doctrine of Christ (Christology) therefore follows logically upon that of divine grace as the cardinal article of the Christian faith, with which the Church stands or falls *(articulus stantis et cadentis ecclesiae)*. While usually this expression is applied to the doctrine of justification, and rightly so, we must not forget that without the vicarious satisfaction of Christ there could be no doctrine of justification by grace, through faith. Hence, as the redeeming work of our Lord is the foundation of the doctrine of divine grace, so it is the foundation also of the doctrine of justification. This becomes evident when we consider that faith justifies only as trust in Christ as the divine Redeemer, who died for our sins (Matt. 16, 13—17; 1 Tim. 2, 6: ἀντίλυτρον ὑπὲρ πάντων), and not as trust in Him as a new "Teacher of ethics," or as a "perfect Ideal," or as a "great Revealer" of the "fatherhood of God," and the like. In view of this fact the paramount importance of the doctrine of Christ is obvious.

The doctrine of Christ is commonly treated under three heads: A. the Doctrine of the Person of Christ *(de persona Christi sive de Christo θεανθρώπῳ);* B. the Doctrine of the States of Christ *(de stationibus exinanitionis et exaltationis);* C. the Doctrine of the Work of Christ *(de officio Christi).* Under these three heads it is possible to group all truths which Holy Scripture reveals concerning our Lord and His work and to refute whatever errors have been voiced against them.

The assumption that the Son of God would have become incarnate even if man had not fallen into sin must be rejected as a useless, yes, dangerous speculation. It is useless, since human reason without divine revelation can never discover what God would have done had man not destroyed his happiness by sinning. It is dangerous, not only because it involves a basic element of pantheism, but also because it ignores the only purpose of Christ's incarnation which Scripture mentions, namely, the salvation of lost and condemned mankind, Matt. 18, 11; 1 Tim. 1, 15; Gal. 4, 5. Augustine: *Si homo non periisset, Filius Hominis non venisset.*

A. The Doctrine of the Person of Christ.

(De Persona Christi.)

1. INTRODUCTION.

Holy Scripture expressly calls Christ true God and ascribes to Him all the divine attributes; but it also calls Christ true man and ascribes to Him all the attributes common to men. Christ is therefore true God and true man, or the God-man ($\vartheta\varepsilon\acute{a}\nu\vartheta\rho\omega\pi\sigma\varsigma$).

For this reason we must reject as unscriptural every doctrine which denies or limits a) the true deity of Christ (Monarchianism, Unitarianism), b) His true humanity (Docetae, Gnostics, Anabaptists), and c) the personal union of the two natures in the one Person *(unio personalis)* together with the resultant doctrines of the communion of the two natures *(communio naturarum)* and the communication of attributes *(communicatio idiomatum)*. The controversies of the Lutherans in defense of the last two doctrines were directed not only against the Calvinists, but also against the papists.

2. THE TRUE DEITY OF CHRIST.

That Christ is true God, coeternal and consubstantial with the Father, is incontrovertibly attested in Holy Scripture. The proofs for the doctrine may be grouped as follows. Scripture ascribes to Christ —

a) The name *God* ($\vartheta\varepsilon\acute{o}\varsigma$, John 1, 1) and *Son of God* ($\upsilon\acute{i}\grave{o}\varsigma$ $\tau o\tilde{v}$ $\vartheta\varepsilon o\tilde{v}$, Matt. 16, 16), and these not in an improper sense, in which they are applied also to creatures ($\vartheta\varepsilon o\grave{i}$ $\lambda\varepsilon\gamma\acute{o}\mu\varepsilon\nu o\iota$, *dei nuncupativi,* 1 Cor. 8, 5; John 10, 35), but in their proper, or metaphysical, sense, so that Christ is said to possess not only divine functions, but also the one divine essence. John 10, 30: "I and the Father are one ($\tilde{\varepsilon}\nu$)"; John 1, 14: "The glory as of the Only-begotten of the Father" ($\delta\acute{o}\xi\alpha\nu$ $\dot{\omega}\varsigma$ $\mu o\nu o\gamma\varepsilon\nu o\tilde{v}\varsigma$ $\pi\alpha\rho\grave{a}$ $\pi\alpha\tau\rho\acute{o}\varsigma$). Even the *nomen Dei essentiale et incommunicabile* Jehovah (יְהֹוָה) is given to Christ, Ps. 97, 1. 7; cp. with Heb. 1, 6;

b) The divine attributes: eternity, John 8, 58; 17, 5; 1, 1; omniscience, John 21, 17; omnipotence, John 10, 28—30;

c) The divine works: creation and preservation, Col. 1, 16. 17; John 5, 17—19; the resurrection of the dead, John 5, 21. 28. 29; miracles performed by His own power, John 2, 11;

d) Divine adoration and worship, John 20, 28; 5, 23; Phil. 2, 9 ff. Thus in every way Scripture describes Christ as equal to God in divine majesty, glory, and honor, Phil. 2, 6.

If modern Subordinationists object that Christ is called God only in the predicate, but never in the subject, we reply a) that this is not true (cp. Heb. 1, 8; John 20, 28) and b) that, if Christ is called God in the predicate, this asserts His deity even more emphatically than if He were called God in the subject, since it is the very function of the predicate to describe the subject according to its true essence, Rom. 9, 5. To this we may add that the term *God,* when used in its proper sense, is never a generic term, but always a proper noun, since it always designates the divine Essence which exists but as one *(una numero essentia divina).*

Again, in reply to the objection that Christ is indeed essentially God, yet only in a secondary sense of the term (Subordinationists), we say that this anti-Scriptural view is based upon a tritheistic or polytheistic conception of God, as if the Holy Trinity consisted of one supreme God and two lesser deities. While it is true that Christ described the Father as greater than Himself, John 14, 28, according to His human nature, in the state of humiliation, Scripture, on the other hand, ascribes to Him the entire divine essence with all its perfections, Col. 2, 3. 9, proving that He is God in the same sense as the Father.

The charge that Christ in that case could not have suffered alone, since the numerically one essence would have drawn into His suffering also the Father (Patripassianism), can be answered thus: We accept the two doctrines (the unity of the divine essence and the exclusion of the Father from Christ's suffering and death) on the authority of Scripture as a part of the great mystery of Christ's miraculous incarnation (1 Tim. 3, 16: ὁμολογουμένως μέγα μυστήριον).

Every denial of Christ's true and essential deity is based, not upon lack of adequate Scripture proof, but upon the rationalistic tendency of the carnal heart, to which the Gospel of Christ is both foolishness and a stumbling-block, 1 Cor. 1, 23; 2, 14. If Christ is not true God, but only a human prophet, Matt. 16, 13 ff., then the entire Gospel of Christ's vicarious redemption is annulled and the Pelagianistic doctrine of work-righteousness must stand; for in that case fallen man has no divine Savior, 1 Cor. 15, 3. 4. 17 f., and therefore is obliged to earn salvation by good works. Yet in this very error the proud, self-righteous mind of unregenerate man glories. (Cp. Luther, St. L., IX, 237 ff. 376 ff.; XVI, 1688 ff.; VII, 1263 ff.)

3. THE TRUE HUMANITY OF CHRIST.

The reason why a detailed proof of Christ's true humanity has become necessary is that errorists have denied Christ's true human nature either a) altogether (*Docetae:* Christ's body was a phantom) or b) in part, by denying His human soul (Arians: The λόγος took the place of His human soul), or His human spirit (Apollinaris: The λόγος took the place of the νοῦς), or His human will (Monothelitism), or His true human birth (Gnostics, Valentinus: The body of Christ was of celestial origin). Christ without a human nature could be the Savior of the world as little as a Christ without a divine nature. 1 John 1, 7: "The *blood* of Jesus Christ, *His Son,* cleanseth us from all sin."

Accordingly Scripture is as emphatic in predicating of Christ true humanity as it is in ascribing to Him true deity. It ascribes to Him a) human names, 1 Tim. 2, 5; John 8, 40; b) human flesh and blood consubstantial with man's, Heb. 2, 14; c) human descent, Rom. 9, 5; Matt. 1, 1 ff.; Luke 3, 23 ff.; Gen. 22, 18, cp. with Gal. 3, 16; d) a really human, though miraculous, conception in the womb of Mary, Luke 1, 42; e) the constituent parts of a human being, John 2, 21; Luke 24, 39; Matt. 26, 38; Luke 23, 46; 22, 42; f) human emotions, Mark 3, 5; 14, 34; g) human physical wants, Matt. 4, 2; John 19, 28; Luke 8, 23; h) human suffering and death, Matt. 27, 46; John 19, 30.

The λόγος therefore did not bring down His body from heaven, but assumed human nature in the body of Mary, so that He was true man, Luke 1, 35. All who deny the true humanity of Christ do so not because the evidence of Scripture is inadequate, but because they allow themselves to be misled by rationalistic ("The finite is not capable of the infinite") or Pelagianistic considerations ("It was not necessary for the Son of God to become the Substitute and Redeemer of man").

Against Pelagianism in every form we hold on the basis of Scripture that the divine Redeemer had to be true man in order that He might perform the stupendous work of redemption, Is. 53, 7—11, fulfil the divine Law in man's place, Gal. 4, 4. 5, and atone for his sin, Is. 53, 1—6. Hence the denial of Christ's true humanity is tantamount to the denial of His vicarious atonement, Heb. 2, 14; John 1, 14.

Christ according to His divine nature is ὁμοούσιος, *consubstantialis,* with the Father; according to His human nature He is ὁμοούσιος, *consubstantialis,* with man, yet not *secundum numerum,* but *secundum speciem.*

The expression *Son of Man* which our Savior usually employed when He spoke of Himself, does not describe Christ as the "Ideal Man," but as the unique Descendant of man, Gen. 3, 15; 26, 4; 28, 14; 2 Sam. 7, 12, in whom the Son of God became incarnate, Is. 7, 14; 9, 6. That is Christ's own explanation of the name which He adopted as His usual designation, as this appears from Matt. 16, 13—17 (cp. v. 16: "the Christ, the Son of the living God"). Hence the "Son of Man" is the *God-man,* foretold in the Old Testament, Dan. 7, 13. 14, who came to destroy the works of the devil, 1 John 3, 8, and who therefore had to be true God, Matt. 9, 2. 4. 6; 12, 8; 26, 63. 64; 25, 31 ff., and at the same time true man, Matt. 8, 20; 11, 19; 17, 12. 22. 23; 20, 18. 19.

Though Christ is true man, consubstantial with all other men, yet His human nature is marked by certain peculiarities *(proprietates individuales)* that are not found in other human beings. Among these peculiarities we note: —

Christ's supernatural conception (extraordinaria conceptio). Christ was not the son of Joseph and Mary (against the Ebionites, Modernists), but was conceived by the Holy Ghost in the womb of Mary, the virgin, Matt. 1, 18; Luke 1, 35 *(conceptio miraculosa).* The *causa efficiens* of the Son of Man was the Holy Ghost; the *materia ex qua,* His virgin mother, Matt. 1, 20. Cp. the Apostolic Creed: *Conceptus est de Spiritu Sancto, natus ex Maria virgine.* If the objection is raised that an inconceivable miracle such as this would violate the "immutable laws of nature," Scripture itself supplies an adequate answer — Luke 1, 34—37. Christ's supernatural conception was a miracle of God's omnipotence and grace, which we should gratefully acknowledge, Luke 1, 38.

Christ's perfect sinlessness (ἀναμαρτησία). While all other men are conceived and born in sin, Ps. 51, 5; John 3, 6; 5, 12—20, the Son of Man was without sin, Is. 53, 9; John 8, 46; Luke 1, 35; 2 Cor. 5, 21; 1 Pet. 1, 19; 2, 22, and had to be without sin to be our Savior, Heb. 7, 26. 27; 1 Pet. 1, 19. Though Scripture ascribes sin to Christ, it expressly explains that this was imputed sin, or our sin charged to Christ, *peccatum imputatum,* Is. 53, 6; 2 Cor. 5, 21.

However, Scripture not only establishes the fact and necessity of Christ's sinlessness, but also explains how it was that He was conceived and born sinless. The cause was not a) that a holy seed

(massa sancta) was preserved and propagated in Israel until the
Savior was born (scholastic theologians), or b) that by way of
evolution Mary developed into a holy person (modern rationalistic
theologians, Olshausen), or c) the immaculate conception of Mary
(immaculata conceptio, proclaimed by Pope Pius IX, December 8,
1854), but the astounding fact that Mary became the mother of
Christ according to His human nature through the Holy Ghost,
Matt. 1, 18: *ἐκ πνεύματος ἁγίου).*

In consequence of His supernatural conception Christ was free
from both original sin *(peccatum originale)* and actual sin *(peccatum actuale).* This truth we derive from all passages that describe
Christ's absolute sinlessness, Heb. 7, 26. 27; 1 John 3, 5, as well as
from those which affirm that He became man not after the order
of nature (Luther: *non ex carne contaminata et horribiliter pol-
luta*), but through the Holy Ghost, Matt. 1, 18; Luke 1, 35. Since
Christ did not descend from sinful seed, He was free from hereditary corruption *(corruptio hereditaria)* and from hereditary guilt
(culpa hereditaria; reatus peccati Adamitici), which is imputed
to all men begotten of sinful flesh, John 3, 6; Rom. 5, 16. 19.

Nevertheless, though Christ's human nature was free from sin,
it was a true human nature, because sin does not belong to the
essence of man (sin being an *accidens*). Hence Christ was indeed
a true man, but one who, so far as His person was concerned, was
not under the Law, but above the Law, Matt. 12, 8.

Since Christ's human nature was received into the *λόγος,*
we must deny that there was in Him even the possibility of sinning, John 8, 46; 1 Pet. 1, 19; the holy Savior *could not sin
(Christus sacerdos impeccabilis).* In spite of this fact we must
not regard the temptation of Christ as mere sham, but as a real
temptation and suffering, which He endured for our salvation,
Matt. 4, 1 ff.; Heb. 2, 18; 4, 15.

The consequences of Christ's sinlessness were —

a) His immortality *(ἀθανασία);* for according to Scripture,
death is the wages of sin, Gen. 2, 17; 3, 17—19; Rom. 5, 12; 6, 23.
Christ died of His own will and power as the Savior of men *(non
aliqua necessitate, sed libera voluntate),* John 10, 18; 1 Cor. 15, 3.
The death of the Sinless One, who Himself was immortal, was the
ransom (Matt. 20, 28; 1 Tim. 2, 6) by which He purchased life
for sinful mankind *(λύτρον, ἀντίλυτρον). Christus mortuus est
propter peccatum imputatum.*

b) Greater natural gifts *(singularis excellentia),* such as wisdom, Luke 2, 52, because there were no disturbing and perverting effects of sin in His body. (Cp. Adam's natural gifts before the Fall, Gen. 2, 19. 20. 23.)

Much has been said concerning Christ's external appearance; but from Ps. 45, 2 we must not infer extraordinary physical beauty nor from Is. 53, 2 extraordinary deformity, since the one passage describes Christ in His beauty as Savior *(Erloeserschoenheit)* and the other in His deep humiliation *(Leidensgestalt).* The evangelists indeed picture the grace of Christ's words, Luke 4, 22, but never any beauty of person. However, let us bear in mind that Christ in His whole state of humiliation suffered the consequences of our sins, so that He always appeared in the form of a servant (μορφὴ δούλου) and in the likeness of men (ἐν ὁμοιώματι ἀνθρώπων), Phil. 2, 7; Rom. 8, 3. His bodily appearance therefore was not like that of man before the Fall, but rather like that of fallen and sinful man (ἐν ὁμοιώματι σαρκὸς ἁμαρτίας). *Similitudo . . . propter assumptas infirmitates peccatrix visa est.*

With respect to the human infirmities which Jesus suffered, Scripture shows that He indeed endured the common, or general, infirmities of men *(infirmitates communes),* such as hunger, thirst, weariness, sorrow, etc., but not the personal infirmities *(infirmitates personales),* such as personal illness, blindness, or any other personal defect; for of these not one instance is recorded.

c) *The impersonality of Christ's human nature* (ἀνυποστασία, ἐνυποστασία). Among the peculiarities of Christ's human nature we note also its want of personality, that is to say, Christ's human nature did not form a distinct person *(carentia propriae subsistentiae).* Christ did not consist of two persons, one divine and the other human, but in Him the divine and the human nature were united into one undivided and indivisible person, 1 Tim. 2, 5. *Humana Christi natura non habet propriam subsistentiam, personalitatem, ὑπόστασιν.*

This fact follows from the peculiar mode of the incarnation *(modus incarnationis).* For when the Son of God became incarnate, He did not assume a human person, but only human nature; in other words, the human nature was received into the person of the λόγος, Gal. 4, 4. 5; John 1, 14; Heb. 2, 14. Accordingly we predicate of Christ's human nature negatively ἀνυποστασία, or the Scriptural truth that it possesses no personality of its own; positively we predicate of Christ's human nature ἐνυποστασία, or the Scriptural truth that the human nature of Christ subsists in the λόγος (*subsistentia humanae naturae in divina natura τοῦ λόγου*).

If the objection is raised against this doctrine that the term *Son of Man* is just as much a designation of a person as is the term *Son of God* and that therefore the human nature of Christ must be regarded as a distinct person, we reply that this conclusion does not hold, since these terms do not designate two different persons, but only one and the same person, who at the same time is both God and man, Matt. 16, 13—17. In the person of Christ there are ἄλλο καὶ ἄλλο, but not ἄλλος καὶ ἄλλος. Of all other men the axiom holds: *Quot humanae naturae, tot personae humanae;* but this axiom is not applicable to Christ, because the Logos assumed human nature into His divine person, Col. 2, 9.

Modern rationalistic theology, which has surrendered the Scriptural doctrine of the impersonality of Christ's human nature, must consequently surrender also the doctrine of the incarnation, since this consisted essentially in the act that the Son of God received into His divine person human nature, so that from the very moment when His human nature was created (*productio*) it was also united (*unitio*) with the λόγος, Luke 1, 43. Ἅμα σάρξ, ἅμα λόγου σάρξ.

As modern rationalistic theology denies the incarnation, so it affirms that the two natures in Christ gradually grew into each other, or coalesced, and that in this way the union (*unitio*) of the two natures was effected. However, Scripture does not teach a union of the two natures in Christ by coalescence, but a union by incarnation, John 1, 14. If modern theology objects to this doctrine on the ground that the union of the Son of God with an embryo cannot be regarded as worthy of God, we answer that this "unworthy conception of God" is clearly stated in Scripture, Luke 1, 35. Again, if it objects that an intimate union such as the incarnation presupposes is unthinkable, we reply that Scripture itself describes the incarnation as a "mystery of godliness," which is "without controversy great," 1 Tim. 3, 16.

In order to emphasize the truth that the Son of God indeed assumed human nature, but not a human person, our dogmaticians say: *Deus assumpsit naturam humanam,* or *humanitatem;* but not: *Deus assumpsit hominem.* In view of the fact that modern rationalistic theology has changed the doctrine of the two natures (*Zweinaturenlehre*) into a doctrine of two persons, this distinction is very important. — The more extreme type of modern theology regards Christ as a mere man, in whom God revealed Himself in a higher degree than in an ordinary man (Ritschl; Modernism); in other words, the difference between Christ and all other men is only one of degree, not of kind.

4. THE PERSONAL UNION.
(De Unione Personali.)

God is at all times essentially and actively present in all creatures, Jer. 23, 23. 24; Eph. 4, 10; and to this union with the Triune God all created things owe their subsistence, Acts 17, 28; Col. 1, 16—18. This union has been fitly called the general union *(unio generalis)* because it embraces all existing things, animate and inanimate, rational and irrational, in the entire realm of nature. In addition to this union, Scripture teaches also a special union *(unio specialis, unio spiritualis),* namely, the most gracious union of the Triune God with the believers *(unio mystica),* by which the communion of saints is the living, spiritual temple of God, John 14, 23; 1 Cor. 3, 16 f.; 6, 17—19; Eph. 1, 22. 23. In the third place, Holy Scripture teaches a sacramental union *(unio sacramentalis),* by which the true body and blood of Christ are really and substantially present in the Lord's Supper and are distributed and received in, with, and under the bread and wine.

From these unions we distinguish the personal union *(unio personalis),* by which the divine and the human nature of Christ are most intimately united in the one person of the God-man (hypostatic union, *unio hypostatica).* Hollaz defines the personal union thus: "The personal union is the conjunction of the two natures, divine and human, subsisting in the one hypostasis (ὑπόστασις, *persona*) of the Son of God, producing a mutual and indissoluble communion of both natures." *(Doctr. Theol.,* p. 296.) This personal union was effected when in His incarnation the λόγος so assumed human nature into His divine person *(actus unitionis)* that in the incarnate Christ (λόγος ἔνσαρκος) God and man are forever one undivided and indivisible person *(status unionis,* ἔνωσις ὑποστατική). This is "the mystery of godliness," of which St. Paul testifies that it is "confessedly great," ὁμολογουμένως μέγα, 1 Tim. 3, 16, or the miracle of all ages.

The personal union is proved incontrovertibly by the personal propositions *(propositiones personales),* that is, by clear Scripture-passages in which with reference to the incarnate Christ it is said

that God is man and man is God. Matt. 16, 13—17: The Son of
Man is the Son of the living God; Luke 1, 31. 32: The Son of
Mary is the Son of the Highest; Jer. 23, 5. 6: The Branch of
David is the Lord, יְהֹוָה, our Righteousness; Rom. 9, 5: The Christ
who comes of the fathers is God, blessed forever; John 1, 14: The
Word was made flesh; Rom. 1, 3. 4: He who was made of the seed
of David is God's Son, our Lord; etc. These personal propositions
can be explained only on the ground that the divine and the human
nature are so intimately and permanently united in the person of
Christ that He is at the same time true God and true man.

The personal, or hypostatic, union of the two natures in Christ
is unique; that is to say, in the entire realms of both nature and
grace there is no other union of God and man like that which
exists in Christ. It may be somewhat illustrated (the union of
soul and body in man; iron glowing with fire); but these unions
are only similar to, not like, the personal union. Thus, while we
can say that in Christ, God is man and man is God, we cannot
say that in man the soul is body or that in iron glowing with fire
the iron is fire.

For this reason the personal propositions have been called
unusual or singular *(propositiones inusitatae),* or propositions for
which there is no analog. Yet, while the personal propositions are
inusitatae (unique), they are real and not merely verbal *(verbales);* proper *(propriae),* not metaphorical, figurative, or tropical *(impropriae et tropicae).* That is to say, in Christ the two
natures are truly united, just as the personal propositions affirm,
so that Christ is God-man (θεάνθρωπος) in the fullest sense of
the term *(persona σύνθετος, persona composita).*

While on the basis of Scripture the Christian Church teaches
the personal union of the two natures in Christ, it emphatically
rejects a) the error of Eutyches (monophysitism), who taught that
the union was effected by a mingling of the two natures into each
other or by confusion or a conversion of the one nature into the
other *(unio per mixtionem et conversionem),* so that by such
mingling, or conversion, a third object *(tertium quiddam)* came
into being; b) the error of Nestorius, who, though affirming
a connection (συνάφεια) of the two natures, nevertheless regarded
them as separate *(Formula of Concord:* "two boards glued together"), thus denying the personal union and in particular the
communion of the natures and the communication of attributes
(Mary is not θεοτόκος).

Against these two errors the Council of Chalcedon (451) declared: "We confess one and the same Jesus Christ, the Son and Lord only-begotten, in two natures (ἐν δύο φύσεσιν) without mixture (ἀσυγχύτως), without change (ἀτρέπτως), [against Eutyches], without division (ἀδιαιρέτως), without separation (ἀχωρίστως), [against Nestorius]." The error of Nestorius was later championed by Zwingli (ἀλλοίωσις), who taught: Wherever Scripture says that Christ has suffered, you must read: The human nature only has suffered.

In refutation of the Eutychian as well as the Zwinglian (Nestorian) error our dogmaticians say: "The two natures in Christ are united a) inconvertibly (the divine nature was not changed into flesh; against Eutyches), b) unconfusedly (the two natures were not mingled into a third object; against Eutyches), c) inseparably and uninterruptedly (against Nestorius); that is to say, the two natures in Christ are never separated by any intervals either of time or place. The union was neither dissolved in death (time), nor is the λόγος after the incarnation anywhere present outside the flesh (place). After the incarnation the Son of God is always and everywhere *Filius Dei incarnatus. Neque caro extra λόγον, neque λόγος extra carnem.* John 1, 14; Col. 2, 9; Rom. 5, 10; etc.

In opposition to all errorists, ancient and modern, the Christian Church confesses that the personal union is —

a. Not *unio nominalis,* a nominal union, as though the Son of Man were God only in name *(Deus nuncupativus).* Christ is true and very God, John 10, 30, so that the personal union is real *(unio realis).* While all Unitarians are willing to *call* Christ God (Ritschl: "For us Christ has the value of God; hence, while the ascription of deity to Christ is not a real judgment [*Seinsurteil*], it is a value judgment [*Werturteil*]"; Harnack: "Christ may be called the Son of God because He proclaimed to men the fatherhood of God"), they strenuously deny that He is God *de facto.*

b. Not *unio naturalis,* a natural union, like that of soul and body, which have been created for each other. The personal union is not a natural union, since it intimately and inseparably unites the Creator and the creature, God and man, into one person *(ens increatum et creatum).*

This union is therefore incomprehensible to human reason, 1 Tim. 3, 16. To render it somewhat intelligible to the human mind, some scholastic theologians said that the Son of God was joined to human nature through the means of the soul *(mediante anima)*, since only in this way two immaterial beings (God and soul are both spirits) can be joined. The soul, however, is just as much a creature as the body, so that the great problem how *God* could be united with a *creature* into one person is hereby not solved. But this view is also unscriptural; for while Christ in death gave up His spirit, Matt. 27, 50; Mark 15, 37; John 19, 30, so that the natural union *(unio naturalis)* of soul and body ceased, the personal union did not cease (Rom. 5, 10: Christ's death was the death of the Son of God). For this reason the personal union cannot be a natural union, or a union *mediante anima.*

c. Not *unio accidentalis,* an accidental union, as when two boards are glued together or a human body is clothed in a garment. An accidental union does not join two things into one in such a manner as the personal union unites the two natures into one person. Of two things accidentally joined together one may be injured and the other not (the garment may be torn, while the body remains unharmed), whereas the human nature in Christ was so joined to the divine that, when the *human nature* suffered, shed blood, and died, *the Son of God* suffered, shed His blood, and died, 1 John 1, 1. 7; 1 Cor. 2, 8; Acts 20, 28.

d. Not *unio sustentativa (nuda παρουσία sive παράστασις),* or a sustaining union by mere divine presence, by which God is present in, and sustains, all creatures, Col. 1, 17; Acts 17, 28. It is true, the divine nature sustained the human in Christ's great suffering, Matt. 26, 42; yet the essence of the personal union does not consist in that sustaining act, but rather in the most intimate conjunction of the two natures in the one person of Christ. Creatures are never assumed into the Godhead in spite of the sustaining presence of God; but through the personal union the human nature of Christ was received into the person of the Son of God.

e. Not *unio habitualis (relativa, σχετική),* a relative union, which indeed places two things into a certain relation with each other, but still leaves them separate essentially. Thus two friends are joined together by the union of mutual love; yet they remain two distinct individuals, separated even by space. But the personal union of the two natures in Christ was not relative (Theodore of Mopsuestia, † ca. 428), since the fulness of the Godhead dwells *in Christ bodily,* Col. 2, 9. The two natures in Christ are *inseparably* joined and by their most intimate and permanent union constitute the one indivisible Christ. While the union effected through friendship may cease, the personal union never ceases.

f. Not *unio essentialis sive commixtiva,* an essential or commingling union, by which through the personal union the two natures coalesced into one nature or essence (Eutychianism).

Since the charge was raised against the Lutherans that they, too, mixed the two natures into each other *(conversio aut confusio aut exaequatio),* the *Formula of Concord* expressly refuted this erroneous accusation, saying (Thor. Decl., VIII, 62 f.) : "In no way is conversion, confusion, or equalization of the natures in Christ or of their essential properties to be maintained or admitted. Accordingly we have never understood the words *realis communicatio,* or communicated *realiter,* that is, the impartation or communion which occurs in deed and truth, of any *physica communicatio vel essentialis transfusio,* physical communication or essential transfusion, that is, of an essential, natural communion or effusion, by which the natures would be commingled in their essence, and their essential properties; . . . but we have only opposed them to *verbalis communicatio* (verbal communication)."

g. Not *unio per adoptionem, a union by adoption* (Adoptionism; Felix of Urgel, Elipandus of Toledo, in the 8th century; condemned by various synods 792—799, mainly at the instigation of Alcuin, † 804), by which Christ according to His human nature has been said to be God's adopted Son *(Filius Dei adoptivus).* Adoptionism is a form of Nestorianism and presupposes two persons in Christ, one divine and the other human, of whom the latter was divinely adopted. In opposition to this error our Lutheran dogmaticians teach that Christ according to His human nature is the "born Son of God," or the Son of God by His very birth *(Filius Dei natus vel ab ipsa nativitate).* The incarnation was not an adoption of a human person by God, but the assumption of human nature into the person of the λόγος.

Eutychianism and Nestorianism (Zwinglianism) are attempts to render the mystery of the incarnation intelligible to human reason, either by mingling or by separating the two natures. But both errors, which equally annul the personal union, in the final analysis deny the vicarious atonement of Christ *(satisfactio vicaria),* since the redemption of lost and sinful mankind could be effected only by the God-man. Eutychianism and Nestorianism both lead to Unitarianism (Modernism), or to the error that Christ was a mere man.

The same may be said of the error of kenoticism, or the doctrine that the Son of God in His incarnation emptied Himself (ἐκένωσεν, Phil. 2, 7) of His divine attributes of omnipotence, omnipresence, and omniscience (Thomasius, Delitzsch, Kahnis, Luthardt, etc.) or of His divine consciousness and personality (Gess, Hofmann, Frank). Through this "self-limitation" of the Son of God the mystery of the incarnation is indeed explained, but at the tremendous cost of denying Christ's true deity. For if God has laid aside His divine attributes, He has laid aside His divine essence and has thus become a mutable being, who cannot be true God.

As we reject kenoticism, so we must reject also the error of autohypostasism (αὐτοϋπόστατος), according to which the Son of Man constituted a separate person (ἰδιοσύστατος), who either gradually coalesced with the divine person of the λόγος (Dorner) or remained separate altogether (Seeberg, Kirn, etc.). If that were true, Christ would be a mere man, in whom God merely worked in an extraordinary measure. If autohypostasism is adopted, the personal union, or the doctrine of Christ's two natures, is surrendered, and extreme Modernism, with its absolute denial of Christ's deity, is the only alternative.

The mystery of the incarnation can never be explained by reason; it must either be believed *in toto* or rejected *in toto*. At this point, as before all mysteries of divine revelation, the theologian stands at the crossroads, and he must choose either the way of Christian faith or that of pagan unbelief.

5. THE COMMUNION OF NATURES.
(De Communione Naturarum.)

A special discussion of the communion of natures *(communio naturarum)* has become necessary because both the Reformed and the papists indeed admit a union of the human nature of Christ with the person (ὑπόστασις) of the λόγος, but deny the real and direct communion of the natures with each other. While they concede the *unio personalis,* they reject the *communio naturarum.* Their opposition to the latter doctrine, which Scripture teaches with great clearness, is based upon the rationalistic axiom: "The finite is not capable of the infinite." *Finitum non est capax infiniti.* The Reformed theologian Danaeus writes: "Nothing whatever that is proper and essential to the Deity can in any way be communicated to a created thing, such as is the human nature assumed by Christ." (Pieper, *Christl. Dogmatik,* II, 135 ff.) Insistence on this principle by Calvinistic theologians is so emphatic that they charge the Lutherans, who on the basis of Scripture affirm the *communio naturarum,* with Eutychianism, or the mingling of the two natures.

However, in denying the *communio naturarum,* the Reformed and the papists contradict and deny their own doctrine regarding the *personal union.* If the finite is incapable of the infinite, then indeed the union of human nature with the person of the λόγος (personal union) is impossible, since the *person* of the Son of God is as infinite as is His divine *nature.* In other words, then there can be no personal union. Then, too, the entire incarnation of the Son of God must be denied as impossible, since this consists essentially in the union of God with man. Hence consistency on the part of the Reformed and papists would demand the rejection of the entire mystery of godliness that "God was manifest in the flesh," 1 Tim. 3, 16. The doctrine of the communion of natures follows directly from that of the personal union, so that they either stand or fall together.

But the Reformed and papistical error is directed also against Holy Scripture. The communion of the two natures of Christ is proved a) from general passages, such as John 1, 14; Heb. 2, 14. 15, etc., which clearly show that the Son of God so joined Himself to the flesh (σάρξ) that His divine nature has true communion with the human nature; b) from special passages, such as Col. 2, 3. 9: "In Him dwelleth all the fulness of the Godhead bodily" (σωματικῶς). From these passages we learn in particular:

a) That the divine nature entered into a true and real union with the human nature, since the fulness of the Godhead dwells in Christ *bodily.* On the basis of this and other passages, Hollaz writes: "The communion of natures in the person of Christ is the mutual participation of the divine and human natures of Christ, through which the divine nature of the λόγος, having become participant of the human nature, pervades, perfects, inhabits, and appropriates this to itself; but the human nature, having become participant of the divine nature, is pervaded, perfected, and inhabited by it" (*Doctr. Theol.,* p. 316 ff.);

b) That in Christ there is not mere contiguity (συνάφεια) of the two natures, but a most profound and intimate interpenetration (περιχώρησις), since the divine nature permeates the human nature, just as the soul permeates the body;

c) That in spite of this most intimate interpenetration there is no mingling, mixture, or change of the two natures, because the fulness of the Godhead dwells in the human nature. As the persons of the Trinity permeate each other without mixture, or as the soul dwells in the body without mingling, so the λόγος pervades the flesh in such a manner that neither of the natures is mingled or mixed with the other (*unio ἀσύγχυτος, ἄμικτος, ἄτρεπτος*);

d) That the divine nature must not be conceived as extending beyond the human, since the fulness of the Godhead dwells *in the body*. In other words, just as the soul is in the living body, but never beyond it, so the λόγος is in the flesh so as never to be beyond or outside it *(neque caro extra λόγον, neque λόγος extra carnem)*;

e) That the communion of the two natures in Christ is inseparable (ἀχώριστος), since they are united permanently (ἀδιαστάτως), or so that they are always mutually present to each other. The doctrine of the communion of natures as taught by the Lutheran theologians is therefore truly Scriptural.

Quenstedt presents the doctrine as follows: "The communion of natures is that most intimate participation (κοινωνία) and combination (συνδύασις) of the divine nature of the λόγος and the assumed human nature by which the λόγος, through a most intimate and profound interpenetration (περιχώρησις), so permeates, inhabits, and appropriates to Himself the human nature personally united with Him that from both, mutually intercommunicating, there arises the one incommunicable subject, namely, one person." (*Doctr. Theol.*, p. 310.) The opposing Zwinglian doctrine (Nestorianism) Quenstedt describes as follows: "[We condemn] the antithesis of the Calvinists, some of whom teach that it is only the person of the λόγος and not at the same time His divine nature that has been united with human nature. . . . Thus they invent a double union, mediate and immediate, saying that the natures are united, not immediately, but through the medium of the person of the λόγος." (*Doctr. Theol.*, p. 316.)

The Reformed theologians object to the communion of natures on the ground that in that case the human nature of Christ must be conceived of as being "very large," since otherwise it could not be everywhere present with the divine nature (local extension); indeed, that in that case it could not be regarded as a true human nature at all, since properties are ascribed to it of which human nature is incapable. In answer to this we say that the human nature of Christ was *not* physically enlarged through the incarnation, but is omnipresent with the divine nature, Matt. 28, 20, not by *local extension,* but by an *illocal mode of presence,* John 20, 19—26; Luke 24, 31, which it possesses besides its ordinary local mode, John 4, 3. 4, by virtue of the personal union.

If the Reformed theologians furthermore ask how this is possible without the destruction of the human nature, we answer that Holy Scripture teaches this to be a fact (John 1, 14; Matt. 28, 18—20), though a great mystery (1 Tim. 3, 16), and that therefore this doctrine must not be denied, but believed. Again, if they affirm that the human nature of Christ received extraordinary finite gifts *(dona finita extraordinaria),* but not truly divine gifts *(dona divina),* we remind them of the Scripture-passages which directly ascribe *divine gifts* to the human nature, 1 John 1, 7; Matt. 9, 6; John 5, 27; Matt. 28, 18. 20. While the human nature performs *actus naturales* (eating, drinking, suffering, dying, etc.) which are common to all men, it performs also *actus personales* (forgiving sins, executing judgment, etc.) which are the direct result of its intimate communion with the divine nature.

As the personal union, so also the communion of natures is proved by such personal propositions as "God is man" and "Man is God"; for these propositions predicate a real communion of the natures in Christ. To the objection of the Zwinglians (Nestorians) that the personal propositions, so far as the communion of natures is concerned *(quoad communionem naturarum),* are only nominal *(propositiones verbales, propositiones tropicae),* we reply that in that case also the incarnation, the personal union, and the entire doctrine of Scripture concerning the person of Christ must be regarded as nominal or figurative; for what is true of a part of a mystery is true of the whole of it. Indeed, if we must regard as nominal or tropical in Scripture everything to which man's blind reason opposes itself, then, in the last analysis, every article of faith must be denied.

Against Eutychianism and Nestorianism the *Formula of Concord* (Art. VIII, 13 ff.) declares: "The two natures were united not as two boards are glued together, so that they *realiter, i. e.,* in deed and truth, have no communion whatever with one another" (against Nestorius and Samosatenus), nor by "a mixing or equalizing of the natures, as when hydromel is made from honey and water, which is no longer pure honey and water, but a mixed drink" (against Eutyches), but as "the soul and body, and fire and iron, which have communion with each other, not by a phrase or mode of speaking or in mere words, but truly and really."

Against the errors of the Calvinists (Nestorians), papists, and Eutychians our dogmaticians have in summary described the permeation of the two natures (περιχώρησις) as follows: It is a) *intima et perfectissima,* intimate and most perfect; b) *mutua,* the divine nature permeating the human and the assumed flesh being completely permeated by the divine nature; c) *inseparabilis* (ἀχώριστος); d) without confusion, mingling, or changing (ἀσύγχυτος, ἄμικτος, ἄτρεπτος), yet so that the two natures of Christ are united continuously (ἀδιάστατοι, *sive sibi mutuo praesentes*) and are never outside each other *(nuspiam ultra, nuspiam extra).*

6. THE COMMUNICATION OF ATTRIBUTES.
(De Communicatione Idiomatum.)

Since the personal union cannot be perfect and permeant (perichoristic) without the participation of properties, the communication of attributes *(communicatio idiomatum)* of the two natures in Christ is the necessary result of the personal union. When the Son of God assumed into His person true human nature, He assumed also the properties which belong to human nature (to be a creature, to be born, to suffer, die, ascend and descend, move about, etc.). All who deny the communication of attributes must deny also the personal union, or the paramount mystery that the Word was made flesh.

Hollaz describes the communication of attributes *(communicatio idiomatum)* thus: "The communication of attributes is the true and real participation of the properties of the divine and human natures resulting from the personal union in Christ, the God-man, who is denominated from either or both natures." *(Doctr. Theol.,* p. 321.)

By the term *properties* (ἰδιώματα, *propria*), which is here used in its wider sense, we understand not only the natural properties themselves, but also what they do and what they suffer (ἐνεργήματα καὶ ἀποτελέσματα, *actiones et passiones*), by which the properties exert themselves (to create — to be created; to give life — to lose life).

While the *idiomata* of the two natures are attributed to the concrete of both natures (Christ — the God-man) or to the concrete of either of the two natures (God — the Son of Man), it does not follow from this that the properties of the one nature become those of the other (God is not mortal; man is not eternal); for by the personal union the two natures are not changed in substance, but each retains the *idiomata* essential or the *idiomata* natural to itself. (*Doctr. Theol.*, p. 313.) Therefore it is only to the person that without further distinction the *idiomata* of the one or the other nature can be ascribed. This truth will be considered more fully later on.

When we speak of the "concrete of the divine nature" we mean such terms as *God, Son of God,* the λόγος, etc.; when we speak of the "concrete of the human nature," we mean such terms as *Man, Son of Man, Son of Mary,* etc.; when we speak of the "concrete of the person," or of both natures, we mean such terms as *Christ, Messiah, Immanuel,* etc., which properly signify the person consisting of both natures.

Although every truth that will be set forth under the head of "Communication of Attributes" is already embraced in the doctrine of the personal union, we nevertheless treat the teachings of Scripture on this score under three distinct heads in order that the doctrine of the communication of attributes may be perceived the more readily and the antithesis of errorists may be refuted the more efficiently. Accordingly we speak of *Three Genera of the Communication of Attributes.*

THE FIRST GENUS (GENUS IDIOMATICUM).

The first genus of the communication of attributes Hollaz describes as follows: "The first genus of *communicatio idiomatum* consists in this, that such properties as are peculiar to the divine or the human nature are truly and really ascribed to the entire person of Christ, designated by either nature or by both natures." (*Doctr. Theol.*, p. 314.) 1 Cor. 2, 8: "They *crucified* the *Lord of Glory*"; Acts 3, 15: "And [ye] *killed* the *Prince of Life*"; Heb. 13, 8: "Jesus Christ, the same yesterday and to-day and forever"; John 8, 58: "Before Abraham was, I am," etc. In all these and similar passages peculiarities of either nature are ascribed to the whole person.

The first genus of the communication of attributes receives its importance from the fact that errorists at all times misinterpreted the Scripture-passages which ascribe human or divine peculiarities to the entire person of Christ. Thus it has been denied that the human *idiomata* "to be born," "to suffer," "to die," may be properly predicated of the Son of God. Nestorius objected to the teaching of the Christian Church by which Mary was called ϑεοτόκος, or "Mother of God." Zwingli resorted to a figure of speech (ἀλλοίωσις) to exclude the Son of God from the suffering and death of Christ. According to Zwingli "Christ suffered" means "The human nature suffered"; "My flesh is meat indeed" means "My divine nature is meat indeed." In short, both Nestorius and Zwingli denied that "the blood of Jesus Christ, His Son, cleanseth us from all sin," 1 John 1, 7, in other words, that the suffering and death of Christ were the suffering and death of God.

Nevertheless Scripture affirms this very fact. God's Son was made of a woman (Gal. 4, 4) and suffered and died (1 Cor. 2, 8); and it is this very fact that *God* suffered and died for us which gives to the blood of Christ the power to cleanse from sin, 1 John 1, 7. Holy Scripture thus ascribes to the entire person of Christ two kinds of properties, one divine and the other human, though in such cases it designates the nature according to which the property in question is ascribed to the whole person. Rom. 1, 3: "His Son, Jesus Christ, our Lord, was made of the seed of David *according to the flesh.*" Sometimes the properties are predicated of the concrete of the divine nature (Son of God, Lord of Glory, Prince of Life), sometimes of the concrete of the human nature (Son of David, Son of Man), and sometimes of the concrete of both natures (Christ, Immanuel, our Lord Jesus Christ), but the attributes are always regarded as belonging to the entire Christ.

In this manner Scripture ascribes to Christ eternity (John 8, 58) and time (Luke 3, 23); the eternal generation from the Father (John 1, 14. 18; Rom. 8, 32) and the birth, in time, of Mary (Gal. 4, 4; Luke 1, 35; 2, 7); omniscience (John 21, 17; 2, 24. 25) and limited knowledge (Luke 2, 52; Mark 13, 32); omnipotence (Matt. 28, 18; Mark 4, 39) and limited power (John 18, 12); life, essential and absolute (1 John 1, 2; John 10, 18; 5, 26), and death and resurrection (Matt. 16, 21; 1 Cor. 2, 8; Acts 3, 15). Both kinds of attributes, the divine and the human, belong to Christ equally, really, and truly, because both natures, the divine and human, really and truly belong to Him. However, the divine attributes belong to Christ according to His divine nature, while the human attributes belong to Him according to His human nature, as Scripture clearly indicates by the diacritical particles *(particulae diacriticae),* as in Rom. 1, 3; 9, 5.

When describing Christ's work of redemption, it is preferable to employ the concrete expressions: "The *Son of God* suffered and died" instead of the abstract: *"Divinity* suffered and died," because these may be taken in the sense of Theopaschitism (Theopassianism). Yet, rightly understood, these terms may be justified. Luther and the dogmaticians of the 16th century employed them frequently in the sense of "Divinity in the flesh." (Cp. Col. 2, 9: "the fulness of the Godhead.") — In passing, we may add that our dogmaticians never asserted that *God in His nature* can suffer and die. What they taught is that Christ, the incarnate Son of God, who is true God and true man, suffered and died *according to His human nature*.

THE SECOND GENUS (GENUS MAIESTATICUM).

The second genus of communication of attributes is that by which the Son of God, because of the personal union, truly and really communicates the properties of His own divine nature to His assumed human nature for common possession, use, and designation (Hollaz). As the *genus idiomaticum,* so also the *genus maiestaticum* follows of necessity from the personal union; for since the human nature has been assumed into the person of the λόγος, it partakes of the entire glory and majesty of the divine nature and therefore also of its divine attributes, John 1, 14; 5, 27; 6, 51. If the incarnation is at all real, then also the communication of divine attributes to the human nature must be real, since by the personal union not only the person, but also the divine nature, which cannot be separated from the person, has entered into communion with the human nature.

Yet this important truth, which Scripture so clearly attests, has been emphatically denied. In particular it has been claimed that the human nature cannot receive divine omnipotence, omniscience, and omnipresence, since the finite is incapable of these infinite properties (Reformed, papists). In fact, as the errorists claim, the human nature would be destroyed if the divine *idiomata* would be forced upon it. Hence by the personal union the human nature of Christ received, not omnipotence, but only very great power; not omniscience, but only very great knowledge; not omnipresence, but only an exalted local presence at the right hand of God. In short, according to the Reformed doctrine the human nature of Christ received not divine gifts, but only extraordinary finite gifts, of which human nature in general is capable. But this denial of the communication of the divine attributes to the human nature is a denial also of the personal union; for if the human nature of Christ could not participate in the divine attributes, it could not be received into the person of the λόγος, so that no incarnation could take place. Practically therefore the Reformed and the papists, by rejecting the doctrine of the communication of attributes, repudiate the doctrine of the incarnation (personal union), though in theory they maintain it.

In opposition to the Reformed and papistic error, Scripture affirms that Christ according to His human nature did in time receive divine omnipotence (Matt. 28, 18: "All power is given to Me"; John 5, 27: "authority to execute Judgment"; 6, 51: power to quicken; cp. also Matt. 16, 27; Acts 17, 31), divine omniscience (Col. 1, 19; 2, 3. 9), divine omnipresence (Matt. 18, 20; 28, 20; John 3, 13; Eph. 1, 23; 4, 10), divine majesty (Matt. 11, 27; Luke 1, 33; John 6, 62; Phil. 2, 6; Heb. 2, 7), divine glory (Matt. 26, 64; Mark 14, 62; Rom. 8, 34; Eph. 1, 20; 4, 10; Heb. 8, 1). In addition to these passages the *genus maiestaticum* is clearly taught in John 1, 14, where it is expressly stated that the glory which was given to the human nature was beheld even in Christ's state of humiliation, and in Col. 2, 9, where the *fulness* of the Godhead is said to dwell bodily in Christ, so that indeed the entire divine essence was communicated to the body, or human nature, of Christ.

In accordance with Scripture we therefore maintain that the human nature of Christ through the personal union came into possession of all the divine attributes of the λόγος, not indeed essentially *(formaliter),* but by communication *(per communicationem);* and just that is what we mean to affirm by the second genus of the communication of attributes.

For further explanation of the *genus maiestaticum* we add the following: —

a. We must distinguish between the possession (κτῆσις) and the use (χρῆσις) of the divine attributes communicated to the human nature. So far as the possession is concerned, the divine properties were communicated to the human nature at one and the same time, namely, at the very moment or act of unition (conception), so that even the infant Jesus was in possession of the entire divine majesty and glory, John 1, 14; Luke 1, 35. Yet Christ refrained from the full use of His imparted majesty during the state of humiliation, though rays of divine omnipotence, omniscience, etc., frequently manifested themselves, John 12, 28; Matt. 3, 17; John 14, 11; 11, 43 f.; Matt. 17, 2 ff. The full and constant exercise of the communicated majesty did not begin until

His exaltation to the right hand of God, Eph. 1, 23; 4, 10; Phil. 2, 9 ff.

b. Reciprocation, which indeed has a place in the first genus, does not occur in the *genus maiestaticum;* for there cannot be a humiliation, emptying, or lessening of the divine nature (ταπείνωσις, κένωσις, ἐλάττωσις), as there is an advancement, or exaltation (βελτίωσις, ὑπερύψωσις), of the human nature. The divine nature is unchangeable and therefore cannot be perfected or diminished, exalted or humiliated. The promotion therefore belongs to the nature that is assumed, not to that which assumes. (Quenstedt.)

Our Lutheran Confessions therefore reject the so-called fourth genus (*genus* ταπεινωτικόν), by which Christ according to His divine nature had laid aside and abandoned in His state of humiliation "all power in heaven and earth." (Cf. *Formula of Concord,* Epit., VIII, 39.) Our Confessions rightly point out that by this "blasphemous perversion" "the way is prepared for the accursed Arian heresy, so that finally the eternal deity of Christ is denied and thus Christ and with Him our salvation are entirely lost." (Cf. the error of kenoticism.)

c. The human nature of Christ, in addition to its essential properties, possessed also more excellent finite gifts than sinful mortals have; these must be ascribed to it because of its perfection and sinlessness, Luke 2, 47. 52. However, in addition to these gifts "truly divine, uncreated, infinite, and immeasurable gifts," or "all the divine attributes" of the divine nature were imparted to Christ according to His human nature through the personal union, Col. 2, 3. 9, for full and external exercise in and after His exaltation, Phil. 2, 9 ff.

d. Since the divine nature communicated to the human nature its own attributes, we ascribe the divine *idiomata* to Christ according to both His divine and His human nature. But to the divine nature we ascribe them essentially, or as inherently belonging to this nature, while to the human nature we ascribe them by way of communication *(per communicationem).* So Scripture speaks: "The fulness of the Godhead dwells bodily in Christ," Col. 2, 9, and so we avoid the error that the communication occurred through "an essential or natural infusion of the properties of the divine nature into the human." This error our Confessions condemn, declaring: "In no way is conversion, confusion, or equalization of the natures in Christ or of their essential attributes to be maintained or admitted." (*Formula of Concord,* Art. VIII, 62 ff.)

On account of the controversies on this matter it is necessary to consider in detail the individual divine properties which according to Scripture were communicated to the human nature.

a. *Omniscience.* According to John 3, 34, the Spirit was given to the human nature of Christ without measure (οὐκ ἐκ μέτρου). Since the Holy Ghost is the Spirit of wisdom and knowledge, Is. 11, 2; 1 Cor. 2, 10. 11, Christ according to His human nature therefore received infinite divine wisdom and knowledge. Hence we distinguish in Christ a twofold knowledge, namely, the infinite divine knowledge which the divine nature communicated to the human nature through the personal union *(actus personalis)* and the knowledge which the human nature possessed as natural and essential *(actus naturalis).* The first is infinite knowledge, or omniscience *(divina omniscientia);* the second, finite knowledge, capable of growth *(scientia naturalis, habitualis, experimentalis).* It is the latter knowledge of which the evangelist speaks; Luke 2, 52: "Jesus increased in wisdom." The infinite, divine knowledge which was communicated to Christ's human nature is attested in Col. 2, 3.

The passage Mark 13, 32 does not deny the communication of infinite, divine knowledge to the human nature, but rather describes the incarnate Christ in His state of humiliation when He abstained from the full use of His communicated attributes. Christ according to His human nature employed His communicated divine gifts only as these were necessary for His redemptive work. The redemption of sinful man, however, did not require the promulgation of the time and hour when the day of Judgment should take place. If the Reformed object that it is impossible to conceive of the communicated, divine knowledge as partly quiescent *(actus primus)* and partly operative *(actus secundus),* we remind them of the fact that the human mind is incapable of understanding the "mystery of godliness," 1 Tim. 3, 16, either in whole or in part. Nevertheless the relation between Christ's operative and inoperative knowledge may be somewhat illustrated by the human soul, which during sleep knows and yet does not know. Both the Reformed and the papists, who deny the communication of divine knowledge to Christ's human nature, must be regarded as errorists on this point *(Agnoetae),* since they affirm that the Son of Man, even in His state of exaltation, is ignorant of many things.

b. *Omnipotence.* That Christ according to His human nature received divine omnipotence is a truth clearly taught in Scripture,

Dan. 7, 13. 14; Matt. 28, 18; Heb. 2, 8. Even in His state of
humiliation He was endowed with almighty power, Matt. 11, 27;
John 13, 3; 3, 35; Is. 9, 6 ff., so that He could heal the sick, Matt.
4, 23; Mark 1, 34; Luke 4, 40, cast out devils, Luke 4, 41; 11, 14,
raise the dead, John 5, 21; 12, 1, and, in short, perform all miracles which according to prophecy the divine Messiah was to accomplish, Is. 35, 4—6; 61, 1. 2; Luke 4, 17—21; Matt. 11, 4—6.

That Christ possessed divine omnipotence also according to
His human nature is proved especially by those passages which
expressly declare that this divine property was given to Him as
the Son of Man, John 5, 26. 27; Matt. 16, 27; Luke 22, 69; Dan.
7, 13. 14; Col. 2, 9. Hence the Son of Man performed His miracles not as a mere agent, acting in the name of His Father
(*instrumentum ἄεργον*), but by His own power (*instrumentum
σύνεργον*), as Scripture expressly points out, John 2, 11; 6, 51—58.

With respect to the passages which state that divine properties
were given to Christ in time, John 5, 26. 27; 13, 3; Matt. 11, 27;
28, 18, the canon of the ancient Christian Church obtains: "Whatever Christ received in time He received according to His human
nature, not according to the divine." In other words, they refer
not to His eternal generation, but to His incarnation. "Whatever
Scripture says that the Word received [in time] . . . it says on
account of His *humanity* and not on account of His *divinity*."
(Athanasius. *Triglot,* p. 1117.)

Besides the infinite, divine power which Christ received according to His human nature, He, in His state of humiliation,
possessed also finite, or limited, power, since to make His redemptive work possible, He did not always and fully exercise the divine
prerogatives communicated to His human nature, 2 Cor. 8, 9; John
10, 17. 18; Phil. 2, 6—8. Only in this way could He "increase in
wisdom," Luke 2, 52, and suffer and die, Phil. 2, 8; though even
in the state of humiliation He did not always conceal His divine
power, John 11, 40—44. The emphatic opposition which the Reformed theologians offer to the Scriptural doctrine of Christ's communicated omnipotence is evident from the statement of Hodge:
"The human nature of Christ is no more omniscient or almighty
than the worker of a miracle is omnipotent." (*Syst. Theol.,*
II, 417.)

c. *Omnipresence.* As Holy Scripture ascribes to Christ's
human nature omniscience and omnipotence, so it ascribes to it
also omnipresence, Matt. 28, 18—20; Eph. 1, 20—23; 4, 10. The

omnipresence of Christ's human nature, however, is taught also John 1, 14 and Col. 2, 9; for these passages declare that wherever, after the incarnation, the λόγος is present, He is present as the λόγος ἔνσαρκος (Filius Dei incarnatus). (Neque λόγος extra carnem, neque caro extra λόγον.)

Our dogmaticians, on the basis of Scripture, very emphatically reject the so-called extra illud Calvinisticum, according to which the λόγος so united Himself with human nature that He indeed altogether inhabits it, yet at the same time, because He is immense and infinite, exists and works also altogether outside the human nature. The extra Calvinisticum is not only unscriptural, but also self-contradictory.

While the Reformed regard the whole doctrine of the communication of attributes as preposterous, they condemn in particular the Scriptural truth of Christ's communicated omnipresence as a monstrous figment (monstrosum figmentum) or a monster of impiety (impium monstrum). (Cp. Pieper, Christliche Dogmatik, II, 183 ff.) Denying the personal presence of Christ's human nature, they affirm a presence only of its efficacy, and they charge their Lutheran opponents with teaching the nonsensical view of ubiquity, or of the local extension of the human nature, though the Lutheran theologians have always rejected this as a puerile fancy; for they explain the omnipresence of Christ's human nature not by way of local extension, but by way of His illocal, supernatural mode of presence.

All the arguments of the Reformed against Christ's omnipresence which are based upon Christ's ascension into heaven, His sitting at the right hand, His second advent, etc., as if these acts presupposed a mere local presence, rest upon a childish conception of God and heavenly matters. Equally groundless is the argument that every real body must always be contained in space, so that Christ's human nature must be viewed as always occupying space. The universe certainly is a created material body; yet it is not in space, but in God, Acts 17, 28.

As the human nature received divine omniscience and omnipotence in the first moment of the personal union, so also divine omnipresence. This does not mean that the human nature through the personal union lost its natural properties in such a manner that the body of Christ ceased to be at any particular place; for the omnipresence of the human nature was not "physical, diffusive, expansive, gross, local, corporeal, and divisible," but divine and supernatural. Our dogmaticians rightly distinguish between Christ's simple omnipresence (*nuda adessentia, praesentia partialis, ἀδιαστασία*) and His triumphant omnipresence (*omnipraesentia totalis, omnipraesentia modificata*), which is always connected with divine dominion. The first mode Christ possessed in the state of humiliation, John 1, 14; Col. 2, 9; John 3, 13, since after the incarnation the λόγος is never outside the flesh. The latter mode Christ possesses since His exaltation, Eph. 1, 20—23; 4, 10.

Besides the divine omnipresence, which was communicated to it through the personal union (*actus personalis, praesentia illocalis, supernaturalis, repletiva*), the human nature of Christ, in His state of humiliation, possessed also a local mode of presence (*actus naturalis, praesentia localis*), Luke 2, 12.

On the basis of Holy Scripture our dogmaticians thus ascribe to the human nature of Christ three modes of presence, namely, a) *praesentia localis, praesentia circumscriptiva,* b) *praesentia illocalis, praesentia definitiva,* John 20, 19, and c) *praesentia repletiva, divina, supernaturalis,* Eph. 1, 23; 4, 10. (Cf. *Christl. Dogmatik,* II, 195 ff.) To these modes of presence may be added the *praesentia sacramentalis,* according to which Christ's body is truly present in the Lord's Supper, Matt. 26, 26.

The "sitting at the right hand of God" must not be referred to a "circumscribed or physical locality," since, as Gerhard rightly comments, "the right hand of God is not a bodily, circumscribed, limited, definite place, but the infinite power of God and His most efficacious majesty in heaven and earth, or the most efficacious dominion by which God preserves and governs all things," Ps. 18, 35; 44, 3; 108, 6; 63, 8, etc. So also Hollaz writes: "To sit at God's right hand means, by virtue of the personal union and the exaltation following this, to govern all the works of God's hands most powerfully, most efficaciously, and most gloriously, 1 Cor. 15, 25 27; Ps. 110, 1. 2; Heb. 2, 7. 8." (Cp. *Doctr. Theol.,* p. 403).

d. *Adoration.* As Holy Scripture ascribes to Christ according to His human nature divine majesty and glory, Col. 2, 9, so it ascribes to Him also divine adoration, John 5, 20—23; Phil. 2, 9—11; Rev. 5, 9. 10. The Reformed and papists, who deny adoration to Christ's human nature on the basis of Is. 42, 8; Jer. 17, 5, show by this denial that in spite of their statements to the contrary they hold the Nestorian doctrine, separate the two natures in Christ, and deny the mystery of the Incarnation (personal union). All

who rightly teach the personal union never regard the human
nature as separate from, but always as united with, the divine
nature in the one, indivisible person of Christ, so that he who
adores the divine nature at the same time adores the human nature,
or the incarnate Christ.

The question has been debated whether, in connection with
the second genus, such abstract expressions as "The human nature
of Christ is quickening" or "The human nature is almighty," etc.,
should not be replaced by the concrete expression "Christ is quickening" or "The Son of Man is almighty," since the former may
mislead the untrained to believe that the human nature apart from
the personal union *(in abstracto reali)* is endowed with such power
or that the human nature possesses divine omnipotence as a special
gift apart from the omnipotence of the divine nature.

Such misunderstandings must certainly be corrected; however,
the use of these expressions should not be condemned, since Scripture itself employs them, John 6, 51; 1 John 1, 7. In addition,
they most emphatically affirm the doctrine of the communication
of attributes, or the Scriptural truth that in Christ the two natures,
with all their attributes, are most intimately united, not only the
so-called operative *(attributa operativa, ἐνεργητικά)*, as omnipotence, omniscience, but also the quiescent *(attributa quiescentia,
ἀνενέργητα)*, as eternity, infinity, immensity, Col. 2, 9; John
1, 14, etc.

Luther writes on this point: "According to the other, the
temporal, human birth, also the eternal power of God has been
given Him; however, in time and not from eternity. For the
humanity of Christ has not been from eternity like the divinity;
but as we reckon and write, Jesus, the Son of Mary, is 1543 years
old this year. But from the instant when divinity and humanity
were united in one person, the man, the Son of Mary, is, and is
called, almighty, eternal God, who has eternal might and has created
and sustains all things *per communicationem idiomatum* for the
reason that He is one person with the divinity and is also true
God." *(Formula of Concord,* Thor. Decl., VIII, 85.)

It must be noted, however, that Scripture, though it ascribes
to the human nature the "fulness of the Godhead," Col. 2, 9, never
predicates directly of Christ's human nature the quiescent attributes (eternity, immensity, infinity), but only the operative attributes (omnipotence, omnipresence, omniscience, etc.). The reason
for this our dogmaticians give as follows: In spite of the per-

sonal union the divine properties remain the essential attributes of the divine nature and never become the essential attributes of the human nature by transfusion. But they are predicated of the human nature in so far as they become active in the human nature as in the body of Christ (the human nature quickens, executes Judgment, etc.). Hence we ascribe divine omnipotence to the human nature not as an essential attribute, but in so far as the Son of God exerts His divine omnipotence in His human nature, which through the personal union is united with His divine nature. On the other hand, those divine properties which within the divine essence remain quiescent and do not exert themselves *ad extra* cannot be predicated directly of the human nature.

To the objection of the Reformed that, unless all divine attributes may be predicated of the human nature, none whatever can be ascribed to it, we reply: —

a. Also in this matter we adhere strictly to Scripture, which indeed ascribes to the human nature of Christ divine omnipotence, omniscience, and omnipresence, but not eternity, infinity, immensity, etc. For this reason the "either-or" of the Reformed must be rejected as anti-Scriptural.

b. But this rationalistic "either-or" is also unreasonable; just as unreasonable indeed as if one would argue: "If the human body, through its union with the soul, is endowed with life, it must likewise become immaterial. But since it does not become immaterial, it does not become alive." Now, as the soul imparts life to the body (an operative attribute), but not immateriality (an inoperative attribute), just so according to Scripture the divine nature of Christ directly exerts in the human nature its operative, but not its quiescent attributes.

Yet Christ's *quiescent* attributes are not entirely excluded from His theanthropic activity; for they are exerted *ad extra* through the *operative* attributes. As God made the world in time through His *eternal* and *immense* omnipotence, so also Christ raised Lazarus from the dead by the *infinite* power of His eternal Godhead.

Moreover, Scripture expressly describes the omnipotence which was communicated to the Son of Man as *infinite*. Dan. 7, 14: "And there was given Him dominion and glory. . . . His dominion is an *everlasting dominion*." In this passage the *quiescent* attribute of eternity is clearly predicated of Christ's *human nature;* for the glory which the Son of Man received is *everlasting*. So also, according to John 17, 5, Christ was glorified with eternal glory; for His human nature, as He says Himself, received the same glory which He, as the preexistent λόγος, had before the world was. (Cp. *Formula of Concord,* VIII, 48 ff.)

THE THIRD GENUS OF THE COMMUNICATION OF ATTRIBUTES.
(Genus Apotelesmaticum.)

Gerhard defines the third genus of the communication of attributes as "that by which in official acts each nature performs what is peculiar to itself, with the participation, however, of the other." 1 Cor. 15, 3; Gal. 1, 4; Eph. 5, 2. The supreme importance of this genus becomes apparent when we consider that Christ could accomplish His work of redemption only because in Him the divine and the human nature were joined together.

Chemnitz writes very aptly on this matter: "This union of the kingship and priesthood of the Messiah was made in the interest of the work of redemption for our sake and for the sake of our salvation. But as redemption had to be made by means of suffering and death, there was need of a human nature. So it pleased God that for our comfort, in the offices of the kingship, priesthood, and lordship of Christ, our assumed nature should also be employed and thus the [official] acts (ἀποτελέσματα) of Christ's offices should be accomplished in, with, and through both." (*Doctr. Theol.,* p. 337.)

The special treatment of this genus has been rendered necessary by the antithesis of the Reformed, who teach that both natures in the work of redemption acted their parts *alone,* each *without* participation of the other. Similarly they claim that the human nature of Christ contributed to the miracles only as a mere or passive instrument (*instrumentum ἄεργον*); that it contributed no more to them than did the hem of the garment which the woman touched, Matt. 9, 20; or than did the human nature of the apostles, Acts 3, 6, or the rod of Aaron, Ex. 8, 16. Calvin called the merit of Christ directly the merit of a man and thus excluded the divine nature from the active acquisition of salvation for men. This is in full accord with the Reformed view according to which the communication of the official acts of Christ (ἀποτελέσματα) cannot be referred to the *communicatio idiomatum.* Practically this means that the human nature of Christ must be excluded from all works of our Savior which involve divine omnipotence, omnipresence, and omniscience. Again, they aver that the omnipresence of Christ in His Church, Eph. 1, 20—23; 4, 10, pertains not to His human nature, but to the divine nature exclusively, so that Christ's human nature is no more present with the Church than is that of Abraham or Paul in glory. For this reason it has become necessary to treat the third genus of the communication of attributes with special emphasis.

By the term *official acts* (ἀποτελέσματα) we understand all functions which Christ as the Savior of all men performed in the state of humiliation and still performs in His state of exaltation, such as dying for the sins of the world, destroying the works of the devil, being present with, and ruling and protecting, His Church, etc. The Scripture-passages which predicate these official works may be grouped as follows: a) such as describe Christ's official functions by a concrete term *(nomen officii concretum)*, as Savior, Mediator, Prophet, King, High Priest, etc.; b) such as describe particular official acts of Christ, as, for example, to bear the sins of the world, John 1, 29; to die for the sins of the world, 1 Cor. 15, 3; to give Himself for our sins, Gal. 1, 4; to give Himself for us an offering and a sacrifice to God, Eph. 5, 2; to destroy the works of the devil, 1 John 3, 8; to bruise the Serpent's head, Gen. 3, 15.

If the question is asked according to which nature Christ performed His official functions for the salvation of the world, we reply on the basis of Scripture: No matter whether, in the particular passages of Holy Writ which predicate the ἀποτελέσματα, the Savior is described according to both natures (1 Tim. 1, 15: Christ Jesus) or according to one nature only, either the divine (Acts 20, 28: God) or the human (Matt. 18, 11: Son of Man), the works of His office are always performed by the entire person according to both natures, inasmuch as each nature contributes that which is proper to it and thus acts in communion with, or with the participation of, the other. (Ἀποτελέσματα sunt operationes ϑεανδρικαί.)

This is the true Scripture doctrine, which also the ancient Church believed and confessed. Athanasius writes: "God the Word, having been united with man, performs miracles, not apart from the human nature; on the contrary, it has pleased Him to work His divine power through it and in it and with it." (*Catalog of Testimonies. Triglot,* p. 1141.) And Leo the Great: "Each nature does what is peculiar to it in communion with the other, namely, the Word working what belongs to the Word [the Son of God] and the flesh executing what belongs to the flesh." (*Ibid.,* p. 1109.)

It is true, Christ indeed suffered and died according to His human nature, yet by virtue of the personal union the divine nature participated in the suffering and death of the human nature; for the human nature was always united with the divine nature, and from this union the holy, vicarious Passion of our Savior received its redemptive value. So Gerhard declares: "The sufferings and bloody death of Christ would have been without a saving result if the divine nature had not added a price of infinite value to the sufferings and death which He endured for us." (*Doctr. Theol.,* p. 336.) And Chemnitz: "If the redemption, atonement, etc., could have been accomplished by the divine nature alone or by the human nature alone, the λόγος would have descended in vain from heaven for us men and for our salvation and become incarnate." *(Ibid.)*

Gerhard is indeed right when, commenting on 1 John 3, 8, he remarks: "The Son of God assumed human nature for the very purpose that in, with, and through it He might accomplish the work of redemption and the several functions of His mediatorial office."

It is for the reason just stated that the third genus must be maintained in its Scriptural purity; for upon it rests the entire comfort which the Gospel of reconciliation proclaims to lost and fallen man. Those who deny this genus rob the Christian believer of the sweetest comfort which he has, namely, of the Gospel truth that "the blood of Jesus Christ, His Son, cleanseth us from all sin," 1 John 1, 7.

Fortunately the opponents of the *genus apotelesmaticum* do not draw the conclusions which their false premises really suggest, but by a strange, yet fortunate, inconsistency retract in practise what they maintain in theory. Hodge, *e. g.,* says at one place: "A soul which is omniscient . . . is not a human soul. The Christ of the Bible and of the human heart is lost if this doctrine be true . . . ; omniscience is not an attribute of which a creature can be made the organ"; but at another place: "Such expressions as *Dei mors, Dei passio, Dei sanguis,* have the sanction of Scriptural as well as Church usage. It follows from this that the satisfaction of Christ has *all the value* which belongs to the obedience and sufferings of the *eternal Son of God,* and His righteousness, as well active as passive, is *infinitely* meritorious." (*Syst. Theol.,* II, 416. 168.) It is this very truth which the Lutherans mean to emphasize by their doctrine of the *genus apotelesmaticum.*

B. The Doctrine of the States of Christ.
(De Statibus Exinanitionis et Exaltationis.)

1. DEFINITION OF CHRIST'S STATE OF HUMILIATION.

The incarnation of Christ consisted essentially in the paramount miracle that the Son of God, with the fulness of the Godhead, entered into an indissoluble personal union with the human nature, John 1, 14; Col. 2, 9. Hence from the very moment of its conception, Luke 1, 35, the human nature of Christ was in possession (κτῆσις) of all divine attributes and of all divine majesty and glory, John 1, 14; 2, 11. However, in order to be able to redeem us by His most holy obedience (active, Gal. 4, 4. 5; passive, Is. 53, 4—6), Christ, from the time of His conception until His revivification in the grave, refrained from the full and constant use (χρῆσις) of His communicated attributes, majesty, and glory, Phil. 2, 6 ff. Throughout His earthly life, till the completion of His work of redemption, He went about in the form of a servant, bearing all the weaknesses and infirmities of human nature after the Fall and being subject to the obligation (Matt. 3, 15; Gal. 4, 4) and curse (Gal. 3, 13) of the divine Law.

This condition of self-renunciation we designate as "Christ's state of humiliation" *(status exinanitionis)*. The humiliation of Christ did not consist essentially in the act of the incarnation, although it was a most gracious condescension for the Son of God to assume our human nature; for while the state of humiliation ceased with His burial, Phil. 2, 8 f., the personal union resulting from the incarnation never ceased, Eph. 1, 20—23; 4, 10. Again, while in the incarnation the Son of God entered into a true and real union with human nature, the state of humiliation does not pertain to Christ's divine, but only to His human nature (against modern kenoticism). Baier defines the state of humiliation as follows: "The state of humiliation consists in this, that Christ for a time renounced, truly and really, yet freely, the plenary exercise of the divine majesty that He might suffer and die for the life of the world." (*Doctr. Theol.*, p. 377.)

The doctrine of Christ's humiliation as set forth in the Confessions of the Lutheran Church is truly Scriptural. Scripture not only clearly establishes the doctrine of the two states of Christ, Phil. 2, 6—11, in general, but also ascribes to His human nature in the days of His flesh full possession of all divine attributes, majesty, and glory, John 1, 14; 2, 11; 5, 17; Matt. 11, 27; Col. 2, 3. 9, etc., while in other passages it presents the same Christ as not using His divine prerogatives, so that the one Christ, who is ineffably rich, was also poor, Matt. 8, 20; 2 Cor. 8, 9; He who is almighty God, John 6, 68. 69; Is. 9, 6, was also weak, Luke 22, 42. 43; He who is the Creator and Lord of all things, John 1, 1—4; Matt. 8, 27. 29, was also subject to man, Luke 2, 51. 52; He who is the Prince of Life, Acts 3, 15; Rev. 1, 18, was also captured and slain by men, Luke 22, 54. 63; 23, 33—37. 46.

These apparently contradictory statements, Scripture explains by the fact that the Son of Man did not always and fully use the divine prerogatives which were communicated to Him as man (John 10, 18: Christ died because He did not use His power to live; Phil. 2, 6—8: Christ died because He humbled Himself). Hence the state of humiliation became possible and real because Christ voluntarily refrained from the complete and uninterrupted use of the fulness of the Godhead, which from the very moment of His conception dwelled in Him bodily.

The reason why our Savior thus abstained from the constant use of His plenary, communicated divine majesty is that according to Scripture He executed the work of redemption through His vicarious satisfaction, Is. 53, 1—6; 2 Cor. 5, 19—21. Had He always and fully used His divine majesty, as He did at His transfiguration and after the resurrection, Matt. 17, 1—8; John 20, 17. 19, He could not have become our Substitute, Phil. 2, 6—8; Is. 53, 1—6, and could not have rendered perfect obedience, Gal. 4, 4. 5; 3, 13, to His heavenly Father in our place. But since He humbled Himself (ἐκένωσεν) by refraining from the full and uninterrupted use of His divine majesty, assuming the form of a servant, appearing in the likeness of men, and so rendering perfect obedience to His Father, Phil. 2, 6--8, He has become our true Redeemer (Jer. 23, 6: "the Lord our Righteousness"), whose poverty is our riches (2 Cor. 8, 9), whose obedience is our redemption (Gal. 4, 4. 5), and whose death is our propitiation (Rom. 3, 24. 25).

Certainly, whenever it was demanded in the interest of His redemptive work, Christ employed His imparted majesty and glory, not only when performing miracles before His great Passion, John 2, 11, or when exercising His prophetic ministry, John 1, 18, but also when, as our great High Priest, He gave Himself for us as an offering, Luke 23, 34; for not only was His human nature sustained by the imparted divine properties in the dreadful agony of His Passion, Matt. 26, 38. 39; 27, 46, but rays of divine glory shone also *ad extra* through the intense gloom of His suffering, John 19, 25—27; Luke 23, 43.

2. ERRONEOUS VIEWS REGARDING CHRIST'S HUMILIATION.

a. The humiliation must not be regarded as identical with the incarnation, for in that case the humiliation would pertain to the divine nature inasmuch as it assumed the human nature (ἐπίδοσις), and the glorification would consist in the putting aside of the human nature. It is true, Christ's incarnation did imply a most wonderful condescension, and sometimes this truth has been expressed even in orthodox circles by the term "humiliation" (exinanitio sensu ecclesiastica accepta). However, when Scripture speaks of the humiliation of Christ in its proper sense (exinanitio sensu biblico accepta), in which it stands in contrast to the exaltation, it means that Christ became man in poverty and wretchedness, or that He assumed the form of a servant (μορφὴ δούλου), though He possessed the form of God (μορφὴ θεοῦ), as Phil. 2, 6. 7 attests. Strong rightly says: "We may dismiss as unworthy of serious notice that view, that it [the humiliation] consisted essentially in the union of the λόγος with human nature; for this union with human nature continues in the state of exaltation." (Syst. Theol., p. 701.)

b. The humiliation of Christ did not consist in this, that the Son of God, for the purpose of becoming incarnate, divested Himself for a time of His operative, or relative, attributes, such as omnipotence, omniscience, and omnipresence, so that the divine nature was reduced, or diminished, by the incarnation. This is the doctrine of the modern kenoticists (Thomasius, Delitzsch, Luthardt, etc.). Extreme kenoticists (Gess, Hofmann, Frank) even claim that the Son of God in His incarnation emptied Himself of *all* divine attributes, or that His divine personality was replaced by a human personality.

Kenoticism therefore undeifies Christ to account for the "true human development" of His human nature. But thereby it contradicts all Scripture-passages which declare, on the one hand, that Christ in His state of humiliation was one with the Father essentially, John 10, 30. 38; 14, 10, so that His *divine mode of subsistence* was not changed by the incarnation, Col. 2, 3. 9; and, on the other hand, that He performed the divine works together with the Father, so that also His *divine mode of operation* was not altered when He became incarnate, John 5, 17—19. The doctrine of kenoticism is therefore rationalistic and anti-Scriptural.

The true human development of Christ, Luke 2, 52, as well as

His answered prayers, Luke 22, 43; John 17, 5, are adequately explained by Scripture when it informs us that our Savior did not always use the divine attributes communicated to the human nature; for since the Son of Man did not always employ His divine majesty, He could ask and receive of the Father just as any other man, Phil. 2, 7.

Modern kenoticism, however, in addition to denying clear Scriptural facts regarding the incarnation, also commits the serious mistake of transforming the incorruptible God (Ps. 102, 26. 27; 1 Tim. 6, 16; Mal. 3, 6) into a being subject to change and thus destroys the very concept of God. Yet even so it does not accomplish its object; for as long as kenoticists affirm a union of God and man, the mystery of the incarnation remains, even if God is conceived as minus some attributes. The mystery of the incarnation can be removed only by rejecting the incarnation in its entirety or by regarding Christ as a mere man, who is without any divine attributes (Modernists).

This fact has been recognized by rationalistic theologians of another type (Dorner, etc.), who, in order to explain the mystery of the incarnation, ascribed to the human nature of Christ independent personal existence. But this rationalistic substitute is as unsatisfactory as is kenoticism; for it destroys the very concept of the incarnation, or of the assumption of human nature into the person of the Son of God. In that case there would be no personal union, but at best only a union by adoption (adoptionism).

c. The humiliation does not consist in the mere concealment of the use of the divine majesty imparted to the human nature (κρύψις τῆς χρήσεως), but in the real renunciation of the full use of the imparted majesty according to the human nature (κένωσις τῆς χρήσεως). In the Cryptist-Kenotist Controversy, 1619—1627, between the Tuebingen theologians (Osiander, Nicolai, and Thummius) and the Giessen theologians (Mentzer and Feuerborn) this question became controverted. The Tuebingen theologians ascribed to the human nature of Christ the sitting at the right hand of the Father even in the state of humiliation, which meant that our Lord made full use even then of the divine majesty, though in a hidden way (κρύψις), whence they were called Cryptists. This position is untenable in the light of the Scripture-passages which ascribe the sitting at the right hand of God to the human nature of Christ in the state of exaltation. The Tuebingen theologians admitted, however, that Christ, in performing His sacerdotal office, or in His suffering and dying, renounced the *full* use of the divine majesty communicated to the human nature. The Giessen theologians, on the other hand, asserted that the human nature of Christ in the state of humiliation was not present with all creatures, and they were inclined to exclude it from the preservation and government of the universe, Christ having thus emptied Himself (Phil. 2, 7) according to His human nature of that much of the divine majesty. For this reason they were called kenotists. But they did not hold with the modern kenoticists that Christ according to His divine nature divested Himself of His divine attributes. They did not teach an *absolute* renunciation of the use of the divine majesty, but freely admitted this use in the case of miracles. Their position is untenable in the face of John 5, 17.

With regard to the terminology which the Church employs in connection with Christ's states of humiliation and exaltation we may note the following: —

a. The *Formula of Concord* employs the expressions *conceal-ment* (κρύψις) and *non-use* of the divine majesty of Christ communicated to the human nature as synonyms. (Thor. Decl., VIII, 26. 65: "This was *concealed* and *withheld* [for the greater part] at the time of the humiliation.") This usage of the two terms is Scriptural; for the humiliation of Christ involved a real concealment of Christ's divine majesty, inasmuch as He was true and very God, Col. 2, 9, and yet appeared as a mere man, John 19, 5. On the other hand, the humiliation of Christ involved also a real renunciation, not indeed of the attributes according to His divine nature, but of the appearance in the form of God (μορφὴ θεοῦ), or of the full use of His imparted divine attributes; for He positively appeared in the form of a servant (μορφὴ δούλου).

b. The expressions "to be in heaven," John 3, 13, and "to sit at the right hand of God," Mark 16, 19, are not synonymous; for the first is predicated of Christ in His humiliation, while the second is the triumphant act of His exaltation.

c. When describing Christ's omnipresence according to His human nature, our theologians have used the expressions *omnipraesentia intima* and *omnipraesentia extima*. The expression *omnipraesentia extima* is used correctly when it is employed as synonymous with *sessio ad dextram Dei*. But when it is understood in the sense that Christ was not present with the creatures during His state of humiliation, it denies the personal union. The terms are used rightly when the one denotes the presence of the

Son of Man before the exaltation and the other His glorious presence after the exaltation.

d. It has been said that Christ before His exaltation, in the state of humiliation, worked *in* and *with* the human nature *(in et cum carne),* but not always *through* the human nature *(non per carnem).* The expression *non per carnem* in this statement is Scriptural if it denotes Christ's *perpetual* and *triumphant* use of the divine majesty imparted to the human nature *(usus plenarius),* or the enthronement of His human nature at the right hand of God. It is incorrect if it is used to deny the Scripture truth that Christ also in His state of humiliation performed His miracles, His prophetic ministry, and His work of preservation and government, John 5, 17; 1, 18, within or through the flesh, John 1, 14; Col. 2, 3. 9; for whatever Christ does after the incarnation He does not outside the flesh *(extra carnem),* but as the God-man, or as the incarnate Christ, 1 John 1, 7; Heb. 9, 14; 2, 8. 9; John 5, 26. 27; Luke 22, 69; Phil. 2, 9; etc., in other words, *within* and thus *through* the flesh.

3. THE SEVERAL STAGES OF THE HUMILIATION.

The humiliation of Christ embraces all events of His earthly life from His conception to His burial, the latter included. Christ's descent into hell *(descensus ad inferos)* must be excluded from His state of humiliation, 1 Pet. 3, 18; Col. 2, 15. The time during which our Lord sojourned on earth, Scripture denominates "the days of His flesh," αἱ ἡμέραι τῆς σαρκός, Heb. 5, 7. Christ's humiliation therefore includes: —

a. *His conception and nativity.* These two events belong to Christ's state of humiliation inasmuch as the incarnation, which in itself was not a humiliation, though a most gracious condescension, took place under extremely humiliating circumstances; for by His incarnation the Son of God took upon Himself the whole misery and wretchedness which sin had brought upon fallen man, 2 Cor. 8, 9; Luke 9, 58; Phil. 2, 6. 7; Matt. 8, 17. Christ was conceived and born as the Savior of the world, Luke 2, 11; for through His most holy conception and birth He atoned for our sinful conception and birth, Ps. 51, 5; Gal. 4, 4. 5. The virgin birth of our Lord is a fact clearly attested by Scripture, Is. 7, 14; Matt. 1, 23; Luke 1, 34. God willed that the Messiah should be the Son of a virgin, Matt. 1, 22. 23; Is. 7, 14, true man, yet without sin, Heb. 7, 26.

Luther writes: "Therefore the Seed of the Woman could not be an ordinary man; for He had to crush the power of the devil, sin, and death; and since all men are subject to the devil on account of sin and death, He most assuredly had to be without sin. Now, human nature does not bear such seed or fruit, as said above; for they are all under the devil because of their sin. . . . So the only means to accomplish the desired end was this: the Seed must be a truly natural Son of the woman, not born, however, of the woman in a natural way, but by an extraordinary act of God, in order that the Scriptures might be fulfilled that He should be the Seed of only a woman, not of a man; for the text [Gen. 3, 15] clearly says that He shall be the Seed of a woman." (St. L., XX, 1796 f.)

Whether our Savior was born *clauso utero* or not we may regard as an open question, though this is possible on account of the communication of attributes. (Cp. *Formula of Concord,* Thor. Decl., VIII, 24; VII, 100.) The denial of the virgin birth of our Savior by rationalists and Modernists (Th. Kaftan: It is "worthless from a religious point of view," *"religioes wertlos"*) is contrary to the express testimony of Scripture and is a result and proof of their unbelief.

The question whether Mary afterwards in her marriage with Joseph had children or not *(semper virgo)* the ancient Church as well as Luther and the older Lutheran dogmaticians have answered in the negative, while the opinions of more recent exegetes are divided on the matter. The question is a purely historical one and may be left open since Scripture does not answer it with sufficient clearness. Cp. Matt. 1, 25; Luke 2, 7; Matt. 12, 46 ff.; 13, 55 ff.; John 2, 12; 7, 3 ff.; Gal. 1, 19. (Cp. Pieper, *Christliche Dogmatik,* II, 366 ff.) Eusebius, III, 11, according to Hegesippus: "Alphaeus (Cleophas) was a brother of Joseph, who after the death of Alphaeus adopted his children, so that these (cousins of Jesus) became brothers of our Savior in the legal sense." According to this view, James, the apostle and brother of the Lord, Gal. 1, 19, and James, the son of Alphaeus, Matt. 10, 3, are identical. Chemnitz (Jerome): *Mariam post partum* (Matt. 1, 25) *aut cum Ioseph concubuisse aut filios ex ipso sustulisse non credimus, quia non legimus, sc. in Scriptura Sacra.* The term *first-born* (Luke 2, 7) does not prove that Mary had other sons.

b. *The circumcision, education, and life of Christ.* As all Jewish male infants were circumcised on the eighth day, so Jesus was made subject to the divine Law by circumcision on the eighth day, Luke 2, 21, although He was the Lord of the Law, Matt. 12, 8; Mark 2, 28. Hence the circumcision of Christ is rightly regarded as a part of His redemptive work.

Though Jesus had no faults that required correction by education, but was rather a pattern of virtue even in His childhood, Luke 2, 51. 52, since He was "holy, harmless, undefiled, and separate from sinners," Heb. 7, 26, He nevertheless by real study increased in wisdom according to the natural knowledge of His human nature *(secundum scientiam naturalem et experimentalem)*, because in His state of humiliation He did not always and fully use the divine omniscience communicated to His human nature, Phil. 2, 6. 7.

In His visible sojourn on earth Christ appeared in the form of a servant and the likeness of man, enduring all troubles, dangers, temptations, reproaches, and hardships that are common to men in general, Matt. 8, 20. He also voluntarily subjected Himself to the civil government, Matt. 17, 27, and appeared ordinarily as a mere man, so that He was regarded as equal or inferior to others, Matt. 9, 14; 16, 13. 14.

c. *The suffering, death, and burial of Christ.* The suffering of Christ extended throughout the days of His visible sojourn on earth, Matt. 2, 13; Luke 2, 1 ff., but culminated in the *passio magna* during the last two days of His earthly life.

The *passio magna* is the extreme anguish which our Redeemer suffered from Gethsemane to Calvary, partly in His soul, partly in His body, by enduring to the end the most extreme and bitter sorrows for the atonement of our sins, Is. 53, 4—6; 2 Cor. 5, 21.

The agony of being forsaken by God, Matt. 27, 46, was the endurance of divine wrath on account of the sins of men in His soul, just as if He Himself had committed the imputed transgressions. Or we may say, it was the endurance of the pangs of hell *(dolores infernales),* which consist essentially in separation from God, Matt. 8, 12; 25, 41; 2 Thess. 1, 9.

Our dogmaticians aptly describe the agony of the *desertio* as the *sensus irae divinae propter peccata hominum imputata.* But it is unscriptural to ascribe to Christ despair *(desperatio)* in His extreme anguish, since despair is wickedness and therefore not in agreement with His sinless character, Ps. 22, 2. 19; Luke 23, 46; Gal. 4, 4. 5.

The death of Christ was a true death, or the separation of His soul from His body, Matt. 27, 50; Mark 15, 37; Luke 23, 46; John 19, 30. In Christ's death not only His soul, but also His body remained in communion with the divine nature *(unio personalis),* so that His death was truly that of the Son of God, Acts 3, 15. The possibility of Christ's death under these circumstances is a mystery so great that He Himself has explained it, John 10, 17. 18. He could die because He did not always and fully use the divine majesty imparted to His human nature.

The honorable burial of Christ and the preservation of His body in the grave Scripture presents as a special prerogative of the Messiah, Is. 53, 9; Ps. 16, 10; Acts 2, 31; 13, 35—37, who after the completion of His redemptive work, Is. 53, 10—12, was to be highly exalted over all things, Phil. 2, 9—11; Eph. 1, 20—23.

Scholastic theologians raised the question whether Christ might be called a true man also while His body was resting in the grave. Quenstedt rightly designates this a *questio curiosa,* based upon a false definition of a human being *(ens vivum, animal).* Scripture clearly affirms that Christ gave Himself for us as a true man, 1 Tim. 2, 5. 6, which includes that He was a true man also in death.

4. THE STATE OF EXALTATION.

Christ's state of exaltation began with His return to life in the grave and exhibited itself to the lower world by His descent into hell, to the world by His glorious resurrection, and to the highest heavens by His ascension and session at the right hand of God the Father.

Our dogmaticians define the state of exaltation as "the state of Christ, the God-man, in which He, according to His human nature, having laid aside the infirmities of the flesh, received and assumed the plenary exercise of the divine majesty" (Baier).

The doctrine of Christ's exaltation is clearly taught in Phil. 2, 9—11; Eph. 1, 20—23; 4, 10; etc. The *Formula of Concord* expressly rejects the error (kenosis) that Christ was exalted according to His *divine nature.* It declares: "[We reject and condemn] when it is taught . . . that all power in heaven and on earth was restored, that is, delivered again, to Christ according to His divine nature, at the resurrection and His ascension to heaven, as though He had also according to His divinity laid this aside and abandoned it in His state of humiliation." The reason for this rejection is given in the words: "By this doctrine not only the words of the testament of Christ are perverted, but also the way is prepared for the accursed Arian heresy, so that finally the eternal deity of Christ is denied and thus Christ, and with Him our salvation, is entirely lost, if this false doctrine were not firmly contradicted from the immovable foundation of the divine Word and our simple Christian [catholic] faith." (Art. VIII, Epit., 39.)

As Christ's humiliation, so also His exaltation took place for our salvation, so that in the doctrine of the two states the entire Gospel of reconciliation is wrapped up, Rom. 4, 25; 2 Cor. 5, 18—21. Our Christian faith rests upon both the crucified and the glorified Christ, 1 Cor. 15, 1—23; Rom. 4, 25.

5. THE SEVERAL STAGES OF CHRIST'S EXALTATION.

a. *The descent of Christ into hell (descensus ad inferos).* The doctrine of Christ's descent into hell rests upon 1 Pet. 3, 18—20, which describes in detail both its nature and purpose. Additional light is shed upon the doctrine by Col. 2, 15. According to 1 Pet. 3, 18 the *descensus ad inferos* consisted in the glorious act of the quickened Christ (ζωοποιηθείς), by which He, with soul and body (against the papists and modern theologians), according to His human nature, went (πορευθείς) to the prison (φυλακῇ) of the evil spirits and the damned (ἀπειθήσασιν) and preached (ἐκήρυξεν) to them. The Greek verb κηρύσσειν does not necessarily mean to "announce salvation," but is a *vox media,* which stands for both Law- and Gospel-preaching; in itself it does not mean more than to proclaim, to announce, to publish. It is used for the preaching of the Law in Matt. 3, 1; Acts 15, 21; Rom. 2, 21; Rev. 5, 2; Luke 12, 3. In 1 Pet. 3, 19, as the context shows, the term manifestly denotes Law-preaching, since Christ here came as a "Herald" (κῆρυξ) to bring the proclamation of His victory to such as had heard the divine Word on earth, yet had refused to accept it (ἀπειθήσασιν). To them Christ therefore appeared as the divine Judge, whose authority they had scorned on earth. That this is the meaning of Christ's appearance in hell is proved·by the very scope of the text; for in the preceding verses the Christians are exhorted to bear suffering at the hand of the ungodly, trusting in the righteous Judge, who will mete out due punishment to all enemies of His Church at His second advent.

The descent of Christ into hell foreshadowed the final judgment of the wicked; and it is for this reason that St. Peter refers to it in this passage.

Hollaz is right when he says: "Christ descended into hell, not for the purpose of suffering any evil from the demons, John 19, 30; Luke 24, 26, but to triumph over the devils, Rev. 1, 18; Col. 2, 15, and to convince condemned men that they were justly shut up in the infernal prison, 1 Pet. 3, 19. The preaching of Christ in hell was not evangelical, but legal, accusatory, terrifying, and that, too, both verbal, by which He convinced them that they had deserved eternal punishments, and real, by which He struck frightful terror into them." (*Doctr. Theol.*, p. 396.)

In opposition to various errorists we hold that it was not the purpose of Christ in descending to hell —

a) To preach the *Gospel* to the evil spirits and their captives (Origen, all teachers of a complete restoration, or *apokatastasis*), or at least to those of the damned who in their earthly life did not have the opportunity to hear the Gospel (Church Fathers, modern theologians). The statement in 1 Pet. 4, 6 that "the Gospel was preached also to them that are dead" does not refer to Christ's preaching in hell, but to the preaching of the Gospel to men while they were still living on earth. This follows from the clause of purpose, "that they might be judged according to men in the flesh." At any rate, the passage does not teach a probation after death.

b) To suffer the pangs of hell (Aepinus, Flacius) or to pay to Satan, as the keeper of the prison, a ransom for the redeemed souls (Origen). For neither was Christ's descent a part of His humiliation, Luke 23, 43—46, nor did Satan have any authority to triumph over man and to hold him captive, 1 John 3, 8; Heb. 2, 14. 15. The passage Acts 2, 24 must not be construed as teaching any suffering of Christ after death; for the expression "pains of death" is equivalent to "power of death," as the context clearly shows.

Against John Parsimonius, who, on the ground that hell is no locality, held that Christ "descended into hell" only in the sense that during His lifetime He suffered the pains of hell, our dogmaticians declared that Scripture teaches us to believe that our Savior descended into hell truly and really, though not by any local movement, since the quickened Christ was no longer in the form of a servant, but in the form of God, and so constantly employed the divine majesty communicated to His human nature.

As John Parsimonius so also the Reformed deny Christ's real descent into hell, some referring the *descensus* to the entire state of humiliation (Sohnius), others to His burial (Bucer, Beza), and still others to the pains which He suffered in His soul during His great Passion (Calvin). In the Lutheran Church the doctrine of Christ's descent into hell was definitely fixed on the basis of Scripture by the adoption of Article IX of the *Formula of Concord.* Hollaz defines the *descensus ad inferos* thus: "The descent of Christ into the lower world is the true, real, and supernatural movement by which Christ, having been freed from the chains of death and restored to life, in His entire person betook Himself to the lower regions that He might exhibit Himself to the evil spirits and to condemned men as the Conqueror of death." (*Doctr. Theol.,* p. 379.)

b. *The resurrection of Christ.* The resurrection of Christ has been defined by Hollaz as "the act of glorious victory by which Christ, the God-man, through the same power as that of God the Father and the Holy Spirit, brought forth His body, reunited with the soul and glorified, and showed it alive to His disciples by various proofs, for the confirmation of our peace, fellowship, joy, and hope in our own future resurrection." (*Doctr. Theol.,* p. 380.) This definition is both Scriptural and complete.

According to Scripture the resurrection of Christ, on the one hand, was the work of God the Father, who acted as its efficient Cause, Eph. 1, 20; Rom. 6, 4. As such our Savior's resurrection was the actual absolution, or justification, of the whole world; for by the resurrection, or justification, of the divine Substitute of man God declared all sinners free from sin, Rom. 4, 24. 25; 10, 9. For this reason Christ's resurrection is the object of justifying faith, 1 Cor. 15, 14. 17. 21. Calov writes of this: "As God punished our sins in Christ, which were placed upon, and imputed to, Him as our Substitute, so also by raising Him from the dead He absolved Him from our sins imputed to Him and therefore also absolved us in Him." (*Biblia Illustr., ad* Rom. 4, 25.)

On the other hand, Scripture describes also Christ Himself as the efficient Cause *(causa efficiens)* of His resurrection, John 2, 19; 10, 17. 18, inasmuch as He is true God and in possession of the same divine power *(una numero omnipotentia)* as the Father and the Holy Ghost, John 5, 19. From this point of view Christ's resurrection is a most powerful proof for His deity and divine Saviorship, John 2, 18—21.

The body of Christ which, reunited with the soul, came forth from the grave was the same body which the Son of God assumed in the body of Mary and which He subjected to suffering and death, John 20, 27. But the risen body of Christ possessed *new properties (idem corpus essentiā, novum qualitatibus).* The natural body (σῶμα ψυχικόν, 1 Cor. 15, 44) had become a spiritual body (σῶμα πνευματικόν, 1 Cor. 15, 44), that is, a glorified body (σῶμα τῆς δόξης, Phil. 3, 21).

The resurrection of Christ occurred *clauso sepulchro,* or through the closed and sealed tomb, Matt. 28, 1—6. This truth is denied by the Reformed theologians because they reject the communication of attributes, John 20, 19.

The eating of the food by the risen Savior, Luke 24, 43, occurred not from necessity, but from free will; not for the nourishment of His body, but for the strengthening of the faith of the disciples.

With regard to the purpose of the resurrection, Hollaz says correctly that Christ rose again in order to manifest the victory which He had obtained over death and the devil, Acts 2, 24; Heb. 2, 14. 15, and to offer and apply to all men the fruits of His Passion and death, Rom. 4, 25; 1 Pet. 1, 3. 4; John 11, 25. 26; 14, 19; 2 Cor. 4, 14; 1 Thess. 4, 14; Rom. 6, 4; 2 Cor. 5, 15. For this reason the doctrine of Christ's resurrection is fundamental for the entire Christian religion.

c. *The forty days between Christ's resurrection and ascension.* The information which Holy Scripture gives with regard to the forty days between Christ's resurrection and ascension is only fragmentary. After His triumphant victory over death our Savior no longer associated with His disciples as He did in the days of His flesh, Luke 24, 44, yet He continually appeared to them, Acts 1, 3; 1 Cor. 15, 4—8, conversed and ate with them, Luke 24, 41—43, and convinced them that He was the Christ, the Son of God, John 20, 19—31.

d. *The ascension of Christ.* Christ's ascension may be viewed either in a wider sense, including His sitting at the right hand of God, Acts 2, 33. 34; Eph. 4, 10, or in a narrower sense, embracing only the visible elevation of Christ on high, Luke 24, 51; Acts 1, 9—11. In this article we use the term in the latter signification.

In contradistinction to the resurrection the ascension occurred before witnesses, Acts 1, 9—14. Essentially it consisted in a local movement upward *(motus localis),* until the Savior was received by a cloud, Acts 1, 9.

The heaven into which Christ ascended is not only the heaven of the blessed saints (John 14, 2: *domicilium beatorum ascensionis terminus ad quem proprius*), but also the *right hand of God (coelum maiestaticum).* God's right hand is not a definite place, but His omnipotent power, which fills heaven and earth, Matt. 26, 64; Ex. 15, 6; Heb. 1, 3; 8, 1; 12, 2; Ps. 139, 10; Eph. 1, 20—23.

The purpose of the ascension was, a) with respect to Christ Himself, His public and triumphant certification as the Savior of the world, or His solemn enthronement according to His human nature, John 6, 60—62, and, b) with respect to all believers, the most glorious assurance that they, too, shall follow Christ into heaven, John 14, 2 f.; 17, 24.

The Reformed regard heaven as created space, in which Christ's human nature is enclosed *(Christus comprehensus et circumscriptus),* so that, according to His human nature, He is present neither in the Lord's Supper nor anywhere else outside the heavenly place in which His human nature is shut in. Acts 3, 21 does *not* prove the error of the Reformed. (Cf. *Formula of Concord,* Thor. Decl., VII, 119.)

Hollaz gives the following comprehensive definition of Christ's ascension: "The ascension is the glorious act of Christ by which, after having been resuscitated, He betook Himself, according to His human nature, by a true, real, and local motion, according to His voluntary determination *(per liberam oeconomiam)* and in a visible manner unto the clouds and thence in an invisible manner into the common heaven of the blessed and to the very throne of God, that, having triumphed over His enemies, He might occupy the kingdom of God, Acts 3, 21, reopen the closed paradise, Rev. 3, 7, and prepare a permanent inheritance for us in heaven, John 14, 2." *(Doctr. Theol.,* p. 380.)

e. *Christ's sitting at the right hand of God.* Since the right hand of God is His omnipresent power and operation, Ps. 139, 9. 10; 118, 15. 16, Christ's sitting at the right hand of God the Father is His full and incessant use of the divine majesty communicated to the human nature for universal and most glorious government in the kingdoms of power, grace, and glory, 1 Cor. 15, 25. 27; Ps. 110, 1; Heb. 2, 7. 8. Christ's session at the right hand of God is therefore His exaltation, according to His human nature, to the sovereign lordship and rule over all things, Eph. 1, 20—23; 4, 10; 1 Pet. 3, 22; Acts 3, 21. (Cp. *Formula of Concora,* Thor. Decl., VIII, 27.)

Concerning the participation of the human nature in the omnipotent operation of the divine nature in the states of humiliation and exaltation, we may note the following: As the divine majesty ($\delta \delta \xi a$) was always in the human nature after the incarnation, John 1, 14; Col. 2, 9, yet revealed itself in a peculiar way through the human nature at the transfiguration, Matt. 17, 1—8, so also the omnipotent operation of the divine nature was always in the human nature after the incarnation, yet revealed itself most gloriously after its exaltation to the right hand of God.

The sitting of Christ at the right hand of God may be defined in all its aspects as "the highest degree of glory, in which Christ, the God-man, having been exalted as to His human nature to the throne of divine majesty, most powerfully and by His immediate presence governs all things which are in the kingdoms of power, grace, and glory for the praise of His own name and the solace and safety of the afflicted Church." (Hollaz, *Doctr. Theol.*, p. 381.)

The special comfort for the believer which attaches to Christ's triumphant session at the right hand of God is beautifully expressed by the *Formula of Concord* in the following words (Thor. Decl., VII, 78 f.): "We hold . . . that also according to His assumed nature and with the same He [Christ] can be, and also is, present where He will, and especially that in His Church and congregation on earth He is present as Mediator, Head, King, and High Priest, not in part, or one half of Him only, but the entire person of Christ is present, to which both natures belong, the divine and the human; not only according to His divinity, but also according to and with His assumed human nature, according to which He is our Brother and we are flesh of His flesh and bone of His bone, even as He has instituted His Holy Supper for the certain assurance and confirmation of this, that also according to that nature according to which He has flesh and blood He will be with us and dwell, work, and be efficacious in us."

f. *Christ's second advent.* The doctrine of Christ's visible and glorious return for the final Judgment will be considered under the head of Eschatology, where it properly belongs.

C. The Doctrine of Christ's Office.
(De Opere sive Officio Christi.)

The incarnation of the Son of God took place in order that the work of redemption, decreed by God from eternity, might be accomplished, John 17, 4; 3, 16; Matt. 18, 11; Luke 19, 10; 1 Tim. 1, 15. The *Augsburg Confession* declares (Art. III): "The Word, that is, the Son of God, did assume the human nature in the womb of the blessed Virgin Mary . . . that He might reconcile the Father unto us and to be a Sacrifice, not only for original guilt, but also for all actual sins of men." Hence, whatever Christ in His state of humiliation did as the God-man, Luke 1, 30. 31; Matt. 1, 21 25; Luke 2, 21, and what He still does as such in His state of exaltation belongs to His divine office, or work.

Of the mediatorial office of Christ Quenstedt writes: "The mediatorial office is the function, belonging to the whole person of the God-man and consisting of theanthropic actions, by which function Christ in, with, and through both natures perfectly executed, by way of acquisition and application, and is even now executing, all things that are necessary for our salvation." (*Doctr. Theol.*, p. 338.) More briefly expressed, Christ's mediatorial work embraces all that He did to effect our salvation and all that He still does to make salvation available to men.

If the question is asked, Since when did Christ execute His mediatorial office? we reply: a) Not only since the time of His baptism, which was indeed the solemn induction into His public mediatorial ministry, but b) from the very moment of His incarnation, since His conception, birth, circumcision, filial obedience, etc., were accomplished for the salvation of sinful and lost mankind, Gal. 4, 4. 5; 1 John 3, 8.

Those who assume that the Son of God became incarnate for reasons other than the redemption of mankind (Socinians, Pelagians, Schleiermacher, modern theologians: "Christ came as the second Adam to perfect creation") oppose Scripture, which expressly teaches that Christ came into the world only to save sinners, John 3, 16; 1 Tim. 1, 15; 1 John 4, 9. 10.

If it is asked why the λόγος waited four thousand years before He became incarnate, we have no other answer in Scripture than that it so pleased God, Gal. 4, 4. 5.

As the Savior of sinful mankind, Christ had to accomplish three distinct works: a) He had to teach men the way of salvation, Luke 4, 18; John 1, 18; Heb. 1, 1; Matt. 17, 5. b) He had to reconcile the world unto God, 2 Cor. 5, 18. 19; Matt. 20, 28; Rom. 5, 10; 1 John 2, 2. c) He had to rule over the Church as its Head and over all things as the sovereign King of the universe, Luke 1, 33; Eph. 1, 20—23; John 18, 33—37. Hence we speak of the threefold office of Christ: a) the prophetic (*munus propheticum*), b) the sacerdotal (*munus sacerdotale*), and c) the kingly (*munus regium*). As the divine Prophet, Priest, and King the

Messiah was pictured already in the Old Testament, Deut. 18, 15—19; Ps. 110; 2, 6—12.

All actions performed by Christ, our Prophet, Priest, and King, are *theanthropic* actions; in other words, all things necessary for our salvation are executed by Christ according to *both* natures.

While the three offices were never divided, or separated, in Christ, we hold to the classification just given *(munus triplex)* for the sake of greater clearness in presenting Christ's work, though some dogmaticians combine the prophetic office with the sacerdotal, obtaining in this way only two offices of Christ.

A. THE PROPHETIC OFFICE OF CHRIST.
(De Munere Prophetico.)

1. THE EXECUTION OF THIS OFFICE IN THE STATE OF HUMILIATION.

In His state of humiliation Christ did not teach as did the prophets of Israel, but as the unique Prophet sent by God *(Propheta κατ' ἐξοχήν, Propheta omnibus excellentior,* Luke 7, 16; John 4, 19; 6, 14, that is to say, immediately *(αὐτοπροσώπως)* and by His own authority, John 7, 46; 1, 18. Our Lord did not receive His divine doctrines by divine inspiration, 2 Pet. 1, 21, but possessed them as the omniscient Son of God, Matt. 23, 8. 10; Luke 24, 19; 4, 32; Matt. 7, 29; John 6, 63. Nor did He possess His divine knowledge merely according to His divine nature; for through the personal union (communication of attributes) also His human nature participated in the omniscience of His divine nature, Col. 2, 3. 9. *(In Christo igitur Deus ipse munere prophetico fungitur,* Heb. 1, 2.) Augustine: *"Doctor doctorum Christus, cuius schola in terra et cathedra in coelo est."*

With respect to the *message* which Christ proclaimed, Scripture declares very plainly that He announced *Himself* as the divine Savior from sin, death, and the power of the devil, Matt. 4, 17; John 6, 40; 3, 14. 15; Matt. 20, 28; John 6, 51—65. As Paul preached Christ and Him Crucified as his central message, 1 Cor. 2, 2; 2 Cor. 4, 5, so our divine Savior centered His entire preaching in the astounding Gospel-truth of salvation through His vicarious death, Luke 18, 31—34; Matt. 16, 21—23; Mark 8, 27—33. Again, as St. Paul proclaimed salvation by grace through faith in the crucified and risen Christ, so also Christ Himself published the Gospel of salvation by grace through faith in Him, Matt. 11, 28; John 6, 29. 32. 33. 35.

It is true, our divine Lord, as the Prophet whom God raised up like unto Moses, Deut. 18, 15, promulgated also the divine Law, Matt. 5—7, not, however, a new law (Modernists), but the same Moral Law which God had published in the Old Testament, Matt. 22, 34—40, the fulfilling of which is love, Rom. 13, 10. Even the Sermon on the Mount, Matt. 5—7, was not a new law, but only the right explanation of the Moral Law in opposition to the false interpretations of the scribes. The commandment of love was taught so explicitly in the Old Testament, Lev. 19, 18, that the Jews at the time of Christ fully understood it, Luke 10, 27. The "new commandment," John 13, 34, was new only with regard to its peculiar application to Christ's followers and the motives with which it was enforced (Luther: "new through the new spiritual powers"); for His disciples were to love one another in imitation of their divine Master, in whom they believed.

In opposition to all errorists who affirm that Christ was essentially a new Lawgiver (Pelagians, Arminians, Semi-Pelagians, Modernists, papists: Christ proclaimed as a new law the evangelical counsels, *consilia evangelica:* chastity, poverty, and obedience) the Church declares on the basis of Scripture: "Christ was indeed a Teacher of the Law, but not a new Lawgiver." *(Christus quidem fuit legis doctor, sed non novus legislator.)* Yet, though Christ preached also the divine Law, the administration of His prophetic office consisted properly in His proclamation of the Gospel of salvation through faith in His atoning suffering and death, John 1, 17.

2. THE EXECUTION OF THE PROPHETIC OFFICE IN THE STATE OF EXALTATION.

In His state of exaltation Christ no longer proclaims the Gospel immediately ($a\dot{v}\tau o\pi\varrho o\sigma\dot{\omega}\pi\omega\varsigma$), but mediately, through the ministerial work of the Church, John 20, 21; Matt. 28, 19. 20; Mark 16, 15. 16; 2 Cor. 13, 2. 3; 2 Tim. 1, 9—11. Nevertheless also in His state of exaltation He remains the true Prophet and Teacher of His Church, Col. 3, 16; Eph. 4, 10—12, so that His Word alone should be preached to men, John 8, 31. 32; 1 Pet. 4, 11; 1 Tim. 6, 3—5. All who preach their own wisdom in place of God's Word are not Christian ministers, but false prophets ($\dot{a}\nu\tau\dot{\iota}\chi\varrho\iota\sigma\tauo\iota$), whom believers should avoid, Matt. 15, 7—9; 7, 15; Rom. 16, 17. 18; 1 John 2, 18. Dr. A. Strong rightly says: "All modern prophecy that is true is but the republication of Christ's message, the proclamation and expounding of truth already revealed in Scripture." (*Syst. Theol.*, p. 389.) Of all false prophets the Pope at Rome is the most insidious and pernicious, since he perverts the Word of God and opposes the prophetic office of Christ under the pretense that he is the viceregent and vicar of the exalted Lord. For this reason he is *the Antichrist* (ἀντίχριστος κατ' ἐξοχήν), 2 Thess. 2, 3 ff.

Also in the Old Testament the Son of God, or the preexistent λόγος, was the true Teacher and Prophet of the Church; for it was He who conversed with the saints of old and revealed to them the truth of salvation. This important fact Scripture teaches by declaring a) that it was the Spirit of Christ that inspired the prophets who prophesied of the grace that should come, 1 Pet. 1, 10—12, and b) that it was the Son of God who revealed to Israel the saving truths of God, John 12, 41; cp. Is. 6, 1 f.; 1 Cor. 10, 4. Luther: "Almost in all places in the Old Testament Christ is revealed to us under the name of God." (St. L., II, 853.)

B. THE SACERDOTAL OFFICE OF CHRIST.
(De Munere Sacerdotali.)

The grace of God which Christ proclaimed as the divine Prophet He Himself secured as the divine Priest of men. Hence those who deny, or pervert the Biblical doctrine of, the sacerdotal office of our Savior, must deny and pervert also His prophetic office. Rationalists of every type who reject the vicarious atonement of Christ (*satisfactio vicaria*) cannot regard Him as the true Prophet of grace and forgiveness, but must consider Him merely a Teacher of morality, who came into the world to induce men to secure salvation by their own works and righteousness. In short, if Christ is not the divine Priest, neither is He the divine Prophet in the Biblical sense.

The sacerdotal office of Christ, who is called Priest (כֹּהֵן לְעוֹלָם, ἱερεὺς μέγας, ἀρχιερεύς) both in the Old and in the New Testament (Ps. 110, 4; Zech. 6, 13; Heb. 5, 6; 8, 4; 10, 21; etc.), is that work of the God-man by which He reconciled the world unto God, 2 Cor. 5, 19. Holy Scripture describes both the manner (*modus reconciliationis*) and the means (*medium reconciliationis*) by which this gracious work was accomplished. Its consistent testimony is that Christ offered Himself, or laid down His life, as a ransom for the sins of the world, John 17, 19; 1 Tim. 2, 6; 1 John 2, 2; John 1, 29.

To the sacerdotal office of Christ belongs also His intercession, which will be considered later. A complete definition of Christ's sacerdotal office is given by Quenstedt, who writes: "The priestly office of Christ is composed of two parts, satisfaction and intercession. For, in the first place, He made an absolutely perfect satisfaction for all the sins of the whole world and earned salvation. In the second place, He anxiously interceded, and still intercedes and mediates, on behalf of all, for the application of the acquired salvation. That the Messiah would perform these functions of a priest is clearly predicted, Is. 53, 12." (*Doctr. Theol.,* p. 347.)

In particular, the purchase-price for our sins (*pretium, λύτρον*) was Christ's blood shed on Calvary, 1 John 1, 7; Heb. 10, 29; 13, 20. Of this Luther writes: "The blood which flowed from the side of our Lord Jesus is the treasure of our redemption, the payment and atonement for our sins. For through His innocent suffering and death and through His holy and precious blood, shed upon the cross, our dear Lord Jesus Christ paid our entire debt of eternal death and damnation, in which we all are because of our sins. The same blood of Christ intercedes for us before God and cries to God without ceasing: Grace! Grace! Forgive! Forgive! Indulgence! Indulgence! Father! Father! and secures for us divine grace, forgiveness of sins, righteousness, and salvation. Thus the blood of Jesus Christ, our only Mediator and Advocate, cries forever and ever without ceasing, so that God the Father regards such crying and interceding of His beloved Son and is gracious to us poor, miserable sinners, Zech. 9, 11." (Expl. of John 19, 34; St. L., VIII, 965 ff.)

In the Old Testament the priests offered lambs and goats for the sins of the people, Heb. 10, 4; Christ, however, the great High Priest, Heb. 7, 26. 27, sacrificed Himself, He being both Priest and Sacrifice in one person, Heb. 9, 12—14; Eph. 5, 2. (*Christus semetipsum sacrificavit.*) This is the golden theme of the whole Bible: the astounding message of reconciliation (*ἱλασμός*) through the holy blood of the divine Victim Jesus Christ, Acts 10, 43; Luke 24, 25—27.

Christ executed His sacerdotal office by rendering perfect obedience to His Father, who out of pure love offered up His only-begotten Son for the redemption of the world, John 3, 16; 1, 29. Scripture accordingly describes Christ's redemptive work as obedience to God (*obedientia*). The vicarious obedience of Christ comprises: a) His *active obedience (obedientia activa),* by which our divine Substitute placed Himself under the obligation of the divine Law, fulfilling it in our stead by His perfectly holy life, Gal. 4, 4. 5; Rom. 5, 19; Matt. 3, 15, and b) His *passive obedience (obedientia passiva),* by which He placed Himself under the curse of the Law and suffered and died for the sins of the world, Heb. 9, 12; Eph. 5, 2; Is. 53, 4—6. Thus by His holy life and His innocent death Christ secured for us that divine merit *(meritum Christi)* which is our righteousness before God unto salvation, Rom. 3, 22—25; 2 Cor. 5, 19—21.

The prepositions ἀντί, ὑπέρ (Matt. 20, 28; 2 Cor. 5, 14), translated in our Authorized Version with "for," do not merely mean "for the benefit of," but rather: "in place of." They express the fact that Christ suffered and died in our stead, or as our true Substitute. Luther rightly says: "Christ suffered death, malediction, and damnation, just as if He Himself had broken the whole Law and deserved every sentence pronounced by the Law on criminals." (St. L., XII, 236.)

Since Christ by His most perfect obedience has paid the penalty of our sin and expiated our guilt, He has freed us also from the dreadful consequences which sin, both original and actual, has brought upon us, such as a) death, 2 Tim. 1, 10; b) the power of the devil, Heb. 2, 14; c) the dominion of sin, Titus 2, 14; etc. All these infinite spiritual blessings are comprised in the expression "the redemption of the human race," which Hollaz defines as "the spiritual, judicial, and most costly deliverance of all men, bound in the chains of sin, from guilt, from the wrath of God, and from temporal and eternal punishment, accomplished by Christ, the God-man, through His active and passive obedience, which God, the most righteous Judge, graciously received as a most perfect ransom (λύτρον), so that the human race, introduced into spiritual liberty, may live forever with God." (*Doctr. Theol.,* p. 346.)

Objections to the Scriptural doctrine of the redemption of lost mankind through the perfect obedience of Christ (active and passive) have always been raised by the proud, self-righteous carnal heart of man, 1 Cor. 1, 23. While some critics denied the necessity and validity of Christ's active obedience ("As a man Christ obeyed the divine Law for His own good"; Anselm, Aepinus), others violently attacked the necessity and validity of His passive obedience (Rationalism, Unitarianism, Modernism). In the interest of denying Christ's vicarious satisfaction it has been claimed: **a)** that the term redemption (ἀπολύτρωσις) means simply liberation and not the purchasing of sinners by the payment of an adequate

ransom; b) that the idea of satisfaction conflicts with the gratuitous remission of sins; c) that God cannot transfer the crime
of one to another and punish an innocent Substitute for guilty
man, etc.

All these objections contradict the clear doctrines of Scripture,
which teaches: a) that Christ's redemption was indeed effected
by the payment of the price of His blood, 1 Cor. 6, 20; 1 Pet. 1,
18. 19; Gal. 3, 13; Eph. 1, 7; Titus 2, 14; Heb. 9, 12. 15; Rev.
5, 9; b) that the mercy of God in remitting sin is indeed gratuitous in the sense that no satisfaction is required of us; but it is
not gratuitous *absolutely*, since it required the satisfaction of
Christ, Rom. 3, 24; Eph. 1, 7; and c) that God indeed transferred
the sins of man upon Christ and punished Him in our stead,
Is. 53, 4—6; John 1, 29; Gal. 3, 13.

Gerhard very exhaustively classifies the Scriptural statements
which describe Christ's sacerdotal work and in particular His vicarious satisfaction as follows: a) Christ is our Mediator, 1 Tim.
2, 5; Heb. 8, 6; 9, 15; 12, 24; b) Christ is our Redeemer, Is. 53,
4—6; Luke 1, 68; Rom. 3, 24; 1 Cor. 1, 30; Eph. 1, 7; Col.
1, 14; 1 Tim. 2, 6; Heb. 9, 12. 15; c) Christ is the Propitiation
(ἱλασμός) for our sins, 1 John 2, 2; 4, 10; Rom. 3, 24. 25; d) by
Him we are reconciled to God, Rom. 5, 10. 11; 2 Cor. 5, 18. 19;
Eph. 2, 16; Col. 1. 20; e) Christ gave His life as λύτρον καὶ
ἀντίλυτρον for us, Matt. 20, 28; Mark 10, 45; Titus 2, 14; 1 Pet.
1, 18. 19; Heb. 9, 15; f) Christ was made sin for us, 2 Cor. 5, 21;
Rom. 8, 3; g) Christ became a curse for us, Gal. 3, 13; h) Christ
took upon Himself our sins and their punishment, Is. 53, 4—6;
John 1, 29; 1 Pet. 2, 24; i) Christ shed His blood for our sins,
Matt. 26, 28; 1 John 1, 7; Heb. 9, 12; j) Christ blotted out the
indictment against us, Col. 2, 14; k) Christ freed us from the curse
of the Law, Gal. 3, 13; 4, 5; l) Christ freed us from the wrath of
God, 1 Thess. 1, 10; m) Christ freed us from eternal condemnation, 1 Thess. 5, 9. 10; n) in Christ we are righteous and beloved,
2 Cor. 5, 21. (*Doctr. Theol.*, p. 357.)

Hence, if any one denies the vicarious satisfaction which
Christ, as the divinely appointed High Priest, made for the sins
of the world, he denies the very heart of the Biblical message of
redemption. Remove from the Bible the atoning work of Christ,
and nothing of the Gospel is left. It is for this reason that Christ's
sacerdotal office constitutes the very core of Christian theology.

1. THE VICARIOUS ATONEMENT.
(Satisfactio Vicaria.)

The Scriptural doctrine of Christ's redemption made for all men is known in ecclesiastical terminology as His vicarious satisfaction *(satisfactio vicaria)*, or vicarious atonement *(stellvertretende Genugtuung)*. Synonyms of this term used in Scripture are: propitiation (ἱλασμός, 1 John 2, 2); mercy-seat (ἱλαστήριον, Rom. 3, 25); reconciliation (καταλλαγή, Rom. 5, 10; 2 Cor. 5, 18); redemption (ἀπολύτρωσις, Eph. 1, 7; Col. 1, 14); ransom (λύτρον, Matt. 20, 28), all of which declare that the redemption of Christ was made by the payment of an adequate price for the captives.

The term *vicarious satisfaction* in particular is used to express the following truths: a) God, according to His perfect justice *(iustitia legislatoria, normativa)*, demands of all men perfect obedience to His Law, and His wrath is upon all *(iustitia vindicativa)* who do not fulfil it, Gal. 3, 10; b) Christ, by His perfect (active and passive) obedience, has satisfied the demands of divine justice in man's stead, Gal. 4, 4. 5; 3, 13; 1 Pet. 3, 18, and has thus turned the wrath of God into grace, or favor, Rom. 5, 10; c) through Christ's satisfaction all men were reconciled unto God, 2 Cor. 5, 18—21; that is to say, God is no longer angry with sinners and no longer imputes to them their transgressions, but has graciously forgiven them all their sins, Rom. 5, 10. 18. 19.

The *Formula of Concord* thus emphasizes this comforting doctrine: "Since it is the obedience, as above mentioned, . . . of the entire person, it is a complete satisfaction and expiation for the human race, by which the eternal, immutable righteousness of God, revealed in the Law, has been satisfied and is thus our righteousness, which avails before God and is revealed in the Gospel and upon which faith relies before God, which God imputes to faith, as it is written, Rom. 5, 19; 1 John 1, 7; Hab. 2, 4; Rom. 1, 17." (Thor. Decl., III, 57.) So also the *Apology* says: "The Law condemns all men; but Christ, because without sin He has borne the punishment of sin and has been made a victim for us, has removed that right of the Law to accuse and condemn those who believe in Him, because He Himself is the Propitiation for them, for whose sake we now are accounted righteous. But since they are accounted righteous, the Law cannot accuse or condemn them, even though they have not actually satisfied the Law." (Art. III, 58.)

2. OBJECTIVE AND SUBJECTIVE RECONCILIATION.
(Reconciliatio Obiectiva, Subiectiva.)

The reconciliation which Christ effected through His vicarious suffering and death is fittingly called *objective reconciliation*. This was accomplished over nineteen centuries ago when our divine Substitute died on Calvary, 2 Cor. 5, 18. 19; Rom. 5, 10. For then the demands of divine justice were fully satisfied, God's wrath was turned into grace, and universal pardon was proclaimed to all sinners, John 19, 30; Rom. 5, 16. 18. 19. Reconciliation (justification) was thus secured without any work or merit on the part of sinful man, just as creation was accomplished without man's cooperation. Objective reconciliation is therefore not brought about through man's faith, but rather, just because it exists, man can now be justified by faith.

The objective reconciliation which Christ effected through His death was publicly proclaimed and offered to the world by God through Christ's glorious resurrection; for this is the actual absolution, or justification, of the whole world, Rom. 4, 25. The objective reconciliation, or justification, of the whole world is moreover announced to all sinners in the Gospel, for which reason the Gospel is called the Word of Reconciliation (λόγος τῆς καταλλαγῆς), 2 Cor. 5, 19. Luther: "The Gospel is a proclamation of Christ, true God and man, who by His death and resurrection has atoned for the sins of all men and conquered death and the devil." (St. L., XIV, 88.)

The *objective reconciliation* of Christ, or the absolution or justification of the whole sinful world, is appropriated by the individual believer through faith in the Gospel promises of forgiveness and thus becomes *subjective reconciliation,* 2 Cor. 5, 20. That is to say, the individual sinner obtains for himself through faith the forgiveness which Christ has secured for all men by His suffering and death. Saving, or justifying, faith may therefore be defined as a penitent sinner's personal trust in the reconciliation effected for the entire world. Saving faith does not justify inasmuch as in itself it reconciles God, but inasmuch as it seizes and obtains the reconciliation which already exists and is freely offered in the Gospel to all sinners. The *Apology* says: "Faith properly so called is that which *assents to the promise.*" (Art. IV [II], 113.) And the *Formula of Concord:* "Faith does not justify because it is so good a work, so illustrious a virtue, but because it apprehends and

embraces the merits of Christ in the promise of the Gospel."
(Thor. Decl., III, 13.)

The distinction between objective and subjective reconciliation
(justification) must be diligently observed; for all who reject the
objective reconciliation of Christ cannot teach justification by grace
through faith without the deeds of the Law. As soon as the Scriptural truth that "God was in Christ, reconciling the world unto
Himself, not imputing their trespasses unto them," 2 Cor. 5, 19, is
denied, the doctrine of salvation by work-righteousness must follow
(Arminianism, Semi-Pelagianism, Modernism), since in that case
the sinner must himself reconcile God by his good works. From
beginning to end the entire comfort of sinners longing for salvation rests upon the objective reconciliation which Christ has made
on Calvary. Their own subjective reconciliation, or justification,
is but the blessed fruit of that amazing deed of love.

3. REJECTION OF ERRORS PERTAINING TO CHRIST'S VICARIOUS ATONEMENT.

The vicarious satisfaction of Christ is repudiated by all who
deny the condemning wrath of God *(iustitia Dei vindicativa);* for
if God had not been angry at man's sin, there would have been no
need for the atoning death of our Savior. (Cf. the antichristian
views of the Unitarians, Modernists, Ritschl, Harnack, etc.) The
objections of all rationalists to the Gospel fact of redemption ("God
could forgive sin without the death of Christ by a mere fiat of
His sovereign will"; "It is an unworthy conception of God to regard Him as so angry over sin that Christ had to die for sinful
man"; "Christ died merely to reveal God's love to man"; "It
would be an act of injustice for God to punish the sinless Savior
for sinful man"; "The idea of God's reconciliation through Christ's
vicarious atonement is unethical or too juridical") are all refuted
by passages of Scripture which affirm the very truths that are
denied by these objectors on rationalistic grounds, Is. 53, 4—6;
2 Cor. 5, 18—21. Among the errors by which Christ's vicarious
atonement is rejected, either in its entirety or in part, we enumerate
the following: —

a. *The error of acceptilation (acceptilatio).* Christ's vicarious
satisfaction was not sufficient in itself, but was accepted as such by
God's sovereign volition (*per liberam [gratuitam] acceptationem;*
Duns Scotus, Calvin, Arminians). Cp. Heb. 9, 11—14; 1 John
1, 7; Acts 20, 28; 2 Cor. 5, 18—21.

b. *The error of work-righteousness* as taught in varying forms and degrees by Pelagians, Semi-Pelagians, Arminians, synergists, Modernists, etc. — If man can either in whole or in part secure reconciliation by his good works, it would not have been necessary for the Son of God to become man and suffer and die in his stead. Cp. Gal. 3, 10—13; Rom. 8, 3. 4; etc. Quenstedt: *"Filius Dei non venisset nec humanam naturam assumpsisset, si homo in statu integritatis perstitisset."*

c. *The error of denying the active obedience of Christ* (Anselm, Parsimonius, modern theologians). If Christ had not fulfilled the Law in our stead, we ourselves would have to fulfil it and thus earn salvation, at least in part. Cp. Gal. 4, 4. 5; Rom. 5, 18.

d. *The error that Christ by His suffering and death paid the ransom-price to Satan* (Origen). According to Scripture, Christ indeed has given Himself an offering and a sacrifice, but to God, to satisfy the claims of His perfect justice *(iustitia Dei legislatoria et vindicativa).* Cp. Eph. 5, 2; 2 Cor. 5, 18—21.

e. *The error that Christ made satisfaction only for the sins of the elect* (Calvinists). Cp. 2 Cor. 5, 18—21; 1 John 2, 2; 1 Tim. 2, 6.

f. *The errors implied in the various theories regarding Christ's death which rationalists substitute* for the Scriptural doctrine of the vicarious atonement. 1) *The Accident Theory.* Christ's death was an accident as unforeseen and unexpected as the death of any other martyr (Modernists). Cp. Matt. 16, 21; Mark 9, 30—32; John 10, 17. 18, etc. 2) *The Martyr Theory.* Christ gave up His life for a principle of truth as any other martyr (Modernists). Cp. 1 Tim. 2, 6; 1 John 2, 2. 3) *The Moral-example Theory* (moral-influence theory, moral-power view of atonement). Christ's death has an influence upon mankind for moral improvement. The example of His suffering softens human hearts and helps man to reform, repent, and better his condition (transformation of character, Horace Bushnell). Cp. Rom. 5, 12—18; 1 John 1, 7. 4) *The Governmental Theory.* God made an example of suffering in Christ in order to exhibit to man that sin is displeasing in His sight; or: God's government of the world makes it necessary for Him to show His wrath against sin (Hugo Grotius; New England Theology). 5) *The Declaratory Theory.* Christ died to show men how much God loves them (Ritschl). While the death of Christ indeed exhibits the great love of God for fallen man, the purpose of His death was primarily to redeem lost mankind, John 3, 16;

1 John 4, 10. 6) *The Guaranty Theory.* Reconciliation is based, not on Christ's expiation for sin, but on His guaranty to win followers and conquer their sinfulness (Schleiermacher, Kirn, Hofmann).

All these man-made theories of the atonement deny Christ's vicarious satisfaction and are based on the same leading thought: salvation by works, or salvation through personal sanctification.

g. *The error of restitution* (ἀποκατάστασις). Christ died also for the fallen angels, so that they, too, will be restored to holiness and perfection in the consummation of all things. Cp. Matt. 25, 41. 46.

h. *The error involved in the papistic Mass,* which purports to be the "unbloody repetition of the sacrifice of Christ, necessary for propitiation." We reject the Mass as a blasphemous denial of the efficacy of Christ's *one* complete and perfect redemption, Heb. 7, 26. 27; 9, 12; 10, 14; John 19, 30.

4. THE PRIESTLY INTERCESSION OF CHRIST.

The sacerdotal office of Christ embraces two parts: a) satisfaction and b) intercession.

Already in His state of humiliation Christ interceded for men *(intercessio terrestris),* John 14, 16; 17, 9; Heb. 5, 6—10. From the nature of Christ's intercessions these are divided into two classes: a) *general intercessions (intercessio generalis),* Luke 23, 34, which were made for men in general; and b) *special intercessions (intercessio specialis),* John 17, 9 ff., which were offered up for believers.

However, Christ remains a Priest also after His exaltation, Heb. 7, 24. 25, and in this state He administers His priestly office, not by repeating His atoning work, Rom. 6, 9. 10; Heb. 9, 12—15; 7, 26. 27, but by interceding for the elect of God *(intercessio coelestis).* This perpetual intercession of the exalted Christ has *no atoning value (intercessio Christi in statu exaltationis non est satisfactoria),* but merely *applicative* value *(intercessio Christi in statu exaltationis est applicatoria),* Heb. 7, 24. 25; 1 John 2, 1; Rom. 8, 34; that is to say, it relates to the gathering and preservation of the Church, or to the salvation of the elect *(Christus est Mediator reconciliationis),* Rom. 8, 34; Heb. 7, 25; 1 John 2, 1.

According to Scripture the heavenly intercession of our glorified Mediator is both real *(intercessio realis),* that is, He presents to the Father perpetually the holy blood which He shed for the sins of the world (Chemnitz: *Ostendit vultui Dei, quae stigmata pro redemptione nostra accepit,* Heb. 9, 12), and verbal *(intercessio verbalis),* that is, He actually prays for men, Heb. 7, 25; Rom. 8, 34; 1 John 2, 1, though this must be understood in a manner becoming the exalted Lord, who sits at the right hand of God *(intercessio incomprehensibilis).*

In contradistinction to the intercession of the Holy Spirit *(intercessio Spiritus Sancti),* Rom. 8, 26. 27, the exalted Christ intercedes as the God-man *(intercessio ϑεανδρική)* and on the basis of His own merits *(merito ipsius intercessoris),* while the intercession of the Holy Spirit *(intercessio ϑεική,* Rom. 8, 27, "according to the will of God," κατὰ ϑεόν) rests on the ground of Christ's redemption *(merito alterius),* Gal. 4, 4—6.

The constant intercession of the exalted Savior at the right hand of God gives the believer the most certain assurance of his final salvation, Rom. 8, 34—39.

The Unitarians (Modernists) deny Christ's vicarious satisfaction and therefore reject Christ's intercession, which is based upon His atonement. According to the Unitarian view, Christ's only function as priest is to inspire men by precept and example to become their own saviors. The papists supplement Christ's intercessory work with the intercessions and merit of the saints and thus deny the Scriptural truth that Christ is the only Mediator between God and man, 1 Tim. 2, 5. 6.

C. THE KINGLY OFFICE OF CHRIST.
(De Munere Regio.)

The kingly office of Christ is described in all those passages of Holy Scripture in which it is said that to Him in time universal dominion has been communicated, Eph. 1, 20—23; Matt. 11, 27; 28, 18; Ps. 2, 6. 8; 8, 6; 1 Cor. 15, 27; etc. The universal character of Christ's rule is emphatically stated in Scripture; for it teaches very clearly that the dominion of the Son of Man extends a) to all nations and peoples, Dan. 7, 13. 14; b) to all things on earth, in the air, and in the sea, Ps. 8, 6—8; and c) even to the enemies of Christ, Ps. 110, 2. In short, from the glorious reign of Christ nothing is excluded except God Himself, 1 Cor. 15, 27. Hence the kingly office of Christ has been very aptly defined as "the theanthropic function of Christ whereby He divinely controls and governs, according to both natures, the divine and the human (the latter as exalted to the right hand of majesty), all creatures whatever in the kingdoms of power, grace, and glory by infinite majesty and power" (Quenstedt).

Also in His state of humiliation Christ was a true King, possessing and exercising divine power, not only according to His divine nature (essentially), but also according to His human nature (by way of communication), as was shown in the article on the second genus of the communication of attributes *(genus maiestaticum).* To the incarnate Christ, Scripture ascribes government, Is. 9, 6, kingship, John 18, 37, divine power, Matt. 28, 18, etc., in an absolute degree, that is to say, in the same manner as to God Himself. But the full and constant use of the divine dominion communicated to the human nature was not exercised by our Savior until His exaltation at the right hand of God, Eph. 1, 20—23; 4, 10; Phil. 2, 9—11.

On the basis of clear Scripture-passages our dogmaticians speak of Christ's threefold kingdom, of *power,* of *grace,* and of *glory.* However, this threefold division must not be understood as if there were three separate kingdoms over which our Lord rules. In reality the dominion of Christ is one, though it exerts itself in different spheres, according to the different character of those who are governed. *(Pro diversa ratione eorum, quos rex Christus sibi subiectos respicit et diversimode gubernat.* Baier.) Thus Christ rules over all unbelievers, apostate angels, and irrational creatures by means of His omnipotent power *(regnum potentiae),* Ps. 2, 9 f.; 45, 5; 8, 6—8; 97, 7. 10; 1 Tim. 6, 14—16; Rev. 17, 14.

In a general way all creatures *as such* belong to Christ's Kingdom of Power because the *regnum potentiae* is essentially the realm of nature *(regnum naturae).*

All who in true faith have accepted Christ's Gospel of reconciliation, 1 Cor. 15, 1, He most graciously rules through His revealed Word *(regnum gratiae),* John 8, 31. 32. To the Kingdom of Grace belong only those who have been justified by faith or who by faith are true members of the Christian Church on earth *(ecclesia militans),* the latter term being a synonym of the former, Rom. 5, 1. 2; Acts 5, 14. While Satan works in all unbelievers as in "children of disobedience," Eph. 2, 2, the exalted Christ exercises His gracious dominion in all who by faith acknowledge Him as their Lord, John 14, 23.

All true believers, who in this life were subject to Christ in His Kingdom of Grace, will forever be His subjects in the Kingdom of Glory *(regnum gloriae),* which is the continuation of the Kingdom of Grace in perfection, Acts 7, 55. 56; 1 Pet. 5, 4; 1 John 3, 2. Then the adherents of the Church Militant *(membra ecclesiae militantis)*, Rom. 8, 17, will be members of the Church Triumphant *(membra ecclesiae triumphantis)*, Rom. 5, 2; John 17, 24. To point out the inestimable blessings of Christ's Kingdom of Grace and the ineffable bliss of His Kingdom of Glory is the real burden of Christian preaching, the purpose of which is not only to make sinners partakers of eternal life, but also to fill them with an ardent longing for heaven, 1 Cor. 1, 7; Rom. 8, 23; Titus 2, 13; 2 Pet. 3, 13; Phil. 3, 20.

In this world the Kingdom of Power serves the Kingdom of Grace, Matt. 28, 18; Rom. 8, 28; for in both kingdoms the same Lord governs all things to His glory, Eph. 1, 20—23, with the same almighty power, Eph. 1, 19; 1 Pet. 1, 5, sustaining the present world for the sake of His elect, Matt. 24, 22; 2 Pet. 3, 9, and protecting His Church Militant against all attacks of the gates of hell, Matt. 16, 18.

While the dominion of our Lord Jesus Christ is one, yet His Kingdom of Grace must not be confounded with His Kingdom of Power. Christ Himself thus distinguishes His Kingdom of Grace from the kingdoms of this world, John 18, 36. Although the Kingdom of Grace (the Church) is in the world, it is not of this world, 1 John 2, 5; John 17, 16. The world is only the domicile of the Kingdom of Grace, John 17, 11. 15; 1 Tim. 2, 1—4, which is not built and maintained after the manner of earthly kingdoms, Mark 16, 15. 16. The kingdoms of this world are formed and preserved through the divine institution of civil government, Rom. 13, 1—4, while the Kingdom of Grace is founded and sustained alone through the means of grace (the Word and the Sacraments), Matt. 28, 19. 20.

But not only must the Kingdom of Grace be distinguished from the Kingdom of Power, but Scripture likewise distinguishes it from the Kingdom of Glory, 1 John 3, 2; Rom. 8, 24. 25, though formally the two cannot be separated, John 5, 24; 3, 36; Col. 3, 2—4; Gal. 4, 26. They agree in having the same Lord and the same blessings of divine grace, but differ a) with respect to the mode of perceiving divine things; for while in the Kingdom of Grace all divine knowledge is mediate, that is, is obtained through faith in the Word *(cognitio abstractiva)*, John 8, 31. 32, in the Kingdom of Glory it is immediate, that is, it is received through beatific vision *(cognitio intuitiva)*, 1 Cor. 13, 12; and b) with respect to the different external conditions of the members of the two kingdoms; for while the condition of the Church Militant is one of distress and tribulation, Acts 14, 22, that of the Church Triumphant is one of supreme glory, Rev. 7, 17; 21, 3. 4.

The doctrine of Christ's kingly office is an article of faith; that is to say, on the basis of Scripture we *believe* that Christ rules most gloriously in His kingdoms of power, grace, and glory. In the Kingdom of Power we indeed see the objects of Christ's reign, but not Christ's ruling scepter, Heb. 2, 8. Indeed, quite frequently it appears as if Satan were ruling this world, and not God. In Christ's Kingdom of Grace the means indeed are perceptible, for we hear the Gospel and see the external Sacraments; yet the kingdom itself is invisible to us, since it is internal, or in the hearts of men, Luke 17, 20. 21; 1 Pet. 2, 5. But in spite of the opposition of the devil, Matt. 16, 18, of false teachers, 2 Tim. 2, 17—19, and of the world, John 16, 33, we believe that the Christian Church, or the Kingdom of Grace, will exist on earth till the end of time, Matt. 28, 20. The Kingdom of Glory, which will be revealed in the Lord's own appointed time, Acts 1, 7, is, however, always the object of the Christian's fondest hope, 1 John 3, 2; Rom. 5, 2; 8, 24. 25, and for its coming he continually waits and ardently prays, Phil. 3, 20.

ERRORS REGARDING THE KINGLY OFFICE OF CHRIST.

With respect to the kingly office of Christ all those err from the divine truth who deny the Scriptural doctrine concerning His divine person and His divine work. Of the many errorists we mention the following: —

a. The papists and Reformed, who separate the human nature from the divine nature by denying the communication of attributes and consider Christ to be King only according to His divine nature, Matt. 28, 18; 11, 27; Phil. 2, 9—11; etc.

b. The modern kenoticists, who deny the divine kingship of Christ in His state of humiliation and claim that Christ, when becoming incarnate, completely emptied Himself (ἐκένωσεν) of the divine attributes of omnipotence, omniscience, and omnipresence. In that case Christ could not be King even according to His divine nature, Col. 2, 3. 9; John 1, 14.

c. The Subordinationists, who deny that Christ according to His divine nature is consubstantial (ὁμοούσιος) with the Father and hence exclude Him from the eternal divine reign, whereas Scrip-

ture ascribes to Him an everlasting dominion, Luke 1, 33; Eph.
1, 21. — The subjection of which St. Paul speaks in 1 Cor. 15,
27. 28 refers to the change of Christ's present mode of rule, which
is mediate and hidden, into a mode of rule which is immediate,
revealed, and common to Christ together with the Father and the
Holy Ghost.

d. All who reject Christ's rule in His Church by substituting
human doctrine and ordinances for Christ's Word and ordinances,
Matt. 23, 8; 15, 9, as, for example, all false prophets, 1 John 2, 18,
and, above all, the Papacy, 2 Thess. 2, 4, or the Antichrist.

e. All who intermingle the *regnum naturae* and the *regnum
gratiae*, or State and Church (papists, Reformed, and other enthusiasts).

f. All chiliasts, or millenarians, who teach the establishment
by Christ of a dominion which is neither a Kingdom of Grace nor
a Kingdom of Glory, but a caricature of both, namely, a reign of
thousand years in duration, which will either precede or follow
His second advent (premillenarians; postmillenarians). We reject the figment of millennialism, because, contrary to Scripture,
it a) changes Christ's spiritual kingdom into a visible, or earthly,
kingdom and b) directs the hope of all Christians, not to the perfect glory of heaven, 1 Cor. 1, 7; Phil. 3, 20. 21; John 17, 24, but
to a future earthly glory, which Scripture clearly repudiates, Matt.
24, 1—42.

g. All Modernists, who deny Christ's vicarious atonement; for
if Christ is not the great High Priest, He is neither the glorified and exalted King of heaven and earth. The Christ of Modernism is a mere man, who could never rule with power at God's
right hand.

h. All advocates of work-righteousness (papists, Arminians,
etc.); for all who endeavor to be justified by the Law are fallen
from grace, Gal. 5, 4, and hence cannot acknowledge Christ as their
gracious and glorious King. Those who reject Christ's *regnum
gratiae* must likewise reject His *regnum gloriae*. Luther: "All
who do not have Christ for their King and are not adorned with
His righteousness are, and forever will be, in the kingdom of the
devil, in sin and in death." (St. L., V, 148.)

THE DOCTRINE OF SOTERIOLOGY.
(Soteriologia.)

The purpose of the doctrine of soteriology is to show how the Holy Spirit applies to the individual sinner the blessed salvation which Christ has secured for all mankind by His vicarious atonement. The subject is treated under various heads: The Appropriation of Salvation, *Applicatio Salutis a Christo Acquisitae;* The Appropriating Grace of the Holy Spirit, *Gratia Spiritus Sancti Applicatrix;* The Way of Salvation, *Via Salutis, Ratio Consequendi Salutem;* The Order of Salvation, *Ordo Salutis,* etc. In German the following terminology is used: *Die Heilsaneignung; Der Heilsweg; Die Heilsordnung; Die aneignende Gnade des Heiligen Geistes,* etc.

A general survey of the doctrine of soteriology embraces the following truths. The salvation, or forgiveness of sins, which Christ has procured for all men by His vicarious atonement, Luke 1, 77; Rom. 5, 10; 2 Cor. 5, 19, is offered to the sinner in the means of grace, that is to say, in the Gospel and the Sacraments, 2 Cor. 5, 19; Luke 24, 47. Through this most gracious and efficacious offer of forgiveness, faith is wrought in the heart of the sinner, Rom. 10, 17, which accepts, or appropriates, the merits of Christ proffered in the means of grace.

The means of grace thus perform a twofold function: they offer and confer forgiveness *(media oblativa sive dativa),* and they produce faith *(media operativa sive effectiva). Media dativa ex parte Dei gignunt fidem sive medium ληπτικόν ex parte hominis.*

By creating faith in the heart of the sinner through His almighty power, 1 Cor. 2, 14; Eph. 1, 19. 20, the Holy Spirit converts and justifies him, Acts 16, 31; Rom. 5, 1f. Now the sinner no longer flees from God, but turns to Him as to His reconciled, gracious Lord, Acts 11, 21.

As soon as the sinner by faith accepts God's general pardon, or the objective justification, the pardon becomes effective in his case, and he is personally justified (subjective justification). By accepting Christ's righteousness, he has made it his own and is therefore regarded as righteous before God, Rom. 4, 3; Ps. 32, 1. 2.

Justification (a forensic, not a medical act) is thus by grace alone, without works, Rom. 3, 28. It puts the believer in possession of all the merits or blessings secured by Christ's perfect obedience. The justified sinner has entered into *the state of grace and peace (status gratiae, status pacis),* in which he is assured of his present and final salvation, Rom. 5, 1—5, his final salvation being guaranteed by God's grace and truth, Rom. 5, 1—11; 8, 38. 39; 1 Cor. 1, 8. 9. *Iustificatio est res gratis promissa propter Christum, quare sola fide semper coram Deo accipitur. (Apology,* Art. III, 96.)

Justification effects the *mystical union (unio mystica),* by which the Holy Trinity, in particular the Holy Spirit, dwells in the believer, Gal. 3, 2; Eph. 3, 17; John 14, 23; 1 Cor. 3, 16; 6, 19. The *unio mystica* is a peculiar indwelling, which is distinct from God's general presence with all creatures *(unio generalis),* since God dwells *essentially* in the believer. Yet it is not a pantheistic transformation of the essence of the believer into the essence of God. It is the result of justification, not the cause of it, Gal. 3, 2; Eph. 3, 17.

Justification produces sanctification. To teach that sanctification produces justification means to champion the basic papistic error of justification by works, Rom. 7, 5. 6; 2 Cor. 3, 6; Gal. 2, 20; 3, 2. 3; Rom. 3, 28.

Justification makes the sinner a member in the Christian Church *(regnum gratiae),* Eph. 1, 17—23; Acts 4, 4; 2, 41, and in the Kingdom of Glory *(regnum gloriae),* Luke 23, 43; John 11, 25.

In this connection Holy Scripture also teaches that we owe the possession and enjoyment of all these blessings to the eternal election of grace, Eph. 1, 3 ff.; Rom. 8, 28—30; 2 Tim. 1, 9; Acts 13, 48.

In the *ordo salutis* the relation of the various articles to one another must be rightly observed. Christ's vicarious satisfaction and the reconciliation of God with the world form the basis of all soteriological teachings, while the article of the sinner's justification by faith is the central and chief article of the Christian religion. Sanctification follows justification as its *effect.* To justification *sola fide* all other doctrines of Scripture stand in relation of cause and effect, of *antecedens et consequens.* Right here lies the fundamental difference between the Christian religion and all man-made religions. Christianity teaches sanctification as the effect of justification by grace through faith; all man-made religions reverse the process and teach justification by works, or by sanctification.

Luther says: *"In corde meo iste unus regnat articulus, scilicet fides Christi, ex quo, per quem et in quem omnes meae diu noctuque fluunt et refluunt theologiae cogitationes.* (Erl. Ed., I, 3. Cf. *Christl. Dogmatik,* II, 473—503; also Dr. Engelder, *Dogmatical Notes.)*

THE DOCTRINE OF SAVING FAITH.
(De Fide Salvifica.)

1. THE NECESSITY OF FAITH.

Through His vicarious atonement *(satisfactio vicaria)* Christ has secured for guilty and condemned mankind a perfect reconciliation with God *(reconciliatio, καταλλαγή)*, because He, in man's stead, has fulfilled the demands of the divine Law and made satisfaction for the sins of the world *(obedientia activa, obedientia passiva)*. In Christ Jesus, therefore, God is gracious toward all sinners and absolves them from all guilt (objective justification, *iustificatio obiectiva*).

This comforting fact God announces to the world through the ordained means of grace (the Word and the Sacraments) and demands at the same time faith in the message of reconciliation, 2 Cor. 5, 19—21; Acts 2, 38; 16, 31; 10, 42. 43; 13, 39; 26, 27—29. It is God's declared will that all men should appropriate to themselves by faith the saving grace which has been secured for them by the divinely appointed Savior, Mark 1, 14. 15; Acts 16, 31. Those who refuse to believe the reconciliation effected by Christ are lost in spite of the fact that also for them salvation has been obtained, Mark 16, 15. 16; John 3, 16. 18. 36; 2 Pet. 2, 1. For this reason we affirm that faith is needed for the acquiring of salvation *(necessitas fidei ad salutem consequendam)*. The rationalistic views that God is gracious toward sinners without Christ's vicarious satisfaction and that man can obtain eternal life by his own works or good conduct (Modernists) are emphatically denied by Scripture, Gal. 3, 10; 5, 4. Holy Scripture knows but one way to salvation, namely, by grace, through faith in the redemption of Christ, Rom. 3, 22—25.

Our dogmaticians are therefore right when they declare that salvation is perfect so far as the acquisition and intention are concerned *(ex parte Dei),* but not as regards its application by man *(ex parte hominis),* since this must be accomplished through faith. *Salus perfecta est quoad acquisitionem et intentionem, non quoad applicationem, quae fide fieri debet.* The meaning of this statement is that salvation indeed has been secured for all men, but that the individual sinner must appropriate it unto himself by faith, Mark 16, 15. 16. *Fides ex parte hominis ad salutem consequendam necessaria est.*

2. THE NATURE OF SAVING FAITH.

If we keep in mind that salvation has been gained for all mankind through the vicarious satisfaction of Christ and that this salvation is offered to all men through the means of grace, it is clear what constitutes saving faith.

a. Saving faith is not *general belief* in the existence of God or in the divine Law of God; for this belief is held also by the heathen, Rom. 1, 19. 20. Nor is saving faith mere knowledge of *(notitia historica),* or mere assent *(assensus historicus)* to, the general truths of the Gospel, namely, that Christ lived and died for men; for this faith *(fides historica, fides generalis)* is found also in devils, Luke 4, 34; Jas. 2, 19, and in unbelievers, John 8, 43. 45. So also saving faith *(fides qua iustificans)* is not mere knowledge of, nor is it mere assent to, the teachings of Scripture in general (Romanists, Arminians, Unitarians). The Law, for instance, is *not* the object of saving faith, since sinners are justified without the deeds of the Law, Rom. 3, 28; Eph. 2, 8. 9. Nor is "Scripture in general" the object of saving faith, though true believers, of course, accept the entire Bible as the Word of God; for Scripture itself testifies that a sinner is justified before God only through his trust in the objective atonement made by Christ, Rom. 3, 24. While it is true that no man can be saved who rejects the inspired Word of God, it is also true that man's justification is brought about only through his personal confidence in the divine promises of the Gospel. *Fides salvifica (iustificans) est certa persuasio de venia peccatorum per Christum obtinenda.*

b. Saving faith *(fides iustificans)* is therefore personal trust *(fides specialis),* or cordial confidence *(fiducia cordis),* in the wonderful message of the Gospel that God for Christ's sake is gracious to all who believe in the atoning blood of His Son shed on Calvary for the sins of the world, Gal. 2, 20; 1 John 1, 7. Hence saving faith is found only in a heart that says: "I believe that Jesus Christ . . . is my Lord, who has redeemed me, a lost and condemned creature, purchased and won me from all sins, from death, and from the power of the devil, not with gold or silver, but with His holy, precious blood and with His innocent suffering and death." In other words, saving faith has for its object the forgiveness of sins which was secured by Christ's perfect obedience and is now offered to all sinners in the Gospel, Mark 16, 15. 16; Luke 24, 47. All who reject God's gracious offer of forgiveness for Christ's sake will perish in unbelief, even though they assent to the divine Law or to "Scripture in general." Luther: "You must rely with constant trust on this, that Christ died for your sins; such a faith justifies you." (St. L., VIII, 1376.)

In order to describe saving faith more fully, our dogmaticians have said: a) Saving faith is always *fides specialis,* or the special faith by which an individual believes that for Christ's sake his sins are remitted him. The very nature of God's general promise in the Gospel calls for this individual application, Gal. 2, 20; Job 19, 25. The Church of Rome forbids this application as presumptuous. (Cf. *Concil. Trid.,* Sess. VI, Can. 14.) b) Saving faith is always *fides actualis,* or the *apprehension* of the divine promise *by an act* of the intellect and will. Synonymous terms of *fides actualis* are found in Scripture, Is. 55, 5. 6; John 6, 44; Gal. 3, 27; Matt. 11, 12. 28. The scholastic theologians defined faith as an "idle habit" *(otiosus habitus),* which Luther condemned as a "mere verbal monstrosity, giving no sense." Also a weak faith and the longing for grace in Christ must be regarded as *fides actualis,* or true faith. c) Saving faith is always *fides directa,* or faith which concerns itself directly with the divine promise set forth in the Gospel. d) Saving faith is not in every case *fides reflexa,* reflex, discursive faith, by which the believer reflects on, and is conscious of, his faith. The faith of infants is true faith, Matt. 18, 6, though the *fides reflexa* is wanting; they have *fides specialis,* which is *fides actualis,* which is *fides directa.* (Cf. Dr. Engelder, *Dogmatical Notes; Christl. Dogmatik,* II, 508 ff.)

Hollaz rightly distinguishes between special faith and general faith as follows: "General faith is that by which man . . . believes all things to be true that are revealed in the Word of God. Of this species of faith we are not now speaking because we are treating of faith as the means of salvation. . . . Special faith is that faith by which the sinner applies to himself individually the universal promises in reference to Christ, the Mediator, and the grace of God accessible through Him and believes that God desires to be propitious to him and to pardon his sins on account of the satisfaction of Christ made for his and all men's sins." (*Doctr. Theol.,* p. 419.) So also the *Augsburg Confession* (XX, 23) writes: "Men are also admonished that here the term *faith* does not signify merely the knowledge of the history, such as is in the ungodly and in the devil, but signifies a faith which believes not merely the history, but also the effect of the history, namely, . . . that we have grace, righteousness, and forgiveness of sins through Christ." And the *Apology* (Art. XIII [VII], 21) says: "And here we speak of special faith, which believes the present promise, not only that [faith] which in general believes that God exists, but which believes that the remission of sins is offered."

From the above it is clear why the Law must be excluded as an object of saving faith. The divine Law has no promises of grace attached to it, but promises life and salvation on the basis of its complete fulfilment, as a reward of personal merit, Luke 10, 28; Gal. 3, 12. If the objection is raised that faith itself is called obedience (ὑπακοή) in Scripture, Rom. 1, 5; Acts 6, 7, we reply that faith is indeed obedience, yet not to the Law, but to the Gospel, Rom. 10, 16. Faith is obedience inasmuch as it accepts the gracious promises of God made in the Gospel. But obedience to the Gospel and obedience to the Law are opposites; for the first excludes the works of men, Gal. 2, 16, while the second demands them, Gal. 3, 12. It is for this reason that the Law cannot be the object of faith. Those who make the Law the object of faith, or, what is the same, who define saving faith as obedience to the divine Law, teach salvation by works and thus lapse into paganism. They deny the very essence of Christianity, namely, the fundamental doctrine of salvation by grace.

It is true, saving faith, which appropriates the grace of God in Christ, manifests itself both in ready acceptance of the Word of God and in constant obedience to the Law; but these manifestations of saving faith do not constitute the reason why it saves. They are rather the fruits and proofs that true faith, which justifies and saves without works, Rom. 3, 28; Eph. 2, 8. 9, exists in the heart, John 8, 47; 13, 35.

That faith is essentially *(formaliter)* trust of the heart *(fiducia cordis)*, or sincere confidence in the grace of God offered to all sinners for Christ's sake in the Gospel, is strenuously denied by the papists. The Council of Trent declares (Sess. VI, Can. 12): "If any one should say that justifying faith is nothing else than trust *(fiducia)* in the divine compassion which forgives sins for Christ's sake, or that we are justified alone by such trust, let him be accursed."

But the teaching that is here anathematized, namely, that saving faith is essentially *fiducia cordis,* is a clear doctrine of Scripture, Rom. 4, 3—5; 10, 9. The expressions "to believe in or on" (πιστεύειν εἰς τὸν υἱόν, John 3, 16. 18. 36; εἰς Χριστόν,

Gal. 2, 16) cannot mean anything else than "to place one's confidence in," "to put one's trust in," the Son, or Christ.

The *Apology* is therefore right when it says (III, 183): "Faith is not only knowledge in the intellect, but also confidence in the will; *i. e.,* it is to wish and to receive that which is offered in the promise, namely, reconciliation and remission of sins." And again (IV [II], 48): "Faith which justifies is not merely a knowledge of history, . . . but it is to assent to the promise of God, in which, for Christ's sake, the remission of sins and justification are freely offered." Wherever the Scriptural doctrine that faith is essentially trust, or confidence, in the promises of the Gospel is repudiated, the pagan doctrine of work-righteousness needs must follow.

3. CONCERNING THE TERMS "KNOWLEDGE," "ASSENT," AND "CONFIDENCE."

Since faith has been described as knowledge *(notitia),* assent *(assensus),* and confidence, or trust *(fiducia),* it is necessary to explain these terms and to point out their relation to one another. The following may serve to elucidate the terminology: —

a. If knowledge and assent are conceived as historic faith *(fides historica),* they are not really parts of saving faith; for also devils and unbelievers have both. Of historic faith, or of such a faith as merely knows, and regards as true, the "history" of Christ, Luther writes (XI, 126): "This is a natural work, without grace." "Of such a faith Scripture, the Word of God, does not speak," that is, when it treats of saving faith.

Nevertheless, while the *fides historica* is not a part of saving faith, it is a necessary prerequisite of saving faith, since the Holy Spirit engenders saving faith only in those hearts which know and understand the Gospel of Christ, Rom. 10, 17. The so-called "implicit faith" *(fides implicita, fides carbonaria)* of the papists, according to which the "faithful" simply believe "what the Church teaches," though they themselves are ignorant of the doctrine, is an absurdity; for without knowledge there can be no true faith. When Christ sent out His apostles to make believing disciples of all nations, He expressly commanded them to preach the Gospel to every creature, Mark 16, 15. 16; Matt. 28, 19. 20, thus showing that saving faith must be rooted in knowledge of the Gospel. The Lutheran dogmatician Scherzer writes very aptly: "He lies who says that he believes what the Church teaches if he does not know what she teaches. For no one can believe what he does not know."

b. However, if the term *notitia* is understood in the sense of true *spiritual* knowledge of Christ, which the Holy Ghost works through the Gospel *(notitia spiritualis)* and the term *assensus* is conceived as *spiritual* assent to the promises of the Gospel, which the Holy Ghost likewise works through the Gospel *(assensus spiritualis),* then both these terms include the *fiducia cordis,* or the sincere confidence of the heart in the grace of God offered in the Gospel. In other words, in that case the terms are synonymous. This fact is obvious from the Scriptural usage of the terms; for at one time it ascribes salvation to knowledge, John 17, 3; 2 Cor. 4, 6; Phil. 3, 8; Luke 1, 77, at another to assent, 1 John 5, 1. 5; 3, 23, and again to confidence, John 3, 16. 18. 36. In all these cases knowledge, assent, and confidence are synonyms of saving faith, so that each may be used without the other to describe the *fiducia cordis* by which a sinner is saved. The Lutheran dogmatician Buddeus rightly says: "Knowledge without assent and assent without confidence is not that knowledge nor that assent which constitutes justifying faith." Luther: "Faith is a living, bold *trust in God's grace,* so certain that a man would die a thousand times for it." *(Trigl.,* p. 941.)

4. WHY SAVING FAITH JUSTIFIES.

Saving faith is never without good works, Gal. 5, 6. Indeed, it is itself a most excellent virtue, by which God is supremely glorified as the Lord of love, who because of His grace in Christ Jesus receives and absolves penitent sinners, Rev. 14, 7. But though faith is itself a most precious work and the unfailing source of constant good works, it does not save as a good work or as the source of good works, but solely as the means *(medium ληπτικόν),* by which the believer apprehends the grace of God and the merits of Christ which are offered to him in the Gospel. Again, although faith is an act of both the intellect and the will of man, — for not the Holy Ghost, but the believer himself trusts in the mercy of God, — yet it does not justify inasmuch as it is an act or work of man.

These two truths are of the greatest importance for the right understanding of the Christian doctrine of salvation by faith *(sola fide).* Our dogmaticians have embodied them in the statement: "Faith does not justify in itself, that is, as an act or habit of believing, nor through the works which it produces, but in view of its object, namely, because it apprehends the grace secured by Christ and offered in the Gospel."

Hollaz writes: "Justifying faith is the receptive organ and, as it were, the hand of the poor sinner by which he applies and takes to himself, lays hold of, and possesses, those things which are proffered in the free promise of the Gospel. God, the supreme Monarch, extends from heaven the hand of grace, the grace obtained by the merit of Christ, and in it offers salvation. The sinner, in the abyss of misery, receives as a beggar in his hand of faith what is thus offered to him. The offer and the reception are correlatives. Therefore the hand of faith, which seizes and appropriates the offered treasure, corresponds to the hand of grace which offers the treasure of righteousness and salvation." (*Doctr. Theol.*, p. 420.)

So also the *Formula of Concord* (Thor. Decl., III, 11. 38) says: "Faith is the gift of God by which we apprehend aright Christ, our Redeemer, in the Gospel." "It is faith alone, and nothing else whatever, which is the means and instrument by which the grace of God and the merit of Christ in the promise of the Gospel are embraced, received, and applied to us." This important truth is taught in all passages of Scripture in which saving faith is placed in opposition to human works, Rom. 3, 28; 4, 5; Eph. 2, 8. 9.

All who teach and believe that saving faith justifies inasmuch as it is a good work itself or the source of good works (papists, Arminians, rationalists, Modernists) have fallen from grace and renounced the Christian faith. Luther: "Christ alone justifies me over against my evil works and without my good works. If I regard Christ in this way, then I apprehend the right Christ." (St. L., IX, 619.)

5. FAITH VIEWED AS A PASSIVE ACT OR A PASSIVE INSTRUMENT.

Because saving faith does not itself produce the righteousness (grace, justification, forgiveness of sins) by which the sinner is saved, but merely accepts the merits that have been secured for the world by Christ's obedience and are offered to all men in the Gospel, our dogmaticians have called it a passive act *(actus passivus)* or a passive instrument *(instrumentum passivum)*. J. A. Osiander thus writes: *Receptio alicuius rei non est actio, sed passio.* And Dannhauer: *Fides patitur sibi benefieri.*

These expressions are Scriptural; for in his conversion man

does not himself contribute anything, but only receives everything as a free gift of God. However, saving faith may be called an *actus passivus,* or an *instrumentum passivum,* also in view of the fact that it is engendered and preserved not by man himself, but solely through the gracious operation of the Holy Ghost, Eph. 1, 19; Phil. 2, 13. In other words, the penitent sinner does not believe in Christ by his own reason or strength, but trusts in Him for salvation only because the Holy Ghost has called him by the Gospel, enlightened him with His gifts, and sanctified him. The *Augsburg Confession* says (Art. XVIII, 9): "Although nature is able in a manner to do the outward work, . . . yet it cannot produce the inward motions, such as the fear of God, trust in God, chastity, patience, etc." In this sense faith is called a passive act or a passive instrument.

However, these expressions must not be understood as if saving faith were not in itself essentially an act of the believer *(actus apprehendendi).* To deny the activity of faith in this sense would mean to deny the essence of faith; for saving faith is by its very nature an act of trusting, or confiding, by which the believer appropriates to himself the grace offered to him in the Gospel. So Holy Scripture itself describes faith when it speaks of it as "receiving the atonement," Rom. 5, 11, or "receiving Christ," John 1, 12.

To express the fact that faith is essentially an act of trusting in the Gospel, our dogmaticians have said that saving faith is *fides actualis,* or *active confidence.* Moreover, they teach on the basis of Scripture (Rom. 9, 30; Col. 2, 6; Is. 55, 5. 6; 2, 2. 3; John 6, 44; 2 Cor. 6, 1; Gal. 3, 27) that to believe means "to desire grace," "to seek Christ," "to stretch out the hand toward Christ," "to embrace Christ," "to come to Christ," "to approach Christ," "to run toward Christ," "to cleave to Christ," "to hold to Christ," "to join oneself to Christ," etc. (Cf. *Christl. Dogmatik,* Vol. II, p. 518 ff.)

All who deny that saving faith is essentially an act of apprehending *(actus apprehendendi)* and regard it merely as an "inactive quality" *(otiosa qualitas)* or as a mere "ability to believe" *(potentia credendi)* deny faith altogether; for a faith that does not trust in Christ is not faith at all, but a mere fancy. In fact, if faith is said to save sinners inasmuch as it is a good quality, then salvation is based upon good works, since in that case faith saves as a human virtue.

Luther very strenuously affirmed that the act of apprehending divine grace is the outstanding characteristic of that true faith which is wrought by the Holy Ghost, whereas a mere faith of the head (historic faith) or a mere knowledge of the facts of salvation does not lay hold of the merits of Christ offered to the sinner in the Gospel. Saving faith, then, is always an act of the believer, though it is an act wrought by the Holy Ghost. Luther: *"Fides est habere* VERBUM *in corde et non dubitare de Verbo."* (*Christl. Dogmatik,* II, 522.)

6. CONCERNING THE EXPRESSIONS "TRUE FAITH" AND "LIVING FAITH."

With regard to these expressions considerable confusion prevails in common theological parlance. *True faith* is personal trust, or confidence, in God's gracious forgiveness of sins for Christ's sake. The term thus stands in contradistinction to implicit faith (*fides implicita),* or assent to the doctrines of the Church, though these may not be known to the person, and to historic faith (*fides historica),* or mere knowledge of, and assent to, the general doctrines of the Bible. Neither a *fides implicita* nor a *fides historica* can justify a sinner; for saving faith is always personal trust in the gracious promises of the Gospel. With regard to the term *living faith (fides viva)* we must bear in mind that faith is "living" (*viva)* only because it apprehends the merits of Christ offered in the means of grace. Faith never becomes true or living by the good works that follow it. Through the performance of good works faith only *manifests* itself as true and living *before men.* We may say therefore that every true faith is living faith; and again, that every true faith reveals itself as living by proper fruits. These distinctions must be carefully observed in order that the element of works may not be injected into justifying faith, Rom. 4, 4. 5.

7. FAITH AND THE ASSURANCE OF SALVATION.

Since saving faith is the believer's trust in the perfect righteousness which Christ has secured for all men by His vicarious satisfaction and which therefore exists even before a person believes, it is clear that a believer is in full possession of divine pardon, life, and salvation from the very moment in which he puts his trust in Christ; for in that very moment all the merits of Christ's suffering and death are imputed to him, Acts 16, 31. For this reason the believer is also certain of his salvation; for saving faith is in its very nature the truest and greatest certainty. If papists and Romanizing Protestants deny that the believer may be sure of his salvation, it is because they teach that salvation, in part at least, depends on the believer's good works, in other words, because they intermingle justification with sanctification. It is evident that all who reject the *sola gratia* and make salvation depend on man's character, righteousness, and good works must deny also the certainty of salvation. Work-righteousness always produces doubt and uncertainty, while personal trust in the vicarious atonement of Christ and His objective justification always effects a most joyous assurance of salvation in the believer's heart. From this follows the rule that, if a believer wishes to be sure of his salvation, he must unflinchingly adhere to the gracious promises of the Gospel. As soon as he turns away from them, he will be lost in a sea of doubt.

The certainty of salvation, which is produced through the Gospel, is not natural *(fides humana),* but supernatural and spiritual *(fides divina),* since it is wrought in the heart of the believer by the Holy Ghost through the means of grace. By nature all men seek salvation by works. Hence the certainty of salvation which the unregenerate claim to possess is based upon their compliance with the divine Law, Luke 18, 11. Such certainty, however, must be condemned as sinful presumption, since all who would be justified by the Law are under the curse, Gal. 3, 10. True certainty, on the other hand, which trusts divine grace without works, is the gift of the Holy Ghost, 1 Cor. 2, 4. 5.

8. CAN THE BELIEVER BE SURE OF POSSESSING SAVING FAITH?

In the controversies on faith the question has been propounded whether a Christian may be sure of possessing true faith. The question has been emphatically denied by Romanists and Romanizing Protestants, while Holy Scripture very strenuously affirms it, 2 Tim. 1, 12; 4, 7.

It is true, a believer may not always be *conscious of his faith.* Saving faith *(fides directa, fides actualis)* need not always be *conscious* faith *(fides reflexa),* or faith which is perceived by the believer. *(Fides reflexa et discursiva, qua homo renatus credit et sentit se credere.)* Thus Christian adults, while asleep or engrossed with their daily occupation, indeed possess direct faith, which truly apprehends the grace of God in Christ Jesus, yet not reflex and discursive faith. That is to say, they meditate neither on their act of faith nor on their state of faith. For the time being faith with all that it implies has passed out of their direct consciousness. They may even be in a condition of *coma,* not being able to reflect on spiritual things at all; or they may be in a state of trial *(in statu tentationis),* when they believe themselves to be without faith because they have lost the sense, or feeling, of faith *(sensus fidei).* In all such cases saving faith truly exists, though the believer is not conscious of it. Even in baptized infants, faith is not a mere potentiality to believe *(potentia credendi)* or an inactive quality *(otiosus habitus),* but *fides actualis,* or actual trust in, and active apprehension of, divine grace *(actus appre-hendendi),* as Christ directly testifies (Matt. 18, 6: οἱ μικροὶ οἱ πιστεύοντες εἰς ἐμέ).

However, the doctrine regarding reflex faith must not be abused in the interest of carnal security and indifferentism; for it is God's will that all believers should be sure of their state of faith and grace, Rom. 5, 1. 2. If Christians entertain doubts concerning their faith, such doubts should be removed. This necessitates the preaching of the Law in order to show that unbelief and doubt are sinful and displeasing to God, John 8, 46; Matt. 14, 31. But above all the preaching of the Gospel is necessary, Rom. 5, 20; 8, 15—17, which alone works certainty of faith, John 8, 31. 32, and dispels all doubts.

It is well to remind the doubting, fearing Christian also of the fact that even the desire to be saved through Jesus Christ is already actual, or direct, faith; for such a desire is never found in the natural, unregenerate heart, 1 Cor. 2, 14, but is the gift of the Holy Spirit, Eph. 1, 19; Rom. 8, 23. The *Formula of Concord* rightly says (Thor. Decl., II, 14): "To all godly Christians who feel and experience in their hearts a *small spark or longing for divine grace (scintillula aliqua et desiderium gratiae divinae)* and eternal salvation this precious passage [Phil. 2, 13] is very comforting; for they know that God has kindled in their hearts this beginning of true godliness and that He will further strengthen and help them in their great weakness to persevere in true faith unto the end." (Cf. Matt. 17, 20: Ἐὰν ἔχητε πίστιν ὡς κόκκον σινάπεως.)

Because the assurance which a believer has concerning His state of grace *(certitudo gratiae)* is not found in man's heart by nature, but is engendered in him by the Holy Spirit, it is rightly said that such certainty rests upon the testimony of the Holy

Ghost *(testimonium Spiritus Sancti).* The testimony of the Holy Spirit is both internal *(testimonium Spiritus Sancti internum)* and external *(testimonium Spiritus Sancti externum).* The internal, or direct, witness of the Holy Spirit is nothing else than faith, which assures the believer that he is a child of God, consoles and strengthens him in all adversity and temptation, and preserves him in the hope of eternal life, Rom. 8, 15. 16; 1 John 5, 10; Phil. 1, 6. The internal testimony of the Holy Spirit is therefore not something that exists without faith or by the side of faith, but it is faith itself, 1 John 5, 10. Cp. the *Apology (Trigl.,* p. 154, § 113, German text): "But *faith,* properly so called *(proprie dicta),* is when my heart and *the Holy Ghost in the heart says:* The promise of God is true and certain. Of this *faith* Scripture speaks."

The *external testimony* of the Holy Spirit consists in this, that God through the means of grace works in the believer manifest *fruits* of faith, such as love for God and His Word, John 8, 47; 1 Thess. 1, 3—6; 2 Thess. 2, 13—15, and love for the neighbor, 1 John 3, 14, which bear witness to his state of grace, Gal. 5, 22—24. This external witness of the Holy Ghost, which occurs only in true believers, must be distinguished from the carnal trust which the unregenerate put in their external "good works," which carnal trust in their "dead good works" proves convincingly that they are self-righteous and therefore not children of God, Luke 18, 10—14.

Every true believer in Christ therefore is sure of his state of grace and salvation; for the Holy Spirit, who through the Gospel has engendered faith in him, assures him by that very faith that he is a child of God and an heir of eternal life, Rom. 8, 15—17.

9. THE FAITH OF INFANTS.

That saving faith *(fides directa, fides actualis)* is found not only in adults, but also in regenerate infants is proved in Scripture by the following: a) Scripture directly ascribes to such children saving faith, Matt. 18, 6; 1 John 2, 13; Ps. 8, 2; b) Scripture ascribes to them the fruit and effect of saving faith, namely, eternal life, Mark 10, 14. The example of John the Baptist, Luke 1, 41—44, who was filled with the Holy Ghost while yet in the womb of his mother, proves that children can believe before they have reached the years of discretion, though in this case the ordinary means of grace (the Word and the Sacraments) were not applied. If from this exceptional case the conclusion is drawn that it is not necessary for us to apply in every instance the means of grace to infants, we answer that God has indeed bound us to the use of these means, Mark 16, 15. 16; Matt. 28, 19. 20, but that He Himself is not bound to them.

While it is impossible for us to describe in detail the faith of infants, we must hold that it is nevertheless an active trust in the divine promises of grace, or an active apprehension of the merits of Christ, Matt. 18, 6; Ps. 71, 6. *Fides infantium fides actualis est, non habitus otiosus vel mera potentia.* Gerhard rightly remarks: "We are not solicitous about the *mode* of this faith, but we simply acquiesce in the fact that infants really believe." (*Doctr. Theol.,* p. 549.)

10. THE USE OF THE TERM "FAITH" IN SCRIPTURE.

Holy Scripture does not always use the term *faith* in the same meaning. In some passages it denotes *faithfulness,* or *trustworthiness,* as found both in God and in man. Faith in this sense is applied to God in Rom. 3, 3 and to the regenerate in Gal. 5, 22. Faith in the sense of faithfulness is in believers a fruit of justifying faith and belongs into the article of sanctification and not into that of justification. In other words, faith justifies and saves, not as faithfulness, or trustworthiness, that is to say, not as a good work in the regenerate, but as the receiving means (*medium λητττικόν*) by which the believer appropriates to himself the grace of God and the merits of Christ offered to him in the Gospel. In its proper sense, that is, regarded as the means by which the believer receives divine grace, faith always denotes *trust* in the merciful promises of God in Christ Jesus, Mark 16, 15. 16; 1, 14. 15; 9, 23. 24; Heb. 11, 1. Or we may say, justifying faith in this sense is always *fides passiva,* which saves not in view of its own worth as a virtue, but in view of its *object,* namely, the grace of God and the merits of Christ, which it appropriates. Cf. the *Apology:* "Faith justifies and saves, not on the ground that it is a work in itself worthy *(opus per sese dignum),* but only because it receives the promised mercy." (*Trigl.,* p. 137.)

In a few passages of Scripture, such as Acts 6, 7; Gal. 1, 23; Jude 3. 20; etc., the term *faith* denotes the Christian doctrine *(fides. quae creditur),* or the Gospel of salvation by grace through faith in Christ. Faith in this sense is called objective faith *(fides obiectiva)* in contradistinction to justifying faith, which is termed subjective faith *(fides subiectiva),* since it is found in the heart of the individual believer. To understand this use of the term *faith,* we must remember that *personal trust* in the grace of God for Christ's sake *(fiducia)* is indeed the central article of the entire Christian religion, so that in this case the Christian doctrine receives its name from its chief characteristic. Whenever our dogmaticians speak of *fides, quae creditur,* they mean the doctrine of salvation which must be believed; when they speak of *fides, qua creditur,* they mean justifying or saving faith, that is, the receiving means of salvation *(medium ληπτικόν).* — In passing, it may be said that some exegetes aver that πίστις in the New Testament is never employed in an objective, but only in a subjective sense, so that πίστις always denotes the *fides, qua creditur,* never the *fides, quae creditur.* (Cp. *Christl. Dogmatik,* Vol. II, p. 540 ff.)

With respect to the terminology of the Church on this point we may note, by way of review, the following: 1) *Implicit faith* is alleged assent to doctrines though these may not be known to the individual *(fides carbonaria, Koehlerglaube:* "I believe what the Church teaches"). 2) *Explicit faith (fides explicita)* is assent to doctrines distinctly known. 3) *Justifying, or saving, faith* is personal trust in the gracious remission of sin for Christ's sake. 4) *Direct faith* is faith which lays hold of the grace of God in Christ Jesus. Justifying faith is always direct. 5) *Reflex, or discursive, faith* is faith by which the regenerate perceives that he believes. Infants, and adults while asleep or unconscious, have direct faith, but not reflex or discursive faith. 6) *General faith (fides generalis)* is assent to all truths revealed in God's Word. 7) *Special faith (fides specialis)* is justifying faith, or personal trust in the grace of God for Christ's sake. The object of general faith is the *whole Bible;* that of special faith is the *promise of the Gospel* concerning the grace of God and the remission of sins through Christ's vicarious satisfaction. 8) *A false, or vain and dead, faith* is called faith only equivocally, because it is nothing but an empty boast or a bold presumption upon the mercy and grace of God made by impenitent men (Hollaz). 9) Faith is said to be *weak, or infirm,* when either the knowledge of Christ is weak or the confidence in Christ is infirm. 10) Faith is *strong* when either the knowledge of Christ, or the trust in Him, is strong. 11) *Objective faith* is the doctrine which is believed. 12) *Subjective faith* is the faith by which one believes. 13) *Historic faith* is mere knowledge of Christ without personal trust in Him. 14) *General assent* is that by which the Gospel promises are regarded as true. 15) *Special assent* is that by which the individual believer regards the gracious promises of the Gospel as applying to him personally. 16) Saving faith is always *fides actualis,* that is, an active confiding on the part of the believer in the grace of God.

All these terms express truths that should be kept in mind in connection with the doctrine of saving faith. Let the student, however, remember that some of these terms have not always been used in precisely the same sense, so that their definitions as given by different dogmaticians may vary.

CONVERSION, OR THE BESTOWAL OF FAITH.
(De Conversione.)

1. SCRIPTURAL BASIS OF THE DOCTRINE.

According to the express teaching of Holy Scripture it is impossible for fallen man to satisfy the demands of divine justice and to atone for his transgressions by good works, Ps. 49, 7. 8; Matt. 16, 26. On the contrary, all who seek to appease God by the works of the Law remain under the curse and condemnation of the divine Law, Gal. 3, 10. In fact, man by nature is so blinded and corrupted by sin, 1 Cor. 2, 14; Eph. 2, 1, that his carnal heart is enmity against God, Rom. 8, 7, and therefore unable rightly to love and worship Him, 1 Cor. 10, 20; Eph. 2, 12. Man by nature is thus incapable of saving himself, Rom. 3, 10—20.

However, what man was unable to do God in His infinite mercy has accomplished for him, Rom. 8, 3. 4. Through the most perfect obedience of His beloved Son, Gal. 4, 4. 5; Is. 53, 4—6, He has reconciled the world unto Himself, 2 Cor. 5, 19; 1 John 2, 2, and since He has blotted out the handwriting of the Law which was against sinful mankind, Col. 2, 13. 14, He now offers to all sinners the merits of Christ through the means of grace (the Gospel and the Sacraments), earnestly desiring *(vocatio seria)* that all men should accept the most gracious forgiveness which He offers in Christ Jesus, 2 Cor. 5, 20. 21. This is the Scriptural basis of the doctrine of conversion. In other words, conversion is possible only because Christ by His suffering and death has secured salvation for lost mankind, John 1, 29, and because God in His indescribable grace offers this salvation to all sinners as a free gift, Eph. 2, 8. 9.

2. THE SCRIPTURAL DEFINITION OF CONVERSION.
(De Forma Conversionis.)

Conversion (*conversio, ἐπιστροφή, μετάνοια*) does not consist in a person's attempt to make amends for his sins and to appease the wrath of God by works; nor is it mere sorrow *(contritio)* over, or disgust at, sin or a solemn resolution on the part of man to improve his life by good works; for all these things even the unconverted may do, Matt. 27, 3. 4; 1 Sam. 24, 16—22. But conversion is essentially the bestowal of faith *(donatio fidei)* in the divine promise of salvation for Christ's sake upon a sinner who from the divine Law has learned to know and lament his sins, Mark 1, 14. 15.

This is the true Scriptural definition of conversion as it is described in Acts 11, 21: "A great number *believed* and *turned* unto the Lord" (πολύς τε ἀριθμός ὁ πιστεύσας ἐπέστρεψεν ἐπὶ τὸν κύριον). The turning to God, or conversion, of the great number, as here related, was accomplished by faith in "the preaching of the Lord Jesus," v. 20. That is to say, the Lord Jesus was preached; a great number believed the Gospel of Christ and thus turned unto the Lord.

In accord with this and other passages, John 1, 45—50; Acts 8, 34—38; 16, 30—34, Luther defines conversion as follows: "To convert oneself to God means to believe that Christ is our Mediator and that we have eternal life through Him." (Cp. St. L., XIII, 1101; V, 590. Pieper, *Christl. Dogmatik,* II, 545 ff.) So also our dogmaticians declare that conversion takes place in that moment when the Holy Spirit engenders faith in the heart of the penitent sinner. Hollaz describes conversion as "the act of grace by which the Holy Spirit excites in the sinner sincere grief for his sins by the Word of the Law and enkindles true faith in Christ by the Word of the Gospel." (*Doctr. Theol.,* p. 466.)

In short, a person is truly converted only when he believes that God has graciously forgiven his sins for Christ's sake; or we may say: A converted person is a true believer in the divine-human Christ, the only Savior from sin. For this reason we must reject all definitions which identify conversion with a mere "change of mind" or with a mere "moral improvement of life" *(reformatio vitae)* as these have been given by ancient and modern rationalists (Pelagians, Unitarians, Modernists, etc.). We readily admit that also an unconverted person may improve his life externally *(iustitia civilis),* that he may suppress this or that vice and cultivate this or that virtue, 1 Tim. 5, 8; but unless a person penitently receives the grace of God offered to him in Christ Jesus, he remains spiritually lost in spite of such change of conduct, Luke 18, 10—14. His outward "good works" will be duly rewarded in this life *(in regno potentiae);* but since he is outside the Kingdom of Grace *(regnum gratiae),* he is without God, Eph. 2, 12, and without hope of salvation, Mark 16, 15. 16. To this truth the whole Bible bears witness. Luther: "God does not desire to be gracious to any people, either Jew or Gentile, unless they are con-

verted, that is to say, unless they believe God with all their heart."
(St. L., III, 1697.)

Because the Scriptural doctrine of conversion is of such eminent importance, it must be guarded against all error. To this end the Christian theologian must not only rule out all unscriptural doctrine on this point, but he must see to it that the terminology which he employs is in agreement with Scripture. Let him therefore consider the following points from the outset: —

a. Any teaching which makes of conversion a meritorious work, performed by man (papists: penance; Unitarians: a moral change) or the product of man's power, either in whole or in part (Pelagianism, synergism), destroys the Christian faith and frustrates the sinner's conversion and justification.

b. The two essential elements in conversion are contrition and faith, Mark 1, 15; Acts 16, 30. 31; Jer. 3, 13. 14. Contrition (*terrores conscientiae*), however, does not form the beginning of, or one half of, conversion, nor does it produce a better spiritual condition in the sinner; the terrified sinner hates God all the more because of his knowledge of sin and flees from Him. Contrition belongs to conversion only for the reason that faith cannot find entrance into the proud and secure heart; it is "the indispensable preparation for conversion." Contrition is the effect of the preaching of the Law, which by itself cannot save a single sinner, Gal. 2, 16. (Cf. the contrition of Judas, Matt. 27, 3—5.)

c. Pietists and Methodists demand a fixed degree of contrition; but what is required is "that a person not only dreads the temporal effects of his sins, but also regards himself as lost forever on account of his sins, Luke 18, 13."

d. Even the kindling of the first spark of faith in the sinner's heart, or his longing after the grace of God in Christ, constitutes conversion. (Cf. *Formula of Concord*, Thor. Decl., II, 54. 14.)

e. Conversion in a wider sense embraces sanctification, which is the inevitable *result* of conversion in the narrow sense (*donatio fidei*). Much confusion and error has been caused by not keeping the two uses of the term separate.

f. The Scriptural doctrine of conversion is perverted 1) by the papists (conversion through man's voluntary reception of grace and its gifts, by which the unjust man becomes a just man); 2) by all rationalists (Unitarians, Modernists), who define conversion as the "moral reformation" of the sinner; 3) by the synergists, who condition God's forgiveness on faith as an "ethical act"; and 4) by all errorists who make the hatred of sin and the purpose to amend one's life the constitutive element of conversion or who (Pietists, Methodists) claim that sorrow for sin from love toward God moves God to be gracious.

g. Conversion does not take place by stages, or degrees, but instantaneously; for while the preparation for conversion (*motus praeparatorii,* which are chiefly the terrors of conscience, wrought by the Law) may extend over a period of time, conversion proper, or the kindling of faith, is effected in a moment. There is no intermediary state (*status medius*) in which man is semidead or semiliving, John 3, 18. The synergists advocate the intermediary state, progressive, or successive, conversion, for the purpose of introducing at some stage of the process man's cooperation. On the other hand, all enthusiasts (Pietists, Methodists) go beyond Scripture in denying that one is genuinely converted who cannot fix the exact moment of his conversion.

h. The term *repentance* is sometimes used for *contrition and faith* (conversion) and sometimes for contrition alone. — In Christians, repentance (*conversio continuata, poenitentia stantium*) continues until death because of the evil which is ever present with them, Rom. 7, 21; Heb. 12, 1. The believer therefore turns daily with a contrite heart to the Gospel of the forgiveness of sins. Perfectionism denies this continued conversion, Matt. 18, 3.

i. The conversion of those who had fallen from grace (David, Peter; Jer. 3, 12; John 3, 7; Gal. 4, 19) is identical with the first conversion. The Calvinists, who, contrary to Luke 8, 13; Matt. 12, 43 ff.; Gal. 5, 4; 1 Tim. 1, 20; 1 Cor. 9, 27; 10, 12, teach that true believers can never lose faith, do not acknowledge *renewed conversion (conversio reiterata, poenitentia lapsorum)* and therefore prevent it. The same is true of Perfectionism.

j. Conversion is not a *substantial change,* that is, not the creation of a new essence of the soul (Flacius, Weigel), but the complete transformation of the soul, or the creation of new qualities in man, 2 Cor. 5, 17; Ps. 51, 10. To teach the latter, does not mean to teach mysticism (rationalists), but to affirm the true doctrine of Holy Scripture on conversion.

k. Conversion is not a *mechanical action;* for in conversion God works in man as in a rational creature and not as in a "stone or block" *(Formula of Concord),* Joel 2, 12.

l. Conversion is not by coercion; that is to say, God does not convert a person *against his will* (by irresistible grace: Calvinism); for conversion consists in this, that "God makes willing persons out of the unwilling" (Augustine; *Formula of Concord,* Epit., II, 15).

m. Our Confession rightly condemns as expressions that "do not conform to the form of sound doctrine" the following: "God draws, but He draws the willing"; "In conversion the will of man is not idle, but also effects something"; and: "Only be willing, and God will anticipate you" (*Formula of Concord,* Thor. Decl., II, 86). In accord with Scripture it describes the divine action in conversion as a "drawing of the Holy Ghost" (Thor. Decl., II, 88), John 6, 44; 12, 32.

n. In conversion man is only the *subiectum patiens,* or the *subiectum convertendum;* that is to say, man "does or works nothing, but only suffers" (*Formula of Concord,* Thor. Decl., II, 89. 90).

o. Against synergism our Confession declares on the basis of Scripture: "Before the conversion of man there are only *two* efficient causes, namely, the Holy Ghost and the Word of God, as the instrument of the Holy Ghost, by which He works conversion." (*Formula of Concord,* Epit., II, 19.)

Some of these points will be considered at greater length later on under their proper heads. We group them here in order to show how necessary it is to guard the Scriptural doctrine of conversion against error and to point out how essential it is to define conversion correctly. (Cf. *Christl. Dogmatik,* II, 542 ff.; Dr. Engelder, *Dogmatical Notes.*)

3. THE STARTING-POINT AND THE TERMINUS OF CONVERSION.
(Terminus a quo; Terminus ad quem Conversionis.)

Since conversion consists essentially in the bestowal of faith in Christ, it is obvious that the *terminus a quo* of conversion is unbelief, while its *terminus ad quem* is true confidence in Christ Jesus, Acts 26, 18: ἐπιστρέψαι ἀπο σκότους εἰς φῶς; 2 Cor. 3, 14—16. Quenstedt: *Conversio prima est infidelium, . . . et sic notat conversionem ab infidelitate ad fidem.*

Only then is a sinner converted when in place of infidelity, which by nature is found in every human heart, 1 Cor. 2, 14, there is found in him faith in the gracious promises of God for Christ's

sake *(propter Christum)*.   As long as a person is without faith
in Christ, he is unregenerate, or unconverted, no matter whether
in the sight of man he is a criminal or a saint, an illiterate or
a sage.   Upon all who are without Christ, Scripture pronounces
the verdict that they are without God in this world and have no
hope, Eph. 2, 12.

However, as soon as a person believes in Christ, his conversion,
or return to God, has been fully accomplished, even though his
faith should be a mere spark *(scintillula)*.   Of all who believe in
Christ, St. Paul writes: "But now in Christ Jesus ye who some-
time were *far off* are made nigh by the blood of Christ," Eph. 2, 13.
According to these words it is faith in Christ that distinguishes
those who are "far off," or the unregenrate, from those who are
"made nigh," or the regenerate.   In other words, as the apost e
clearly teaches, conversion takes place through faith in the blood
of Christ.

Unless this truth is constantly borne in mind, it is impossible
to avoid the mistake of regarding the unconverted as converted,
or *vice versa,* the converted as unconverted.

Properly speaking, the starting-point of conversion is unbelief,
its terminus, saving faith in Christ, and its essential feature, the
kindling of faith (donatio fidei).   However, since unbelief is always
joined with spiritual darkness, the dominion of Satan, idolatry,
the state of sin, etc., also these factors may be said to constitute
the starting-point of conversion.   On the other hand, faith is
always joined with spiritual life, communion with God, the keeping of the divine commandments, etc., and therefore also these
things may be said to be the terminus of conversion.   Thus Scripture itself speaks of conversion as a turning from darkness to light,
from the power of the devil to God, Acts 26, 18, from idolatry to
the worship of the living God, Acts 14, 15; 1 Thess. 1, 9, from
transgression to the keeping of the divine Law, Ezek. 18, 21, etc.

In all these passages unbelief and faith are described according
to their outward manifestation, or fruits, so that we may rightly
say: All who are in spiritual darkness, or under the dominion of
Satan, or in the power of sin, or in the thraldom of idolatry are
unconverted, while those who have spiritual life, are in communion
with God, and possess new spiritual powers to keep the commandments of God are truly converted.   But it must not be forgotten
that to be converted, in its proper and narrow sense, always means
to come to faith in the Gospel of Christ, the Savior of sinners,

Acts 11, 20. 21; 1 Pet. 2, 25, whereas spiritual life, communion with God, and the keeping of the divine commandments are, properly speaking, *fruits,* or *effects,* of conversion. A person truly performs the will of God only after his will has been inclined, or turned, to God through faith in Christ, in other words, *after he has been converted.*

4. THE EFFICIENT CAUSE OF CONVERSION.
(Causa Efficiens Principalis Conversionis.)

The question concerning the efficient cause of conversion has been answered in three different ways. In the first place, it has been said that man himself is the cause of his conversion (Pelagianism). Again, it has been claimed that both God and man cooperate in bringing about the conversion of man, the sinner either beginning the work and God completing it (Semi-Pelagianism, Arminianism), or God making the beginning and the enlightened and awakened sinner himself completing it (synergism).

With regard to Semi-Pelagianism and synergism the *Formula of Concord* says (Epitome, II, 10. 11): "We reject also the error of the Semi-Pelagians, who teach that man by his own powers can *make a beginning* of his conversion, but *without the grace of the Holy Ghost cannot complete it;* also, when it is taught that, although man by his free will before regeneration is *too weak to make a beginning* and by his own powers to turn himself to God and from the heart to be obedient to God, yet, if the Holy Ghost, by the preaching of the Word, has made a beginning and therein offered His grace, *then the will of man from its own natural powers can add something* [synergism], though little and feebly, to this end, can help and cooperate, qualify and prepare itself for grace, and embrace and accept it, and believe the Gospel." According to this clear, decisive statement the Lutheran Confession on the basis of Scripture rejects both Pelagianism and synergism and supplies a third answer to the question concerning man's conversion, namely, *God alone* is the efficient Cause of conversion (divine monergism), while the sinner *(subiectum convertendum)* conducts himself *mere,* or *pure, passive.*

Of this the *Formula of Concord* says (Thor. Decl., II, 87): "The conversion of our corrupt will, which is nothing else than a resuscitation of its spiritual death, is only and solely the work of God, just as the resuscitation in the resurrection of the body must be ascribed to God alone, as has been fully set forth above and proved by manifest testimonies of Holy Scripture." The doctrine of conversion here set forth is that of Holy Scripture, which teaches expressly that, if a sinner is converted, this is due, not to any efforts of his own, but alone to the effectual working of divine grace, Eph. 1, 19. The Scriptural proof for this truth may be stated as follows: —

a. Scripture positively ascribes conversion, or the engendering of faith in man's heart, exclusively *to God,* John 6, 44; Rom. 1, 5—7; Col. 1, 12. 13; in particular, to His grace, Phil. 1, 29; Eph. 2, 8. 9, and omnipotent power, Eph. 1, 19; 2 Cor. 4, 6. Moreover, it depicts conversion as a new birth from God, John 1, 12. 13; 1 John 5, 1, or a spiritual resurrection, Col. 2, 12. 13. All these passages describe conversion as an act of divine grace (monergism) and exclude from it man's operation or cooperation.

b. Scripture expressly denies to unconverted man the power to know or to believe the Gospel, 1 Cor. 2, 14; John 6, 44, and charges him with the offense of resisting the good and gracious will of God, which earnestly desires his regeneration, up to the very moment when he is converted, 1 Cor. 2, 14; Rom. 8, 7. Hence also these passages describe conversion as an act of divine grace and exclude from it man's operation or cooperation. Both positively and negatively Scripture therefore declares itself for divine monergism and against all forms of Pelagianism and synergism. Luther: "We rightly honor God if we acknowledge that we are not saved by our merits and put our trust in His mercy." (St. L., XI, 2217.)

That God alone is the efficient Cause of conversion is clear also from the very nature of conversion *(forma conversionis).* As we have seen, conversion consists essentially in this, that the terrified and penitent sinner believes in Christ and with such faith indeed as strenuously repudiates all work-righteousness and trusts for salvation in nothing else than in the merits of Christ. But such faith in Christ implies a complete and absolute change of the sinner's heart and mind. By nature man is addicted to work-righteousness and desires no other way of salvation than that of relying on his good works.

But if that is the case, then the change in his heart by which he repudiates all works and clings alone to Christ's merits cannot come from man; for by nature he detests and opposes the Gospel way of salvation, 1 Cor. 2, 8. 14; 1, 23. The change must therefore be of God, as indeed it is. The *Apology* writes correctly

(Art. III, 144 ff.) : "This opinion of the Law inheres by nature in men's minds; neither can it be expelled, unless when we are divinely taught. But the mind must be recalled from such carnal opinions to the Word of God."

Against the Scriptural doctrine that God alone works and effects conversion it has been claimed that man by nature is indeed unable to believe the Gospel, to desist from opposing the Holy Spirit, to prepare himself for grace, and to observe a proper conduct toward the calling and sanctifying operation of God; but this, it is claimed, he certainly can do as soon as he is endowed with spiritual powers.

To this objection we reply that, if a person is able to do these spiritual works with powers granted to him by the Holy Ghost, he is already converted; for in that case his heart is completely changed, his will is conformed to God and divine things, his mind no longer regards the Gospel as foolishness, but as divine wisdom, and the crucified Savior, the world's only spiritual Hope, is no longer a stumbling-block to him. In other words, in that case man exhibits every characteristic of a converted person, or of a believer.

Of the unregenerate, or unconverted, the *Formula of Concord* rightly declares (Thor. Decl., II, 7) : "The natural free will according to its perverted disposition and nature is *strong and active only with respect to what is displeasing and contrary to God.*" Of conversion it says (*ibid.*, § 83) : "Conversion is such a change through the operation of the Holy Ghost in the intellect, will, and heart of man that by this operation of the Holy Ghost man can accept the offered grace." Our Confession thus supports the Scriptural doctrine that the endowment of a person with spiritual powers is the very essence of conversion. *(Donatio virium spiritualium est ipsa conversio.)*

That God alone is the efficient Cause of conversion is the proper scope of Article II of the *Formula of Concord.* As it correctly points out, man with respect to his conversion is not active, but *pure passivus* (purely passive), that is, "he does nothing whatever towards it, but only suffers what God works in him" (Thor. Decl., II, 89). *(Hominem in conversione sua pure passive sese habere, id est, pati id, quod Deus in ipso agit. . . .)* In other words, man's capacity for conversion must be regarded as entirely passive *(capacitas passiva, non capacitas activa).* His spiritual cooperation therefore begins only after he has been converted.

Our Confession says (Thor. Decl., II, 90) : "The intellect and will of the unregenerate man are nothing else than *subiectum convertendum,* that is, that which is to be converted, it being the intellect and will of a spiritually dead man in whom the Holy Ghost works conversion and renewal, toward which work man's will that is to be converted does nothing, but suffers God alone to work in him, until he is regenerate; and then he works also with the Holy Ghost that which is pleasing to God in other good works that follow."

Hence there are not three efficient causes of conversion *(tres causae efficientes conversionis),* namely, the Holy Spirit, the Word, and the assenting will of man, as Melanchthon and his synergistic followers erroneously affirmed, but only two, the Holy Spirit and the Word of God. In his conversion man is like a block or stone, indeed, much worse than a block or stone, since by reason of his natural enmity against God, 1 Cor. 2, 14; Rom. 8, 7, he resists the operations of the Holy Spirit until he is converted.

The *Formula of Concord* says of this (Thor. Decl., II, 59) : "A stone or block does not resist the person who moves it, nor does it understand, and is sensible of, what is being done with it, as man with his will so long resists God the Lord until he is converted. . . . He can do nothing whatever towards his conversion . . . and is in this respect much worse than a stone and block; for he resists the Word and will of God, until God awakens him from the death of sin, enlightens and renews him."

It is true, conversion does not take place without a complete inner change of the heart; for the sinner experiences the terrors of conscience *(terrores conscientiae),* and through the operation of the Holy Spirit he believes the Gospel, which formerly, in his state of unbelief, he rejected. But neither the effects of the Law upon his heart nor his faith in the Gospel promises are due to his own efforts; for over against both the Law and the Gospel he is purely passive and only suffers "what God works in him" (*ibid.,* § 89). "Man of himself, or from his natural powers, cannot do anything or help towards his conversion, and . . . conversion is not only in part, but altogether an operation, gift, present, and work of the Holy Ghost alone, who accomplishes and effects it by His power and might, through the Word." *(Ibid.)*

In these clear and unmistakable words the *Formula of Concord* defends divine monergism against synergism. Its doctrine is:

"Conversion is alone the work of the Holy Ghost, who operates by means of the Word of God." *(Solus Deus convertit hominem.)*

To the charge that our Confession rather overemphasizes this point, we reply that the writers of the *Formula of Concord* were fully persuaded that the adoption of synergism by the Lutheran Church would completely destroy the foundation of the Reformation and lead the purified Church back to Pelagianism, the fundamental error of the Papacy. A synergistic Lutheran Church, they perceived, could not teach the *sola gratia* in its Scriptural truth and purity. Hence, when they warded off the attacks of the synergists, they fought against foes who "flew at the throat" of Christianity. (Cp. Luther's words addressed to Erasmus: *"Unus tu et solus cardinem rerum vidisti et ipsum iugulum petisti."* Also Dr. F. Bente's statement: "Genuine Lutheranism would have been strangled if synergism had emerged victorious from this great controversy of grace versus free will." *Concordia Triglotta,* Histor. Introd., p. 128.)

5. THE MEANS OF CONVERSION.
(Causae Instrumentales Conversionis.)

Though God alone is the Cause of conversion, yet He does not convert men immediately, or by immediate operation, but through definite, ordained means. This truth our Lutheran Confession maintains against all forms of enthusiasm (Calvinism, Anabaptism, etc.). The *Formula of Concord declares* (Thor. Decl., II, 4): "Moreover, both the ancient and modern enthusiasts have taught that God converts men and leads them to the saving knowledge of Christ through His Spirit, without any created means and instrument, that is, without the external preaching and hearing of God's Word."

In these words the *Formula of Concord* points out the *means* by which the Holy Spirit works conversion, or regeneration, in the human heart, namely, by "the external preaching and hearing of God's Word." As aforesaid, conversion in its proper sense is nothing else than that a person, terrified by the Law on account of his sins, becomes a believer in Christ, trusting for salvation in the divine promises of the Gospel. The Gospel is therefore the *object* of converting faith; but it also is the *means* of conversion. Through the same means by which God offers to man the merits of Christ *(vis evangelii dativa vel collativa)* He also works in man faith in the proffered grace *(vis evangelii effectiva vel operativa).*

This truth is clearly taught in Holy Scripture, *e. g.,* Rom. 10, 17: "Faith cometh by hearing and hearing by the Word of God"; Jas. 1, 18: "Of His own will begat He us with the Word of Truth"; 1 Thess. 1, 5: "Our Gospel came not unto you in word only, but also in power and in the Holy Ghost and in much assurance"; 2 Thess. 2, 13. 14: "God hath chosen you to salvation through sanctification of the Spirit and belief of the truth, whereunto He called you by our Gospel"; 1 Thess. 2, 13: "Ye received the Word of God, . . . not as the word of men, but as it is in truth, the Word of God, which effectually worketh also in you that believe."

These passages prove that the Gospel is not a "dead letter," but a living witness, full of power, John 6, 63, because the Holy Spirit is always active and operative through it to inscribe its divine promises into the human heart, Gal. 3, 1—5; Rom. 1, 16; Is. 55, 11.

Luther writes on this point: "Such is the efficacy of the Word whenever it is seriously contemplated, heard, and used that it is bound never to be without fruit, but always awakens new understanding, pleasure, and devoutness and produces a pure heart and pure thoughts. For these words are not inoperative or dead, but creative, living words." (*Large Catechism,* Third Commandment, § 100.) The Gospel is therefore the effective means by which the Holy Spirit works faith, or conversion, in man.

Because the Gospel is connected with Baptism, Acts 2, 38, and the Lord's Supper, Matt. 26, 26—28, also the Sacraments are effective means *(media salutis; Gnadenmittel),* through which the Holy Spirit either works faith (Baptism: Titus 3, 5) or strengthens faith (Lord's Supper: 1 Cor. 11, 26), in other words, through which He either converts sinners (infants) or confirms and preserves in faith those who are already converted (baptism of adults; Lord's Supper).

While the Gospel is the proper means by which the Holy Ghost works faith, or conversion, in man, the divine Law is used by God to *prepare the sinner for conversion.* Saving faith can never exist in a person who has not previously been convinced of his exceeding sinfulness and his state of wrath and damnation, Ps. 34, 18; 51, 17; Is. 66, 2; Acts 2, 37—41; 16, 27—31.

True repentance therefore comprises both contrition *(contritio; terrores conscientiae),* which is effected by the Law, and faith *(fiducia),* which is wrought by the Gospel. Hence, in order that sinners may be converted, the preaching of the Gospel must be preceded or accompanied by that of the Law, Rom. 3, 19. 20. In other words, the proclamation of the Law and the Gospel must always go hand in hand, both in their proper connection and with the proper distinction of their functions and purposes, Luke 24, 47.

The *Formula of Concord* says (Thor. Decl., V, 24—26): "These two doctrines [the Law and the Gospel], we believe, . . . should ever and ever be diligently inculcated in the Church of God, . . . although with the proper distinction of which we have heard, in order that through the preaching of the Law and its threats . . . the hearts of impenitent men may be terrified and brought to a knowledge of their sins and to repentance; but not in such a way that they lose heart and despair in this process, but that . . . they be comforted and strengthened again by the preaching of the holy Gospel concerning Christ, our Lord, namely, that to those who believe the Gospel, God forgives all their sins through Christ, adopts them as children for His sake, and out of pure grace, without any merit on their part, justifies and saves them."

Hollaz writes in the same tenor: "Conversion, taken in a special sense [conversion proper], is that act of grace by which the Holy Spirit excites in the sinner sincere grief for his sins by the Word of the Law and kindles true faith in Christ by the Word of the Gospel that he may obtain remission of sins and eternal salvation." (*Doctr. Theol.*, p. 466.)

The preaching of the Law is supported and furthered also by the crosses and afflictions, Luke 15, 14—18; Acts 16, 26—30; Ps. 119, 71, which come upon men and by the manifold earthly blessings by which God calls sinners to repentance, Rom. 2, 4. For this reason the peculiar dealings of God with men have been called *concio legis realis,* that is, a preaching of the Law by act. However, neither the manifestation of God's wrath nor of His goodness may take the place of the preaching of the divine Word; for this alone is the means through which the Holy Ghost operates in man toward his conversion, Mark 16, 15. 16.

To the objection that divine monergism in conversion makes the use of external means unnecessary (Calvinism, enthusiasm) we reply that divine monergism certainly excludes *human cooperation,* but not the employment of the divinely appointed means.

Of this the *Formula of Concord* writes (Thor. Decl., II, 46): "This doctrine concerning the inability and wickedness of our natural free will and concerning our conversion and regeneration, namely, that it is a work of God alone and not of our powers, is abused in an unchristian manner both by enthusiasts and Epicureans; . . . for they say that, since they are unable from their own natural powers to convert themselves to God, they will always strive with all their might against God or wait until God converts them by force against their will; or since they can do nothing in these spiritual things, but everything is the operation of God the Holy Ghost alone, they will *regard, hear, or read neither the Word nor the Sacrament, but wait until God, without means,* instils into them His gifts from heaven, so that they can truly feel and perceive in themselves that God has converted them." Luther: *"Deus non dat interna nisi per externa. Spiritum Sanctum non mittit absque Verbo."*

6. THE INTERNAL MOTIONS IN CONVERSION.
(Motus Interni, quibus Conversio Absolvitur.)

Whenever a sinner is converted to God, distinct motions, or movements, occur in his heart. In the first place, alarmed on account of his sins, which the divine Law has made known to him, Rom. 3, 20, he experiences the terrors of conscience *(terrores conscientiae),* that is, true fear and anguish of heart, Acts 16, 29. 30. The terrors of conscience *(terrores incussi conscientiae agnito peccato),* though necessary, are not meritorious in themselves, Matt. 27, 3—5. In spite of his knowledge of sin and the wrath of God the alarmed sinner, as long as he hears nothing of the Gospel, remains unconverted. However, when the Gospel is preached to him, the Holy Spirit engenders in his heart true faith *(fiducia cordis)* in the gracious promises of forgiveness, and it is through this second motion, that is, through implicit trust in Christ, that he is converted, Acts 16, 31—34.

These two motions, contrition and faith, are found in every person who is truly converted, Ps. 32, 1—5. Where they do not occur, genuine conversion has not taken place.

The *Formula of Concord* writes (Thor. Decl., II, 70): "In genuine conversion a *change, new emotion,* and *movement* in the intellect, will, and heart must take place, namely, that the heart perceive sin, dread God's wrath, turn from sin, perceive and accept the promise of grace in Christ, have good spiritual thoughts, a Christian purpose and diligence, and strive against the flesh. *For where none of these occurs or is present, there is also no true conversion."*

However, where contrition and faith are present in the heart, there conversion has taken place, even though the believer's knowledge of sin and his trust in divine grace are yet weak. Scripture nowhere demands a specific degree of contrition or faith, though, of course, the regenerate should strive to grow in knowledge of both sin and grace, Col. 1, 9—11; 2 Pet. 3, 18. True contrition may be said to exist in every case where a penitent sinner regards himself as eternally lost on account of his sins, Acts 16, 30.

True love of God is not a part of contrition; love is a *fruit* of faith, Gal. 5, 22, or the effect of conversion. But saving faith exists in the heart as soon as the penitent sinner *longs for,* or *desires,* divine grace in Christ Jesus, that is to say, as soon as he has a mere spark of faith *(scintillula fidei),* as Holy Scripture clearly teaches, Is. 42, 3; Mark 9, 24. The *Formula of Concord* says (Thor. Decl., II, 14): "To all godly Christians who feel and experience in their hearts a small spark or longing for divine grace and eternal salvation this precious passage [Phil. 2, 13] is very comforting; for they know that God has kindled in their hearts this beginning of true godliness and that He will further strengthen and help them in their great weakness to persevere in true faith unto the end."

7. CONVERSION IS INSTANTANEOUS.
(Conversio Momentanea Est.)

In the discussion of the subject of conversion the question whether conversion is successive *(conversio successiva)* or instantaneous *(conversio momentanea)* has been given much consideration. Since conversion takes place through the kindling of faith in the heart by the Holy Ghost, it is clear that it occurs in a moment *(conversio momentanea),* namely, in that moment when the Holy Spirit through the means of grace engenders faith in the contrite sinner. Hence, as soon as the penitent sinner possesses the first spark or longing of faith, he is already fully converted. *(Conversio temporis momento fit, . . . veluti ἐν ῥιπῇ ὄμματος.* Calov.)

Conversion may be said to be successive *(conversio successiva)* only in case certain acts *(actus praeparatorii)* which commonly precede it are regarded as a part of conversion. To these *actus praeparatorii* belong the inculcation of the divine Law, the conviction of the sinner of his guilt and condemnation, the incitement of the *terrores conscientiae,* and the like. Properly speaking, however, these acts of the Holy Ghost only *prepare* the sinner for conversion, but do not convert him; for conversion, properly speaking, occurs only in that moment when the Holy Spirit through the Gospel changes the alarmed and despairing sinner into a rejoicing believer in Christ.

For this reason we must not speak of a middle state *(status medius)* between conversion and non-conversion *(homo renascens, homo in statu medio constitutus),* since this is both unscriptural and synergistic. It is unscriptural; for Holy Scripture recognizes only two classes of men, the converted and the unconverted, or what is the same, believers and unbelievers, John 3, 18. 36; Mark 16, 16; 1 Pet. 2, 25. According to Scripture it is impossible for a person to be in a middle state even for a moment, for there is no middle ground between belief and unbelief, between life and death, Luke 11, 23.

Theologians who in opposition to Scripture reject the instantaneous character of conversion and explain it as a long-drawn-out process, during which the sinner is first enlightened, then awakened, and finally brought to the decision to accept Christ, commonly do so in the interest of synergism, that is to say, to support their erroneous views that the awakened sinner in the final analysis must convert himself with spiritual powers bestowed upon him by the Holy Ghost (Latermann).

As a matter of fact, the objections of modern rationalistic theologians to the instantaneous character of conversion are really not directed against the *conversio momentanea,* but against the *sola gratia;* for synergistic rationalism regards conversion both as an act of divine grace and as an act of human meritorious effort. It champions the doctrine of "successive conversion" and of "the middle state" since according to its erroneous view God endows the sinner only with the potentiality, or ability, to believe and not with faith itself. Faith, it is claimed, is man's own free, conscious, and deliberate self-determination *(Selbstbestimmung),* accomplished through spiritual powers granted to him by God. From this it is clear that the onslaught upon the Scriptural doctrine of instantaneous conversion is, in the last analysis, directed against divine monergism in conversion, or against the *sola gratia.*

It goes without saying that what is here said of synergism is true also of Arminianism. Both insist upon successive conversion because both hold that man in the last instance must convert himself. *Hominis voluntas in conversione non est otiosa, sed agit aliquid.* Against this error the *Formula of Concord* testifies (Thor. Decl., II, 62): "No *modus agendi,* or no way whatever of working something good in spiritual things, can be ascribed to man before his conversion."

8. THE GRACE OF CONVERSION IS RESISTIBLE.
(Gratia Conversionis Resistibilis Est.)

Although the conversion of man is a work of God's omnipotent power, Eph. 1, 19; 2 Cor. 4, 6, divine converting grace nevertheless is not irresistible *(gratia irresistibilis),* as the Calvinists teach, but resistible *(gratia resistibilis),* as Holy Scripture affirms, Matt. 23, 37; Acts 7, 51. The reason for this is evident. Though God is irresistible whenever He deals with man according to His sovereign power *(in nuda maiestate),* Matt. 25, 31. 32, He can be resisted whenever He exercises His omnipotent power through means, Matt. 11, 28; 23, 37. Both in His Kingdom of Power and in the Kingdom of Grace the means by which He purposes to bless man can be rejected. Thus life, the greatest of God's earthly gifts, though created and sustained by divine omnipotence, can nevertheless be destroyed by man. Similarly spiritual life, or conversion, though offered through the means of the omnipotent Word of God, can be rejected by man through malicious resistance.

Maintaining the resistibility of converting grace *(gratia conversionis),* the confessional Lutheran Church disavows both Calvinism and synergism. Denying the universality of grace, the Calvinists declare that the elect are regenerated by irresistible grace, while to the non-elect only common grace is granted. The synergists, on the other hand, conclude from the resistibility of grace that, as the sinner can reject the divine grace offered to him, so also he can cooperate with the Holy Spirit in his conversion, by rightly using the spiritual powers granted to him. Both errors are opposed to the clear teaching of Holy Scripture on this point, 1 Tim. 2, 4; Phil. 2, 13.

9. TRANSITIVE AND INTRANSITIVE CONVERSION.
(Conversio Transitiva; Conversio Intransitiva.)

On the basis of Holy Scripture our dogmaticians speak of transitive and intransitive conversion *(conversio transitiva; conversio intransitiva).* In other words, God is said to convert man, and again, man is said to convert himself (Jer. 31, 18, הֲשִׁיבֵנִי;

Acts 3, 19, μετανοήσατε; Jer. 24, 7, וְיָשֻׁבוּ). Between the two, however, there is no real distinction (realis distinctio), since man converts himself only when God converts him.   Both expressions
therefore describe one and the same act, of which God alone is the
efficient Cause.   The expressions must therefore not be understood
in the synergistic sense as though God began while man himself
accomplished or completed conversion.   While the expression "intransitive conversion" ("Man converts himself") is Scriptural, it
must not be forgotten that in conversion God "worketh in man
both to will and to do," Phil. 2, 13.

Baier's remark on the point is truly Scriptural.   He writes:
"The word conversion is taken in a double sense in the Scriptures,
inasmuch as at one time God is said to convert man and at another
that man is said to convert himself, although as to the thing itself
(quoad rem) the action is one and the same (una et eadem)."   That
God alone works conversion is abundantly proved in Scripture, Jer.
31, 18; John 6, 44; Eph. 1, 19; etc.   These passages do not allow
even a modified form of synergism (Man's conversion depends on
his necessary condition of passiveness and submissiveness toward
the Gospel call; cp. Latermann, Dieckhoff, etc.).

10. CONTINUED CONVERSION.
(Conversio Continuata.)

On the basis of Scripture our dogmaticians speak also of
continued conversion, that is, of that conversion which continues
throughout the life of the believer, Matt. 18, 3.   The need of continued conversion is based upon the fact that the regenerate are
not fully sanctified, but retain the Old Adam, Heb. 12, 1; Rom.
7, 21. 23, so that because of the sinfulness of their flesh and the
manifold actual sins flowing therefrom they must live in "daily
repentance," Rom. 6, 3—6.   It is this "daily repentance" with
which "continued conversion" (continued regeneration, resuscitation, illumination) must be identified. (Poenitentia continuata sive
quotidiana est dolor hominis iam conversi de residua ad peccandum
proclivitate et vitiositate.)

Holy Scripture distinguishes sharply between the first conversion (conversio prima), by which the unregenerate becomes
a believer in Christ, and the continued conversion (conversio
secunda) of the believer, 1 Pet. 2, 25 (cp. also v. 10), which extends
throughout his life, Ps. 51, 1—12.   The conversio prima is complete when the believer is endowed with the first spark of faith

(scintillula fidei), while his *conversio secunda* is never complete as long as he lives in this world, Rom. 7, 24. In the first conversion man is purely passive *(mere passivus),* but in the second he cooperates with the Holy Ghost according to the "new man" (ἔσω ἄνθρωπος; καινὸς ἄνθρωπος, Eph. 4, 24), implanted in him in his first conversion, Gal. 5, 17. 24; Rom. 7, 22. 25. The second conversion must never be mingled with the first, as some synergists have done in the interest of denying the *pure passive* of the first conversion, by which the unregenerate becomes a believer. (Cp. Pieper, *Christl. Dogmatik,* II, 559 ff.)

11. REITERATED CONVERSION.
(Conversio Reiterata.)

It is a clear doctrine of Scripture that believers in Christ may fall from grace, or lose their faith, Luke 8, 13. 14; 1 Tim. 1, 19. This is proved also by the examples of David and Peter. This truth must be emphasized over against the Calvinists, who affirm that believers, when committing mortal sins, lose indeed the exercise of faith *(exercitium fidei),* but not faith itself.

Our Lutheran Confession strongly condemns this Calvinistic doctrine as unscriptural and pernicious. It says (*Smalcald Art.,* III, 42): "If certain sectarists would arise . . . holding that all those who had once received the Spirit or the forgiveness of sins or had become believers, even though they should afterwards sin, would still remain in the faith and such sin would not harm them: . . . I have had before me many such insane men, and I fear that in some such a devil is still remaining." On the other hand, it must be maintained that those who have fallen from faith may again be converted *(conversio reiterata). (Poenitentia iterata lapsorum, qui ad meliorem frugem redeunt.)* This truth we hold against the ancient Novatians and their modern followers. (*Augsb. Conf.,* XII, 9.)

However, when the sinner has committed the sin against the Holy Ghost, reiterated conversion is impossible, Matt. 12, 31—32; 1 John 5, 16. Since, however, man can only in rare cases definitely know who has committed the sin against the Holy Ghost, it is the duty of the Christian Church to preach repentance and faith to all men as it has opportunity, Ezek. 18, 23—32; 3, 16—21.

With regard to the Terministic Controversy, which occurred in the Lutheran Church early in the 18th century and in which the Pietists, on the basis of such passages as Matt. 3, 7 ff.; 7, 21;

20, 1—16; 2 Pet. 2, 20; Heb. 6, 4 ff., defended "terminism," that is, the doctrine that only a limited term *(terminus peremptorius salutis)* is accorded to an individual for salvation, while the orthodox Lutherans, on the basis of Luke 23, 40 ff.; Rom. 5, 20; Is. 65, 2, affirmed that God desires the salvation of every sinner throughout his life and that, if there is a shortened term of grace *(terminus gratiae peremptorius),* this is due only to the sinner's self-hardening against the means of grace, the rule just stated suffices: The Church should not withhold, but bestow, the grace of the Gospel as long as men are ready to receive it, Mark 16, 15.

12. OBJECTIONS AGAINST DIVINE MONERGISM IN CONVERSION.

Among the numerous objections which have been raised against the Scriptural doctrine that God alone converts man *(Solus Deus convertit hominem)* the following deserve special notice: —

a. *Since God in His Word demands repentance, or conversion, of man* (Acts 16, 31; Mark 1, 15), *he must be able, at least in part, to convert himself.* To this we reply that from the divine demand no conclusion may be drawn with respect to man's ability to comply with God's will. *A debito ad posse non valet consequentia.*

On the contrary, the divine commands and exhortations are the means by which God works that which He demands. Thus through the commands of the Law *(admonitiones legales)* He humiliates man and works in him true knowledge of sin, Luke 10, 28; Rom. 3, 20, while through the Gospel exhortations *(admonitiones evangelicae)* He works in him true faith, Matt. 11, 28. As an analog of the divine method of working through His omnipotent Word that which He wills we may cite the resurrection of Lazarus, John 11, 43. 44 (cp. also Acts 3, 6) and the work of creation, Gen. 1, 3 ff. Hence we must not reason: "Why command men to do what they are utterly unable to do? Why bid a man believe when he cannot?" but rather regard both the *ac monitiones legales* and the *admonitiones evangelicae* as the efficient means by which God accomplishes His beneficent purpose of saving sinners. That the synergistic argument *A debito ad posse valet consequentia* is untenable Scripture clearly shows, Matt. 11, 28, cp. with John 6, 44.

With regard to the conditional clauses, Rom. 10, 9, it may be said that these point out, not *real conditions,* but the *means* by which God accomplishes man's salvation. Thus the statement "If thou shalt believe in thine heart, . . . thou shalt be saved," means nothing else than "By faith thou shalt be saved."

b. *Unless man cooperates in his conversion, his conversion becomes an act of coercion* (COACTIO), *or force; in other words, in that case man is converted by irresistible grace, an assumption which Scripture condemns.* To this we reply that this objection ignores the very nature of conversion, which consists in the divine act by which God through the means of grace changes the unwilling into such as are willing, John 6, 44. Conversion is not an act by which God thrusts upon the sinner what he does not desire or forces him to receive what he does not want, but it is a gracious divine drawing (John 6, 44: Ἑλκύσῃ), by which He works in him "both to will and to do," Phil. 2, 13. Luther rightly remarks that God, in converting man, does not draw him as the hangman draws a criminal to the gallows, but by "softening and changing his heart" through the means of grace. *"Es ist ein freundlich Locken und An-sich-Ziehen, wie sonst ein holdseliger Mann die Leute an sich zieht."* (St. L., VII, 2287 ff.)

c. *God works the ability to believe, but not the act of faith, or He prepares man for conversion, but does not accomplish it, since the final decision rests with man himself.* To this we reply that according to Holy Scripture the very act of faith is God's work and gift, Phil. 1, 29; Eph. 1, 19. 20; Phil. 2, 13. We concede indeed that God works in man the ability to believe, but as soon as this ability has been bestowed upon the sinner, he is no longer spiritually dead, but alive in Christ, or what is the same, then he is already converted. Spiritual death in that case has been removed, and in its place spiritual life has been implanted in the heart.

So the *Formula of Concord* understands the well-known statement, which synergists so often have quoted in their favor (Thor. Decl., II, 83): "Conversion is such a change through the operation of the Holy Ghost in the intellect, will, and heart of man that by this operation of the Holy Ghost man *can accept* the offered grace" *(qua homo potest oblatam gratiam apprehendere).* According to the *Formula of Concord* the person who "can accept the offered grace" is already regenerate; for it states definitely (Thor. Decl., II, 85): "The man who is not regenerate resists God altogether and is entirely a servant of sin, John 8, 34; Rom. 6, 16. The regenerate man, however, delights in the Law of God after the inward man." Hence our Confession cannot be quoted as favoring the modified doctrine of the later synergists, who affirmed that man can convert himself by using rightly the new spiritual powers communicated to him by God (Latermann, a disciple of George Calixtus, † 1662), or what is the same, that he can convert himself after God has bestowed upon him the ability to believe.

d. *Unless man cooperates in his conversion, not he himself, but the Holy Spirit in him does the believing; in other words, in that case not man, but the Holy Ghost is the subject of faith.* However, if this argument were correct, it would apply also to the natural life of man, for God "giveth to all life and breath," Acts 17, 25. Yet though God is the sole Author and Preserver of human life, Acts 17, 28, every sane person agrees to the fact that man himself lives, moves, works, eats, weeps, rejoices, etc.; in other words, that the life, movement, and activity of a person are his own.

e. *If man can resist divine grace and so hinder his salvation,* Matt. 23, 37, *then he can also assist divine grace and so make his salvation possible.* Expressed more briefly, the argument reads: *If man can damn himself, then he can also save himself.* To this argument we reply that this conclusion does not follow. For while Scripture ascribes to man the power to destroy himself, Hos. 13, 9; Acts 7, 51, it emphatically denies that he can save himself, 1 Cor. 2, 14; Rom. 8, 7; Phil. 2, 13. Hence from the statement "Ye would not" we must not conclude with respect to the regenerate "Ye would." What is true in the realm of grace is true also in the realm of nature. Man by suicide can destroy his life, but the life so destroyed he is unable to restore. So in the realm of conversion there is no *capacitas volendi* corresponding to man's *capacitas nolendi.*

f. *If man is unable to cooperate in his conversion, then conversion is not a "moral" process.* In order to meet this argument properly, we must bear in mind that the expression "moral" is ambiguous. We admit that conversion is a "moral" act inasmuch as in conversion God does not deal with man as with an inanimate creature (a block or stone), but rather as with a personal moral being endowed with reason and will. Taken in this sense, conversion may indeed be called a moral process; for in conversion the Holy Spirit enlightens the intellect, changes the will, and sanctifies the heart. However, conversion is no "moral process" in the synergistic sense, that man in his conversion cooperates with divine grace toward his regeneration; for Scripture, on the one hand, denies to man any power to convert himself, 1 Cor. 2, 14;

John 6, 44; Eph. 2, 1. 5, and, on the other, positively declares that God is the sole Cause of his conversion, Eph. 1, 19. 20; 2, 10; 2 Cor. 4, 6; John 1, 12. 13. For this reason the *Formula of Concord* rightly affirms (Thor. Decl., II, 87): "The conversion of our corrupt will, which is nothing else than a resuscitation of it from spiritual death, is *only and solely the work of God,* just as also the resuscitation in the resurrection of the body must be ascribed to God alone."

g. *Conversion is a "free" process in man. (Homo libere se convertit.)* To this argument we reply that, if the term "free" is used in opposition to coercion, its application to conversion is justified, because conversion is that act of God by which He changes the unwilling into willing. *(Ex nolentibus gratiam volentes gratiam facit.)* But the term "free" may not be applied to conversion in the synergistic sense, that man before conversion is "neutral," so that he can decide either for or against grace *(ut possit velle aut non).* With regard to man's relation to God and His kingdom there is no neutrality; for man is either with or against Christ, Matt. 12, 30; Luke 9, 50. Luther writes: "Here there is no middle road; for we are necessarily either under the strong tyrant the devil, in his captivity, or under the Redeemer Christ in heaven. . . . Hence every man lives either with Christ against the devil or with the devil against Christ." (St. L., VII, 172.)

h. *Man can cooperate in his conversion since he is capable of civil righteousness (iustitia civilis, probitas naturalis).* In answer to this argument we say that, while man by nature is indeed capable of civil righteousness *(iustitia civilis),* he is of himself incapable of spiritual righteousness *(iustitia spiritualis).* He may indeed refrain from gross sins outwardly, but inwardly he cannot truly love God nor rightly keep His commandments, since with all his external righteousness he does not believe the Gospel of Christ, but rather hates and resists it, 1 Cor. 2, 14. The Pharisees gloried in their civil righteousness; yet Christ judged of them: "The publicans and harlots go into the kingdom of God before you," Matt. 21, 31. In spite of their "civil righteousness" the "princes of this world . . . crucified the Lord of Glory," 1 Cor. 2, 8. Even to the "best" Jews, Christ Crucified is a stumbling-block, and to the "best" Gentiles He is foolishness, 1 Cor. 1, 23, until they are converted, 1 Cor. 1, 24.

i. *Man is able to cooperate in his conversion since he can use the means of grace externally, that is, attend church, read the*

Bible, etc. We readily admit that man by nature can externally use the means of grace, as also the *Formula of Concord* declares (Thor. Decl., II, 53): "This Word man can externally hear and read, even though he is not yet converted to God and regenerate; for in these external things, as said above, man even since the Fall has to a certain extent a free will, so that he can go to church and hear or not hear the sermon." Yet this external use of the means of grace does not presuppose any ability on the part of men to repent of their sins and believe in Christ; for even while they read or hear the Word, "the veil is upon their hearts," 2 Cor. 3, 15, which veil is "done away in Christ," v. 14, that is, through faith in Christ, wrought by the Holy Spirit, vv. 16—18.

j. If God alone works conversion in man, then it cannot be maintained that He really desires the salvation of all men; for actually He does not convert all. To this we reply that Holy Scripture teaches both the *sola gratia* and the *gratia universalis;* that is, God alone converts and saves sinners, and He earnestly desires to save all sinners. Both doctrines must therefore be taught side by side without any modification or qualification of either of them. It is true, if this is done, the theologian is confronted with the perplexing problem, which human reason cannot solve, "Why, then, are not all saved?" *(Cur alii, alii non? Cur alii prae aliis?)* Calvinism solves the mystery by denying the *universalis gratia;* synergism, by denying the *sola gratia,* whereas the theologian who is loyal to Scripture does not attempt any solution of the mystery at all, just as little as he endeavors to solve the mysteries involved in the doctrines of the Holy Trinity, the personal union, the real presence, etc. Reason indeed argues thus: Since all men are in the same state of guilt *(in eadem culpa)* and only God, who earnestly desires to save all men *(universalis gratia),* can save sinners *(sola gratia),* the actual conversion of all men must needs follow. But the true theologian does not recognize reason as his principle of faith *(principium cognoscendi);* he is bound to Scripture as the only source and rule of faith, which, however, does not explain this *crux theologorum.*

Scripture indeed affirms that God is the sole Cause of man's conversion and salvation, Phil. 2, 13; Eph. 1, 19. 20, and, on the other hand, that unregenerate man is the sole cause of his damnation, Matt. 23, 37; Acts 7, 51; Hos. 13, 9. But it does not explain why of two sinners who are in the same guilt (David, Saul; Peter, Judas) the one is saved and the other is not. For this reason we reject the argumentation of Melanchthon: "Since the promise is universal and there are no contradictory wills in God, it necessarily follows that there is in us a certain distinguishing cause *(aliqua discriminis causa)* why Saul is rejected and David accepted; that is, there is in these two a certain dissimilar action *(aliqua actio dissimilis)*." This synergistic explanation indeed satisfies human reason, for it explains why one is saved and another is lost; but it denies the *sola gratia* and thus repudiates the central doctrine of Scripture.

The *Formula of Concord* clearly points out the true position which the theologian must take when he faces the mystery of election and conversion. It says (Thor. Decl., XI, 54—58): "Thus there is no doubt that God most exactly and certainly foresaw before the time of the world, and still knows, which of those that are called will believe or will not believe. . . . However, since God has reserved this mystery for His wisdom and has revealed nothing to us concerning it in His Word, much less commanded us to investigate it with our thoughts, but has earnestly discouraged us therefrom, Rom. 11, 33 ff., we should not reason in our thoughts, draw conclusions, nor inquire curiously into these matters, but should adhere to His revealed Word, to which He points us. . . . Likewise when we see . . . that one is hardened, blinded, given over to a reprobate mind, while another, who is indeed in the same guilt, is converted, etc., — in these and similar questions Paul (Rom. 11, 22 ff.) fixes a certain limit to us how far we should go, namely, that in the one part we should recognize God's judgment (for He commands us to consider in those who perish the just punishment of God and the penalties of sins). For they are all well-deserved penalties of sins when God so punishes a land or nation for despising His Word that the punishment extends also to their posterity," etc.

13. THE PERNICIOUS CHARACTER OF SYNERGISM.

While both the gross synergists (Melanchthon: "The assenting will of man is an efficient cause of conversion") and the subtle synergists (Latermann, modern evangelical Protestantism in general: "Man's will is able to decide for salvation through new powers bestowed by God") profess to teach salvation by grace, they in reality disavow the Scriptural doctrine of salvation by grace and inculcate salvation by work-righteousness. Both the gross and the subtle synergists, in the final analysis, ascribe man's salvation in part to his good conduct, his decision for Christ, his self-determination, his omission of malicious resistance, etc. Hence synergism does not acknowledge the doctrine of grace in the sense of Scripture and the Christian Church. On the contrary, it represents a return to the camp of Semi-Pelagianistic Romanism, which Luther and the Reformers so ceaselessly and zealously condemned. (Cp. Luther's address to Erasmus in reply to his *Diatribe: "Unus tu et solus cardinem rerum vidisti et ipsum iugulum petisti."*) The *Apology* says (Art. III, 144): *"Verum opera incurrunt hominibus in oculos. Haec naturaliter miratur humana ratio, et quia tantum opera cernit, fidem non intelligit neque considerat, ideo somniat haec opera mereri remissionem peccatorum et iustificare. Haec opinio legis haeret naturaliter in animis hominum, neque excuti potest, nisi quum divinitus docemur."*

However, since synergism denies the monergism of divine grace *(sola gratia)*, it really renders the conversion of a sinner impossible, since man is saved solely by grace, through faith, without the deeds of the Law, Rom. 3, 24—28; Eph. 2, 8. 9. Indeed, those who have been truly converted and have become children of God by trusting solely in Christ *(sola fide)* will fall from grace and lose their saving faith if they espouse the pernicious error of synergism, Gal. 5, 3. 4. 9. 11. 12.

Lastly, synergism involves its champions in hopeless contradictions and creates endless doctrinal confusion in all circles in which it is insisted upon; for even while it affirms man's cooperation in conversion, that is, his own efforts as necessary for regeneration and salvation, it again stresses grace as the sinner's only hope. Synergism is therefore an affirmation and a denial at the same time, a blending of grace and nature, which, consistently carried out, destroys "the central Christian truth of justification by grace alone and, with it, the assurance of a gracious God and of eternal salvation — the supreme religious concern of Luther and the entire Lutheran theology." (Cp. Dr. F. Bente's Historical Introduction on the Synergistic Controversy, *Concordia Triglotta,* p. 124 ff.)

Synergism derives its doctrine "not from any clear statements of the Bible, but by a process of anti-Scriptural and fallacious reasoning" *(ibid.);* and it is all the more dangerous and pernicious since "it reduces man's cooperation to a seemingly harmless minimum and clothes itself in ambiguous phrases and apparently pious and plausible formulas" *(ibid.).* Its line of reasoning is: "Since all who are not converted or finally saved must blame, not God, but themselves for rejecting grace, those, too, who are converted must be credited with at least a small share in the work of their salvation, that is to say, with a better conduct toward grace than the conduct of those who are lost." *(Ibid.)* This, however, in its final effect, overthrows the entire Gospel of free grace. It was for this reason that Luther and all confessional Lutherans so emphatically inculcated the monergism of divine grace. "The restoration of this wonderful truth, taught by St. Paul, made Luther the Reformer of the Church." *(Ibid.)*

Also in its modern subtle form, synergism teaches that conversion is the product, in part, of man's *natural* powers; for it is the unconverted sinner who must make the right use of the new powers granted to him by grace, decide in favor of conversion, cease wilful resistance, and the like. In its *most subtle* form, synergism makes conversion hinge on the non-occurrence of wilful resistance in a given moment or on a favorable condition and the consequent good attitude and conduct of natural man.

The theory that the Holy Ghost removes man's *natural* resistance, but that the sinner himself must suppress all *wilful* resistance is Pelagianism pure and simple; for it ascribes spiritual powers to the unconverted. It is true, also dogmaticians like Gerhard, Quenstedt, Calov, etc., used the unscriptural expression that election took place *intuitu fidei;* but they repudiated the synergistic concept logically inherent in this phrase and taught that non-resistance is in no sense man's own work, but rather the work of God, which unconverted man can only resist. (Cf. Dr. Pieper, *Conversion and Election;* Dr. Engelder, *Dogmatical Notes.*)

14. SYNONYMS OF CONVERSION.

In order that the way of salvation *(ordo salutis),* so clearly and simply set forth in God's Word, may be presented in its Scriptural purity and truth, the theologian must fully understand in what relation conversion stands to regeneration, vivification, resuscitation, illumination, vocation, repentance, etc., all of which are terms which Scripture employs to describe the divine act of grace, by which the sinner is delivered from the power of darkness and translated into the kingdom of Christ, Col. 1, 13. Actually all these terms, in their restricted sense, are synonyms of conversion, so that the distinction between them and conversion is only nominal, or logical, and not at all real. The difference which they represent lies only in the point of view from which they depict the sinner's return to God.

a. *Regeneration (regeneratio)*. Regeneration in its strict sense describes the new birth, John 3, 5. 6, which the sinner undergoes in his conversion, or the bestowal of new spiritual life through faith in Christ. According to Scripture every person is born of God who believes that Jesus is Christ, 1 John 5, 1. The term therefore in its proper application is synonymous with conversion, Acts 11, 21. Hence we may say that the sinner who is converted is also regenerated, and *vice versa,* since the two terms designate one and the same act of the Holy Ghost, John 1, 12. 13. Luther writes: "Whoever believes in Christ . . . is born again, or born anew." (St. L., VII, 1862.)

The instrumental means of regeneration is the Word of God, in particular the Gospel of Christ, 1 Pet. 1, 23, as also Baptism, Titus 3, 5, since the latter is water "comprehended in God's command and connected with God's word," that is, with the gracious divine promise of remission of sins, Acts 2, 38.

b. *Vivification, or resuscitation (vivificatio, resuscitatio)*. Both terms designate the transplanting of the sinner from the state of spiritual death into the state of spiritual life, Eph. 2, 1—9, through faith in Christ Jesus, Col. 2, 11—13. Hence also these terms are synonyms of conversion. The *Formula of Concord* affirms (Thor. Decl., II, 87): "The conversion of our corrupt will is nothing else than a resuscitation of it from spiritual death."

In an unscriptural sense the term has been employed by both synergists and Pietists to denote a state, or condition, in which the sinner is indeed awakened to a sense of his guilt and to a desire for salvation through Christ, but is not yet converted because he has not yet decided to accept divine grace *(status medius)*. However, according to Scripture all who are thus truly awakened (vivified, resuscitated) are already converted, Eph. 2, 5—8.

It is true, the term *awakened* may be used correctly in the sense that a sinner has been alarmed by the Law, though not yet brought to faith in Christ through the Gospel. In that sense Felix, Acts 24, 25, and the jailer at Philippi, 16, 30, may be said to have been awakened. If used in this way, the "awakening" of the sinner belongs to the preparatory acts of conversion *(actus praeparatorii),* or to the assisting grace of God *(gratia assistens),* which reacts upon the sinner merely from without *(extrinsecus),* as our dogmaticians have said.

The great mistake which the Pietists and synergists made was that they applied the term *awakened* to those who were not only terrified by the divine Law, but possessed already "the first beginnings of faith" *(prima initia fidei),* in other words, who were already converted. The *awakened,* they maintained, were neither converted nor unconverted. Such a synergistic middle state *(status medius),* however, Scripture does not acknowledge, as we have shown above. On the contrary, according to Scripture every penitent sinner who has the *prima initia fidei (scintillula fidei)* is truly converted, as the *Formula of Concord* rightly teaches (Thor. Decl., II, 14).

c. *Illumination (illuminatio).* This term designates the transfer of man from his natural state of spiritual darkness into a new state of spiritual light, Eph. 5, 8. Illumination, in its strict sense, therefore is synonymous with conversion; for it consists essentially in the gracious act of God by which He "opens the eyes of the spiritually blind, turns them from darkness to light and from the power of Satan unto God that they may receive forgiveness of sins and inheritance . . . by faith," Acts 26, 18. Both illumination and conversion occur through faith in the Gospel of Christ; both have the same *terminus a quo,* namely, darkness, and the same *terminus ad quem,* namely, faith. This is proved by the word of Christ: "I am come a Light into the world that whosoever believeth on Me should not abide in darkness," John 12, 46. Hence, as long as a person is an unbeliever, he is not enlightened, or illuminated. With respect to this point the Pietists were right in opposing their orthodox opponents, who ascribed even to unbelieving ministers a certain illumination, or rather an allumination *(alluminatio);* for illumination can be predicated only of true believers in Christ.

d. *Vocation (vocatio).* The term *vocation* in Scripture sometimes denotes merely the proclamation of the Gospel, or the extending of the divine invitation of salvation to sinners. In this sense all men are called who hear or read the gracious message of the Gospel, Matt. 20, 16; 22, 14. However, in most passages of Scripture the word designates not merely the gracious offer of salvation through the Gospel, but the effectual calling of sinners to spiritual life, or their actual transfer from the kingdom of Satan to the kingdom of Christ. In this sense the term *vocation* is synonymous with conversion. The called (κλητοί) are the converted, that is to say, true believers, who by faith have appropriated unto themselves the gracious promises of the Gospel, Rom. 1, 5. 6; 8, 30; 1 Cor. 1, 2. 26; 2 Tim. 1, 9, etc.

e. *Repentance (poenitentia).* The term *repentance* (μετάνοια) is used in both a narrower and a wider sense. The *Formula of Concord* thus writes (Thor. Decl., V, 7. 8): "The term *repentance* is not employed in the Holy Scriptures in one and the same sense. For in some passages of Holy Scripture it is employed and taken for the entire conversion of man, as Luke 13, 5; 15, 7. But in this passage, Mark 1, 15, as also elsewhere, where repentance and faith in Christ, Acts 20, 21, or repentance and remission of sins, Luke 24, 46. 47, are mentioned as distinct, to repent means nothing else than truly to acknowledge sins, to be heartily sorry for them, and to desist from them" (*i. e.,* from outward motives of fear and punishment; cp. Judas).

Thus the term denotes: a) contrition, or the knowledge of sin wrought by the Law *(terrores conscientiae);* this is the meaning of the word in all those passages in which repentance is distinguished from remission of sins, Luke 24, 47; b) contrition and faith, or the entire conversion of man, Luke 13, 5. In the latter sense the term *repentance* is a synonym of conversion.

Baier writes of this distinction (III, 310): "Although repentance is sometimes used in a stricter sense for that part of conversion which is called contrition, yet often it is employed for the entire conversion." So also the *Augsburg Confession* describes repentance when it says (Art. XII): "Repentance properly consists of these two parts: One is contrition, that is, terrors smiting the conscience through the knowledge of sin; the other is faith, which is born of the Gospel, or of absolution, and believes that for Christ's sake sins are forgiven, comforts the conscience, and delivers it from terrors."

The *Augsburg Confession* rightly adds that the good works which are bound to follow repentance are the *fruits* of repentance. *Deinde sequi debent bona opera, quae sunt fructus poenitentiae.*

This important truth must be held against the error of the Romanists, who maintain that repentance consists of contrition, confession, and satisfaction *(contritio cordis, confessio oris, satisfactio operis).* The papistic error, according to which human satisfaction for all transgressions constitutes the essential part of repentance, is a total denial of the Scriptural doctrine of repentance, Mark 1, 15, since it bases forgiveness of sins upon the good works of the penitent sinner. According to papistic teaching not only the *confessio oris* and the *satisfactio operis,* but also the *contritio cordis* must be regarded as a meritorious act of the sinner. Hence repentance, in the Roman Catholic sense of the term, is altogether a work of man.

This fact explains why Luther so vehemently inveighed against the papistic conception of repentance, insisting, on the basis of Scripture, that repentance indeed always produces good works, but is never the foundation upon which the forgiveness of sins rests. Cp. the *Apology,* Art. XII (V), 16 ff.: "For the following dogmas are clearly false and foreign not only to Holy Scripture, but also to the Church Fathers: 1. that from the divine covenant we merit grace by good works wrought without grace; 2. that by attrition we merit grace; 3. that for the blotting out of sin the mere detestation of the crime is sufficient; 4. that on account of contrition, and not by faith in Christ, we obtain remission of sins," etc.

The Romanistic conception of contrition, with its emphasis on the good works of the penitent, renders impossible not only true faith in Christ, or trust in His merits, but also true contrition *(contritio passiva),* or the *terrores conscientiae,* which God works in man through the Law. As long as a sinner "repents" in the sense of Roman Catholic work-righteousness, it is impossible for him to believe in Christ and to be saved, Gal. 5, 4.

———————

JUSTIFICATION BY FAITH.
(De Iustificatione.)

---

1. DEFINITION OF JUSTIFICATION.

As soon as a contrite sinner believes the divine promises of grace which for Christ's sake is offered to him in the Gospel, or as soon as he puts his trust in the vicarious satisfaction which Christ has made for the sins of the world by His perfect obedience, he is justified, or declared righteous before God, Rom. 3, 23. 24. This is the so-called *subjective justification,* Rom. 4, 6, or the personal application, through faith, of the merits which Christ has secured for the whole world by His substitutionary atonement *(objective justification),* 2 Cor. 5, 19 ff.

Holy Scripture quite simply describes the act of justification negatively as a "forgiving of sins," or a "covering of sins," or a "non-imputation of sins," Rom. 4, 6—8, and positively as the "counting of faith for righteousness," Rom. 4, 5; Gal. 3, 6; Rom. 4, 3. Subjective justification may therefore be defined as the act of God by which He removes from the believer the sentence of condemnation to which he is subject because of his sin, releases him from his guilt, and ascribes to him the merit of Christ. Baier defines justification as "the act by which the sinner, who is responsible for guilt and liable to punishment *(reus culpae et poenae),* but who believes in Christ, is pronounced just by God, the Judge." *(Doctr. Theol.,* p. 424.)

By subjective justification we therefore do not understand "a moral condition existing in man or a moral change which he experiences, but only a divine judgment upon man, by which his relation to God is reversed." *(Ibid.)* Hollaz rightly says: "Justification is a judicial and at the same time a gracious act by which God, reconciled by the satisfaction of Christ, acquits the sinner who believes in Christ of the offenses with which he is charged and accounts and pronounces him righteous." *(Doctr. Theol.,* p. 428).

When defining justification by faith, we must bear in mind that justification by faith without works is based upon the justification of the whole world, secured by Christ's vicarious satisfaction and offered to all men in the Gospel, Acts 10, 43. Because of the objective justification (reconciliation) subjective justification takes place "freely," Rom. 3, 24, no work on the sinner's part being necessary to complete the justification of Christ. If the vicarious satisfaction of Christ is denied, no room is left for justification by faith. On the other hand, the perfect redemption effected by Christ leaves no room for the papistic justification by works. The Gospel contains full pardon for every sinner, and as soon as he accepts the pardon by faith, he is justified subjectively.

All who deny that the means of grace impart the forgiveness of sins (enthusiasts, Reformed, modern Lutheran theologians) and who make, not the redemptive work, but the "person of Christ" or His "historical reality," the object of faith, teach justification without faith by works, that is to say, by something in man, or by *gratia infusa*. However, that "faith is counted for righteousness," Rom. 4, 5, means that faith justifies, not considered in itself, but *because of the object which it apprehends,* namely, the promise of the Gospel.

It is not Scriptural to say one must make only Christ or only His merit and not also the objective justification the object of justifying faith. — Only the direct promise of the Gospel can give us perfect assurance of the forgiveness of our sins. A justification by works from its very nature cannot but be productive of doubt. (Cf. Rom. 4, 16.) The "theology of doubt" *(monstrum incertitudinis)* of papist theology is a necessary concomitant of the theology of work-righteousness. (Cf. Council of Trent, Sess. 6, Can. 13.)

The Roman Catholic sect is the greatest enemy of the Christian Church; for all Christians live, move, and have their being in the doctrine of justification by faith. But this doctrine the papacy does not permit its adherents to accept and believe. It rather reviles and curses the Scriptural doctrine of justification by faith (cf. Council of Trent, Sess. 6, Cans. 9, 11. 12. 20) and trains its followers to seek salvation by works. The Church of Rome has murdered thousands bodily for their adherence to the doctrine of justification by faith and millions spiritually by teaching them to trust in justification by works.

The Roman Catholic claim that the majority of modern Protestant teachers are advocates of the Catholic doctrine of justification by works is well founded. Those who deny the vicarious satisfaction and teach salvation through "morality" or through an "ethical act" or through faith as a "moral act" or "force" constitute a large majority among Protestants. Yet the doctrine of justification by faith, without works, has been believed and will be believed by all true members of the Christian Church to the end of time, Rom. 1, 16. 17; 3, 21. 22; 4, 3; Rev. 7, 14. (Cf. Dr. Engelder, *Dogmatical Notes.*)

2. JUSTIFICATION BY FAITH ALONE.
(Sola Fide.)

According to the express teachings of Holy Scripture the believer is justified by faith alone *(sola fide),* without the deeds of the Law, Rom. 3, 28; 4, 5; Phil. 3, 9. Positively, Scripture affirms this truth by ascribing justification directly to faith, Rom. 3, 21—24, and negatively, by excluding from justification every work of man as a meritorious cause, Rom. 3, 27. Indeed, Scripture emphatically declares that all who would be justified by works are under the curse, Gal. 3, 10, and it illustrates this fact by examples which leave no doubt as to the necessity of excluding human works from justification, Rom. 4, 1—3; Luke 18, 9—14.

According to Scripture the attempt on the part of man to secure justification by his own efforts is "zeal not according to knowledge," Rom. 10, 2, and the insistence upon good works as necessary for salvation "a doctrine of the flesh," Gal. 3, 2. 3. On the other hand, it is the characteristic teaching of the Christian religion, which is of God, that sinners are justified before God solely by faith, without works, Gal. 1, 8; 5, 4. 5. Hence we must exclude from the act of justification not only a) all good works which God works in men in His Kingdom of Power *(iustitia civilis),* Rom. 2, 14. 15, but also b) all spiritually good works, which flow from faith, Rom. 4, 2. 3; for the exclusive particles *(particulae exclusivae),* such as "without the Law," "without works," "not of works," etc., Rom. 3, 28; 4, 5; Eph. 2, 8. 9, debar from the act of justification all human works whatsoever.

The *Formula of Concord* says (Thor. Decl., III, 9) : "Concerning the righteousness of faith before God we believe . . . that poor sinful man is justified before God, that is, *absolved and declared free and exempt from all his sins* and from the sentence of well-deserved condemnation, . . . without any merit or worth of our own, also *without any preceding, present, or any subsequent works,* out of pure grace, because of the sole merit, complete obedience, bitter suffering, death, and resurrection of our Lord Christ alone, whose obedience is reckoned to us for righteousness."

Moreover, as the *Formula of Concord* shows, Holy Scripture also points out the reasons why human works must be excluded from justification, namely, a) because God wishes to demonstrate the glory of His grace in the unmerited salvation of sinful mankind, Eph. 2, 9; 1, 6. 7, and b) because He, in His infinite grace, has purposed to provide for lost mankind a salvation of which the sinner, on the basis of His gracious promise, may be absolutely sure and certain, Rom. 4, 16.

By teaching that justification is by faith, without the deeds of the Law, Holy Scripture rejects the papistic errors a) that justification is based upon infused grace *(gratia infusa),* or upon some good quality in man; b) that justification is a medical act *(actus medicinalis),* by which the sinner is made righteous through sanctification; c) that there are degrees *(gradus)* in justification, so that one believer is more justified than another; and d) that the believer cannot be sure of his salvation *(monstrum incertitudinis).*

Positively, by its doctrine of *sola fide,* Scripture affirms a) that justification is based upon God's gracious disposition in Christ Jesus *(gratuitus Dei favor propter Christum),* or upon divine grace, which is outside of man, "in God's own heart," though revealed and offered to him in the Gospel *(Media gratiae instrumenta iustificationis sunt);* b) that justification is a forensic act *(actus forensis),* by which God declares the sinner who believes in Christ to be righteous; c) that justification has no degrees, but is instantaneous and complete, the believer being justified as soon as he trusts in Christ for righteousness; d) that faith justifies not as a virtue or good quality in man, but solely as the instrument, or means, by which the believer lays hold of the perfect righteousness of the divine-human Savior; and e) that the believer may be sure of salvation, because salvation rests not upon his own worthiness, but upon the imputed merits of Christ.

The doctrine of justification which the Reformers set forth in Art. IV of the *Augsburg Confession* is therefore truly Scriptural. It reads: "Men cannot be justified before God by their own strength, merits, or works, but are freely justified for Christ's sake, through faith, when they believe that they are received into favor and that their sins are forgiven for Christ's sake, who by His death has made satisfaction for our sins. This faith God imputes for righteousness in His sight, Rom. 3 and 4." By pronouncing upon this comforting doctrine of Scripture its anathema, the Church of Rome has proved itself to be the Church of Antichrist.

The doctrine of justification by faith, without the deeds of the Law, presupposes as necessary postulates a) objective justification, or the doctrine that Christ through His vicarious atonement has secured reconciliation for the whole world; b) universal grace *(gratia universalis),* or the doctrine that God earnestly desires the salvation of all men; c) salvation by grace alone *(sola gratia),* or the doctrine that the sinner is saved without any preceding, present, or subsequent human works; d) the means of grace *(media gratiae),* or the doctrine that the Word of God and the Sacraments are the gracious means by which God offers and conveys to men the forgiveness of sins and righteousness which Christ has secured by His death (*media δοτικά*).

All who deny these doctrines (Romanists, Calvinists, synergists) cannot consistently teach the Scriptural doctrine of justification by faith, since the rejection of these teachings invariably leads to the teaching of work-righteousness.

3. THE DOCTRINE OF JUSTIFICATION THE CENTRAL DOCTRINE OF THE CHRISTIAN RELIGION.

It requires little proof to show that the article of justification by faith is the central doctrine *(articulus fundamentalissimus, articulus stantis et cadentis ecclesiae)* of the entire Christian religion; for it is the preeminent teaching of Holy Scripture, to which all the sacred truths of the Gospel converge. What the Word of God tells us of Christ's incarnation, suffering, death, resurrection, etc., is only the foundation of this paramount doctrine; for Christ became incarnate, suffered, died, rose again, etc., in order that sinners, who could not be saved by their own efforts, might be justified by grace, through faith in His vicarious atonement. Hence those who deny the Scriptural doctrine of justification by faith deny the entire Christian religion; for they are compelled to teach the paganistic way of salvation by works, by which the Gospel of Christ is annulled.

It is for this reason that Scripture so emphatically insists upon the clear and unadulterated proclamation of salvation by faith in Christ, John 3, 16; Rom. 3, 23—28; 1 Cor. 2, 2ff.; Gal. 2, 21; 5, 4; Eph. 2, 8. 9; Phil. 3, 8. 9; Gal. 1, 8. 9; 3, 1—3; 5, 4; etc. The entire polemics of Scripture culminates in the refutation of all heresies that pervert the article of justification through faith in Christ, John 8, 24; Acts 10, 42. 43; Gal. 1, 6—10; Phil. 3, 2—9, etc. Its supreme warnings and exhortations to the believer center in the appeal to continue in the faith of the Lord Jesus Christ, 2 Tim. 3, 8; Titus 2, 1—15; Heb. 4, 14—16; 1 Pet. 4, 1—5; 1 John 5, 10 ff., etc. All its teachings either point forward to it *(articuli antecedentes),* Luke 24, 25—27, or back to it *(articuli consequentes),* Rev. 5, 9—14. It is the paramount theme of the Old Testament, Is. 53, 4—6, and of the New Testament, 2 Cor. 5, 19—21.

In short, the doctrine of justification by faith in the crucified and risen Christ is the entire Gospel. Wherever it is believed, there the Church of Christ, the communion of saints, exists; wherever it is not believed, there can be no Christian Church, since this has for its members only those who believe that Christ died for them and rose again, Mark 16, 15. 16; 1 Cor. 15, 3. 4. Hence the Christian pastor must so administer his office that unfailingly he teaches this doctrine in its truth and purity and exposes and rejects all errors that are contrary to it, Acts 26, 22. 23; Titus 1, 9.

This is the clear demand which our Lutheran Confessions make of all who would serve as ministers of Christ's holy Gospel. Thus the *Smalcald Articles* (II, 4. 5) declare: "Since it is necessary to believe this and it cannot be otherwise acquired or apprehended by any work, law, or merit, it is clear and certain that this faith alone justifies us, as St. Paul says, Rom. 3, 26. 28. Of this article nothing can be yielded or surrendered (nor can anything be granted or permitted contrary to the same), even though heaven and earth, and whatever will not abide, should sink to ruin. *For there is none other name under heaven given among men whereby we must be saved,* says Peter, Acts 4, 12. *And with His stripes we are healed,* Is. 53, 5. And upon this article all things depend which we teach and practise in opposition to the Pope, the devil, and the [whole] world. Therefore we must be sure concerning this doctrine and not doubt; for otherwise all is lost, and the Pope and devil and all things gain the victory and suit over us." Cp. also Art. II, 1: "Of this article nothing is to be surrendered or conceded because the first article does not allow it."

The *Formula of Concord* writes in the same vein (Art. III, 6): "This article concerning justification by faith, as the *Apology* says, is the *chief article in the entire Christian doctrine,* without which no poor conscience can have any firm consolation or can truly know the riches of the grace of Christ, as Dr. Luther also has written: 'If this only article remains pure on the battle-field, the Christian Church also remains pure and in goodly harmony and without any sects; but if it does not remain pure, it is not possible that any error or fanatical spirit can be resisted.'"

This firm stand of our Lutheran Confessions on the doctrine of justification by faith is taken also by our Lutheran dogmaticians, of whom Chemnitz, for example, writes (*Loc. Th.*, II, 216): "This one point mainly distinguishes the Church from all heathen and superstitions, as Augustine says: 'The Church distinguishes the just from the unjust, not by the law of works, but by the law of faith.' Yes, this article is, as it were, the citadel and chief bulwark of the entire Christian doctrine and religion, which being either obscured or adulterated or subverted, it is impossible to retain the purity of the doctrine in other points. But if this doctrine remains untouched, all idolatries, superstitions, and perversions in all the other doctrines destroy themselves." (*Doctr. Theol.*, p. 440 f.)

Actually all true Christians, no matter how much they may be lacking in Christian knowledge and discernment on other points, hold to the doctrine of justification by faith, since all "are children of God *by faith in Christ Jesus*," Gal. 3, 26—28; cp. also 3, 7. Those who repudiate this article are *extra ecclesiam* (Gal. 3, 10), or, as Luther says, "either Jews or Turks, papists or heretics." Every true Christian confesses with Luther: "I believe that Jesus Christ, true God . . . and also true man, . . . is my Lord, who has redeemed me, a lost and condemned creature," etc. This truth we find attested especially in the many Christian hymns, which are the expressions of the personal faith of hundreds of Christians, who, though living at different places and times and belonging outwardly to different denominations, repeat the same joyous refrain: "By grace are ye saved, through faith," Eph. 2, 8.

4. THE CHRISTIAN TERMINOLOGY BY WHICH THE DOCTRINE OF JUSTIFICATION BY FAITH IS GUARDED AGAINST ERROR.

a. *"By grace, for Christ's sake, through faith."* These terms are used to exclude from the article of justification all works of men, either preceding, present, or following. The *Formula of Concord* writes (Thor. Decl., III, 25): *Ad iustificationem enim tantum haec requiruntur atque necessaria sunt: gratia Dei, meritum Christi et fides."*

The expression *by grace* ascribes salvation alone to God's gracious disposition in Christ *(gratuitus Dei favor)* and excludes from justification as a meritorious cause the so-called "infused grace" *(gratia infusa)* of papistic theology. The expression *for Christ's sake* means as much as "for the sake of Christ's vicarious satisfaction," "since He has made satisfaction for us to the Law and paid for our sins" (*Formula of Concord,* Thor. Decl., III, 14).

Justification for Christ's sake must be maintained a) against the papists, who regard infused grace *(gratia infusa),* love, etc., as a cause of justification; b) against all enthusiasts, who base justification not upon the merits of Christ, but upon the "Christ in us," or upon His indwelling and sanctifying influence in the heart (Osiander); and c) against all modern rationalistic theologians, who reject the forensic character of justification as too "juridical" and define it as an ethical process, or a transformation of man *(Umgestaltung der Menschheit)* through the sanctifying influence of the Holy Spirit *(actus medicinalis).*

The expression *by faith* designates faith as the receiving means *(medium ληπτικόν),* by which the believer appropriates to himself the merits of Christ offered to him in the means of grace *(media δοτικά).* All three expressions together affirm the Scriptural truth "that all our righteousness is to be sought outside the merits, works, virtues, and worthiness of ourselves and of all men and rests alone upon Christ the Lord" (*Formula of Concord,* Thor. Decl., III, 55).

This truth must be defended against all errorists who substitute for the objective righteousness of Christ, which is outside the sinner, a righteousness which is within man as the ground for his justification (papists, enthusiasts, religious experimentalists [*Erlebnistheologen*], etc.).

b. *"Justification not a physical or medical, but a forensic, or judicial, act."* The meaning of these expressions is that justification does not consist essentially in the inward transformation of the sinner, or in his sanctification, but rather in the divine act by which God declares a sinner righteous for Christ's sake. That is to say, justification is not essentially a change by which man is *made* just, but a change whereby he is *declared* just on account of the perfect righteousness of Christ which he appropriates by faith. The change which follows justification is the fruit of faith and properly belongs into the doctrine of sanctification, not into that of justification.

When we speak of justification as a forensic, or judicial, act, we must note, however, that there is a distinctive difference between the judgment of the civil courts and that of God. The civil courts justify, or declare righteous, the just and condemn the wicked. Those who justify the wicked and condemn the just are an abomination to the Lord, Prov. 17, 15. But God, in the act of justification, justifies the ungodly, Rom. 4, 5, and this on the valid ground that Christ by His perfect obedience has paid the debt for the wicked, Is. 53, 5. 6; 2 Cor. 5, 21.

The *Apology* declares (Art. III, 185): "Moreover, in this passage [Rom. 5, 1] *to justify* signifies, according to forensic usage, to acquit a guilty one and to declare him righteous, but on account of the righteousness of another, namely, of Christ, which righteousness of another is communicated to us by faith. Therefore, since in this passage our righteousness is the imputation of the righteousness of another, we must here speak concerning righteousness otherwise than when in philosophy or in a civil court we seek after the righteousness of one's own work."

This distinction is important; for if God would justify only the just and condemn all the unjust, as do the civil courts, not a single sinner would be saved, Luke 18, 14; Gal. 3, 10, since in spite of all their moral efforts all men remain unrighteous before God, Is. 64, 6. The papistic doctrine that God can justify only those who really are just, either in whole or in part, cancels the entire Gospel-message of justification by faith. Luther rightly called this doctrine "the venom of Satan" and the "most pestilential pest (*pestilentissima pestis;* St. L., V, 517), since it deprives the sinner of all true consolation and robs God of the honor which is due Him as the gracious Lord, who freely forgives sin for Christ's sake, Rom. 3, 28; Eph. 2, 7—9.

It is necessary to emphasize this truth because not only all Romanizing Protestants (Andrew Osiander, Schwenkfeld, Weigel), but also Arminians and synergists deny the *actus forensis* in its Scriptural sense.

That the verb δικαιοῦν means "to declare righteous" and not "to make righteous" is incontestably proved not only by its consistent usage in Scripture, but also by the exclusive particles *(particulae exclusivae)* which in Scripture are commonly joined with this term, Rom. 3, 23—28; 4, 5—8. These show that justification is not a healing or sanctifying process *(actus medicinalis),* by virtue of which the sinner is enabled to merit salvation by good works, but rather a forensic act, by which God for Christ's sake declares him to be righteous, though in himself he is unworthy and unrighteous, Rom. 4, 5.

c. *"By faith alone" (sola fide).* Luther's insistence upon the *sola fide* was well motivated. His papistic opponents were willing to concede that the sinner is saved by faith; but they refused to admit that he is justified solely by faith *(sola fide).* They well understood that by this expression the Reformer did not mean to exclude from justification God's grace, Christ's merit, and the means of grace as God's means of conferring the righteousness which Christ by His vicarious satisfaction has secured for the world *(media δοτικά).* But they knew that by this term the Lutherans meant to define faith merely as a receiving means *(medium ληπτικόν; medium aut instrumentum)* of the righteousness of Christ offered to the sinner in the Gospel; and to this definition they persistenly objected. When they declared that the sinner is "saved by faith," they defined faith as a virtue or good quality *(bona qualitas),* implanted into him by God *(gratia infusa),* so that, after all, "salvation by faith" means "salvation by works" *(fides, quae per caritatem operatur).*

The *sola fide* of Luther therefore served the purpose of denying this Semi-Pelagianistic error. Positively, it affirmed that faith saves merely as an *instrumentum,* or *medium;* negatively, that in the article of justification faith must not be considered as a good work or quality.

The Lutherans were fully justified in their contention that their opponents, since they denied the *sola,* denied also the *fide;* in other words, that their doctrine of justification was in direct opposition to that of Scripture, Rom. 3, 28; 4, 5, which excludes from justification all human works.

Thus the *sola fide* has become the shibboleth of the Reformation; and to-day it still is the slogan of the confessional Lutheran Church to proclaim to the world its chief article of faith, namely, that a sinner is justified before God gratuitously, by His grace *(δωρεὰν τῇ αὐτοῦ χάριτι),* apart from works of the Law *(χωρὶς ἔργων νόμου),* Rom. 3, 21—28. The *Catholic Encyclopedia, sub* "faith," says: "By leaving out the obnoxious sola [alone], the article [Art. IV of the *Augsburg Confession*] might be glossed in Catholic sense." (Cp. *Christl. Dogmatik,* II, 643 ff.)

d. *"Justification does not require even the presence of good works."* *(Neque* PRAESENTIA *operum ad iustificationem requiritur.)* This statement must be understood in the light of the important truth "that faith is never alone, yet always justifies alone" *(Fides nunquam est sola, sed iustificat sola).* This truth is clearly taught in Scripture. On the one hand, saving faith is always followed by works, Rom. 5, 1—5; Gal. 5, 6; Jas. 2, 20; on the other hand, faith never saves inasmuch as it is productive of good works, Rom. 3, 28; 4, 5.

Of this the *Formula of Concord* writes (Thor. Decl., III, 41): "Good works do not precede faith, neither does sanctification precede justification. But first faith is kindled in us in conversion by the Holy Ghost from the hearing of the Gospel. This lays hold of God's grace in Christ, by which the person is justified. Then, when the person is justified, he is also renewed and sanctified by the Holy Ghost, from which renewal and sanctification the fruits of good works then follow. . . . This should not be understood as though justification and renewal were sundered from one another in such a manner that a genuine faith could exist and continue for a time together with a wicked intention, but hereby only the order . . . is indicated how one precedes or succeeds the other. For what Luther has correctly said remains true nevertheless: Faith and good works well agree and fit together (are inseparably connected); but it is faith alone, without works, which lays hold of the blessing; and yet it is never and at no time alone."

The statements "Good works are required in justification," or "Good works are necessary for salvation," must be condemned as both wrong in themselves and as favoring the Pelagianistic doctrine of human cooperation in conversion. It is against such erroneous statements as these that the Lutheran Church confesses: "Justification does not require even the presence of good works."

e. *"Justification has no degrees."* (*Iustificatio non admittit gradus, non fit successive, non recipit magis et minus.*) This Lutheran statement is directed against the doctrines of the papists and Romanizing Protestants, who, while mingling sanctification into justification, assume that justification is successive, or gradual, inasmuch as divine grace in man (*gratia infusa sive inhaerens*) operates toward perfection by degrees, so that a person's justification actually depends on his progress in sanctification.

Against this error the confessional Lutheran Church teaches on the basis of Scripture that justification is instantaneous and therefore complete as soon as the sinner believes in Christ, Rom. 4, 7; Luke 18, 24; Rom. 5, 1. Luther thus writes: "Justification does not come in pieces, but in a heap."

It is true, there are degrees with respect to faith, for the faith of one Christian is strong while that of another is weak; but also a weak faith justifies as much as does the strong, since even a weak faith is trust in Christ's righteousness. Luther rightly says (St. L., XI, 1840) : "Therefore we are all alike in Christ through faith. St. Peter may have a stronger faith than I, yet it is nevertheless the same faith in Christ. . . . Who receives Him [Christ] receives Him entirely, no matter whether he receives Him weakly or strongly."

f. *"Forgiveness of sin is the entire justification, not merely a part of it."* This truth our Confessions affirm time and again. The *Apology* writes (Art. IV [II], 76) : "To attain the remission of sins is to be justified, according to Ps. 32, 1: 'Blessed is he whose transgression is forgiven.'" And the *Formula of Concord* states (Epit., III, 7) : "According to the usage of Holy Scripture the word *justify* means in this article to absolve, that is, to declare free from sins"; and again (Thor. Decl., III, 30) : "The righteousness of faith before God consists alone in the gracious reconciliation, or the forgiveness of sins."

This truth is taught by St. Paul in Rom. 4, 5—8, where he describes the justified as such whose sins are covered, or forgiven. Those of our dogmaticians who divide justification into two parts, namely, imputation of Christ's righteousness and forgiveness of sins, do this for the sake of clarity. In reality the imputation of Christ's righteousness is the necessary prerequisite of forgiveness; in other words, God, by imputing to the sinner Christ's perfect righteousness, forgives his sins. In the divine verdict of justification the two acts really coincide; or we may say, they constitute one act, namely, that of justification.

Scripture, when referring to the cause of justification, sometimes mentions Christ (Rom. 3, 22), then again Christ's righteousness (Rom. 5, 18), or Christ's death and blood (1 Cor. 2, 2), or His resurrection from the dead (Rom. 10, 9), or His name (1 John 5, 13), etc. But all these phrases express the same truth, namely, that a sinner is justified on account of Christ's vicarious suffering and death, which God freely offers to all men in the Gospel. For the sake of clearness our dogmaticians usually distinguish between the causes of justification as follows : *Divine grace is causa impulsiva interna; Christ* (His vicarious satisfaction), *the causa impulsiva externa sive meritoria; the Gospel, causa instrumentalis ex parte Dei.* These distinctions help us to understand the great truth that God most graciously forgives the sins of all who by faith appropriate to themselves Christ's righteousness offered in the means of grace. And such forgiveness is justification.

5. JUSTIFICATION ON THE BASIS OF WORKS.

In some places, Scripture teaches also a justification on the basis of works, namely, the justification before men. When we speak of justification in this signification, we use the term in a wider sense. The true justification, which is before God (ἐνώπιον θεοῦ) and by which a sinner becomes a child of God, is by faith, without the deeds of the Law, Rom. 3, 20—22. However, such faith is known only to God; before men it remains invisible. For this reason God justifies His believing saints before men by their works; that is to say, He proves their faith and justification by their fruits, Luke 7, 47; John 13, 35; Matt. 12, 37; 25, 34—40. So also all Christians should recognize their state of grace by the fruits which the Holy Spirit has wrought in their hearts, 1 John 3, 14; 2, 3. 4; 2 Pet. 1, 10; Matt. 6, 14.

The *Apology* remarks very correctly (Art. III, 154): "Christ often connects the promise of the remission of sins with good works, not because He means that good works are a propitiation, for they follow reconciliation; but for two reasons. One is, because good fruits must necessarily follow. Therefore He reminds us that, if good fruits do not follow, the repentance is hypocritical and feigned. The other reason is, because we have need of external signs of so great a promise, because a conscience full of fear has need of manifold consolation. As therefore Baptism and the Lord's Supper are signs that continually admonish, cheer, and encourage desponding minds to believe the more firmly that their sins are forgiven, so the same promise is written and portrayed in good works in order that these works may admonish us to believe the more firmly." The justification on the ground of works thus coincides with the external testimony of the Holy Ghost *(testimonium externum sive indirectum),* which we distinguish from His internal testimony *(testimonium internum sive directum),* or faith.

However, justification by faith and justification by works must not be mingled together, Gal. 3, 10. By the former the sinner obtains salvation; by the latter he is proved an heir of salvation. In order to make this matter clear, Luther sometimes speaks of inward and outward forgiveness. By the former he means justification before God; by the latter, justification before men. By the former a sinner becomes a child of God; by the latter he is proved a child of God. It is the basic error of Romanism to regard justification by works as the ground of a sinner's justification and thus to make salvation depend on good works.

It is evident that the doctrine of justification by faith *(sola fide)* cannot be taught in its purity unless the Scriptural distinction between the Law and the Gospel is observed. The Law must never be mingled with justification, since this gracious act of God belongs entirely in the Gospel. But the Law is mingled with justification whenever the latter is based, either in whole or in part, upon some natural or spiritual virtue in man or when faith is said to justify as a "good quality" or as the source of sanctification or as compliance with the demands of the Law or as the beginning of the Christian's new life, etc. In short, the Law is mingled with justification whenever justification is grounded, in whole or in part, on human works (Pelagians, synergists, Arminians).

Such mingling of the Law with justification destroys, of course, the blessed consolation which God has intended to bestow upon men by the glorious doctrine of justification by faith. While the doctrine of justification by faith gives the believer full assurance of salvation, that of justification by works removes this assurance; for it takes salvation out of the gracious hand of God and places it in man's own sinful and impotent hand. It is a significant fact that all errorists who deny the *sola fide* deny also the Scriptural truth that a believer may be sure of his salvation.

Foremost among these errorists is the Pope, whom Luther exposed as the Antichrist, showing him to be such not because of his unholy works, but mainly because of his shameful perversion of the Scriptural doctrine of salvation by grace through faith in Christ. Luther's assertion as to the Pope's being the Antichrist spoken of in 2 Thess. 2 is correct; for to this day the anathema of the Council of Trent upon all true Christians who adhere to the Scriptural doctrine of justification by faith is upheld by the Church of Rome.

6. THE EFFECTS OF JUSTIFICATION.
(Effectus Iustificationis.)

As soon as a person has been justified by faith, he is in possession of all the spiritual blessings which Christ has secured for the world by His vicarious atonement, 1 Cor. 3, 21; Rom. 5, 1—5. Having by faith received the adoption of sons, Gal. 4, 5; John 1, 12, he is an heir of God and a joint-heir with Christ, Rom. 8, 17, so that he lacks no spiritual gift whatsoever, 1 Cor. 1, 4—7; Eph. 1, 3—8. Of the spiritual blessings which justification confers we may mention in particular: —

a. *The state of grace (status gratiae).* The justified believer is no longer under wrath,. Eph. 2, 1—3, but in that blessed state where he has peace with God *(pax conscientiae)*, Rom. 5, 1. Through faith in Christ he is sure not only of divine grace in the present life, but also of eternal salvation in the life to come *(spes vitae aeternae)*, Rom. 5, 2. The certainty of divine grace and eternal life through faith must be maintained against all Semi-Pelagians (papists) and synergists, who assert that a believer cannot be sure of salvation. As a matter of fact all those who uphold the "monster of uncertainty" *(monstrum incertitudinis)* thereby show that they are ignorant of what justification in its Scriptural sense really means.

The "monster of uncertainty" is the unfortunate result of the mingling of justification and sanctification, or of the fatal error that salvation depends, at least in part, on human works. The objections against the certainty of salvation which have been raised also within the external Lutheran Church are utterly devoid of Scriptural ground; for such passages as 1 Cor. 10, 12; Rom. 11, 20, etc., upon which these objections are founded, are designed not to intimidate the believer, but rather to warn those who are carnally secure and indifferent. Hence doubts with respect to the certainty of salvation must not be regarded or commended as a virtue, but must be condemned as unbelief, Rom. 4, 16; 8, 17. 37—39.

b. *The indwelling of the Holy Ghost and of the Holy Trinity (inhabitatio Spiritus Sancti sive Dei triuni essentialis).* Through faith the justified believer receives the Holy Spirit, who dwells in his heart as in His holy temple, Gal. 3, 2; 1 Cor. 3, 16, strengthening his faith and moving him to continuous childlike prayer, Gal. 4, 6; Rom. 8, 15. 16.

But according to Scripture not only the Holy Spirit, but also the entire Holy Trinity dwells essentially in the believer, John 14, 23. This wonderful union of God with the believer is called *unio spiritualis,* or *unio mystica,* 1 Cor. 6, 17; Eph. 5, 30—32. While through the mystic union the substance of the Christian is not transformed into that of God, as mystics at all times have affirmed (Weigel, Schwenkfeld), we nevertheless maintain on the basis of Scripture that God Himself *(unio essentialis)* and not merely His gifts *(dona Dei;* papists, Calvinists), dwells in the believer.

With equal emphasis we at the same time reject the error of Andrew Osiander, who taught that the essential indwelling of Christ is the believer's righteousness before God; for Christ is our Righteousness inasmuch as He has redeemed us by His vicarious atonement and not inasmuch as He, with His essential righteousness, is found within us. In other words, our righteousness before God is Christ's perfect obedience *(obedientia activa et passiva; iustitia aliena)*, which we appropriate through faith, Rom. 3, 24; 5, 18. 19.

c. *Sanctification, or renewal (sanctificatio vel renovatio).* By sanctification, or renewal, we understand the inward transformation of the believer through the Holy Ghost *(mutatio hominis interna per actum physicum vel medicinalem)*, by which he is removed from the service of sin and made fit for the service of God in a new spiritual life *(iustitia inhaerens; iustitia vitae)*.

These inward spiritual changes occur in the very moment in which a person is justified by faith; for they are the unfailing fruits of justification, Rom. 6, 1—11. Before a person is justified, neither sanctification nor good works are to be found in him, Eph. 2, 1—3; but after justification he is continually being sanctified and actuated to good works through faith in Christ, Eph. 2, 10; Gal. 5, 6. For this reason sanctification and good works are indications *(indicia)* of the accomplished justification, 1 Thess. 4, 9; John 14, 15, though they are never a cause of justification, Eph. 2, 8. 9.

d. *The Christian liberty (libertas Christiana).* By Christian liberty we mean the believer's absolute freedom from every form of human tyranny in spiritual matters, Gal. 5, 1—4. In other words, the justified believer is no longer a servant of men, 1 Cor. 7, 23, to heed and obey human doctrine, but he is a servant of God, Rom. 6, 22, and of Christ, 1 Cor. 3, 23, whose Word is the only rule of his faith, John 8, 31. 32. In relation to God all Christians are subordinate, for they all are equally bound to His Word and subject to His will, 1 John 5, 3; Matt. 22, 38—40; but in relation to one another they are brethren, Matt. 23, 8, who are alike obedient to their divine Master, Luke 17, 10, and subservient to one another in love, Gal. 5, 13. 14.

Hence in the Christian Church not the word of man must prevail, but only the Word of God. Christian liberty thus consists in the believer's freedom from the doctrines of men, Matt. 15, 9, and his unswerving attachment to Christ and His Word.

e. *Membership in the Christian Church and possession of all its gifts and blessings.* The Christian Church is the communion of saints, that is, of all true believers in Christ, 1 Cor. 1, 1. 2; Eph. 1, 1; 2, 20; Acts 5, 14. Hypocrites, or nominal Christians, are not members of the Church, though in this life they are outwardly joined with the visible Church. The rights and privileges of the Church, commonly called the Office of the Keys *(potestas clavium)*, that is, the peculiar church power to administer the means of grace, to forgive and retain sins, to preach the Word of God in its purity, to call and ordain ministers, etc., belong to all believers and not merely to the clergy, Matt. 16, 19; cp. with 18, 18; 28, 19. 20; 1 Cor. 3, 21, as will be shown later.

THE DOCTRINE OF SANCTIFICATION AND GOOD WORKS.

(De Sanctificatione et Bonis Operibus.)

1. DEFINITION OF SANCTIFICATION.

The justification of a sinner is immediately followed by his sanctification, or renovation, Rom. 5, 1—5. That is to say, the justified sinner turns from sin and serves God in good works, Rom. 12, 1. 2; 1 Thess. 4, 3—7; 5, 23; 1 Pet. 1, 15; Rom. 13, 13. 14. As many other theological terms, so also that of sanctification (ἁγιασμός, ἁγιωσύνη) is used in a wider and a narrower sense.

In its wider sense, sanctification embraces all acts of divine grace by which the Holy Spirit turns a person from sin to holiness and from the service of Satan to the holy, happy service of God, Heb. 13, 12; Acts 26, 18. In other words, sanctification in its wider sense includes every work of God by which He separates a sinner from the lost and condemned world and makes him His own, such as the bestowal of faith, justification, sanctification in its narrower sense, or the inward change in man by which he becomes holy, his preservation in faith to the end, and his final glorification on the day of Judgment, 2 Thess. 2, 13; 1 Pet. 1, 2.

In the wider sense of the term Christians are designated in Scripture *called saints* (κλητοὶ ἅγιοι), Rom. 1, 7; 1 Cor. 1, 2, or persons whom God has graciously endowed with faith, justified, and transplanted into His kingdom, in which He purposes to preserve them through faith unto the Day of our Lord Jesus Christ, Phil. 1, 3—6. In its wider sense Luther uses the term *sanctification* in his Large Catechism (Art. III, 40. 41), where he says: "I believe that the Holy Ghost makes me holy, as His name implies. But whereby does He accomplish this, or what are His method and means to this end? Answer: By the Christian Church, the forgiveness of sins, the resurrection of the body, and the life everlasting." So also Quenstedt writes: "Sanctification is sometimes employed in a wider sense *(late)* and includes justification, as Eph. 5, 26; Heb. 10, 10; otherwise, however, it is used in a strict sense *(stricte),* and thus coincides with renovation in its strict sense, as in Rom. 6, 19. 22; 1 Thess. 4, 3. 4. 7."

In its narrower, or strict, sense, sanctification denotes the inward spiritual transformation of the believer, which follows upon, and is inseparably joined with, justification, Rom. 6, 22;

2 Cor. 7, 1. Of the order between justification and sanctification the *Formula of Concord* writes (Thor. Decl., III, 40. 41): "In the same manner the order also between faith and good works must abide and be maintained and likewise between justification and renewal, or sanctification. For good works do not precede faith, neither does sanctification precede justification. But first faith is kindled in us in conversion by the Holy Ghost from the hearing of the Gospel. This lays hold of God's grace in Christ, by which the person is justified. Then, when the person is justified, he is also renewed and sanctified by the Holy Ghost, from which renewal and sanctification the fruits of good works then follow."

To reverse this order and make sanctification in its narrower sense the cause of justification (Papism) means to give up the central article of the Christian faith and to base salvation on work-righteousness, Gal. 5, 4. Justification and sanctification are indeed indissolubly *(nexu indivulso)* joined together; yet the two must not be mingled with each other. *Justification is the source of sanctification.* To teach the reverse means to teach the antichristian doctrine of work-righteousness and thus to thwart both justification and sanctification.

The righteousness of faith *(iustitia imputata),* by which a person becomes a Christian, is outside of man; for God declares the ungodly to be just for Jesus' sake, Rom. 4, 5. Sanctification, however, takes place within man, and by it he is transformed into a holy man *(iustitia inhaerens),* 2 Cor. 7, 1. Inherent righteousness, or the righteousness of life, is not at all a part of imputed righteousness, Phil. 3, 9, but follows justification, Rom. 6, 14; Titus 3, 7. 8.

In ecclesiastical language sanctification and renovation (renewal) are commonly used as synonyms. Sanctification is renewal inasmuch as the believer thereby enters upon a new life; renewal is sanctification inasmuch as the new life of the believer is a holy life. Our Confession at times also distinguishes between sanctification and good works as between cause and effect *(antecedens et consequens).* In that case sanctification is conceived as the principle of holiness from which all good works flow, Gal. 5, 25. 26. 22.

Properly speaking, however, the good works of the believer coincide with his sanctification, since the latter, viewed concretely *(in concreto),* occurs by way of performing individual good works, the believer either suppressing that which is evil or accomplishing that which is praiseworthy. Sanctification, viewed concretely, is never an idle state or quality *(status otiosus; habitus otiosus),* but a continued act, or a ceaseless activity, since the Holy Spirit is always operative in the believer, Titus 2, 11; Gal. 5, 22—25.

Of faith, which is the direct causative principle of sanctification, Luther rightly says: "Oh, it is a living, busy, active, powerful thing that we have in faith, so that it is impossible for it not to do good unceasingly! Nor does it ask whether good works are to be done; but before the question is asked, it has wrought them and is always engaged in doing them. . . . Faith is a living, bold trust in God's grace, so certain that a man would die a thousand times for it. . . . And on account of this, man becomes ready and cheerful, without coercion, to do good to every one, to serve every one, and to suffer everything for love and praise to God, who has conferred this grace on him, so that it is impossible to separate works from faith, yea, just as impossible as it is for heat and light to be separated from fire." (*Formula of Concord*, Thor. Decl., Art. IV, 10 ff.)

2. THE EFFICIENT CAUSE OF SANCTIFICATION.
(Causa Efficiens Sanctificationis.)

As God by His almighty power engenders faith in man, Eph. 1, 19; John 6, 29, so also He works in the believer sanctification as the *fruit* of faith, 1 Thess. 5, 23. 24; 1 Cor. 3, 16; 6, 19; Eph. 2, 10. Nevertheless there is this distinction between conversion and sanctification, that in the former man is purely passive *(pure passive se habet)*, while in the latter he cooperates with the Holy Ghost *(active se habet sive cooperatur)*.

However, this cooperation must be rightly understood. It is not coordinate with the operation of the Holy Ghost, but subordinate to it. In other words, man cooperates in sanctification *dependenter a Deo;* that is to say, he works because and inasmuch as the Holy Ghost works in him, Rom. 8, 14: ὅσοι πνεύματι θεοῦ ἄγονται; Gal. 5, 16—18: εἰ δὲ πνεύματι ἄγεσθε. Hence every new spiritual impulse which the believer has, and every new good work which he does, is prompted and executed in him through the gracious power of the Holy Spirit, Phil. 1, 6; 2, 13.

The *Formula of Concord* writes of this very correctly (Thor. Decl., II, 65): "As soon as the Holy Ghost, . . . through the Word and the holy Sacraments, has begun in us this His work of regeneration and renewal, it is certain that through the power of the Holy Ghost we can and should cooperate, although still in great weakness. But this . . . does not occur from our carnal, natural powers, but from the new powers and gifts which the Holy Ghost has begun in us in conversion, as St. Paul expressly exhorts that as workers together with Him we receive not the grace of God in vain, 2 Cor. 6, 1. But this is to be understood in no other way than that the converted man does good to such an extent and as long as God by His Holy Spirit rules, guides, and leads him and that, as soon as God would withdraw His gracious hand from him, he could not for a moment persevere in obedience to God. But if this were understood thus, . . . that the converted man cooperates with the Holy Ghost in the manner as when two horses together draw a wagon, this could in no way be conceded without prejudice to the divine truth."

Hence not only conversion, but also sanctification depends entirely upon God's grace, 2 Cor. 5, 17. 18; 3, 5: ἡ ἱκανότης ἐκ τοῦ θεοῦ. This great truth, so clearly revealed in Scripture, should prompt the believer continually to perfect sanctification, Rom. 6, 14; 2 Cor. 7, 1; Heb. 12, 1. 2.

3. THE INNER MOTIONS OF SANCTIFICATION.
(Motus Interni Sanctificationis.)

Through faith in Christ the believer becomes a new creature, Eph. 4, 24; Col. 3, 10; 2 Cor. 4, 16; 5, 17, who consents to God's will, Rom. 7, 22, and lives wholly unto God, in the newness of the spiritual life into which he has entered, Rom. 6, 1—11.

Nevertheless, while the believer thus serves God according to the inward, or new, man which has been implanted in him in his conversion, Eph. 4, 24; Rom. 7, 22. 25, there remains in him also the old man, or the corruption of his nature, Eph. 4, 22; 2 Cor. 4, 16; Rom. 6, 6; 7, 18, so that according to the old man he is subject to sin, Rom. 7, 18—24, and continually opposes, and struggles against, the Spirit, Gal. 5, 17: ἡ σάρξ ἐπιθυμεῖ κατὰ τοῦ πνεύματος.

Sanctification therefore occurs in the believer in this manner, that after his inward, or new, man he combats the flesh with its affections and lusts, Gal. 5, 24, resists its evil desires, prevents its wicked designs, and performs that which is pleasing to God, contrary to the promptings of his perverse nature. Such is the combat of the spirit against the flesh which Scripture so earnestly demands of all believers. Negatively they by faith always put off the old man (παλαιὸς ἄνθρωπος), and positively they continually put on the new man (καινὸς ἄνθρωπος), which after God is created in true righteousness and holiness, Eph. 4, 24; Col. 3, 10.

The "old man" is the corrupt nature, or mind; the "new man," the mind conformed to God's will. While the believer is perfectly holy in so far as he is a new man, Rom. 6, 1—11; Eph. 4, 24; 1 John 3, 9, the old man is and remains thoroughly corrupt, Rom. 7, 18. Sanctification is effected not by reforming, Rom. 8, 13; Gal. 5, 24, but by crucifying and mortifying him, Matt. 18, 8. 9.

With regard to the struggle of the spirit against the flesh the Christian must note the following: —

a. The constant struggle between the two natures in the believer does not prove that he has fallen from grace, as many true Christians in hours of trial are inclined to think, but, on the contrary, it is a proof that he is living in the state of grace, Rom. 7, 22—25. There is spiritual death only when the struggle against the flesh has ceased, Rom. 8, 13.

b. Since the old man in the believer always remains corrupt, so that according to the flesh Christians are no better than unbelievers, who have never been born again, John 3, 5. 6, the believer must not be surprised if he is tempted by his carnal nature to commit even gross sins, Rom. 7, 18; 1 Thess. 4, 3—7. On the other hand, this fact should induce him to continue without ceasing to mortify the deeds of his body and to crucify the flesh, Rom. 8, 13; Gal. 5, 24; Col. 3, 5; 1 Cor. 9, 27; Matt. 18, 8. 9.

c. The struggle against the carnal nature is both difficult and painful, since it is directed against the believer's own evil flesh, Heb. 12, 1. Yet the good fight of faith against the flesh must go on to the end, 1 Tim. 6, 12; 2 Tim. 4, 7. It is of great comfort to believers that even the greatest saints in the Bible were obliged continually to wage war against their evil flesh, Rom. 7, 24.

d. Scripture assures the believers that in their struggles against the flesh they will finally obtain the victory provided they adhere to God's Word and thus permit the Holy Spirit to work effectually in their hearts, John 15, 7. 8; Eph. 6, 17; Rom. 8, 37; Luke 18, 26. 27; 2 Cor. 12, 10; 4, 8 ff.; etc. It is understood that with such steadfast use of God's Word there must be joined also ceaseless, fervent prayer, Matt. 26, 41; Eph. 6, 18.

e. It is an important rule of Christian combat always to substitute for the evil impulse and desire of the flesh the corresponding holy impulse and desire of the inward man. In other words, when the Christian is tempted to murmur against God, let him praise and give thanks; when he is troubled with impure thoughts, let him strive the more after that chastity which the holy Savior de-

mands of His disciples; if he is weary in well-doing, let him follow
the more zealously the goal of goodness which is set before him, etc.
However, to accomplish this, he must know the Word of God and
like Christ meet every temptation to evil with proper passages from
Scripture, Matt. 4, 1—11.

In conclusion, we may add what Luther says on this important
matter (Holman transl., Vol. III, p. 31): "This life is not righteousness, but growth in righteousness; not health, but healing;
not being, but becoming; not rest, but exercise. We are not yet
what we shall be, but we are growing toward it; the process is not
yet finished, but it is going on; this is not the end, but it is the
road; all does not yet gleam with glory, but all is being purified."
*"Dass also dies Leben nicht ist eine Froemmigkeit, sondern ein
Frommwerden, nicht eine Gesundheit, sondern ein Gesundwerden,
nicht ein Wesen, sondern ein Werden, nicht eine Ruhe, sondern
eine Uebung: wir sind's noch nicht, wir werden's aber. Es ist
noch nicht getan und geschehen, es ist aber in Gang und Schwang.
Es ist nicht das Ende, es ist aber der Weg; es gluehet und glaenzt
noch nicht alles, es fuegt sich aber alles."*

4. THE MEANS BY WHICH SANCTIFICATION IS ACCOMPLISHED.

The means by which the old man is mortified and the new
man is strengthened is the Word of God; properly speaking, however, not the Law, but the Gospel. The Law indeed reveals sin,
Rom. 3, 20, but it cannot free the sinner from the curse and dominion of sin, Rom. 7, 5—13. However, also in the process of sanctification the Law must be diligently used by the believer as a means
to prepare the way for the Gospel in showing the exceeding sinfulness of sin, as also to point out what works are truly pleasing to
God, 1 Cor. 6, 1—10. Thus the believer uses the Law as a mirror
(Rom. 3, 20) that "he may be led to the knowledge of his sins";
as a curb (1 Cor. 9, 27) "to restrain his intractable carnal heart as
though by certain bars"; and as a "fixed rule (Ps. 119, 9) according to which he regulates and directs his whole life."

The *Formula of Concord* aptly declares (Epit., VI, 4): "For
although they [the believers] are regenerate and renewed in the
spirit of their mind, yet in the present life this regeneration and
renewal is not complete, but only begun, and believers are, by the
spirit of their mind, in a constant struggle against the flesh, that
is, against the corrupt nature and disposition which cleaves to us

unto death. On account of this Old Adam, which still inheres in the understanding, the will, and all the powers of man, it is needful that the Law of the Lord always shine before them [mirror] in order that they may not from human devotion institute wanton and self-elected cults [rule]; likewise, that the Old Adam also may not employ his own will, but may be subdued against his will, not only by the admonition and threatening of the Law, but also by punishments and blows [curb], so that he may follow and surrender himself captive to the Spirit, 1 Cor. 9, 27; Rom. 6, 12; Gal. 6, 14; Ps. 119, 1 ff.; Heb. 13, 21 (Heb. 12, 1).''

While the Law thus reveals sin (mirror), restrains the flesh outwardly (curb), and guides the Christian to good works (rule), the power to accomplish sanctification and to do good works comes alone from the Gospel, Rom. 12, 1; 1 John 4, 10. 11. According to Scripture it is the Gospel which inscribes the Law in the heart and enables the believer to keep it, Jer. 31, 31 f. While it is true that through the Law externally good works *(iustitia civilis)* may be produced in men since they are made to fear God's wrath and punishments, it is alone the Gospel that produces spiritually good works *(iustitia spiritualis),* or works which flow from true faith in Christ and true love to God. (Cp. Luther, St. L., XII, 318 ff.)

With respect to the chastisements with which God visits His saints on earth, such as poverty, sickness, sorrow, etc., we may say that, while these do not in themselves sanctify the believers, yet they are the means by which God induces them to meditate on His Word, so that through the study of the Law they learn that they indeed deserve the chastening trials of God, and through the study of the Gospel they again comfort themselves with the abiding love of their heavenly Father, Rom. 8, 35—39. Also the blessings with which God endows His saints on earth should lead them to repentance, Rom. 2, 4, namely, by moving them to search the Holy Scriptures, in which the glory of divine grace shines forth in the face of Christ Jesus and from which they constantly draw strength for greater faith and holier service, Ps. 119, 9—16. 105—112.

5. THE NECESSITY OF SANCTIFICATION AND GOOD WORKS.

In the Lutheran Church the question has been debated with great ardor whether it is correct or not to say: "Good works are necessary" (Cp. *Formula of Concord*, Art. IV.) Those who denied the query did so because they understood the word *necessitas* in the sense of coercion, so that the statement "Good works are necessary" was interpreted by them to mean: "Believers are coerced to do good works." This declaration they rightly regarded as unscriptural, and so they objected to the emphatic demand of Luther and the Gnesio-Lutherans that "good works are necessary."

While the *Formula of Concord* admits the truth that "good works are done by believers, not through coercion, but from a willing mind, sanctified by faith," it nevertheless insists that the statement "Good works are necessary" is Scriptural. It therefore says (Thor. Decl., Art. IV, 3): "It has been urged by some that good works are not necessary, but are voluntary [free and spontaneous] because they are not extorted by fear and the penalty of the Law, but are to be done from a voluntary spirit and a joyful heart."

And again (IV, 14. 15): "As regards the necessity or voluntariness of good works, it is manifest that in the *Augsburg Confession* and its *Apology* the expressions are often used and repeated that good works are necessary; likewise, that it is necessary to do good works, which also are necessarily to follow faith and reconciliation; likewise, that we necessarily are to do and must do such good works as God has commanded. Thus also in the Holy Scriptures themselves the words *necessity, needful,* and *necessary,* likewise *ought* and *must,* are used concerning what we are bound to do because of God's ordinance, command, and will, as Rom. 13, 5; 1 Cor. 9, 9; Acts 5, 29; John 15, 12; 1 John 4, 21. Therefore the expressions or propositions mentioned . . . are unjustly censured and rejected in this Christian and proper sense, as has been done by some; for they are employed and used with propriety to rebuke and reject the secure, epicurean delusion by which many fabricate for themselves a dead faith or delusion, which is without repentance and without good works, as though there could be in a heart true faith and at the same time the wicked intention to persevere and continue in sins, which is impossible; or as though one could indeed have and retain true faith, righteousness, and salvation even though he be and remain a corrupt and unfruitful tree, whence no good fruits whatever come, yea, even though he persist in sins against conscience or purposely engage again in these sins, — all of which is incorrect and false."

In this way the *Formula of Concord,* on the one hand, excludes all possible misunderstanding of the terms *necessity, must, ought,* etc., and, on the other, establishes on Scriptural grounds the true necessity of sanctification and good works. What Holy

Scripture teaches concerning the necessity of sanctification and good works may be stated as follows: —

a. Sanctification and good works are *not necessary for salvation*. This truth is expressly taught in Scripture, which ascribes salvation entirely to divine grace in Christ, Eph. 2, 8. 9; Rom. 4, 6, excluding at the same time most vigorously, through the use of *exclusive particles (particulae exclusivae): "without Law," "without works," "by grace,"* all works of men, either preceding or following justification, Titus 3, 3—7.

Roman Catholic theologians teach the necessity of good works for justification and salvation (Council of Trent, Sess. VIII, Can. 24). While the Jesuits claim that salvation is gained by good works alone, others maintain that salvation is obtained through Christ *and* good works (the Council of Trent). However, both parties nullify grace and lead the sinner to hell. Modern rationalistic theologians likewise teach the necessity and meritoriousness of good works for salvation; this error is a corollary of the erroneous doctrine of justification by works.

The *Formula of Concord* rightly says (Thor. Decl., IV, 22—24): "Here we must be well on our guard lest works are drawn and mingled into the article of justification and salvation. Therefore the propositions are justly rejected *that to believers good works are necessary for salvation, so that it is impossible to be saved without good works.* For they are directly contrary to the doctrine *de particulis exclusivis in articulo iustificationis et salvationis* (concerning the exclusive particles in the article of justification and salvation), that is, they conflict with the words by which St. Paul has entirely excluded our works and merits from the article of justification and salvation and ascribed everything to the grace of God and the merit of Christ alone, as explained in the preceding article. Again they . . . take from the afflicted, troubled consciences the comfort of the Gospel, give occasion for doubt, are in many ways dangerous, strengthen presumption in one's own righteousness and confidence in one's own works; besides, they are accepted by the papists and in their interest adduced against the pure doctrine of the alone-saving faith. Moreover, they are contrary to the form of sound words, as it is written that *blessedness is only of the man unto whom God imputeth righteousness without works,* Rom. 4, 6."

While our Confession emphatically condemns the gross error of Majorism, namely, that good works are necessary for salvation, or to acquire salvation, it rejects with equal vigor as unscriptural also the later modified form of Majorism (Major, Menius) that good works are necessary to *preserve* faith or salvation. As salvation is not bestowed upon man on account of his works, so it is neither preserved by him through his works, but alone by the Holy Ghost, through the Gospel and faith, Phil. 1, 6; 1 Pet. 1, 5; 2 Tim. 1, 12—14; 2 Thess. 3, 3.

The *Formula of Concord* rightly rejected the error of Majorism because its evil source was the synergism of Melanchthon (*Loci* of 1535: "Good works are the *causa sine qua non,* and hence they are necessary for salvation), which Luther so vehemently condemned, compelling his colleague at the same time to retract his false doctrine. Cp. Dr. Bente, "Historical Introductions to the Symbolical Books," *Trigl.,* pp. 112 ff.: "This is the very theology of Erasmus, nor can anything be more opposed to our doctrine"; also: "To say that the new obedience is the *causa sine qua non contingit vita aeterna* means to tread Christ and His blood under our feet."

While it is true that evil works destroy faith, Eph. 4, 30; 5, 5; 1 Cor. 6, 9 ff.; Gal. 5, 21; Rom. 8, 13; Col. 3, 5. 6, it is not true that good works preserve faith. As a matter of fact, if works, even the best, are mingled into the article of justification and salvation, faith is destroyed and salvation rendered impossible, Gal. 3, 10; 5, 4.

It is true, the good works of believers are tokens *(indicia, testimonia)* of their faith and state of grace *(testimonium externum Spiritus Sancti de fide et statu gratiae);* but they are not the *causa sine qua non,* much less the *causa efficiens salutis.* Those who teach that good works preserve faith deny the cardinal doctrine of justification and salvation as taught in Scripture and the Lutheran Confessions and maintain the Semi-Pelagianistic error of the papists that faith saves inasmuch as it works by love *(fides caritate formata).* In other words, having rejected the *sola fide,* they base salvation on work-righteousness.

Concerning the Scripture-passage Heb. 12, 14, by which Majorism endeavored to prove its false doctrine, it may be said: 1) This passage presupposes faith and therefore also the possession of salvation, Eph. 2, 8. 9; John 5, 24; for the words are addressed to believing Christians, who should follow holiness because they already possess salvation, Heb. 12, 1. 2; Col. 3, 1 ff.; 2 Cor. 7, 1. 2) They are a warning against carnal security, as the whole context shows, and thus are a part of the divine Law *(sunt phrases legales),* which must be applied to Christians who pervert faith *(contra fucatam fidem)* by neglecting sanctification, Heb. 12, 15—17. The above passage therefore does not belong in the article of justification and salvation; in other words, it must not be used to mingle the Law into the Gospel, which was the fatal error of Majorism.

But even in the realm of the new obedience, or sanctification, it is wrong to declare: "Good works are necessary for salvation." The new obedience of the Christian is essentially the fulfilling of the Law, Rom. 13, 8—10, and as we cannot say: "The fulfilling of the Law is necessary for salvation," so we can neither say that the new obedience (good works) is necessary for salvation. Majorism therefore must be condemned in both its original and modified form, both when it is applied to the article of justification and to that of sanctification. The Majoristic assertion "Good works are necessary for salvation" is intrinsically wrong and opposed to sound doctrine.

In opposition to Majorism, Amsdorf asserted that "good works are injurious to salvation."

The *Formula of Concord* acknowledges that this statement originally meant to express the truth that good works are injurious to salvation *provided the sinner puts his trust in them.* In this sense, our Confession admits, good works are injurious to salvation.

Its declaration reads (Thor. Decl., Art. IV, 37): "As regards the proposition that good works are said to be injurious to salvation, we explain ourselves clearly as follows: If any one should wish to drag good works into the article of justification or rest his righteousness or trust for salvation upon them, to merit God's grace and be saved by them, to this not we say, but St. Paul himself says, and repeats it three times, Phil. 3, 7 ff., that to such a man his works are not only useless and a hindrance, but also *injurious.* But this is not the fault of the good works themselves, but of the false confidence placed in the works, contrary to the express Word of God."

On the other hand, the *Formula of Concord* condemns the proposition of Amsdorf on three grounds: 1) because "in believers good works are indications *(indicia)* of salvation when they are done *propter veras causas et ad veros fines* (from true causes and for true ends," Phil. 1, 28); 2) because "it is God's will and express command that believers should do good works, which the Holy Ghost works in believers"; and 3) because God "promises to them a glorious reward in this life and in the life to come." For these reasons we must not say *"simpliciter* and flatly": "Good works are injurious to believers for, or as regards, their salvation"; but "this proposition is censured and rejected in our churches because as a flat statement it is false and offensive, by which discipline and decency might be impaired and a barbarous, dissolute, secure, epicurean life be introduced and strengthened." *(Ibid.)*

b. The statement "Sanctification and good works are necessary" is Scriptural and must therefore be maintained. Scripture speaks of the new obedience as a necessity, ἀνάγκη, Rom. 13, 5; δεῖ, Acts 5, 29. Christian believers *"must needs* be subject to governments"; they *"ought* to obey God rather than men." These Scriptural expressions must never be weakened or modified, but should be taught in their full meaning and force. Whenever misinterpretations occur, these must be corrected; but the requirements of the divine will should not be altered by man, nor should His Word be changed to please the carnal heart. Sanctification *must* be followed by the believer, and good works *must* be done by him, because God demands this *(necessitate voluntatis et praecepti sive mandati divini),* 1 Thess. 4, 3; 1 John 3, 23.

The *Formula of Concord* is very insistent in inculcating the necessity of sanctification and good works. It says (Thor. Decl., IV, 31. 32): "The false epicurean delusion is to be earnestly censured and rejected, namely, that some imagine that faith and the righteousness and salvation which they have received can be lost through no sins or wicked deeds, not even through wilful and intentional ones, but that a Christian, although he indulges his wicked lusts without fear and shame, resists the Holy Ghost, and purposely engages in sins against conscience, yet none the less retains faith, God's grace, righteousness, and salvation. Against this pernicious delusion the following true, immutable, divine threats and severe punishments and admonitions should be often repeated and impressed upon Christians who are justified by faith: 1 Cor. 6, 9; Gal. 5, 21; Eph. 5, 5; Rom. 8, 13; Col. 3, 6."

While the *Formula of Concord* thus emphasizes the necessity of good works, it at the same time stresses the fact that it understands this necessity not as a *necessitas coactionis* (a necessity of coercion), but as a *necessitas ordinis, mandati et voluntatis Christi ac debiti nostri* (a necessity of Christ's ordinance, command, and will, and of our obligation), since it is true that "truly good works should be done willingly or from a voluntary spirit by those whom the Son of God has made free," Ps. 110, 3; 54, 6; 2 Cor. 9, 7;

Rom. 6, 17. It says (Thor. Decl., IV, 16. 17): "When this word *necessity* is employed, it should be understood not of coercion, but only of the ordinance of the immutable will of God. *(Vult enim mandatum Dei, ut creatura suo Creatori obediat.)"*

If the question is asked for whose sake believers should do good works, the answer is: 1) For God's sake, whom they serve with holy works, Rom. 12, 1. 2; 2) for their own sake, namely, that they may have true indications *(indicia, testimonia)* of their state of grace, 1 John 3, 14; Matt. 6, 14. 15; 1 Pet. 2, 9, since the new obedience and good works of believers are really the *testimonium Spiritus Sancti externum;* 3) for the sake of the children of the world, to whom believers should prove the truth and power of the Gospel by a holy life, so that thereby they may be induced to hear the Word of God and be saved, 1 Pet. 2, 12; 3, 1. 2; Matt. 5, 13—16.

Yet this new obedience does not flow from the coercion of the Law, Rom. 7, 22, though the Law serves also the believer as a mirror, curb, and guide, Ps. 1, 2; 119, 1; 1 Cor. 9, 27; Rom. 7, 18. 19; Deut. 12, 8. 28. 32, — a fact that must be maintained against every form of Antinomianism (John Agricola, ca. 1535),— but from faith in the precious Gospel of Christ, which inscribes the Law into the heart, Jer. 31, 31 ff., and thus makes the believer willing to, and zealous of, every good work, Ps. 110, 3; 2 Cor. 9, 7; 1 Pet. 5, 1—4. The terms *willing* and *free,* etc., must, however, not be interpreted in the sense "that it were optional with them [the believers] to do or to omit them [good works] or that they might or could act contrary to the Law of God and none the less could retain faith and God's favor and grace." *(Formula of Concord,* Thor. Decl., Art. IV, 20.)

6. THE IMPERFECTION OF CHRISTIAN SANCTIFICATION IN THIS LIFE.

While justification is complete and therefore admits of no degrees, sanctification, on account of the remaining sinfulness of the flesh, Rom. 7, 24, is never complete, or perfect, in this life, Phil. 3, 12—14, but gradual and susceptible of constant growth, Eph. 4, 15. 16; Col. 2, 19. This truth, which is so prominently impressed upon believers by Scripture, is of the greatest importance for the proper understanding of their Christian duties.

Of the imperfection of Christian sanctification in this life, Quenstedt writes: "Renovation [sanctification] in this life is partial and imperfect, admitting degrees, and therefore never attains the highest pinnacles of perfection. For sin remains in the regenerate, affecting their self-control, and the flesh lusts against the Spirit; wherefore our renovation progresses from day to day and is to be continued through life, 2 Cor. 4, 16. The want of perfection in renovation does not arise from the impotency of God, who renews, but from the weakness of man, who is the recipient of divine action." (*Doctr. Theol.*, p. 490.)

And again: "Renovation is increased by godly acts and frequent efforts. If these are intermitted or diminished, a diminution follows, so that at one time there is an increase, at another a decrease. The Holy Scriptures expressly affirm that the renovation of the regenerate in this life ought continually to increase and grow, Eph. 4, 16."

These quotations show how earnestly our Lutheran dogmaticians stress the imperfection of Christian sanctification and the daily need of the believer to strive after progress in the grace of holiness. Our Lutheran teachers indeed acknowledge the fact that the regenerate, according to the new man, are spiritual, 1 Cor. 2, 15; 14, 37; Gal. 6, 1, but, on the other hand, they affirm that the regenerate are also carnal, Rom. 7, 14, namely, so far as their evil flesh (σάρξ) is concerned, Rom. 7, 22. 23.

Hollaz comments on this as follows: "When a renewed man is called spiritual, the reason why he is so denominated is derived from that which is preponderant, namely, from the prevailing spirit (the inward or new man); but when the same (the renewed man) is called carnal, the reason is derived from that which is subordinate, namely, from the flesh, which is indeed subdued, but yet rebels and resists and with which the justified person, placed in the way of life, is continually carrying on war." (*Doctr. Theol.*, p. 491.)

The doctrine of the imperfection of Christian sanctification is well supported by Scripture. From the viewpoint of their imperfections it admonishes believers "to grow up into Christ in all things," Eph. 4, 15; "to abound in every good work," 2 Cor. 9, 8; "to abound in the work of the Lord," 1 Cor. 15, 58; "to increase in the knowledge of God," Col. 1, 10; "to be strengthened with all might . . . unto all patience and long-suffering with joyfulness," Col. 1, 11; "to increase and abound in love one toward another and toward all men," 1 Thess. 3, 12; "to abound yet more and more in the knowledge and in all judgment," Phil. 1, 9; "to abound more and more in pleasing God," 1 Thess. 4, 1; etc.

All these exhortations show that the Christian believer, according to the old man (παλαιὸς ἄνθρωπος), who is still in him, is very imperfect indeed and that his whole life must be a perpetual effort to overcome his evil inclinations, struggle against sin, and accomplish that which is good in the sight of God.

The *Formula of Concord* aptly remarks (Thor. Decl., II, 68): "Since we receive in this life only the first-fruits of the Spirit and the new birth is not complete, but only begun in us *(regeneratio nondum sit absoluta, sed solummodo in nobis inchoata),* the combat and struggle of the flesh against the spirit remains even in the elect and truly regenerate men; for there is a great difference perceptible among Christians, not only in this, that one is weak and another strong in the spirit, but each Christian moreover experiences in himself that at one time he is joyful in spirit and at another fearful and alarmed; at one time ardent in love, strong in faith and hope, and at another cold and weak."

In order to impress this point, our dogmaticians have said: "The righteousness of faith, or our imputed righteousness, is perfect or complete; the righteousness of life, or our inherent righteousness, is imperfect, begun, and incomplete." *Iustitia fidei sive imputata perfecta sive consummata est, iustitia vitae sive inhaerens imperfecta, inchoata, non consummata.* (Baier.)

There is, then, in the believer a constant warfare between his new man (νοῦς, ἔσω ἄνθρωπος, καινὸς ἄνθρωπος) and between his flesh (σάρξ), as St. Paul clearly shows Rom. 7, 25. (Cp. Luther, St. L., XV, 1552.)

The doctrine of the imperfection of Christian sanctification must be held and defended in all its Scriptural truth and force against the error of perfectionism (papists, Unitarians, Arminians [Limborch], enthusiasts [Weigel, Schwenkfeld, etc.], Methodists, Finney of Oberlin, etc.).

While the error of perfectionism is taught in different forms, so that we must carefully distinguish between various types of this delusion (papistic, Methodist, Oberlin, etc.), the *Formula of Concord* adequately defines this false doctrine in a general way when it writes (Epit., II, 12): "[We reject also the error that] man, after he has been born again, can perfectly observe and completely fulfil God's Law," "that a Christian who is truly regenerated by

God's Spirit can perfectly observe and fulfil the Law of God in this life" (Epit., XII, 25).

That, in general, is the essence of perfectionism. It is based on the unscriptural premise that only those transgressions that are done consciously and deliberately are truly to be called sins. Cp. Wesley: "I believe a person filled with love of God is still liable to involuntary transgressions. Such transgressions you call sins if you please; I do not." Strong, *Syst. Theol.*, 878. Cp. also *The Decisions of the Council of Trent,* Sess. V, *Decretum de peccato originali,* 5.

In its consequences, perfectionism means defection from the article of justification by faith *(sola fide),* because saving faith can dwell only in a contrite heart, which by daily repentance (contrition and faith) lays hold of the merits of Christ to cover its sins. In other words, a true believer never denies his sinfulness (original and actual), but always confesses his sins before God, Ps. 32, 5; 38, 1ff.; 51, 1ff.; 90, 8; 143, 2, etc. In view of this fact, perfectionism must be condemned as a species of self-righteousness, Luke 18, 11. 12, which is as offensive as it is pernicious. Its culmination is found in the blatant boast of Romanism that there are saints whose supreme holiness even produces supererogatory works *(opera supererogationis),* that is, works which are more than sufficient and can therefore be dispensed to others who are lacking in perfection.

Against perfectionism Scripture attests that, "if we say that we have no sin, we deceive ourselves, and the truth is not in us"; indeed, that, "if we say that we have not sinned, we make Him a liar, and His Word is not in us," 1 John 1, 8. 10. It is true, the same apostle who wrote these words said also: "Whosoever is born of God doth not commit sin; for His seed remaineth in him; and he cannot sin because he is born of God," 1 John 3, 9. However, in this passage he describes the believer according to the new man ("because he is born of God") and not according to his corrupt nature ($\sigma\acute{\alpha}\varrho\xi$), from which all his transgressions after conversion flow. The believer indeed "has sin," 1 John 1, 8. 10, and he is forgiven and cleansed from all unrighteousness, 1 John 1, 9, only if he confesses his sins. At the same time he, as a new creature in Christ, is no longer under the dominion of sin "that he should obey it in the lusts thereof," Rom. 6, 12. 14. When a true believer sins, it is not his regenerated self or the new man in him that sins, but his Old Adam, or his corrupt flesh.

St. John, in the passage just quoted (1 John 3, 9), thus supports St. Paul, who says of himself: "Now, then, it is no more I that do it, but sin that dwelleth in me," Rom. 7, 17. This he explains further by saying: "For I delight in the Law of God after the inward man; but I see another law in my members, warring against the law of my mind and bringing me into captivity to the law of sin which is in my members," Rom. 7, 22. 23. Perfectionism can therefore be proved neither by 1 John 3, 9 nor by Rom. 6, 14.

In passing, we may say that the error of perfectionism is itself an outgrowth of the evil nature (σάρξ), or the conceited reason of man, which refuses to humble itself before God, Luke 18, 9; 2 Pet. 2, 18. 19; 1 Pet. 5, 5. 6.

The fact that sanctification in this life is gradual and incomplete *(renovatio inchoata, imperfecta)* must not be abused by the Christian in such a manner that he makes no efforts towards sanctification. On the contrary, it should constantly move the believer to strive after holiness in the fear of God. While perfect sanctification is impossible in this life, it should nevertheless be the Christian's supreme goal.

That is God's will, 1 Cor. 1, 30; 2 Thess. 2, 13; Heb. 12, 14; 1 Thess. 4, 3—7; etc. His demand is that the believer "cleanse himself from *all* filthiness of the flesh and spirit, *perfecting* holiness in the fear of God," 2 Cor. 7, 1, and that he be "holy in all manner of conversation," 1 Pet. 1, 15. Negatively, the believer should put off *every* sin; positively, he should put on *every* virtue; for only a life of perfect holiness becomes him as a saint of God in Christ Jesus, Col. 1, 10; Phil. 4, 8; cp. also Col. 3; Eph. 5 and 6; Rom. 12—15; etc. Thus Holy Scripture not only multiplies its exhortations to holiness, but also sets before the believer the lofty standard of perfection, Matt. 6, 24; Luke 14, 25—35; Matt. 7, 13. 14; 18, 8. 9; etc. The life of faith means a life of absolute self-denial and self-mortification, 1 Cor. 9, 25. 27.

In fact, God in His holy Word demands of the believer so perfect a degree of sanctification that the question indeed forces itself upon the trembling, penitent heart: "Who, then, can be saved?" Matt. 19, 25. Christ's reply to this query: "With men this is impossible; but with God all things are possible," Matt. 19, 26, confirms the truth taught in so many passages of Scripture that the standard of Christian perfection which God has set is so high that only His grace can save us, Eph. 2, 8. 9.

In view of these facts the unspeakable folly of perfectionism becomes obvious. That this doctrine was ever taught in the Church is due to the pernicious mingling of Law and Gospel, which always occurred when Christians apostatized from the Word of God and resorted to doctrines of the flesh. Papism, Arminianism, Unitarianism, etc., teach perfectionism because, on the one hand, they have weakened the stern demands of the divine Law and, on the other, have dimmed the perfect glory of God's grace in Christ Jesus. First they taught salvation by work-righteousness; after this pagan doctrine had become rooted in their system of teaching, the "epicurean delusion" of perfectionism was bound to follow. First their conceited reason said: "I can do good works to merit salvation"; then it arrogantly added: "I can do more good works than are required for salvation."

Accordingly we must not say: "If the doctrine of sinless perfection is a heresy, the doctrine of contentment with sinful imperfection is a greater heresy" (A. J. Gordon; cp. *Christl. Dogmatik,* Vol. III, p. 40), but rather: "Both are intolerable heresies, which render salvation impossible."

However, in the final analysis, perfectionism itself is neglect and repudiation of Christian sanctification, since the self-sufficient perfectionist, denying his exceeding sinfulness, refuses to follow the course which God in His Word prescribes for Christian sanctification. True sanctification occurs only when a believer by daily sincere repentance *(poenitentia quotidiana, poenitentia stantium)* humbly beseeches God to forgive his manifold sins for Christ's sake and then, in the strength of faith and trusting in the grace of God, renews his fight against sin and his consecration to holiness. True sanctification thus presupposes continual study of the Law for the purpose of obtaining an ever greater knowledge of sin and of God's demands, continual meditation on the Gospel for an ever greater assurance of forgiveness, and continual mindfulness of the goal which the pilgrim of Christ *(homo viator)* must attain on his road to heaven, his real home *(homo comprehensor,* Phil. 3, 20. 21). The life of true sanctification is a life in Christ, unto God, by the power of the Holy Spirit, in view of the hope of eternal glory *(sub specie aeternitatis;* Heb. 13, 14: τὴν μέλλουσαν [πόλιν] ἐπιζητοῦμεν).

With regard to the argument of the perfectionists that God does not command the impossible, Matt. 5, 48, we reject this as a fallacy and declare: *A praecepto ad posse non valet consequentia.*

With respect to the Scripture-passages which perfectionists adduce to support their error, we may say in summary: 1 John 3, 9 describes the Christian according to the new man; Phil. 3, 15 speaks of the Christian's striving after perfection; Heb. 5, 13. 14 sets forth the perfection of maturity; Matt. 5, 48 commands love like God's, not regarding quantity, but quality; Col. 2, 10 teaches the perfection of justification.

In conclusion, we wish to remind the reader once more of the important fact that the article of sanctification can be kept pure only in case the article of justification is taught in its Scriptural purity. Those who err with respect to justification must err also with regard to sanctification.

To this great truth the *Formula of Concord* directs attention when it says (Thor. Decl., III, 22): "When we teach that through the operation of the Holy Ghost we are born anew and justified, the sense is not that after regeneration no unrighteousness clings any more to the justified and regenerate in their being and life, but that Christ covers all their sins, which nevertheless in this life still inhere in nature, with His complete obedience. But irrespective of this they are declared and regarded godly and righteous by faith and for the sake of Christ's obedience, . . . although on account of their corrupt nature they still are and remain sinners to the grave. . . . Nor, on the other hand, is this the meaning, that without repentance, conversion, and renewal we might or should yield to sins and remain and continue in them."

And again (*ibid., 32*): "It is also correctly said that believers, who in Christ through faith have been justified, have in this life first the imputed righteousness of faith and then also the incipient righteousness of the new obedience, or of good works. But these two must not be mingled with one another or be both injected at the same time into the article of justification by faith before God. For since this incipient righteousness or renewal in us is incomplete and impure in this life because of the flesh, the person cannot stand with and by it . . . before God's tribunal, but before God's tribunal only the righteousness of the obedience, suffering, and death of Christ, which is imputed to faith, can stand, so that only for the sake of this obedience is the person (even after his renewal, when he has already many good works and lives the best . . . life) pleasing and acceptable to God and is received into adoption and heirship of eternal life." (Cp. *Christl. Dogmatik,* III, p. 41 ff.; also Luther, St. L., XV, 1551. 1554.)

7. THE DOCTRINE OF GOOD WORKS.
(De Bonis Operibus.)

We shall treat the doctrine of good works under three heads:
a) Definition of Good Works; b) The Works of the Heathen; and
c) The Christian's Growth in Good Works.

A. DEFINITION OF GOOD WORKS.

Good works, according to Holy Scripture, are the fruits of
justifying faith, 1 John 5, 4; Gal. 2, 20; 5, 6; Heb. 11, 4—39.
Hence, when we speak of good works in the strict Scriptural sense
of the term, we include every thought, desire, word, and deed which
a believer does through faith in Christ Jesus. The element of
faith is therefore rightly stressed in all definitions which our dogmaticians have given of good works.

Hollaz defines good works thus: "Good works are free acts of
justified persons, performed through the renewing grace of the
Holy Spirit according to the prescription of the divine Law, true
faith in Christ preceding, to the honor of God and the edification
of men." (*Doctr. Theol.*, p. 493.) So also the *Augsburg Confession* says (Art. XX, 28—30): "It is only by faith that forgiveness of sins is apprehended, and that for nothing. And because
through faith the Holy Ghost is received, hearts are renewed and
endowed with new affections, so as to be able to bring forth good
works. For Ambrose says: *'Faith is the mother of a good will
and right doing.'*" Faith in Christ is therefore the true source
from which all truly good works flow.

In opposition to the false definition of good works current in
papistic theology Hollaz emphasizes the fact that also the "internal
affections of the heart and the movements of the will" which flow
from faith must be regarded as good works. He writes: "By works
here are understood not only external visible actions (which proceed from the hand or tongue), but internal affections of the heart
and movements of the will and thus the entire obedience and
inherent righteousness of the regenerate. A distinction is therefore to be made between internal and external good works. The
former are seen by the eyes of God alone and comprise the inner
thoughts of the mind, the movements of the will, and the pure
affections of the heart (such as love, the fear of God, confidence
toward God, patience, humility). The latter are seen not only
by God, but likewise by man and manifest themselves by outward
demeanor, words, and actions." (*Doctr. Theol.*, p. 493.)

It is necessary to remember this point whenever the doctrine of good works is being considered; for otherwise one's definition of good works may become too narrow and exclude from their sphere many elements that properly belong to it.

Our Lutheran dogmaticians were compelled to set forth and defend the Scriptural doctrine of good works especially in opposition to the papistic perversion of it. For this reason they were obliged, in the first place, to determine the true *norm* of Christian good works. According to Scripture the norm, or standard, of good works is a) neither man's own will (Col. 2, 23: "will-worship"; cp. Luther, St. L., I, 866 ff.); b) nor the will of other men (Ezek. 20, 18: "neither observe their judgments"; Col. 2, 16: "Let no man judge you"); c) nor the will of the Church (Matt. 15, 9: "teaching for doctrines the commandments of men"); d) nor even the "good intention" of man, 1 Sam. 15, 22; John 16, 2; Acts 26, 9; but e) alone the revealed Word and will of God (Deut. 5, 32: "Ye shall observe to do as the Lord, your God, hath commanded you"; Matt. 4, 10: "Thou shalt worship the Lord, thy God, and Him only shalt thou serve"). *(Bona opera sunt actiones, quae secundum Dei legem e fide proficiscuntur.)* To disregard the Word of God as the norm of good works is tantamount to apostasy from God and therefore to gross idolatry, 1 Sam. 15, 22. 23.

Luther rightly remarks: "Scripture calls it a most horrible sorcery, idolatry, and idol-service not to listen to the Word of God, but to purpose to do something without or against God's Word; and this is indeed a most dreadful verdict, especially when you see how common this is and how much it is done in the world." (St. L., I, 866.)

This judgment is true. All who put as a source and rule of faith the commandments of men in the place of God's Word degrade themselves by becoming "slaves of men," 1 Cor. 7, 23; in fact,. by their unlawful obedience they really honor men as gods. Even the *sufferings (das Kreuz)* of Christians dare be imposed only by God, 1 Pet. 3, 17, and should not be self-chosen, 1 Pet. 4, 15. 16. 19: (πάσχοντες κατὰ τὸ θέλημα τοῦ θεοῦ).

Quenstedt is right in saying: "The directing norm according to which good works are to be done and judged is the word of the divine Law, which offers an absolutely perfect rule of righteousness and divine holiness and prescribes both what should be done and what should be omitted." (II, 1387; cp. *Christl. Dogmatik,* III, 45.) "Truly good works are not those which every one contrives himself from a good intention or which are done according to traditions of men, but those which God Himself has prescribed and commanded." (*Triglot*, p. 939.)

By setting up false standards of "good works" (man's own devotion, the commandments of the Church, the infamous system of morals established by the Jesuits), the Church of Rome proves that it is the Church of Antichrist. Luther rightly condemned the fictitious holiness of the monks and nuns and praised the true holiness of works performed by all believers in the humblest calling as works hallowed by God's commandments. (St. L., IX, 952 ff.)

The rule just stated is not weakened by the fact that God in His Word commands subjects to be obedient to the civil government and children to their parents, Eph. 6, 1 ff.; Col. 3, 20; Rom. 13, 1—7, provided, of course, that the government and parents do not command anything that is in opposition to His own commandments, Acts 5, 29. All lawful commands of governments and parents are God's own commandments since He Himself has given them authority to rule. The same applies to Christian ministers whenever in the name of God and by authority of His Word they command or exhort their hearers to do what God enjoins upon them, Heb. 13, 7; 1 Thess. 5, 12. 13; 1 Tim. 5, 17. 18. In all other cases, however, Christians should not recognize as a norm of their works the will or commandments of other men, Matt. 15, 9; Gal. 2, 3. 5. 11—14. Under given circumstances it even becomes the sacred *duty* of Christians to renounce human norms and standards, namely, in all cases where these conflict with the Word of God, Gal. 5, 1—3.

So, then, the norm of good works is not the will of men, Matt. 15, 9; not conscience, John 16, 2; Acts 26, 9 ff.; not the Law of Moses as given to the Jews, containing both ceremonial and political elements designed only for the Old Testament, Lev. 11; Num. 15, 32 ff., cp. with Col. 2, 16. 17; not the special commandments given to individual persons, Gen. 22, 1 ff.; not the Church, Matt. 23, 8; Mark 7, 7; but only the Moral Law of God, or His "immutable will," as this is revealed to us in clear passages of the Old Testament and the New Testament, Matt. 22, 37—40; Rom. 13, 10. Men may err; conscience is fallible; the temporary laws of the Old Testament have been abolished; the special commandments were limited to individuals; the Church itself is subject to God's Word; but the Moral Law, or the immutable will of God, stands forever as the norm and rule of Christian life, John 12, 48.

In his *Large Catechism,* Luther writes very emphatically on the norm of good works: "Therefore I constantly say that all our life and work must be ordered according to God's Word if it is to be God-pleasing and holy. Where this is done, this commandment [the Third Commandment] is in force and is being fulfilled. On the contrary, any observance or work that is practised without God's Word is unholy before God, no matter how brilliantly it may shine, even though it be covered with relics, such as the fictitious spiritual orders, which know nothing of God's Word and seek holiness in their own works." (*Triglot,* p. 607, §§ 92. 93. Cp. also Luther's sermon on Titus 2, 13; St. L., IX, 952 ff.)

On the basis of Scripture our dogmaticians have always pointed out against the Romanists that the "good intention" of the doer can never make any work good, nor can it change an evil work into a good work.

Though the Moral Law, or the immutable will of God, as revealed in Holy Scripture, is the norm of good works, yet it is not their *source;* for truly good works of Christians are not "works of the Law," but "fruits of the Spirit." Between the two the *Formula of Concord* rightly distinguishes as follows (Epit., VI, 5. 6): "The works which are done according to the Law are, and are called, works of the Law as long as they are only extorted from man by urging the punishment and threatening of God's wrath. Fruits of the Spirit, however, are the works which the Spirit of God, who dwells in believers, works through the regenerate and which are done by believers so far as they are regenerate (spontaneously and freely), as though they knew of no command, threat, or reward; for in this manner the children of God live in the Law and walk according to the Law of God, which St. Paul in his epistles calls the Law of Christ and the Law of the mind, Rom. 7, 25; 8, 7; 8, 2; Gal. 6, 2."

As the *Formula of Concord* here correctly teaches, all good works of the regenerate flow from a willing spirit, or from love toward God. This is a clear doctrine of Scripture, Ps. 110, 3; 54, 6; Rom. 6, 18; 7, 22 ff.; 2 Cor. 9, 7. In fact, every work which does not flow from love toward God is a transgression of God's Law; for "love is the fulfilling of the Law," Rom. 13, 8—10. It is for this reason that Luther so emphatically begins his explanations of the Ten Commandments with the words: "We should fear and love God"; for by these words he indicates the true source from which all obedience to the Law must come.

From this it is clear that true obedience to the divine Law is rendered only by true Christians, whom the Holy Spirit has endowed with spiritual powers through faith, Phil. 4, 13. Unbelievers perform only externally good works, as these flow either from natural love toward those whom they serve (parents, children, country, etc.) or from ambition or love of fame and praise, as also from the desire to earn salvation by good works. Because of their remaining evil nature also the regenerate may be misled to do good works from these motives. But all "good works" which are done after the flesh are sinful and worthless before God. *(Opera bona non-renatorum coram Deo sunt peccata.)*

However, after the inward man, or as new creatures in Christ, believers perform good works from love and gratitude toward Him who is their Father in Christ Jesus, 1 John 4, 19. Such spiritual works are not designed to earn heaven, but are prompted by the joyful assurance that in Christ they already have heaven, Rom. 12, 1. (Cp. Luther, St. L., XII, 136.) Luther therefore is right in saying that first the person must be good before his works can be good; that is to say, a person must be sanctified through faith in Christ before his works can please God.

So also the *Apology* says (III, 4): "After we are justified by faith and regenerated, we begin to fear God, to love, to ask and expect assistance of Him. . . . We begin likewise to love our neighbors, because our hearts have spiritual and holy emotions. These things cannot take place unless, being justified by faith and regenerated, we receive the Holy Spirit." This is the meaning also of the theological axiom: "Good works must not only be good, they must also be done in a good manner" *(bene fieri debent),* i. e., they must be done in faith, Heb. 11, 6.

Though the good works of believers flow from faith, they nevertheless are not perfect in themselves, since they are tainted by the sin and corruption which still cleaves to their flesh, Rom. 7, 14—19. Their good works are either not done entirely and exclusively according to the norm of the divine Law (other motives or considerations prompting their actions), or they are not done with an altogether free and willing spirit, they being prompted in part by the threats of the Law, Rom. 7, 22. 23. For this reason the good works of the believers are qualitatively deficient, or not as perfect as God desires them to be, Gal. 6, 8.

To this we must add also a deficiency in quantity, for the Christian never performs so many good works as he should, Gal.

6, 9. 10; 2 Cor. 8, 7. 10. 11; 1 Cor. 16, 1. 2. The good works of the regenerate are therefore never "good" in the strict sense of the term, or, what is the same, they never measure up to the perfect standard of the divine will, Rom. 7, 24. 25. If they are accepted as good by God, it is only because the perfect righteousness of Christ, which the believer appropriates by faith, covers their imperfections. In other words, God mercifully forgives their inadequacy for Christ's sake, 1 John 2, 1. 2.

The *Formula of Concord* thus writes (Thor. Decl., IV, 8): "Nor is there a controversy as to how and why the good works of believers, although in this flesh they are impure and incomplete, are pleasing and acceptable to God, namely, for Christ's sake, by faith, because the person is acceptable to God." And again (Thor. Decl., VI, 22): "But how and why the good works of believers, although in this life they are imperfect and impure because of sin in the flesh, are nevertheless acceptable and well-pleasing to God is not taught by the Law, which requires an altogether perfect, pure obedience if it is to please God. But the Gospel teaches that our spiritual offerings are acceptable to God through faith for Christ's sake, 1 Pet. 2, 5; Heb. 11, 4 ff."

So also Quenstedt declares: "The works of the regenerate, in themselves considered, are not perfectly good, but are rendered sordid and polluted by the stain of sin; but in Christ they are perfectly good, and in such a sense that what is not done in them is pardoned through and on account of Christ, and what they lack in perfection is compensated for by the imputation of the most perfect obedience of Christ." (*Doctr. Theol.*, p. 493.) The fact, then, remains that the blood of Jesus Christ, God's Son, must cleanse us also from the sinfulness of our good works, 1 John 1, 7.

B. THE WORKS OF THE HEATHEN.

Since St. Paul, in his Epistle to the Romans, avers that the heathen "by nature do the things contained in the Law," Rom. 2, 14. 15; cp. also 1, 19. 20. 32, it is necessary to consider the question in what sense also the heathen or the unregenerate can do good works. While it is true that, properly speaking, only those works can be called good that flow from faith and true love of God, Heb. 11, 6, we may nevertheless apply the term "good" to all works of the unregenerate that are done according to the norm of the divine Law written in their hearts, Rom. 2, 15; 1, 32, such as feeding the hungry, clothing the naked, helping the oppressed, being diligent in one's calling, etc. Luther once said that, viewed externally, these works frequently surpass those of the believers; for "Alexander the Great, Julius Caesar, and Scipio accomplished greater deeds than ever a Christian" (St. L., II, 461 ff.).

But despite this fact both Luther and our Lutheran Confessions declare that the difference between the good works of believers and unbelievers is one of kind and not one of degree; that is to say, the good works of the unregenerate do not properly belong in the class of Christian good works at all, but are good only outwardly (quoad materiale), not inwardly (quoad formale). Luther says: "Cursed are all works which are not done in love." (St. L., X, 407; cp. also VII, 1862.)

The works of unbelievers are indeed also actuated by God, not, however, in His Kingdom of Grace (regnum gratiae), where the Holy Spirit produces spiritually good works (iustitia spiritualis) through the means of grace, but in His Kingdom of Power (regnum potentiae), where God, for the purpose of preserving this world, effects civilly good works (iustitia civilis), or externally good works (opera externa), through His divine Law inscribed in the heart of man. These externally good works (iustitia civilis) are necessary for the welfare of human society, and hence God rewards them with temporal blessings in His Kingdom of Power. In this sense, then, the works of the unregenerate may be called good; they are done according to the divine norm and accomplish much temporal good in the domain of the earthly life.

But when these works are considered with regard to the source from which all spiritually good works flow, namely, faith, a regenerate heart, the new life in Christ, etc., we cannot call them good at all, but must condemn them as utterly sinful. The reason for this is evident. Holy Scripture declares without qualification that all unregenerate persons are "dead in trespasses and sins," Eph. 2, 1; "alienated from the life of God through the ignorance that is in them," Eph. 4, 18; "without God and having no hope in this world," Eph. 2, 12; and addicted to "dumb idols," 1 Cor. 12, 2, so that what they sacrifice "they sacrifice to devils and not to God," 1 Cor. 10, 20.

It is significant that both Romanists and Romanizing Protestants regard the works of "moral heathen" as good, meritorious, and even as saving. This proves that they understand neither the Law nor the Gospel. They regard the works of the heathen as good because they themselves teach the pagan doctrine of work-righteousness and have thus fallen from grace.

Since, therefore, the unregenerate are in a state of spiritual ignorance and hopelessness, they certainly are unable to do good works from spiritual motives. Moreover, as they themselves displease God, Titus 1, 16; Ps. 53, 1—3, so also their works displease Him, since they are evil, Matt. 12, 33; Luke 6, 43. 44. Hence with respect to the good works of the unregenerate we maintain this distinction: In the sphere of God's Kingdom of Power (*regnum potentiae*), or of earthly matters, they may be called good; in the sphere of His Kingdom of Grace (*regnum gratiae*), or of spiritual things, they are sin (Augustine: "glittering vices").

This is the clear teaching of our Confessions. The *Augsburg Confession* (Art. XVIII) declares: "Although nature is able in a manner to do the outward work, [for it is able to keep the hands from theft and murder,] yet it cannot produce the inward motions, such as the fear of God, trust in God, chastity, patience, etc."

The *Apology* says (Art. IV [II], 33 ff.): "If the carnal mind is enmity against God, the flesh certainly does not love God; if it cannot be subject to the Law of God, it cannot love God. If the carnal mind is enmity against God, the flesh sins even when we do external, civil works. If it cannot be subject to the Law of God, it certainly sins even when, according to human judgment, it performs deeds that are excellent and worthy of praise. The adversaries consider only the precepts of the Second Table, which contain civil righteousness that reason understands. Content with this, they think that they satisfy the Law of God. In the mean time they do not see the First Table, which commands that we love God, that we declare as certain that God is angry with sin, that we truly fear God, that we declare as certain that God hears prayer. But the human heart without the Holy Ghost either in security despises God's judgment or in punishment flees from, and hates, God when He judges. Therefore it does not obey the First Table. Since, therefore, contempt of God and doubt concerning the threats and promises inhere in human nature, men truly sin even when, without the Holy Ghost, they do virtuous works because they do them with a wicked heart, according to Rom. 14, 23. . . . For such persons perform their works with contempt of God, just as Epicurus does not believe that God cares for him or that he is regarded as heard by God. This contempt vitiates works seemingly virtuous, because God judges the heart."

The *Formula of Concord,* quoting Luther, writes (Thor. Decl., II, 43): "Herewith I [Luther] reject and condemn as nothing but error all dogmas which extol our free will, as they directly conflict with this help and grace of our Savior Jesus Christ. For since outside of Christ death and sin are our lords and the devil [is] our god and prince, there can be no power or might, no wisdom or understanding, whereby we can qualify ourselves for, or strive after, righteousness and life; but we must be blinded people and prisoners of sin and the devil's own to do and to think what pleases them and is contrary to God and His commandments."

Since, then, all works which do not flow from faith in Christ are, spiritually considered, sin before God, it is obvious why man by nature cannot qualify himself for grace or cooperate in his conversion and why therefore conversion is alone the work of God (monergism of divine grace). Those errorists who teach man's cooperation in conversion (Pelagians, Semi-Pelagians [papists], Arminians, synergists) deny also the Scriptural truth that the good works of the unregenerate are, spiritually considered, sin before God. The Council of Trent (Sess. VI, Can. 7) has even anathematized those who on the basis of Scripture affirm this doctrine. *(Si quis dixerit, opera omnia, quae ante iustificationem fiunt, quacumque ratione sint, vere esse peccata vel odium Dei mereri — anathema sit.)*

Among modern Protestant theologians, Hofmann assumed that also the heathen will finally be justified on the basis of their good works which they did in agreement with conscience (*Schriftbeweis,* I, 470ff.). We reject this unscriptural doctrine as a figment of reason, Eph. 2, 12. If Unitarians [Modernists] ascribe to the unregenerate good works in the strict sense of the term, this is only consistent with their general unbiblical system of belief; for they themselves boast of good works though they are outside the Church (*extra ecclesiam)* and can therefore produce nothing but evil works before God, Heb. 11, 6.

C. THE CHRISTIAN'S GROWTH IN GOOD WORKS.

It is the will of God, clearly revealed in Holy Scripture, that Christian believers should perform good works in abundance, 1 Tim. 6, 18; 2 Cor. 8, 7; 9, 8—11. Their abounding in good works is the inevitable effect of the abundance of divine mercies which they have received in Christ Jesus, 2 Cor. 8, 9. Holy Scripture accordingly describes true Christians as regenerated per-

sons, who consecrate themselves entirely to the holy, grateful service
of God in Christ Jesus, Rom. 12, 1; Is. 60, 6—9.

Luther's comment on the last passage is apposite. He says:
"Where there are true Christians, they give themselves and all they
have to serve Christ and His own." (St. L., XII, 312.) This new
mind and disposition all believers indeed possess according to their
new or inward man, Gal. 2, 20; Ps. 110, 3. However, since their
flesh remains corrupt even after conversion, they are always in
danger of abusing the doctrine of justification by grace in the
interest of neglecting good works. This was the case already in
the early Apostolic Church, as the numerous exhortations of
St. Paul clearly prove, Gal. 5, 13; 6, 6—10; Titus 3, 14.

When Luther restored the Gospel in its apostolic purity, he
was obliged to publish similar admonitions (St. L., XI, 216 f.;
X, 456 ff.), and to-day the situation in the Christian Church is very
much the same. Instead of abounding in good works, Christians,
impelled by their evil flesh, quite commonly are remiss in performing the good works which God gives them occasion to do
(negligence in church-work, in prayer, in Christian giving, in personal missionary work, etc.).

It is for this reason that Scripture everywhere stresses not only
the *quality,* but also the *quantity* of the Christians' good works,
insisting on constant growth in the grace of doing the good God
demands of them, 2 Cor. 8, 7. 20; 9, 8. 11. According to Scripture,
believers should be "zealous of good works," Titus 2, 14; 2 Cor.
8, 4; should not "be weary in well-doing," Gal. 6, 9; should "do
good unto all men as they have opportunity," Gal. 6, 10; should
"redeem the time" in doing good works, Eph. 5, 16; should be
"careful to maintain good works," Titus 3, 8; etc. In short,
Scripture multiplies its exhortations and unweariedly repeats its
admonitions that believers should bring forth fruits of faith in
abundance (cp., for instance, the closing chapter of St. Paul's
epistles).

In addition to this, Scripture insists that Christian ministers
should constantly urge their parishioners to "maintain good works,"
Titus 3, 8. 14; "to do good, be rich in good works, ready to distribute, willing to communicate, laying up in store for themselves
a good foundation against the time to come," 1 Tim. 6, 17—19.
Christian pastors are therefore Christ's watchmen, 1 Pet. 5, 1—4,
who are in duty bound to produce, through preaching the divine
Word, such works as please God both by their quality and quantity.

For this purpose they are to employ the Law and the Gospel: the Law to point out what good works are, Matt. 22, 37—40, and the Gospel to make men willing to do good works, Rom. 12, 1; Heb. 13, 20. 21.

It is indeed very necessary for Christian ministers to pay unceasing attention to this important function of their holy office. Moved by love for Christ, they must strive also in this matter to give their congregations a maximum of consecrated service, attending to their sacred duty of making their parishioners zealous of good works with unwearying zeal. While faithless prophets and pastors are "dumb dogs, sleeping, lying down, loving to slumber," Is. 56, 10, true ministers of Christ, after the example of their Lord and His apostles, perpetually seek to make their parishioners so minded in all things as God would have them be, 1 Cor. 15, 10; 1 Tim. 4, 15; 2 Tim. 4, 2, and, in particular, fruitful in every good work, Titus 3, 8. 14.

Of this fact Luther reminds all true *ministri Dei et ecclesiae* when he writes (St. L., X, 5): "For this reason, my dear pastors and ministers, note that our office has now become an altogether different thing than it was under the Pope; for now it has become serious and salutary. But just for this reason it involves much more toil and trouble, danger and trial, and there is in addition little gratitude or reward in the world. But Christ will be our Reward if we labor faithfully."

The Christian minister must therefore urge the performance of good works for his own sake, namely, in order that he may be found faithful as a good steward of Jesus Christ, 1 Cor. 4, 1. 2; 2 Cor. 6, 3—10. But he must urge good works also for the sake of his congregation, namely, in order that they who have been entrusted to his care may please God by many praiseworthy deeds, Titus 2, 11—14. To accomplish this, he must urge good works, not feebly or timidly, but joyfully, decidedly, and forcefully, ever mindful of the fact that Christ Himself constantly and zealously admonished His hearers to be fruitful in all good works, Matt. 5, 13—16. To this end he must also rightly distinguish between justification and sanctification; for it is impossible to inculcate true sanctification unless the right relation of justification to sanctification is ever kept in mind, 2 Tim. 2, 15.

It is a most serious mistake to imagine that insistence upon justification leads to neglect of sanctification. On the contrary, wherever justification is not rightly inculcated, there can be no true sanctification; for justification supplies not only the motive, but also the power for sanctification. Hence, if the Christian minister would move his hearers to do good works, he must constantly point them to the grace of God, by which the regenerate have been endowed with all spiritual blessings in heavenly places in Christ, Eph. 1, 3—7; Rom. 12, 1; 2 Cor. 8, 9.

Luther is right in saying (St. L., XII, 318 ff.): "A preacher of the Law forces by means of threats and punishments; a preacher of grace draws and moves by means of the divine goodness and mercy revealed [to man]; for he wants no unwilling works nor any unwilling service; indeed, he wants nothing else than a glad and joyous service of God. He who does not permit himself to be moved and drawn by the sweet and lovely words of God's mercy, given and granted to us so abundantly in Christ, so that he joyfully and lovingly does all this to God's glory and the welfare of the neighbor, amounts to nothing, and love's labor is lost upon him. . . . It is not man's, but God's mercy that has been given to us and that St. Paul would have us consider to urge and move us."

With respect to the *tithe* which God enjoined upon the Jews in the Old Testament, Lev. 27, 30, we must remember, on the one hand, that also this provision belonged to the Ceremonial Law, which has been abolished by Christ, Col. 2, 16. 17, so that it is no longer binding upon Christians in the New Testament; on the other hand, however, the abolition of the law of tithing must not be abused by Christians in the interest of neglecting liberal giving, since also in the New Testament God exhorts His saints to give continually and liberally, 2 Cor. 9, 6. 7.

But while God in the New Testament desires constant and liberal giving just as much as He desired this in the Old Testament, He accomplishes His purpose not through commands and threats, but through appeals to the love of His saints, which is rooted deeply in His own manifestation of grace and mercy in Christ, 2 Cor. 8, 7—10.

To this distinction between the Old and the New Testament, Luther calls attention when he writes (St. L., XII, 337): "In the Old Testament it was commanded that [the Jews] over and above all the annual tithes which they had to give to the Levites had to contribute a special tithe every third year for the poor, the widows and orphans, etc. Now, such giving is neither expressly determined in the New Testament, nor is demanded by specific laws; for this is a time of grace, in which every one is admonished to do this willingly, as St. Paul writes, Gal. 6, 6."

St. Paul himself explains this difference, saying: "Even so we, when we were children, were in bondage under the elements of the world; but when the fulness of the time was come, God sent forth His Son, made of a woman, made under the Law. . . . Wherefore thou art no more a servant, but a son; and if a son, then an heir of God through Christ," Gal. 4, 3—7. Because in Christ Jesus believers are children of God, they are no longer under ceremonial laws, to be compelled to do God's will by coercion; but being under grace, they grow by faith in the grace of willing Christian service, 2 Cor. 8, 9, loving Him because He first loved them, 1 John 4, 19; Gal. 6, 6—10. That does not mean that the Law should not be urged upon Christians or that neglect of Christian giving should not be reproved, Gal. 6, 7; but it does mean that the Christian pastor, when inculcating Christian liberality, must constantly refer to the grace of God that has appeared in Christ Jesus, our Lord, in order to stimulate Christian giving, Titus 2, 11—15. It is only at the foot of the blood-stained cross of Calvary that the believer learns the art of Christian giving.

8. THE REWARD OF GOOD WORKS.

Holy Scripture teaches very distinctly that a sinner is not justified by good works, Rom. 3, 23—28; 4, 4. 5; Gal. 2, 21; 3, 10; etc. Good works are therefore "not necessary for salvation." But neither are good works "necessary to preserve faith," since the believer is preserved in faith unto salvation by the power of God, Phil. 1, 6; 1 Pet. 1, 5. Hence all who do good works in order to earn salvation by them are under the curse; for they are fallen from grace, Gal. 3, 10. 11; 5, 4. Holy Scripture, moreover, affirms that good works flow from faith alone or from the triumphant assurance of the believer that God already has bestowed heaven on him as a free gift of grace for Christ's sake, so that they are done freely, cheerfully, and willingly, without any coercion whatsoever, and without any thought of meriting even the least grace by them, Gal. 2, 20. In view of these facts it would seem to be out of place to speak of any reward of Christian good works.

Nevertheless Scripture itself in many places most emphatically assures the believers that their good works shall be liberally rewarded. "Great is your reward in heaven," Matt. 5, 12; Luke 6, 23. 35; "Every man shall receive his own reward according to his own labor," 1 Cor. 3, 8; "God is not unrighteous to forget your work and labor of love," Heb. 6, 10. In these and many other passages Holy Scripture speaks distinctly of a reward that shall be bestowed upon believers on account of their good works. This reward is granted both in this life, 1 Tim. 4, 8, and in the life to come, Luke 14, 14.

How are we to understand these statements of Scripture? Do they annul the doctrine of justification by grace through faith (sola fide)? In order to avoid any error of man's conceited reason on this point, we must remember two facts: In the first place, though Scripture speaks of a reward of Christian good works, it nevertheless teaches that this reward is of grace (Gnadenlohn) and not of merit, Rom. 4, 4. Luther, in his exegesis of Gal. 3, 22, explains this matter correctly when he says that, since the world does not reward believers for their good works, but rather hates them on account of them, Acts 5, 40; Rom. 8, 36; 1 Cor. 4, 13, God is so kind as to attach to them special promises of gracious rewards. (Cf. St. L., IX, 443.) So also the Apology says (Art. III, 244): "In the preaching of rewards, grace is set forth" ("In praedicatione praemiorum gratia ostenditur").

So, then, we maintain on the basis of Scripture the two doctrines: a) The believer in Christ shall receive for his good works an abundant reward of grace (praemium gratiae), ὁ μισθὸς ὑμῶν πολύς, Matt. 5, 12; but b) all who demand a reward on account of their good works shall not only forfeit God's reward of grace, but also lose their salvation, Gal. 5, 4.

These two doctrines are clearly set forth also in Matt. 19, 27—30; 20, 1—16, where Christ, on the one hand, promises to His believing apostles a sure reward of grace and, on the other, declares that, whenever the demand of a reward is made on the basis of merit, "the first shall be last," Matt. 20, 16, that is, the first, or the self-righteous, shall be entirely rejected.

In the second place, God's free promises of reward made to His saints serve the excellent purpose of prompting the individual believer zealously to perform good works, Matt. 5, 12; Luke 6, 23. 35. To this truth the Apology points when it says (Art. III, 78): "By these praises of good works (Matt. 5, 10) believers are undoubtedly moved to do good works" ("His praeconiis bonorum operum moventur haud dubie fideles ad bene operandum)."

Luther stresses this point when he remarks that in all passages of Scripture which speak of the reward of the believer (Gen. 15, 1: "Thy exceeding great Reward"; Rom. 2, 6. 7, etc.) the godly are incited, comforted, and encouraged to continue, remain and conquer in doing what is good and in enduring what is evil, so that they may not become weary and dispirited." (St. L., XVIII, 1810 f.)

The gracious promises of reward which Scripture offers to believers therefore deny the doctrine of salvation by works or merit and confirm that of salvation by grace. This truth the Christian believer must always bear in mind, especially since both the papists and modern rationalistic Protestants misuse the Scriptural doctrine of God's gracious reward of Christian good works in the interest of work-righteousness.

Luther states the matter very clearly when he writes (St. L., VII, 677 ff.) : "Then learn to reply correctly to those passages in which merit and reward are spoken of [saying]: I indeed hear that Christ says: 'Blessed are the poor in spirit; for theirs is the kingdom of heaven,' and: 'Blessed are ye when men persecute you for My sake, for great is your reward in heaven,' etc. But by these words He does not teach me the foundation upon which I should rest my salvation; but He [by these words] gives me a promise, [showing me] what comfort I should have in my suffering and Christian life. These two things you must not mingle into each other nor brew together; nor must you make a merit of that which God gives me freely in Christ through Baptism and the Gospel. For He does not say here that I could earn such things or that I no longer need Christ or Baptism, but rather that those are Christ's true disciples to whom He here preaches and who for His sake must suffer many things, so that they do not know how they may comfort themselves. Since people do not suffer them on earth, they should therefore in heaven all the more possess all things." (Cp. also Dr. Pieper's excellent presentation of the doctrine, *Christl. Dogmatik,* III, 64 ff.)

9. THE GREAT VALUE OF GOOD WORKS.

Although good works have no value so far as the justification of a sinner is concerned, since salvation is not by works, but by grace, Rom. 3, 28; Eph. 2, 8. 9, it is incorrect to declare that good works are of no value whatsoever. To say that good works have no value whatever, as the Anabaptists at Luther's time claimed, is both anti-Scriptural, since Scripture with great earnestness inculcates good works, Eph. 2, 10; Matt. 5, 13—16, and unreasonable, since even conscience, on the basis of the divine Law inscribed in the human heart, prompts a person to do what is good, Rom. 2, 14. 15. Over against the enthusiasts, Luther (St. L., IX, 442 ff.) emphasized the truth that outside the article of justification good works indeed could not be praised enough (*"Extra causam iustificationis nemo potest bona opera a Deo praecepta satis magnifice commendare"*).

Against the Anabaptists, Luther wrote (St. L., XIV, 310 ff.) : "See how nobly they teach regarding good works, saying that they would give away all their good works for a farthing! By this they want to be our apes and imitate our doctrine, having heard that we teach that good works do not make a sinner pious, do not blot out sins, and do not reconcile us to God. To this the devil adds his supplement and despises good works, so much so that he would sell them all for one farthing. . . . We teach that to reconcile God, to make pious, to blot out sin is so high, great, and glorious a work that alone Christ, the Son of God, could do it and that this is really a pure, special, peculiar work of the one true God and His grace, in comparison with which our works are nothing and can do nothing. But that for this reason good works should amount to, and be worth, nothing, who ever has taught or heard such a thing except out of the lying mouth of the devil? I would not give one of my sermons, not one of my lectures, not one of my writings, not one of my Lord's Prayers, indeed, not even the least of the good works I have done or yet do for all the goods of the world; yes, I regard it [each of these good works] greater than my own life, which certainly is dearer to every one, and must be dearer, than the whole world; for each is a good work which God has done through and in me. But if God has done it, and if it is God's work, what is the whole world compared with God and His work? And though I am not made pious through such works, — for that can be done alone through Christ's blood and righteousness, without works, — nevertheless they are done to the praise and glory of God and to the benefit and weal of my neighbor, so that not even a single one of them could be paid for by the whole world or compared with those of the world. And this fine rabble would take only a farthing for them! Oh, how well Satan has hidden himself here! Who could not detect him here?"

This high estimate of the value of Christian good works is in full agreement with the clear teaching of Scripture. Christian good works are indeed of great value, and this for the following reasons : —

THE DOCTRINE OF SANCTIFICATION AND GOOD WORKS.

a. They are done according to the *norm of God's Law.* While all works that are not done according to God's will are worthless and displeasing to God, those which are accomplished according to His will are esteemed by Him as infinitely precious in His sight, Rev. 2, 2 ff.

b. They are *God's own works in us;* for He is the efficient Cause *(causa efficiens)* of all Christian good works, Phil. 2, 13; 2 Cor. 3, 5; 1 Cor. 12, 6—11; Eph. 2, 10. While all "good works" that are done by men to merit salvation are condemned in Scripture as "works of the flesh," Gal. 3, 2. 3. 10, the good works of believers are praised and glorified in Holy Scripture as "fruits of the Spirit," Gal. 5, 22. 23, which God Himself works in them to His glory, Eph. 2, 10; Col. 1, 5. 6; 1 Tim. 6, 17—19; Titus 2, 11—14; etc.

c. They are *tokens and testimonies (testimonia Spiritus externa)* of the state of grace into which the believer has been placed through faith in Christ, Luke 7, 47; 1 John 3, 14. As such they are of great value to the believer himself, Rev. 2, 19, and to all other men, Matt. 5, 16.

d. They are *imperishable,* following the believer into eternal life, where they are rewarded most graciously, Rev. 14, 13; Matt. 5, 12; 19, 29; 10, 42; Gal. 6, 9, while all earthly works will be consumed by fire on the Last Day, Matt. 24, 35; 1 Cor. 7, 31; 2 Pet. 3, 10.

e. On account of the good works of believers, of which the preaching of the Gospel is the foremost, God defers Judgment Day, Matt. 24, 14; 1 Pet. 2, 9. For this reason Christians should at all times be most diligent in performing good works, Gal. 6, 10; Eph. 5, 16; Col. 4, 5, and Christian ministers should constantly inculcate them, Titus 3, 8; 1 Tim. 6, 17 ff.

f. The performance of good works is the real objective of the Christian's life on earth. As soon as a person has become a believer in Christ, he no longer belongs to this world, but to the kingdom of heaven, Phil. 3, 20; John 5, 24. But God wants His saints to live on earth for a while in order that they may serve Christ, publish His Gospel, and perform many good works to the praise of His name, Matt. 5, 13—16. From all this it is evident that Christian good works *(opera spiritualia)* are indeed of the greatest value. Luther says (St. L., I, 867): "The works which we do in our calling through faith in the Son of God shine before God, the holy angels, and the whole Church."

10. PERVERSION OF THE DOCTRINE OF GOOD WORKS.

Since the Church of Antichrist claims to be the true promoter of good works (Cardinal Gibbons: "The Catholic Church is a society for the sanctification of its members") and condemns the Church of the Reformation as one which, stressing unduly the doctrine of justification, habitually neglects sanctification, it is necessary to point out that the Church of Rome is not a promoter, but rather a perverter of the doctrine of good works.

The charge that Luther disparaged good works was made already in the early stages of the Reformation (Edict of Worms, 1521: "Luther teaches an unbound, self-willed life, which excludes all divine laws and is altogether bestial"). This unjust and untrue accusation is continued to this day despite the fact that both by word and deed it has been proved a malicious lie. As a matter of fact, just because Luther taught the true doctrine of justification, he taught also the true doctrine of sanctification, that is to say, he vigorously and ceaselessly insisted upon good works as fruits and proofs of the living faith of the true believers.

On the other hand, the Papacy, so far as it lies in its power, renders the performance of Christian good works impossible because it anathematizes the basic article of the Christian faith, the doctrine of justification by grace, from which all truly good works flow. True Christian good works are the fruits of justification by faith; hence wherever this doctrine is abolished and anathematized, good works in the sense of Christ and the Bible are out of the question. The Roman Catholic Church indeed insists upon works, but these are not "good," but pagan works, since they are done for the purpose of earning salvation, Gal. 3, 10; 5, 4. Whenever Christian good works do occur in the Church of Antichrist, it is only because individual believers reject for their part the pagan doctrine of work-righteousness taught them by their priests and believe in the gracious forgiveness of their sins for Christ's sake without the deeds of the Law, Rom. 3, 28. This faith puts them in a position where they can perform truly good works.

We condemn the "good works" of Romanism particularly for two reasons. In the first place, they involve a malicious denial and rejection of the sufficiency of Christ's redemptive work, being done to *merit righteousness* before God *(meritum de congruo, meritum de condigno)*. But good works done for this purpose insult and mock God, who in His Word offers to all sinners through faith the entire, perfect righteousness which His beloved Son has secured for the world by His vicarious satisfaction (*satisfactio vicaria*). This is the clear doctrine of Scripture; for St. Paul writes emphatically: "If righteousness comes by the Law, then Christ is dead in vain," Gal. 2, 21. The "good works" of the papists are therefore "under the curse," Gal. 3, 10. When Cardinal Gibbons (*The Faith of Our Fathers,* p. 35) describes the Catholic Church as "*a society for the* SANCTIFICATION *of its members,*" he attests officially that it is in principle an antichristian and pagan sect, which like all heathen cults bases salvation upon good works.

Luther is right in saying (St. L., IX, 443): "The works which are done outside of faith, no matter how holy they may appear according to their external aspect, are sinful and under the curse. For this reason those who desire to earn grace, righteousness, and eternal life by them do not only fall short [of these blessings], but also heap sin upon sin. In this way the Pope, the man of sin and the son of perdition, does good works and all who follow him. In this manner also all self-righteous persons and heretics, who have fallen from the Christian faith, do their works."

That the entire process of sanctification in the Roman Catholic Church proceeds along unscriptural and antichristian lines is proved by the fact that this Church has perverted and condemned Christ's Gospel (Council of Trent, Sess. VI, Cans. 11. 12. 20) and persecuted its adherents (Luther was officially called "the evil foe in the form of a man," "a wild, voracious boar," "a most rapacious beast," "whose memory ought to be blotted out of the communion of Christ's believers"), contrary to the express exhortation of Christ, Luke 10, 16; John 13, 20; Phil. 2, 29. The "good works" of the Papacy must therefore be condemned as a sanctimonious fraud, which Antichrist perpetrates for the purpose of deceiving the simple (2 Thess. 2, 9: "lying wonders").

In the second place, we repudiate the good works of the Roman Catholic Church because they are not done according to the norm of the divine Law; in other words, they are not done in the sense that God has commanded them. On the contrary, they are the products of "commandments of men" and thus fall under the condemnation of our Lord: "In vain they do worship Me, teaching for doctrines the commandments of men," Matt. 15, 9. Papistic sanctification is not Christian sanctification at all, but only a caricature of that true sanctification which God demands of His children as the fruit of faith.

According to Scripture the regenerate, justified by faith, serve God cheerfully and gratefully in every calling in which He has called them, either in the Church or without, Rom. 15, 16; 1 Cor. 7, 20 ff.; Col. 3, 23. 24; Eph. 6, 7; 1 Tim. 2, 15. However, the Church of Antichrist prescribes new norms of good works (the evangelical counsels, *consilia evangelica,* obedience, poverty, chastity) and in addition invents a new anti-Scriptural, antichristian purpose of good works, namely, that of earning salvation.

Ordinary Catholic Christians are taught to earn salvation as much as lies in their power by means of the "second board" *(tabula secunda),* that is, through penance *(poenitentia),* which formally consists in doing the "good works" of *contritio cordis, confessio oris,* and *satisfactio operis.* The preferred class of papistic "good-workers" (monks, nuns, etc.), in addition to *poenitentia,* cultivate the *consilia evangelica,* by which they are able to earn not only sufficient, but even superabundant merits *(opera supererogationis),* which, upon payment of a certain price, the Pope administers to the "poor souls" in purgatory. (Council of Trent, Sess. VI, Can. 30.) The wickedness of the papistic teaching is apparent to every Christian believer who has tasted the sweetness of the Gospel and knows the Biblical doctrine of justification by faith. As papistic justification (by way of sanctification) is diametrically opposed to Biblical justification, so also papistic sanctification is diametrically opposed to Biblical sanctification; it is a sanctification of the flesh, or the carnal heart, not that of the Spirit, Gal. 3, 1—3.

The pernicious doctrine of work-righteousness as presented by the Roman Catholic Church culminates in the perversions of the Jesuits, by which manifest transgressions even cease to be sins and become eminently good works if they are commanded by the superiors of the order.

The *Index Generalis* declares expressly: "The superiors may obligate [members] to sin by virtue of the obedience (which is due them), provided this will confer great benefits." *"Superiores possunt obligare ad peccatum in virtute obedientiae, quando id multum conveniat."* (Cp. *Index Generalis,* Vol. II, *sub Obedientiae et Obedire;* also, *Christl. Dogmatik,* III, p. 80 ff.) This blasphemous disavowal of God's Word and tyrannizing of consciences is but the inevitable result of the papal rejection of God's Word as the only source of faith *(principium cognoscendi)* and its frightful enslaving of consciences in general as this is practised throughout the Church of Antichrist (cp. the demand of *sacrificium intellectus et voluntatis*).

The Pope demands implicit obedience of all members of his Church, both in articles of faith and in matters of life, so that every Catholic sins mortally who rests his decisions on doctrine or life upon his own conscience or Holy Scripture. (Cp. Council of Trent, Sess. IV; Luther, St. L., XIX, 341 ff.; IX, 1235 ff.)

Holy Scripture demands that every thought ($\pi\tilde{\alpha}\nu$ $\nu\acute{o}\eta\mu\alpha$) be brought into captivity to the obedience of Christ, 2 Cor. 10, 5; but the Pope demands that every thought of his deluded followers be brought into captivity to the obedience of his own perverted mind. It was in view of these abhorrent perversions that Luther called the Papacy a *confluxus* of all heresies and affirmed that the Papacy at Rome was founded by the devil.

It is true, all heretics teach ungodly doctrines; but the Pope not only adorns his ungodly doctrines with the name of Christ and the Christian Church, but also claims to be Christ's vicar upon earth and as such the infallible teacher of divine truth. Just that is the chief characteristic of Antichrist. To be a real papist means to believe ungodly doctrine and to do evil works contrary to God's Word, for salvation's sake.

As the Church of Rome, so also modern rationalistic Protestantism perverts the doctrine of good works. While the Church of Antichrist is swayed by the pernicious error of Semi-Pelagianism, rationalistic Protestantism corrupts itself by the equally pernicious errors of Arminianism and synergism. The result is the same in both cases.

As Romanism rejects the doctrine of justification, which is the necessary postulate of good works, so also rationalistic Protestantism, in both Lutheran and Reformed circles, rejects this central doctrine of Scripture. Since the forensic conception of justification, as taught by Luther and the Lutheran Confessions, is regarded as too "juridical" and not sufficiently "ethical," it is consigned to the scrap-heap of theological oblivion, and the sinner is taught to cooperate in his conversion and thus to rely on his good works for salvation. As a result also modern rationalistic Protestantism teaches justification by way of sanctification, or salvation by good works. The old Melanchthonian (Majoristic) claim that "good works are necessary for salvation" is thus revived as a dogma of the Church. Thus work-righteousness lands modern Protestantism in the camp of Semi-Pelagian Romanism, and both are enemies of the Gospel of Christ.

11. SANCTIFICATION AND THE CHRISTIAN LIFE.

We shall treat this subject under three heads: a) The Christian Life and the Cross; b) The Christian Life and Prayer; and c) The Christian Life and the Hope of Eternal Life.

A. THE CHRISTIAN LIFE AND THE CROSS.

A special section on cross and tribulation in a Christian dogmatics is fully justified, since Scripture itself devotes much attention to this important subject. Accordingly some of our Lutheran dogmaticians (Quenstedt and Calov) have embodied the subject in their description of the Christian life; and it is well for us to follow their example.

The topic is surely worthy of careful consideration. Through faith in Christ the regenerate are indeed in a most blessed state. God is "for them," Rom. 8, 31; they are God's children and heirs of eternal life, John 1, 12. 13; Gal. 3, 26; Rom. 8, 17; the holy angels minister to them, Heb. 1, 14; in God's Word they have abundant comfort for every trouble in life and strength for every vexing question pertaining to their salvation. However, in spite of all this the glory which is theirs in Christ Jesus is not yet revealed, 1 John 3, 2. They walk in the same lowliness, humiliation, and suffering which characterized Christ's own life on earth, 1 Pet. 4, 1. This life of sorrow and tribulation Scripture fitly calls the cross *(crux)* of the Christians, Matt. 10, 21. 38; 16, 24; Luke 14, 27. (Cp. also Luther, St. L., XII, 729 ff.)

1. *What the Christian cross implies.* Holy Scripture never applies the term *cross* to the tribulations of the ungodly, Ps. 32, 10; 34, 21; 16, 4. It is only the Christian who is said to bear a cross, and this indeed as he exercises his Christian calling in the world. Luther writes (St. L., XII, 544 ff.): "A Christian, in so far as he is a Christian, is subject to his dear holy cross, so that he must suffer either from other people or from the devil himself, who torments and terrifies him with tribulation, persecution, poverty, sickness, or inwardly in his heart by means of his poisonous darts." Especially when Christians faithfully bear witness to Christ and His Gospel, or when they lead a holy life according to the Word of God, they must always expect to endure trials and bear crosses, Matt. 10, 25. Hence by cross we mean that suffering which Christians suffer for Christ's sake, Matt. 10, 16—22.

It is true, also the regenerate are still sinners, and for this reason they deserve not only temporal punishments, but also eternal damnation, Rom. 7, 24. However, since they live in daily repentance and by faith receive constant forgiveness of all their sins, the punishments which God in His fatherly love metes out to them are not punishments in the strict sense of the term, since they do not flow from divine wrath, but rather gracious chastenings *(castigationes paternae),* which are designed for their temporal and eternal good, Rom. 8, 28; Heb. 12, 6; 1 Cor. 11, 32; Is. 26, 16.

But it is not on account of their sins that Satan and the wicked world trouble the regenerate. Luther says very aptly (St. L., XIII, 434 ff.) : "The evil Foe and the world are not angry with Christians because they are sinners and stumble and fall now and then. No indeed; the devil and the world gladly tolerate this and even approve of it. But on account of the Word and their faith [they hate them], namely, because they hope in the Son of God, comfort themselves with His death and resurrection, fear God, and wish to live according to His will, earnestly desiring that through their confession also others may come to the knowledge of Christ and faith; that neither the devil nor the world can endure, and for this reason they constantly torment the Christians."

However, the Christian cross is occasioned not only by the devil and his servants, the children of the world; it comes also from the flesh of the Christians, which constantly lusts against the Spirit and thus always tempts and troubles them. For the Christian to bear his cross therefore implies ceaseless warfare against the flesh, Gal. 6, 12; 5, 17; uninterrupted self-denial, Matt. 16, 24; renunciation of everything that interferes with his following of Christ, Luke 14, 33; repudiation of his own carnal wisdom in spiritual matters, Matt. 11, 25. 26; cheerfully and willingly foregoing the peace and quietness of life, Matt. 10, 34; Luke 12, 51; making nothing of the esteem of the world, Matt. 5, 11; Luke 6, 22; 1 Pet. 4, 14; relinquishing the friendship and the love of even father and mother, sister and brother, Matt. 10, 35—37; Luke 12, 52. 53; being willing to lose his earthly possessions, 1 Cor. 7, 30; Matt. 19, 21. 22; indeed, hating his own life, Luke 14, 26. The Christian cross-bearer must therefore ceaselessly fight the good fight of faith against his own flesh, Gal. 5, 24; Col. 3, 5; Rom. 6, 6.

2. *The close connection (nexus indivulsus) between Christianity and the cross.* Cross-bearing is so intimately connected with the Christian profession that all who refuse to take upon themselves and bear their cross cannot be regarded as true Christians, Matt. 10, 38. 39; Mark 8, 34. 35; Luke 9, 23. 24. 57—62;

Rom. 8, 17; Luke 14, 25—35. Luther's remarks on this matter are indeed pertinent. He writes (St. L., II, 467): "He who is no *crucianus,* if I may so speak, is also no *Christianus.* That is to say, he who does not bear his cross is no Christian, for he does not conform to Christ, his Master."

In spite of this it remains true that a Christian should not impose crosses upon himself (1 Pet. 3, 17: εἰ θέλοι τὸ θέλημα τοῦ θεοῦ; 1, 6: εἰ δέον) or upon others, Rom. 13, 10; Matt. 22, 37—40; for he knows neither whether the chosen cross is salutary nor whether God will grant him power to bear it, 1 Cor. 10, 13. Luther rightly called those who impose crosses upon themselves "work-saints" *(Werkheilige)* and "the devil's own martyrs *(des Teufels Maertyrer),* by which he meant to say that, since they want to earn heaven by their crosses, they suffer at the instigation of the devil (St. L., IX, 1130).

3. *How Christians should regard their crosses.* Because cross-bearing is a most painful burden to the flesh of the regenerate, they often labor under the false impression that God is dealing unjustly and cruelly with them in making them suffer as He does, indeed, that He has forgotten them or has even become their enemy, Lam. 5, 20; Ps. 13, 1; Job 30, 21; Is. 49, 14. For this reason some "in time of temptation" lose their faith and fall away from God, Luke 8, 13. Scripture therefore is very explicit in explaining the true nature and purpose of Christian cross-bearing, Heb. 12, 6—11; 1 Cor. 11, 32. Christian cross-bearing is a testimony of the Holy Spirit *(testimonium Spiritus Sancti externum)* that God's saints do not belong to the condemned world, but to Christ and that they are joint heirs with Him, if they faithfully suffer with Him, Rom. 8, 16. 17; 1 Pet. 4, 14; Matt. 5, 11. 12. Their cross therefore always points to the glory which shall be revealed in them, Rom. 8, 18; 2 Thess. 1, 5—7; 2 Cor. 4, 7. 8. It is the characteristic (Luther: *Hoffarbe*) of Christ's pilgrims who are on their way to heaven (Luther, St. L., XII, 718 ff.), and for this reason they should truly rejoice in their sufferings for Christ's sake, Matt. 5, 12; Luke 6, 23, knowing that, as they suffered with Him, they shall also be glorified with Him, 1 Pet. 4, 13; 3, 14. 15. Thus the apostles at Jerusalem rejoiced in their persecutions, Acts 5, 41, and above all St. Paul thus rejoiced in his sufferings, Acts 16, 25; Rom. 5, 3.

In their cross-bearing Christians may rejoice all the more, since they know that God has not only accommodated their cross to their ability to bear, but also actually aids them in bearing it, 1 Cor. 10, 13; 2 Cor. 12, 9. Hence the cross of the individual Christian is never too heavy for him; it is apportioned in mercy and proportioned to his measure of faith, 2 Cor. 4, 17.

4. *The benefits of Christian cross-bearing.* Everything that God assigns to His believing saints on earth is of eternal value, Rom. 8, 28. So also the cross which believers bear is of incalculable benefit to them. It points them to heaven, Acts 14, 22; renders them humble before God, 2 Cor. 12, 7; teaches them implicit trust in divine grace, 2 Cor. 12, 8. 9; strengthens their faith, 1 Pet. 1, 6. 7; moves them to prayer, Ps. 18, 6; Is. 26, 16; crucifies their old man and destroys the body of sin, Rom. 6, 6; 1 Pet. 4, 1; and turns their view from this present, perishable world to the eternal, imperishable life to come, 2 Cor. 4, 18. By their patient and faithful cross-bearing believers also encourage others to be steadfast in their trials and to continue in the hope of the glorious promises of the living God, 2 Cor. 1, 6; 1 Thess. 1, 6. 7. The lesson of Christ's glorious cross is best taught by him who has victoriously borne his own cross, 2 Cor. 1, 4; 12, 10. (Cp. Luther, St. L., IX, 1131.)

5. *The strength to bear the cross.* Even the truest and best believer cannot bear the cross laid upon him by his own power, 2 Cor. 12, 7—9. Patient cross-bearing therefore always presupposes and necessitates divine grace, 2 Tim. 1, 8; 2 Cor. 4, 7. In particular, the Christian cross-bearer receives strength to bear his cross from the gracious assurance of the forgiveness of all his sins, Rom. 5, 1—5; from his sure hope of eternal life, Rom. 8, 18; from his new, spiritual life with Christ in God, Col. 3, 3. 4; from God's glorious promises of a gracious reward in heaven, Matt. 5, 12; in short, from his abiding, sanctifying faith in the divine human Christ, who loved him and gave Himself for him, Gal. 2, 20.

Luther rightly remarks that a person who is not sure of eternal life and does not look for that blessed hope (Titus 2, 13) can be neither submissive nor patient (St. L., IX, 956), while Christians, whose conversation is in heaven, have power to rejoice even in their greatest tribulations.

Of St. Paul Luther writes (St. L., XII, 717ff.): "Behold how he [St. Paul] turns his back upon the world and looks forward to the coming revelation, just as though he saw no trouble or misery whatever upon earth, but only joy. Indeed, if we should suffer ever so much, what does all our suffering amount to, he says, when we compare it with the unspeakable joy and glory which shall be revealed in us? . . . Thus St. Paul regards all the suffering of this earth as a little drop and a small spark, but of the glory which we are looking for he makes an infinite ocean and a great fire. And in calling it a 'glory that shall be revealed in us,' he indicates why it is that we suffer so unwillingly, namely, because our faith is yet weak, so that we do not look to the glory, still hidden in this life, which shall be revealed in us. For if it were a glory that we could see with our eyes, then indeed we should be fine, patient martyrs."

Luther closes this fine paragraph with the pertinent remark that because of the blindness of our miserable, weak flesh we cannot comprehend the great, surpassing goodness and grace to which God calls us by laying upon us our Christian crosses, "the Holy Spirit must be our Teacher in this matter and put such comfort into our hearts." To this every true Christian cross-bearer agrees. Unless the Holy Spirit grants us grace to bear our cross, we shall never possess enough power to bear it, not even the lightest.

6. *Christian cross-bearing and the Christian's sin.* In connection with this subject the question has been raised whether also the sin which still cleaves to the Christian believer may be considered a part of the cross which he must endure. This query must be answered in the affirmative; for whenever the believer sins, he does something that he abominates, Rom. 7, 15. A true Christian earnestly deplores the fact that he is so "sold under sin," Rom. 7, 14, that he constantly commits the sins that he does not wish to do, Rom. 7, 15, and so he fervently beseeches God to deliver him from "the body of this death," Rom. 7, 24. For this reason our dogmaticians rightly say that also the evil flesh, which is sold under sin, Rom. 7, 17—19, belongs to the cross which believers must bear in this life. (Cp. Luther, St. L., XII, 727. 728. 735.)

B. THE CHRISTIAN LIFE AND PRAYER.

1. *The intimate connection (nexus indivulsus) between the Christian life and prayer.* As long as a person remains in his natural state of sin and wrath, he fears and therefore also flees God, Heb. 2, 15; Gen. 3, 8. But as soon as he by faith has entered into the new, spiritual life, he begins to commune with God, Rom. 8, 15. This spiritual communion of the believer with God we call prayer.

Christian prayer has rightly been defined as "the communion

of a believing heart with God," Ps. 27, 8. While words of the mouth are not absolutely necessary to make a "communion with God" a prayer, Is. 65, 24; Rom. 8, 26. 27, yet they must not be regarded as superfluous, Acts 7, 59; 16, 25.

Since Christian prayer is the fruit of the believer's faith in the gracious forgiveness of his sins for Christ's sake, it is continuous, 1 Thess. 5, 17, because the regenerated heart, led and moved by the Holy Spirit, is habitually turned toward God and therefore also in ceaseless communion with Him, Rom. 8, 14. 15.

Hence a Christian prays even when he is not aware of it, as when he is occupied with his work or when in great tribulation he considers himself incapable of praying. (Cp. Luther, St. L., IX, 922.) As the natural pulse beats ceaselessly as long as there is life in a body, so the pulse of prayer is beating constantly as long as a person has spiritual life.

Luther rightly (St. L., VIII, 363) says: "Wherever there is a Christian, there is also the Holy Spirit, who does nothing else than pray ceaselessly. For although he [the Christian] does not always move his mouth or utter words, nevertheless his heart always moves and beats, just as his pulse and his natural heart, with such ceaseless sighings as: Dear Father, Thy name be hallowed, Thy kingdom come, Thy will be done among us and all men, etc. . . . Hence you cannot find a single Christian who does not always pray, just as little as you can find a living person without a pulse, which never stands still, but always beats, though the person may sleep or do something else, so that he does not take notice of it."

The simple division of prayer into supplication and thanksgiving is adequate, since also the intercessions that are to be made for governments and for all men (1 Tim. 2, 1—3; Jer. 29, 7), for believers (Eph. 6, 18), and for unbelievers and enemies (Matt. 5, 44; Luke 23, 34; Acts 7, 59) come under the head of supplications. (Cp. Luther, St. L., X, 2204.)

2. *What Christian prayer presupposes.* Christian prayer presupposes much more than the "absolute feeling of dependence upon God" (Schleiermacher) or "faith in the general providence of God" (Ritschl). Even the heathen perceive that they are dependent upon a Supreme Being, and to some extent they, too, have faith in a divine providence, Acts 17, 23. 26—28; yet St. Paul affirms that what they sacrifice they sacrifice to devils and not to God, 1 Cor. 10, 20.

As a matter of fact, when a Christian prays, a most intimate communion takes place between a creature who is dust and ashes, Gen. 18, 27, and, what is more, a sinner and by nature an enemy of God, Rom. 8, 7; 5, 8, and the sovereign, majestic Creator, Ps. 5, 1—7. In order that a sinner, blind, dead, and unworthy as he is by nature, may rightly commune with God as a dear child communes with its loving father, he must be regenerated, or born again, John 3, 5. 6.

Christian prayer therefore always presupposes true faith in Christ, or faith in the gracious forgiveness of all sins for Christ's sake. Holy Scripture describes as true prayers only those which are offered in the name of Christ, John 16, 23; 14, 13. 14. If a prayer is to be a true prayer, it must flow from faith in Christ, John 6, 29; 14, 6. No other prayer can be addressed to God with true confidence, Rom. 5, 1—5, which is a basic characteristic of Christian prayer, Jas. 1, 6. 7; Rom. 14, 23. Luther is indeed right when he says (St. L., VIII, 362; IX, 922 ff.) that no one can offer a prayer outside the name of Jesus (such as are the prayers of the Turks, Jews, monks, and hypocrites), while, if a prayer is offered in Jesus' name, even one letter is valid and pleasing to God.

True, also the heathen and all those in the visible Church who reject Christ's vicarious atonement pray with a certain earnestness and devotion; but such religious emotions flow from the flesh and not from true faith. Their author *(causa efficiens)* is not the Holy Ghost, who always glorifies Christ in those in whom He operates, John 16, 14, but the devil, who "worketh in the children of disobedience," Eph. 2, 2. Ritschl condemned his own rationalism (denial of Christ's vicarious atonement) when he said: "The prayer to God as our Father in Christ Jesus distinguishes the Christian religion from all others."

The truth of this statement is borne out by the study of comparative religion. Christianity alone teaches its followers to pray to the Father in heaven in the name of His divine Son, who by His vicarious death secured reconciliation for all sinners. All religions which have their origin in the depraved flesh of man inculcate prayer on the ground of the sinner's own righteousness, or good works. Hence all who do not pray in the name of Jesus know neither to whom to pray nor how rightly to pray; their prayers are vain repetitions, spoken without faith and confidence, and are never heard, Matt. 6, 7. This is true both of the prayers of the heathen (prayer-mills of the Buddhists) and of the apostate

Christians (the rosaries of the Romanists). It is only the true believer who prays in the name of Christ, that is, with perfect trust in the divine grace for the sake of Christ, Dan. 9, 16—19, and without any confidence in his own merit or worthiness.

All prayers of unchristian and anti-Christian lodges, which deny the Holy Trinity and Christ's deity and vicarious atonement, are pagan and idolatrous and as such an abomination in the sight of God. For a Christian to hold membership in such lodges means to deny the divine Savior and His vicarious atonement and to give great offense to professing Christians. A Christian can therefore not hold membership in a lodge without endangering his soul's salvation.

Luther writes (St. L., VIII, 361 ff.): "Wherever there is the Spirit of grace, there He brings it to pass that we can and dare, aye, indeed, that we must begin, to pray. . . . For before we become Christians and believe, we do not know what and how we should pray. Although a person prays ever so earnestly [viewed externally], yet [before conversion] the Spirit of grace is not there. . . . There is [then] no faith in divine grace and mercy for Christ's sake, and the heart always remains uncertain, so that it must ever doubt whether it is heard; it deals with God only on the ground of its own holiness or that of others, without Christ, as if God should humble Himself before it and be prevailed upon to bestow His grace or help for our sake and thus become our servant or debtor. To do this means not to merit grace, but wrath; it is not a prayer, but rather a mockery of God."

3. *What Christian prayer works and bestows.* Since God preserves the world only for the sake of His saints, more especially, in order that they may preach the Gospel for a witness unto all nations, Matt. 24, 14, and since all true Christians pray in perfect agreement with God's good and gracious will, which sustains and governs all things, 1 John 5, 14, we may say that their prayers sustain and govern *(instrumentaliter)* the whole universe. That is the clear doctrine of Scripture, which assures us that all things occurring in the Kingdom of Power and in the Kingdom of Grace are mediated through Christian prayer.

In particular, because of Christian prayer "the Word of the Lord has free course," 2 Thess. 3, 1; through it God opens to His servants "a door of utterance to speak the mystery of Christ," Col. 4, 2—4; Eph. 6, 19. 20; through it all ministers of the Word are "delivered from them that do not believe," Rom. 15, 30—32;

through it the peace of the world is preserved, Jer. 29, 7; as a result of it Christians lead a quiet and peaceable life in all godliness and honesty, 1 Tim. 2, 1—3; through it the godly are preserved from the wicked, Ps. 55, 24; 2 Pet. 2, 7, etc. Whatever Christ works as the *causa efficiens* He works through His Christians as through instrumental causes *(causae instrumentales),* as He Himself testifies, Acts 1, 8; 1 Cor. 3, 9.

Luther writes on this point (St. L., VIII, 350 ff.) : "We must not separate the Head from its members, that is, Christ from His apostles and all Christians. Every single Christian is such a one as the Lord Jesus Christ Himself was while He was upon earth, and he accomplishes such great things that he can rule the world in divine things, help and profit every one, and do the greatest works that are done upon earth. For he is regarded higher by God than the whole world, so that for his sake God gives and sustains to the world all things that it has; indeed, if no Christians would be upon earth, no city and no country would have peace; then surely on a single day all things that are upon earth would be destroyed by the devil. That grain grows in the field and the people prosper, enjoy food, peace, and protection, for all this they must thank us Christians. For while it is true that we are poor beggars, as St. Paul writes 2 Cor. 6, 10, we are nevertheless such as make many rich; as possessing nothing and yet possessing all things. In short, it is true, what kings, princes, lords, citizens, and peasants have in the world they have not because of their golden hair, but because of Christ and His disciples. Therefore the Christians are truly helpers and saviors, yes, lords and gods of the world, as also God said to Moses, Ex. 7, 1: 'I have made thee a god to Pharaoh.' "

4. *What Christian prayer asks for.* Since Christians, when praying in the name of Jesus, pray according to God's will, their prayers include all things which God Himself wills and has promised to give them. It is for this reason that Christ has said: "All things, whatsoever ye shall ask in prayer, believing, ye shall receive," Matt. 21, 22; Mark 12, 24; John 14, 13. 14; 16, 23; Matt. 7, 7. 8. The words "all things whatsoever" must not be limited, but taken in their full force, since the will of the believer always coincides with the good and gracious will of God.

It is true, in so far as believers are still flesh, they often do not will what God wills; but because they are new creatures in Christ, the will of the flesh is suppressed, and their prayers are offered up to God according to the rule of Christ: "Not My will, but Thine, be done." As Christians acknowledge the Word of God as the only source and rule of their faith, so they also acknowledge solely the will of God as the norm of their petitions, 1 John 5, 14.

From this follows the general rule that, whenever believers pray for temporal blessings, they pray conditionally, Matt. 26, 39; but if they pray for spiritual blessings, they pray unconditionally, since God has promised to grant them His grace, forgiveness of sins, life, and salvation under all circumstances, 2 Cor. 12, 9.

Unconditional prayers for earthly blessings belong in the domain of heroic faith (fides heroica). But the heroic prayer should not be attempted unless the believer is fully assured that he has heroic faith (cp. Luther's supplication for the restoration of Melanchthon's health).

Of all prayers the Lord's Prayer is the best, since it was given to us by our Lord Jesus Christ and embraces all spiritual and bodily needs of the believer. Luther says: "There is no nobler prayer on earth than the Lord's Prayer; for it has the glorious promise that God gladly hears it; and we should not exchange all the blessings of this earth for it."

The prayers to the departed saints are foolish, Is. 63, 16; 1 Kings 8, 39; Acts 10, 25. 26; idolatrous, Matt. 4, 10; and blasphemous; indeed, an insult to God's perfect grace secured by the merits of Christ, 1 Tim. 2, 5. 6; 1 John 2, 1. 2; Rom. 8, 31. 32. 34.

While no prayers should be offered to angels, Rev. 19, 10; 22, 8. 9, Christ as the Son of Man, or Christ according to His human nature, should be given divine worship because of the unio personalis, Matt. 16, 16. 17.

Extemporaneous prayers may be abused as much as prayers that are read from prayer-books; if the latter are exposed to the danger of mechanical recital, the former are liable to that of vain repetition, as experience proves. Whenever a Christian prays, he should bear in mind that he is in the presence of the holy, sovereign God, Dan. 9, 18.

With respect to the forms and ceremonies to be observed when a Christian prays, we may quote Luther's directions as in full accord with God's Word. Luther writes (St. L., VIII, 748): "It does not matter whether we stand, kneel, or lie prostrate; for all these, being external matters, are unnecessary since they are neither commanded nor forbidden, as also others, for instance, lifting up the head and eyes to heaven, folding the hands, and smiting upon

one's breast. Yet they should not be despised, since Scripture, yes,
Christ Himself, praises them, Eph. 3, 14; 1 Tim. 2, 8; John 17, 1.
So also it is not wrong if, for instance, one who is binding sheaves
in a field or who is lying in bed should pray only with the heart."

C. THE CHRISTIAN LIFE AND THE HOPE OF ETERNAL LIFE.

The Christian life is lived in constant joyous expectation of
Christ's second and final Advent, Titus 2, 13. (Cp. Luther's great
sermon on this passage; St. L., IX, 930 ff.) As the believers in the
Old Testament always waited for Christ's gracious coming in the
flesh, Luke 1, 67—79; 2, 29—32, so the believers in the New Testament await with true joy and patience His glorious coming to
judge the quick and the dead, Luke 21, 28.

This cheerful, hopeful expectation of the day of Judgment is
a characteristic of the true Christian, 1 Cor. 1, 7; Titus 2, 13;
Phil. 3, 20. According to Scripture, Christians, on the one hand,
"call on the name of the Lord Jesus Christ" (ἐπικαλούμενοι εἰς
τὸ ὄνομα κυρίου Ἰησοῦ Χριστοῦ), Acts 9, 14. 21; 1 Cor. 1, 2;
2 Tim. 2, 22, and, on the other, they "wait for the revelation of our
Lord Jesus Christ" (ἀπεκδεχόμενοι τὴν ἀποκάλυψιν τοῦ κυρίου
Ἰησοῦ Χριστοῦ), 1 Cor. 1, 7.

The precious hope of their perfect final salvation through the
glorious return of their Lord motivates their entire Christian life.
It makes them diligent in the performance of good works, Matt.
24, 45 ff.; 25, 14 ff.; Luke 12, 15 ff.; ardent in the preaching of the
Gospel, Matt. 24, 14; cautious and circumspect in their earthly
life, Titus 2, 12—14; watchful against carnal security, Matt.
24, 36 ff.; satisfied with their pilgrimage on earth, 1 Pet. 2, 11;
Heb. 13, 14; careful in the use of earthly things, 1 Cor. 7, 31;
kind toward all men, Phil. 4, 5; ready at all times to receive the
Lord at His coming, Matt. 25, 1 ff.; unmindful of the tribulations
of their brief earthly life, Rom. 8, 18; joyful in cross-bearing,
Rom. 8, 18; Luke 6, 23; Matt. 5, 12; 1 Pet. 2, 12. 13; and triumphant in death, 1 Thess. 4, 13—18.

In short, the inspiring hope of their Lord's glorious advent
constantly moves them to walk worthy of their high calling in
Christ, Eph. 4, 1 ff.; Col. 1, 10 ff.; 1 Cor. 16, 22; 1 Pet. 4, 7; Jas.
5, 8; Phil. 4, 5. Christians should lead godly lives also in view of
death, Phil. 1, 21—23; Ps. 90, 12; but above all the Christian
life is oriented to the last advent of Christ with its glorious eternal
salvation (sub specie aeternitatis).

It is true, also in hoping, waiting, and living for the glorious return of their Lord, believers are not perfect; therefore they must strive after perfection from day to day. Luther very fittingly calls it a "Christian art and true masterpiece" for a believer "to turn his back upon the world, which is made to pass away, and to keep his view persistently on the future life, which remains eternally and into which he properly belongs."

He writes: "This is rightly taught, but not easily learned; this is truly proclaimed, but not easily believed; this is correctly impressed upon the heart, but not easily followed; this is well said, but not easily done. . . . It is a part of our weakness [of the flesh] that we always fear death, mourn, and doubt if things turn out badly. This is a proof that we do not await the blessed hope as we should."

Again: "If the heart does not direct and prepare itself for that imperishable life, but cleaves to this temporal, perishable life, it does not understand what Baptism, the Gospel, Christ, and faith really mean. We have not been baptized unto this life; we are not called Christians because we are citizens, peasants, lords, servants, maids, rulers, or ruled, laborers, and housekeepers, but we are baptized unto this, and for this purpose we hear the Gospel and believe in Christ, that we may set aside all these vocations . . . and turn from this world to another existence and life, where there is neither lord nor servant, maid nor mistress, woman nor man, but where we are altogether equal and one in Christ Jesus, Gal. 3, 28, which equality begins in this life through faith, but is made perfect in vision in the life to come. . . . Unto this eternal life we are baptized, unto this Christ has purchased us by His death and blood, and for this purpose we have received the Gospel."

THE DOCTRINE OF PRESERVATION.

(De Perseverantia.)

One of the most important questions relating to the Christian life is that concerning the believer's preservation in faith to the end. (Cp. Luther, St. L., IX, 1807.) Our Savior Himself urges us to consider this question when He reminds us of the great truth that only "he that endureth to the end shall be saved," Matt. 10, 22; 24, 13. The emphasis in these passages rests upon the verb *endure,* so that Christ's words are a most earnest exhortation addressed to His followers to endure to the end.

This earnest admonition implies that many do not endure in faith, and that again suggests the weighty query, How can the believer endure in faith unto the end? In answer to this question Holy Scripture stresses two vital facts: 1) All who endure in faith to the end do so alone by divine grace; or we may say, Christian preservation is solely the work of God's omnipotent grace. 2) All who fall from faith do so through their own fault; in other words, the only cause of apostasy is man's wilful rejection of God's Word and his malicious opposition to the operation of the Holy Spirit in the divine Word. These truths must be maintained and defended against both Calvinism and synergism.

a. *Against Calvinism.* Calvinism teaches persistently that it is impossible for those who have once been endowed with faith to lose it again, even if they should commit enormous crimes *(peccata enormia).* Its claim is that, while the exercise of faith *(exercitium fidei)* may cease, faith itself never ceases. Calvin: *Tenendum est, quantumvis exigua sit ac debilis in electis fides, quia tamen Spiritus Dei certa illis arrha est ac sigillum suae adoptionis, nunquam ex eorum cordibus deleri posse eius sculpturam.* (*Inst.,* II, 2, 12.)

The doctrine of the inamissibility of faith is taught by the Calvinists to remove the uncertainty which the individual Reformed believer must feel with respect to his state of grace in view of the fact that he dare not believe in universal grace *(gratia universalis).*

Luther, on the other hand, who affirmed the *gratia universalis,* taught also the Scriptural doctrine of the amissibility of faith, 1 Cor. 10, 12; Luke 8, 13; Is. 1, 2. The *Augsburg Confession* (Art. XII) teaches: "They condemn the Anabaptists, who deny that those once justified can lose the Holy Ghost." Those who were troubled about their state of grace, Luther comforted with the gracious promises of God in Christ Jesus, revealed and offered in the Gospel to all sinners, Titus 2, 11, and not with any "past or present experience of Christ's presence and indwelling in the heart," as the Calvinists do.

Luther's method alone is Scriptural; for not only does the Gospel truly comfort all alarmed sinners, but it is also the divine means by which those who have fallen from grace may be restored to faith in Christ, Rom. 10, 17.

It goes without saying that all who deny the *gratia universalis* are unable to console despairing sinners with the gracious Gospel promises. Since they teach particular grace *(gratia particularis),* it is impossible for them to assure the individual sinner that God's grace is seriously meant for him. By a fortunate inconsistency the practise of Calvinistic preachers is often better than is their theory.

b. *Against synergism.* As the Calvinistic doctrine of final perseverance is unscriptural, so also is that of the *synergists.* While the Calvinists deny the *gratia universalis,* the synergists deny the *sola gratia.* Hence they are compelled to prompt the sinner to rely for salvation, in part at least, on his own worthiness. The statement that "good works are necessary to preserve faith," which the *Formula of Concord* so vigorously rejects, is a real expression of synergistic cooperation. It is synergistic doctrine that, as the sinner must do his share to become a believer, so he also must do his part to persevere in faith. In the final analysis therefore synergism teaches, in common with Calvinism, that the Christian assurance of the believer depends on something in his own heart, be it the experience of Christ's indwelling (Calvinism) or his good conduct, or works (synergism). Both Calvinism and synergism therefore ascribe to man the ability to persevere in faith unto the end.

In contradistinction to this error Holy Scripture affirms that the believer owes his perseverance alone to the grace and power of God. In other words, divine monergism is responsible also for the believer's preservation unto salvation, Phil. 1, 6 ; 1 Pet. 1, 5 ; John 10, 28—30. Scripture thus takes the salvation of the believer out of his own weak and helpless hands and places it into the almighty, faithful hand of God, 1 Thess. 5, 24 ; 2 Thess. 3, 3.

Even while Scripture exhorts Christian believers to work out their salvation with fear and trembling, it assures them at the same time that it is God which "worketh in them both to will and to do of His good pleasure," Phil. 2, 12. 13. Hence this passage cannot be employed in the interest of synergism, since the last clause absolutely excludes every synergistic claim.

The connection between the two verses is quite clear. In the first, the apostle addresses the secure and indifferent, who neglect sanctification; in the second, he reproves the pharisaic spirits, who through their deceitful self-trust make salvation depend on their own power to sanctify themselves. In fact, this self-trust, or self-righteousness, is the real cause why temporary believers lose their faith. In this way Peter fell from faith. His defection occurred because he believed himself capable of greater faith and constancy than his fellow-disciples, Mark 14, 29; and even the earnest admonition of the Lord did not shatter his self-confidence, Mark 14, 30. Peter thus fell through his own sinful self-confidence, and had it not been for divine grace, he never would have regained faith, Luke 22, 32; John 21, 15—17. Synergism, which expressly teaches such self-confidence, is therefore a most pernicious error; it is a doctrine which; consistently followed, must occasion, or lead to, apostasy. Against synergism Luther, in his defense of divine monergism, rightly said that perseverance depends not upon the will of man, but upon the sustaining grace of God *(Perseverantia est non volentis hominis, sed sustentantis Dei)*.

As Calvinism cannot comfort a believer with real assurance of salvation, so also synergism fails to supply the believer with an adequate foundation on which he may rest his hope of everlasting life with certainty. Its consolation is only the sinking sand of the believer's own worthiness. But woe to the person who trusts in that, 1 Cor. 4, 4! In fact, he who trusts in his own works for salvation has fallen from grace, Gal. 5, 4, and is under the curse of God, Gal. 3, 10. On the other hand, the Scriptural truth that we are kept by God's power through faith unto salvation, 1 Pet. 1, 5, affords the believer abiding comfort even in the severest trials; for he knows that in the hands of almighty God his salvation is absolutely secure. The doctrine of the *sola gratia* not only produces, but also strengthens and preserves, true Christian faith.

Some synergistic theologians have claimed that divine grace and power indeed preserve the believer's faith against all external foes, but not against his own flesh (Meyer, Philippi). But this claim is void of Scriptural foundation. When Christ assured His disciples that "no one shall pluck them out of His hands," John 10, 28. 29, this promise certainly included the foe within as much as that without. So also the other promises of Scripture regarding perseverance are universal in their scope, Phil. 1, 6; 1 Pet. 1, 3—5; 5, 10; 2 Thess. 3, 3. Hence the Christian believer should be assured that, as God did not omit anything to prepare salvation for him, so also He omits nothing by which this salvation is *finaliter* attained. In other words, divine grace relates not only to justification and sanctification, but also to the perseverance of the believer unto eternal salvation.

Doubts regarding salvation arise only when men intermingle Law and Gospel, that is to say, when they apply the Scripture-passages that are meant as a warning against carnal security, 1 Cor. 10, 12; Rom. 11, 20, to penitent sinners, who in the anguish of their hearts cry out for the comfort of the Gospel, Rom. 7, 24, or when they urge despairing souls to assure themselves of salvation by their good works. Penitent sinners who long for comfort should listen to no other message than that of God's justifying, sanctifying, and preserving grace, Matt. 11, 28; Is. 55, 1—3.

The warnings set forth in Holy Scripture against defection, 1 Cor. 10, 12; Rom. 11, 20. 21; Heb. 3, 12, etc., enforced by examples of temporary believers (Saul, Demas) do not militate against the blessed assurance of the Gospel that God will graciously keep the believer in faith to the end, Phil. 1, 6, but rather sustain it. These warnings belong to the Law and must not be misused to nullify the Gospel promises. St. Paul, though aware of the possibility of his becoming a castaway, 1 Cor. 9, 27, was nevertheless fully persuaded of his perseverance, Rom. 8, 38. 39; 2 Tim. 4, 7. God warns us against defection through the Law in order that we may beware of carnal security, which destroys the certainty of salvation, and cling to the Gospel, which bestows and nourishes the assurance of salvation.

The precious Gospel truth concerning the certainty of the believer's salvation does not engender spiritual pride, but fosters true humility and suppresses the carnal security of the flesh. Also with the growth of the believer's certainty of salvation his gratitude toward God and his zeal in good works increase, and these are divine blessings which both despair and carnal security destroy.

Since it has pleased God to bestow His grace upon men by the means of grace, it is self-evident that the believer will persevere in faith only if he faithfully uses the divine means of grace (the Word and the Sacraments). Christians who desire to remain steadfast in their faith and sure of their salvation must therefore continually dwell in the sanctuary of sanctuaries, the divine Word, where God offers and imparts to them constant grace and strength for abiding with Christ in true faith, Rom. 1, 16; 10, 17; John 8, 31. 32. 51.   To the diligent and conscientious use of the Word of God must be joined also ceaseless, ardent prayer, John 16, 23. 24; Matt. 26, 41; Eph. 6, 17. 18; 1 Thess. 5, 17, since God has promised to bestow His blessings only upon those who continue in prayer, Luke 11, 13; Jas. 1, 5. 6; 4, 2.

With respect to the question *(crux theologorum),* "Why do not all believers persevere in faith" *(Cur alii, alii non)?* the Christian theologian has no other answer than that given in Hos. 13, 9. Those who persevere in faith do so alone by divine grace; those who fall from faith must blame themselves for their apostasy (unbelief; self-righteousness; malicious neglect or rejection of the means of grace).   If a comparison is instituted between two individual persons, such as Saul and David, Judas and Peter, the Christian theologian at this point humbly acknowledges a mystery which he is incapable of explaining, since Scripture itself does not answer the perplexing question why Saul perished in unbelief and David repented or why Judas died in despair and Peter was rescued from perdition.

The advice of the *Formula of Concord* with regard to this matter is Scriptural and sound (Thor. Decl., XI, 57—63): "As regards these things in this disputation which would soar too high and beyond these limits, we should with Paul place the finger upon our lips and remember and say, Rom. 9, 20: 'O man, who art thou that repliest against God?'"

THE DOCTRINE OF THE MEANS OF GRACE.
(De Mediis Gratiae.)

---

1. DEFINITION OF THE TERM.

In order to offer and convey to men the merits which Christ has secured for the world by His death on the cross, 2 Cor. 5, 21; Rom. 5, 18, God employs certain external, visible means through which the Holy Spirit works and preserves faith and thus accomplishes the sinner's salvation.

That is the clear teaching of our Confessions. The *Formula of Concord* thus writes (XI, 76): "The Father will not do this [draw any one to Himself] without means, but has ordained for this purpose His Word and Sacraments as ordinary means and instruments." The *Smalcald Articles* (Part II, Art. VIII, 3): "In those things which concern the spoken, outward Word we must firmly hold that God grants His Spirit or grace to no one except through or with the preceding outward Word." The *Augsburg Confession* (Art. V, 2): "They [our churches] condemn the Anabaptists and others who think that the Holy Ghost comes to men without the external Word, through their own preparations and works."

Our dogmaticians define the means of grace as "*media externa a Deo ordinata, quibus Deus gratiam a Christo acquisitam hominibus offert et fidem ad gratiam accipiendam necessariam in hominibus efficit et conservat.*" As divinely ordained means of grace they acknowledge, on the basis of Scripture, only the Word (the Gospel) and the Sacraments, Baptism and the Lord's Supper, the latter two as the visible Word *(Verbum visibile).*

According to Scripture these divinely ordained means have a twofold function or power, namely, a) an exhibiting, offering, or conferring power *(vis exhibitiva, dativa, collativa)* and b) an effective, or operative, power *(vis effectiva sive operativa).* The first consists in this, that the Holy Spirit through the means of grace earnestly offers to those who hear or read the Word the grace of God *(Dei favor)* and the righteousness of Christ *(meritum Christi);* the second, that He through the means of grace actually works, strengthens, and preserves in the hearts of men a living faith in the gracious forgiveness of their sins, so that they are converted, justified, sanctified, and finally glorified.   For this reason we rightly call the means of grace *media communicationis remissionis peccatorum sive iustificationis ex parte Dei.*

This doctrine of the means of grace the conceited reason of man has corrupted in a twofold manner. On the one hand, it has declared that means of grace are unnecessary for salvation (Zwinglianism: The Holy Spirit requires no wagon [*vehiculum*] for His divine operations); and, on the other, it has added to the two Sacraments ordained by Christ additional sacraments (Romanism: penance, confirmation, marriage, the ordination of priests, extreme unction). In the final analysis every perversion of the doctrine of the means of grace is made in the interest of the doctrine of work-righteousness.

2. THE MEANS OF GRACE IN GENERAL.

The doctrine of the means of grace is understood properly only when it is considered in the light of Christ's redemptive work *(satisfactio vicaria)* and the objective justification, or reconciliation, 2 Cor. 5, 19. 20, which He secured by His substitutionary obedience *(satisfactio vicaria).* If these two doctrines are corrupted (Calvinism: denial of *gratia universalis;* synergism: denial of *sola gratia*), then also the Scripture doctrine of the means of grace will become perverted. Calvinism thus regards the means of grace as unnecessary; synergistic rationalism (Arminianism), as mere incentives for virtuous efforts to obtain salvation. Hence, if the doctrine of the means of grace is to remain intact, the entire doctrine of the vicarious redemption of Christ must be taught in its Scriptural truth and purity. This becomes evident as we study the doctrine of the means of grace in detail.

According to Holy Scripture the preeminent means of grace is the Word of Reconciliation, 2 Cor. 5, 19, or the Gospel of Christ, Rom. 1, 16. The divine Law, or the immutable will of God, though in itself it is the inspired Word of God no less than the Gospel, nevertheless is not a means of grace, since it offers to the sinner only wrath and condemnation, Gal. 3, 10, not grace and the forgiveness of sins. In contradistinction to the Gospel, which is properly "the ministration of righteousness," 2 Cor. 3, 9, the Law is the "ministration of condemnation" *(ibid.).* For this reason the divine Law is rightly excluded from the means of grace.

The Gospel is a means of grace, not only inasmuch as it offers grace to the sinner, but also because it actually absolves him from all sins. Luther very correctly says: "The Gospel is a general absolution; for it is a promise which, according to God's will and command, all in general and every one in particular should accept." (St. L., XXI b, 1849.)

Moreover, the Gospel is a true means of grace in every form in which it is presented to the sinner, no matter whether it is preached publicly (Mark 16, 15. 16; Luke 24, 47), or whether it is read (John 20, 31; 1 John 1, 3. 4); whether it is directly pronounced as an absolution, either in public or in private (John 20, 23; 2 Cor. 2, 10: "To whom ye forgive anything, I forgive also") or expressed by a symbol (John 3, 14. 15; crucifix), or whether it is considered in the heart (Luke 2, 51; Rom. 10, 8), etc. In short, no matter how the Gospel is brought before the minds of men, it is always a true means of grace, offering to them, and conferring upon them, the grace of God through faith in Christ Jesus.

Some modern theologians have argued that the Gospel is effective only when it is proclaimed or preached (the Dorpat school; Volck, etc.); but the passage on which they base their contention (Rom. 10, 17) does not support their claim, since the words "by hearing" (ἐξ ἀκοῆς) do not exclude other modes of receiving the divine Word, John 20, 31; 1 John 1, 4. The Word of God is always efficacious when it is applied, because it is spirit and life, John 6, 63. Our old dogmaticians rightly say that the Word is supernaturally endowed with efficacy, that is to say, it has an active, supernatural, and truly divine force or power of producing supernatural effects, *i. e.,* of converting, regenerating, and renewing the minds of men. (*Doctr. Theol.,* p. 501.)

This supernatural power, which must not be compared with the natural force which inheres in every human word and especially in every eloquent human discourse, is always inherent in the divine Word, because the Holy Spirit is indissolubly connected with it, so that we must never regard the divine Word as being without divine efficacy or as being in itself a "lifeless instrument" which the Holy Spirit employs efficaciously only under certain conditions, whenever it pleases Him.

On the contrary, wherever the divine Word is, there also is the divine Spirit; and whenever a person uses the Word of God in any form, God is divinely operative in it, 1 Cor. 2, 4. God's operation upon a person who reads the written Word is therefore not an "operation from a distance" *(actio in distantia),* but an operation which is directly mediated through the divine Word

(Rom. 10, 17: πίστις ἐξ ἀκοῆς). Christ Himself commands us not
only to hear the Gospel, but also to "search the Scriptures," John
5, 39. 46, thus asserting efficacy of the Word also when it is
being read.

With regard to the efficacy of the divine Word and the power
of the Holy Spirit, who works through the Word, Quenstedt writes
(I, 183) : "The Holy Ghost does not by Himself do something and
the Word of God by itself something else, but they produce the
one effect by one and the same action." That is Scripture doctrine,
Rom. 1, 16; 1 Cor. 2, 4.

Since God has connected His most gracious promise of forgiveness with Baptism and the Lord's Supper, these also are true
and efficacious means of grace, namely, by virtue of the divine
promises that are attached to them.

Of Baptism, Scripture teaches expressly that it is "for the
remission of sins," εἰς ἄφεσιν ἁμαρτιῶν, Acts 2, 38, and "for the
washing away of sins," ἀπόλουσαι ἁμαρτίας, Acts 22, 16; Eph.
5, 26; 1 Cor. 6, 11.

In the Lord's Supper Christ offers to the communicant the
body and blood shed for the remission of sins, Luke 22, 19. 20;
Matt. 26, 26—28, so that also in this Sacrament we have God's
gracious offer of pardon for the sake of Him who died and shed
His blood as a ransom for sinners.

Since the sacred actions of Baptism and the Lord's Supper,
to which the divine promises are attached, can be perceived by
the eye, they are called the "visible Word" (Verbum visibile), or
"Sacraments."

The Apology explains this expression correctly when it says
(Art. XIII [VII], 5) : "These rites have God's command and the
promise of grace, which is peculiar to the New Testament. For
when we are baptized, when we eat the Lord's body, when we are
absolved, our hearts must be firmly assured that God truly forgives
us for Christ's sake. . . . But just as the Word enters the ear
in order to strike our heart, so the rite itself strikes the eye in
order to move the heart. The effect of the Word and of the rite
is the same, as it has been well said by Augustine that a Sacrament
is a visible word, because the rite is perceived by the eyes and is,
as it were, a picture of the Word, signifying the same thing as
the Word."

In order that we may rightly understand the doctrine of the
Sacraments, we must bear in mind that all means of grace have

THE DOCTRINE OF THE MEANS OF GRACE.

the same purpose and effect; that is to say, on the one hand, they offer to men God's gracious forgiveness of sins *(vis collativa);* on the other, they engender and strengthen faith *(vis effectiva).*

The divine pardon proclaimed in the Gospel is therefore the same as that offered and conveyed by Baptism or the Lord's Supper, so that we do not obtain one-third of God's forgiveness through the Gospel, another third through Baptism, and a last third through Holy Communion. Scripture expressly describes the whole forgiveness of sins which God purposes to give to sinners for Christ's sake as mediated through the Gospel, Rom. 1, 16, or through Baptism, Acts 2, 38; 22, 16, or, again, through the Lord's Supper, Matt. 26, 28.

In short, by whatever means God offers grace to men, He always offers His entire grace and not merely a part of it, so that every means of grace instituted by God conveys to the believer His full forgiveness with life and salvation. The *Augsburg Confession* (Art. V) says: "For through the Word and Sacraments, as through instruments, the Holy Ghost is given, who works faith when and where it pleases God." For this reason it is unscriptural to attribute to the various means of grace specific functions in an exclusive sense, as, for example, to Baptism the working of regeneration, to Holy Communion the implanting of the resurrection body, and even physical benefits.

It is true, Holy Scripture indeed ascribes to Baptism the power of regeneration, for it calls this Sacrament "a washing of regeneration and renewing of the Holy Ghost," Titus 3, 5; but it ascribes the same regeneration also to the Gospel, 1 Pet. 1, 23: "Being born again by the Word of God," and no less to Holy Communion, Matt. 26, 28: "This is My blood, shed for the remission of sins," since it is the gracious assurance of the forgiveness of sins that works regeneration. The *Augsburg Confession* (Art. XIII) therefore teaches that "the Sacraments were ordained to be signs and testimonies to *awaken* and *confirm* faith in those who use them," the same as the Gospel itself. (Cp. *Apology,* Art. XIII [VII], 3—5.

All who deny that the Sacraments offer to the sinner the same grace and pardon that are proffered to him in the Gospel pervert the Scriptural doctrine of the means of grace and, in particular, that of the Sacraments. Those who ascribe to the Sacraments a lesser or partial grace do so in the Calvinistic interest of reducing the value of the Sacraments ("Sacraments are mere signs or memorials"), while those who ascribe to them "a physical operation" do this in the interest of the Romanistic error of an operation without faith, or *ex opere operato, sine bono motu utentis.*

According to the Calvinistic conception the means of grace are not necessary for salvation; according to the papistic view the Sacraments require no receiving means (*medium ληπτικόν*) on the part of the sinner, since grace is infused by mere physical contact with the Sacrament. Both errors equally corrupt the comforting doctrine of Scripture regarding the divine way of applying to the sinner the forgiveness of sins which Christ has secured for him by His perfect obedience. Calvinism substitutes for the Scriptural way (through means, by faith) the man-made way *of faith without means* (faith through immediate divine operation), while Romanism substitutes the man-made way *of means without faith (operation by physical contact, ex opere operato).*

In both cases God's application of forgiveness to the sinner (through the means of grace, by faith) is obstructed by man-made impediments; for in the first instance God's conferring means (*media δοτικά*) are removed, and in the second, faith, or man's receiving means (*medium ληπτικόν*), is taken away, so that in neither case God's forgiveness is received by the sinner.

If, despite their errors, Reformed and papistic believers do receive forgiveness of sins, it is only because they, by the grace of God, correct their unscriptural theory by a Scriptural practise. In other words, the Reformed believer, in spite of the false Calvinistic teaching, faithfully clings to, and uses, the means of grace, while the papistic believer, in spite of the pernicious *ex-opere-operato* doctrine, confides in the gracious promises which are conveyed to him in the means of grace. (Cp. *Apology,* Art. XIII [VII], 18—23.)

When we consider the relation of faith to the means of grace, we must bear in mind that faith is not an essential part of the means of grace, nor does their efficacy depend on faith. The blessed promise of the means of grace always stands, and their power remains unimpaired, despite the unbelief of man. Yet the means of grace and faith are correlatives. The *Apology* says (Art. XIII [VII], 20): "The promise is useless unless it is received by faith." This truth we must hold against the Reformed. (Cp. Hodge: "The efficacy of the Sacraments is not due to their inherent virtue, but is conditioned on the presence of faith in the recipient." *Syst. Theol.,* III, 501.) Hodge should have said: "The Sacraments do

THE DOCTRINE OF THE MEANS OF GRACE.

not profit without faith, since faith is the receiving means of their promises and blessings."

If the question is put, "Why did God ordain so many means of grace when one suffices to confer upon the sinner His grace and forgiveness?" we quote the reply of Luther who writes *(Smalcald Articles,* IV) : "The Gospel not merely in one way gives us counsel and aid against sin; for God is superabundantly rich in His grace. First through the spoken Word, by which the forgiveness of sins is preached in the whole world, which is the peculiar office of the Gospel. Secondly through Baptism. Thirdly through the holy Sacrament of the Altar. Fourthly through the power of the keys and also through the mutual conversation and consolation of brethren, Matt. 18, 20."

The Scriptural explanation that "God is superabundantly rich in His grace" should induce us gratefully to consider and use *all* the means of grace with equal esteem and keep us from perverting the doctrine of the means of grace by setting one against the other or by denying the necessity of any or all of them. Also in the corruption of the doctrine of the means of grace the conceited reason of man reveals its ingrained blindness and perversity.

With respect to the number of the Sacraments there can be no controversy among theologians as long as they adhere to Scripture as the only rule of faith. If by the term *sacrament* we mean a sacred act in which the divine *command* and *promise* are attached to visible signs, or elements, prescribed by God Himself, there are only two Sacraments, namely, Baptism and the Lord's Supper. To these two sacred acts the term *sacrament* ought to be confined, since otherwise confusion is bound to follow.

The additional "sacraments" of the Roman and Eastern Catholic churches (confirmation, penance, ordination of priests, marriage, extreme unction) are not commanded in Scripture; in their perverted forms (Catholic penance, for example, is not Scriptural repentance) they are "commandments of men," Matt. 15, 9, and therefore "vain worship." Marriage, which likewise is a "Catholic sacrament," is indeed instituted by God, but to it is attached only the promise of propagation, Gen. 1, 28, not that of forgiveness of sins.

In conclusion, we may say that, since the term *sacrament* is a *vox ἄγραφος,* or only an ecclesiastical term *(vox ecclesiastica),* it must not be taken amiss if orthodox teachers who adhere to the principle of Scripture *(principium cognoscendi)* occasionally em-

ploy the expression in a wider sense, as, for example, the *Apology*
does (Art. XIII [VII], 4 ff.) : "Therefore Baptism, the Lord's
Supper, and Absolution, which is the Sacrament of Repentance, are
truly Sacraments."

In this *wider* use the term *sacrament* comprises all "rites which
have the command of God and to which the promise of grace has
been added." (*Ibid.*, 3.) In other words, the visible, divinely prescribed earthly elements (water, bread, and wine) are in that case
not regarded as *essential* parts of a sacrament. Since absolution has
both a divine command and a promise, it may be called a sacrament
in a wider sense.

However, to avoid confusion, our dogmaticians discourage the
use of the term *sacrament* in this case, and they consistently speak
only of two Sacraments, namely, Baptism and the Lord's Supper.
So also our Confessions speak whenever they employ the term in
its strict, or real, meaning.

3. ERRONEOUS DOCTRINES REGARDING THE MEANS OF GRACE.

The Scriptural doctrine of the means of grace has been grossly
perverted by Romanists, Calvinists, and synergistic (Arminian-
istic) rationalists. On account of the importance of the matter we
shall consider their outstanding errors in detail.

a. *The error of Romanism.* Romanism indeed teaches that
Christ by His death has secured grace for sinners. Hence it
emphatically rejects the doctrine that a sinner may be justified and
saved "without divine grace through Christ" (Council of Trent,
Sess. VI, Cans. 1. 2. 3. 10. 22). According to papistic doctrine this
divine grace, secured by Christ, is designed for all men, so that
the Council of Trent repudiates without reserve the particular grace
(gratia particularis) of Calvinism (Sess. VI, Can. 17).

In view of these facts the Roman Catholic Church ought to
espouse the Lutheran doctrine of justification by grace through
faith in Christ's vicarious atonement; yet Rome has expressly
anathematized this cardinal doctrine of the Christian Church.

To understand this attitude, we must remember what Roman
Catholic theologians understand by the terms "divine grace," "justifying grace," etc. According to papistic doctrine, Christ died for
the sins of the world in order that God can infuse into the sinner
(with his own constant cooperation) so much grace *(gratia infusa)*
that he is enabled truly to merit justification and salvation

(Council of Trent, Sess. VI, Cans. 4. 32) either *de congruo* (by desiring, or striving after, the good) or *de condigno* (by actually accomplishing meritorious works). In other words, according to Roman Catholic doctrine, Christ has secured for sinners so much grace that they by divine gracious assistance (infusion of divine powers) can earn salvation themselves.

From this it follows that according to Roman Catholic doctrine the *media gratiae* are not divinely appointed means by which God offers and conveys to the sinner by faith the entire obedience of Christ, but rather means by which the sinner through infused grace is put into a position to earn salvation by his own efforts. The entire doctrine of the means of grace is thus perverted in the interest of work-righteousness.

However, since reliance on works always leaves a sinner uncertain with regard to his state of grace and salvation (and such uncertainty Rome declares to be a particular Christian virtue; Council of Trent, Sess. VI, Cap. 9, Can. 13), the number of "sacraments" has been multiplied (confirmation, penance, ordination, marriage, extreme unction), so that the sinner through *many* "sacraments" may receive the maximum of *gratia infusa* and so multiply works for salvation (Council of Trent, Sess. VII, Cans. 3. 4).

Especially the "sacrament of penance" is designed for the production of good works on a large scale (crusades, pilgrimages, indulgences, monkery, etc.). In fact, there is no limit to the good works which a Catholic may do by diligently using the "sacrament of penance." Yet despite all these works he may never be sure of salvation, in consequence of which his Christian life remains a perpetual striving after salvation by means of good works. Even the Sacraments cannot give him comfort in his trouble of sin; for though they are said to "infuse grace," and this *ex opere operato, sine bono motu utentis* (of themselves, without any good intention on the part of the recipient), they do not impart forgiveness of sins, life, and salvation. The Romanistic doctrine of the Sacraments is therefore a radical perversion of the Scriptural doctrine of the means of grace.

b. *The error of Calvinism.* Since Calvinism denies the *gratia universalis* and insists that the grace of God in Christ Jesus is particular *(gratia particularis),* that is, designed for, and confined to, a limited number of men (the elect), it is obliged to teach that there are no real means of grace for the non-elect. On the

contrary, for all those whom God has predestinated to eternal condemnation the means of grace become "means of damnation," as
Calvin asserts. *"Est universalis vocatio, qua per externam Verbi
praedicationem omnes pariter ad se invitat Deus, etiam quibus
eam in mortis odorem et gravioris condemnationis materiam pro-
ponit."* (*Inst.,* III, 24, 8.)

It is true, Calvin ascribes the damnation of the non-elect also
to their own rejection of divine grace, which is offered to them in
the "universal call" of God through the preaching of the external
Word; but this is one of the many inconsistencies of Calvinistic
soteriology. In reality, according to the Calvinistic view, there
is no divine grace for the non-elect, and hence there is no occasion
for them to despise or reject it. He writes: "Only the elect experience the inward power of the Spirit and receive, in addition to
the outward signs, also the *res* or *virtus sacramenti."* (*Inst.,* III,
24, 15; *Consens. Tigur.,* c. 16.)

In short, according to Calvin there is no saving grace for the
non-elect, even though at times he charges the *reprobi* and *impii*
with rejection of divine grace. In Calvin's case this mode of speech
is only a meaningless repetition of the language of orthodox Christianity, which rightly speaks of a rejection of divine grace on the
part of the *improbi* and *impii,* since on the basis of Scripture it
teaches that divine grace is universal and the divine call to salvation therefore serious. Grace can be rejected by men only in case
it is seriously offered to all *(vocatio seria),* as our dogmaticians
have always pointed out.

However, in the final analysis, Calvinism acknowledges no
means of grace even for the *elect.* Calvin distinctly advises the
believer not to judge his election and salvation according to the
universal Gospel call *(vocatio universalis),* which is extended
through the external Word *(per externam praedicationem),* but
only according to the special call *(vocatio specialis),* which consists in *inward illumination* by the Holy Ghost. From the strict
Calvinistic point of view this direction is quite consistent, since
even true believers dare not build their hope of salvation on the
call and promise of the Word; for this is extended also to the
non-elect as "a savor of death unto death" and might therefore
deceive them. Consequently the Reformed *pii* and *electi* have no
other way of judging their election and salvation than that of
the inward illumination of the Holy Ghost *(interior Spiritus
illuminatio),* or of infused grace.

However, even this inward illumination of the believer occurs, according to the Calvinistic view, not through the preaching of the Gospel, but immediately. ("In the working of regeneration all second causes are excluded." — "The infusion of a new life into the soul is the immediate work of the Spirit." — "The truth [the Gospel] attends the work of regeneration, but is not the means by which it is effected." Hodge, *Syst. Theol.*, II, 684 sq.)

From this it follows that Calvinism can recognize no means of grace by which God offers and seals salvation to men and engenders faith or works regeneration. In other words, Calvinism must reject the means of grace as "second causes," or means by which regeneration is effected. Its denial of the *gratia universalis* consistently destroys the Scriptural doctrine of the means of grace, leaving no signs and testimonies whatever *(signa et testimonia)* of God's gracious will toward the sinner by which faith is created or strengthened.

It is true, Calvinism speaks of the Word and the Sacraments also as "signs," "symbols," etc., of divine grace *(signa, symbola, tesserae, sigilla; Conf. Helv., II, c. 19; Conf. Belgica, Art. 33).* But as long as it holds that divine grace is particular and that the same signs may be "signs of salvation" and "signs of condemnation," the believer must forever remain in doubt regarding his state of grace, since he cannot determine whether the *signum* or *sigillum* in his case means salvation or damnation. Hence he is obliged to put his hope for salvation in the *interior illuminatio,* or in the inward illumination of his heart; and that, after all, is nothing else than the *gratia infusa.*

However, the case is still more serious. The Calvinistic denial of universal grace and of the Scriptural doctrine of the means of grace destroys also the Scriptural doctrine of saving *faith* and saving *grace.* A faith that does not rely solely on the gracious promises of the Gospel is not true faith in the sense of Scripture, but only a mere fancy *(Einbildung).* According to the express teaching of the Bible saving faith is engendered through the preaching of the Gospel and consists essentially in reliance upon the Gospel promises, Rom. 10, 17; Mark 1, 15; 16, 15. 16. Every other kind of trust is confidence in a man-made foundation and therefore a fictitious faith.

But right here Calvinism and Romanism meet to disavow the Scripture doctrine of saving faith. Romanism, on account of its rejection of the *sola gratia,* is forced to trust in infused grace *(gratia infusa, i. e.,* sanctification, good works) for salvation; Calvinism, on account of its rejection of the *gratia universalis,* is likewise compelled to trust in sanctification for assurance of salvation *(interior illuminatio).* Romanism makes the mistake of claiming that divine grace is infused into the sinner *ex opere operato,* or without faith on the part of man; Calvinism makes the equally great mistake of teaching that the Holy Spirit works regeneration or faith immediately, or without the means of grace. The departure from Scripture in either case is evident and, consistently maintained, makes saving faith impossible, since it assigns to it a false foundation, *sc. gratia Dei in nobis,* or the sanctified heart.

However, saving faith and saving grace are correlatives, and he who perverts the one is bound to pervert also the other. As Romanism and Calvinism pervert the doctrine of saving faith by resting faith upon a good quality in man, so they also pervert the doctrine of saving grace *(gratia salvifica).* Both regard saving grace not as God's gracious disposition toward the sinner for Christ's sake *(Dei favor gratuitus),* but rather as God's gracious sanctifying operation in the heart, known in the one case as *gratia infusa* (Romanism) and in the other as *interior illuminatio* (Calvinism).

This is true despite the fact that many Reformed theologians expressly state that the object of the sinner's trust is the *Dei favor gratuitus.* What they teach in theory they retract in practise, especially whenever they are obliged to comfort a sinner who is alarmed about his state of grace. Since they deny universal grace and the objective reconciliation of the whole world through the death of Christ, they must point the sinner who is looking for assurance of salvation to divine grace as this is active in his heart, or to "the present experience of Christ's presence and indwelling, corroborated by active service and purity of life" (Strong). For additional assurance they point, moreover, to the supposed fact that the Holy Ghost, once granted to the believer, can never be lost. But both these doctrines are man-made, and so the assurance of salvation derived from them is likewise man-made and therefore nugatory and vain.

c. *The error of synergism.* What has been said of Romanistic Semi-Pelagianism may be said also of synergism (Arminianism). Romanism denies the *sola gratia;* synergism does the same. Both ascribe salvation in part to the virtuous efforts of man to apply himself to, or to decide for, grace. And though neither synergism nor Arminianism regards the means of grace as working *ex opere operato,* yet they both consider them, not simply as God's conferring means (*media δοτιχά*), **by which He** graciously offers salvation and engenders and strengthens faith, but rather as incentives by which the sinner is induced to convert himself through the divine powers communicated to him.

But here again it must be said that a faith which does not trust exclusively in the grace of God for Christ's sake is not true faith in the sense of Scripture, Gal. 5, 4; 3, 10, but the very opposite of faith, namely, wilful repudiation of the Gospel, Rom. 4, 4. 5. In its final result therefore also synergism perverts the doctrine of the means of grace and renders saving faith impossible.

d. It is almost superfluous to mention the fact that all errorists who deny the vicarious satisfaction of Christ (*satisfactio vicaria*) cannot teach the Scriptural doctrine of the means of grace. Since they refuse to accept the reconciliation secured by Christ's substitutionary death, they are obliged to reconcile God by "trying to keep the commandments of God," and this leaves no room for any divine means of grace as *media remissionis peccatorum sive iustificationis,* Eph. 1, 7; Gal. 5, 4. Modernism is paganism, veiled by, and decked with, Christian terminology, which destroys the very heart of the Christian religion, namely, justification by grace through faith in the atoning blood of Christ, Rom. 3, 23—28.

e. What is true of Modernism is true to a great extent also of enthusiasm, or the belief that the Holy Spirit works outside of, and apart from, the divinely ordained means of grace (*extra illud enthusiasticum*)

This error presents itself in many different forms. One form is that of Zwinglianism: "The Holy Spirit requires no wagon (*vehiculum*) to enter, and work in, the hearts of men; hence faith is not the fruit of the Gospel, but of the immediately working Spirit" (*immediate operantis Spiritus*). Quakerism is another and more extreme form of enthusiasm: "God gives His Spirit without the means of His Word, so that even those may be saved who have never heard of the historic Christ." But the error of enthusiasm is advocated also by those modern theologians who teach that faith may be awakened through "the person of Christ" or His "historical manifestation" (*"die geschichtliche Erscheinung"*), apart from the Gospel-message of His vicarious death. Saving faith certainly trusts in the historic Christ, but the historic Christ is the Christ of the gospels, who shed His blood on the cross for the sins of the world, 1 John 1, 7; Gal. 3, 13; 2, 20. And this Christ, the only Savior of sinners, whose merits are earnestly offered to all men in the means of grace, modern rationalistic theology rejects.

That modern experimentalism (experience-theology; *Erlebnistheologie*) is enthusiasm pure and simple requires no further proof. A faith that is not engendered by the Holy Ghost through the means of grace is not true faith, but self-delusion, 1 Tim. 6, 3. 4. The different forms of enthusiasm (Muenzer, Zwingli, Hodge, the Pietists, modern experimentalists) differ not in kind, but only in degree. When modern experimentalists say: "The Christian lives not by the means of grace, but through the personal fellowship with God which he experiences in Christ" (A. Harnack); or: "The man who is inwardly overcome by the power of the person of Jesus experiences in this same inner transaction God's forgiveness of his sins" (W. Hermann), they prove by these clear statements that they reject the means of grace just as all other enthusiasts reject them. Faith is indeed an experience; but it is the Gospel that must produce this faith, or this experience, John 8, 31. 32; 17, 20. Whenever men look for the grace of God outside the Gospel, they overthrow the very foundation of faith.

Among the arguments by which enthusiasts of all types have attempted to justify their disavowal of the means of grace, we may note the following: —

a. The means of grace are superfluous, since the Holy Spirit requires no means (Zwingli: *dux vel vehiculum*) to enter and work in man's heart. *Answer:* Holy Scripture clearly teaches that the Holy Spirit will ordinarily not deal with men without means, John 17, 20; Rom. 10, 17; Eph. 2, 20; etc.

b. Since regeneration is the work of God's almighty power, it cannot be effected through means. *Answer:* Holy Scripture teaches that regeneration is the work of God's almighty power working through means, Eph. 1, 19; Rom. 10, 17; Titus 3, 5. For this reason Hodge should not write: "If the Gospel and the Sacraments save, it is no longer God who saves." (*Syst. Theol.*, II, 683. 685. Cp. the following *reductio ad absurdum:* "If bread sustains life, it is no longer God who sustains life.")

c. It is an unworthy conception of God to regard Him as bound to means when dealing with men. *Answer:* Since it has pleased God to employ means both in the realm of nature and that of grace, it is unbecoming to us to judge Him.

d. If God actually operated through means of grace, then all to whom the means are applied would have to be saved. *Answer:* This argument does not hold since grace, operating through means, can be resisted, Matt. 23, 37; Acts 7, 51.

e. The means of grace are superfluous since saving faith rests on Christ. *Answer:* We admit that saving faith rests on Christ; but unless faith rests on the means of grace, it does not rest on Christ, John 8, 31. 32; 17, 20; 1 Tim. 6, 3ff.

f. Many rely upon the fact that they are baptized and thus sink into carnal security. *Answer:* In spite of this fact Scripture teaches the efficacy of Baptism, Acts 2, 38; 1 Pet. 3, 21.

g. Holy Scripture teaches that we are saved alone by faith in Christ; therefore Baptism does not regenerate. (Cp. Hodge, *Syst. Theol.*, III, 1600.) *Answer:* Scripture teaches both: Faith saves, and Baptism saves. The two statements do not exclude, but include each other.

h. The passage John 3, 8 is opposed to the doctrine of the means of grace. *Answer:* This passage describes the mysterious character of the work of the Holy Spirit, but it does not say that the Holy Spirit works without means; cp. v. 5; John 6, 45; Eph. 3, 6; 1 Pet. 1, 23; John 17, 20.

Enthusiasts thus pit their rationalist conceptions of what is possible and proper for God to do against the clear Scripture-passages which assert that God has appointed and uses the means of grace for the powerful operation of His grace, Is. 55, 11; Jer. 23, 29; Acts 2, 38; 20, 32; Rom. 10, 17; 1 Pet. 1, 23; 3, 21, etc. (Cp. Dr. Engelder, *Dogmatical Notes.*)

The Scriptural doctrine of the means of grace is of such weighty importance that all Christians have reason to examine themselves whether on this point "they are in the faith," 2 Cor. 13, 5. If Christians neglect the means of grace (the hearing of the Word and the use of the Sacraments), they are in danger of falling from faith and losing their salvation, John 8, 43—47. All Christians, too, are constantly threatened by self-righteousness, since the *opinio legis* by nature inheres in their flesh, Gal. 3, 1—3. Also with respect to the doctrine of the means of grace Christ's earnest admonition "Watch and pray that ye enter not into temptation," Matt. 26, 41, must be constantly heeded.

In the Lutheran Church the *Pietists* directed the alarmed sinner not to the Word and the Sacraments, but to their own prayers and wrestlings with God in order that he might win his way into a state of grace. They also instructed the believer to base his assurance of grace not on the objective promise of the Gospel, but on the right quality of his contrition and faith and on his *feeling* of grace. In both cases they taught Reformed (enthusiastic) doctrine. Moreover, because they based salvation on what is really a *gratia infusa,* they championed papistic doctrine. (Cp. Luther, St. L., XI, 453 ff.; XIX, 943 ff.)

As we warn our hearers against the subjectivism of the sects, which makes the validity of the divine pardon offered in the means of grace and their efficacy dependent on the hearer's subjective attitude, we must strenuously uphold the objective nature of salvation, that is to say, the objectivity and reality of the vicarious atonement, as not being conditioned on any act of man and the objective nature of the means of grace as offering forgiveness of sins outright to men and exercising their power in every case where they are applied. What Dr. Walther writes on this point deserves our constant, diligent attention. He says: "The characteristic feature of our dear Evangelical Lutheran Church is her objectivity, which means that all her doctrines by their very nature keep man from seeking salvation in himself, in his own powers, aspiration, performance, and condition and lead him to seek his salvation outside of himself, while the characteristic feature of all other churches is their subjectivity, they all leading man to ground his salvation upon himself." (Cp. *Lehre und Wehre,* 36, 19.) By nature all men are enthusiasts, and it is only through the diligent use of the means of grace that the believer obtains strength to overcome the temptation to renounce the means of grace. (Cp. Luther, St. L., XI, 455 ff.; also Dr. Engelder, *Dogmatical Notes.*)

In this connection we must warn our hearers also against the error of making faith its own object; that is to say, believers must never base their faith upon their faith. Faith must be based alone on the Gospel, never on anything within man *(aliquid in nobis)*. Luther writes very aptly: *"Es ist gar viel ein ander Ding den Glauben* HABEN *und sich auf den Glauben* VERLASSEN." We are certainly required to believe, but only because by faith the promise of the Gospel is accepted, never because faith in itself, as a good quality, could reconcile God. To ask a person first to establish the fact that he has faith and then to permit him to trust in divine grace is a Calvinistic error, not Lutheran practise. Passages such as Mark 16, 15. 16; Acts 16, 31; Rom. 10, 9, etc., which have been quoted to support the Reformed error, in reality command us to look away from ourselves and to cling to the objective Gospel promises of grace and salvation.

4. THE IMPORTANCE OF THE DOCTRINE OF THE MEANS OF GRACE.

In Reformed, as in rationalistic circles in general, the doctrine of the means of grace is commonly regarded as of no importance whatever. American Fundamentalism, for instance, stresses the doctrines: a) that the Bible is the Word of God; b) that Christ is the God-man, who died for the sins of the world; c) that the sinner is saved through faith in Christ's blood; d) that Christ will gloriously return in His own appointed time; e) that Christ rose from the dead, and f) that there will be a final resurrection of all the dead. But Fundamentalism has no room at all in its system of theology for the Scriptural doctrine of the means of grace.

On the other hand, Luther is being charged by modern theologians with having attached undue importance to this doctrine, following in this matter too closely the pattern of the Church of Rome. As a matter of fact, the great Reformer's emphasis on the true doctrine of the means of grace was a real departure from, and a most decisive repudiation of, Romanism. He did not teach the doctrine of the means of grace because "he was still bound by the fetters of scholastic traditionalism," but because Scripture itself attaches supreme significance to this doctrine. In the final analysis it was Luther's loyalty to the Scriptural doctrine of *sola gratia* and *sola fide* that moved him to espouse and maintain the Biblical teaching of the means of grace. Without it he could not have taught the central article of the Christian faith, the so-called material principle of the Reformation, namely, justification by grace through faith in the *satisfactio vicaria* of Christ.

That the doctrine of *sola fide* stands and falls with that of the means of grace we have already pointed out. Romanism has rejected the Scriptural doctrine of the means of grace, and it has also rejected the *sola fide*. Calvinism, though avowing the *sola fide* in theory, denies it in practise; for on account of its denial of universal grace it is obliged to comfort the alarmed and doubting believer with the experience of his "inward illumination," or sanctification. Hence also in this case the perversion of the doctrine of the means of grace leads practically to the denial of the *sola fide*. The same may be said of enthusiasm and of rationalism in general. In every case the one error goes hand in hand with the other. The perversion of the doctrine of the means of grace always leads to the perversion of the central article of the Christian faith, namely, the doctrine of justification by faith without works. From this it is clear that the doctrine of the means of grace is indeed of the greatest importance for the preservation of the true Christian faith. Those who consistently disavow this doctrine must disavow also the very heart of the Christian religion.

Scripture itself stresses the doctrine of the means of grace as one of fundamental importance. In the first place, it teaches expressly that regeneration, or conversion, occurs solely through the means of grace, that is, through the Word (1 Cor. 2, 4. 5; 1 Pet. 1, 23; Rom. 10, 17) and the Sacraments (Acts 2, 38; Matt. 28, 19. 20; 1 Pet. 3, 21; etc.). In the second place, it affirms most definitely that all who reject the means of grace forfeit salvation, Luke 7, 30; John 8, 47; 1 Cor. 10, 21. 22; 11, 26—29. In the third place, it shows clearly and emphatically that contempt for the means of grace is not a little sin, which God readily condones, but rebellion against the Lord of mercy and grace, 1 Cor. 1, 22. 23, which He punishes with eternal damnation, 1 Cor. 1, 18—21. 26—29; Mark 16, 15. 16.

It is a plain doctrine of Scripture that all who will not receive God's grace as it is proffered to sinners in the means of grace shall not receive it at all, Matt. 10, 14. 15; Acts 13, 46. 51. Hence the statements of the Reformed: "There is no place for the use of means"; "Nothing intervenes between the volition of the Spirit and the regeneration of the soul" (Hodge, *Syst. Theol.*, II, 417. 684. 685, etc.); *"Tractatus internus est immediate operantis Spiritus"* (Zwingli, *De Providentia,* opp. IV, 125); *"Dux vel vehiculum Spiritui non est necessarium"* (Zwingli, *Fidei Ratio,* p. 24), must be condemned as a virtual rejection of God's grace in Christ Jesus as this is freely offered to sinners in the means of grace. As long as Calvinists maintain that "the influence of the Holy Spirit is directly upon the human spirit and is independent of the Word" (Shedd, *Dog. Theol.,* II, 501), confessional Lutheranism must refuse them the hand of Christian fellowship and regard them as perverters of God's way of salvation. (Cp. Pieper, *Christl. Dogmatik,* III, 156—223.)

5. THE MEANS OF GRACE IN THE FORM OF ABSOLUTION.

On the basis of clear Scripture-passages, Luther taught that the whole Gospel is nothing else than God's free absolution of all sinners for Christ's sake, 2 Cor. 5, 19—21; Rom. 4, 25. On this fundamental truth the great Reformer based his entire doctrine regarding absolution, or the application of the general Gospel promises of forgiveness to individual persons, either in private confession *(Privatbeichte)* or in the general confession *(allgemeine Beichte)*.

As Luther, so also the Lutheran Confessions inculcate the doctrine of absolution with great emphasis. The *Smalcald Articles* (Art. VI) declare: "The keys are an office and power given by Christ to the Church for binding and loosing sin." And the *Apology* (Art. XII) says: "The power of the keys administers and presents the Gospel through absolution, which proclaims peace to men and is the true voice of the Gospel"; Art. XI: "We should believe the absolution and regard it as certain that the remission of sins is freely granted us for Christ's sake"; Art. VI: "We also retain confession, especially on account of the absolution, as being the word of God which by divine authority the power of the keys pronounces upon individuals." Similarly the *Small Catechism:* "Confession embraces two parts. The one is that we confess our sins; the other, that we receive absolution, or forgiveness, from the confessor as from God Himself and in no wise doubt, but firmly believe, that our sins are thereby forgiven before God in heaven."

Absolution has been well defined as "that *special form* of administering the Gospel according to which a minister of the Church or any other Christian forgives one or more persons, upon their confession, their sins." (Cp. Luther, St. L., XVI, 1795; X, 1235.) Luther: *"Was ist die Absolution anders denn das Evangelium einem einzelnen Menschen gesagt, der ueber seine bekannte Suende Trost dadurch empfahe?"* Hence absolution is nothing else than the Gospel individualized, or applied to individuals, Matt. 9, 2; Luke 7, 48, just as it is done in the Sacraments. What the Gospel offers to all men, absolution offers to the individual.

The Scriptural doctrine of absolution has always been a stumbling-block to those who rejected the true doctrine of the means of grace. Zwingli said: "The assurance of our spirit that we are sons of God comes from the Spirit, not from the speaking confessor." The Pietists even averred: "The confessional chair is a devil's chair, a *Satansstuhl.*" Because the Scriptural doctrine of absolution was not distinguished by them from that of Romanism, which indeed is a perversion of the Scriptural truth, it was branded as a "commandment of Antichrist," etc.

The true doctrine of absolution, however, is firmly founded upon Scripture. Christ's words are clear and unmistakable:

"Verily I say unto you, Whatsoever ye shall bind on earth shall be bound in heaven, and whatsoever ye shall loose on earth shall be loosed in heaven," Matt. 18, 18. Again: "Whosesoever sins ye remit, they are remitted unto them, and whosesoever sins ye retain, they are retained," John 20, 23. (Cp. also Matt. 9, 8; 2 Cor. 2, 10.)

From these passages it is evident: a) that all who have received the Holy Ghost, that is to say, all true believers, are to remit or forgive sins; b) that this forgiveness relates to distinct persons ("whosesoever sins"); c) that all sins so forgiven by men are forgiven also before God in heaven ("they are remitted unto them").

It must be well understood that in absolution the forgiveness of sins is not merely announced to, or invoked upon, men, but actually conferred and conveyed, John 20, 23, just as this is done in the Gospel in general, Luke 24, 47. Moreover, it is God who absolves from sin in absolution. There is not a twofold absolution, one pronounced by God and the other by man; but the absolution spoken by men is God's absolution, pronounced by men in His stead. (Cp. Luther, St. L., XIX, 945.) The *Augsburg Confession* therefore rightly says (XXV): "Our people are being taught that they should highly prize the absolution as being the *voice of God* and pronounced by God's command." While the confession to the minister is an institution of the Church, the pronouncing of absolution to all who desire it is an institution of God. — *Auricular confession* is an antichristian abomination. (Cp. Luther, St. L., XI, 582 ff.)

The absolution practised in the Roman Catholic Church is a caricature of the absolution instituted by Christ. Luther therefore rightly denounced it as "altogether Pelagianistic, enthusiastic, and antichristian" (St. L., XIX, 943), because it is conditioned on the contrition, plenary confession, and satisfactions made by the applicant. Besides, absolution in the Roman Catholic Church is made dependent on the "intention" of the priest. — Another infamous feature of papistic absolution is the "erring key," which means that the absolution of the priest gives no assurance whatever that the sins are forgiven before God in heaven. Thus papistic absolution is utterly without consolation and assurance of salvation. But just that is what Roman Catholic theology desires: *the sinner should not be sure of the forgiveness of his sins and of his salvation.*

In opposing the Lutheran and Scriptural doctrine of absolution, Zwingli applied his supposed figure of speech, the so-called *alloeosis,* also to these words of the Savior, substituting for the personal pronoun *"ye"* the *"Holy Ghost,"* so that they really mean: "Whosoever sins the Holy Ghost remits, they are remitted." Zwingli's contention was that, when the Savior said: "Whosoever sins *ye remit,"* this was done out of pure divine friendship *("aus lauter goettlicher Freundschaft").* "Though Christ ascribes the binding and remitting to the disciples, yet this is solely the work of the operating Spirit; . . . hence there is attributed to the names of the apostles out of pure divine friendship what is solely the work of the Spirit." (Cp. *Christl. Dogmatik,* III, p. 225 ff.)

The followers of Zwingli unanimously agreed to his doctrine and likewise denied the Biblical doctrine of absolution. The reason for this is not hard to find. Zwinglianism (Calvinism) teaches the errors of particular grace ("saving grace only for the elect") and of the immediate operation of the Holy Spirit *(immediata Spiritus Sancti operatio);* but these two errors render absolution in the sense of Scripture impossible. According to Calvinism, no man can forgive the sins of any individual sinner, since, on the one hand, he cannot know whether the sinner is an elect or not, and because, on the other, this is the exclusive business of the Holy Spirit.

In Lutheran circles the doctrine of absolution was disavowed by both the Pietists and the synergists. Pietism misunderstood the real meaning of the divine Gospel promises (denial of objective reconciliation), while synergism, with its insistence on human cooperation in conversion, bases the remission of sins partly on man's own good conduct, so that neither he who absolves nor he who is absolved can know in any given case whether the absolution is effective. In both cases these Lutheran teachers erred because they departed from the doctrine of Scripture and the Lutheran Confessions (rejection of the objective justification and of the *sola gratia*).

Those who claim that the Lutheran doctrine of absolution is a "Romanistic leaven" *("roemischer Sauerteig")* fail to perceive the radical difference between the Biblical doctrine of absolution which the Lutheran Church advocates and the unbiblical doctrine of the Church of Antichrist. According to the papistic conception, absolution can be granted only by the priests (in severe cases only by the bishop or the Pope) upon adequate satisfaction rendered by the penitent individual *(contritio cordis, confessio oris, satis-*

factio), the priest acting as judge to decide whether the satisfaction is sufficient. Absolution in that case depends on the sinner's own worthiness, obtained by performing humanly prescribed penances, which are adjudged by human standards or values. The Roman Catholic doctrine of absolution is therefore in the fullest sense of the term a "commandment of men" (Matt. 15, 9) and as such cannot mediate forgiveness, but rather leaves the sinner under the curse, Gal. 3, 10; 5, 4.

Scripture, on the other hand, teaches: a) that the Office of the Keys *(potestas clavium),* that is, the peculiar power to forgive or retain sins, belongs to all Christians, John 20, 23; Matt. 18, 18; 16, 19, so that every believer may absolve from sin as effectually as does a priest or bishop; and b) that absolution is based neither upon contrition (either fictitious or genuine) nor upon any satisfaction which the sinner renders for his sins (Roman Catholic doctrine), but alone upon the perfect reconciliation which Christ has made for all men by His vicarious obedience and upon God's command (John 20, 21; Luke 24, 47) to preach remission of sins in His name among all nations. Absolution is therefore nothing else than the individual application of divine pardon for Jesus' sake. Hence it should not be doubted or rejected, but rather be received in true faith, just as the divine promises of God must be believed which the Gospel proclaims in general to all sinners.

From this it is also clear why, as Luther so emphatically says, *every Christian* may absolve. His right to absolve is as certain as that of preaching the Gospel, 1 Pet. 2, 9; in fact, absolution is only a special form of preaching the Gospel of grace and reconciliation.

If Romanists and Romanizing Protestants aver that the power of remitting and retaining sins was granted by Christ only to the clergy, John 20, 22. 23, they fail to observe that our Lord on that occasion addressed not only the Twelve, but also other disciples; cp. John 20, 19. 24; Luke 24, 33. Dr. A. Spaeth, *e. g.,* writes: "When this power was conveyed by the Lord, the apostles were not all present; nor were those present on this occasion all apostles. John clearly distinguishes between the Twelve (v. 24) and the disciples (v. 19). And Luke tells us distinctly that others were gathered with the disciples on that evening, Luke 24, 33. Luther therefore is right in saying: 'This power is given to all Christians. Whosoever hath the Holy Spirit, to him this power is given, that is, to him who is a Christian.' " *(Annotations to the Gospel according to St. John;* cp. *Christl. Dogmatik,* III, 227 ff.)

While some object to the doctrine of absolution on the ground of its being a "Romanistic leaven," others do so because they say it is God's exclusive prerogative to forgive sins. For this reason they regard it as blasphemous to ascribe to any man the power to forgive or retain sins. To this stricture we reply that it is indeed God's prerogative to forgive sins; however, He does not exercise this prerogative immediately (by direct announcement), but mediately, through the Gospel, which He commands His believing disciples to proclaim to every creature, Mark 16, 15. 16; Matt. 28, 19. 20. Hence God forgives sins through the very Word which believers preach in His name, 2 Sam. 12, 13; Luke 24, 47. Even when a person reads the divine Gospel promises and thus applies the absolution of the Gospel to himself, he receives forgiveness of sins not immediately *(interior Spiritus illuminatio),* but mediately, through the Word of the prophets and apostles, Eph. 2, 20.

To the objection that the doctrine of absolution may mislead men both to carnal security and carnal pride *(Priesterstolz)* we reply that the abuse of a thing does not annul its right use. If the doctrine of absolution is not to be taught because it is subject to abuse, then we must neither preach the Gospel in general nor administer the Sacraments in particular, since these are likewise subject to abuse. In passing, we may remark that the doctrine of absolution can produce carnal security or spiritual pride only if it is proclaimed in a perverted form (Romanism). Absolution in the sense of Scripture always presupposes contrition and faith.

To the objection that a minister cannot forgive sins because he does not know if the recipient is "worthy" or not we reply: Absolution does not depend on any worthiness in man, but on God's grace in Christ Jesus, which has appeared to all men and should therefore also be proclaimed and offered to all. This is done both by the preaching of the Gospel in general and by the special promulgation of the Gospel in the form of absolution. Those who announce the grace of God in Christ Jesus to men never make a mistake; for there is no *clavis errans,* or *Fehlschluessel.* The words of absolution are always as true as is the Gospel itself, of which absolution is only a special application. If any one fails to receive the forgiveness announced and proffered in absolution, the fault is his alone and not that of the absolution. For Christ's sake God has graciously remitted the sins of the whole world, 2 Cor. 5, 19. 20, and absolution is nothing else than the proclamation of this gracious forgiveness to the individual. Every one who believes this glorious fact is in actual possession of complete pardon.

Every objection to the Biblical doctrine of absolution is therefore based upon a misunderstanding of what absolution really is; and absolution is misunderstood because men fail to comprehend the objective reconciliation which Christ made by His vicarious atonement. And this, again, they fail to comprehend because they base a sinner's salvation, in part at least, on his own worthiness and not exclusively on God's grace and Christ's vicarious obedience *(sola gratia, sola fide)*, offered to all men as a free gift in the means of grace.

As soon as a believer understands that absolution is only the application of the general pardon offered and conveyed by the Gospel, he readily understands also why Baptism and the Lord's Supper must be regarded as forms of private absolution. In both Sacraments God offers individually that grace which Christ has secured for the whole world by His death, Acts 2, 38; Matt. 26, 26—28, and which is received by faith in His gracious Gospel promises. No matter in what manner the Gospel is applied to men, whether by general proclamation, or through Baptism, or the Lord's Supper, or the act of absolution, the sinner is always absolved, that is, his sin is forgiven; for the same joyous, comforting message is heard alike in them all: "Be of good cheer; thy sins be forgiven thee," Matt. 9, 2.

From this it is evident that absolution should not be pronounced *conditionally* ("If you truly repent and truly believe, your sins are forgiven"), but always *unconditionally* ("Thy sins be forgiven thee"). It is true, forgiveness is received only by faith, and true faith dwells only in a contrite heart. From this point of view Luther correctly says that "every absolution has the condition of faith"; but he adds: "yet only in so far as it receives the absolution and says yes to it" (St. L., XXIb, 1847ff.). On the other hand, Luther most emphatically repudiates the doctrine that the forgiveness is based upon a person's contrition and faith inasmuch as these are good or meritorious works.

If contrition and faith were meritorious acts, then indeed absolution would have to be pronounced conditionally. Since forgiveness, however, does not rest on any good work in man, but only on God's gracious disposition toward the sinner in Christ Jesus, no condition whatever attaches to it. God actually forgives every sinner his transgressions for Christ's sake, and this glorious truth should be announced to every sinner, and every sinner should believingly trust in it.   Hence, as neither Baptism nor the Lord's Supper is conditional ("I baptize you in case you truly believe"; "'Take, eat; this is My body,' if you truly believe"), so neither absolution is conditional.   God's forgiveness is truly offered to every sinner in every form of Gospel-preaching; for man's unbelief never makes the faith of God without effect, Rom. 3, 3.   In all cases therefore absolution is to be pronounced unconditionally.

If, according to the custom of the Lutheran Church, the pronouncement of absolution is preceded by the questions: "Do you heartily repent of your sins, believe on Jesus Christ, and sincerely and earnestly purpose by the assistance of God the Holy Ghost henceforth to amend your sinful lives?" this is not to render absolution conditional, but merely to warn the secure and to comfort the penitent.

It is clear that the Scriptural doctrine of absolution can be maintained only by those who adhere to the Biblical doctrine of justification by grace, through faith in Christ Jesus.   Romanism, synergism, and Calvinism err with regard to the doctrine of absolution just because they deny either the *sola gratia* or the *gratia universalis*.   Where these two doctrines are denied, God's amnesty must be based upon a condition in man; but where God's amnesty is made to rest upon "certain conditions" on the part of the sinner, absolution in the Scriptural sense becomes impossible. (Cp. *Christl. Dogmatik,* III, 223—248.)

6. THE MEANS OF GRACE IN THE OLD TESTAMENT.

The Gospel of Jesus Christ, that is, the gracious message of the forgiveness of sins through faith in the promised Savior, was the divine means of grace also during the whole time of the Old Testament, Acts 15, 11.   This is the clear testimony of Scripture, which tells us: "To Him give all the prophets witness that through His name whosoever believeth in Him shall receive remission of sins," Acts 10, 43.   In the promised Christ, Abraham believed, John 8, 56, and of Him Moses wrote, John 5, 46.   St. Paul expressly assures us that all New Testament believers are "Abraham's children," Gal. 3, 7, and "Abraham's seed," Gal. 3, 29, because they believe as Abraham did.

In particular, the New Testament Scriptures declare that the Christian doctrine of justification by grace, through faith, without

the deeds of the Law, is "witnessed by the Law and the prophets,"
Rom. 3, 21. The entire fourth chapter of the Epistle to the
Romans is designed to prove that the doctrine of justification by
faith is a doctrine of the Old Testament. Even after the Mosaic
covenant was established, the Gospel of Christ as a means of grace
was still in force, Gal. 3, 17.

It is true, when the promised Messiah appeared in the fulness
of time, the Jews did not believe in Him; but this was not due
to lack of adequate testimony concerning Him, but to their contempt for the clear witness of Moses, John 5, 45—47. So also the
weak faith of the disciples in the crucified and risen Savior was
owing to their disregard of the clear prophecies of the Old Testament, Luke 24, 25. For the same reason also modern rationalistic
theology denies the incontestable fact that ever since the Fall the
Gospel of Christ has been the true means of grace by which sinners
have become children of God through faith in the divine promise.
It repudiates the Messianic character of clear Messianic prophecies,
Gen. 3, 15; 4, 1; etc., just because it refuses to believe the witness
of the prophets and, what is worse, that of Christ Himself and
of His holy apostles, Luke 24, 25. In short, rationalism cannot
find Christ and His vicarious atonement in the Old Testament
because it does not believe the Gospel so clearly set forth in the
New Testament.

As the Gospel of Christ, so also the Circumcision and the
Passover were means of grace, offering and conveying forgiveness of sins. To the act of circumcision was attached the divine
promise of grace: "I will be their God," Gen. 17, 8, that is, their
gracious God, who out of pure love freely forgives sin. This is
evident from the fact that in the New Testament St. Paul calls
the sign of circumcision "a seal of the righteousness of faith,"
Rom. 4, 11. Of the Passover, Scripture distinctly says that it
mediated grace to the Israelites; for they were spared in the
plague, not as Jews, but because the passover lamb was killed and
its blood was sprinkled on the lintel and the two side-posts, Ex. 12,
21—27. For this reason God commanded: "And ye shall observe
this thing for an ordinance to thee and to thy sons forever,"
Ex. 12, 24. Hence both to Circumcision and to the Passover was
attached the divine promise of grace, and we therefore rightly speak
of them as the Sacraments of the Old Testament.

Luther writes: "It is a mistake [to believe] that the Sacraments of the New Testament differ from the Sacraments of the

Old Testament according to their force and meaning [namely, as divinely appointed means of grace]. . . . Both our and the fathers' signs, or Sacraments, have attached to them a word of promise, which demands faith and cannot be fulfilled by any other work. Therefore they are signs, or Sacraments, of justification." (St. L., XIX, 62 ff.) Thus also in the Old Testament the Gospel and the Sacraments (Circumcision and the Passover) offered and conveyed to the believers divine grace and forgiveness. In other words, their function was precisely the same as is that of the means of grace instituted by Christ in the New Testament.

7. THE MEANS OF GRACE AND PRAYER.

In connection with the doctrine of the means of grace the question has been discussed whether also prayer may be classified among the means of grace. The query has been affirmed by the Calvinists. Hodge thus writes: "The means of grace, according to the standards of our Church, are the Word, Sacraments, and *prayer.*" (*Syst. Theol.*, III, 466; cp. p. 708.) However, while the term *means of grace* is a *vox ἄγραφος* and as such its meaning is not fixed by Scripture, so that we may employ it in various meanings, it is confusing to apply it to prayer in the same sense as it is applied to the Gospel and the Sacraments.

The Word and the Sacraments are, as Luther expresses himself, "God's work upon us," that is, means by which God deals with us; while prayer is the means by which the believer deals with God. Prayer, properly speaking, is a fruit of Christian faith and not the means by which faith is engendered. Through the Word and the Sacraments, God offers and conveys to us His grace and pardon. Through prayer we sue for temporal and spiritual blessings or render thanks to God for gifts received.

Hence, when without further qualification prayer is called a means of grace, the distinctive difference between it and the Word and the Sacraments is ignored, just as also their various purposes are confused. Moreover, if prayer is regarded as a means of grace, then the error must follow that through prayer, or through a work of man, forgiveness of sins and salvation can be merited.

As a matter of fact, those who regard prayer as a means of grace actually declare that God is thereby reconciled. They therefore urge sinners who seek assurance of salvation to pray, whereas they ought to point out to them the grace of God in Christ Jesus, which is offered to all men in the Gospel and the Sacraments, and exhort them to put their trust wholly in the divine promises of pardon and peace.

If the objection is raised that Christ Himself practically makes prayer a means of grace by teaching us to pray: "Forgive us our sins," Luke 11, 4, we reply that believers indeed receive forgiveness of sins as also all other blessings of God by way of prayer, yet not because prayer is properly a means of grace, but simply because a true Christian prayer is an expression of faith in the divine promises. Properly speaking, it is not the prayer itself, that is, the speaking of words, but the Christian faith, of which the prayer is a manifestation, which secures forgiveness. Hence, whenever a true believer prays, he does not regard his prayer as another means of grace, in addition to the Word and the Sacraments, but his prayer rests upon the divine promises that are offered to him in the means of grace. What he really prays for is that God would be gracious to him and forgive his sins for Christ's sake as He has promised to do in His blessed Gospel.

Whenever a person prays on the supposition that his prayer is a meritorious work, on account of which God forgives sins, his prayer is not offered in the name of Jesus, but contrary to the direction of Jesus. It is not a manifestation of faith, but a manifestation of unbelief; it is not a good work at all, but an abomination in the sight of God, Gal. 3, 10. To such a prayer the words of Christ apply: "When ye pray, use not vain repetitions, as the heathen do; for they think that they shall be heard for their much speaking," Matt. 6, 7.

That the Calvinists regard prayer as a means of grace is quite intelligible from their point of view. Because they deny universal grace, they are unable to comfort an alarmed sinner with the general promises of grace offered in the Gospel; for these, according to Calvinistic doctrine, pertain only to the elect. Hence they must look for other means than the Gospel and the Sacraments by which to assure the terrified sinner of salvation, namely, acts of devotion (among which are prayers) that produce a sense or feeling of grace *(sensus gratiae)*. Such assurance, however, since it rests upon human endeavors, is only imagination and not true Christian assurance, as has already been pointed out.

However, not only Calvinists, but also synergists and Arminians regard prayer as a means of grace and also urge the alarmed sinner who desires assurance of salvation to seek this through prayer (Reformed revivalists, Lutheran Pietists). What underlies this unscriptural advice is the denial of the *sola gratia* and, along with this, the repudiation of the objective reconciliation secured by Christ's vicarious atonement and of the means of grace as the true conferring means (*media δοτικά*), by which God freely offers Christ's perfect righteousness to all men. From all this it is clear what a fatal mistake it is to regard prayer as a means of grace. Those who pray with the understanding that their supplications are meritorious means, which secure grace and salvation, have practically rejected the Gospel of Christ and lapsed into paganism.

THE LAW AND THE GOSPEL.

(De Discrimine Legis et Evangelii.)

While the doctrines so far treated necessitated a constant reference to, and discussion of, the Law and the Gospel, so that practically everything has been said on this subject that need be said, nevertheless it is not superfluous to set forth the Scriptural teachings concerning the Law and the Gospel under a special head. Modern rationalism, just as Romanism and Zwinglianism (Zwingli: "In itself the Law is nothing else than a Gospel"; cp. *Concordia Triglotta,* p. 161 ff.), has practically abolished the distinction between the Law and the Gospel, so that the two teachings are continually mingled into each other and the Biblical way of salvation is completely obscured (denial of the *sola fide;* salvation by work-righteousness).

Confessional Lutheranism, on the other hand, regards the "distinction between the Law and the Gospel as a special brilliant light *(clarissimum quoddam lumen),* which serves to the end that God's Word may be rightly divided and the Scripture of the holy prophets and apostles may be properly explained and understood" *(Formula of Concord,* Thor. Decl., V, 1), and therefore assigns to the subject a prominent place in every orthodox dogmatic treatise. Despite this fact, however, Antinomianism, which is a perversion of the Scriptural doctrine of the Law and the Gospel, has caused confusion also within Lutheran circles (John Agricola, the Philippists, Poach, Otto, etc.), so that it is indeed necessary to give the matter adequate consideration. For these reasons we here treat the subject more fully under a special head.

1. DEFINITION OF LAW AND GOSPEL.

Scripture itself distinguishes very clearly between the Law and the Gospel and likewise our Lutheran Confessions. According to the *Formula of Concord* (Thor. Decl., V, 17) the Law, in its strict or proper sense *(lex proprie accepta),* is "a divine doctrine in which the righteous, immutable will of God is revealed, what is to be the quality of man in his nature, thoughts, words, and works, in order that he may be pleasing and acceptable to God; and it threatens its transgressors with God's wrath and temporal and eternal punishments." More briefly the Epitome of the *Formula of Concord* (V, 3. 4) defines the divine Law in its proper sense as "a divine doctrine which teaches what is right and pleasing to God and reproves everything that is sin and contrary to God's will," so that "everything that reproves sin is, and belongs to, the preaching of the Law."

On the other hand, the Gospel, in its strict or proper sense (*evangelium proprie acceptum*), is defined by the same Confession as "such a doctrine as teaches what man who has not observed the Law and therefore is condemned by it is to believe, namely, that Christ has expiated, and made satisfaction for, all sins and has obtained and acquired for him, without any merit of his, ... forgiveness of sins, righteousness that avails before God, and eternal life." (Epitome, V, 5.)

This distinction between the Law and the Gospel is clear and Scriptural, so that we may describe as divine Law everything in Scripture that demands of man perfect obedience to God, Gal. 3, 12, pronounces His curse upon all transgressors, Gal. 3, 10, renders all the world guilty before God, Rom. 3, 19, and mediates knowledge of sin, Rom. 3, 20; and as Gospel everything that offers grace, peace, and salvation to the sinner, Rom. 1, 16. 17; 10, 15; Acts 20, 24; Eph. 6, 15; 1, 13.

It is true, both terms (Law and Gospel) are used in Scripture also in a wider sense, so that the term *Law* denotes the entire revelation of God as this is set forth in His Word, Ps. 1, 2; Is. 2, 3, and the term *Gospel* the entire divine doctrine, Mark 1, 1. This is done by way of synecdoche, so that the whole is named after a part (Gerhard: *"ut ex parte digniori et potiori totum intelligatur"*).

This peculiar use of the term *Gospel* is recognized also by our Lutheran Confessions; for we read in the *Formula of Concord* (Thor. Decl., V, 3 ff.): "The term *Gospel* is not always employed and understood in one and the same sense, but in two ways in the Holy Scriptures. ... For sometimes it is employed so that there is understood by it the entire doctrine of Christ, our Lord. ... Furthermore the term *Gospel* is employed in another, namely, in its proper sense, by which it comprises ... only the preaching of the grace of God."

2. FEATURES THAT ARE COMMON TO BOTH THE LAW AND THE GOSPEL.

If we compare the two doctrines with each other, we find that they have several important elements in common. In the first place, both the Law and the Gospel are the divinely inspired Word of God. This point is essential. While the function of the Law is entirely different from that of the Gospel, it is nevertheless just as much God's holy and inspired Word as is the Gospel, Matt.

22, 37—40; Rom. 3, 21. In the second place, both doctrines, the Law as well as the Gospel, pertain to all men, so that they must always be taught side by side till the end of the world. So the *Formula of Concord* teaches: "From the beginning of the world these two proclamations . . . have been ever and ever inculcated alongside of each other in the Church of God, with a proper distinction. . . . These two doctrines, we believe, . . . should ever and ever be diligently inculcated in the Church of God even to the end of the world." (Thor. Decl., V, 23. 24.)

The fact "that the Law and the Gospel must ever and ever be inculcated alongside of each other" must be maintained against Antinomianism, which, claiming that repentance (contrition) must be preached from the Gospel, denied that the Law should be inculcated in the New Testament. John Agricola taught: "The Decalog belongs in the court-house, not in the pulpit"; that is to say, the Law is a matter of the State, not of the Church. Modified forms of Antinomianism were advocated and defended by Poach, Otto, etc., who said: "The Law must not be inculcated upon the *regenerate.*" The Philippists, on the other hand, claimed: "Unbelief must be reproved from the Gospel." (Cp. *Triglot,* Hist. Intr., p. 161 ff.) The errors of Antinomianism are adequately refuted in Articles V and VI of the *Formula of Concord,* which show clearly and convincingly that Antinomianism is neither Scriptural nor reasonable.

Luther rightly characterizes the ingrained folly of Antinomianism when he writes: "They want to do away with the Law, and yet they teach [divine] wrath, something the Law alone must do. Hence they do nothing but cast aside the poor word *Law,* but confirm the wrath of God, which is indicated and understood by this term, not to speak of the fact that they wring Paul's neck and place the last first." (St. L., XX, 1618 ff.)

Again: "Is it not blindness, yea, worse than blindness that he [Agricola] does not want to teach the Law without and before the Gospel? He is trying something that is impossible. How can one preach forgiveness of sins before sins are there [*i. e.,* known]? How can one announce life before death is there [*i. e.,* known]? . . . For grace must wage war, and be victorious in us, against the Law and sin, lest we despair." (St. L., XX, 1659. 1656.)

Dr. Bente (*Triglot,* Hist. Intr., p. 161) says of Antinomianism that it "was a veiled effort to open once more the doors of the Lutheran Church to the Roman work-righteousness which Luther had expelled." He writes: "When Luther opposed Agricola, the father of the Antinomians in the days of the Reformation, he did so with the clear knowledge that the Gospel of Jesus Christ with its doctrine of justification by grace and faith alone was at stake and in need of defense. 'By these spirits,' said he, 'the devil does not intend to rob us of the Law, but of Christ, who fulfilled the Law' (St. L., XX, 1614)."

As a matter of fact, the Antinomians, in the final analysis, based their faith in the gracious forgiveness of sins on their renewal, or sanctification, particularly on the repentance that results from true love produced by the preaching of the Gospel. In this manner they intermingled justification and sanctification and restored the Romanistic doctrine of work-righteousness (justification by means of sanctification; *gratia infusa*).

3. THE LAW AND THE GOSPEL CONSIDERED AS OPPOSITES.

It was Luther who again proclaimed to the world that the Law and the Gospel are as widely distinct as they possibly can be, separated from each other more than opposites *("inter se longissime distincta et plus quam contradictoria separata sunt")*. (St. L., IX, 447.) This must not be regarded as an extreme and "mis-understandable" statement (Thomasius, *Dogmengeschichte,* II, 425); for it is a reaffirmation of the truth which Scripture itself teaches.

When we compare the two doctrines according to their contents, we find that they absolutely contradict each other. The Law demands perfect obedience of man in every way and condemns all who are disobedient, while the Gospel demands nothing, but freely offers to all sinners grace, life, and salvation for Christ's sake. The same sinners whom the Law consigns to everlasting damnation the Gospel, for Jesus' sake, assigns to everlasting glory in heaven, Rom. 5, 18—21. The Law requires works, Luke 10, 28; the Gospel declares that the sinner "is justified by faith, without the deeds of the Law," Rom. 3, 28.

St. Paul strikingly contrasts the Law and the Gospel when he writes: "There is no difference; for all have sinned and come short of the glory of God, being justified freely by His grace, through the redemption which is in Christ Jesus," Rom. 3, 22—24. According to these words the Law condemns, while the Gospel justifies. (Cp. also Gal. 3, 10—14.)

The same difference between the Law and the Gospel becomes evident when we consider their promises, which, too, are absolutely contradictory. The promises of the Law are conditional (*promissiones conditionales*); those of the Gospel are promises of pure grace (*promissiones gratuitae*). That is to say, the Law promises life to the sinner provided he obeys it perfectly, Gal. 3, 12; Luke 10, 28; but the Gospel promises him life and salvation "without the deeds of the Law," "without works," "freely," "by grace" (*particulae exclusivae*), so that indeed "the *ungodly* are justified," Rom. 4, 5. In other words, the Law justifies persons who are in themselves *just,* Gal. 3, 21, while the Gospel justifies persons who in themselves are *unjust,* Rom. 4, 5.

The so-called Gospel imperative (*imperativus evangelicus,* Acts 16, 31) is "concentrated Gospel." When St. Paul commanded the keeper of the prison at Philippi: "Believe on the Lord Jesus Christ, and thou shalt be saved," he preached faith into his heart. So also the "command" of 1 John 3, 23 is not a legal command, but a most gracious invitation, expressed in the strongest manner, to accept the Gospel offer of forgiveness. The faith demanded by the Gospel is described in Scripture as the very opposite of any human achievement, Eph. 2, 8. 9.

From this it is evident that the conditions of the Law, Luke 10, 28, are *real* conditions, demanding absolute fulfilment of the imposed obligations, Gal. 3, 12, while those of the Gospel (Rom. 10, 9: "If thou shalt believe, thou shalt be saved") merely indicate the means by which God applies to the sinner life and salvation (*modus applicationis*). The statement "If thou shalt believe, thou shalt be saved" means only this: Without any works or worthiness on thy part thou art saved alone by faith in the Lord Jesus, whom God has raised from the dead. Rom. 3, 23—28.

Since, then, the Law and the Gospel, considered according to their contents and promises, are absolute contradictions (*plus quam contradictoria*), we must clearly distinguish between the two spheres to which each belongs in the economy of salvation. That is the only correct way of removing the "insuperable difficulty" which confronts us as we view these two *contradictoria* according to their Scriptural presentation.

The Law must indeed be preached in its full rigor and severity, and nothing dare be taken away from it, Matt. 5, 17. 18; Gal. 3, 10; Rom. 1, 18; 3, 9—19; but it must be proclaimed for no other purpose than to bring the sinner to a clear knowledge of his sin and condemnation, Rom. 3, 20. That is the proper sphere of the Law, as Scripture plainly shows, 2 Cor. 3, 9: "the ministration of condemnation." It is a message of wrath and as such "our schoolmaster unto Christ that we might be justified by faith," Gal. 3, 24.

However, when the Law has accomplished its purpose and the contrite sinner cries out in fear: "What must I do to be saved?" Acts 16, 30, then the proclamation of the Law must cease and that of the Gospel must set in, Acts 16, 31; for, while it is the function of the Law to terrify the secure sinner, it is the function of the Gospel to comfort the contrite sinner with the grace of God in Christ Jesus, John 3, 16; Rom. 10, 4. This sharp distinction between the two spheres of the Law and the Gospel is always observed in Scripture, 2 Sam. 12, 13; Acts 2, 37—39; 1 Cor. 5, 1—5; 2 Cor. 2, 6—8.

Luther writes: "The Law has its goal, just how far it must go and how much it must accomplish, namely, 'unto Christ,' to terrify the impenitent with God's wrath and disfavor. In the same manner also the Gospel has its work and function, namely, to preach forgiveness of sins to the troubled conscience. . . . Now, where conscience is rightly awakened, duly feels its sins, and is in agony of death, . . . there it is high time to know how to separate the Law from the Gospel and to put each in its place." (St. L., IX, 798 ff.)

Generally speaking, then, the Law belongs to the sphere of sin and the Gospel to that of grace; the first is the message of repentance (contrition), the second that of remission of sins, Luke 24, 47. Both must be taught in their Scriptural purity and truth; the rigor and severity of the Law must not be diminished, nor must the sweetness and winsomeness of the Gospel be modified, for only in that way can the divine message of sin and grace enter the sinner's heart and transform it.

The Law and the Gospel differ from each other also with respect to their *principia cognoscendi*. While the Law is written in the hearts of men, Rom. 2, 14. 15, and may thus, in part at least, be known even without the revealed knowledge of Scripture, the Gospel is the "hidden wisdom of God," made known to man by special revelation, 1 Cor. 2, 7—12; Rom. 16, 25, so that not a single person can know it unless it is revealed to him, Mark 16, 15; Rom. 10, 14. 15. 17. This is demonstrated and proved by the fact that all man-made religions are "religions of the Law," or of good works, while the Christian religion, which is taken from the Bible

as its only source, is a "religion of faith." Moreover, all men who
are addicted to the natural religion of good works reject the religion of faith as foolishness, 1 Cor. 1, 23; 2, 14, until through the
Gospel the Holy Spirit has removed from them the *opinio legis,*
2 Cor. 3, 15. 16.

In the course of the Antinomian controversy the question was
debated whether the sin of unbelief must be reproved from the
Law (Gnesio-Lutherans) or from the Gospel (Philippists). The
answer of the Gnesio-Lutherans was adopted and embodied in the
Formula of Concord (cp. Arts. V and VI). The Philippists were
perhaps misled by the consideration that, since the divine Law is
ignorant of Christ and of faith in Him, it cannot reprove the sin
of unbelief. But the question is readily settled if we bear in mind
the specific spheres and functions of the Law and the Gospel; for
while the Law always judges, condemns, and reproves, the Gospel,
in its proper sense, never judges, condemns, and reproves. It is
therefore against the very nature of the Gospel to reprove.

The statement "The Gospel reproves sin" (Melanchthon) can
be defended only if the term *Gospel* is used in its wider sense, as
denoting the entire doctrine of Christ. However, that the Gospel
in its strict sense does not reprove either the sin of unbelief or any
other sin is obvious from the fact that, if the Gospel would be
properly a message of reproof and condemnation, salvation would
be absolutely impossible; for in that case there would be no message of salvation in which sinners, who by nature are all unbelievers, might trust. The Gospel saves, Rom. 1, 16, just because it
has only a saving and not a reproving or condemning function.
Unintentionally, yet actually, the Philippists changed the Gospel
into Law by ascribing to it in its proper sense a reproving office.

The *Formula of Concord* concedes that the Gospel (or rather
the Gospel facts, namely, Christ's suffering and death) may indeed
be used to depict the great wrath of God on account of man's sin,
just as Christ Himself so used it, Luke 23, 31. Yet when the
Gospel is employed in this manner, it performs not its own and
proper office *(proprium suum officium),* but a foreign office *(alienum opus).* Our Confession (Thor. Decl., V, 12) says: "Yea,
what more forcible, more terrible declaration and preaching of
God's wrath against sin is there than just the suffering and death
of Christ, His Son? But as long as all this preaches God's wrath
and terrifies men, it is not yet the preaching of the Gospel nor
Christ's own preaching, but that of Moses and the Law against the

impenitent. For the Gospel and Christ were never ordained and given for the purpose of terrifying and condemning, but of comforting and cheering those who are terrified and timid." The last truth here stressed must never be left out of mind; for the Gospel in its proper sense never reveals sin or terrifies the sinner, but always shows divine grace and consoles the alarmed sinner.

In concluding this chapter, we may call attention to the fact that the Law and the Gospel are only different aspects of God Himself in His relation to the sinner. The Law shows God as He condemns the sinner on account of his sin *(Deus propter peccata damnans),* while the Gospel describes Him as freely forgiving and justifying the sinner for Christ's sake *(Deus propter Christum absolvens et iustificans).* This fact the Christian theologian must always bear in mind when he determines the spheres and functions of the Law and the Gospel.

4. THE CLOSE CONNECTION BETWEEN THE LAW AND THE GOSPEL.

While the Law and the Gospel are radically distinct from each other so far as their content is concerned, they nevertheless must be closely conjoined in their practical application. Luther writes of this (St. L., IX, 454): "Although these two [doctrines] are most remote so far as their content *(re ipsa)* is concerned, yet at the same time they are most intimately linked together in one and the same heart. Nothing is more fastly bound together than are fear and faith, Law and Gospel, sin and grace. They are indeed so united that one is swallowed up by the other *(absorbeatur).* Therefore there can be no mathematical conjunction which is like to this."

This close connection of the Law and the Gospel becomes apparent when we consider the sinner's conversion. As we have shown in a previous chapter, conversion takes place in the very moment when a penitent sinner personally trusts in the gracious promises of the Gospel; or we may briefly say, his conversion is effected through the Gospel. However, in order that the Gospel may accomplish its comforting and saving function, the Law must first convict the sinner of his sin and guilt, terrify and humble him, and cause him to despair of his own efforts to save himself, Rom. 3, 19. 20. 23. 24. Thus the conversion of a sinner requires and presupposes the preaching of both the Law and the Gospel. The Law must first point out to the sinner his spiritual death in order that

he may rejoice in the spiritual life which the Gospel gives. The
Law must convince him of God's righteous demand in order that
he may be willing to accept by faith the free gifts of the Gospel.
The Law must proclaim sin in order that the Gospel can proclaim grace.

When speaking of the second use of the divine Law, our
dogmaticians rightly distinguish between its *usus elenchticus* (the
revealing and convicting of sin, Rom. 3, 20) and its *usus paedagogicus* ("our schoolmaster to bring us unto Christ," Gal. 3, 24).
However, it must be borne in mind that the Law itself does not lead
to Christ, but only to despair. But it serves the coming to Christ
(compulsus indirectus) by pointing out to the sinner his need.
When the Law has terrified the sinner, Christ is at hand to proclaim to him the comfort of the Gospel. That the Law by itself
does not produce any moral change and improvement in the sinner's heart, predisposing it for the reception of the Gospel, is
taught in such passages as 2 Cor. 3, 6 b; Rom. 7, 5. 8. The Gospel
must therefore go hand in hand with the Law if the sinner is to
be converted and saved.

This intimate connection between the Law and the Gospel the
Antinomians denied when they tried to relegate the Law out of
the Church. But in the final analysis their opposition to the Law
was opposition to the Gospel; for as Luther rightly says (St. L.,
XX, 1646): "If the Law is removed, no one can know what Christ
is or what He has done when He fulfilled the Law for us." The
great Reformer clearly perceived that "the devil through this enthusiasm (Antinomianism) meant to remove not the Law, but
Christ, the Fulfiller of the Law" (XX, 1614).

Again, the close connection of the Law and the Gospel becomes apparent also when we consider the sanctification of the
believer. It is true, according to the inward, or new, man the
believer does not require the Law, 1 Tim. 1, 9, since, as a new creature in Christ, he has the divine Law written in his heart, Jer.
31, 33; Ezek. 36, 26, and obeys it as cheerfully and willingly as
Adam did before the Fall, Ps. 110, 3. The *Formula of Concord*
rightly declares (Thor. Decl., VI, 17): "But when a man is born
anew by the Spirit of God and liberated from the Law, that is,
freed from this driver, and is led by the Spirit of Christ, he lives
according to the immutable will of God comprised in the Law and,
so far as he is born anew, does everything from a free, cheerful
spirit."

THE LAW AND THE GOSPEL.

However, the situation becomes quite different when we view the believer according to the flesh, which still cleaves to him, Rom. 7, 14—24. According to the old man the believer neither knows the Law thoroughly nor does he fulfil it willingly, Rom. 7, 15, but he constantly opposes and transgresses it, Rom. 7, 18.

Luther says (St. L., IX, 881): "According to the spirit the believer is righteous, without any sin whatsoever, and does not require the Law; but according to the flesh he still has sin. . . . Since, then, sin still exists [in us], Scripture judges us to be equal to the unrighteous and sinners, so that according to the flesh we must have the Law just as much as they."

So also the *Formula of Concord* remarks (Thor. Decl., VI, 18 ff.): "Since believers are not completely renewed in this world, but the Old Adam clings to them even to the grave, there also remains in them the struggle between the spirit and the flesh. Therefore they delight indeed in God's Law according to the inner man, but the law in their members struggles against the Law in their mind; hence they are never without the Law and nevertheless are not under, but in the Law and live and walk in the Law of the Lord and yet do nothing from constraint of the Law."

Together with the Gospel the believer must therefore also use the divine Law, namely, a) as a curb, to crucify his evil flesh, Rom. 8, 7; 1 Cor. 9, 27; b) as a mirror, which constantly reveals his sins, Rom. 7, 7. 13; Gal. 5, 19—21; and c) as a rule, according to which he must regulate and direct his whole life, Gal. 5, 22—25. Hence even the regenerate must continually employ the Law in close connection with the Gospel: the Law to curb his flesh outwardly, the Gospel to destroy it inwardly; the Law to point out good works, the Gospel to give him power to do good works; the Law to show him his sins, the Gospel to teach him how he may be cleansed from sin.

There is, of course, no contradiction between such passages as 1 Tim. 1, 9: "The Law is not made for a righteous man" and those which apply the Law in all its uses to the Christian, *e. g.*, Rom. 7, 23. 24; 1 Cor. 9, 27; etc. In the former passage the Christian is described according to the new man; in the latter, according to his old, corrupt nature. Luther rightly says: *"Ein Christ ist zwischen zwei Zeiten geteilt. Sofern er Fleisch ist, ist er unter dem Gesetz; sofern er Geist ist, ist er unter der Gnade."* (Cp. St. L., IX, 452. 880.)

Conversion and sanctification are therefore the result of the *cooperation of the Law and Gospel.* The preaching of the Law alone results in hypocrisy or despair; the preaching of the Gospel alone results in indifference and security. (Cp. Luther, St. L., V, 988; also Dr. Engelder, *Dogmatical Notes.*)

For the sake of completeness we may here add that our dogmaticians speak of a fourfold use of the divine Law, each of which applies also to the believer. The Law holds in check the flesh of the Christian and coerces it to external discipline *(usus politicus);* it reveals to him, and convinces him of, his sin *(usus elenchticus);* it is his schoolmaster to bring him unto Christ *(usus paedagogicus);* it furnishes him with a safe rule of life *(perpetua vivendi regula,* Matt. 5, 17; *usus didacticus).*

5. THE ART OF DISTINGUISHING BETWEEN THE LAW AND THE GOSPEL.

While it is comparatively easy to distinguish between the Law and the Gospel in theory, it is extremely difficult to apply the distinction in practise. Luther very correctly remarks that the true distinction between the Law and the Gospel in practise lies beyond the natural powers of man and can be accomplished only through the operation of the Holy Ghost. The reason for this is to be found in the natural disposition of man, who persistently clings to the *opinio legis,* that is to say, to the desire to save himself by work-righteousness. To this basic error also the believer is subject, namely, in so far as he is flesh. Hence he is constantly tempted to misapply the Law and the Gospel, so that he must ceaselessly pray God for illumination by His Holy Spirit, Ps. 143, 10.

However, still more difficult is the task of the Christian pastor, who must rightly divide the Word of Truth in his official capacity as a minister of Jesus Christ, 2 Tim. 2, 15. Here the words of Luther hold: "Whoever knows well this art of dividing the Law from the Gospel, him put in the first place and call him a doctor of Holy Scripture." The Christian minister must constantly teach the Law and the Gospel side by side, with proper regard for both their distinction and their connection, so that the secure are terrified and the terrified are comforted. He must never commingle the two doctrines, but teach the Law in all its severity and the Gospel in its full sweetness.

Those who earnestly apply themselves to this task will readily agree with Luther, who says (St. L., IX, 798 ff.) : "Without the Holy Ghost it is impossible to make this distinction [*sc.,* between the Law and the Gospel]. I know it from my own experience and also daily perceive it in others how hard it is to separate the doctrine of the Law from that of the Gospel. Here the Holy Ghost must be the Master and Teacher, otherwise no man on earth will be able to understand or teach it. The art is easily taught; it can be quickly said that the Law is a word and doctrine different from the Gospel; but to distinguish them practically and to apply the art is labor and sorrow."

But while it is very difficult to distinguish the Law from the Gospel, it is absolutely necessary to do so, since without a proper distinction of the two doctrines there can be no saving faith and therefore also no true Christianity. Luther draws attention to this fact when he writes (St. L., IX, 798 ff.) : "If a mistake occurs at this point, it is impossible to tell a Christian from a heathen or a Jew; so important is the distinction."

Luther's reason for this verdict is not hard to understand. The cardinal doctrine of the Christian faith is that of justification by grace, through faith *(sola gratia; sola fide)*. In order to teach this doctrine in its Scriptural purity, it is necessary to exclude from it every demand of the Law, or every good work. As Luther says, justification must not be made to depend even on a pious Lord's Prayer if the full truth of the Christian doctrine is to be preserved. If at this point the severity of the divine Law is modified and the Gospel of divine grace in Christ is not presented in all its Scriptural sweetness, the sinner will never be truly contrite, nor will he cast himself entirely upon the mercy of God in Christ Jesus for his salvation. In short, unless the Gospel is strictly distinguished from the Law, it is impossible to teach justification by faith.

From this it furthermore follows that it is also impossible to comfort a sinner with the assurance of salvation if Law and Gospel are commingled. In other words, if in the article of justification the Law is mingled into the Gospel, so that man's salvation is made to depend on his fulfilment of God's righteous demands, he must forever doubt his state of grace; for it is then taken out of the almighty hand of God and placed into his own impotent hands. The mingling of the Law and the Gospel at this point therefore deprives a person of the greatest blessing which Christianity offers to the world, namely, the *certitudo gratiae et salutis* by faith in Christ Jesus, for whose sake God freely justifies the sinner who comes short of the glory of God; Rom. 3, 23. 24.

Luther says of this (St. L., IX, 619): "It is impossible that Christ and the Law should be able to dwell together in the heart; for either Christ or the Law must depart." What Luther means is this: Man trusts for salvation either in works or in Christ; or, what is the same, he desires to be saved either by the Law or by the Gospel. Between the two there is no middle ground. But woe to the sinner who trusts for salvation in the Law, Gal. 3, 10; 5, 4! Since he is unable to keep it, he is forever under its curse. Thus the mingling of the Law and the Gospel deprives the sinner of that true comfort which alone can sustain him in life and console him in death — the sure hope of salvation through faith in Christ Jesus.

Lastly, without the proper distinction between the Law and the Gospel it is also impossible to understand the Scriptures. The *Formula of Concord* directs attention to this point by calling the distinction between the Law and the Gospel "a special brilliant light, which serves to the end that God's Word may be rightly divided and the Scriptures of the holy prophets and apostles may be properly explained and understood" (Thor. Decl., V, 1). This statement of our Confession is no exaggeration; for, on the one hand, Scripture clearly says: "This do, and thou shalt live," Luke 10, 28, and, on the other: "A man is justified by faith, without the deeds of the Law," Rom. 3, 28. These statements are in themselves contradictory, just as contradictory as are yes and no. To remove the difficulty, the Antinomians endeavored to banish the Law from the Church to the court-house, so that within the Church nothing should be taught but the Gospel alone. But this procedure is unscriptural; for it is God's express will, set forth in His Word, that the Law (Moral Law) should be proclaimed without any qualification or abridgment to the end of time, Matt. 5, 18.

Modern rationalistic theologians try to do away with the contradiction by changing the Gospel into a law; but upon all who in this way empty the Gospel of its glorious content, God's Word pronounces the divine curse, Gal. 1, 8; 6, 14. In short, the contradiction must not be removed by discarding either of the two doctrines, but by properly distinguishing between the two and assigning each to its proper sphere. If that is done, we can readily understand why, on the one hand, Scripture says: "The man that doeth them (*sc.* the works of the Law) shall live in them," Gal. 3, 12, and, on the other: "A man is not justified by the works of the Law, but by the faith of Jesus Christ," Gal. 2, 16; for in that case we remember that the Law has been given us that we might come to the knowledge of our sins, Rom. 3, 20, and the Gospel, that we might obtain forgiveness of sins. In short, if we properly distinguish between the Law and the Gospel, the Bible will be to us a clear book; if we do not, it will forever remain dark and incomprehensible.

The truth of this statement is proved by the false attitude of the Romanists and of Protestant synergists toward the vital question of certainty of salvation *(certitudo salutis)*. These errorists commingle the Law and the Gospel by denying the *sola gratia* and teaching, either directly or indirectly, salvation by works. In consequence they maintain that a believer cannot be sure of his salvation *(monstrum incertitudinis)*. This means wilful rejection of a clear Scripture doctrine, Rom. 8, 38. 39; yet they attempt to base their false claim on Scripture, 1 Cor. 10, 12. They fail, however, to distinguish between the Law and the Gospel. Misled by their basic error, they forget that passages such as 1 Cor. 10, 12; Heb. 12, 14, etc., are Law, designed to warn and terrify the secure and indifferent, while passages such as Rom. 8, 38. 39; John 10, 27—29; 3, 16—18, etc., are Gospel, intended for the comfort of the contrite and penitent. According to the old man, believers always need the warnings of the Law, while according to the new man they rejoice in the sure hope of salvation held out to them in the precious Gospel, Rom. 5, 1—5. It is therefore absolutely necessary that the believer in general, as he privately judges his own state of grace, but especially the Christian minister, as he officially proclaims the divine way of salvation, clearly and sharply distinguish between Law and Gospel, 2 Tim. 2, 15.

But this can be done only when God bestows His grace upon us and keeps us in His grace. His Holy Spirit must teach and lead us to distinguish between the Law and the Gospel and to apply both in the right order. Without the illumination and guidance of the Holy Ghost no one can appeal from the condemnation of the Law to the blessed Gospel promises of forgiveness of sins, life, and salvation and trust in them. That is the Spirit's gracious work in us, Eph. 1, 19. 20; Phil. 1, 29; Col. 2, 12, just as perseverance in faith, by constant trust in the Gospel promises, is God's work in us, 1 Pet. 1, 5. Again, though the Law accuses and condemns man, nomism, which makes the Law the means of salvation by way of sanctification, is so deeply rooted in his flesh that as a born legalist he trusts in the works of the Law for salvation and refuses to appeal from the Law to the Gospel, which to the flesh is both a stumbling-block and foolishness, 1 Cor. 1, 23. Hence God must help and save us, working in us both to will and to do, Phil. 2, 13. Without His grace we can do nothing also in the matter of making the proper distinction between the Law and the Gospel. (Cp. Luther, St. L., IV, 2077 f.; IX, 446 ff.; XXII, 760 f.; V, 1171.)

6. BY WHOM THE PROPER DISTINCTION BETWEEN THE LAW AND THE GOSPEL IS SET ASIDE.

The proper distinction between the Law and the Gospel is set aside and hence Law and Gospel are commingled by —

a. *The Romanists,* who mingle the Law and the Gospel in the interest of their pernicious teaching of work-righteousness and of the uncertainty of salvation. The Council of Trent expressly anathematizes the doctrine that the "Gospel is the absolute and unconditional promise of eternal life, without the condition that he [man] must first keep the Law" (Sess. VI, Can. 20).

b. *The Calvinists,* who deny the *gratia universalis* and the operation of the Holy Ghost through the divinely appointed means of grace. In consequence of these errors they do not proclaim the universal Gospel promises of grace to all sinners, but condition the sinner's salvation on his compliance with the prescribed conditions on which God will accept the sinner. According to Charles Hodge the "external call" is "a promise of acceptance in the case of all those who comply with the conditions," while the Gospel is "a proclamation of the *terms on which God is willing to save sinners* and an *exhibition of the duty of fallen men* in relation to that plan" (*Syst. Theol.,* II, 642). Thus, in the final analysis, the Calvinists commit the same fatal mistake as the Romanists.

c. *The synergists,* who deny the *sola gratia* and make salvation depend on the sinner's own decision for grace. According to synergism the Gospel is a message of God promising grace to all who will apply themselves to grace. Synergism is therefore a return to the Pelagianistic camp of Romanism.

d. *All Modernists,* who deny the *satisfactio vicaria;* for, since they deny the vicarious atonement of Christ, they must teach salvation by works or the sinner's own atonement for his sins.

e. *Certain modern theologians,* who affirm a "higher unity" *("hoehere Einheit")* between the Law and the Gospel. According to their opinion the difference between the Law and the Gospel is one only of degree, not one of kind; for both, as it is falsely claimed, demand of the sinner moral works. In that case the Gospel, in the final analysis, is only a modified Law. This erroneous view, of course, completely annuls the distinction between the two doctrines. It converts the Gospel into Law and makes the sinner's salvation depend on his own obedience.

Luther, who is represented by these errorists as favoring this pernicious opinion, in reality distinguished between the Law and the Gospel as *plus quam contradictoria.*

In closing this chapter, we may call attention to the fact that in all cases where the Law and the Gospel are mingled into each other the purpose is always the same, namely, to eliminate the "foolish preaching" of the crucified and risen Savior as man's only hope of salvation and to confirm the pagan doctrine of salvation by works *(opinio legis).*

The result of all error in theology is, in the final analysis, the elimination of "the Lamb of God, which taketh away the sin of the world," John 1, 29. Luther says very correctly (St. L., XX, 873): "Whoever denies, blasphemes, or dishonors Christ in one point or article can teach or honor Him rightly in no other place."

In a more subtle way the Law and the Gospel are commingled by all who weaken the rigor of the Law, teaching that God is satisfied if men obey it as much as they can; by all who inject legal elements into the Gospel, depriving it of its sweetness; and by all who proclaim the Law to terrified sinners and the Gospel to such as are secure and carnally indifferent. The Law and the Gospel may thus be commingled with respect to their nature and contents, with respect to their functions, and with respect to the persons dealt with. But whenever the Law and the Gospel are commingled, the doctrine of justification by grace and the certainty of salvation are destroyed. In fact, where the distinction between the Law and the Gospel is not known and practised, there no man can become or remain a Christian. Luther's words therefore deserve careful consideration: "This distinction between Law and Gospel is the supreme art in Christianity, which all who glory in, and bear, the Christian name may and should understand." (St. L., IX, 798.)

THE DOCTRINE OF HOLY BAPTISM.
(De Baptismo.)

1. THE DIVINE INSTITUTION OF BAPTISM.

Baptism is not a mere church rite, but a divine ordinance *(institutio divina)*, which is to be in force till the end of time and must be observed by all Christians, Mark 16, 15. 16; Matt. 28, 19. 20. The command to baptize was given by Christ as emphatically as was that of preaching the Gospel, a fact which the apostles duly recognized, Acts 2, 38; 10, 48. This must be maintained despite the fact that it was St. Paul's special mission to evangelize rather than to baptize, 1 Cor. 1, 14. 15; for throughout his epistles he teaches both the necessity and the efficacy of Baptism, Rom. 6, 3. 4; Gal. 3, 27; Titus 3, 4—7; etc. Hence, if Quakers, the Salvation Army, and other enthusiasts reject Baptism as a mere "ceremony, which is not binding on the conscience," they reject God's own institution and ordinance. However, their rejection of Holy Baptism is only a corollary to their repudiation of the doctrine of the means of grace in general.

Modern rationalistic theologians (Holtzmann) deny the divine institution of Holy Baptism, though they admit that Baptism was a common practise in the early Christian Church. But all their arguments (Paul baptized only in exceptional cases, 1 Cor. 1, 14; Peter himself did not baptize, Acts 10, 48; Jesus did not baptize, but only taught, John 3, 22; 4, 2) cannot overthrow the clear words of Matt. 28, 19. 20 and Mark 16, 15. 16, where the divine institution of Holy Baptism is unmistakably taught.

Modern rationalizing theologians of a more conservative tendency indeed admit the divine institution of Baptism, but object to the so-called "legalistic character" of this ordinance. In reply to this rather vague argument we say that the Church's obligation to baptize is no more "legalistic" than is its duty to proclaim the Gospel. If men can be saved without Baptism, the reason is not that Baptism is "more legalistic" than is the proclamation of the Gospel, but that God in His infinite grace offers to the sinner already through the Word of the Gospel His entire grace with complete pardon. However, this fact does not make Baptism superfluous; for God, who is "superabundantly rich in His grace," wishes to give us "counsel and aid against sin *not merely in one way*" *(Smalcald Art.,* Part III, Art. IV). Assuredly, our blessed

Lord, who has instituted Baptism, does not want us to despise this holy and salutary Sacrament, Luke 7, 30.

The divine command to baptize always calls for water as the visible element that should be used in this Sacrament, John 3, 23; Acts 8, 36, so that the employment of any substitute renders Baptism invalid. All those of whose baptism we can obtain no reliable proof must be regarded as not having been baptized. (Cf. Luther, St. L., X, 2128 ff.)

While the use of water in Baptism is necessary, the manner in which it is applied *(modus applicandi)* is optional, since the Greek verb βαπτίζειν means not only to immerse, but also to wash (cf. Luke 11, 38; Mark 7, 3, where βαπτίζεσθαι means as much as νίπτεσθαι, or wash). Therefore our Lutheran Catechism rightly holds that to *baptize* means to "apply water by washing, pouring, sprinkling, or immersing." To those who insist that Baptism must be by immersion because it symbolizes burial into death, Rom. 6, 3. 4, our dogmaticians reply that Baptism signifies not only burial, but also the washing away of sins, Acts 22, 16, the outpouring of the Holy Ghost, Titus 3, 5. 6, and the sprinkling with the blood of Christ, Heb. 10, 22, cp. with Ex. 24, 8; Heb. 9, 19; 1 Cor. 10, 2, so that any one of the different modes of applying the water symbolizes its meaning.

If the objection is made that immersion is necessary because the entire person must be cleansed by Baptism, we answer that the cleansing power of Baptism does not lie in the amount of water used, but in the Sacrament itself, so that whoever receives it in any form is completely cleansed, John 13, 9. 10.

In passing, we may remind the reader that usually those who insist upon immersion because "Baptism must symbolize the burial into death" deny the very efficacy of the Sacrament to bury the baptized into Christ's death, that is, to secure for him the benefits of Christ's vicarious death. While they insist upon the form, they reject the essential part of Baptism; they retain the shell, but discard the kernel.

All objections to the divine institution of Holy Baptism have their source in man's conceited, unbelieving reason, which wilfully sets aside Holy Scripture as the only source and rule of faith. When men declare that Baptism is superfluous — just as are all the means of grace — because only the "baptism of the Spirit and fire" is required (Quakers); or because it is a "Jewish ceremony" (Salvation Army); or because Baptism is a mere church rite

(Modernists; rationalistic theologians); or because it was meant only for the primitive Church (Socinians); or because the Trinitarian formula of Matt. 28, 19 is an interpolation, since the concept of the Trinity, as expressed in this passage, was foreign to the mind of the primitive Church (modernistic theologians; cp. 2 Cor. 13, 14; Titus 3, 4—7; 1 Pet. 1, 10—12); or because the account of St. Matthew is unhistorical, since Christ did not rise from the dead; or because, in view of 1 Cor. 1, 14; John 3, 22; 4, 2, the passage Matt. 28, 19 cannot be regarded as a baptismal command issued by Christ, they prove that they wilfully set themselves against Holy Scripture and exalt their blind reason above the Word of God.

2. WHAT MAKES BAPTISM A SACRAMENT.
(De Forma Baptismi.)

In order that there may be a valid baptism, there must be application of water to an individual; for water and its application are essential elements of this sacred ordinance. But water alone does not make Baptism a Sacrament. As Luther rightly says in his Catechism: "Baptism is not simple water only, but it is the water comprehended in God's command and connected with God's word." St. Augustine expresses the same truth in the words: "When the Word is connected with the element, then the act becomes a Sacrament" (Accedit Verbum ad elementum et fit sacramentum); that is to say, the act becomes a Sacrament when it is performed according to Christ's institution. While the application of water is important, it is really the word of Christ connected with the application that makes Baptism "a washing of regeneration and renewing of the Holy Ghost."

The nature of this word of Christ is twofold. In the first place, it is a command (Matt. 28, 19 [lit.]: "Going therefore, disciple all the nations [make disciples of all the nations], baptizing them"). As the apostles were to go, so they were to make disciples by baptizing. The command to baptize is therefore very clear.

In the second place, the divine word connected with Baptism is a promise (Matt. 28, 19: "into the name [εἰς τὸ ὄνομα] of the Father and of the Son and of the Holy Ghost"). What these words express is that Baptism is not an empty ceremony, but an efficacious means of grace, by which the baptized enters (through faith, of course, and not merely ex opere operato) into communion with the Triune God. The words therefore are a most gracious promise and as such explain why the apostles could "make disciples by baptizing."

The baptismal promise is stated more clearly in Mark 16, 16 as follows: "He that believeth and *is baptized shall be saved.*" In Rom. 6, 4 the promise is put still more definitely: "We are buried with Christ by Baptism into death" (*sc.* Christ's death). In Gal. 3, 27 St. Paul declares that they who have been baptized into Christ *have put on Christ,* namely, His righteousness and merits (justification).

Baptism is therefore correctly defined as water comprehended in God's command and connected with God's promise of forgiveness of sins, life, and salvation.

It has been pointed out (Tertullian, *De Bapt.,* c. 5) that some heathen religions had their own established baptisms *(Sacris quibusdam [nationes exterae] per lavacrum initiantur Isidis alicuius aut Mithrae).* These baptisms were man-made and therefore inefficacious; but Christ, the omnipotent, omniscient Lord, established by His divine command that true Baptism (a divine means of grace) through which the baptized enters into communion with the true God and all His spiritual blessings of grace and forgiveness (καθαρισμός, λουτρὸν παλιγγενεσίας καὶ ἀνακαινώσεως πνεύματος ἁγίου, Titus 3, 5 f.).

Since Christ commanded His holy apostles and thus the entire Christian Church to baptize "in the name of the Father and of the Son and of the Holy Ghost," this form of Baptism *(Taufformel)* must be employed by the Christian believers whenever they administer the holy Sacrament. This is not disproved by the fact that Scripture sometimes speaks of Baptism as performed "in" or "into the name of Christ" (Acts 2, 38: ἐπὶ τῷ ὀνόματι Ἰησοῦ Χριστοῦ; 8, 16: εἰς τὸ ὄνομα κυρίου Ἰησοῦ; 10, 48: ἐν τῷ ὀνόματι Ἰησοῦ Χριστοῦ; Gal. 3, 27: εἰς Χριστόν; Rom. 6, 3: εἰς τὸν Χριστόν).

The baptism "by authority of," or "into the name of," Christ does not stand in opposition to the baptism into the name of the Triune God, since, on the one hand, Christ instituted the Sacrament, and, on the other, those who are baptized enter into communion with the Triune God only through faith in Christ. The two series of passages are therefore not exclusive, but inclusive; that is to say, he who is baptized is baptized by Christ's command into the Triune God through Christ Himself. In other words, we must never separate Baptism from Christ; it exists only because Christ commanded it, and it is efficacious only because it rests on His vicarious atonement, by which He secured all the spiritual blessings that are offered in Baptism.

This is the clear doctrine of St. Paul, who writes: "Christ also loved the Church and gave Himself for it that He might sanctify and cleanse it *with the washing of water by the word,*" Eph. 5, 25. 26. Baptism is therefore a sanctifying and cleansing water by virtue of the word (Gospel) connected with it, in which Christ freely offers to all men the merits which He secured when "He gave Himself" into death for the sins of the whole world. Every true baptism consequently is always in relation to Christ and because of this also in relation to the Holy Trinity.

Zoeckler, in his commentary on Acts 2, 38, rightly remarks that the apostles, when baptizing "in the name of Jesus," no doubt used the form prescribed in Matt. 28, 19, quoting in this connection the Διδαχή (7, 2. 3). This was in full accord with their constant insistence on the Triune God as the only true and living God and the Source and Author of all spiritual blessings, 2 Cor. 13, 14; Eph. 1, 2—14; 1 Pet. 1, 2—4.

It is immaterial whether the minister uses the formula "I baptize thee in the name of the Father, Son, and Holy Ghost" (Lutherans, Roman Catholics) or the one employed by the Greek Catholic Church: "This servant is baptized in the name of the Father, Son, and Holy Ghost." Even such a formula as "I baptize thee in the name of the Holy Trinity" is valid. But it must be borne in mind that the most fitting formula is that which comes closest to the words of institution. No minister should change the formula established in the Church, since deviations are bound to cause doubt and arouse disputation.

The question as to how we must regard baptismal acts performed by anti-Trinitarian heretics "in the name of the Father and of the Son and of the Holy Ghost" has been clearly and unanimously answered by all Christian teachers. Already St. Augustine reports that at his time heretics frequently baptized in the name of the Triune God, but that such a baptism was not recognized as valid by the Church.

Rejecting such a baptism is done on Scriptural grounds; for while it is true that in this case the name of the Holy Trinity is used, it is also true that such a use of God's name is only mockery and blasphemy, since these heretics do not believe in the God whose name they employ. Our dogmaticians therefore rightly contend that in all these cases God's Word is lacking, so that there is a "baptism" without the Word of God, and consequently no true baptism.

This case, of course, differs from one where an unbelieving minister (a hypocrite) serves a *Christian congregation;* in that case his personal unbelief does not invalidate Baptism, since he, when administering Baptism, serves as the representative of the Christian Church.

It goes without saying that every baptism should be absolutely certain, so that the baptized may truly comfort himself with the covenant of grace established in Holy Baptism. In all cases of uncertainty the person in question must therefore be baptized. But this is not to be regarded as a *second* baptism or as a *repetition* of baptism, since an uncertain baptism is really no baptism. In conclusion we may say that we accept as valid all acts of baptism performed within and by professed Christian congregations.

3. BAPTISM A TRUE MEANS OF GRACE.

Baptism, according to Scripture, is not a mere ceremony or church rite, but a true means of grace *(aqua divino mandato comprehensa et Verbo Dei obsignata),* by which God offers and conveys to men the merits which Christ secured for the world by His vicarious satisfaction, Acts 2, 38. Luther in his Catechism therefore says: "Baptism works forgiveness of sins, delivers from death and the devil, and gives eternal salvation to all who believe this, as the *words* and *promises* of God declare." (Mark 16, 15. 16.) Very aptly our dogmaticians have called Baptism "a means of justification" *(medium iustificationis sive remissionis peccatorum),* which belongs into the Gospel, not into the Law. That is to say, Baptism does not save as a work which *we* perform unto God (not as the fulfilment of an obligation), but rather as a work of God in which *He deals with* and blesses us. "There is here no work *done by us,* but a treasure which *He gives us.*" (Luther, *Triglot,* p. 741.)

Baptism bestows nothing else than what also the Gospel offers and imparts; it works forgiveness of sins, Acts 2, 38, washes away sin, Acts 22, 16, sanctifies and cleanses, Eph. 5, 26, regenerates and saves, Titus 3, 5; 1 Pet. 3, 21, etc. Moreover, what the Holy Spirit does through the Gospel, working and strengthening faith, Rom. 1, 16; 1 Cor. 2, 4, He does also through Baptism, 1 Pet. 1, 23; Titus 3, 5. In fact, Baptism confers all divine spiritual blessings just because it is water connected with the Gospel promises of grace and salvation. As these divine promises are efficacious whenever they are heard or read, so they are efficacious also when they are applied in Baptism. "By the Word such power is imparted to Baptism that it is a laver of regeneration." (Luther, *Triglot,* p. 739.)

The distinctive difference between Baptism and the Gospel in general is this, that God's *individual offer of grace* in Holy Baptism through its application by water to the individual person becomes the *visible Word (Verbum visibile).* The *Apology* (Art. XIII [VII], 6) rightly remarks: "Just as the Word enters the ear in order to strike our heart, so the rite itself strikes the eye in order to move the heart. The effect of the Word and of the rite is the same, as it has been well said by Augustine that a Sacrament is a *visible word,* because the rite is received by the eyes and is, as it were, a picture of the Word, signifying the same thing as the Word. Therefore the effect is the same."

The truth just stated must be maintained against both Romanists and Calvinists. The papists indeed teach that through Baptism grace is bestowed upon the baptized *(gratia infusa),* but they err in claiming that this occurs *ex opere operato,* that is, without faith on the part of the person who is baptized. Against this error the *Apology* testifies (XIII [VII], 18 ff.): "This is absolutely a Jewish opinion, to hold that we are justified by a ceremony, without a good disposition of the heart, *i. e.,* without faith. . . . We teach that in the use of the Sacraments faith ought to be added, which should believe these promises and receive the promised things there offered in the Sacrament. The promise is useless unless it is received by faith."

The Council of Trent (Sess. VII, Can. 8) expressly anathematizes the Scriptural doctrine (Rom. 4, 11) that divine grace offered in the Sacraments is received only by faith. The Church of Antichrist therefore makes it impossible for its followers to obtain grace, since Holy Scripture teaches that faith is the only effectual means by which forgiveness of sins, life, and salvation can be secured, Mark 16, 15. 16; Rom. 4, 20—25. Its doctrine of Baptism is designed not to confer grace, but to deprive the sinner of grace; not to comfort him, but to impress upon him the *monstrum incertitudinis gratiae.*

The Church of Rome pretends to be the true defender of Christian Baptism, but in reality it despises and invalidates it. According to Roman Catholic doctrine, Baptism completely destroys original sin, so that the remaining evil lust in the flesh *(concupiscentia vel fomes)* is no longer sin, a doctrine which is entirely opposed to Scripture, Rom. 7, 17—20. But to this error Romanism adds another, namely, that those who through mortal sins have fallen from grace may return to it, not indeed by faith in the baptismal promises, but by means of the "second board," namely, through penance, or the performance of *contritio cordis, confessio oris, satisfactio operis.* The Roman Catholic doctrine of Baptism is therefore designed from beginning to end to support the papistic doctrine of salvation by works.

In agreement with the Romanists are all Romanizing Protestants who claim that Baptism indeed works regeneration, but without actually kindling faith. They thus regard baptismal grace as conferred without a receiving means on the part of man, whereas Scripture teaches very clearly that there can be no regeneration without faith in the forgiveness of sins secured by Christ, John 1, 12. 13; 3, 5. 14. 15; 1 John 5, 1, and offered and conveyed to men by the means of grace. The Lutheran Church, on the other hand, teaches correctly that Baptism is a means of regeneration for the reason that it offers and conveys forgiveness of sins and works and strengthens faith through its gracious Gospel offer. All (Romanists and Romanizing Protestants) who deny that Baptism is *primo loco* a means of justification by faith in the proffered grace intermingle Law and Gospel by making Baptism a means of sanctification, not by faith, but by works.

The Scriptural doctrine concerning the efficacy *(efficacia, virtus)* of Baptism is rejected *in toto* by the Reformed. According to the Zwinglian view, Baptism is not a means *(vehiculum)*, but only a *symbol* of forgiveness and regeneration *(factae gratiae signum)*, the Holy Ghost working regeneration in man by immediate operation. ("Efficacious grace acts immediately.") *"Non affert gratiam baptismus."* (Zwingli, *Fidei Ratio,* Niemeyer, p. 25.)

Water, according to the Calvinistic doctrine, simply cannot do such great things. (Boehl: *"Das Wasser kann solche hohe Dinge nicht tun." Dogmatik,* p. 560.) This Luther admits to be true when he writes: "It is *not the water* indeed that does them." But then follows his classic explanation: "[It is not the water indeed that does them,] but the word of God [the conferring means] which is in and with the water, and faith [the receiving means], which trusts such word of God in the water. For without the word of God the water is simple water and no Baptism. But with the word of God it is a Baptism, that is, a gracious water of life and a washing of regeneration in the Holy Ghost, as St. Paul says, Titus, chapter third."

According to Luther, Baptism therefore "works forgiveness of sins, delivers from death and the devil, and gives eternal salvation to all who believes this," just because the words and promises of God in Baptism so declare or because Baptism is not simple water only, but water comprehended in God's command and connected with God's word (promise).

Luther thus makes the efficacy of Baptism depend entirely on the Gospel promises which are connected with the water, Matt. 28, 19; Mark 16, 15. 16; Acts 2, 38; for on these promises the faith of the baptized rests. "Faith must have something upon which it stands and rests." (Luther, *Triglot*, p. 739.)

Zwingli's denial of the efficacy of Baptism was the result of his refusal to believe the promises which God has joined to the Sacrament. While Luther said that he would with joy and thanksgiving pick up a blade of straw if God had connected with this act such promises as are given in Baptism (St. L., XVI, 2296), Zwingli persistently repeated his rationalistic argument that "water cannot do such great things" and that he "never read in Scripture that the Sacraments offer and distribute grace" *(Fidei Ratio,* Niemeyer, pp. 24. 25), though he certainly knew such clear passages as Acts 2, 38; 22, 16; Eph. 5, 26; Titus 3, 5; etc. Luther was a true theologian, loyal to Scripture *(Schrifttheolog),* while Zwingli, just like his followers (Boehl, etc.), argued away the efficacy of Baptism on rationalistic grounds.

As the Reformed deny that Baptism is a *means of regeneration (initiationis et regenerationis sacramentum),* so they also deny that it is a means by which a person is joined to the spiritual body of Christ, namely, the Church, 1 Cor. 12, 13, and by which the sanctification of the regenerate, namely, the crucifying of the old man and the raising up of the new man, is effected, Rom. 6, 1—11. According to the Reformed view these things are only *symbolized* by Baptism. Zwinglianism (Calvinism), as said before, is therefore a denial of the efficacy of Baptism *in toto.* Every blessing which Scripture ascribes to this Sacrament is consistently denied on the strength of the rationalistic axiom: "Water cannot do such great things; it is the Spirit who must accomplish them."

From the rationalistic viewpoint this rejection of the efficacy of Baptism by the Reformed is quite intelligible. As Calvinism acknowledges no means of grace whatever in the Scriptural sense

("Efficacious grace acts immediately"; "Nothing intervenes between the volition of the Spirit and the regeneration of the soul"), so it also rejects the special means of grace known as the Sacrament of Baptism.

Baptism is a *medium remissionis peccatorum et regenerationis* also in the case of adults who have already been regenerated through the Gospel. Our dogmaticians declare that such "adults receive an increase of those gifts by Baptism" (Gerhard), since they are confirmed and kept in their faith through the baptismal confirmation of the Gospel-promise. Baptism, like the Gospel itself, the seed of regeneration, 1 Pet. 1, 23, engenders faith not only at conversion, but continuously, Rom. 10, 17.

All other blessings of Holy Baptism, such as sanctification, or the continued renewing begun in Baptism, Titus 3, 5, the crucifying of the old man, the revival of the new man, Rom. 6, 3—6, etc., result from the justification and regeneration which it works. So also the implanting into the body of Christ, which is effected by Baptism, 1 Cor. 12, 13, is the necessary concomitant of its imparting of faith and the working of forgiveness of sins. Luther writes: "Therefore, if you live in repentance, you walk in Baptism, which not only signifies such a new life, but also produces, begins, and exercises it. For therein are given grace, the Spirit, and the power to suppress the old man, so that the new man may come forth and become strong." (*Large Catechism, De Baptismo,* 75.) It is Baptism therefore that enables us to keep our baptismal vow.

In connection with Baptism, Lutheran dogmaticians have discussed also the question whether a *materia coelestis* (a heavenly element) may be said to exist in this Sacrament, just as in the Lord's Supper the *materia coelestis* is the body and blood of Christ. While some (Gerhard, Calov, Quenstedt) affirmed the question ("The *materia coelestis* in Baptism is the word of God, the Holy Spirit, Christ's blood, the Holy Trinity," etc.), others (Baier, etc.) suggested that it is better not to speak of a *materia coelestis* in Baptism, especially since the Holy Ghost, the word, the Holy Trinity, etc., may be called a *materia coelestis* not in a strict *(stricte loquendo),* but only in a wider sense (Hollaz). The point is well taken; for in Baptism there is, properly speaking, no celestial element that corresponds to the body and blood of our Lord in the Holy Supper.

Between the word and the water in Baptism there exists so

intimate a union that we must not distinguish between a *baptismus internus et externus.* "There is but *one* Baptism and *one* washing." (*Saxon Visitation Articles; Triglot,* p. 1153.) Cp. also [We reject the false and erroneous doctrine of the Calvinists] "that Baptism is an outward washing of water, whereby an inner washing [ablution] from sins is only signified." (*Triglot,* p. 1155.)

4. THE USE OF BAPTISM.

While the Lord's Supper should be used frequently by the believer, 1 Cor. 11, 26, Scripture nowhere commands that Baptism should be applied to one and the same person oftener than once. On the contrary, Baptism, once applied, should comfort and exhort the believer throughout his life, 1 Pet. 3, 21; Gal. 3, 26. 27; Rom. 6, 3 ff. For this reason the apostles in the New Testament again and again remind Christians of their Baptism, 1 Cor. 1, 13; 6, 11; 12, 13; Rom. 6, 3 ff.; Eph. 4, 5; Col. 2, 11. 12; Titus 3, 5. 6; 1 Pet. 3, 21; etc., and urge them to heed not only its sweet comfort, but also its great significance for sanctification. *Baptismus semper exercendus est.* (*Large Catechism, De Baptismo,* 65.)

The daily repentance of the Christian believer *(poenitentia stantium)* is nothing else than a constant penitent return to the covenant of grace which God has established with him in Baptism, or the continuous apprehension by faith of the gracious promises of forgiveness, life, and salvation offered and conveyed to him in this precious Sacrament. So also the repentance of the apostates from the Christian faith *(poenitentia lapsorum)* is only a return to their baptism *(reditus ad baptismum),* not their laying hold of the "second board" *(secunda tabula)* of the papistic penance *(satisfactio operis).* This truth the Christian minister must always inculcate upon his hearers, especially when he is called upon to instruct and confirm catechumens.

Confirmation is not "a confirmation of Baptism" nor "a Sacrament which supplements and perfects Baptism," but only a public profession of loyalty to the true God, who in Baptism establishes His covenant of grace with men. It is the believer's public reply to his baptism, or his public confession of Christ, who has cleansed him in Baptism, Eph. 5, 26; Matt. 10, 32. Confirmation, of course, was not instituted by Christ; yet we retain it as a laudable, useful Christian custom (though not as a Sacrament), because it so vividly reminds the believer of His baptism and the exceeding grace which God conferred on him in that priceless Sacrament.

5. WHOM THE CHURCH SHOULD BAPTIZE.
(Obiectum Baptismi.)

Holy Scripture teaches that both adults and children should be baptized. With respect to adults, Scripture expressly points out that only such should be baptized as believe in, and confess, Christ, Acts 2, 41; 8, 36—38. Children are to be baptized if they are brought to us for baptism either by their parents or by such as have parental authority over them, Mark 10, 13—16. The Lutheran Church has always condemned the unscriptural papistic practise of baptizing children without the knowledge or against the will of the parents (baptism in secret). We therefore baptize only such children as are offered for baptism by those who have parental authority over them.

That infants should be baptized is a clear doctrine of Scripture (cp. Mark 10, 13—16 with Col. 2, 11. 12). We may outline the Scripture evidence for infant baptism as follows: a) Infants are flesh born of flesh and as such are lost in sin, Ps. 51, 5; John 3, 5. 6. b) It is God's will that also infants should be regenerated and saved, Mark 10, 13—16, by their being brought to Christ, Luke 18, 15—17. c) The means by which infants are brought to Christ is Baptism, Titus 3, 5. 6; 1 Pet. 3, 21; Col. 2, 11. 12. Hence infants are to be baptized.

Scripture expressly records that in the primitive Christian Church believers were baptized "with their whole house," 1 Cor. 1, 16; Acts 11, 14; 16, 15. 33. All those who deny that this included infants must furnish the evidence for their contention.

To the objection that infant baptism is not mentioned in the Bible and that hence it was not practised in apostolic times we rejoin that this argument does not apply, since infant baptism may not have been mentioned just because it was so self-evident.

From Col. 2, 11. 12 we know that Baptism in the New Testament took the place of Circumcision, a Sacrament which was administered to male infants on the eighth day. This fact alone argues for pedobaptism, especially since our Lord commanded His apostles to baptize, and thus make disciples of, *all nations* ($\pi\acute{a}\nu\tau a$ $\tau\grave{a}$ $\check{\epsilon}\vartheta\nu\eta$), an expression which ordinarily includes children.

In short, both directly and indirectly Scripture inculcates infant baptism, so that the Christian Church need not be troubled on this point by the groundless objections of enthusiasts and fanatics, who base their opposition to pedobaptism chiefly on the supposition that infants cannot believe.

Scripture declares expressly that little children *can* believe, Matt. 18, 2—6; Mark 10, 13—16; Luke 18, 15—17; 1 John 2, 13. Nor is their faith a mere "potential faith" *(potentia credendi),* but actual faith *(fides actualis),* or direct faith, which truly apprehends the promises offered in Baptism.

If the objection is raised that it is impossible for us to conceive of direct faith in infants, we reply that it is also impossible for us to conceive of a direct faith in adults while they are asleep or in a coma. The question, however, is not whether we can comprehend the mysteries of faith by reason, but whether they are actually taught in Scripture.

With respect to infant baptism it is proved by history that its practise was general in the second century. Origen (in *Epist. ad Rom. V:* "*Ecclesia ab apostolis traditionem accepit etiam parvulis baptismum dare*") quotes it as a general custom, while Tertullian, though disapproving of it himself on heretical grounds, testifies to its universal prevalence.

With regard to infants of Christian believers who die without Baptism, it is best to commend them to God's infinite mercy, who has power to work faith also without the ordained means of grace (Luke 1, 44, cp. with Luke 1, 15; cp. also the female infants in the Old Testament, who were not circumcised). With respect to the infants of unbelievers and heathen we dare not affirm that they are saved, Eph. 2, 12. Here rather we confront the unsearchable judgments of God, Rom. 11, 33, concerning which the *Formula of Concord* warns us "that we should not reason in our thoughts, draw conclusions, nor inquire curiously into these matters." (*Trigl.,* p. 1081.)

The christening of all *res inanimatae* (bells, ships) is a mockery of Holy Baptism and ought to receive the emphatic disapproval of all earnest Christians.

From 1 Cor. 15, 29 it cannot be argued that Baptism may take place for the benefit of such as have died without this Sacrament (Mormons). The Greek preposition ὑπέρ in this passage has no doubt a *local,* not a vicarious, signification. While "baptism for the dead" was practised by some heretics, church history records no instance where this was in use within the ancient Christian Church. We therefore reject the practise as unchristian. That the just shall live by *his* faith and not by that of another is a clear doctrine of Scripture, Mark 16, 16; John 3, 15—18, and in itself a conclusive argument against this heretical practise.

6. THE ADMINISTRANTS OF BAPTISM.
(Causa Ministerialis Baptismi.)

As all spiritual blessings which Christ has secured by His vicarious death belong to all believers, 1 Cor. 3, 21. 22, directly and immediately (that is, without the mediation of a clerical estate), so also Baptism. For this reason the question as to who should administer the Sacrament of Baptism (administrants of Baptism) becomes very simple. In the absence of called and ordained pastors every Christian believer has not only the privilege, but also the duty to baptize (emergency baptism; lay baptism). In organized Christian congregations the called and ordained pastors administer the Sacrament by virtue of their office in the name of the believers who called them.

The Calvinists, who discountenance baptism by laymen, especially by women, claiming that only ordained ministers can rightly administer the Sacrament, go beyond, indeed against, Scripture, 1 Cor. 3, 21. The real reason why they take this stand is that they erroneously believe Baptism is not necessary, since salvation does not depend upon "water baptism," but upon the grace of election and of the divine covenant. (Cf. Alting, *Syllabus Controversiarum etc.*, p. 263; cp. Pieper, *Christl. Dogmatik,* III, p. 323.) Their argument that laymen, by baptizing, presume to exercise the functions of the public ministry is only a pretext; what motivates their objection to lay baptisms is really their repudiation of the means of grace. Their claim is that baptismal acts performed by laymen have no efficacy *(Baptismi nullam vim esse).* But actually, according to their principle, by which they reject the means of grace, Baptism is not efficacious under any circumstances, since it does not effect regeneration, but only symbolizes it.

7. THE NECESSITY OF BAPTISM.

While Baptism is no *adiaphoron,* but a divine institution and ordinance, we must not regard it as absolutely necessary in the sense that no one can obtain forgiveness of sins and be saved who has not received this Sacrament. *"Necessitas baptismi non est absoluta."* The reason for this is that already the preaching of the Gospel offers divine grace with forgiveness of sins, life, and salvation so completely and perfectly that any one who believes its promises is in possession of all spiritual blessings.

This truth Luther and all Lutheran dogmaticians consistently maintained against the papistic theologians, who endeavored to prove the absolute necessity of baptism, though they modified their doctrine somewhat by teaching that all infants that die without baptism suffer only negatively (*poena damni, i. e.,* they do not behold God), not positively (*poena sensus, i. e.,* they do not experience the torments of the damned). Hodge's claim that also the Lutheran theologians teach the absolute necessity of baptism (*Outlines,* p. 502) ignores the fact that it is true Lutheran doctrine that "not the lack, but only the contempt of Baptism damns" *(Contemptus sacramenti damnat, non privatio).*

While the confessional Lutheran Church has always emphasized the absolute necessity of faith in the forgiveness of sins for Christ's sake *(sola fide),* it has never taught the absolute necessity of baptism. To those who try to prove the absolute necessity of baptism from John 3, 5 we reply that Christ here rebuked the pharisaic contempt for Baptism; for of the Pharisees and lawyers we are told expressly that they "rejected the counsel of God against themselves, being not baptized of him," John the Baptist, while of "all the people and the publicans" the holy writers declare that they "justified God" (*i. e.,* acknowledged God's counsel of salvation), "being baptized with the baptism of John," Luke 7, 29. 30. As Christ, so also we must insist upon the necessity of baptism *(necessitas praecepti; necessitas medii)* over against all who despise this holy Sacrament, repeating the words of our Lord: "Except ye be born again of water and of the Spirit, ye cannot enter into the kingdom of God." This emphatic preaching of the divine Law must not be weakened under any circumstances where the pastor deals with such as show contempt for Baptism.

8. REGARDING BAPTISMAL CUSTOMS.

Every baptismal act is valid in which water is applied to a person in the name of the Triune God. However, in the course of time many customs and ceremonies have attached themselves to this important Sacrament. These Gerhard (*Locus de Baptismo,* §§ 258—269) divides into three classes, namely, a) such as are based upon the divine command; b) such as were established by the apostles; and c) such as were added later.

However, when we speak of baptismal customs and ceremonies, we ought to exclude all acts commanded by God (the application of water in the name of the Triune God) and consider only the usages which were developed in the course of time within the Church. What God has established by divine command does not lie on the same level as that which has been added by men.

According to Dr. C. F. W. Walther (*Pastorale*, p. 130 ff.), the recognized customs and ceremonies of Baptism are the following: a) the reference to original sin; b) the giving of the name; c) the so-called "small exorcism"; d) the sign of the cross; e) a prayer and the benediction; f) the "large exorcism"; g) the reading of Mark 10, 13—16; h) the laying on of hands; i) the Lord's Prayer; j) the renunciation and the Apostles' Creed; k) the use of sponsors; l) the covering of the child with the baptismal garment; m) the final blessing. All these usages are in themselves only *res indifferentes* (adiaphora), which may be employed or omitted without injury to the sacramental action; nevertheless, as the *Formula of Concord* aptly remarks (Epit., X, 5), "herein all frivolity and offense should be avoided, and especial care should be taken to exercise forbearance towards the weak in faith, 1 Cor. 8, 9; Rom. 14, 13."

The reference to original sin is important; for by directing attention to this sin, the necessity of Holy Baptism is pointed out. The giving of the name is both comforting and hortative; for, on the one hand, it reminds the baptized that, since God has established His covenant with him who is thus personally named, he may at the remembrance of his sins always comfort himself with the assurance of baptismal grace; and, on the other, that he must continually walk in the newness of life, which the washing of water by the word signifies, Rom. 6, 4. The exorcism has been quite generally discarded; wherever it is retained, care must be taken to show that it does not refer to any bodily obsession, but to the spiritual thraldom which Satan exercises over all men by nature, Eph. 2, 2. 3.

Since the use of sponsors often causes difficulties to the Christian minister, it is well for him to give adequate instruction on this point in due time. It goes without saying that only fellow-believers can be asked to fulfil the sacred obligations of godparents (*e. g.*, the Christian training of the child in case of the parents' death), so that in Lutheran churches only fellow-Lutherans may serve as sponsors. Heterodox friends of the baptized may serve only as witnesses to the holy act of baptism. If such heterodox persons are professed enemies of the true faith, they ought not to be admitted even as witnesses; for they may afterwards hinder the baptized in his Christian faith, 1 Cor. 15, 33. If among those who have been asked to serve as sponsors there are none who may be admitted as godparents, the pastor, treating them all as mere witnesses, must not obligate them to fulfil the duties of true Christian sponsors. The Roman Catholic doctrine that the sponsors enter into a spiritual relationship with the baptized is not based upon Scripture, but upon anti-Scriptural tradition.

The renunciation (*abrenuntiatio Satanae*) in connection with the Apostles' Creed points out the *effect* of Holy Baptism; for through this means of grace the baptized is transplanted from the kingdom of Satan into that of Jesus Christ, our Lord, John 3, 5. The questions which are asked at this point are directed to the baptized, not to the sponsors, though these answer them in the name of the child; for whoever is baptized (including also infants) is baptized upon his own faith and not upon that of his sponsors or upon a potential future faith.

This faith Baptism itself works as a means of regeneration, Titus 3, 5, through the Gospel, Rom. 1, 16. 17, with which it is connected, Mark 16, 15.-16; for wherever the Gospel is proclaimed, there the Holy Spirit is present to work faith and regeneration, 1 Cor. 2, 4. 5; Rom. 10, 17; Jas. 1, 18; 1 Pet. 1, 2—5.

Scripture teaches very plainly that God's grace, offered in the conferring means (*media δοτικά*), is apprehended only through faith as the receiving means (*medium ληπτικόν*), so that we must reject as a pernicious error any doctrine claiming that Baptism works *ex opere operato*, Acts 16, 31; Rom. 1, 16. 17, or without faith.

That also infants (*τὰ βρέφη*) can believe is clear from Jesus' own words, Matt. 18, 6; Luke 18, 15ff.; 2 Tim. 3, 15.

Speaking of infant baptism in general, Luther rightly says (St. L., XI, 497): "The baptism of infants, and the comfort we derive from it, rest upon the word: 'Suffer little children to come unto Me and forbid them not; for of such is the kingdom of God.' He has spoken this, and He does not lie. Hence it must be right and a Christian act to bring little children unto Him, which can be done in no other way than through Baptism. For this reason it must also be certain that He blesses them and that He gives the kingdom of heaven to all who come to Him in this way; for He adds: 'Of such is the kingdom of God.'"

Speaking more specifically of the faith of infants, Luther rightly argues that we can be more certain of the faith of infants than of that of adults because the latter may wilfully resist, which wilful resistance is not found in little children. (St. L., XI, 496 f.)

If the objection is raised that it is rather strange to ask for a profession of the infant's faith and then to demand the answer from the sponsors, we reply that this is a public confession of our sincere belief that the child indeed has faith, though it is unable to make public profession of it. The confession is the more necessary since there are so many who deny that infants can have true faith, Matt. 18, 6, though they claim to be believing Christians (Calvinists).

To the suggestion that the questions "Do you believe in God the Father, Son, and Holy Ghost?" etc., should indeed be put to adults, but not to infants, we reply that the Church has not two kinds of Baptism (some sects: Children are "sprinkled," while adults are "baptized," *i. e.,* immersed), but, as St. Paul declares, only one (Eph. 4, 5: "one Lord, one faith, one Baptism"). (Cp. St. L., XI, 490.)

The question "At what time during the baptismal act is faith engendered in the child?" need not give us much concern. So Luther treats this query. His contention is that we bring little children to Baptism upon the command of our Lord, no matter whether they believe "either before or in baptism" (St. L., XI, 489). Since the divine command has been given, Mark 10, 13—16; Luke 18, 15—17, we must bring our little children to Jesus and trust Him to bless them when and how He wills. (St. L., XI, 495.)

However, since no human ceremony is properly a part of Baptism and therefore has no divine promise attached to it, it is correct to say that faith is engendered in that moment when the water is applied to the infant in the name of the Triune God. If before this solemn act the question is put to the child, "Do you believe in God the Father, Son, and Holy Ghost?" this is done by way of anticipation to emphasize the Scriptural truth and Christian confession that Baptism is indeed a *medium iustificationis,* or the means of regeneration, by which faith is engendered.

In conclusion we may remark that the Scriptural doctrine of infant faith is a test of a person's faith in God's Word. If at this point we consult reason, we shall deny that little children can believe and like the erring disciples rebuke those who bring infants to Jesus to have them baptized, Luke 18, 15. However, in that case Jesus "is much displeased" also with us and reprovingly commands us: "Suffer the little children to come unto Me and forbid them not; for of such is the kingdom of God," Mark 10, 14.

Indeed, then He warns us, too, that we shall not enter the kingdom of God unless we receive it "as a little child," Mark 10, 15. Also with respect to the faith of regenerate infants, Christ exhorts us: "Be not faithless, but believing. . . . Blessed are they that have not seen and yet have believed," John 20, 27—29.

9. THE BAPTISM OF JOHN THE BAPTIST.

Our Lutheran dogmaticians (Chemnitz, Gerhard, Aegidius Hunnius, etc.) have always identified the baptism of John with that of the Christian Church so far as its *purpose* and *efficacy* are concerned. Modern theologians have censured this "essential and complete identification" of the two (Thomasius, *Dogmatik,* IV, 10). However, our older dogmaticians based their teaching on firm Scriptural ground; for according to Scripture John's Baptism was a true means of grace, possessing both the *vis dativa* and *vis effectiva* of Christian baptism.

The holy evangelists tell us expressly that John preached the "Baptism of repentance for the remission of sins," Mark 1, 4; Luke 3, 3, just as St. Peter on Pentecost, following the instructions of our Lord, preached Baptism "for the remission of sins," Acts 2, 38. For this reason John's baptism must be regarded as identical with that which Christ instituted at a later time, as our older dogmaticians rightly affirmed.

Since John the Baptist was the way-preparer for Christ and appeared in the name of the Lord, Luke 1, 76—79, his baptism was no less by divine command than was his preaching, John 1, 32—36; 5, 33—35. Hence also John's baptism was "water comprehended in God's command and connected with God's word" and as such a true means of grace.

To-day the question is, of course, of no practical importance, since the baptism of John is no longer in use. But the early Christian Church had to reckon with it, and Scripture records an instance where "certain disciples" who had been baptized "unto John's baptism" were at St. Paul's instigation "baptized in the name of the Lord Jesus," Acts 19, 1—6. The reason why this was done is quite evident. While the baptism of John was a true Sacrament, it was valid only during the time of preparation, until Christ should appear and finish His work. After Pentecost therefore the baptism of John no longer had any value, just as the Old Testament Sacrament of Circumcision, though still practised by the Jewish Christians, became a mere ceremony. (Kretzmann, *Popular Commentary,* Vol. 1, 630.)

Moreover, we may not be wrong in assuming that the "certain disciples" at Ephesus had not been baptized by John himself, but by some of his followers, who discarded their master's command to join Jesus as "the Lamb of God," John 1, 35—37; Matt. 9, 14. 15; Luke 5, 33. The "disciples of John," refusing to accept Jesus as the promised Savior, had therefore degenerated to a Judaistic sect, so that their baptism, properly speaking, was no longer "the baptism of John," but a godless "opposition baptism." (Acts 19, 2: "We have not so much as heard whether there be any Holy Ghost"; cp. with John 1, 33: "The same is He which baptizeth with the Holy Ghost.") John's witness of Christ evidently was no longer known to them.

There is yet another way of interpreting this passage, according to which Paul did not baptize these "certain disciples" at all, but merely laid his hands on them, whereupon they received the Holy Ghost. According to this interpretation, v. 5 gives the words of Paul, and not those of Luke, so that Paul here relates what the people did when they heard John the Baptist urging them to believe on Christ Jesus. In other words, when the people heard the preaching of John the Baptist concerning Christ, they were baptized in the name of the Lord Jesus, a fact which Paul here quotes to confirm the baptism of John. This simple interpretation has much in its favor, though it is quite commonly rejected by modern exegetes.

For the sake of completeness we may add that our older dogmaticians carefully distinguish the *baptismus fluminis,* or the "water baptism," which Christ instituted for the remission of sins, Matt. 28, 19; Mark 16, 15. 16, from the *baptismus flaminis,* or the outpouring of the gifts of the Holy Ghost, Acts 1, 5, and from the *baptismus sanguinis,* or martyrdom, Matt. 20, 22. It is understood, of course, that only the first is a true Sacrament and that in all other cases the term *baptism* is employed in a wider, or figurative, sense.

THE DOCTRINE OF THE LORD'S SUPPER.

(De Coena Sacra.)

1. THE DIVINE INSTITUTION OF THE LORD'S SUPPER.

The Lord's Supper is no less a divine institution and ordinance *(institutio divina)* than are Baptism, Matt. 28, 19, and the preaching of the Gospel, Mark 16, 15. 16. The Holy Supper, which our Lord instituted in the same night in which He was betrayed, was to continue in use till the end of time (Luke 22, 19: "This do in remembrance of Me"; 1 Cor. 11, 25: "This do ye, as oft as ye drink it, in remembrance of Me"). So the holy apostles and the primitive Christian Church understood the divine command, 1 Cor. 10, 16—22; 11, 17—34, and celebrated Holy Communion accordingly.

The divine institution of the Lord's Supper requires emphasis, since to-day certain enthusiasts (Quakers, the Salvation Army) reject the Holy Supper "as a mere ceremony not commanded by our Lord." In doing this, these enthusiasts are thoroughly consistent. Inconsistent enthusiasts (Calvinists) repudiate only the oral reception of the body and blood of Christ in Holy Communion *(manducatio oralis)* on the ground that "the flesh profiteth nothing" (a misapplication of John 6, 63), while the Quakers reject the Sacrament altogether, on the ground that "the kingdom of God is not meat and drink" (a misapplication of Rom. 14, 17) and that no man must judge the Christian "in meat or in drink" (a misapplication of Col. 2, 16).

According to Quakerian doctrine the true Lord's Supper is eaten and drunk in the heart (a misapplication of Rev. 3, 20). Quakerism teaches, moreover, that Christ celebrated the first Supper only for the benefit of His "weak disciples," so that this was meant for perpetuation as little as was "foot-washing," John 13, 5, or "the anointing of the sick with oil," Jas. 5, 14. 15, or "the abstaining from blood and from things strangled," Acts 15, 29. But the Quakers are not the only offenders in this respect.

Modern rationalistic theologians (B. Weiss, Juelicher, Spitta) have endeavored to disprove the divine institution of the Lord's Supper by arguments no more valid than are those which Quakerism employs ("Only Paul and Luke cite the words: 'This do in remembrance of Me,'" etc.). Cremer, on the contrary, rightly remarks that no fact in the New Testament is better attested than is the divine ordinance of the Holy Supper (RE,[3] I, 33).

In contradistinction to Holy Baptism, which is the *sacramentum initiationis,* or the Sacrament by which faith is engendered, the Lord's Supper is the *sacramentum confirmationis,* that is, the Sacrament by which faith is strengthened. Gerhard: *Per baptismum in foedus Dei recipimur; per usum sacrae coenae in eo conservamur. Per baptismum fides et reliqua Spiritus dona in nobis accendentur; per usum sacrae coenae augentur et confirmantur.*

Baptism therefore rightly precedes Holy Communion. On Pentecost, St. Peter urged the penitent Jews to be baptized, but not to receive the Lord's Supper, Acts 2. This fact is of great practical importance; for persons who desire to receive Holy Communion should first be baptized before they are admitted to the Lord's Table. (Cp. Col. 2, 11. 12: Baptism in the New Testament has taken the place of Circumcision; and in the Old Testament only the circumcised were admitted to the Passover, Ex. 12, 48.)

The names which are applied to this Sacrament are either given in Scripture directly (the breaking of bread, *κλάσις τοῦ ἄρτου,* Acts 2, 42; the Lord's Supper, *δεῖπνον κυριακόν,* 1 Cor. 11, 20; the Lord's Table, *τράπεζα κυρίου,* 1 Cor. 10, 21), or suggested by Scripture (Eucharist, *εὐχαριστήσας,* Mark 14, 23; Communion, 1 Cor. 10, 16; *Abendmahl* or *Nachtmahl,* 1 Cor. 11, 23). In the writings of the Church Fathers this Sacrament is also called "religious service" (*σύναξις*), "love-feast" (*ἀγάπη*), "liturgy" (*λειτουργία*), "sacrifice" (*θυσία*), "offering" (*προσφορά*), "mystery" (*μυστήριον*), "thanksgiving" (*εὐχαριστία, εὐλογία*), etc., and in those of the Latin fathers "mass" *(missa), coena Domini, sacramentum altaris,* etc.

As long as the names of the Sacrament are not used to express unscriptural doctrine, no controversy ought to be waged about them (cp. Luther, St. L., XX, 174 ff.). Luther at times employed the name *mass,* though he expressly rejected the papistic doctrine of the Mass, and he defended this use against his fanatic opponent Carlstadt. Modern German theologians (Holtzmann, Noesgen, etc.) frequently employ the term *Herrenmahl,* which is the equivalent of our English expression "Lord's Supper."

2. THE RELATION OF THE LORD'S SUPPER TO THE OTHER MEANS OF GRACE.

As the Gospel in its proper sense and Holy Baptism are means of justification and remission of sins *(medium iustificationis sive remissionis peccatorum),* so also is the Lord's Supper. That is to say, the Lord's Supper is not Law or a work which men perform for God, but pure Gospel, or a most gracious work, by which Christ deals with men, offering to all communicants the grace and merits which He obtained for the world by His death on the cross. The Lord's Supper is therefore a true means of grace, by which the Holy Spirit assures all communicants that they have a gracious God, who freely forgives their sins for Christ's sake.

This truth is taught in the words of institution: "Take, eat; this is My body, which is given for you"; and: "Take, drink; this is My blood, which is shed for you." Quite manifestly these words express the gracious Gospel-message that we need not atone for our sins, since Christ Himself has atoned for them by shedding His blood for us on the cross, and that we obtain full possession of these heavenly gifts by accepting in true faith the blessed Gospel offer which He makes to us in Holy Communion.

Luther well says (St. L., XIX, 346): "The mass [the Lord's Supper] is not a work or sacrifice [which men must render], but a word and sign of divine grace, which God employs on our behalf to establish and strengthen in us faith toward Him." So also the *Apology* declares (Art. XXIV [XII]): "The Sacrament was instituted for the purpose of being a seal and testimony of the free remission of sins, and accordingly it ought to admonish alarmed consciences to be truly confident and believe that their sins are freely remitted." The *Smalcald Articles* similarly classify the Lord's Supper among the means of grace, "by which the forgiveness of sins is preached" (Part III, Art. IV).

In common with Holy Baptism and private absolution *(Privatabsolution)* the Lord's Supper offers forgiveness of sins, life, and salvation to sinners *individually,* so that the same grace which the Gospel proclaims to all is announced and offered *personally* to every one who attends the Lord's Table. But the Lord's Supper has one characteristic which is not found in any other means of grace. In this Sacrament Christ confirms and seals His gracious forgiveness of sins by imparting *His own body and blood,* which the communicant receives in, with, and under the bread and wine, 1 Cor. 10, 16; 11, 27—29. The Lord's Supper thus has a true *materia coelestis* (the body and blood of Christ), which the Sacrament of Baptism has not, and through the gift of this "heavenly matter" Christ assures the communicant of the gracious forgiveness of his sins.

The Lord's Supper is therefore a most salutary Sacrament, in which every believer should greatly rejoice. But, alas! this precious Sacrament has been most shamefully perverted by men who exalted their conceited reason above the Word of God. The Romanists have not only mutilated it *(sub una specie)*, but have also changed it from an efficacious means of grace to an anti-Scriptural "unbloody sacrifice" (transubstantiation; the papistic sacrifice of the Mass for the sins of the living and the dead; cp. Luther, St. L., XIX, 1303). The Calvinists (Zwinglians), on the other hand, denied the real presence of the body and blood of our Lord in the Holy Supper and blasphemously charged the Lutherans, who maintained the true Scriptural doctrine concerning the *realis praesentia,* with cannibalism, Thyestean banqueting, and the like (cp. *Formula of Concord,* Thor. Decl., VII, 67: *duos pilos caudae equinae et commentum, cuius vel ipsum Satanam pudeat; excrementum Satanae, quo diabolus sibi ipsi et hominibus illudat).*

Other errorists, also going beyond Scripture, ascribe to the Lord's Supper a "physical" or "natural" operation *(physische Wirkung, Naturwirkung)* and thus turn the attention of Christians from the real purpose and function of the Holy Supper. It is the confutation of these errors that makes a more lengthy and detailed treatment of the doctrine of Holy Communion necessary.

3. THE SCRIPTURAL DOCTRINE OF THE LORD'S SUPPER.

The following three doctrines have been taught within Christendom concerning the Lord's Supper: —

a. In the Holy Supper there is only body and blood of our Lord Jesus Christ, that is to say, in the Eucharist the bread and wine are changed (transubstantiated) into the body and blood of our Lord *(transubstantiation;* established by the Lateran Council of 1215 as a dogma of the Roman Catholic Church and confirmed by the Council of Trent, Sess. XIII, Can. 2).

b. In the Holy Supper the bread and wine are only symbols or bare signs of the absent body and blood of Christ *("Abesse Christi corpus et sanguinem a signis tanto intervallo dicimus, quanto abest terra ab altissimis coelis"*; cp. *Formula of Concord,* Thor. Decl., VII, 4. 5; also the *Consensus Tigurinus,* XXII, Niemeyer, p. 196, where the Lutheran doctrine is rejected as "preposterous").

c. In the Holy Supper a peculiar union (the sacramental union) occurs by virtue of Christ's institution between the bread and the wine, on the one hand, and the body and blood of Christ, on the other, and because of this union all communicants *(manducatio generalis)* receive in, with, and under the bread and wine in a supernatural, incomprehensible manner Christ's true body and blood *(manducatio oralis)* as a pledge of the gracious remission of their sins.

This union is neither personal, as is the union of the two natures in Christ, nor mystical *(unio mystica),* as is that between Christ and the believer, but sacramental, that is to say, the *unio sacramentalis* takes place only in the Holy Supper *(praesentia sacramentalis).* It is neither natural nor local, but illocal, supernatural, and incomprehensible, yet real.

This doctrine has always been maintained by confessional Lutheranism as the true doctrine of Scripture. It is set forth in Luther's *Small Catechism:* "The Sacrament of the Altar is the true body and blood of our Lord Jesus Christ under the bread and wine, for us Christians to eat and to drink, instituted by Christ Himself"; in the *Augsburg Confession* (Art. X): "Of the Supper of the Lord they teach that the body and blood of Christ are truly present and are distributed to those who eat in the Supper of the Lord; and they reject those that teach otherwise"; in the *Formula of Concord* (Epit., VII, 6. 7): "We believe . . . that in the Holy Supper the body and blood of Christ are truly and essentially present and are truly distributed and received with the bread and wine. We believe . . . that the words of the testament of Christ are not to be understood otherwise than as they read, according to the letter, so that the bread does not signify the absent body and the wine the absent blood of Christ, but that on account of the sacramental union they [the bread and wine] are truly the body and blood of Christ."

If we compare the three tenets with Holy Scripture, we find that indeed only the Lutheran doctrine can be proved to be Scriptural. That transubstantiation does not occur in the Lord's Supper is shown by St. Paul in 1 Cor. 11, 27; 1 Cor. 10, 16, where he declares that the earthly elements (bread and wine) remain such even after the consecration. The contention of the Romanists that only "the external appearance and taste" *(visus et gustus corporeus)* of the earthly elements remain while their substance has disappeared is a "sophistical subtlety." In 1 Cor. 10, 16 and 1 Cor. 11, 28 St. Paul declares the very opposite to be true; for he speaks of the consecrated bread as still being bread, etc.

Luther is indeed right when he says *(Smalcald Articles,*

Part III, Art. VI) : "As regards transubstantiation, we care nothing about the sophistical subtlety by which they teach that bread and wine leave or lose their own natural substance and that there remain only the appearance and color of bread and not true bread. For it is in perfect agreement with Holy Scripture that there is and remains bread, as Paul himself calls it, 1 Cor. 10, 16 : 'The bread which we break'; and 1 Cor. 11, 28 : 'So let him eat of that bread.' "

Closely connected with the pernicious doctrine of transubstantiation are the papistic errors of the "sacrifice of the Mass," by which Christ's body "is continually offered up in an unbloody manner for the sins of the living and the dead," of the "adoration of the host" (*corpus Christi* festivals; Eucharistic Congresses), and of *sub una specie,* that is, the prohibition of the cup to the laity (cp. the pernicious doctrine of concomitance: with the consecrated host the communicant receives both the body and blood of our Lord). For these three papistic errors not even a shred of proof is found in Holy Scripture; indeed, the Word of God is strictly opposed to them, Heb. 10, 10—14; Matt. 26, 27; 1 Cor. 11, 24—26.

The Reformed doctrine ("The body and blood are absent from the Lord's Supper, but are received spiritually, or by faith") is disproved by the words of institution, where Christ says distinctly: "Take, eat, this is My body; take, drink, this is My blood." In other words, our Lord declares expressly of the bread which is eaten that it is His body and of the wine which is drunk that it is His blood. Chemnitz rightly affirms that, when Christ says: "Eat, drink," *He directly prescribes the way, or mode, of the receiving (modus sumptionis),* so that we indeed receive His body and blood with the mouth (oral reception; *manducatio oralis*).

Chemnitz, of course, does not champion a "Capernaitic," or natural, eating and drinking of the Lord's body and blood; for he teaches distinctly that, while the bread and wine are received in a *natural manner,* the body and blood of our Lord are received in a supernatural, incomprehensible manner. According to the words of institution the reception of Christ's body and blood with the mouth is true and real.

The words of institution, it is true, demand also a spiritual eating or drinking, or *faith in the words* "Given and shed for you for the remission of sins." This is proved directly by Christ's command: "This do in remembrance of Me." But what the words of institution declare in particular is that "in, with, and under the bread and wine Christ presents His true body and blood to be truly and substantially eaten and drunk by us." In other words, the words of institution say: *"That which I offer you, which you are to receive and eat, is not only bread, but also My body. That which I offer you, which you are to receive and drink, is not only wine, but also My blood."*

The papistic doctrine makes of the bread a "sham bread" *(Scheinbrot),* teaching that the bread is transubstantiated into Christ's body, while that of the Reformed makes of the body a "sham body," claiming that the bread is only a *symbol* of Christ's *absent* body. The Lutheran doctrine, on the contrary, affirms that the bread remains real bread also after the consecration, but that Christ's true body is substantially present in, with, and under the bread on account of the sacramental union. That is to say, Lutheranism accepts the words of institution as they read, or in their literal sense. It avers that our Lord, when instituting the Holy Supper, employed a mode of speech which is readily intelligible, namely, the so-called *locutio exhibitiva,* according to which only that object is named to which attention should be directed *(synecdoche).*

Our Savior said: "This [the bread] is My body; this [the wine] is My blood," directing the attention of the disciples not to that which was visible, namely, the bread and wine, but to that "which was exhibited through the medium of the bread and wine, namely, His body and blood." This is proved also by the words which He added: "which is given" and "which is shed"; for they show that Christ, when instituting the Holy Supper, had in mind His *real* body and His *real* blood.

Hollaz writes: "In the former proposition ('This is My body') the demonstrative pronoun *this* denotes the entire *sacramental complex,* consisting of bread and the body of Christ; in the latter proposition ('This is My blood') it likewise denotes the entire complex, consisting of . . . the wine and the blood of Christ, mysteriously united. Because the pronoun *this* is employed with regard to both the bread and the body, the Romish doctrine of transubstantiation is excluded. The substantive verb *is* connects the predicate with the subject and denotes that that which is offered in the Holy Supper is really and truly not only bread, but also the body of Christ." *(Doctr. Theol.,* p. 559. Cp. also Luther, St. L., XX, 1034 ff.)

To the objection of the Reformed (Hodge, *Syst. Theol.,*

III, 662) that, "if the bread is literally the body of Christ, it is no longer bread; for no one asserts that the same thing can be bread and flesh (or body) at the same time," we reply that this is a premise which not even the Calvinists concede. For although Scripture applies the same *locutio exhibitiva* to Christ (Luke 1, 35: "The Holy Thing which shall be born of thee shall be called the Son of God"), they nevertheless admit that Christ is not only true God, but also true man. (Cp. also Matt. 16, 16.) For this reason their argument "If the words of Christ are to be taken literally, they teach the doctrine of transubstantiation" (Hodge) is untenable. As the *locutio exhibitiva* in Luke 1, 35 does not exclude the existence of the true human nature in Christ, so the *locutio exhibitiva* in Matt. 26, 26—28 does not exclude the existence of true bread and wine in the Lord's Supper.

It has been pointed out that "the Reformed were not agreed among themselves" (Hodge). This well-known Reformed theologian says (*Syst. Theol.*, III, 626) that "there were three distinct types of doctrine among them, the Zwinglian, the Calvinistic, and an intermediate form, which ultimately became symbolical, being adopted in the authoritative standards of the Church." But Shedd, another Calvinistic theologian, admits (*Dogm. Theol.*, II, 569) that "the difference between Zwingli and Calvin upon sacramentarian points has been exaggerated."

In the final analysis all Reformed theologians were in full agreement with one another with respect to the "sacramentarian points." Their difference related to *expressions* rather than to *doctrines;* for they all held that Christ's body has only a local and visible mode of presence *(praesentia localis)* and, since it is now locally included in heaven, cannot be really present in the Holy Supper.

The *Formula of Concord* (Thor. Decl., VIII, 2) says: "When Dr. Luther . . . had maintained the true, essential presence of the body and blood of Christ in the Supper with solid arguments from the words of institution, the objection was urged against him by the Zwinglians that, if the body of Christ were present at the same time in heaven and on earth in the Holy Supper, it could be no real, true human body; for such majesty was said to be peculiar to God alone and the body of Christ not capable of it."

Calvin denied the real presence in the sense of the Lutheran teachers as much as did Zwingli, as also Hodge admits. Of this the *Formula of Concord* declares (Thor. Decl., VII, 5): "Afterwards, when they were forced by Christ's words to confess that the body of Christ is present in the Supper, they still understood and declared it in no other way than spiritually, that is, of partaking through faith of His power, efficacy, and benefits, because, they say, through the Spirit of Christ, who is everywhere, our bodies, in which the Spirit of Christ dwells here upon earth, are united with the body of Christ, which is in heaven."

Calvin's accommodation to the Lutheran terminology was done mainly in the interest of effecting a pan-Protestant union between the Reformed and the Lutherans. Dr. F. Bente is right when he says: "Calvin's doctrine was nothing but a polished form of Zwingli's crude teaching, couched in phrases approaching the Lutheran terminology as closely as possible." (*Concordia Triglotta*, Hist. Introd. XVIII, pp. 174 ff.)

However, while the Reformed agreed with respect to the doctrine that Christ's body is absent from the Holy Supper and is therefore received only spiritually by the believing communicant, they disagreed with regard to the *interpretation* of the words of institution. Carlstadt asserted that the word *this* does not refer to the bread, but to the body of the present Christ, who "pointed to His own body" while pronouncing the words of institution. ("I have always explained it thus that Christ pointed to His body when He said, 'This is My body.'" St. L., XX, 2325.)

Zwingli, on the other hand, explained the words of institution by taking the verb *is* in the sense of *signify (significat)*, so that the meaning is: "This signifies or represents My body."

Calvin (Oecolampadius), again, sought the figure of speech in the words "My body," explaining them as follows: "That which I give you is the sign of My body *(signum corporis).*" While Carlstadt's explanation of the words of institution was soon rejected as absurd even by Reformed scholars (Schenkel), those of Zwingli and Calvin, though just as arbitrary, were generally accepted.

Against Zwingli's contention that the verb *is* means as much as *signifies* Krauth (*Cons. Ref.*, p. 619) rightly declares: "Language itself would commit suicide if it could tolerate the idea that the substantive verb *is* shall express not substance, but symbol." On this point compare also Luther, St. L., XX, 909 ff.; also Meyer on 1 Cor. 10, 16, who, though personally favoring the Reformed interpretation, nevertheless declares: "'Εστί never means anything else than *est;* never does it mean *significat;* it is a copula, always expressing that which is *(die Kopula des Seins).*"

The passages adduced by Zwingli in proof for his doctrine (John 10, 9; 15, 5; 1 Cor. 10, 4; Luke 8, 11; Matt. 13, 38; 11, 14; Gal. 4, 24) do not support his claim. When, for example, it is said that "Christ is the Door," the verb *is* does not mean *signify,* but *is;* since in the realm of heavenly things Christ actually is what a door is in the realm of earthly things. In other words, as the door admits a person into a house, so Christ admits a person into heaven. Consequently the figure of speech *(tropus)* in the statements quoted is not to be sought in the verb *is,* but in the predicate noun (door, rock, vine, etc.). Luther is right when he says that no man can ever prove that in a single Scripture-passage, indeed in all the languages of the world, *is* means as much as *signifies* (St. L., XX, 905 ff.).

Dr. Krauth writes very correctly (*Cons. Ref.,* 618 ff.) : "A more dangerous falsity in interpretation than the assumption that the word *is* may be explained in the sense of *signify* or *be a symbol of* is hardly conceivable. Almost every doctrine of the Word of God will melt under it. 'The Word was God' would mean: 'The Word signified, was a symbol of, God.' 'God is a spirit' would mean: 'God is a symbol of a spirit.' When it is said of Jesus Christ: 'This is the true God,' it would mean that He is the symbol, or image, of the true God. By it Christ would cease to be the Way, the Truth, and the Life and would be a mere symbol of them. . . Creation, redemption, and sanctification would all fuse and be dissipated in the crucible of this species of interpretation. It would take the Bible from us and lay upon our breasts, cold and heavy, a Swedenborgian nightmare of correspondences."

Among the Reformed theologians who rejected Zwingli's interpretation we may note Keckermann († 1609) and John Piscator († 1625). Piscator thus writes: "In the copula *is* there can be no trope" *(in copula* EST *non posse esse tropum).*

However, must we then not adopt Calvin's interpretation? Calvin, as said before, interpreted the words of institution to read: "This is the sign of My body *(signum corporis).*" In other words, he affirmed that the words "My body" and "My blood" must be explained figuratively. Against this claim the Lutherans assert that the words do not allow a figurative interpretation, since Christ here speaks of that body *which was given into death and of that blood which was shed for the remission of sins* (Luther, St. L., XX, 1046 ff.).

Hollaz says: "It is readily inferred that in the Eucharist

with the consecrated bread there is given us to eat not a *typical* body or a *figurative* one, such as was the body of the paschal lamb, so far as it shadowed forth and prefigured the body of Christ; not a *mystical* body, which is the Church, Eph. 1, 23; not the *sign of a body,* for that was not crucified for us; but the true and personal body of Christ, belonging to the Son of God." (*Doctr. Theol.,* p. 561.)

Even Beza, the pronounced Calvinist, affirmed that the term *body* here cannot stand for *sign of the body,* since Christ describes as the *materia* the body which was given and the blood which was shed. For this reason the word *body* must be taken to denote the true, substantial, or essential body of Christ. (Beza, *Hom. 2, De Coena: "Confiteor hic nullum tropum esse, quia* SIGNUM *proprie* EXPONI *necesse fuit, ne* FALLEREMUR.")

Beza also rejected the explanation that in the words of institution the words *body* and *blood* indicate the *fruit and effect* of Christ's death, an explanation which even Hodge adopted ("To receive the body and blood as offered in the Sacrament . . . is to receive and appropriate the sacrificial *virtue,* or *effects,* of the death of Christ on the cross." *Syst. Theol.,* III, 646).

Of this sort of explanation Beza states: "It would certainly be absurd to interpret the words *body* and *blood* with respect to the *fruit* and *effect* of the death of Christ" (*Epist. 5 ad Alemannum,* p. 57, ed. Geneva). Beza himself rejected the doctrine of the real presence, which the Lutherans taught so strenuously, but he likewise rejected the interpretation of Calvin as absurd and impossible. (Cp. *Christl. Dogmatik,* III, 368 ff.)

Calvin's error is fully refuted by St. Paul, who teaches (not that the word *body* is to be interpreted as *sign of body,* but) that the bread is the communion (κοινωνία) of the body and the cup (wine) the communion of the blood of Christ, 1 Cor. 10, 16, so that, "whosoever shall eat this bread and drink this cup of the Lord unworthily shall be guilty of the *body and blood of the Lord,"* 1 Cor. 11, 27; and who also says that "he that eateth and drinketh unworthily eateth and drinketh damnation to himself, not discerning the *Lord's body,"* 1 Cor. 11, 29. This explanation, given by divine inspiration, decides the matter once for all and establishes the truth of both the sacramental union and the oral reception.

Some Reformed theologians (Keckermann, Zanchi, Bucanus, etc.) assumed that the trope, or figure of speech, must be sought not in particular expressions of the words of institution, but rather in the entire statement ("This is My body"; "This is My blood"). However, in the final analysis their explanation is the same as that of Calvin *("Panis est symbolum sive signum corporis Christi").*

It goes without saying that, if the entire statement must be interpreted figuratively, then all the words ought to be interpreted tropically and not merely a few individual words. Krauth calls attention to this when he writes (*Cons. Ref.,* p. 608 ff.) : "The word *eat* they [the Reformed] have interpreted literally; though why the eating ought not to be done symbolically, or mentally, to correspond with the symbolical, or mental, character of the body they cannot say. Certainly there are plenty of instances of a figurative use of the word *eat,* while there are none of such a use of the word *is.* The Quakers are more consistent."

In summary, it is clear that the Reformed have no Scriptural ground whatever for the *figurative* interpretation of the words of institution. Their doctrine is based alone on the rationalistic axiom that (as Luther says) "Christ's body must be at one place bodily and palpably, as a peasant is in his coat and trousers" (St. L., XX, 950. 953. 1776), since it has only a local and visible presence *(localis et visibilis praesentia).*

Calvin expressly styled the Lutheran doctrine of the illocal and repletive presence of Christ's human nature (John 20, 19; Eph. 1, 20—23; 4, 10) a ridiculous notion *(stultum commentum),* because in that case the human nature of Christ would be destroyed. In his *Inst.,* IV, 17. 29 (tr. by John Allen) he says: "It is essential to a real body to have its particular form and dimension and to be contained within some certain space. Let us hear no more, then, of the ridiculous notion which fastens the minds of men and Christ Himself to the bread."

At this point the Calvinists argue as rationalistically as when they deny the *gratia universalis* on the ground that not all are actually saved or when they deny the true communion of natures in Christ *(realis communio)* on the ground that the finite is not capable of the infinite *(Finitum non est capax infiniti).* (Cp. Oecolampadius against Luther: "Our reason is that the body of Christ is in heaven; that is certain and cannot be wrong." St. L., XX, 591 ff.)

This rationalistic interpretation of Scripture, Calvin employs quite consistently. According to Calvin, Christ did not appear before His disciples through closed doors (John 20, 19), but opened the door and so came to them quite naturally. Again, Christ did not vanish out of the sight of the two disciples at Emmaus (Luke 24, 31), but merely closed their eyes, so that they could not see Him. Moreover, the right hand of God is not God's majesty and omnipotent power, as Scripture distinctly teaches, Is. 48, 13; Ps. 89, 13. 14; 118, 15. 16; 20, 6; Ex. 15, 6. 12, but a definite place where Christ is enclosed till the end of the world. The omnipresence of Christ, so strongly attested in Matt. 28, 20, Calvin predicates only of the divine nature of Christ.

As an ingrained rationalist, Calvin also argues that Christ's human nature would become *locally extended,* or infinite (immense) if omnipresence (the real presence) would be ascribed to it. Hence, with the exception of sinlessness, Calvin avers, we must predicate of the human nature of Christ nothing that cannot be predicated of any other human nature. Calvinism on this point is therefore as rationalistic as is Unitarianism; the difference between the two is only that, while Unitarianism unfortunately is consistent, denying the entire supernatural content of Scripture, Calvinism fortunately is inconsistent and does not draw all the conclusions which its rationalistic premises demand.

Against the Calvinists, who charged the Lutherans with teaching a local extension of Christ's body *(ubiquitas localis, extensio localis),* our dogmaticians declared: "We indeed affirm the communicated omnipresence of Christ's human nature *(ubiquitas personalis et supernaturalis, i. e., omnipraesentia),* but no *local extension (ubiquitas localis).* The doctrine of the (local) ubiquity, which the Calvinists ascribed to the Lutherans, is a Calvinistic figment, fabricated for the purpose of ridiculing and disproving the Lutheran doctrine of the real presence.

Since the Calvinists cannot prove their erroneous doctrine against the real presence, to which they cling so tenaciously, from the words of institution, they resort to John 6, 53—56. Their argument is: Since the eating of the flesh and the drinking of the blood of Christ in this passage must be understood spiritually, or of faith, the same is true also of the words of institution. But that the two passages are not parallel and do not treat of one and the same matter is obvious from the fact that Christ in John 6, 53—56 guarantees eternal life to all who "eat His flesh and drink His blood," while in the Holy Supper the body of Christ may be eaten to damnation, 1 Cor. 11, 29.

The Lutheran dogmaticians therefore teach that in John 6,

53—56 Christ indeed speaks of faith (this against the Romanists, who use this passage to support their error of transubstantiation), while in Matt. 26, 26—28 and all parallel passages He speaks of a true sacramental eating (this against the Reformed). (Cp. *Christl. Dogmatik,* III, 384 ff.)

Against the claim that, since the words of institution have led to so much controversy, they cannot be regarded as adequate to determine the doctrine of the Lord's Supper, we reply that this principle in the final analysis would render impossible the use of all Scripture, since the entire Bible has always been in controversy. The argument therefore does not hold. Against the charge that the words of institution are too *difficult* to be a *sedes doctrinae,* we reply that they are difficult only if one refuses to believe what they say. Our dogmaticians have always emphasized the fact that the words of institution are clear in themselves and that only the conceited reason of unbelieving men makes them obscure.

That the Calvinists, in spite of their violent opposition to the Lutherans, were not sure of their ground is shown by their union-istic spirit. Calvin, on the one hand, condemned the Lutheran doctrine as an "incantation of Satan" *(diaboli incantatio);* yet he as well as Zwingli demanded that the Lutherans regard them as brethren and maintain Christian fellowship with them. Of this Melanchthon writes: "They urged us very much to call them brethren. But behold their folly! Although they condemn us (as false teachers), they nevertheless desire that we should regard them as brethren." (St. L., XVII, 1956.) Such unionism wantonly discards the Word of God and proposes to establish agreements suitable to reason, but condemned by Scripture, Rom. 16, 17; Titus 3, 10. It is therefore just as rationalistic as is the rejection of the Scriptural doctrine of the real presence.

Against the misconstructions which the Reformed have put on the Lutheran doctrine of the sacramental union our dogmaticians have said (Hafenreffer): "The sacramental union is a) not a tran-substantiation of the bread into the body of Christ; b) it is not a consubstantiation, or *commixture* of the two substances, but in both the bread and the wine the substance of the body and blood of Christ remains unmixed; c) nor is it a *local* or *durable adhesion* or *conjunction* to the bread and wine apart from the use of the Supper; d) nor is it an *impanation,* that is, the inclusion of some small corpuscle lying hid under the bread; e) nor is it, finally, a *personal union* of the bread and body of Christ, such as exists between the Son of God and the assumed humanity." (*Doctr. Theol.*, p. 571.)

Quenstedt adds another thought to clear up the Scriptural doctrine of the sacramental union. He writes: "We say that only the *body* of Christ is united with the bread, and only the *blood* is united with the wine, and (both are) *sacramentally* received by the mouth of the body. But *the whole Christ* is received *spiritually,* by the mouth of faith." (*Doctr. Theol.*, p. 570.)

4. THE LUTHERAN DOCTRINE AND THE WORDS OF INSTITUTION.

It has been said that the various doctrines concerning the Lord's Supper are only the results of different "interpretations" of the words of institution. Properly speaking, however, the Lutheran doctrine is not an "interpretation" of the words of institution, but merely the simple and plain presentation of the Scripture doctrine set forth in these words.

The papists indeed require much "interpretation" to demonstrate that the bread is *transubstantiated* into the body, that the *cup must be withheld* from the laity (concomitance), and that the whole sacramental act must be performed as an *unbloody sacrifice* for the sins of the living and the dead. It certainly requires a good deal of misinterpretation and "eisegesis" to prove these gross perversions from clear Scripture-passages which teach quite the opposite, 1 Cor. 10, 16; Luke 22, 19. 20; Heb. 9, 11—15.

Similarly the Reformed have proved by their many divergent views that it is indeed "labor and sorrow" for them to establish their error on the basis of Scripture. They must show by much painful "interpretation" that the words "This is My body, given for you; this is My blood, shed for you" do not mean what they say, but rather what the rebellious reason of doubting Zwinglians wants them to say, namely, that the faith of the believer must elevate itself to heaven and there unite spiritually with Christ, whose human nature, they say, is enclosed in heaven.

In particular they must explain away 1 Cor. 10, 16 and 11, 27—29. They must furthermore explain why Christ did not say in the words of institution what according to their view He should have said. Then they must explain why the Lord's Supper is at all necessary if it is no more than a symbol of a faith-union, which takes place also outside the Sacrament. In short, they are confronted with the impossible task of proving the absence of

Christ's body when Scripture so emphatically teaches and proves the real presence.

The Lutherans, on the contrary, take the words in their simple meaning, just as they read, and trust that Christ, who has made the promise, is able also to fulfil it. In this they follow the time-honored hermeneutic rule that we must not depart from the literal meaning of the text unless the text itself compels us to do so. The Lutheran doctrine therefore rests on Scriptural ground and is in agreement not only with the words of institution, but also with every other passage of Scripture that treats of the Holy Supper.

Against the claim of the Lutherans that their doctrine rests upon the literal sense of the words of institution, the Reformed (including Hodge, *Syst. Theol.,* III, 662) have set up the counter-claim that the Lutherans, too, "have given up the literal sense" of the words. This accusation is based upon the fact that the Lutherans admit that "the cup is used metonymically for the wine in the cup." To this we reply that we indeed admit this metonymy (synecdoche), the container ("this cup") being named for the thing therein contained; for Scripture itself tells us: "And they all drank of it," Mark 14, 23. What the disciples drank was not the goblet, but the wine in the cup. In other words, Scripture itself establishes the metonymy in this case. But that point is beside the question, since the literal interpretation, upon which the Lutherans insist, does not apply to the expression *cup,* but rather to the statements: "This *is* My body"; "this *is* My blood." The bread *is* indeed Christ's body, and the wine *is* His blood, yet not, as the papists teach, because of *transubstantiation,* but on account of the *sacramental union (propter unionem sacramentalem).*

Again, the Reformed seek to substantiate their indictment against the Lutherans ("They have given up the literal sense") by referring to their explanation "in, with, and under." But the use of this expression does not involve a departure from the literal sense of the words of institution; it is but an amplification of the literal sense of the words. Hodge does the same thing when he amplifies the words "who is in the bosom of the Father," John 1, 18, thus: "who is, was, and ever shall be in the bosom of the Father." What Hodge here writes is correct, and neither a Reformed nor a Lutheran theologian would charge him at this place with using "figurative language." The phrase "in, with, and under" fittingly serves the purpose of repudiating the papistic error of transubstantiation and of affirming, in opposition to the error of the Reformed, the Scriptural doctrine of the sacramental union.

However, Hodge bases his charge on yet another point. He writes: "If the words of Christ are to be taken literally, they teach the doctrine of transubstantiation. . . . If the bread is literally the body of Christ, it is no longer bread; for no one asserts that the same thing can be bread and flesh (or rather, the body of Christ) at the same time." This argument we already considered when we spoke of the *locutio exhibitiva;* for there we showed that not even Hodge is willing to concede in another point (Luke 1, 35: "The Holy Thing shall be called the Son of God") what he here demands. But Hodge's argument: "If the bread is the body of Christ, it is no longer bread, but only body" does not follow; for St. Paul, by divine inspiration, assures us that the bread remains bread even after consecration, 1 Cor. 10, 16. The argument of Hodge therefore directs itself not against Luther, but against Scripture. To the charge that it is a blasphemy to say that "the bread is Christ's body" we answer that Christ Himself makes this statement, so that the decision in this matter rests with Him. Holy Scripture never blasphemes God, but always glorifies Him.

It is a common charge that the Lutheran doctrine of the real presence rests not on the words of institution, but rather on the doctrine of the person of Christ. This charge is absurd, for the very opposite is true. The Lutherans would never have drawn into the discussion of the doctrine of the Holy Supper that of the person of Christ had not their opponents compelled them to prove that the body of Christ can really be present in the Lord's Supper.

Because the Reformed predicated of the body of Christ only a local and visible presence, the Lutherans were forced to show that Scripture ascribes to the Son of Man not only a local *(praesentia localis, circumscriptiva),* but also an illocal *(praesentia illocalis, invisibilis, definitiva)* and a peculiar divine presence *(praesentia divina et repletiva).* The first is predicated of Christ in John 4, 4; the second, in John 20, 19; the third, in Eph. 4, 10 (to name only a few Scripture-passages). When Lutherans therefore read Matt. 28, 20, they do not think of Christ's presence according to His divine nature only, as do the Calvinists, but also of the presence of His human nature by reason of its communicated *praesentia illocalis, divina, repletiva.* The whole divine-human Christ is present with His Church to the end of time.

5. DIFFERENT ACCOUNTS OF THE WORDS OF INSTITUTION.

Every Bible student knows that the words of institution are not quoted in precisely the same manner by all the sacred writers. Modern exegetes have therefore gone to much trouble to ascertain the original words *(ipsissima verba)* which Christ employed when He instituted the holy Sacrament. However, Cremer rightly says (RE.[3] I, 35): "Which the *ipsissima verba* are cannot be determined." Yet from the different accounts we must not conclude that the Bible is not verbally inspired (cp. Kahnis, *Dogmatik,*[7] I, 666 ff.), but rather that "Christ at the institution of the Sacrament did not repeat the words in the same stereotyped form" (Noesgen), so that all the holy writers quote them correctly, though they cite them in various ways.

After all, however, there is no actual difference between the various accounts with respect to the doctrine that is taught in the words of institution. The words concerning the bread unanimously affirm the same truth: "This is My body," Matt. 26, 26; Mark 14, 22; Luke 22, 19; 1 Cor. 11, 24. The words concerning the cup show a greater variation, though they also affirm one and the same doctrine. Matthew and Mark directly denote the blood as the sacramental gift (Matt. 26, 28: "This is My blood of the new testament, which is shed for many for the remission of sins"; Mark 14, 24: "This is My blood of the new testament, which is shed for many"). On the other hand, the words of Luke and St. Paul designate directly the object *(finis)* of the Holy Supper as a means of grace, namely, the "new testament," or "remission of sins" (Luke 22, 20: "This cup is the new testament in My blood, which is shed for you"; 1 Cor. 11, 25: "This cup is the new testament in My blood").

That the *new testament* (New Covenant) is essentially God's gracious *remission of sins* is clear from direct Scripture-passages (cp. Jer. 31, 31—34 with Rom. 11, 27: "This is My covenant unto them when I shall take away their sins"; also with Heb. 8, 8—12; 10, 16. 17). The old testament was the covenant of the Law, which imputed sin and pronounced damnation (2 Cor. 3, 9: "the ministration of condemnation"); but the new testament is the covenant of the Gospel, which forgives sin and announces salvation through the blood of Christ (2 Cor. 3, 9: "the ministration of righteousness"). "Righteousness" here denotes the *iustitia imputata,* or the forgiveness of sins for Christ's sake; for it stands in contrast to "condemnation." Luther writes regarding this point (St. L., XX, 278 ff.) : "What else is the new testament than the forgiveness of sins, secured for us by Christ and offered to us in the Sacrament?"

The words "in My blood" (Luke, St. Paul) show the reason why the cup is the new testament, or the forgiveness of sins; for the cup is the new testament on account of the blood of Christ which is offered in it (Luther: *"meines Blutes halben"*; Chemnitz: *propter sanguinem meum;* Meyer: *"vermoege meines Blutes"*).

If the objection is raised that in the statement "This cup is the new testament by virtue of My blood" the verb "is" must be taken in the sense of "signify," we refer the reader to such passages as John 11, 25: "I am the Resurrection and the Life," and 6, 63: "My words are spirit, and they are life." According to the first passage, Christ does not merely signify, but actually is, the Resurrection and the Life, inasmuch as these heavenly gifts are found in Him and are offered to us by Him. According to the second passage the words of Christ do not merely signify spirit and life, but actually are spirit and life, because these heavenly gifts are contained in them and are offered to us by them. In the same way the cup does not merely signify the new testament, but actually is the new testament, or the forgiveness of sins; for with the shed blood of Christ which is therein contained it truly offers the forgiveness which our Savior secured for us by His death on the cross. (Cp. *Christl. Dogmatik,* III, 410 ff.)

This is the clear doctrine which Scripture inculcates in the words of institution and which accordingly the Lutheran Church teaches and confesses without any regard for the objections of man's doubting reason on this point. According to the Lutheran doctrine the words of institution, no matter how they are quoted, all express the same sublime truth, namely, that in, with, and under the bread and wine, as by true *vehicula et media collativa,* the communicant receives Christ's true body and blood for the gracious remission of his sins *(ad veniam peccatorum impetrandam).*

6. THE MATERIAL ELEMENTS IN THE LORD'S SUPPER.

The Lutheran Church confesses with the ancient Christian Church "according to the words of Irenaeus that in this Sacrament there are two things, a heavenly and an earthly" (*Formula of Concord,* Thor. Decl., VII, 14). The heavenly elements *(materiae coelestes)* are the true body and blood of Christ. So the *Formula of Concord* says: "With the bread and wine the body and blood

·of Christ are truly and essentially present, offered, and received."
The earthly elements *(materiae terrenae)* in the divinely instituted
action *(actio)* of the Holy Supper are true bread and wine. As
in Baptism we dare not employ another material element than
water, so also in Holy Communion we dare not depart from the
·elements *(elementa, species)* which Christ has definitely fixed.
That Christ used bread is clear from the words of institution,
Matt. 26, 26; that He used wine (οἶνος) is proved by the expression
·"*this fruit of the vine*" (ἐκ τούτου τοῦ γεννήματος τῆς ἀμπέλου),
Matt. 26, 29.

While heretics in the ancient Church frequently used substitutes for wine (Encratites: milk, honey, unfermented grape-juice),
the Christian Church has always condemned such surrogates as not
permissible. The argument that the expression "the fruit of the
vine" is a generic term, which embraces all products of the vine
and therefore also grape-juice does not hold, since Christ used the
expression in question as a special term for wine, which was invariably used by the Jews at their sacred festivals. Quite manifestly the expression γέννημα τῆς ἀμπέλου is the Greek for פְּרִי הַגָּפֶן,
which even to-day the orthodox Jews use in their consecration of
the Kiddush cup ("Blessed art Thou, Lord, our God, King of the
world, Creator of *the fruit of the vine*": בָּרוּךְ אַתָּה יְיָ אֱלֹהֵנוּ מֶלֶךְ
הָעוֹלָם בּוֹרֵא פְּרִי הַגָּפֶן.).

The objection against the use of wine in the Holy Supper
would never have been raised, had not fanaticism declared the use
of wine objectionable in general, contrary to the clear words of
Scripture, 1 Tim. 5, 23; Eccl. 9, 7; Ps. 104, 15.

With respect to the wafers *(Hostien)*, which are in use in the
Lutheran Church, the Christian minister must carefully instruct
his people that these are bread in the true sense of the term, but
in themselves not a better *materia terrena* than is ordinary bread.

It is necessary for the sacramental union that the material
elements should really be distributed *(distributio)* and received
(sumptio) by the communicants; for the sacramental union occurs
only in the sacramental action and not outside it. *Ipsa sacramentalis unio non fit nisi in distributione.* Hence the "consecrated
host" used by the Romanists for adoration is not Christ's true body,
but a mere piece of bread, and its worship is idolatry. *Panis
extra usum a Christo institutum non est corpus Christi.*

The axiom of the ancient Christians and the Lutheran
Church: "Nothing has the nature of a Sacrament apart from the

use instituted by Christ" *(Nihil habet rationem sacramenti extra usum a Christo institutum)* is based directly on the words of institution ("Eat, drink") and is therefore Scriptural. (Cp. *Formula of Concord,* Thor. Decl., VII, 85.)

Whether the bread is received directly with the mouth as offered by the pastor or first taken in the communicant's own hand is immaterial (adiaphoron); some Reformed erroneously contended that the latter alone is correct.

Also the "breaking" of the bread must be regarded as an adiaphoron, though some Reformed theologians insisted upon this act, since according to their view the breaking of the bread signifies the death of Christ on the cross (whose bones, however, were not broken, John 19, 33. 36). At the first Communion the "breaking" was accidental; the bread was broken in order that it could be distributed, Luke 24, 30; 1 Cor. 10, 16.

As the material elements which Christ used should not be changed, so also the celestial elements must be left intact. That is to say, we must not designate as the *materia coelestis* anything else than Christ's body and blood. In particular, we must not regard as the *materia coelestis* —

a) The "entire Christ," or "Christ's person" (Calvinists, Romanists, some modern Lutheran theologians), since Christ expressly offers us His *body* and *blood* to eat and to drink. Beyond the words of institution ("This is My body; this is My blood") we dare not argue with respect to any sacramental presence of Christ. "Only His body and blood are united with the elements and are received orally." (Luthardt.) The papistic doctrine of "concomitance" (with the body the communicant receives the blood) is as unscriptural as is that of transubstantiation.

b) Nor must we substitute for Christ's body and blood as the *materia coelestis* merely the benefits of Christ *(beneficia),* or the efficacy of His body and blood *(virtus),* or His merits *(merita),* etc. (Reformed and modern theologians). While it is true that we receive all of Christ's blessings by faith, it is true also that they were not "given and shed" for us, so that in the Lord's Supper we do not receive them orally with the mouth (oral reception).

c) Again, the *materia coelestis* is not the Holy Ghost or His supernatural operation (Calvin). Even Beza declared that it is absurd to substitute for the body and blood of Christ in the Sacrament the Holy Spirit and His divine operation, since these were not given into death for us.

d) Furthermore, the *materia coelestis* is not the spiritual fellowship with Christ and the engrafting of the believer into His body, the Church. While spiritual fellowship is indeed a fruit and effect of the Sacrament upon all who believe the divine promise, it is not the *materia coelestis* for the reason aforementioned.

e) Lastly also the glorified body of Christ, or the glorified Christ, is not the *materia coelestis,* as Calvin and some modern theologians claimed, since our Lord designates as such only the *body* that was given and the *blood* which was shed. The glorification of Christ has nothing to do with His real presence in Holy Communion, which rests entirely a) on His divine promise: "Take, eat; this is My body," and b) on the fact of the personal union, by which the human nature of Christ received truly divine attributes (omnipresence), so that it really can be present in the Lord's Supper. In other words, the real presence rests upon the fact that Christ's body is the body of the Son of God.

In short, we must not substitute for the body and blood of Christ as *materia coelestis* anything which our Lord has not Himself named in the words of institution, since this would be unscriptural and, besides, would cause confusion. The sacramental union consists only in the union of the bread with the body and of the wine with the blood.

While the papists reject the Scriptural doctrine of the sacramental union *in toto* and substitute for it transubstantiation, the Calvinists, on the other hand, profess to teach the *unio sacramentalis.* However, they understand by this term nothing more than the union of the *believer* with the *absent Christ* by faith, so that in reality their sacramental union is only significative, representative, or symbolical *(unio significativa, repraesentativa, symbolica).*

Their sacramental union is therefore no more of a real union than is that produced by a glance at a crucifix or at a picture of Christ, which, by the recalling of our Savior to our memory, makes Him present in our minds. The Calvinists also frequently speak of their sacramental union as *unio vera, realis, substantialis,* etc.; yet in spite of this fact they deny the substantial presence *(realis praesentia)* of Christ's body in the Sacrament, so that, after all, they teach no sacramental union at all.

The Lutherans, on the contrary, regard the sacramental union between the bread and the body and between the wine and the blood as so real and intimate that in the sacramental act the communicant receives Christ's true body and blood in, with, and under the bread and wine *(manducatio oralis)*, the bread and wine indeed in a natural manner *(manducatio naturalis)*, but the body and blood in a supernatural, incomprehensible manner.

The Lutherans very strenuously reject the charge that the real presence implies a *local inclusion,* or an impanation, or consubstantiation *(localis inclusio, impanatio, consubstantiatio)*. The *Formula of Concord* thus says (Thor. Decl., VII, 64) : "For this command ['Eat and drink'] cannot be understood otherwise than of oral eating and drinking; however, not in a gross, carnal, Capernaitic, but in a supernatural, incomprehensible way."

The accusation that the Lutherans teach a natural, or Capernaitic, eating and drinking has been preferred against them both by Reformed and non-Reformed theologians (Harnack, Frank, etc.). (Cp. *Christl. Dogmatik,* III, 423 ff.) However, not only Luther (St. L., XX, 811) and the Lutheran Confessions (*Formula of Concord,* Thor. Decl., VII, 16), but also all Lutheran dogmaticians at all times have repudiated this erroneous doctrine in unmistakable terms.

7. WHAT MAKES THE LORD'S SUPPER A SACRAMENT.
(Forma Coenae Sacrae.)

Because the Lord's Supper is a Sacrament which should be celebrated till the end of time, 1 Cor. 11, 26, we must deal also with the important question, What produces the true presence of the body and blood of Christ in the Holy Supper? According to the Reformed view there can be no true Sacrament unless the communicants have true faith in Christ. In other words, it is the faith of the believer that makes the eating and drinking a true Sacrament.

In refutation of this error the *Formula of Concord* writes (Thor. Decl., VII, 74) : "Not the word or work of any man produces the true presence of the body and blood of Christ in the Supper, whether it be the merit or recitation of the minister or the eating and drinking or faith of the communicants; but all this should be ascribed alone to the power of Almighty God and the word, institution, and ordination of our Lord Jesus Christ."

Also Luther, whom the *Formula of Concord* here quotes, affirms: "His [Christ's] command and institution have this power and effect, that we administer and receive not mere bread and wine, but His body and blood, as His words declare: "This is My body,' etc.; 'This is My blood,' etc., so that it is not our work or speaking, but the command and ordination of Christ that makes the bread the body and the wine the blood from the beginning of the first Supper even to the end of the world." (*Ibid.*, 77.)

Again: "Thus here also, even though I should pronounce over all bread the words 'This is Christ's body,' nothing, of course, would result therefrom; but when in the Supper we say, according to His [Christ's] institution and command: 'This is My body,' it is His body, not on account of our speaking or word uttered, but because of His command, that He has commanded us thus to speak and to do and has united His command and act with our speaking." (*Ibid.*, 78.)

This doctrine is Scriptural; for neither the faith of man (Reformed) nor the power of the priesthood (Romanists) nor any magic influence of the spoken word makes the eating or drinking a Lord's Supper, or Sacrament, but only Christ's institution and command: "This do ye."

The *Formula of Concord* stands on solid Scripture ground when it declares: "The true and almighty words of Jesus Christ which He spake at the first institution were efficacious not only at the first Supper, but they endure, are valid, operate, and are still efficacious, . . . so that in all places where the Supper is celebrated according to the institution of Christ and His words are used, the body and blood of Christ are truly present, distributed, and received because of the power and efficacy of the words which Christ spake at the first Supper. . . . As Chrysostom says in his *Sermon concerning the Passion:* 'Christ Himself prepares this table and blesses it; for no man makes the bread and wine set before us the body and blood of Christ, but Christ Himself who was crucified for us. . . . Just as the declaration Gen. 1, 28: "Be fruitful and multiply and replenish the earth," was spoken only once, but is ever efficacious in nature, so that it is fruitful and multiplies, also this declaration ["This is My body; this is My blood"] was spoken once, but even to this day and to His advent it is efficacious and works so that in the Supper of the Church His true body and blood are present.'" (*Ibid.*, 75. 76.)

The charge of the Calvinists that the Lutherans, like the Romanists, attribute the real presence in the Lord's Supper to the word and authority of man is therefore absolutely false.

Just because the Lutherans teach that the true presence of Christ's body and blood in the Holy Supper depends on Christ's institution and command, they, in accord with the ancient Christian Church, 1 Cor. 10, 16, retain the words of institution for the *consecration* (*consecratio, εὐλογία*) of the material elements. Calvin, who opposed the papistic consecration as a "magic incantation," emphatically denied the necessity of the consecration on the ground that it has nothing to do with the sacramental action.

In opposition to this unscriptural notion (cp. 1 Cor. 10, 16) the *Formula of Concord* (Thor. Decl., VII, 79—82) insists upon the recitation of the words of institution for three reasons: a) "that obedience may be rendered to the command of Christ"; b) "that the faith of the hearers concerning the nature and fruit of this Sacrament may be excited, strengthened, and confirmed"; and c) "that the elements of bread and wine may be consecrated or blessed for this holy use."

Even Hodge (*Syst. Theol.,* III, 618) declares that "the bread and the cup were blessed" in order that "the bread and wine might be symbols of His body and blood," though, according to 1 Cor. 10, 16, he should have said: "that the bread might be the communion of the body and the wine the communion of the blood." Hodge at least admits that the blessing (consecration) related to the sacramental act, not merely to the persons, as Calvin taught.

The Lutherans rightly insist upon the use of the words of institution in the Holy Supper no less than in Holy Baptism. While they do not regard the accidental omission or mispronunciation of a word or an unintentional error that may occur during the consecration as an offense by which the whole Sacrament is invalidated, they demand that "the words of institution are to be publicly spoken or sung distinctly and clearly and should in no way be omitted." (*Formula of Concord,* Thor. Decl., VII, 79.)

The question whether or not the mere good intention of the celebrants could sufficiently consecrate the material elements can hardly be treated seriously. It belongs to the *curiosae quaestiones* which we answer best by not paying any attention to them.

Since the Lord's Supper is a Sacrament not by the faith or work of man, but only through the institution and command of our Lord, it follows that also unworthy guests, or unbelieving communicants, receive Christ's true body and blood *(manducatio generalis)*. This truth Scripture states expressly in 1 Cor. 11, 27. 29, so that the Reformed, who deny the *manducatio indignorum,* repudiate a clear teaching of Scripture. However, just as they reject the *manducatio indignorum,* so they also reject the *manducatio dignorum,* that is, the oral reception of Christ's body and blood by the believer.

According to Reformed teaching Christ's body is not at all present in the Holy Supper, and therefore it is orally received neither by the worthy nor by the unworthy. Zwingli: *"In eucharistia nihil aliud est quam commemoratio." — "Quanto fides est maior et sanctior, tanto magis contenta est spirituali manducatione."* In the Wittenberg Concordia (1536) Luther expressly insisted that his Sacramentarian opponents should acknowledge the *manducatio indignorum;* for by this test he could ascertain whether they agreed to the doctrine of the real presence or not.

Because it is solely the institution and command of Christ which makes the Lord's Supper a Sacrament, a means of grace, it follows also that neither the papists nor the Calvinists have that true Holy Communion which our Savior instituted. Their "supper" lies entirely outside the institution of our Lord *(extra usum a Christo institutum)* since it is neither based upon it nor is in accord with it.

Concerning the Mass of the Romanists the *Formula of Concord* writes (Thor. Decl., VII, 86. 87): "If the institution of Christ be not observed as He appointed it, there is no Sacrament. . . . And the use, or action, here does not mean chiefly faith, neither the oral participation only, but the entire external, visible action of the Lord's Supper instituted by Christ, the consecration, or words of institution, the distribution and reception, or oral partaking of the consecrated bread and wine, [likewise the partaking] of the body and blood of Christ. Apart from this use, when in the papistic Mass the bread is not distributed, but offered up or inclosed, borne about, and exhibited for adoration, it is to be regarded as no Sacrament."

Similarly Luther writes of the private masses *(Winkelmessen)* (St. L., XIX, 1265): "In the private Mass we find not only the abuse, or sin, that the priest acts and receives unworthily; but even if the priest should be holy and worthy, nevertheless the very essence of Christ's institution is removed *(tamen ipsa substantia Christi sublata est);* the real ordinance and institution of Christ they take away and create their own ordinance. . . . Hence no one can or should believe that there is Christ's body and blood because His institution is not there."

With respect to the "supper" of the Reformed some Lutheran dogmaticians (Fecht, Dannhauer, etc.) judged that they have the true Holy Communion which Christ instituted, so that they receive Christ's body and blood whenever they partake of it. This argument was based upon the fact that the Calvinists retain the words of institution. But the "supper" of the Calvinists lies outside the institution of Christ, since they expressly *renounce* the words of institution by declaring that the doctrine of the real presence is an "abomination" and that they do not come together to perpetrate such an offense, but only to celebrate a "memorial feast" in remembrance of Christ's death. Zwingli: "Should we want to be cannibals *(anthropophagi)?*" From this it is clear that the "supper" of the Reformed is without the word and promise of Christ, so that it cannot be a true Lord's Supper.

Luther's verdict on this point is very emphatic. He writes: "Our present opponents of the Sacrament have nothing but bread and wine; for they have not the words and the appointed ordinance of God, but they have perverted and changed them according to their own self-conceived notion." (*Formula of Concord,* Thor. Decl., VII, 32.)

While we rightly reject the Reformed "supper" as no Lord's Supper at all, we acknowledge their Baptism as valid, since their errors with respect to this Sacrament relate not to its essence, but only to its fruit and effect. (Cp. Dr. Walther, *Pastorale,* p. 181.)

With respect to the question whether the sacramental union *(unio sacramentalis)* occurs directly upon the consecration and before the distribution and reception *(ante usum),* a point on which John Saliger (pastor in Luebeck and Rostock) insisted, the *Formula of Concord* judges rightly (Thor. Decl., VII, 83. 84): "This blessing, or the recitation of the words of institution of Christ, alone does not make a Sacrament if the entire action of the Supper as it was instituted by Christ is not observed; . . . but the command of Christ 'This do' (which embraces the entire action or administration in this Sacrament . . .) must be observed unseparated and inviolate, as also St. Paul places before our eyes the entire action of the breaking of bread or of *distribution and reception,* 1 Cor. 10, 16."

This decision is of great practical importance; for only the consecration in connection with the actual distribution and reception, as Christ has appointed this, guarantees us the real presence of Christ's body and blood in the Lord's Supper. If the elements are only consecrated, but not distributed and received, there is no Lord's Supper.

This truth Quenstedt ably defended against Bellarmine's contention that Christ's body must be present by virtue of the consecration even without the distribution, since Christ says: "This is My body." He replied that Christ said: "This is My body" of that bread of which He first had said: "Take and eat" (II, 1268). Hence Christ's body and blood are really present with the consecrated earthly elements only when we eat and drink them. "*Ad externam actionem requiritur consecratio, distributio et sumptio.*" (*Formula of Concord,* VII, 86.)

8. THE PURPOSE OF THE LORD'S SUPPER.
(Finis cuius Coenae Sacrae.)

Of the design of the Holy Supper we had to speak already in an earlier chapter, since the purpose of this Sacrament is most intimately connected with its essence *(forma).* On account of the importance of this matter we here repeat what was said before for the sake of greater clearness and emphasis.

In his Small Catechism, Luther summarizes the purpose of the Holy Supper under the question: "What is the benefit of such eating and drinking?" as follows: "That is shown us by these words, 'Given and shed for you for the remission of sins'; namely, that in the Sacrament forgiveness of sins, life, and salvation are given us through these words. For where there is forgiveness of sins, there is also life and salvation." The great Reformer here points out that Christ's explanation "which is given for you" and "which is shed for you" (Luke 22, 19. 20) is added to the words "This is My body; this is My blood" to show the benefit, or object, of the eating and drinking, or of the Holy Supper.

It is true, these words also *describe* the body and blood of Christ as His real and true body and blood. At the same time, however, they also show the *purpose* of the eating and drinking; for as the body was given into death and the blood was shed for the remission of our sins, so in the Holy Supper they are offered and imparted to the communicant for the remission of his sins. It is because of this fact that some of the sacred writers (Luke and St. Paul) say directly: "This cup is the new testament in My blood," Luke 22, 20; 1 Cor. 11, 25; for these words mean: "With this body and blood I offer to you the new testament, or the gracious forgiveness of sins." The peculiar gift of the Lord's Supper is therefore, as Luther rightly says, forgiveness of sins, life, and salvation, or precisely the same blessing which the Gospel conveys generally and Baptism individually. Baptism offers this gift through the application of water; the Lord's Supper, through the reception, by the communicant, of Christ's body and blood in, with, and under the bread and wine.

In this connection it may be pointed out that both Reformed and modernistic theologians (Harnack) accuse Luther of having so emphasized the *real presence* that he lost sight of the final purpose of the Lord's Supper, namely, the apprehension of the merits of Christ by faith. But this is one of the manifest misrepresentations, of which the student of church history finds so many. It is true, Luther did place emphasis on the doctrine of the real presence, but for the simple reason that this was the chief *status controversiae* in his conflict with the Sacramentarians. As a matter of fact, however, he regarded the real presence only as a means to the end. He insisted upon the true presence of Christ's body and blood in the Sacrament in order that he might the more clearly and assuredly proclaim its comfort and declare its benefit, namely, the gracious forgiveness of sins.

Luther did not put the real presence in place of the *sola fide,* as Harnack erroneously claims, but rather taught that the *sola fide* is the only means by which God's gracious forgiveness of sins, offered in the Lord's Supper, can be obtained. He thus writes in the *Small Catechism:* "He that believes these words ["Given and shed for you for the remission of sins"] has what they say and express, namely, the forgiveness of sins." Luther furthermore stressed the Scriptural doctrine that the oral reception of Christ's body and blood is useless, yes, harmful, without faith, 1 Cor. 11, 29. In the *Small Catechism* he says: "But he that does not believe these words or doubts is unworthy and unprepared; for the words 'For you' *require all hearts to believe."*

It is Luther's doctrine, voiced by him from beginning to end, which the *Formula of Concord* declares when it says (Thor. Decl., VII, 53): "There is no doubt that also these words of Luke and Paul: 'This cup is the new testament in My blood,' can have no other meaning than that which St. Matthew and St. Mark give: 'This' (namely, that which you orally drink out of the cup) 'is My blood of the new testament,' whereby I establish, seal, and confirm with you men this My testament and New Covenant, namely, *the forgiveness of sins."* In all his discussions on the subject, Luther never lost sight of the gracious forgiveness of sins which Holy Communion offers and conveys. To him the Lord's Supper was a "dear and blessed Holy Supper" just because Christ has joined to His body and blood the gracious promise "Given for you; shed for you." (St. L., XIX, 1292.)

In connection with this point we may discuss also the question regarding the *specific object* of the communicant's faith. The communicant of course must believe that Jesus Christ, true God and true man, died for his sins. Moreover, he must believe that this same Christ communicates to him in Holy Communion His true body and blood; for every one who refuses to believe this is an unworthy guest and eats and drinks damnation to himself, "not discerning the Lord's body," 1 Cor. 11, 29. But even faith in the real presence is not yet saving faith. As Luther rightly says, the worthy communicant believes in the words "Given and shed *for you.*" That is to say, if any one wishes to be a worthy communicant, he must believe that *he personally* receives forgiveness of sins, life, and salvation by receiving Christ's body and blood, given and shed for him.

That is the pivotal point in the whole doctrine of the Lord's Supper. Luther argues this point under the question: "Who, then, receives such Sacrament worthily?" He writes in his *Small Catechism: "He* is truly worthy and well prepared *who has faith* in these words: 'Given and shed *for you* for the remission of sins.'" As Luther points out, these words are a direct promise of forgiveness to every communicant; and all who wish to be worthy communicants must put their trust in this divine promise. In other words, they must believe what Scripture says concerning both the *essence* and the *object* (purpose) of Holy Communion.

The doctrine that Christ in the Holy Supper offers forgiveness of sins to the communicant is rejected by the papists. The Council of Trent directly anathematizes all who designate the gracious offer of forgiveness as the chief purpose of the Lord's Supper (Trid., *De Sacrosancto Eucharistiae Sacramento,* Can. 5). Similarly Carlstadt regarded it as "a base and abominable injury for our Christians to *seek forgiveness of sins* in the Sacrament" (S. L., XX, 94). Zwingli and Calvin likewise voiced a warning against the thought that "the visible sign, while being offered, produces also the grace of God" *(Consensus Tigurinus).*

From the viewpoint of Calvinism this warning is quite intelligible; for according to the Reformed view the Lord's Supper cannot offer grace to all sinners, since, on the one hand, divine grace is not intended for all (denial of the *gratia universalis*) and, on the other, there are no means of grace, which offer, seal, and convey forgiveness of sins, life, and salvation. ("In the work of regeneration all second causes are excluded." "Nothing intervenes between the volition of the Spirit and the regeneration of the soul." "The infusion of a new life into the soul is the immediate work of the Spirit.")

However, in view of this fact the Calvinists have no right to speak of the Holy Supper as a sign, seal, and pledge (*signum, tessera, pignus*) of divine grace secured by Christ Jesus, since to them it is only a "memorial feast," celebrated in remembrance of Christ's death.

The gracious forgiveness of sins, with life and salvation, is the foremost gift of the Holy Supper; all other blessings (*beneficia*) offered therein are only its concomitants. Among these blessings we may mention the gracious effects of this Sacrament, such as the strengthening of faith, the union with Christ and with His spiritual body, the Church, growth in sanctification, furtherance in love toward God and the neighbor, increase in patience and in the hope of eternal life, greater joy in confessing Christ, 1 Cor. 11, 26, etc. Incidentally the Lord's Supper also serves the purpose of distinguishing Christian believers from the heterodox and the ungodly.

All these blessed effects are due to the fact that the Lord's Supper is a *medium iustificationis,* or a means by which we receive forgiveness of sins; for in proportion as the believer is assured of the forgiveness of his sins, his faith is strengthened, his love is increased, and his hope of eternal life is confirmed. Assured of his adoption as God's child in Christ Jesus, he also struggles against sin and lives unto Him who died for him and rose again. In short, he loves God because He first loved him, 1 John 4, 19.

All those who deny that the Lord's Supper is primarily a means of justification, or of forgiveness (Romanists, Calvinists, etc.), really render these gracious effects of the Holy Supper impossible. They change this beneficial "work of God upon us" into "a human work for God," or, what is the same, they convert the Gospel-message of Holy Communion into one of Law and good works and so leave the communicant under the curse, Gal. 3, 10. Indeed, as unworthy guests, who trust in their own righteousness, they eat and drink damnation to themselves, 1 Cor. 11, 29.

How thoroughly the Romanists have perverted the doctrine of the purpose of the Lord's Supper may be learned from the following decisions of the Council of Trent: *"Si quis dixerit, prae-*

cipuum fructum eucharistiae esse REMISSIONEM PECCATORUM, *anathema sit."* (Sess. XIII, Can. 5.) *"Si quis dixerit, in missa non offerri Deo verum et proprium* SACRIFICIUM, *anathema sit." "Si quis dixerit, missae sacrificium* . . . NON ESSE PROPITIATORIUM, . . . *non pro peccatis, poenis, satisfactionibus et aliis necessitatibus offerri debere, anathema sit."* (Sess. XXII, Cans. 1. 3.) Yet despite this emphasis on the sacrifice of the Mass the *Roman Catechism* (II, C. IV, Qu. 41) declares that in the Eucharist only the venial sins are forgiven.

As the Romanists, so also the Calvinists deny that in the Lord's Supper Christ offers and imparts forgiveness of sins. Zwingli: *"Coena dominica mortis commemoratio est, non peccatorum remissio."* Strong: "It *symbolizes* the death of Christ for our sins." — "Baptism and the Lord's Supper tell the story of redemption." *(Watchman-Examiner.)*

9. WHO MAY BE ADMITTED TO THE LORD'S SUPPER.
(Finis cui Coenae Sacrae.)

Christian ministers are only "stewards," not lords, of the mysteries of God, 1 Cor. 4, 1. For this reason they must administer the means of grace (the Gospel and the Sacraments) just as Christ has instituted them, 1 Cor. 4, 2; Matt. 28, 20. Ministers or congregations departing from Christ's institution in administering the Holy Supper reject His authority, oppose His will, misuse the precious Sacrament, and therefore "come together unto condemnation," 1 Cor. 11, 29—34. — Concerning the right administration of the Lord's Supper Holy Scripture teaches the following truths: —

a. Not open, but close communion must be practised by the Christian Church, since it is God's will that only believers should approach the Lord's Table, 1 Cor. 11, 26—28. While the Gospel should be preached to believers and unbelievers alike, Mark 16, 15. 16, the Lord's Supper is designed only for the regenerate, as Christ's words of institution and the normative practise of the holy apostles prove, 1 Cor. 10, 16; 11, 26—34.

Luther writes on this point (St. L., XI, 615): "So Christ has done; the preaching [of the Gospel] He permitted to go to every one in a heap, as afterwards also the apostles did, so that all heard it, whether they were believers or unbelievers. . . . So also we must do. But we should not cast the Sacrament among the people in a heap. If I preach the Gospel, I do not know whom it strikes; but here I must be sure that it has struck him who goes to the Sacrament. So I must not be in doubt, but know assuredly that he to whom I give the Sacrament has comprehended the Gospel and rightly believes."

The doctrine of close communion must be maintained not only against Reformed sects, but also against Lutheran errorists. (Cp. *Geschichte der Luth. Kirche,* by A. L. Graebner, sub *Abendmahl; Lehre und Wehre,* 1888, pp. 257 ff. 302 ff.)

b. Of Christians only those may be admitted to the Lord's Table —

1. Who are already baptized;

2. Who are able to examine themselves, 1 Cor. 11, 28. This excludes children, unconscious persons, patients in a coma, and all persons who are not *compos mentis* (insanity);

3. Who believe that in Holy Communion they receive Christ's body and blood in, with, and under the bread and wine for the gracious remission of their sins, Matt. 26, 26—28. This excludes all Reformed, rationalists, etc., who deny the real presence, as well as all papists (Romanizing Lutherans), who teach that the Sacrament works *ex opere operato* and so deny that faith is the *medium ληπτικόν* of the proffered forgiveness of sins;

4. Who may do so without giving offense to others, 2 Cor. 6, 3; Matt. 18, 7. This excludes all those 1) who live in gross sins, 1 Cor. 5, 11; 2) who refuse to forgive and be reconciled, Matt. 18, 15—17. 35; 5, 23. 24; and 3) who are guilty of unionism or syncretism, Rom. 16, 17; 2 John 10. 11. The Sacrament must be withheld from all who are connected with erring churches and unchristian or antichristian cults, Eph. 4, 1—6; 5, 7—11; 2 Cor. 6, 14—18.

Since lodgery is a pagan cult, based upon work-righteousness, and as such denies the very purpose of Holy Communion, namely, the imparting of the forgiveness of sins through faith in Christ *(sola fide),* it is self-evident that lodge-fellowship is inconsistent with the true profession of the Christian faith. Lodge members should therefore be excluded from Holy Communion a) because, as members of antichristian cults, they deny the specific teachings of the Christian religion (the Holy Trinity, the deity of Christ, His vicarious atonement, salvation by grace, etc.) and b) because they give offense to confessing Christians by going to the Lord's Supper while holding membership in antichristian societies, Matt. 10, 32—39.

Because the Holy Supper may be received to judgment (1 Cor.

11, 29 : *κρίμα)*, the Christian minister must not only urge all communicants diligently to examine themselves, 1 Cor. 11, 28, but also aid them in their self-examination. To this end he should retain both the confessional service and the Lutheran custom of "announcing for Communion" *(Beichtanmeldung)*, which gives him an opportunity to deal individually with those who desire to attend the Lord's Table.

However, while the pastor should not admit to Holy Communion any unworthy guest, he must take care not to restrain from it any who are entitled to it. In general, it may be said that all baptized Christians who heartily repent of their sins, truly believe in Jesus Christ, regard the ordinance of Holy Communion as Christ instituted it, are open to Christian instruction on every point of doctrine and life, are able to examine themselves, lead a Christian life, and purpose to amend their lives by the aid of the Holy Spirit should be admitted to the Lord's Table.

Since the sacramental worthiness consists essentially in true faith, which this Sacrament strengthens and increases, also the weak in faith should be admitted to it, Matt. 11, 28; John 6, 37; in fact, these should be urged to come to the Lord's Table.

In all cases where the pastor, who is responsible for the conscientious administration of his office not only to his congregation, but also to God, 1 Cor. 4, 1. 2, would become a partaker of another man's sin, 1 Tim. 5, 22, if he accepts him as a guest at the Lord's Table, he is in duty bound to suspend a church-member from Holy Communion (cp. the case where a person refuses to be reconciled to his brother, Matt. 5, 23—25; 18, 28 ff.; Luke 17, 3).

Suspension from Holy Communion is not equivalent to the ban, or the official excommunication of the sinner by the congregation, 1 Cor. 5, 13, but the pastor's solemn declaration that the member in question for the time being cannot receive Holy Communion as a worthy guest. The suspended member may of course appeal from the pastor's judgment to that of the congregation, but in case the congregation wrongly decides against his correct decision, the Christian minister should allow himself to be expelled from office rather than lift the suspension which he has imposed in accordance with God's Word.

While the confession (either public or private) is not divinely instituted, it should be retained, especially on account of the absolution pronounced in it. (Cp. Luther, St. L., X, 1655; XI, 585—590.) All other questions pertaining to this subject belong to the domain of Pastoral Theology.

10. THE NECESSITY OF THE LORD'S SUPPER.

While all Christians should frequently attend the Lord's Table in the manner which Scripture prescribes, 1 Cor. 11, 26—29, we cannot speak of an *absolute necessity* of the Lord's Supper. The spiritual eating of Christ's body, John 6, 53, or faith in Christ *(sola fide),* is indeed absolutely necessary for salvation; but the sacramental eating of His body is not absolutely necessary. Also here the words of St. Augstine apply: "Not the privation, but the contempt of the Sacrament condemns" *(Contemptus sacramenti damnat, non privatio).*

However, let the Christian minister conscientiously remind his parishioners that indifference to, or neglect of, Communion implies contempt of the Sacrament and that contempt for the Lord's institutions is tantamount to apostasy. (Cp. Luther, *Large Catechism,* "The Sacrament of the Altar," 42 ff.: "Such people as deprive themselves of, and withdraw from, the Sacrament so long a time are not to be considered Christians.")

THE DOCTRINE OF THE CHRISTIAN CHURCH.

(De Ecclesia.)

We shall treat this subject under two heads: a) The Church Universal; b) Local Churches.

A. The Church Universal.

(De Ecclesia Universali.)

1. DEFINITION OF THE TERM.

Through the efficacious means of grace, Is. 55, 10. 11; Rom. 10, 17, the Holy Ghost continually gathers into the kingdom of heaven such as truly believe that they are saved alone by faith in the vicarious atonement of Christ, the divine-human Savior of the world, Acts 2, 44—47; 5, 42; 11, 21; 13, 48. The *communion of believing saints* which the Holy Ghost thus gathers through the Gospel we call the Church (קָהָל, מִקְרָא, עֵדָה, συναγωγή, ἐκκλησία, *communio sanctorum, congregatio vere credentium, coetus fidelium*), after the example of Scripture, Eph. 5, 24—27. The Christian Church accordingly consists of all those who truly believe the Gospel, that is, God's gracious message that for the sake of Christ's vicarious satisfaction they freely (χάριτι) have forgiveness of sins, life, and salvation; or, more briefly expressed, who believe in Christ, the Lamb of God, which takes away the sin of the world, John 1, 29.

This definition of the term *Church* is important in view of the many errors that have been maintained on this point. According to Scripture only faith in the Christ *(fiducia cordis)* who died for the sins of the world makes a person a member of the Church, not the external connection with a local church, nor the external use of the means of grace, nor the external profession of the Christian faith, nor the administration of offices in visible churches, nor the effort to imitate Christ's example by outwardly following Him, Acts 5, 14. Hence the statements of our dogmaticians, *Sola fides in Christum membra ecclesiae constituit; Christiani sunt ecclesia,* are truly Scriptural; for only a true believer in Christ is a member of His holy Church, Acts 16, 31.

It is true, as soon as a person believes in Christ, his sanctification, or renovation, begins as the inevitable effect and fruit of justification, 2 Cor. 5, 17. 18. For this reason Holy Scripture frequently describes the true members of the Church according to their sanctified nature, 1 Cor. 6, 15—20; 1 Pet. 2, 5, or according to the holy works which they do through faith, 1 Pet. 2, 9—25. But the regenerate are members of the Church not inasmuch as they are sanctified by the Holy Ghost or inasmuch as through His power they bring forth fruits of faith, John 15, 4. 5, but only because they trust in Christ for salvation without works, Rom. 3, 28; 4, 3—5. In other words, as we are justified *sola fide,* so also we are members of Christ's Church *sola fide.* Of justification by faith, Luther rightly says that this article alone begets, nurtures, builds, preserves, and defends the Church of God and that without it the Church of God cannot exist even for an hour (St. L., XIV, 168).

From this it follows that all unbelievers and hypocrites *(mali et hypocritae)* who outwardly belong to visible churches are really outside the pale of the Christian Church. They are never a part of the Church *(non sunt pars ecclesiae),* although they outwardly hold membership in local congregations *(ecclesiae admixti sunt secundum societatem externam).* The true members of the Church are joined to it through their inward, spiritual communion of faith with the Triune God, by reason of which they are God's house, 1 Tim. 3, 15; God's temple, 1 Cor. 3, 9; 2 Cor. 6, 16; the temple of the Holy Spirit, 1 Cor. 6, 19; Christ's body, Eph. 1, 23; children of God, John 11, 52; Gal. 3, 26—29; etc. On the other hand, unbelievers according to Scripture are not God's house, or temple, but the workshop of Satan, who "worketh in the children of disobedience," Eph. 2, 1—3. With respect to the definition "The Church is the communion of the elect," which was used by Huss and commended by Luther (St. L., V, 1234 ff.), we accept this as truly Scriptural, 1 Pet. 2, 9, since the true believers in Christ are the elect of God. (Baier: *"Homines illi, quos Deus iuxta aeternum suum decretum fide et gratia sua donavit, collective sumpti dicuntur ecclesia."* III, 614.)

That the Christian Church consists solely of true believers in Christ is a doctrine which our Lutheran Confessions firmly maintain against the erroneous tenets of the papists: *"Ecclesia est regnum divinum, unicum veritatis salutisque fundamentum, a Christo in orbe terrarum conditum,* QUOD PONTIFEX MAXIMUS PER EPISCOPOS SECUNDUM CANONES ADMINISTRAT."

Thus the *Augsburg Confession* writes (Art. VIII): "The Church properly is the congregation of saints and true believers." The *Apology* (Art. VII [VIII], 5): "The Church is not only the fellowship of outward objects and rites, as other governments, but it is originally a fellowship of faith and of the Holy Ghost in hearts." Again (*ibid.*, § 16): "The Church, which is truly the kingdom of Christ, is properly the congregation of saints. For the wicked are ruled by the devil and are captives of the devil; they are not ruled by the Spirit of Christ." According to the *Apology* (*ibid.*, §§ 17—19) "the kingdom of Christ is not yet revealed, so that wicked men are mingled with the Church and hold offices; but the wicked are not the kingdom of Christ; for that is always the kingdom which He quickens by the Spirit."

The Lutheran Church thus professes the Scriptural doctrine that all true believers are members of the Church, while unbelievers are not members, even though they are outwardly joined to a visible church. While it sincerely believes and confesses that it is the true visible Church, it at the same time holds that all sincere believers in erring churches are truly members of Christ's Church (*ecclesia invisibilis*). According to the Lutheran doctrine, faith is so absolutely the means by which a person is joined to the Church that not even the ban, or the excommunication from a local church, in case it is unjustly executed, can annul his membership in the Church of Christ.

It is self-evident that such adults as have not yet been baptized, but have come to faith in Jesus Christ are true members of the Church, since Baptism is not absolutely necessary, as was pointed out in a previous chapter. On the other hand, it is likewise true that a sincere believer never despises the ordinances of Christ, Luke 7, 29. 30, so that a true member of the Church neglects neither Baptism nor the Lord's Supper.

2. ERRONEOUS DOCTRINES CONCERNING THE CHURCH.

It is obvious that all who err with regard to the distinctive doctrines of the Christian religion must err also with respect to the doctrine of the Church. Of all errors concerning the Church the foremost is that the Church is an "outward polity" (*externa politia*, "*aeusserliche Polizei*," "*Heilsanstalt*") "of the good and wicked" (*Apology*, VII [VIII], 13 ff.), to which persons are joined by their external membership.

Closely related to this error, which pertains to the essence (*forma*) of the Church, is that regarding its *purpose*, namely, that the Church is a "society for the sanctification of its members" or that it is an organization whose object is to save souls by means of good works. These basic errors are not incidental, but rather the result of the rejection of the fundamental Christian article of justification by grace, through faith.

In fact, all who repudiate the *satisfactio vicaria,* the efficacy of the means of grace, and the *sola fide* must of necessity regard the Church as a sort of reform school in which men are to learn how to be good and so to merit salvation. On the other hand, the Biblical doctrine of the Church is built up on the central doctrine of justification by grace, through faith, so that it stands or falls with that doctrine. In particular it rests —

a. *Upon Christ's vicarious satisfaction.* According to Scripture the Church consists of all those who believe in the Christ who died for the sins of the world. All who refuse to believe this are outside the Church, 1 Pet. 2, 8. This doctrine is opposed by all rationalists (Photinians, Socinians, Unitarians, Modernists, etc.), who reject the doctrine of salvation by faith in Christ's blood, 1 John 1, 7, as an "obnoxious blood-theology" and to whom the Gospel of the crucified Christ is both foolishness and a stumbling-block, 1 Cor. 1, 23. Hence they have no other way of defining the Church — if they at all care for a church — than as "a free society of rational beings for the realization of earthly and heavenly happiness, conditioned by man's religious illumination and virtue" (Roehrs).

More simply defined, the Church, according to all rationalistic theologians, is a society of men who wish to secure happiness in this world and the next by means of religious devotions and other good works. In their estimation the Church is only a "moral or ethical society" and embraces as members all who are willing to perform the duties which it imposes.

As all rationalists in general, so also the rationalistic papists in particular regard the Church as a pious society of men sanctifying themselves by good works. According to the papistic doctrine a person does not become a member of the Church through faith in Christ, but through his professed willingness to obey the instructions of God and the Church (Council of Trent, Sess. VI, Can. 20), or through the performance of good works prescribed by the Church (Sess. VI, Can. 32). This basic error really places the papists *extra ecclesiam;* for Scripture testifies that all who are of the works of the Law are fallen from grace, Gal. 5, 4, and are under the curse, Gal. 3, 10.

The antichristian attitude of the Church of Rome is moreover proved by the fact that it has pronounced its anathema upon the true Christian Church, namely, upon all who believe that they are justified alone by grace, through faith in Christ (Council of Trent, Sess. VI, Cans. 11. 12), defining at the same time the "true Church" (*sc.* the Roman Catholic Church) as "the congregation of men under the rule of duly called pastors and especially of the one vicar of Christ upon earth, the Roman Pontiff" *(coetus homi-num . . . sub regimine legitimorum pastorum ac praecipue unius Christi in terris vicarii, Romani pontificis,* Bellarmine). Officially Rome thus makes it impossible for its followers to be members of Christ's holy Church.

If Catholics despite the pernicious rationalism of their Church are members of Christ's Church, it is because in their *terrores con-scientiae* they renounce its doctrine of work-righteousness and, contrary to its will and command, believe the *sola fide.* We there-fore recognize the papistic Church as Christian, not inasmuch as it rejects the Christian doctrine in its official theology (decisions and canons of the Council of Trent), but inasmuch as, quite incon-sistently with its general theological system, it professes the Apostles' Creed, which acts as a corrective in the case of individual Catholics. Officially Roman Catholicism is not Christian, but pagan, because it professes as its cardinal dogma salvation by works.

Since also many modern "positive" theologians (Hofmann, Kirn) repudiate the *satisfactio vicaria,* they, too, err in their defi-nition of the Christian Church. According to Kirn the Church is "the communion of the religious and moral life determined by the spirit of Christ" (*Ev. Dogmatik,* p. 118) ; that is to say, the communion of all who lead a moral life in the spirit of Christ. This, in the last analysis, reduces the Church to an "ethical society."

Because the Calvinists deny the *gratia universalis* and the efficacy of the means of grace as the *media iustificationis,* they also cannot define the Church rightly as the communion of all true believers in Christ, but must regard it theoretically as the "com-munion of the elect" and practically as the communion of all who possess the *gratia infusa,* or the immediate operation and indwelling of the Holy Ghost in their hearts. All true members of the Church in Calvinistic denominations *repudiate the gratia particularis* and in their spiritual distress hold to God's gracious promise which He offers to all sinners in the Gospel. It is on account of this fact that they are members of Christ's Church.

b. *Upon the doctrine of the means of grace.* By this we mean that without the means of grace there can be no Church. According to the clear teaching of Scripture a person becomes a true member of Christ's Church only by appropriating to himself the merits of Christ, Rom. 4, 3; Acts 10, 43—48. But unless the merits of Christ are offered to the sinner by God through His conferring means (the Word and the Sacraments), man cannot appropriate them at all. The Reformed error of "immediate grace" *(Efficacious grace acts immediately)* must be rejected as unscriptural, Rom. 10, 13—17; Acts 2, 38. The Calvinists repudiate the means of grace and thus render faith and justification and consequently the existence of the Church impossible.

For the means of grace some modern "positive" theologians substitute the "Christian experience" *(Erlebnistheologie);* but the Bible does not recognize the Christian experience as a means of grace. It is rather a fruit of faith. Hence there is only one way in which a person may become a member of Christ's Church, namely, by faith in the divine promises of grace offered in the Gospel and in the Sacraments, 2 Cor. 5, 19—21.

c. *Upon faith as the receiving means (medium ληπτικόν).* This is evident from the fact that only those are members of the Church who believe in Christ, Mark 16, 15. 16; Acts 16, 31. All who deny faith as the *medium ληπτικόν* of God's proffered grace are unable to define the Church in its Biblical sense, as the communion of true believers. Those who regard the Sacraments as working *ex opere operato* (Romanists, Romanizing Protestants) are obliged to define the Church as a communion of men who, by the aid of the Holy Spirit, endeavor to lead a moral life; for with the rejection of the *sola fide* only good works remain as the means of justification *(medium iustificationis).*

d. *Upon the sola fide.* This follows from what has been said before. The Church is the communion of true believers; but true believers are those only who hope to be saved by grace, through faith, without works, Rom. 3, 28; 4, 3—5. For this reason all Pelagians, Arminians, and synergists are compelled either to renounce their doctrine of work-righteousness or to abandon the Scriptural definition of the Church. The history of the Christian dogma proves that quite consistently they abandon the latter and thus regard the Church as the congregation of all who seek salvation by works. (Cp. *Christl. Dogmatik,* III, 464 ff.) That they take this unfortunate step is quite logical; for only those can rightly define the Church as the communion of believers who adhere to the Scriptural doctrine of justification by faith *(sola gratia).*

3. THE PROPERTIES OF THE CHRISTIAN CHURCH.
(Attributa Ecclesiae.)

According to Holy Scripture the Christian Church has certain undeniable characteristics for the very reason that it is the communion of all true believers *(communio omnium fidelium)*. We may classify these characteristics as follows: —

a. *The Church is invisible. (Ecclesia est invisibilis.)* This follows from the fact that saving faith, which constitutes the means by which a person becomes and remains a member of the Church, is unseen of man, 1 Kings 8, 39; 19, 18; Rom. 11, 3—5; Acts 1, 24. The invisibility of the Church is, however, predicated only with respect to men, not with respect to God. Of men the words of Christ in Luke 17, 20. 21 hold; to God St. Paul's words in 2 Tim. 2, 19 apply (cp. John 10, 14. 27. 28).

All who affirm that the Church is either wholly (papists) or partly (modern Lutheran theologians) visible destroy the Scriptural concept of the Church and change it from a communion of believers to an "outward polity of the good and wicked" *(externa politia bonorum et malorum; aeussere Anstalt; Heilsanstalt)*, in which the believers only play a more or less important rôle.

Occasionally Lutheran theologians to-day speak of *two* aspects of the Church, a visible aspect: the Word and the Sacraments, and an invisible one: the true members of the Church. But it is logically incorrect to describe the marks of the Church *(notae ecclesia)* as an essential part of the Church. It is true, the Gospel and the Sacraments are true *marks* of the Church; for the Church is never found where these are not in use. Moreover, the Gospel and the Sacraments are also the *means* by which the Church is established and preserved; for without the means of grace there can be no believers, Is. 55, 10 ff.; Rom. 10, 17; Matt. 28, 19. 20; Mark 16, 15. 16. But to call the means of grace a part of the Church or the Church itself is an absurdity.

The Church is the communion of believers, and since the faith of an individual is invisible to man, we rightly say: *Ecclesia est invisibilis*. Accordingly we must regard every one who professes the Christian faith and adorns this profession with a Christian life as a true member of the Church. To go beyond this and endeavor to ascertain the faith of an individual in any other way, Scripture expressly forbids, 1 Cor. 4, 5, since it is God's prerogative to know them that are His, 2 Tim. 2, 19; Col. 3, 3; 2 Cor. 5, 4. 5.

Even in case we could really identify the *living* members of the Church, the communion of saints in its entirety would still be invisible to us; for not until Judgment Day will Christ reveal His Church in glory, Matt. 25, 34; Col. 3, 4; 1 John 3, 2.

To the objection of the Romanists, who aver that the Church is "a gathering of men so visible and palpable as is that of the Roman people or the kingdom of Gaul or the republic of Venice" (Bellarmine), but that an invisible Church of true believers is a mere "Platonic idea" or a "figment of the mind," we reply that this communion of saints is so real that God knows and lovingly acknowledges all its members as His, 2 Tim. 2, 19; John 10, 27. 28, preserves this Church against the gates of hell, Matt. 16, 18, makes it the chief concern of His divine providence, Rom. 8, 28; Matt. 24, 22—24, and will finally receive it into eternal glory, Luke 12, 32.

On the other hand, the Church of Rome is not Christ's Church at all, but a human organization, founded upon commandments of men, Matt. 15, 9, and controlled by a deceiver, whom Scripture calls the Antichrist and the son of perdition, 2 Thess. 2, 3. 4, so that it is indeed outside the true Church *(extra ecclesiam)* both in this world, Gal. 5, 4; 3, 10, and in that to come, Gal. 4, 30.

b. *The Church is one. (Ecclesia una est.)* The unity of the Christian Church, which is expressly taught by Christ, John 10, 16, is based upon its unity of faith in the one Savior, Eph. 4, 3—6; for since the Church is the communion of believers, it is composed only of such as believe that they, being lost and condemned sinners, Rom. 3, 23. 24, are saved solely by grace, through faith in the atoning death of Christ, Rom. 3, 28. All who do not profess this Christian faith are not members of the Church, but outside the Church, 1 John 2, 23; 5, 12; Gal. 5, 4; 3, 10. Of the true members of the Church St. Paul says: "Ye are all one in Christ Jesus," Gal. 3, 28, so that the statement of our dogmaticians *Omnes Christiani de evangelio consentiunt* is indeed true.

c. *The Church is holy. (Ecclesia sancta est.)* This is true, 1) because all believers by faith possess Christ's perfect righteousness *(iustitia fidei imputata,* Phil. 3, 8. 9), and 2) because through faith they produce holy works *(iustitia vitae),* Rom. 6, 14. According to the imputed righteousness (justification) believers are perfect in the sight of God; according to their *iustitia vitae* they remain imperfect *(iustitia inchoata, imperfecta)* throughout their lives, Phil. 3, 12—16.

d. *The Church is universal, or catholic. (Ecclesia est universalis sive catholica.)* This is true; for the Church embraces all believers at all times and in all places, Acts 10, 43; John 8, 56; Rom. 4; Gal. 3, 6 ff. Even in the Old Testament the saints of God were such only because they believed in Christ Jesus, the promised Savior of the world, Rom. 3, 21. 22; 4, 3 f.

e. *The Church is apostolic. (Ecclesia apostolica est.)* This is true because all true members of the Church till the end of the world believe in Christ through the word of the apostles, John 17, 20; Acts 2, 42; Eph. 2, 20; Rom. 16, 17 f. "APOSTOLICA *dicitur ecclesia, quod doctrinam apostolicam fide amplectitur et integram tenet."* The Romanists and Episcopalians trace the apostolic character of the Church to the "apostolic succession"; but the doctrine of "apostolic succession" is manifestly anti-Scriptural, since Scripture does not draw a distinction between bishops and presbyters, or elders, Acts 20, 17. 28; Titus 1, 5—7. In addition, it urges all Christians to avoid those who teach any other doctrine than that taught by the blessed apostles, Rom. 16, 17; Gal. 1, 6—8, even if they claim to possess apostolic authority, 2 Cor. 11, 12—14; Gal. 2, 4 f.; 2 Pet. 2, 1. 2.

f. *No salvation outside the Church. (Extra ecclesiam nulla salus.)* All who desire to be saved must be members of Christ's Church. The papists apply this axiom wrongly to the Church of Antichrist, of which we may rather say: *Intra ecclesiam nulla salus,* namely, in so far as the members of this Church believe what Antichrist teaches, Rev. 13, 1—9; 14, 8—12; 20, 10. The axiom *Extra ecclesiam nulla salus* is true of Christ's Church because only those have life and salvation who believe in the Gospel of Christ and through this faith are members of the Church, John 3, 16—18. 36. The Church of Antichrist, on the other hand, makes salvation depend on the keeping of the Law (Council of Trent, Sess. VI, Can. 20) and thus leaves its members under the divine curse, Gal. 3, 10.

4. THE GLORY OF THE CHRISTIAN CHURCH.

The members of the Christian Church enjoy the high privilege of being subject only to Christ, their divine Lord and Master, 1 Cor. 3, 23; Matt. 23, 8, and not to any human teacher, 1 Cor. 7, 23; Matt. 15, 9. The Pope at Rome is the Antichrist for the very reason that he sits in the temple of God, exalting himself above all that is called God, 2 Thess. 2, 3. 4, that is, because he makes his own word the rule and standard of faith and life. It is true, God at all times bestows special gifts upon certain members of the Church and calls these as teachers of their fellow-believers, Eph. 4, 11—13. But such teachers of the Church are to inculcate only *His* Word, 1 Pet. 4, 11; Jer. 23, 16. 18, and not their own.

According to Scripture all teachers who preach their own word and doctrine are "proud know-nothings," or "conceited dolts," whom the Church should reject and shun as perverters and cor- rupters, 1 Tim. 6, 3—5, indeed, as seducing spirits, teaching doc- trines of devils, 1 Tim. 4, 1—3; Col. 2, 18—23. Even the holy apostles did not command obedience in so far as they were human beings, 1 Cor. 3, 21—23, but their word must be heard and heeded solely because of its being God's Word, given by divine inspiration, 1 Cor. 4, 1; 2, 12. 13.

Christian ministers are not mediators between God and the believers (priests); for all Christians have access to God's throne through the one Mediator, Christ, in whom they believe, Rom. 5, 1. 2; Eph. 3, 12; Heb. 4, 16. In fact, all believers are the imme- diate possessors of all gifts and blessings which Christ has secured for His Church, such as the means of grace and the keys of the kingdom of heaven, Matt. 16, 19; 18, 18; John 20, 23; 1 Cor. 5, 3—5. 13. Theirs alone is the privilege to preach the Gospel and to administer the Sacraments, in short, to execute the entire Office of the Keys, so that the called and ordained pastors exercise their ministerial functions only in the name of the church which has called them.

To the objection of the Romanists that in Matt. 16, 18 Christ builds His Church on Peter, Luther rightly replies that "all Chris- tians are Peters on account of the confession of Christ which Peter here made; this confession is the rock upon which Peter and all Peters are built." The above words of our Lord cannot be referred to the person of Peter either as the primary apostle or as the repre- sentative of the apostles; for, as the context shows, Peter here did not act as an apostle at all, but only as a believing Christian. That not Peter himself was meant to be the rock upon which the Church is built, but his Christian confession, is unmistakably indi- cated by the words of the text (Πέτρος, πέτρα).

Luther is right in saying that in this passage Christ clearly distinguishes between Peter and his confession; for had He meant to make Peter the rock of the Church, He should have said: "Thou art Peter, and upon thee will I build My Church." (Cp. Luther, St. L., XX, 282; XVIII, 1375 ff.)

Among modern Protestant exegetes some (*e. g.,* Meyer) refer the term πέτρα to the person of Peter, as if this apostle were here given the primacy among the apostles *(primus inter pares),* though they deny the conclusions which the papists draw from this premise with reference to the Roman Pontiff. Other modern exegetes rightly refer the words to Peter's confession (Lange, Ewald, Wieseler).

Whether the term πέτρα refers to Christ Himself or to the confession of Christ is immaterial, since the Church that is built upon the confession of Christ is built upon Christ Himself.

As believers possess all spiritual gifts and blessings of God in Christ Jesus, so they possess also all temporal gifts and blessings of God, so that indeed all things present and things to come are theirs, 1 Cor. 3, 21—23, as children of God and coheirs with Christ, Rom. 8, 14—17.

5. HOW THE CHURCH IS FOUNDED AND PRESERVED.

Since saving faith, by which a person becomes a member of the Church, is solely the work of God, Eph. 1, 19. 20; 1 Pet. 1, 5; John 1, 13, the Church owes its existence and preservation entirely to divine grace, Ps. 100, 3; 1 Pet. 2, 9. 10.

Synergism, which makes man's faith depend in part on his meritorious efforts, therefore undermines the very foundation of the Church.

The means, or instrument, by which God gathers and sustains His Church is the Gospel in all its various forms of application (the Word and the Sacraments), through which the Holy Ghost engenders and preserves faith, Rom. 10, 13—17; 1 Pet. 1, 23—25. (Cp. Luther, St. L., V, 990 ff.; VI, 21 ff.)

Calvinism, which denies the efficacy of the means of grace and teaches the creation of faith by the immediate operation of the Holy Spirit, therefore removes the very foundation on which the Church rests. Fortunately the practise of Calvinists is more Scriptural than is their theory; for, unlike the consistent Quakers, they use and apply the means of grace; that is to say, they preach the Gospel and retain the Sacraments, though not in their Scriptural purity.

Believers are instrumental causes *(causae instrumentales)* of the Church inasmuch as they preach the Gospel and administer the Sacraments, Is. 40, 9; Mark 16, 15. 16; Matt. 28, 20.

In this sense the visible Church on earth is the mother of all believers *(mater fidelium),* who like Isaac are children of the promise, Gal. 4, 26—28. Luther thus declares (St. L., IX, 573ff., especially 575ff.) : "Sarah, or Jerusalem, is our free mother, namely, the Church, Christ's bride, by which we all are born. But she bears children without ceasing till the end of the world by the ministry of the Word, that is, by teaching and spreading the Gospel; for that is what *to bear* means. The Church should do nothing else than teach the Gospel in its truth and purity and thus bear children."

From this follows that the State (civil government) is not a sort of maid *(ancilla ecclesiae)* that must assist the Church in its divine work of winning souls for Christ. While both the papists and the Calvinists intermingle Church and State in principle and practise, the Lutherans, on the basis of Scripture, oppose every attempt to mingle the two. According to Lutheran doctrine the mingling of the two produces only harm, never any good (cp. church conditions in all European state churches). The Church loses nothing of its dignity or power by being independent of the civil government. On the contrary, its freedom from the restrictions of the civil law enables it to attend to its sacred duty of proclaiming the Word the more efficiently.

On the other hand, however, the independent constitution of the Church *(die freikirchliche Verfassung)* must not be interpreted as a sort of means of grace, which in itself makes it more effective in saving souls. Its success depends entirely on the testimony of the Gospel in its full truth and the administration of the Sacraments according to Christ's institution. That is both its privilege and its power.

With regard to the existing forms of government (absolute monarchies; limited monarchies; republics; Zwingli favored the republic; Calvin the oligarchy) the *Augsburg Confession* (Art. XVI) rightly affirms: "The Gospel teaches an eternal righteousness of the heart. Meanwhile it does not destroy the State or the family, but very much requires that they be preserved as ordinances of God and that charity be practised in such ordinances. Therefore Christians are necessarily bound to obey their own magistrates and laws, save only when commanded to sin; for then they ought to obey God rather than men, Acts 5, 29." The *Augsburg Confes-*

sion does not favor any particular form of government, but teaches that Christians must acknowledge, and be subject to, all "powers that be," Rom. 13, 1—7; Matt. 22, 21; 1 Pet. 2, 13. 17; 1 Tim. 2, 1—3; Jer. 29, 7.

While Christian believers who have been chosen to fill governmental offices must not conceal or deny their faith, but as earnest Christians witness the more faithfully to the truth of the Gospel, Acts 17, 34; Rom. 16, 23, wherever they have an opportunity, nevertheless they must carefully distinguish between the provinces of the Church and of the State, bearing in mind, on the one hand, that the State cannot be governed by God's Word or "Christian principles," but only by reason and common sense *(lex naturalis)*, while, on the other, the Church is governed alone by God's Word and not by any dictates of reason or by the external coercion of laws. In other words, though Christians should put into the service of Christ also the influence which is theirs because of their high station in life, just as they so use their money and other talents, they must not intermingle the Church and the State in the interest of either of the two.

During the Reformation the prevailing conditions prevented Luther from carrying into effect his clear principle regarding the separation of Church and State; yet he never ceased to declare this principle as the only correct and Scriptural one. (Cp. *Christl. Dogmatik*, III, 481 f.)

B. Concerning Local Churches.
(De Ecclesiis Particularibus.)

1. DEFINITION OF THE TERM.

What has been said so far related to the Church Universal, or to the Church in its primary sense, namely, the "one fold," John 10, 16, or the communion of believers, Matt. 16, 18, which the Holy Ghost continuously gathers through the preaching of the Gospel, Rom. 11, 2—5. However, Scripture applies the term *Church* also to local congregations, 1 Cor. 16, 19; 1, 2; 11, 16; Acts 8, 1; Rom. 16, 16, which therefore are known as local churches *(ecclesiae particulares)*. Such local churches are assemblies of believers, or Christians grouped together at one place, to preach the Gospel and administer the Sacraments, in short, to execute the Office of the Keys, Acts 20, 28; 14, 23. 27; 1 Tim. 3, 5; Matt. 18, 17; 1 Cor. 14, 23.

With respect to the relation between the Church Universal and the local churches, Scripture teaches clearly that these are not two different churches or two different kinds of churches, but the Church Universal consists of all true believers who are found in the local churches. Since it is God's will that all believers should be joined to local churches, all cases where an individual believer on account of special circumstances temporarily does not hold membership in a local church must be regarded as exceptional and hence require no consideration in this connection. Local churches therefore are true believers, or true members of the Church Universal, who are joined together in a visible communion for the purpose of executing the Office of the Keys, or the peculiar church-power which Christ has given to His Church on earth. This point must be clearly understood; for local churches, in the proper sense of the term, consist only of true believers.

All hypocrites, who are not members of the Church Universal, are likewise not truly members of local churches, Matt. 24, 32; 22, 12—14; 20, 10—16; 13, 47—48. Their connection with the local churches is only external and accidental. Accordingly, when St. Paul addressed the local church at Corinth ("the church of God which is at Corinth"), he addressed its members as "those that are sanctified in Christ Jesus, called [to be] saints, with all that in every place call upon the name of Jesus Christ, our Lord," 1 Cor. 1, 2. This description certainly does not apply to the hypocrites (*mali et hypocritae*) who were joined to the church outwardly (*ecclesiae admixti secundum societatem externam*).

Again, when hypocrites manifest themselves as such, Christ distinctly commands that they should be excommunicated, Matt. 18, 15—18; for since they are not members of the Church, they should not disgrace or injure the local congregation by their presence, 1 Cor. 5, 6—13.

· Lastly, all the divinely imposed obligations of the local churches presuppose that those who fulfil them are true believers; for these Christian duties can be performed rightly only by persons who are truly regenerate; *e. g.*, mutual instruction and admonition, Col. 3, 16. 17; church discipline, Matt. 18, 15—18; 1 Cor. 5, 1—13; preservation of the true doctrine and spiritual guardianship over the teachers, Rom. 16, 17; Col. 4, 17; preaching the Gospel, 1 Pet. 2, 9; Christian conduct in the fear of God, 1 Pet. 3, 8—17; etc. Before hypocrites can become members of the local churches, they must first "repent and be converted," Acts 3, 19.

We therefore rightly define local churches as assemblies of true believers, who are gathered at a certain place for the purpose of preaching the Gospel and administering the Sacraments. If in a general way we apply the term also to heterodox congregations or even to antichristian cults, this is done in a wider sense, either by way of synecdoche, because also in heterodox local churches there may be members of the Church Universal, or improperly *(improprie), i. e.,* according to the common mode of speaking (unchristian cults).

2. THE DIVINE INSTITUTION OF LOCAL CHURCHES.

The question whether local churches exist by divine institution or command, so that believers living at one place must either organize such churches where they do not exist or join them where they do exist, is of great importance.

To the objection of those who deny this point on the ground that membership in the Church Universal is sufficient for salvation and that Christ has given His followers no direct command to establish or to join local churches, so that local churches are free organizations, founded by men as the practical needs of believers in this world have made them necessary, we reply that it is indeed God's will and appointment —

a) That all believers living at one place should establish in their midst the public ministry and make diligent use of it by hearing and learning God's Word as it is proclaimed by the divinely called ministers, Eph. 4, 3—6; Acts 2, 42—47; 14, 23; 20, 28; 1 Cor. 12, 28; 1 Pet. 5, 2. 3; Titus 1, 5;

b) That they should together celebrate Holy Communion, 1 Cor. 11, 26; 10, 17, and exercise the duties of Christian fellowship and love, 1 Cor. 11, 33; 1, 10; Acts 6, 1—6; Col. 3, 15. 16;

c) That they should not only privately reprove an erring brother, Matt. 18, 15. 16, but also as a church, or congregation, rebuke and discipline impenitent sinners, Matt. 18, 17; 1 Cor. 5, 13.

From all this it follows that it is indeed God's will and ordinance that Christians should establish and maintain local churches; for without them these Christian obligations, enjoined so definitely, cannot be performed.

This principle is in full accord with the practise of the apostles and their followers, who consistently gathered the believers into local churches and commonly instructed, admonished, and comforted them as such in their epistles, 1 Cor. 1, 2; Rom. 1, 7; Gal.

1, 2; Eph. 1, 1; Phil. 1, 1; Acts 20, 28; 14, 23; 1 Cor. 5, 13;
2 Cor. 2, 6—8; Titus 1, 5; Rev. 1—3.

For this reason we rightly insist that the ban, or excommunication, Matt. 18, 17; 1 Cor. 5, 13, should be declared by local
churches and not by assemblies of Christians which have not been
divinely instituted. Among such bodies we may classify all conferences, synods, and similar convocations which are established for
the furtherance of Christ's kingdom and cause. Yet even with
respect to synods, conferences, and similar organizations, Christians
must always be guided by the rule of Christian love, 2 Cor. 13, 11;
1 Cor. 16, 14; Rom. 13, 10.

3. ORTHODOX AND HETERODOX CHURCHES.

It is God's will and command that all believers should hear,
learn, and proclaim only the pure Word which He Himself has
given them in Holy Scripture, Jer. 23, 30—32; 1 Tim. 6, 3—5.
All who pervert the Word of God and teach their own doctrine in
place of God's revealed truths, Matt. 15, 9, Scripture condemns as
false prophets, Matt. 7, 15, teachers, both of fables and of damnable
heresies, 1 Tim. 1, 3—7; 2 Pet. 2, 1, ungodly men, Jude 3. 4, men
of corrupt minds and reprobate concerning the faith, 2 Tim. 3,
1—8, deceivers and antichrists, 2 John 7, whom all Christians must
avoid, Rom. 16, 17; 2 John 10, as conceited ignoramuses, 1 Tim. 6,
3—5, who are under God's curse, Gal. 1, 8, etc. As Holy Scripture
condemns all sinful conduct, 1 Cor. 5, 9—11; Rev. 21, 8; 22, 15,
so it likewise condemns every corruption of the Christian faith, as
this is set forth in God's Word, Gal. 3, 10; 5, 10—12; Rev. 22,
18. 19; Matt. 18, 6. 7; 5, 19.

All churches that tolerate and follow such perverters of the
divine truth are known as heterodox churches *(ecclesiae hetero-
doxae, ecclesiae impurae)*, while churches that teach the Word of
God in its truth and purity and administer the Sacraments according to Christ's institution are orthodox, or pure, churches *(ecclesiae
orthodoxae, ecclesiae purae)*.

This distinction all sincere Christians must carefully observe,
especially at this time, when the spirit of indifferentism is alarm-
ingly spreading in so many churches and there is a manifest tendency to discard the Christian doctrine (abrogation of creeds) and
to reorganize the churches on a "broader basis of social service"
(applied Christianity; the gospel of social service). The program
of present-day Modernism calls for the abolition of every confes-

sional basis and is therefore in opposition to the direct commission which Christ gave to His Church, Mark 16, 15; Matt. 28, 20; 10, 32—39.

In order that believers may rightly distinguish between orthodox and heterodox churches, the following points must be kept in mind.

In the first place, a church is orthodox, or pure *(ecclesia vera seu pura)*, not simply when it acknowledges the divine truth in general through confessions which are in accord with Scripture, but when it actually teaches the divine truth without qualification and prevents or suppresses all error. In other words, a church must be pure, or orthodox, not only in principle, but also in practise, so that it earnestly reproves and disciplines all who teach false doctrine. But this is not all. If a church wishes to be truly orthodox, it must not only teach in conformity with Scripture, but also insist upon a practise that is in strict accord with whatever the Word of God inculcates (conditions of church-membership, attendance at Holy Communion, regulation of the Christian life of its members, opposition to religious indifferentism and unionism, etc.). A church which is orthodox in theory only, but not in practise cannot be considered as being truly orthodox, since it disregards Holy Scripture in its insistence upon the proper application of the divine truth to life, 1 Cor. 5, 13; 11, 20—22; 6, 1—6; 14, 34—40; etc.

In the second place, an orthodox church does not become heterodox *(ecclesia corrupta)* through errors which *accidentally* occur in its midst; for it is only the *toleration* of false doctrine and an unscriptural practise that make a church heterodox. Even in the churches established by the apostles, errorists arose, who succeeded in spreading false doctrines, Acts 20, 30; Gal. 1, 6—9; 1 Cor. 15, 1—19; but they were reproved and condemned.

Hence a church becomes impure, or heterodox, only when it ceases to apply God's directions given in Rom. 16, 17; 2 John 10. 11; Matt. 18, 17; etc., and so permits error and ungodliness to exist side by side with truth or even to gain the ascendency over truth.

Heterodox churches are *sects,* inasmuch as they adhere to error, which separates them from the Church. *"Ecclesia quatenus impura, non est ecclesia."* They are *churches* inasmuch as they still adhere to the Christian truth and are thus joined to the Church, provided, of course, their errors do not deny the fundamental articles of the Christian faith, in which case they cease to be heterodox churches and become antichristian cults (cp. Calvinism with Unitarianism; 1 Tim. 6, 20. 21; 2 Tim. 2, 16—18).

Although heterodox churches, in the common sense of the term, still adhere to the fundamentals of the Christian faith and so harbor true believers in their midst, nevertheless all Christians who recognize their error are in duty bound to sever their connection with them, since, on the one hand, one error is bound to produce others, Gal. 5, 9, and, on the other, the toleration of a recognized falsehood is a denial of the divine truth, Matt. 10, 32—36, and this is incompatible with the true Christian profession, Rom. 16, 17; 2 Cor. 6, 14—18.

4. HETERODOX CHURCHES AND TRUE DISCIPLESHIP.

Heterodox churches do not exist by the will of God, Matt. 28, 20, but against His will, Jer. 23, 29—40; 1 Cor. 3, 15—17. God permits them to exist partly to prove the faith of His true disciples, 1 Cor. 11, 19, and partly to punish the indifferentism, ingratitude, and infidelity of the ungodly, 2 Thess. 2, 11. 12.

Hence Christians should view the existence of heterodox churches not with indifference, but with horror, since every error is an offense (σκάνδαλον), which not only provokes God to anger, Deut. 32, 5. 6; 28, 15—68, but also endangers the salvation of all who are brought into contact with it, 1 Cor. 15, 33; 2 Tim. 2, 16. 17.

Nevertheless true believers may be found even in heterodox churches, not inasmuch as they are heterodox, — for falsehood always opposes itself to saving faith, — but inasmuch as by the grace of God they still retain the fundamentals of the Gospel.

Our Savior Himself, while denouncing the religion and worship of the Samaritans, John 4, 22, still acknowledged the true discipleship of individual believing Samaritans, Luke 17, 16; 10, 33. So also Luther, though he condemned the Papacy as an institution founded by the devil, still recognized true believers (the baptized children; adults who adhered to the *sola gratia* against the teachings of the Pope) also in this corrupted Church. Similarly the great Reformer held that there were true believers among the followers of Zwingli and Calvin because they adhered to them in ignorance. (St. L., IX, 44.)

The confessional Lutheran Church, though ever insisting upon the prerogative of being the true orthodox Church, has never identified itself with the *una sancta ecclesia, extra quam nulla est salus,* but has always taught that the Church Universal is the communion of all believers who put their hope of salvation alone in Christ's vicarious atonement. (Cp. Walther, *Kirche und Amt,* pp. 95—113; 160 ff.) Dr. Walther writes: "Whoever binds salvation to membership in any visible Church annuls the article of justification by grace alone, through faith in Christ."

5. THE INADMISSIBILITY OF SPIRITUAL FELLOWSHIP WITH HETERODOX CHURCHES.
(Religious Unionism.)

What has just been said should not lead any one to regard religious unionism (syncretism, *Unionismus, Religionsmengerei*) as permissible, much less as laudable. The words "with charity toward all" apply indeed to all men, for Christians are commanded to love all men, Matt. 22, 39; 5, 44; 1 John 3, 17. 18; but they do not mean that Christians should countenance false prophets and their errors, Matt. 7, 15; Gal. 1, 8. 9. The direction of Scripture with regard to this point is both clear and emphatic, Rom. 16, 17; Gal. 5, 9; 2 John 10. 11; Titus 3, 9—11; 1 Tim. 1, 3—7; 2 Cor. 6, 14—18.

To the objection that religious unionism may be justified both because of the principle of Christian charity, Rom. 13, 10; 1 Cor. 13, 7, and in view of Christ's earnest prayer that all believers may be one, John 17, 20. 21, we reply —

a) That it is indeed only a caricature of Christian love to permit any one to grope in spiritual darkness and to endanger his soul's salvation, 2 Cor. 5, 13—15; 1 Cor. 9, 22. 23; 2 Cor. 6, 3—10, so that religious unionism, which in the last analysis is carnal indifferentism, really ignores true Christian love both toward God (faithfulness to His Word) and toward the neighbor (conscientious interest in his avowal of the divine truth);

b) That the unity which the Holy Ghost Himself works through the Word is the unity of faith, John 17, 17. 20. 21. 25. 26; Eph. 4, 3—6; 1 Cor. 1, 10, which Christians must foster by witnessing to the truth.

True unity of faith is indeed commanded by God, 1 Cor. 1, 10, and all Christian believers should therefore do all in their power to effect it. But this unity, which is of the Spirit, is neither established nor furthered by carnal indifferentism and toleration of error, 2 Cor. 6, 14—18; 1 Kings 18, 21. 22. 40.

The peril that lurks in religious unionism is that by an unfortunate consistency in the profession of falsehood one error always produces another. So also carnal indifferentism toward one doctrine is bound to produce carnal indifferentism towards others. Luther says (St. L., XVII, 1180): "Whoever regards his doctrine, faith, and confession as true, right, and certain cannot stand in one stall with others that teach or favor false doctrine." (Cp. XVIII, 1996.)

The contention of modern rationalistic theologians that the "various theological tendencies" (denominational divisions) are intended by God is neither Scriptural nor reasonable.

6. SEPARATISTS, OR SCHISMATICS.

The term *separatism,* or *schism,* denotes a denominational separation of religious groups from existing churches on non-Scriptural grounds, such as ecclesiastical customs, forms, usages, and the like (Donatism). Schisms are therefore opposed to God's Word and are sinful. For practical reasons we distinguish between malicious separatism *(schismatici malitiosi)* and non-malicious separatism *(schismatici non-malitiosi).* The former is caused by, and mingled with, spite and uncharitableness; the latter is the result of ignorance or prejudice and is not joined with intentional disregard of the principle of brotherly love.

To apply the terms *separatists* and *schismatics* to persons who separate themselves from erring churches on account of their unsound doctrine or unscriptural practise is unjustified.

With regard to the right *use* of the doctrine of the Church, the Lutheran Catechism gives the following important directions. We use the doctrine of the Church properly, a) when we take heed to be and remain members of the invisible Church, 2 Cor. 13, 5; John 8, 31. 32; b) when we to this end adhere to the Church of the pure Word and confession and avoid all false churches, Matt. 7, 15; 1 John 4, 1; Rom. 16, 17; 2 Cor. 6, 14—18; and c) when we contribute toward its maintenance and propagation according to our ability, 1 Cor. 9, 14; Gal. 6, 6. 7; 1 Tim. 5, 17. 18; 1 Thess. 5, 12. 13; Mark 16, 15. 16; Matt. 28, 19. 20. These points deserve the constant consideration of every Christian believer and should be inculcated most diligently by the pastor in both his public and his private instruction.

7. THE REPRESENTATIVE CHURCH.
(De Ecclesia Repraesentativa.)

Neither individual persons (Popes, princes, presidents) nor assemblies (church councils, synods, pastoral conferences, parliaments, consistories) have been ordained by our Lord to decide questions of faith or church polity. For all questions of doctrine, Scripture is the only source and norm, 1 Pet. 4, 11, while questions pertaining to the external management of the churches are adiaphora, Acts 4, 32; 15, 22—29; 1, 15—26, which must be decided in brotherly love according to the principle of Christian order and expediency, 1 Cor. 14, 40.

The Pope's claim that he is Christ's vicar on earth, whose decisions on doctrine and life are binding on all Christian consciences (Papa habet omnia iura in scrinio pectoris) proves him to be Antichrist, 2 Thess. 2, 3. 4. Equally condemnable is the ambition of earthly rulers to prescribe to the Church (Caesaropapism).

However, it is not contrary to Scripture to have Christian believers, in certain ecclesiastical affairs, represented by persons duly elected by them. Thus elders may represent local congregations, and special delegates may represent entire groups of local churches at synods or conferences. But such a representative Church (ecclesia repraesentativa) has only so much authority as has been delegated to it by the express declaration of the local churches which it represents. In itself it has not legislative, but only advisory power; that is to say, what the representative Church decides must be in agreement with the will of the churches which it represents and must always be ratified by them.

In accord with this principle the Constitution of the Missouri Synod declares with respect to the relation of Synod to the local churches (chap. IV): "So far as the self-government of the local churches is concerned, Synod is only an advisory body." This declaration rests upon the correct, Scriptural principle that the local church is divinely appointed and is vested not only with the Office of the Keys, but with supreme authority to direct all matters pertaining to church polity, Matt. 18, 15—18; 1 Cor. 5, 11—13; 14, 33—36. (Cp. Luther, St. L., IX, 1253f.; X, 1540ff.; XIX, 958 ff.; Christl. Dogmatik, III, 492—501.)

Hence there is no ecclesia repraesentativa in the sense that either the clergy or church councils or synods or church conventions have authority to "determine controversies of faith and cases of conscience; to set down rules and directions for the better ordering of the public worship of God and government of His Church, . . . which decrees and determinations, if consonant to the Word of God, are to be received with reverence and submission, not only for their agreement with the Word, but also for the power whereby they are made, *as being an ordinance of God, appointed thereunto in His Word*" (Presbyterian Confession of Faith, XXXI).

Synods and councils which arrogate to themselves such authority imitate the papistic practise and set aside the rights and privileges of the local church, which is indeed "an ordinance of God, appointed thereunto in His Word."

Once more, however, let us repeat that local churches have authority neither to set aside God's Word nor to offend against Christian love. In all matters of doctrine and life they are bound to Holy Scripture, and in all cases of church management or church polity *(adiaphora)* their supreme concern must be the highest welfare of the Church, Christian love being the deciding factor in all disputes or differences of opinion.

Synods and councils (Presbyterians, Methodists, Episcopalians) are not a sort of superchurch, but it is the local church that is supreme, because it is an ordinance of Christ. All other questions on this point belong to the domain of Pastoral Theology.

THE DOCTRINE OF THE PUBLIC MINISTRY.
(De Ministerio Ecclesiastico.)

1. DEFINITION OF THE TERM.

The term *ministry (Predigtamt, ministerium)* is used both by Scripture and the Church in a wider and a narrower sense. In its general sense the word denotes every manner of proclaiming the Gospel or of administering the means of grace, no matter whether this is done by Christians in general, to whom the means of grace have been divinely entrusted, or by called and ordained ministers of the Word *(ministri ecclesiae)* in the name of the Christian congregation *(Pfarramt)*.

Accordingly we speak of the Christian ministry in the abstract *(in abstracto)*, that is, distinct from the persons who administer it, and in the concrete *(in concreto)*, or as it is vested in called and ordained pastors, who perform its duties in the name of the local congregations. In this special, or narrow, sense we employ the term ministry in this discussion *(Pfarramt; Predigtamt im engeren Sinn)*.

The Christian ministry in its narrow sense *(in concreto)* presupposes the existence of local churches, for it certainly can be established only where such congregations exist. In this sense the *Smalcald Articles* (Of the Power and Primacy of the Pope, § 67) aptly say: "Wherever the Church is, there is the authority [command] to administer the Gospel. Therefore it is necessary for the Church [German: *die Kirchen*] to retain the authority to call, elect, and ordain ministers. . . . Wherever there is a true church, the right to elect and ordain ministers necessarily exists."

The *Smalcald Articles* voice the clear doctrine of Holy Scripture on this point. When St. Paul had founded Christian churches on the island of Crete, he commanded Titus (Titus 1, 5) to ordain elders, whom in v. 7 he calls *bishops* (ἐπισκόπους), in every city (κατὰ πόλιν), that is, in every city where there were local churches. Again, after St. Paul and Barnabas had established local churches in Asia Minor on their first missionary journey, they, on their return trip, "ordained them elders (πρεσβυτέρους) in every church (κατ' ἐκκλησίαν), commending them to the Lord, on whom they believed," Acts 14, 23. Elders so ordained were expressly commanded to "take care of the church of God," 1 Tim. 3, 5; to "take heed to all the flock over the which the Holy Ghost hath made them overseers," Acts 20, 28; to "feed the Church of God," v. 28b; to "watch . . . and warn every one night and day," v. 31; to be "ensamples to the flock," 1 Pet. 5, 3; etc. In short, they were to serve as divinely appointed pastors in their congregations.

Hence we rightly say that the office of the Christian ministry *(das christliche Pfarramt)* is of divine appointment or command. So also the *Apology* says (Art. XIII, 11) : "The ministry of the Word has *God's command* and glorious promises." Gerhard writes: "The ministry of the Church is a sacred and public office *by divine appointment.*" (XIII, 224.) And Hutter: "The ministry of the Church has been established . . . *by God Himself."* (*Loc. Th.,* 186.) (Cp. *Doctr. Theol.,* p. 606 ff.)

The Christian ministry is called "public," not in view of the place, where its functions are performed, but rather in view of the fact that its functions are executed in the name and by the authority of the congregation, so that even such functions of the ministerial office as are done in private (private Communion; private admonition; private absolution) belong to the *public ministry* (cp. public service; public servants, etc.). So, then, the divine rule obtains: Wherever true believers are found at one place, they must organize and maintain local churches. And wherever there are local churches, they must also by God's will call official pastors or ministers, who in the name of the congregation preach the Gospel and administer the Sacraments, or who in the name of the congregation execute the Office of the Keys. (Cp. Luther, St. L., III, 723.)

2. THE PUBLIC MINISTRY AND THE SPIRITUAL PRIESTHOOD OF ALL BELIEVERS.

It is self-evident that the public ministry *(das Pfarramt)* does not stand in opposition to the general ministry (spiritual priesthood) of all believers, who as spiritual priests have the duty to proclaim the Gospel throughout the world, 1 Pet. 2, 9. The office of the public ministry rather presupposes the spiritual priesthood of all believers; for, on the one hand, the called ministers of the Word must themselves be spiritual priests, or true believers, 1 Tim. 3, 2—7; Titus 1, 5—9; and, on the other, they publicly, that is, in the name of the believers who have called them, administer the duties and privileges which all Christians have as spiritual priests.

The relation between the public ministry and the spiritual priesthood of all believers is therefore obvious. That the two are not identical follows from the fact that Scripture sharply distinguishes between believers in general and shepherds, bishops, or elders (ministers) who are placed over the believer. Thus —

a) All believers are to know and to profess the divine truth, John 6, 45; 7, 38. 39; 1 Cor. 2, 15. 16; 1 John 2, 27; 1 Pet. 2, 9; Col. 3, 16; but the official teachers of the Church must possess a preeminent knowledge of divine truth and a special aptitude to teach, 1 Tim. 3, 1—7; 5, 22; Titus 1, 5—11.

b) While Holy Scripture teaches that all believers are charged with the duties and enjoy the privileges of the Office of the Keys, Matt. 18, 17; 1 Cor. 5, 18, it expressly declares, on the one hand, that God gives to the Church apostles, prophets, evangelists, pastors, and teachers for the work of the ministry, Eph. 4, 11. 12; 1 Cor. 12, 28; Acts 20, 28, and, on the other, that not all believers are apostles, prophets, teachers, 1 Cor. 12, 29; Jas. 3, 1 (διδάσκαλοι).

c) While Holy Scripture declares that "the manifestation of the Spirit is given to every man to profit withal," 1 Cor. 12, 4—12, and that all the members of Christ's body should therefore have abundant honor, 1 Cor. 12, 23—25, it demands that the official teachers of the Church be especially esteemed as such as speak the Word of God, Heb. 13, 7; that they which preach the Gospel should live of the Gospel, 1 Cor. 9, 14; that he who is taught in the Word should communicate unto him that teacheth in all good things, Gal. 6, 6. 7; that the elders that rule well be counted worthy of double honor, especially they who labor in the Word and doctrine, 1 Tim. 5, 17: 18; that believers should know them which labor among them and are over them in the Lord and admonish them, 1 Thess. 5, 12. 13; and that Christians should obey them that have the rule over them and watch over their souls as they that must give account, Heb. 13, 17.

d) Lastly, when St. Paul wrote to the Corinthians: "Let a man so account of us as of the ministers of Christ and stewards of the mysteries of God," 1 Cor. 4, 1, he referred not only to himself, but also to Apollos, 1 Cor. 4, 6, and his other fellow-laborers in the Word, 1 Cor. 3, 21.

We therefore rightly distinguish between believers as spiritual priests and believers as called ministers of Christ and stewards of God's mysteries.

No one distinguished between the spiritual priesthood of all believers and the public ministry more clearly than did Luther.

On the one hand, he writes (St. L., V, 1038): "As soon as we have become Christians through this Priest [Christ] and His priesthood and in Baptism through faith have been engrafted into Him, we have the right and authority to teach and confess the Word, which we have from Him, before everybody, every one according to his calling and station. For though we are not all in the public office or calling, still every Christian should teach, instruct, exhort, comfort, and reprove his neighbor through God's Word whenever and wherever any one is in need of it, as a father and mother must do with their children and servants and a brother, neighbor, citizen, or peasant with another. For a Christian can instruct and admonish another who is yet ignorant or weak in the Ten Commandments, the Creed, the Lord's Prayer, etc.; and whoever hears this is in. duty bound to receive it from him as God's Word and to confess it publicly." (Cf. X, 1590.)

However, on the other hand, Luther also writes (St. L., V, 1037): "Though we all are priests, yet we all neither can nor should for this reason preach, teach, or rule. But from the whole throng we must select and choose some to whom we entrust this office; and whoever conducts it is not a priest on account of his office (which they all are), but a servant of all others. And if he can no longer preach or serve, or if he should no longer desire this, he again steps among the common throng, entrusts his office to another, and is nothing else than an ordinary Christian. Thus you must distinguish between the ministry, or the office of service, and the common priesthood of all baptized Christians. For this office is nothing else than a public service, which is entrusted to one by the whole congregation, who are all priests at the same time." (Cf. X, 1589.)

3. THE PUBLIC MINISTRY IS A DIVINE APPOINTMENT OR ORDINANCE.

The public ministry is a divine appointment or ordinance. This follows, as we have shown —

a) From the practise of the holy apostles, Acts 14, 23, and from their command to their successors to ordain elders, or bishops, Titus 1, 5, so that ministers or pastors (πρεσβύτεροι, ἐπίσκοποι) were regularly appointed at all places where local churches had been established, Acts 20, 17. 18; Titus 1, 5;

b) From the description of the personal qualifications of the public ministers, 1 Pet. 5, 3; 1 Tim. 3, 2—7;

c) From the description of their functions and duties, Titus 1, 9—11; 1 Tim. 3, 5; Acts 20, 28. 21; 1 Pet. 5, 1 ff.; Heb. 13, 17; etc.;

d) From the distinction which Scripture makes between the elders, or bishops, and all other believers, 1 Cor. 12, 28. 29;

e) From the honor and dignity which are ascribed to all who officially teach the Word, Heb. 13, 7; 1 Cor. 4, 1.

We repeat this for the sake of emphasis, since this doctrine, so clearly taught in Scripture and so emphatically set forth by our Lutheran dogmaticians, has been denied also within the external Lutheran Church.

The claim has been made by some, e. g., Hoefling, that the ministry of the Word in its concrete form (Pfarramt) is of human origin or a mere "historical development." They contend that the appointment of elders (πρεσβύτεροι) in the Church, Acts 14, 23; Titus 1, 5 ff., had only a temporary or local significance, since the peculiar conditions prevailing in those early times made bishops, or presbyters, necessary.

To this argument we reply that such a limitation of the apostolic appointment of ministers is nowhere suggested in the text. On the contrary, elders, or bishops, were put in charge of the various churches because it is God's appointment that there should be elders, or bishops (ministers, pastors), who "take heed unto the flock and feed the Church of God," Acts 20, 28—31; "rule well and labor in the Word and doctrine," 1 Tim. 5, 17; "labor among the brethren and are over the believers in the Lord and admonish them," 1 Thess. 5, 12. 13; "watch over their souls as they that must give account," Heb. 13, 17; etc.

Hence it is not optional with believers to organize local churches and to establish the office of the public ministry in their midst, but this must be done because of Christ's institution and ordinance. So also Dr. Walther taught: "The ministry, or pastoral office (Pfarramt), is no human institution, but an office which has been instituted by God Himself." (Kirche und Amt, 193. 211.) The Apology is in full agreement with Scripture when it writes: "Ministerium Verbi habet mandatum Dei."

It is true, Hoefling and his associates admitted that the public ministry is God's institution and ordinance in the sense that everything that is "reasonable," "proper," and "morally necessary" may be called a divine ordinance, 1 Cor. 14, 40. But he denied that the public ministry is divinely commanded or appointed (cp. *Grund-saetze ev. luth. Kirchenverfassung,* Erlangen, 3d ed., 1853) since it resulted merely from an "inner necessity" *("mit innerer Not-wendigkeit")*. For this reason he also denied the conclusions which our Lutheran dogmaticians have rightly drawn from such passages as Acts 14, 23; Titus 1, 5, etc.

However, Hoefling's argument was not based upon any clear Scripture-passage, but upon the unwarranted inference that, if the public ministry is regarded as divinely commanded, then a legalistic or ceremonial element is transferred from the Old to the New Testament, which, however, is not a covenant of commands or laws, but of Christian freedom, Gal. 5, 1—7, and as such incapable of legalistic elements.

But this argument defeats itself by proving too much; for, consistently applied, it would abrogate all divine institutions and ordinances of the New Testament, so that Christians could not be commanded to baptize, to celebrate the Lord's Supper, to preach the Gospel, to follow after holiness, and the like. In that case the New Testament Church ultimately would have to adopt Antinomianism as its only alternative.

The error of Hoefling and his followers originated in their opposition to Romanizing Lutherans (Muenchmeyer, Loehe, Kliefoth, Vilmar, etc.), who claimed that the public ministry is a divine institution in the sense that it has been directly transmitted from the apostles to their successors as a ministerial estate *(geistlicher Stand)* through the rite of ordination.

Hoefling's opponents thus presented as Lutheran doctrine a caricature of the Lutheran doctrine of the divine institution of the public ministry. In addition, they spoke as though the means of grace were truly efficacious only if they are applied by persons who through the rite of ordination have received their office directly from the holy apostles (cp. Romanism; Episcopalianism: the apostolic succession).

Hoefling correctly rejected this Romanizing doctrine, but erred on the other hand by denying the *mandatum Dei* of the public ministry. In order to deny Loehe's *immediate divine establishment* of the public ministry, he regarded it as necessary to deny also its *mediate divine establishment,* or the fact that it is God's institution and ordinance that Christian believers should confer upon called and ordained ministers the public administration of the Office of the Keys.

In the controversy, men like Stroebel *(Zeitschr. f. luth. Th.*

und K., 1852, p. 699) correctly pointed out that it is indeed the divine right [under certain conditions even the unavoidable duty] of every baptized Christian as a spiritual priest to preach the Word of God to his neighbor, to administer the Sacraments, to forgive his sins, to lay on hands, etc., but that he should exercise this right only in case of need on account of God's established order, with which He is well pleased; otherwise he should make use of the office of pastors who are rightly called by Christ through the congregation. Christian congregations should consider that they must not discard the spiritual office (the pastoral office) instituted by Christ nor allow it to be usurped by a foolish mob or by ecclesiastical or worldly tyrants, but that they should always confer it on capable, faithful, and pious men until the Lord's second coming. . . . For it is an illogical conclusion to say: "All who have not received the spiritual office [the pastoral office] directly from the Lord, but through the congregation have received it from men and are therefore servants of men." (Cp. *Christl. Dogmatik,* III, 508—512; also *Lehre und Wehre,* 1870, p. 161 ff. 174; 1855, p. 1 ff.)

4. IS THE PUBLIC MINISTRY NECESSARY?

Although the public ministry (the pastoral office), which is mediately conferred upon pastors through the congregation, is a divine institution, it is not absolutely necessary; for all believers, as spiritual priests, are bound by divine command to preach the Gospel, 1 Pet. 2, 9, and to teach and admonish one another in psalms and hymns and spiritual songs, Col. 3, 16. Already Luther called attention to the fact that "the world may become so utterly epicurean that upon the whole earth there will be no public ministry at all, but that the Gospel will be preserved alone in the [Christian] homes through [Christian] fathers" (St. L., VI, 938). Also through the study of the Bible by individual believers Christ's Church may be preserved and spread on earth.

Hence, as Dr. Walther rightly affirms (*Kirche und Amt,* p. 195), the pastoral office *(Pfarramt)* must not be regarded as a sort of means of grace, which is absolutely necessary for the salvation of men, so that no one can come to faith and receive remission of sins without the service of an ordained pastor. This *absolute necessity* applies only to the use of the Word of God, and in particular to that of the Gospel of Christ, without which no one can ordinarily be saved.

The enthusiasts, who deny the necessity of preaching the

Gospel, claiming that it is the "inner Word" *(Verbum internum)* which saves, reject the clear teaching of Scripture concerning the means of grace and base their doctrine on their speculations. Luther: "We must firmly hold that God grants His Spirit or grace to no one except through or with the preceding outward Word in order that we may [thus] be protected against the enthusiasts, *i. e.,* spirits who boast that they have the Spirit *without* and *before* the Word." *(Smalcald Art.,* Part III, Art. VIII, 3. *Triglot,* p. 495.)

Nevertheless, while the public ministry is not absolutely necessary, it should not be despised. This is done a) when Christians refuse to come to church, claiming that they read the Bible at home, Luke 10, 16; Heb. 10, 23—25 (cp. Luther, St. L., III, 1736); or b) when called and ordained ministers neglect their holy office under the plea that their flock does not require feeding, since, as spiritual priests, they can take care of themselves (cp. Ezek. 3, 17 ff.; 2 Tim. 4, 2 ff.; 1 Tim. 4, 13 ff.; Phil. 2, 21; also Luther, St. L., X, 5); or c) when churches refuse to maintain schools in which Christian ministers or teachers are trained for the holy office (St. L., X, 417. 458 ff.). Contempt for the public ministry is commonly motivated by contempt for Christ and His blessed Gospel, Matt. 10, 22; 24, 9; John 17, 14.

5. THE CALL INTO THE MINISTRY.
(De Vocatione Ministeriali.)

Concerning the necessity of the ministerial call the *Augsburg Confession* declares (Art. XIV): "No one should publicly teach in the Church or administer the Sacraments unless he be regularly called." What is meant by the ministerial call, Hollaz explains thus: "By the divine call is here understood the appointment of a certain and suitable person to the ministry of the Church, with the right to teach in public, to administer the Sacraments, and to exercise ecclesiastical discipline, made by God either alone or by the intervening aid of men." *(Doctr. Theol.,* p. 607.)

Our dogmaticians rightly distinguish between the *immediate* and the *mediate* call *(vocatio immediata, vocatio mediata).* This distinction, which also Luther makes (St. L., XI, 1910 ff.), is Scriptural; for Holy Scripture shows that even the prophets and the apostles (including St. Paul) never preached without a call from God (Ex. 3, 10; Is. 6, 8. 9; 40, 6—9; Jer. 1, 2—10; Mark 16, 15; Matt. 28, 19. 20; John 20, 21—23; Acts 22, 21; Gal. 1, 1; Eph. 1, 1; Col. 1, 1; etc.).

The immediate call is that divine call which is made "without any intervening *judicial (arbitraria)* aid of other men" (Baier). As Hollaz correctly says, "an immediate call is not to be expected in the Church to-day."

The mediate call is no less divine than is the immediate. The difference between the two, as Gerhard explains, is merely this, that the mediate call is effected "through ordinary means" *(per vocationem ecclesiae),* divinely appointed for this purpose, while the immediate call comes from God directly.

The divinity of the mediate call Gerhard establishes from the following facts: a) It is referred to God as its Author, 1 Cor. 12, 28; Eph. 4, 11. b) It is based upon apostolic authority, Acts 14, 23; 20, 28; 1 Tim. 4, 14; 3, 1. 2; 5, 21; 2 Tim. 1, 6; 2, 2; Col. 4, 17. c) It is confirmed by God's gracious promises, 1 Tim. 4, 16; 2 Cor. 3, 6; Eph. 4, 11. 12.

The divinity of the mediate call is amply proved by the fact that Holy Scripture says of the elders, or bishops, who were called mediately: "The Holy Ghost hath made you overseers," Acts 20, 28.

That also the mediate call is truly divine is of the greatest importance both to the ministers themselves and to those whom they serve, 1 Cor. 4, 1; Luke 10, 16; 1 Pet. 5, 2. 3; Jer. 23, 21; Heb. 5, 4; Jas. 3, 1.

Since the mediate call is extended through men (the Church), we must consider also the question who the men are by whom God duly calls His ministers. The Romanists claim that only the *Pope* has authority to create bishops and their assistants. The Episcopalians teach that ordination by the *bishop* confers the highest orders. Romanizing Lutherans hold that Christian ministers owe their pastoral authority to "the estate of the ministry" *(der geistliche Stand),* which is self-propagating. In other cases, princes or ruling bodies in the Church have claimed the right to call and ordain ministers.

However, Holy Scripture ascribes this power to call to all true believers, since to them Christ has entrusted the Office of the Keys, Matt. 18, 17; 1 Cor. 5, 4. 13; 3, 21. Christ's Great Commission, Matt. 28, 19. 20, was meant not only for the apostles, but for all Christians; for He states expressly: "I am with you alway, even unto the end of the world." By virtue of their spiritual priesthood all believers "unto the end of the world" possess the inherent right to preach the Gospel and to administer the Sacraments. Since, then, all Christian believers are entrusted with the means of grace, it is their privilege to call pastors, or ministers, who in their name publicly apply the means of grace. Cp. Luther: "That some are chosen from the multitude is done for the reason that they, as representatives of the congregation, should administer and execute the office [ministerial office], which *they all have."* (St. L., IX, 1174.)

But while the communion of all believers constitutes the Church Universal, it is not to the *ecclesia universalis* as such that Christ has given the power to call and ordain ministers, but rather to the local churches *(ecclesiae particulares),* as is clear from Matt. 18, 17—20; 1 Cor. 5, 13; etc. The *Smalcald Articles* rightly say (Of the Power and Primacy of the Pope, § 67—69): "Wherever there is a true church, the right to elect and ordain ministers necessarily exists." (Cp. also Luther, St. L., XVII, 1074ff.)

Individual persons or representative bodies may duly call ministers for others, but only if they, either directly or by consent, *tacito consensu,* have received authority to do so from those who originally possess the right to call, *principaliter et immediate,* that is, from local churches.

Against the exclusive right of the local congregations to call their ministers various objections have been raised, of which we may note the following: —

a. *Not the local churches, but the apostles (Paul, Barnabas, Titus) "ordained elders in every church,"* Acts 14, 23; Titus 1, 5. To this objection Luther replies (St. L., XIX, 347): "Although Paul commanded Titus to 'ordain elders in every city,' Titus 1, 5, it does not follow that Titus did this in an arbitrary manner; but he, after the example of the apostles, appointed them after their election by the people; otherwise the command of Paul would be in conflict with the general custom of the apostles."

There are indeed weighty reasons why Luther's explanation should be believed and accepted. In the first place, the text (Acts 14, 23) itself suggests the calling of elders by a popular vote ($\chi\varepsilon\iota\varrho\sigma\tau\sigma\nu\acute{\eta}\sigma\alpha\nu\tau\varepsilon\varsigma$, not *constituebant* (Vulgate), but rather *"stimmwaehlen"* (Meyer), that is to say, having chosen them by the raising of hands. In the second place, it was the general custom of the apostles, Acts 6, 2—6, to have the "whole multitude" ($\pi\tilde{\alpha}\nu\ \tau\grave{o}$ $\pi\lambda\tilde{\eta}\vartheta\varsigma$) elect by popular vote the ministers of the churches (Stephen, Philip, etc., Acts 6, 5). For this reason we rightly infer that the verb $\chi\varepsilon\iota\varrho\sigma\tau\sigma\nu\acute{\varepsilon}\omega$ (to stretch forth the hand, to elect by the raising of hands, *"durch Aufheben der Hand abstimmen"*) has this special meaning both in Acts 14, 23 and 2 Cor. 8, 19 ("the brother chosen of the churches": $\chi\varepsilon\iota\varrho\sigma\tau\sigma\nu\eta\vartheta\varepsilon\grave{\iota}\varsigma\ \acute{v}\pi\grave{o}\ \tau\tilde{\omega}\nu\ \grave{\varepsilon}\varkappa\varkappa\lambda\eta\sigma\iota\tilde{\omega}\nu$). The apostles, then, ordained elders not arbitrarily, by their mere apostolic authority (Loehe), but with direct consent and by active cooperation of the local churches.

b. *Not the local churches, but Peter received the Office of the Keys, Matt. 16, 18. 19.* This objection does not hold, since Peter, on this occasion, did not come into consideration as an apostle or as a leader of the apostles *(primus inter pares)*, but merely as a believing follower of Christ, who professed the divine truth (cp. Matt. 16, 17). The rock (πέτρα) upon which Christ built His Church is not Peter's person (Πέτρος), but the confession which Peter as a believer in Christ here made.

So Luther writes: "All Christians are Peters for the sake of the confession which Peter here makes, which [confession] is the rock on which Peter and all Peters are built." (Marginal note to Matt. 16, 18). The "keys of the kingdom of heaven" are the means of grace, in particular the Gospel, which Christ has entrusted to all believers, 1 Pet. 2, 9. And Chemnitz says (*Examen,* 1607, p. 223): "Luther taught from the Word of God that Christ gave and commended the keys, that is, the ministry of the Word and the Sacraments, to the *whole Church.*" Inasmuch as all believers are entrusted with the means of grace, they possess the keys of the kingdom of heaven.

c. *The Lutheran Confessions teach that the public ministry is directly derived from the apostolic office.* To this we reply that, rightly understood, this statement is correct; for although Christian ministers are not apostles in the sense of the chosen Twelve (and St. Paul), who by divine inspiration were infallible teachers of the Word of God both as preachers and as writers of the New Testament canon, yet their office, so far as its content and efficacy are concerned, is precisely the same as was that of the apostles. In other words, Christian ministers to-day preach the same Word of God and administer the same Sacraments as did the apostles; and these means of grace, used by them, are just as efficacious to-day as when they were employed by the Twelve.

This is not a "dogmatic construction," but the clear teaching of Scripture; for when Christ commanded His disciples to preach the Gospel and to administer the Sacraments, Matt. 28, 20; Mark 16, 15. 16, He expressly specified that the ministry of the Word should continue "even unto the end of the world." Rightly understood, that is, excluding all Romanistic and Episcopalian errors on this point (apostolic succession) as well as the false notions of

Romanizing Lutherans (Loehe, Vilmar, Muenchmeyer, etc.), we may therefore say that the public ministry to-day is a continuation of the ministry of the apostles.

To this we may add that the apostles themselves regarded their non-apostolic fellow-ministers, that is, the elders and bishops who with them served the various churches, as equal in rank and office, 1 Cor. 4, 1ff.; 1 Pet. 5, 1ff. (lit.): "The elders (πρεσβυτέρους) among you I exhort as the fellow-elder (συνπρεσβύτερος)."

Yet, while this is true, it is true also that our Confessions, in accord with Scripture, Matt. 18, 17—20; 1 Cor. 5, 13; Rom. 16, 17; 1 Pet. 2, 9, expressly teach that the Office of the Keys belongs to the whole Church and that Christian ministers therefore hold their office by virtue of their call from their churches. The *Smalcald Articles* say (Of the Power and Primacy of the Pope, 67—69): "Wherever the Church is, there is the authority [command] to administer the Gospel. Therefore it is necessary for the Church to retain the authority to call, elect, and ordain ministers. And this authority is a gift that in reality is given to the Church, which no human power can wrest from the Church. . . . Hence, wherever there *is a true church,* the right to elect and ordain ministers necessarily exists. . . . Here belong the statements of Christ which testify that the keys have been given to the Church, and not merely to certain persons, Matt. 18, 20. Lastly, also the statement of Peter confirms this, 1 Pet. 2, 9. These words pertain to the Church, which certainly has the right to elect and ordain ministers since it alone has the priesthood." While, then, all Christian ministers who are duly called are "fellow-elders" (συνπρεσβύτεροι) of the blessed apostles, 2 John 1; 3 John 1; 1 Cor. 3, 5—9, they are elders and bishops (ministers, pastors) not through any "apostolic succession" nor through any "self-propagation of the clerical estate," but solely by virtue of the call which they have received from their churches. In other words, it is alone the divine call extended to them mediately through the local congregation that makes them "fellow-elders" of the apostles.

6. OF ORDINATION.

The ordination of called ministers is not a divine institution, or ordinance, but a church rite; for while it is mentioned, Acts 14, 23, it is not commanded in Scripture. We therefore rightly classify ordination among the adiaphora and affirm that not the ordination, but the call makes a person a minister.

Luther writes (St. L., XVII, 114): "The laying on of hands [ordination] blesses, confirms, and attests this [the call to the office], just as a notary and witnesses attest a worldly matter and as a pastor, when he blesses a bridegroom and bride, confirms or attests their marriage, that is, that they before took each other and publicly announced it."

Similarly also the *Smalcald Articles* declare that ordination is only the public ratification of the call. They say (Of the Power and Primacy of the Pope, 70): "Formerly the people elected pastors and bishops. Then came a bishop, either of that church or a neighboring one, who confirmed the one elected by the laying on of hands; and ordination was nothing else than such a ratification."

For this reason the confessional Lutheran Church does not practise the so-called *absolute ordination,* that is, the ordination of a person who as yet has received no call, since this might create the wrong impression as though by the ordination the ordained person were received into a "spiritual estate" *(ein geistlicher Stand)* and made a consecrated priest, who is eligible for a call by a congregation just because of special virtues conferred by the ordination. (Cp. Walther, *Pastorale,* p. 65.)

It goes without saying that also the right of ordination is originally vested in the local churches, as the *Smalcald Articles* declare: "Wherever there is a true church, the right to elect and ordain ministers necessarily exists."

According to Roman Catholic doctrine only those are Christian ministers (priests) who have been ordained by bishops created by the Pope, while pastors called and ordained by Christian congregations are thieves and murderers (Council of Trent, Sess. XXIII, Can. 4). From the viewpoint of the Papacy this antichristian doctrine is quite intelligible; for according to papistic teaching the "sacrament" of ordination confers *ex opere operato* upon the ordained the Holy Spirit and impresses upon him an "indelible character" *(character indelebilis),* which makes him a priest for all times, even though by gross sins he should render himself unworthy of the sacred office.

But this is not all. Through the ordination the priest, according to Roman Catholic doctrine, receives also the supernatural power to transubstantiate the bread and wine in the Holy Supper into Christ's body and blood and to offer these up as a sacrifice for the sins of the living and the dead (Council of Trent, De Sacram. Ord., Cans. 1—8). This is a power so great that not even the holy angels or the greatest saints are said to possess it. Indeed, this power is superior even to that of the human nature of Christ, which, as they claim, must obey the command of the priest whenever he bids it appear on earth to be sacrificed for the sins of the living and the dead. The papistic doctrine of ordination and the Mass therefore involves an unspeakable blasphemy of Christ and His holy Word.

While the Episcopalians do not acknowledge the Pope as the vicar of Christ on earth, they nevertheless teach that ordination is the only means by which the apostolic succession, and with it the true ministry, can be transmitted.

Finally also the Romanizing Lutherans, who regard the ministry as a "special spiritual estate" *(ein besonderer geistlicher Stand),* which is self-propagating, change the church rite of ordination into a divine institution, or ordinance. These Romanizing Lutherans emphatically deny that the Christian minister receives his office through the call of the congregation, though this doctrine is clearly taught in Scripture.

7. THE CHRISTIAN MINISTRY DOES NOT CONSTITUTE A SPIRITUAL ESTATE.

Attention may be directed to the fact that also Luther, in accommodation to the *usus loquendi,* at times speaks of ministers, that is, of those "who serve in ecclesiastical offices" (St. L., X, 423 ff.), as "priests," "spirituals" *(Geistliche),* a "spiritual estate" *(geistlicher Stand),* etc. He declares, however, that the use of these terms is not only without foundation in Scripture, but also misleading, since according to Holy Scripture all believers are "anointed," 1 John 2, 27, "spiritual," Gal. 6, 1, a "spiritual house" and a "spiritual priesthood," 1 Pet. 2, 5. 9. *"Alle Christen sind wahrhaft geistlichen Stands, und ist unter ihnen kein Unterschied denn des Amts halber allein."* (Cf. *Hutterus Redivivus,* p. 270.)

Luther furthermore declares that the Holy Spirit in the New Testament carefully avoids the application of the name priest *(sacerdos)* to the apostles or their colaborers, while He distinctly applies that term to all baptized Christians. He says (St. L., XIX, 1260): "We are not born [again] in Baptism as apostles, teachers, preachers, pastors, but as *priests.* Then the Church takes one of these regenerate priests and calls and elects him to such functions as all believers should execute because of their [priestly] office." Luther thus rejects the erroneous opinion that ministers, or pastors, constitute a "spiritual estate."

Luther's position is in strict conformity with the teaching of Holy Scripture; for Scripture describes the elders and bishops not as "spiritual" in preference to others, but as ministers (servants) of the believers (*ministrantes inter Christianos*), 2 Cor. 4, 5. It is true, all pastors are also servants of Christ and of God, 1 Cor. 4, 1; Titus 1, 7; 2 Tim. 2, 24; Luke 12, 42; but they are such only as ministers of the Church or because the Church has called them to be "ministers of Christ and stewards of the mysteries of God."

Of this Luther writes (St. L., X, 1590): "Paul calls himself *servum* that is, a servant, and more than once he says: *Servio in evangelio,* I serve in the Gospel. This he does not in order that he may establish an estate or order, a right or a certain dignity, as people to-day would do, but that he might alone praise the office and work and preserve the right and dignity of the priesthood in the congregation."

Similarly Dr. Walther says (*Kirche und Amt,* p. 221): "The public ministry is not a special estate, which exists in contradistinction to the common state of Christians or is holier than it, but it is a ministry of service."

For this reason the churches have also the right and the duty to *watch over the ministry* of their pastors and teachers, Col. 4, 17, and to dismiss them in case they refuse to preach the Word of God in its truth and purity and to adorn it with a holy life, Col. 4, 17; John 10, 5; Matt. 7, 15; Rom. 16, 17. 18. (Cp. Luther, St. L., X, 1591.)

Ministers, of course, hold their office only so long as they administer the functions of the public ministry which they have received through the call.

When describing the manner in which called ministers receive their divine office from the congregation, our dogmaticians have used the verb *confer* (*uebertragen, demandare, deferre, comittere*). They said: "Through the call the Christian congregation *confers* the public ministry upon qualified persons."

This term should not be condemned as objectionable; for it expresses the Scriptural truth that the congregation is the "fountain of all church power" (Hase: *"der Quell aller Kirchengewalt"*) by virtue of the Office of the Keys which Christ has given to His Church, and that pastors exercise the public ministry only in the name and by the authority of the congregation. Those who object to the term have reason to examine themselves whether they fully agree with the Scriptural doctrine of the Office of the Keys. (Cp. *Christl. Dogmatik,* III, 522 ff.)

With respect to the power which Christian pastors possess by virtue of their call our dogmaticians rightly say that *all* power which they have as ministers is conferred upon, or delegated to, them by the congregation, so that their jurisdiction is limited by the call.

The power of the ministry *(potestas ministerialis)* embraces a) the power of preaching the Gospel and administering the Sacraments *(potestas ordinis)* and b) that of remitting and retaining sins *(potestas clavium, potestas iurisdictionis).*

The power of excommunication, commonly called the ban, the pastor must never administer without the congregation, Matt. 18, 17. 18; 1 Cor. 5, 13. It is properly the function of the pastor rightly to guide the congregation in judging each case and, if the sinner under discipline is found to be impenitent, to publish and declare publicly as a servant of the church what the congregation has decided to do, 1 Cor. 5, 1—7. 13.

Again, if the sinner repents, it is the duty of the pastor to urge the congregation to forgive him, 2 Cor. 2, 6—11, and then to publish, or declare publicly, the absolution of the congregation. A ban which a minister executes contrary to God's Word and without the congregation Luther calls a "lying ban" *(Luegenbann).* (Cp. St. L., XIX, 950 ff.)

8. THE POWER OF THE PUBLIC MINISTRY.

Since the pastoral office is the ministry of the *divine Word (ministerium Verbi et sacramentorum, Gnadenmittelamt, potestas clavium),* all believers are in duty bound to obey their pastors just as they obey God Himself, Heb. 13, 17; Luke 10, 16. As long therefore as pastors are true ministers of the Word, their authority *(potestas)* is as great as that of the divine Word. However, as soon as they go beyond God's Word and teach commandments of men, they have no authority at all, and their hearers must refuse them obedience for conscience' sake, Matt. 23, 8; Rom. 16, 17.

Adiaphora *(res mediae),* that is, matters which are neither commanded nor forbidden by God's Word, should not be adjudged by the minister, but by the entire congregation by common consent *(per mutuum consensum).*

Against the claim of the papists that laymen must obey their priests *in all things,* the *Apology* correctly declares (Art. XXVIII, 19. 20): "He that heareth you heareth Me, Luke 10, 16, cannot be understood of *traditions*. For Christ requires that they teach in such a way that (by their mouth) He Himself be heard, because He says: 'He heareth Me.' Therefore He wishes *His own voice, His own Word,* to be heard, not human traditions. Thus a saying which is most especially in our favor and contains the most important consolation and doctrine these stupid men pervert to the most trifling matters, the distinction of food, vestments, and the like. They quote Heb. 13, 17: 'Obey them that have the rule over you.' This passage requires obedience to the Gospel. For it does not establish a dominion for the bishops apart from the Gospel. Neither should the bishops frame traditions contrary to the Gospel or interpret their traditions contrary to the Gospel. And when they do this, obedience is prohibited, according to Gal. 1, 9: 'If any man preach any other gospel, let him be accursed.' "

The minister therefore has no power or jurisdiction whatever *(iure divino)* outside his call and office. His authority is limited to the *potestas clavium* (the Office of the Keys, *Schluesselgewalt*).

9. THE RELATION OF CHRISTIAN MINISTERS TO ONE ANOTHER.

On account of the various ranks and orders which the Papacy has created contrary to God's Word (the Roman Catholic hierarchy), it is necessary to emphasize the Scripture truth that all Christian ministers are equal in rank and dignity, Matt. 23, 8; 1 Pet. 5, 1. As Christian pastors have no power over their congregations outside that which God has given them as ministers of the Word, so by divine right *(iure divino)* they have no power at all over their fellow-ministers. Whatever ranks there are in the Church are only of human right *(iure humano)*.

Luther writes on this point: "Neither is the Pope higher than the bishops nor the bishop higher than all presbyters, according to divine right." This is true Scriptural doctrine.

As the Romanists, so also the Episcopalians and other Romanizing Protestant bodies pervert the Scriptural doctrine regarding the equality of Christian ministers.

With respect to the terms *presbyters* (πρεσβύτεροι) and *bishops* (ἐπίσκοποι) Scripture makes no distinction whatever, but denominates the same persons by both names, Acts 20, 17. 28; Titus 1, 5. 7.

The prohibition of St. Paul to Christians not to be servants of men, 1 Cor. 7, 23, applies also to all attempts at establishing human authority *(Menschenknechtschaft)* in the Church through the inauguration of hierarchism. (Cp. *Christl. Dogmatik,* III, 524 ff.)

10. THE PUBLIC MINISTRY IS THE SUPREME OFFICE IN THE CHURCH.

That the public ministry *(Pfarramt)* is the supreme office in the Church is a thought to which Luther in his writings reverts time and again. But he also shows why the office of the Christian pastor must be regarded as the highest office; it is supreme because of the *Word of God* which it teaches and applies. Luther says (St. L., X, 1592): "If the ministry of the Word is committed to some one, then also all the other offices which are administered in the Church through the Word are given him, namely, the power to baptize, to bless [to administer Holy Communion], to bind and to loose, to pray, to judge and decide. Indeed, the office of preaching the Gospel is the highest of all; for it is the true apostolic office, which lays the foundation for all others, on which all others must build, as, for example, the office of teachers, prophets, and rulers and those of persons who have the gift of healing." (Cp. also X, 1547.)

Of the bishops, who according to 1 Tim. 3, 5 must take care of the Church of God, Luther writes (St. L., XII, 338): "These, then, are those who must take care of all other offices that the teachers may attend to their office and not be negligent, that the deacons may rightly divide the gifts and not be indolent."

Again (X, 1548): "To whom the ministry of the Word is committed, to him is entrusted the highest office in Christendom; hence he may also baptize, administer the Mass [Holy Communion], and attend to all pastoral duties. But if he does not wish to do this, he may adhere alone to preaching and leave the other secondary offices *(Unteraemter)* to others, as Christ and Paul and all apostles did, Acts 6."

As Luther, so also the confessional Lutheran Church teaches that the public ministry (the pastoral office) is the supreme office in the Church, since it deals with the Word, which is Christ's supreme gift to the Church. (Cp. Dr. Walther on the proposition: "The Ministry of the Word the Highest Office in the Church, from which All Other Offices of the Church Flow." *Kirche und Amt,* p. 342 ff.)

11. OF ANTICHRIST.

Holy Scripture employs the term *antichrist* in a wider and in a narrower sense. Used in a wider sense, the term denotes all teachers who supplant the Word of God with doctrines of men, 1 John 2, 18. All false teachers must be regarded as antichrists (ἀντίχριστοι, adversaries of Christ), since our Lord insists that in the Church no other doctrine should be taught than that of Holy Scripture, Matt. 28, 20; John 8, 31. 32; 17, 20; 5, 39; Rom. 16, 17; 1 Pet. 4, 11; 1 Tim. 6, 3 ff.; 2 Tim. 3, 15—17; 2 John 10; Rev. 22, 18. 19. All who disregard this divine command are insurgents and adversaries of God, Luke 11, 23.

In its narrower sense the term ἀντίχριστος, however, denotes the great Antichrist, whose coming is foretold in 2 Thess. 2, 3—12. In 1 John 2, 18 this Antichrist κατ' ἐξοχήν is carefully distinguished from the "many antichrists," and his appearance is represented as a sign of the last times. In him antichristianism culminates, 2 Thess. 2, 7 f.

Since Holy Scripture pictures the Antichrist as the Wicked, of whom all believers must beware and whom therefore they can know, 2 Thess. 2, 8, we must carefully consider the marks by which divine prophecy characterizes him. These unmistakable marks, according to 2 Thess. 2, 3—12, are the following: —

a. *The "falling away"* (ἡ ἀποστασία). That this "falling away" must not be understood in a political sense (Communism and anarchy; the appearance of despotic sovereigns), as some erroneously opined, but in a spiritual or religious meaning, 2 Thess. 2, 10—12 clearly shows. The apostasy is caused by a "strong delusion," the result of which is that men believe lies and are damned through their misbelief. It is therefore "a falling away" from Christ and His Word, 2 Thess. 2, 4.

b. *The "sitting in the temple,"* 2 Thess. 2, 4. The great apostasy from Christ and the Gospel occurs not outside, but within the Church; for "the temple of God" is the Church, 1 Cor. 3, 16 ff.; 1 Tim. 3, 15; 2 Tim. 2, 20. The great apostasy which Antichrist causes is therefore not the spread of paganism or of antichristian cults, but a falling away within the external Church. For this reason it is called also "the mystery of iniquity" (μυστήριον τῆς ἀνομίας), v. 7, that is, a lawlessness which conceals itself by pious words and forms. Nor is this lawlessness only temporary, but it is permanent; for the Antichrist will continue to sit in the temple of God until the Lord's second return, v. 8.

c. *The opposing and exalting above all that is called God.* The Antichrist, who sits in the temple of God, will be in constant opposition to God and His Word, claiming for himself supreme authority in religion ("showing himself that he is God," v. 4). Under the reign of Antichrist the Church will obey neither Christ nor His Gospel, but do only what Antichrist by his alleged divine authority demands. All who are under his rule are bound to submit to him, not to God.

d. *The working of Satan in Antichrist.* While Antichrist is not Satan himself, his "coming is after the working of Satan" (*κατ' ἐνέργειαν τοῦ σατανᾶ,* v. 9); that is, he appears by the deceitful, crafty, and wicked working of Satan and sustains himself in the Church by Satan's power; for with the help of Satan he is able to perform "all power and signs and lying wonders," v. 9. The adjective modifier *lying* in our translation (Greek: *ψεύδους*) belongs to all three nouns: *power, signs, wonders.* As Antichrist teaches doctrines that are lies, so he also performs works that are lies. His rule therefore rests upon his ability, wrought by Satan, to deceive men by all manner of lies.

e. *The revealing and consuming of Antichrist with the Spirit of the Lord's mouth,* v. 8. Antichrist will remain unknown to many ("mystery of iniquity," v. 7); yet in due time he will be revealed and consumed by the spirit of the Lord's mouth, which is God's Word, Is. 11, 4; 49, 2; Rev. 1, 16. Antichrist will therefore be revealed and consumed through the preaching of God's Word. This, however, does not mean the *end* of his wicked reign; for the Lord Himself shall "destroy" him (*καταργήσει,* annul him, put him out of the way) "with the brightness of His coming," v. 8; that is to say, the reign of Antichrist will continue till Judgment Day.

f. *Antichrist's coming and reign are a manifestation of God's wrath* upon all those who "received not the love of the truth that they might be saved," v. 10. His appearance therefore leads to the damnation of many, v. 12, and thus foreshadows God's condemning wrath on Judgment Day, v. 3.

All these marks of Antichrist we witness not in individual deceivers (Arius, Mohammed) nor in individual tyrants (Nero, Napoleon), but in the Papacy. Here, within the external Church of Christ, is the great apostasy (*ἀποστασία*), namely, the rejection of Scripture as the only source and norm of faith and of the central doctrine of the Christian religion, the *sola fide,* "which alone begets, nourishes, builds, preserves, and defends the Church and without which the Church of God cannot exist even for an hour" (Luther; St. L., XIV, 168).

In the Church of Antichrist the doctrine of justification by grace through faith is anathematized, and its Christian defenders are damned as heretics and antichrists (Council of Trent, Sess. VI, Cans. 11. 12. 20).

Here, moreover, the impious opponent of Christ performs lying works, signs, and wonders and "with all deceivableness of unrighteousness" and with "strong delusions" misleads uncounted souls into damnation, Gal. 3, 10; 5, 4.

Here, too, we find the greatest apostasy, *concealed by an outward show of piety,* the most consummate hypocrisy, veiled with the cloak of discipleship, and the most vicious hatred against Christ and His blessed Gospel, hidden under the pretentious names of "vicar of Christ," "viceregent of Christ," etc.

Here, within the Christian Church, we find the crassest paganism (the worship of saints and statues, work-righteousness) and the ruthless shedding of the innocent blood of thousands of martyrs, who in true Christian faith and zeal opposed this antichristian paganism.

Here we find the revealing and consuming of Antichrist by the spirit of the Lord's mouth, that is to say, the branding of the Pope as the Antichrist by the Lutheran Reformation.

Here, lastly, we find that arrogant presumption over against all existing governments, which is a true characteristic of Antichrist, the man of sin and the son of perdition, who "exalteth himself above all that is called God."

Our Lutheran Confession therefore rightly declares that the Pope at Rome is the Antichrist. "The marks [all the vices] of Antichrist plainly agree with the kingdom of the Pope and his adherents. For Paul, 2 Thess. 2, 3, in describing to the Thessalonians Antichrist, calls him *an adversary of Christ,* who opposeth and exalteth himself above all that is called God. . . . He speaks therefore of one ruling in the Church, not of heathen kings, and he calls this one the adversary of Christ, because he will devise doctrines conflicting with the Gospel and will assume to himself divine authority." (*Smalcald Articles; Triglotta,* p. 515, § 39.)

Again (p. 517, § 41): "This being the case, all Christians ought to beware of becoming partakers of the godless doctrine, blasphemies, and unjust cruelty of the Pope. On this account they ought to *desert* and *execrate* the Pope with his adherents as the kingdom of Antichrist, just as Christ has commanded Matt. 7, 15: 'Beware of false prophets.' And Paul commands that godless teachers should be avoided and execrated as cursed, Gal. 1, 8; Titus 3, 10. And in 2 Cor. 6, 14 he says: 'Be ye not unequally yoked together with unbelievers; for what communion hath light with darkness?'" (Cp. also Luther, St. L., XVII, 2191; XVIII 1529 ff.)

The doctrine of our Confession *"papam esse ipsum verum antichristum"* (*Smalcald Articles; Triglotta,* p. 474, § 10) has been denied on the ground that in 2 Thess. 2, 3—12 the apostle is speaking, not of a system of teaching, but of an individual deceiver. But this objection does not hold, since St. Paul here describes "a mystery of iniquity" which was active already in his time and which will endure to the end of time, vv. 7. 8.

If modern Protestant theologians fail to recognize that the Pope at Rome is the Antichrist, it is because they themselves do not understand what an abomination it is to reject God's Word as the only source and standard of faith and to anathematize the doctrine of justification by faith. Since the Papacy destroys the central article of the Christian faith, its outward adherence to the Apostles' Creed is only one of the many lies by which it deceives the unwary. To these lies belong also the many "good works" of which it boasts. Luther rightly says (St. L., XVIII, 1530): "The Papacy is a kingdom which destroys both faith and the Gospel."

The question whether individual Popes may personally be believers in Christ may hardly be answered in the affirmative, since each Pope is the head of an antichristian cult which officially and permanently anathematizes the article of justification by faith. Also the "pious Popes" belong to the "lying wonders" by which Satan deceives those who do not love the truth.

While the doctrine concerning Antichrist is not a fundamental teaching of Scripture, since no one is saved inasmuch as he recognizes the Antichrist, nevertheless we must not regard it as of little importance, since God has imparted this truth to us for doctrine and reproof, 2 Tim. 3, 16. As St. Paul warned his hearers against Antichrist, so to-day Christian ministers should warn their hearers against him, 2 Thess. 2, 3. 5. Hence for a minister to claim that he is unable to recognize Antichrist shows a weakness and dulness in Christian discernment of which he has no reason whatever to be proud, 2 Thess. 2, 13—15.

If discerning believers recognized the Pope as the Antichrist even before the Reformation (Savonarola, Huss, Wyclif), we should do so all the more since God has revealed the Wicked (2 Thess. 2, 8) through His work of the Reformation, by which He restored to His Church both Holy Scripture as the sole source of faith (the formal principle of the Reformation) and justification by grace through faith as the sinner's only hope of salvation (the material principle of the Reformation). Luther: *"Deus impleat vos odio Papae!"*

THE DOCTRINE OF ETERNAL ELECTION.
(De Electione Aeterna sive de Praedestinatione.)

The doctrine of eternal election has been treated by our dogmaticians at various places in their dogmatic treatises (in connection with the doctrine of divine grace, Quenstedt, Hollaz; or with that of salvation in Christ, Baier). If the doctrine of election is taught in its Scriptural truth, it does not matter at what place in a dogmatic treatise it is presented.

Nevertheless, since the doctrine of election is not a central article of faith, but is given, in the main, for the consolation of the believers, and since also, as the *Formula of Concord* observes (Epit., XI, 11), we should proceed in the study of God's predestination "according to the order which St. Paul has observed in the Epistle to the Romans, who first directs men to repentance, to knowledge of sins, to faith in Christ, to divine obedience, before he speaks of the mystery of the eternal election of God," we prefer to place it after the discussion of the doctrines of sin and grace, repentance and faith, so that the student may consider it with all the facts and consolatory promises of the Gospel well in mind.

1. DEFINITION OF THE TERM.

The central teaching of Scripture is the comforting doctrine of God's grace in Christ Jesus toward fallen and lost mankind, Rom. 3, 23. 24; Eph. 2, 8. 9. To this divine grace the Christian owes his conversion, justification, sanctification, and preservation in faith, 2 Tim. 1, 9; Titus 3, 7; 1 Cor. 15, 10. That is the doctrine of the *sola gratia,* which Scripture teaches so plainly and consolingly.

To this doctrine Holy Scripture adds the comforting truth that whatever spiritual blessings God confers upon believers in time He in His infinite grace has decreed to bestow upon them from eternity. Accordingly we find in Scripture also the doctrine of eternal election.

The doctrine of election may be summarized in the words: Election is the eternal act of God with respect to all who are saved, by which, out of pure grace and for Christ's sake *(Praedestinatio gratuita et libera est),* He purposed to endow them in time with the spiritual blessings of conversion, justification, sanctification, and preservation unto life eternal. This definition embraces all divine truths which Scripture presents in connection with the doctrine of eternal election.

The doctrine of election centers in the consolatory message that whatever spiritual blessings God's saints receive in time He has graciously decreed for them from eternity, 2 Tim. 1, 9; Acts 13, 48; 2 Thess. 2, 13. 14; Eph. 1, 3—6; Rom. 8, 28—30.

Thus to God's eternal election of grace, or to His gracious purpose (κατ' ἰδίαν πρόθεσιν καὶ χάριν), without any consideration whatever of their works ("not according to our works"), Scripture ascribes the *vocation,* or *calling,* of the believers, 2 Tim. 1, 9. To God's gracious election, Scripture ascribes their *faith* (Acts 13, 48: "As many as were ordained to eternal life believed," ὅσοι ἦσαν τεταγμένοι εἰς ζωὴν αἰώνιον). To God's gracious election Scripture ascribes their *"obtaining of the glory* of the Lord Jesus Christ" (2 Thess. 2, 13. 14: "Because God hath from the beginning chosen you to salvation," ὅτι εἴλατο ὑμᾶς ὁ θεὸς ἀπ' ἀρχῆς εἰς σωτηρίαν). To God's gracious election ("According as He hath chosen us in Him before the foundation of the world," καθὼς ἐξελέξατο ἡμᾶς ἐν αὐτῷ πρὸ καταβολῆς κόσμου) Scripture ascribes *"all spiritual blessings* in heavenly places in Christ," with which God endows the believers in time, Eph. 1, 3—6. To God's gracious election (τοῖς κατὰ πρόθεσιν κλητοῖς) Scripture ascribes the comforting fact that all things must work together for good to them that love God; for they are called, justified, and glorified because He predestinated them, οὓς δὲ προώρισεν τούτους καὶ ἐκάλεσεν, Rom. 8, 28—30.

Holy Scripture thus traces all the spiritual blessings of conversion, justification, sanctification, and preservation back to God's eternal election of grace in Christ Jesus. In this life and in the life to come believers receive nothing but what God before the foundation of the world decreed to give them in His beloved Son. The believing remnant (τὸ λίμμα) in Israel is a "remnant *according to the election of grace,*" κατ' ἐκλογὴν χάριτος, Rom. 11, 5.

In order that no one may doubt that this election is entirely of grace and in no way of works, the apostle adds: "And if by grace, then is it no more of works; otherwise grace is no more grace," Rom. 11, 6. Indeed, he shows that Israel, which sought salvation by works, did not obtain it; for he writes: "Israel hath not obtained that which he seeketh for; but the *election hath obtained it* (ἡ δὲ ἐκλογὴ ἐπέτυχεν) and the rest were blinded," Rom. 11, 7.

The works of the believers are not a meritorious cause of their election of grace; for the apostle expressly declares: "For the children, being not yet born, neither having done any good or evil, that the purpose of God according to election might stand, not of works, but of Him that calleth (ἵνα ἡ κατ' ἐκλογὴν πρόθεσις τοῦ θεοῦ μένῃ, οὐκ ἐξ ἔργων, ἀλλ' ἐκ τοῦ καλοῦντος), it was said unto her, The elder shall serve the younger," Rom. 9, 11. 12.

So definitely and unmistakably Scripture ascribes all the spiritual and heavenly blessings of the believers to God's eternal election in Christ that no doubt whatever can remain with respect to this truth.

The *Formula of Concord* acknowledges this fact in its full Scriptural content when it writes (Epit., XI, 5): "The predestination, or eternal election of God, extends only over the godly, beloved children of God, *being a cause of their salvation (haec est causa ipsorum salutis),* which He also provides as well as disposes what belongs thereto. Upon this [predestination of God] our salvation is founded so firmly that the gates of hell cannot overcome it, John 10, 28; Matt. 16, 18."

Two basic truths, then, must be borne in mind whenever the article of eternal election of grace is being considered: —

a. God's eternal election of grace did not take place in view of man's foreseen final faith *(electio intuitu fidei finalis),* but rather embraced this faith together with the whole way of salvation *(ordo salutis, media salutis),* such as conversion, justification, sanctification, and final preservation. Hence the believer is not elected because of his foreseen faith *(ex praevisa fide finali);* on the contrary, he has become a believer in time because of his eternal election to salvation. In other words, a person is brought to saving faith in time just because God from eternity has graciously elected him to salvation, Acts 13, 48; Eph. 1, 3—6; Rom. 8, 28—30.

So also the *Formula of Concord* testifies (Thor. Decl., XI, 8): "The eternal election of God, however, not only foresees and foreknows the salvation of the elect, but is also, from the gracious will and pleasure of God in Christ Jesus, *a cause which procures, works, helps, and promotes our salvation and what pertains thereto."*

What· the *Formula of Concord* means by the words "a cause which procures, works, helps, and promotes our salvation and what pertains thereto" it further explains when it says (*ibid.,* 14): "The entire doctrine concerning the purpose, counsel, will, and ordination of God pertaining to our redemption, call, justification, and salvation should be taken together."

That again, as the *Formula of Concord* shows, means that

"God in His purpose and counsel ordained: 1) that the human race is truly redeemed and reconciled with God through Christ ... ; 2) that such merit and benefits of Christ shall be presented, offered, and distributed to us through His Word and Sacraments; 3) that by His Holy Ghost, through the Word, . . . He will be efficacious and active in us, convert hearts to true repentance, and preserve them in the true faith; 4) that He will justify all those who in true repentance receive Christ by a true faith ... ; 5) that He will also sanctify in love those who are thus justified ... ; 6) that He also will protect them in their great weakness . . . and preserve them [for life eternal]; 7) that He will also strengthen, increase, and support to the end the good work which He has begun in them if they adhere to God's Word, pray diligently, abide in God's goodness [grace], and faithfully use the gifts received; 8) that finally He will eternally save and glorify in life eternal those whom He has elected, called, and justified" (*ibid.*, 14—22).

God's eternal election of grace thus embraces the whole order of salvation (*ordo salutis*) by which the sinner comes to faith and is preserved in faith to the end, Rom. 8, 28—30.

b. With respect to the doctrine of election all those are sure to err who reject the *sola gratia* and so teach that a sinner is saved (elected and converted) not by grace alone, but also by some good quality or worthiness in him (*aliquid in homine; aliqua causa discriminis*) which God foresaw and on account of which He elected him (synergism). Similarly also those err with respect to this doctrine who teach that God's eternal election of grace consisted merely in the appointment of the means of grace (*ordinatio mediorum* — election *in a wider sense,* used in this sense by the errorists).

While the *Formula of Concord* clearly states that God's eternal election of grace embraces the way of salvation (*ordo salutis; media salutis*), it emphatically declares that the eternal election of grace was not merely a predestination of the means of salvation, but "of each and every person of the elect who are to be saved through Christ."

Our Confession says (*ibid.*, 23): "In this counsel, purpose, and ordination God has prepared salvation not only in general, but has in grace considered and chosen to salvation *each and every person of the elect* who are to be saved through Christ, also ordained that in the way just mentioned He will by His grace, gifts, and efficacy bring them thereto."

We therefore rightly say that God's eternal election of grace is properly a predestination of *persons* to be saved through faith by the means of grace (Eph. 1, 4: *ἐξελέξατο ἡμᾶς;* 1 Pet. 1, 1: *ἐκλεκτοῖς παρεπιδήμοις*).

Summarizing all points of importance that may be considered under the head "Definition of the Term," we may say: The election of grace is an election of persons *(Personenwahl),* not an election of the means of salvation *(ordinatio mediorum);* nor is it the ordination of the *ordo salutis* nor the divine decree that all who persevere in faith till the end shall be saved, Eph. 1, 4; 2 Thess. 2, 13; Matt. 24, 24. Election is not general (error of Huber), but particular, Eph. 1, 4; Matt. 20, 16. It is an election of individuals *(Einzelwahl),* which must be held against all who teach that election does not refer to individual persons, but to the Church in general, Eph. 1, 4. It does not embrace temporary believers, but only those who actually obtain eternal salvation, Matt. 24, 24; Rom. 8, 28—30.

2. HOW BELIEVERS ARE TO CONSIDER THEIR ELECTION.

The *Formula of Concord* very earnestly urges all believers "to think and speak *correctly* and *profitably* concerning the eternal election, or the predestination and ordination of the children of God to eternal life" *(ibid.,* 13); for "if any one presents the doctrine concerning the gracious election of God in such a manner that *troubled Christians cannot derive comfort from it,* but are thereby *incited to despair,* or that *the impenitent are confirmed in their wantonness,* it is undoubtedly sure and true that such a doctrine is taught *not according to the Word and will of God,* but according to [the blind judgment of human] reason and the instigation of the devil" *(ibid.,* 91).

Since Satan desires to mislead souls into despair or carnal security also by the misapplication of the doctrine of God's gracious election, the *Formula of Concord* gives this advice to all believers: "We should accustom ourselves not to speculate concerning the bare, secret, concealed, inscrutable foreknowledge of God, but how the counsel, purpose, and ordination of God in Christ Jesus, who is the true Book of Life, is revealed to us through the Word" *(ibid.,* 13. 14).

Even Luther complains that the doctrine of eternal election filled him with terror as long as he thought incorrectly and unprofitably of it (St. L., II, 182). Afterwards, however, when he had learned to understand the Gospel of God's free grace in Christ Jesus, the doctrine of election gave him abiding comfort.

In what light, then, should believers consider their election? From a close study of all passages concerned, it is clear that the holy apostles consistently employ the doctrine of election distinctly for the purpose of comforting the believers. In the manner therefore in which they present the doctrine, it never terrifies, but always inspires and consoles.

Indeed, the doctrine of eternal election is used by them to arouse in their hearers supreme joy and sincere thanksgiving to God. (Eph. 1, 3: *"Blessed be the God and Father* of our Lord Jesus Christ."* Rom. 8, 28—30: *"All things work together for good* to them . . . who are called *according to His purpose."* 1 Pet. 1, 2. 3: *"Elect* according to the foreknowledge of God the Father. . . . *Grace* unto you, and *peace,* be multiplied. *Blessed be the God and Father* of our Lord Jesus Christ," etc.)

It is true, our divine Savior used the doctrine of election also for a *warning;* in both cases, however, He had in mind not *true believers,* but the *self-righteous,* who either *demanded salvation* as a due reward for their works, Matt. 20, 1—16, or *rejected His righteousness* and came to the King's wedding without the proper wedding-garment, Matt. 22, 2—14.

Christ's warning "Many are called, but few are chosen" is therefore a most earnest plea to accept the *free salvation of grace* which God has prepared for all sinners in Him. Or we may say: It is the most earnest exhortation to accept with true faith the merits of Christ offered freely to all in the means of grace, the Gospel and the Sacraments.

Christ's words are in this manner properly applied because God's eternal election of grace embraces the means of grace, by which each and every chosen person is saved. Hence, if we wish to be sure of our election and salvation, we *must trust in the grace of God offered to all men in the Gospel* and not confide in our own works, or merits.

From this, then, we learn how we should consider our election properly and for our comfort. Holy Scripture states explicitly that God has elected us *"in Christ Jesus,"* Eph. 1, 3—6, *"to salvation through sanctification of the Spirit,* unto *obedience and sprinkling of the blood* of Jesus Christ," 1 Pet. 1, 2, etc.

In other words, as the *Formula of Concord* rightly says, we should not speculate concerning the bare, secret, concealed, inscrutable foreknowledge of God, but consider our election *in Christ Jesus, who is the true Book of Life.* However, "this Christ calls to Himself all sinners and promises them rest, and He is in earnest [seriously wills] that all men should come to Him and suffer themselves to be helped, to whom He offers Himself in His Word and wishes them to hear it and not to stop their ears or [neglect and] despise the Word. Moreover, He promises the power and working of the Holy Ghost and divine assistance for perseverance and eternal salvation [that we may remain steadfast in the faith and attain eternal salvation]." (Epit., XI, 8.)

Here, then, the *Formula of Concord* points out the true way in which Christian believers should consider their election.

In the first place, they should believe Christ's glorious Gospel invitation to come unto Him and be saved, Matt. 11, 28; John 6, 35—37; 10, 27—29. In other words, they should trust in Christ and sincerely believe that He, for the sake of His blood shed on Calvary, will forgive all their sins and receive them into eternal life, Gal. 2, 20; 1 Tim. 2, 4—6; 2 Tim. 4, 18; 1, 12.

In the second place, from the cross of Calvary, which guarantees everlasting salvation to every believer in Christ, Christians should direct their attention to the eternal grace of God, who before the foundation of the world planned a perfect redemption for the whole world and thus a most sure salvation in the blessed Redeemer *for every lost and condemned sinner (gratia universalis),* Eph. 1, 3—6; 1 Tim. 2, 4; Rom. 8, 28—30; 2 Thess. 2, 13; 1 Pet. 1, 2—5.

Hence, as Christians firmly believe that they are *saved by Christ,* so they should believe also that they are *God's elect in Christ Jesus;* for so Scripture speaks consistently: "God has chosen *you* to salvation," 2 Thess. 2, 13; "He hath chosen *us* in Him," Eph. 1, 4, etc.

Christians should therefore assuredly believe that they are God's chosen saints in Christ Jesus.

Just that is what the *Formula of Concord* means when it writes (Epit., XI, 7): "But the Word of God leads us to Christ, who is the Book of Life, in whom all are written and elected that are to be saved in eternity." As long as believers so view their election in Christ Jesus, it will be to them a cause of great joy and a source of true comfort.

On the other hand, if Christians view their election from reason *(ex rationis nostrae sententia; ex ulla aliqua externa specie)* or from the inscrutable hidden will of God *(ex arcano consilio Dei)*, they will be misled either into despair or into an epicurean life. Of this the *Formula of Concord* writes (Epit., XI, 9) : "Therefore we should judge concerning this our election to eternal life neither *from reason* nor *from the Law of God,* which lead us either into a reckless, dissolute, epicurean life or into despair and excite pernicious thoughts in the hearts of men; for they cannot, as long as they follow their reason, successfully refrain from thinking: If God has elected me to salvation, I cannot be condemned, no matter what I do; and again: If I am not elected to eternal life, it is of no avail what good I do; it is all . . . in vain anyway."

While the *Formula of Concord* condemns the way of judging election from reason, it condemns also what it calls the "sounding of the abyss of God's hidden predestination" (Thor. Decl., XI, 33). Christians attempt to sound the abyss of God's hidden predestination when they ask the very irrelevant question: "If God has elected me to salvation, or if He has elected a few, why did He not elect all?" *(Cur alii prae aliis, cur alii, alii non?)* The same irrelevant question was put to Christ by His disciples when one of them asked: "Lord, are there few that be saved?" That this query was one of the many unbecoming questions which even believers sometimes put in their folly and ignorance, Acts 1, 6. 7, Christ showed by answering the inquisitive disciple: "Strive to enter in at the strait gate; for many, I say unto you, will seek to enter in and shall not be able," Luke 13, 23. 24.

To understand this reproof of Christ, we must remember that the proper scope of Scripture is the salvation of sinners. It therefore confines its instruction to what is needful for men to know in order that they may be saved, John 5, 39 ; 2 Tim. 3, 15. Questions which serve only to satisfy their curious reason, Christians should avoid as conflicting with God's sovereign majesty and their own salvation, Rom. 9, 19. 20 ; 11, 33—36 ; 2 Tim. 2, 15. 16 ; 1 Tim. 6, 3—5.

The *Formula of Concord* rightly declares (Thor. Decl., XI, 33) : "With this revealed will of God we should concern ourselves, follow and be diligently engaged upon it, because through the Word, whereby He calls us, the Holy Ghost bestows grace, power, and ability to this end, and [we] should not [attempt to] sound the abyss of God's hidden predestination, as it is written in Luke 13, 24, where one asks: 'Lord, are there few to be saved?' and Christ answers: 'Strive to enter in at the strait gate.'"

Our Lutheran Confessions thus reject the Calvinistic error of *"absolute election"* and affirm that we are chosen *in Christ* (ἐν Χριστῷ, Eph. 1, 4; ἐν ἁγιασμῷ πνεύματος καὶ πίστει ἀληθείας, 2 Thess. 2, 13). That is to say, our election is based upon *Christ's merit,* and this, together with the sanctification of the Spirit and faith, is so interwoven with the act of eternal election that the use and effect of the means of grace are part and parcel of it.

Hence we must not consider our election *"in a bare manner"* *(nude),* but as "the counsel, purpose, and ordination of God in Christ Jesus, who is the true Book of Life, is revealed to us through the Word" *(ibid.,* 13. 14). "Those who according to the purpose are predestinated to an inheritance hear the Gospel, believe in Christ, pray and give thanks," etc., and so have the Spirit's own testimony "that they are children of God" *(ibid.,* 30. 31).

"The Eleventh Article of the Formula of Concord indeed speaks of God's counsel of redemption, especially in the so-called Eight Points, 13—23. But by doing so, it does not teach an election in a wider sense *(eine allgemeine Wahl, ordinatio mediorum).* By this it rather teaches that election must not be considered *nude,* but in connection with the whole counsel of God, 'pertaining to our redemption, call, justification, and salvation,' § 14." (Dr. Engelder, *Dogmatical Notes.*)

3. THE OBJECTS OF ETERNAL ELECTION.

According to Holy Scripture, God has not elected all men (error of Samuel Huber, † 1624) nor the steadfast believers *(finaliter credentes)* together with the temporary believers (error of the Tuebingen school and some modern theologians, J. A. Osiander, † 1697; Frank), but only those who are actually saved *(praedestinatio est particularis).* This follows from the clear teaching of Scripture that all the elect shall surely be saved *(praedestinatio est immutabilis et infallibilis),* Matt. 24, 24; Rom. 8, 28—30. The *Formula of Concord* writes (Thor. Decl., XI, 23): "God has in grace considered and chosen to salvation *each and every person of the elect who are to be saved.*"

Those who deny the immutability and infallibility of election, teaching that the elect may be lost, make of predestination a mere divine foreknowledge *(praescientia),* which is determined by, or conditioned upon, man's conduct in time. They thus deny the Scriptural doctrine of election *in toto.*

Hence the term *election* is not used in Scripture, as some

erroneously claim, in a *widest sense* (all men are elect), a wider sense (such as will be saved and temporary believers), and in a narrow sense (such as will be saved), but only in one sense, that is to say: "The predestination, or eternal election, of God extends *only over the godly, beloved children of God,* being a cause of their salvation" (Epit., XI, 5).

Quite generally those who used the term *election* in a wider or a general sense erroneously confounded God's eternal plan of salvation with His eternal election of grace.

God's general counsel of grace *(Gottes allgemeiner Gnadenwille, benevolentia Dei universalis)* certainly extends over all sinners, 1 Tim. 2, 4; but His eternal election of grace extends only over such as will be saved, Matt. 20, 16; 22, 14.

The claim that also the *Formula of Concord* teaches an election in a wider sense is based upon the misunderstanding of those paragraphs (Thor. Decl., XI, 15—22) in which it describes the *ordo salutis* embraced in God's eternal election. *(Praedestinatio non est absoluta, sed ordinata, i. e., fundatur in Christo.)*

When determining the objects of eternal election, some dogmaticians erroneously claimed that God's eternal predestination consists in the *general principle, or decree:* "He that shall endure unto the end, the same shall be saved," Matt. 24, 13. While this general principle, or decree, is a truth which Scripture urges with much emphasis, John 3, 18. 36, it must not be confounded with the divine decree of election, since according to Scripture not *general principles,* but *persons* have been chosen to salvation (2 Thess. 2, 13: *you;* Eph. 1, 4: *us*).

For this reason we reject also the following claims: a) that God's eternal election is the ordination of the means of grace *(ordinatio mediorum,* called by some election in a wider sense); and b) that the object of God's gracious election is the *Church in general* (Hofmann, Luthardt, Vilmar, Thomasius). The last claim involves a contradiction, since the Church is properly the "communion of saints" and therefore consists of individual persons.

Holy Scripture, without any qualification whatever, describes *all true believers* as elect saints of God, Eph. 1, 4; 2 Thess. 2, 13; 1 Thess. 1, 4; 1 Pet. 1, 2. Hence all sincere Christians should regard themselves as God's elect through faith in Christ Jesus, Rom. 8, 33. 34. All those who claim that they cannot know whether they are chosen or not or who doubt their election should examine themselves if they really *believe* in Christ as their true and only Savior, 2 Cor. 13, 5.

It is true, the believer can never become sure of his election and salvation as long as he considers the question from the *viewpoint of God's bare foreknowledge,* since no one can definitely know just what God foreknew or foresaw in him *(intuitu fidei finalis).* The opinion that God has elected men in view of their final faith *(ex praevisa fide finali)* is neither Scriptural nor comforting. It is not Scriptural, since there is not a shred of Scripture proof for it. It is not comforting, since it takes the believer into the domain of God's inscrutable and hidden will. For all practical purposes it is an impossible doctrine, lying, as it does, in the province of the unknowable.

The *Formula of Concord* rightly argues with respect to the *intuitu fidei finalis* (Thor. Decl., XI, 54. 55): "There is no doubt that God most exactly and certainly foresaw *(praeviderit)* before the time of the world, and still knows *(et hodie etiam norit),* which of those that are called will believe or will not believe; also which of the converted will persevere [in faith] and which will not persevere. . . . However, since God has reserved this mystery for His wisdom and has revealed nothing to us concerning it in His Word, much less commanded us to investigate it with our thoughts, but has earnestly discouraged us therefrom, Rom. 11, 33 ff., we should not reason in our thoughts, draw conclusions, nor inquire curiously into these matters, but should adhere to His revealed Word, to which He points us."

This admonition is very pertinent; for we are sure of our election and salvation only if in true faith we cling to Christ, who has promised to receive all sinners and to give them rest, Matt. 11, 28. It is only by faith in Christ that we may be sure of our election and salvation.

Again, the believer cannot become sure of his election and salvation as long as he doubts or limits universal grace *(gratia universalis).* The *Formula of Concord* rightly says (Thor. Decl., XI, 28): "If we wish to consider our eternal election to salvation with profit, we must in every way hold sturdily and firmly to this, that, as the preaching of repentance, so also the promise of the Gospel is *universalis* (universal), that is, it pertains to all men, Luke 24, 47."

All who deny the *gratia universalis* (Calvinists) have no foundation on which to rest their faith; for if the promises of the Gospel are limited to only a few (the elect), how can we know whether or not we belong to the chosen few?

However, not only the Calvinists limit the *gratia universalis,* but also the synergists, though in theory they acknowledge the universality of divine grace. Actually, however, the synergists limit God's saving grace to those who do not maliciously resist the Holy Spirit or who cooperate in their conversion. Hence neither Calvinism nor synergism can make any one sure of his election and salvation.

Lastly, the believer cannot be sure of his election and salvation as long as he accounts for the difference why one is saved and the other is not *(Cur alii, alii non?)* by a "different conduct in men" *(aliquid in homine, aliqua actio dissimilis in homine).*

This was the mistake of Melanchthon, who taught (*Loci,* 1548): "Since the promise is universal, and since there are no contradictory wills in God, some cause of discrimination must be in us why Saul is rejected and David accepted; that is, there must be some dissimilar action in these two." So also Pfeffinger (*Quaestiones Quinque,* Thesis 23): "We are elected and received because we believe in the Son." Compare also the synergistic argument in general: "Since man's contempt of God's Word is the cause of his reprobation, man's acceptance of God's grace must be regarded as a cause of his election." (Cp. Dr. Bente's "Historical Introductions to the Symbolical Books," *Concordia Triglotta,* p. 195 ff.) This synergistic conception of election makes predestination *a priori* an election of merit and not of grace, Rom. 11, 5—7.

Against the synergistic error the *Formula of Concord* writes (Thor. Decl., XI, 88): "Therefore it is false and wrong [conflicts with the Word of God] when it is taught that not alone the mercy of God and the most holy merit of Christ, but that also in us there is a cause of God's election *(verum etiam aliquid in nobis causa sit electionis divinae)* on account of which God has chosen us to eternal life. For not only before we had done anything good, but also before we were born, yea, even before the foundations of the world were laid, He elected us in Christ."

However, while neither Calvinism (denial of the *gratia universalis*) nor synergism (denial of the *sola gratia*) can render any person certain of his election and salvation, such certainty is fully obtained by faith in the universal Gospel-promises of free grace; for these most gracious promises offer to all men most seriously and efficaciously *(gratia seria et efficax)* forgiveness of sins, life, and salvation for the sake of Christ, who shed His blood for the sins of the world, 1 John 2, 2; 4, 10. In other words, every Christian should surely believe on the basis of Scripture that Jesus Christ has redeemed him, a lost and condemned sinner, purchased and won him from all sins, from death, and from the power of the devil . . . that he may be His own and live under Him in His kingdom and serve Him in everlasting righteousness, innocence, and blessedness. With respect to the gracious promise of God in Christ Jesus (John 3, 16—18) he should say with true faith: "This is most certainly true!" and rejoice in his election and salvation.

That is the line of argument which St. Paul points out in Rom. 8, 32. 33, where he writes: "He that spared not His own Son, but delivered Him up for us all, *how shall He not with Him also freely give us all things?* Who shall lay anything to the charge of God's elect? It is God that justifieth."

Following the apostle's line of argument, every believer should confidently confess: "If God by grace has given me His only-begotten Son to be my Savior and has renewed my heart by His Holy Spirit through faith, pardoned my sins, and justified me by His grace, who shall prefer against me the charge that I am not His elect? *Since God has justified me in Christ Jesus, I believe with all my heart that He has chosen me in Christ Jesus.*"

The certainty of election and salvation which follows such trust in the divine promises is of course not an *absolute certainty* in the sense that it rests upon a direct or immediate revelation of the Holy Ghost, but it is a *certainty of faith* and so a most blessed certainty; for divine faith is not doubt or uncertainty, but a most *positive assurance* wrought by the Holy Ghost through the Gospel *(fides divina).*

This divine certainty St. Paul describes in these memorable words: "I am persuaded that neither death, nor life, nor angels, nor principalities, nor powers, nor things present, nor things to come, nor height, nor depth, nor any other creature shall be able to separate us from the love of God which is in Christ Jesus, our Lord," Rom. 8, 38. 39. The true believer is persuaded of his election and salvation because the Holy Ghost Himself persuades him of this by faith through the Gospel, 2 Tim. 1, 12.

With respect to the numerous warnings against apostasy, which Holy Scripture addresses also to the believers, we must remember that they pertain to Christians only inasmuch as they are flesh ($\sigma\acute{\alpha}\varrho\xi$). Hence these warnings and admonitions belong to the preaching of the Law, which works knowledge of sin also in the believer, Rom. 3, 20. But they do not pertain to the believer inasmuch as he is a new creature in Christ (2 Cor 5, 17: καινὴ κτίσις) and as such "presses towards the mark for the prize of the high calling of God in Christ Jesus," Phil. 3, 12—14.

As a new man in Christ (καινὸς ἄνθρωπος), who longs for eternal life, Phil. 3, 20. 21, a Christian must entirely forget the threatenings of the divine Law, 1 Tim. 1, 9, and comfort himself with the gracious promises of the Gospel, Rom. 10, 4; Gal. 3, 13; 2, 19; Rom. 6, 14. The warnings of the Law apply to him only inasmuch as sin still cleaves to him, Rom. 7, 18—25; 1 Cor. 10, 12, or inasmuch as he is still inclined to set aside the goal of eternal salvation and to love this present world, 1 Cor. 10, 1—6; 1 John 2, 14—17.

As warnings of the Law we must consider also the frequent references in Scripture to *temporary believers,* Luke 8, 13; Hos. 6, 4; 2 Tim. 4, 10. Temporary believers fall from grace because they disbelieve the Gospel, by which the Holy Ghost engenders and preserves faith, 1 Pet. 1, 5. Hence the fault of their damnation is theirs and not God's, 2 Tim. 1, 13. 14; 2 Thess. 3, 3. God's unqualified promise to all believers reads: "Whosoever believeth on Him shall not be ashamed," Rom. 10, 11.

For this reason Christians should never doubt their election and salvation, but through diligent use of the means of grace hold fast to the hope of eternal life which is in Christ Jesus, John 10, 27. 28.

4. THE RELATION OF FAITH TO ETERNAL ELECTION.

With regard to the important question, which has been in controversy ever since the sixteenth century: "In what relation does faith stand to election?" we must bear in mind that notionally *(notionaliter, begrifflich)* Scripture places faith neither *before* nor *after* election.

Faith was placed *before* election by all the later Lutheran theologians who taught that God elected those who will be saved, in view of their foreseen faith *(intuitu fidei finalis).*

Faith is placed *after* election by the Calvinists, who teach that faith, the same as Christ's redemption, is merely the execution of God's eternal, absolute (arbitrary) decree of predestination.

As a matter of fact, the right relation of faith to eternal election is this, that saving faith, wrought by the Holy Ghost, belongs into election as the *means* by which the object of election is accomplished. In other words, God in His eternal counsel of grace decreed to save His elect saints through faith in Christ Jesus, Eph. 1, 3—8; 1 Pet. 1, 2; or we may say, from eternity He graciously endowed the elect with faith and thereby separated them from the lost world *(massa perdita).*

Of this the *Formula of Concord* writes (Thor. Decl., XI, 44): "God in His counsel, before the time of the world, decided and ordained that He Himself, by the power of the Holy Ghost, would produce and work in us, through the Word, everything that pertains to our conversion." So also Dr. Walther declares: "We teach that God, as He saves us in time through faith, so also from eternity He decreed to save the elect through faith; and just this, according to Scripture, our Confessions, and our doctrine, is the decree of eternal predestination. . . . We believe, teach, and confess according to Scripture and our Confession that God has chosen us to salvation through faith." (*Christl. Dogmatik,* III, 548 ff.)

Since, then, God has chosen the elect unto faith in Christ, we regard the faith which the elect receive *in time,* just as their whole state of grace, which follows such faith, also as the *effect,* or *result,* of their eternal election (2 Tim. 1, 9: "who hath called us according to His own purpose and grace"; Acts 13, 48: "As many as were ordained to eternal life believed"). Faith, then, according to Scripture is rightly viewed both as the *effect* of election and as the *means* by which its purpose is accomplished. Chemnitz writes (*Enchiridion,* p. 109): "The election of God does not follow after our faith and righteousness, but precedes it as a cause of all this." And the *Formula of Concord* says (Thor. Decl., XI, 8): "The eternal election of God . . . is also, from the gracious will and pleasure of God in Christ Jesus, *a cause* which procures, works, helps, and promotes our salvation and what pertains thereto."

From this doctrine of Scripture and the Lutheran Confession the later Lutheran dogmaticians (since Hunnius, † 1603) departed, teaching that God elected such as are saved in view of their foreseen final faith *(intuitu fidei finalis, ex praevisa fide finali).* This view they sought to justify by taking the verb *foreknow* (Rom. 8, 29: προέγνω) in the sense of *knowing before* or *seeing before (nudam scientiam denotans).*

Accordingly they interpreted St. Paul's statement in Rom. 8, 29 thus: "Whose final faith He foreknew or foresaw *(quorum fidem finalem praescivit sive praevidit)* He also did predestinate" (καὶ προώρισεν). This explanation has been adopted by some modern exegetes (Philippi), who accepted the *intuitu-fidei* theory either on synergistic grounds or on account of its supposed greater clearness and fitness.

But to substitute the words *quorum fidem finalem praescivit sive praevidit* for the plain words of the apostle *"whom He did foreknow"* (οὓς προέγνω) is a violation of the text, since it forces upon the statement of the apostle something that it does not express (eisegesis). St. Paul does not say: "whose final faith He foreknew," but: *"whom* He foreknew." The object of "He foreknew" (προέγνω) is not faith, but a certain number of persons, whom the apostle calls "the called according to His purpose," v. 28.

In addition to this, the *intuitu-fidei* theory is directly anti-Scriptural, since Holy Scripture plainly teaches that the faith which the elect receive in time is not the cause, but rather the effect of election, Acts 13, 48; Matt. 24, 21—24.

For *"final faith"* other exegetes substitute in this passage *good works* (Ambrose: *quorum merita praescivit*), or *love* (Weiss, Ebrard), or the *good conduct* (*facultas se applicandi ad gratiam, voluntas non repugnans, sed assentiens,* Melanchthon), in short, some good quality of the elect, which explains why some were chosen and others were not *(Cur alii, alii non?)*.

Over against this synergistic interpretation, Luther, as also the *Formula of Concord,* regarded the verb *to know* or *foreknow* as used in a peculiar sense, which it frequently has in Scripture (Luther: *zuvorversehen,* to *determine beforehand;* the *Formula of Concord: in Gnaden bedenken, graciously to consider; clementer praescire, graciously* to foreknow; Luthardt: *ein aneignendes Zuvorerkennen,* an appropriating foreknowing; others: *sich zu eigen machen,* to make a person one's own; *sich verbinden,* to join some one to oneself).

In this sense γινώσκειν, following the use of the Hebrew יָדַע (cp. Deut. 7, 6 with Amos 3, 2), is used in Gal. 4, 9: "After that ye have known God, or rather are *known of God";* Rom. 11, 2: "God hath not cast away His people which He *foreknew";* 1 Cor. 8, 3: "If any man love God, the same is *known* of Him."

In all these and many other passages of Scripture the verb *to know* or *to foreknow* does not designate mere knowledge, but a knowledge joined with love *(nosse cum affectu et effectu),* so that the person thus known of God is made His own and acknowledged by Him as His own. In this sense we take the verb προέγνω in Rom. 8, 29, since, on the one hand, the direct object of *did fore-*

know is the relative pronoun *whom,* which refers to persons and does not mean "whose faith" or whose "better conduct" He foresaw, and since, on the other, the grammatical antecedent of *whom* (οὕς) is the definite number of God's saints who are "called according to His purpose," v. 28.

The sense of v. 29, then, is: "Whom He did graciously determine beforehand according to His purpose *(welche er aber zuvorversehen hat),* He also did predestinate."

To the objection that this would constitute an inexcusable tautology (Hunnius, Philippi) we reply that this conclusion does not follow.

Even if we should take προγινώσκειν as a synonym of προορίζειν, the sentence would not be tautological, but only progressive in thought; for it would then say: "Whom God did choose before, them also He really did predestinate," *sc.,* "to be conformed to the image of His Son."

In other words, the thought would then indeed be repeated, yet not uselessly, but to connect it with the new and very important truth: "to be conformed to the image of His Son."

However, we may distinguish between the meaning of προγινώσκειν and προορίζειν in this manner: the first verb expresses the loving appropriation of the elect *(die liebende Aneignung der Auserwaehlten);* the second, their predestination to conformity to the image of His Son.

We thus distinguish in God's eternal decree logically a twofold gracious action, namely, first, a loving appropriation of the elect and, secondly, the actual predestination of the elect, though really *(sachlich)* the two coincide.

The doctrine of *intuitu fidei* (the so-called "second form") has no Scriptural foundation whatever, since Holy Scripture teaches directly that nothing moved God to elect His saints to salvation except His infinite grace in Christ Jesus. The reason why "the second form" was introduced into the theology of the Church was that it was regarded as necessary to explain the reason why some were chosen and others not. Its advocates decided to remove the difficulty that, if divine grace is universal *(gratia universalis)* and all men by nature are in equal guilt *(in eadem culpa)* and depend alone on divine grace for salvation *(sola gratia),* it is impossible to explain the mystery why some are predestinated to life and others not (particular election).

Hence the *intuitu-fidei* theory is intelligible only if it is taken in a synergistic sense, that is, if it is understood in the synergistic meaning that by nature not all men are in the same guilt and therefore salvation is not alone by grace.

That is indeed an explanation of the mystery of election, but one that opposes Scripture and denies the fundamental article of the Christian faith, the *sola gratia*. It is the same anti-Scriptural explanation concerning which Luther wrote to Erasmus: "Thou hast seized me by the throat, *Iugulum meum petisti.*"

It is true, not all dogmaticians who taught the *intuitu fidei* were synergists; but the theory lends itself so readily to the support of synergism that it should not be used by those who do not mean to be synergists.

5. THE PURPOSE OF THE DOCTRINE OF ETERNAL ELECTION.

According to Holy Scripture it is not the purpose of the doctrine of eternal election to deny or limit the *gratia universalis* (Calvin and others), but rather to inculcate the *sola gratia*. In other words, it should induce Christian believers, whenever they compare themselves with unbelievers, to ascribe their state of grace not to their own praiseworthy conduct (synergism, Pelagianism), but solely to divine grace in Christ Jesus (divine monergism). This emphasis on the *sola gratia is indeed necessary;* for if Christians ascribe their salvation to their good conduct, or worthiness, even only in part, they are fallen from grace and are under the divine curse, Luke 18, 9 ff.; Gal. 3, 10.

This purpose of the doctrine of eternal election appears already from Israel's election as the people of the Old Testament Church, which was typical of God's eternal election of grace. When God led His people into the land of promise, He expressly declared: "Not for thy righteousness or for the uprightness of thine heart dost thou go to possess their [the heathen nations'] land. . . . Understand therefore that the Lord, thy God, giveth thee not this good land to possess it for thy righteousness; for thou art a stiff-necked people," Deut. 9, 5. 6.

This same thought, "not for thy righteousness," the doctrine of election impresses upon the believer in the New Testament. (2 Tim. 1, 9: "God hath saved us . . . not according to our works, but according to His own purpose and grace"; Eph. 1, 5. 6: "having predestinated us unto the adoption of children by Jesus Christ to Himself according to the good pleasure of His will"; Rom. 11, 6: "If by grace, then it is no more of works.")

It is only when we keep this important truth in mind that we are able to understand chaps. 9—11 of St. Paul's Epistle to the Romans correctly. In these chapters the apostle indeed affirms the universal grace of God, Rom. 10, 21; 11, 32, but condemns the arrogance and pride of the self-righteous, who, when comparing themselves with those who are lost, regard themselves as better than they and so ascribe their salvation to their own worthiness, Rom. 9, 30—33; 11, 18 ff.

In agreement with these statements of Scripture the *Formula of Concord* writes (Thor. Decl., XI, 87. 88): "By this doctrine and explanation of the eternal and saving choice [predestination] of the elect children of God His own glory is entirely and fully given to God, that in Christ He saves us out of pure [and free] mercy, without any merits or good works of ours, according to the purpose of His will. . . . Therefore it is false and wrong [conflicts with the Word of God] when it is taught that not alone the mercy of God and the most holy merit of Christ, but that also in us there is a cause of God's election on account of which God has chosen us to eternal life."

As a warning against self-righteousness our Lord employs the doctrine of eternal election in Matt. 20, 1—16 and Matt. 22, 1—14, where He reproves those who trust in their own righteousness and reject the *sola gratia* and the *meritum Christi* as the sole foundation of their eternal hope.

While the doctrine of God's eternal election in Christ Jesus is therefore a most earnest warning addressed to Christians inasmuch as their flesh inclines to self-righteousness, it is a warning also, addressed to their secure and indifferent hearts, not to despise the means of grace, through which God's grace in Christ Jesus is offered and conveyed to all sinners (Matt. 22, 1—14: "And they would not come").

On this point the *Formula of Concord* writes very correctly (Thor. Decl., XI, 51): "From this article also powerful admonitions and warnings are derived, as Luke 7, 30: 'They rejected the counsel of God against themselves'; Luke 14, 24: 'I say unto you that none of those men which were bidden shall taste of my supper'; Matt. 20, 16: 'Many be called, but few chosen'; also Luke 8, 8. 18: 'He that hath ears to hear, let him hear,' and: 'Take heed how ye hear.'"

Again (Thor. Decl., XI, 41. 42): "Few receive the Word and follow it; the greater number despise the Word and will not come

604 THE DOCTRINE OF ETERNAL ELECTION.

to the wedding, Matt. 22, 3 ff. The cause of this contempt for the Word is not God's foreknowledge [or predestination], but the perverse will of man, which rejects or perverts the means and instrument of the Holy Ghost which God offers him through the call and resists the Holy Ghost, who wishes to be efficacious and works through the Word, as Christ says: 'How often would I have gathered you together, and ye would not!' Matt. 23, 37. Thus many 'receive the Word with joy, but afterward fall away again,' Luke 8, 13. But the cause is not as though God were unwilling to grant grace for perseverance to those in whom He has begun the good work, for that is contrary to St. Paul, Phil. 1, 6; but the cause is that they wilfully turn away again from the holy commandment [of God], grieve and embitter the Holy Ghost, implicate themselves again in the filth of the world, and garnish again the habitation of the heart for the devil. With them the last state is worse than the first, 2 Pet. 2, 10. 20; Eph. 4, 30; Heb. 10, 26; Luke 11, 25."

As Matt. 20, 1—16 and 22, 1—14, so we must view as a most earnest warning also the apostle's admonition to give diligence to make our calling and election sure, 2 Pet. 1, 10. What the apostle here inculcates is that Christians should diligently use the means of grace, walk in obedience to God by faith in Christ Jesus, and so through the witness of the Holy Spirit (testimonium Spiritus Sancti) become subjectively sure of their state of grace and election, Gal. 5, 22—25.

However, while it is a manifest purpose of the doctrine of eternal election to warn and exhort Christians to adhere to the *sola gratia* and not to despise the means of grace (Law-preaching addressed to Christians according to their Old Adam [παλαιὸς ἄνθρωπος], Eph. 4, 22—24), the proper scope of the doctrine is to bless all Christian believers with true comfort and abiding consolation. In this manner Scripture employs the doctrine of election preeminently, Eph. 1, 3—6; Rom. 8, 28—30; 1 Pet. 1, 2—6; for the proclamation of the *sola gratia (sola fide)* is by its very nature the sweetest and most consoling Gospel truth, John 3, 16—18.

In particular, the doctrine of God's eternal election in Christ Jesus comforts the Christian believer in two ways: It shows him a) how very earnestly God desires the eternal salvation of every Christian, and b) how God at all times preserves His Church on earth against the fury of Satan, the onslaughts of the wicked world, and the deceitfulness of the believer's own corrupt flesh (σάρξ).

The *Formula of Concord* speaks very fittingly of this precious comfort when it says (Thor. Decl., XI, 45. 46): "Thus this doctrine affords also the excellent, glorious consolation that God was so greatly concerned about the conversion, righteousness, and salvation of every Christian and so faithfully purposed it . . . that, before the foundation of the world was laid, He deliberated concerning it and in His [secret] purpose ordained how He would bring me thereto [call and lead me to salvation] and preserve me therein; also, that He wished to secure my salvation so well and certainly that, since through the weakness and wickedness of our flesh it could easily be lost from our hands or through craft and might of the devil and the world be snatched and taken from us, He ordained it in His eternal purpose, which cannot fail or be overthrown, and placed it for preservation in the almighty hand of our Savior Jesus Christ, from which no one can pluck us, John 10, 28."

Again (*ibid.*, 48. 49): "Moreover, this doctrine affords glorious consolation under the cross and amid temptations, namely, that God in His counsel, before the time of the world, determined and decreed that He would assist us in all distresses [anxieties and perplexities], grant patience [under the cross], give consolation, excite [nourish and encourage] hope, and produce such an outcome as would contribute to our salvation. Also, as Paul in a very consolatory way treats this, Rom. 8, 28. 29. 35—39, that God in His purpose has ordained before the time of the world by what crosses and sufferings He would conform every one of His elect to the image of His Son and that to every one His cross shall and must work together for good, because they are called according to the purpose, whence Paul has concluded that it is certain and indubitable that neither tribulation nor distress, nor death, nor life, etc., shall be able to separate us from the love of God which is in Christ Jesus, our Lord."

Lastly (*ibid.*, 50): "This article also affords a glorious testimony that the Church of God will exist and abide in opposition to all the gates of hell and likewise teaches which is the true Church of God, lest we be offended by the great authority [and majestic appearance] of the false Church, Rom. 9, 24. 25."

While the *Formula of Concord* thus points out, and impresses, the consolatory nature of the doctrine of eternal election to life, it shows also that, "when this consolation and hope are weakened or entirely removed by Scripture [by false Scriptural interpretation, as that of Calvinism and synergism], it is certain that it is understood and explained contrary to the will and meaning of the Holy Ghost" (*ibid.*, 92), so that, "if any one presents the doctrine concerning the gracious election of God in such a manner that troubled Christians cannot derive comfort from it, but are hereby incited to despair or that the impenitent are confirmed in their wantonness, it is undoubtedly sure and true that such a doctrine is taught not according to the Word and will of God, but according to [the blind judgment of human] reason and the instigation of the devil" (*ibid.*, 91).

To the believing Christian who rejoices in the sweet consolation of the blood-stained cross of Calvary and in its radiant light and glory views his own certain election and salvation "this doctrine gives no cause either for despondency or for a shameless, dissolute life" (*ibid.*, 89).

6. HOLY SCRIPTURE TEACHES NO ELECTION TO DAMNATION.

Calvinism argues very seriously that, since God has elected some to eternal life, He also must have elected others to eternal damnation. In other words, there must be an election of wrath (*eine Zornwahl*) to correspond to the election of grace (*"die notwendige Kehrseite,"* the necessary reverse side).

The Lutheran denial of an eternal reprobation to damnation (*electio aeterna, qua Deus . . . alios ad interitum praedestinavit*) Calvin rebuked with the harshest terms (*inscite nimis et pueriliter; plus quam insulse, Inst.*, III, 23, 1).

So also the followers of Calvin designate the Scriptural position of the *Formula of Concord* on predestination as "untenable ground" (Hodge, *Syst. Theol.*, II, 325). Shedd entirely ignores the Lutheran position and divides all Christians into Calvinists (denial of universal grace) and Arminians (denial of the *sola gratia*). In his system of theology there is no room for the Scriptural doctrine of eternal election as the Lutheran Church confesses it (*Dogm. Theol.*, I, 448).

However, Holy Scripture knows of no "reverse side" of God's eternal election of grace; for while the one (election unto eternal life) is clearly taught in many passages, the other (election unto eternal damnation) is plainly repudiated.

In Acts 13, 48 we are indeed told: "As many as were ordained to eternal life believed," but this passage does not add: "As many as were ordained to eternal damnation believed not." **On the contrary,** it cites as the true reason why the others did not believe their wilful and perverse rejection of the proffered grace (v. 46: "Seeing ye put it from you and judge yourselves unworthy of everlasting life, lo, we turn to the Gentiles"). The reason why some do not believe is stated clearly by Christ when He says of them: "Ye would not," Matt. 23, 37. 38.

In accord with this verdict of Holy Scripture the Lutheran Church teaches: All who are saved are saved by grace; but all who are lost are lost through their own perverse opposition to the Holy Ghost, Hos. 13, 9. Calvinism indeed declares that also to those whom He from eternity has reprobated to damnation God offers a certain kind of grace (common grace), while to His elect He offers "irresistible grace"; but this is only a new error, designed to confirm the error of eternal reprobation. Calvinism thus teaches contradictory wills in God; for by the outward call, extended to the non-elect, He wills their salvation, while according to His eternal decree of reprobation *(horribile decretum),* by which He reprobated the non-elect to damnation, He does not desire to save them. Scripture, on the contrary, plainly teaches that also those who reject the divine offer of grace are seriously called, Acts 13, 38—41; Matt. 23, 37. 38: *vocatio seria.*

Moreover, the fact that God hardens the hearts (Ex. 10, 1; 5, 1—23) of those who first harden themselves *(voluntas Dei consequens)* does not prove an eternal reprobation to damnation; for Scripture tells us expressly that the divine act of obduration is a measure of wrath and punishment which occurs as a "recompense" (εἰς ἀνταπόδομα, Rom. 11, 9) for their resistance and rejection of divine grace. *"Verstockung ist immer eine Folge der Selbstverstockung."*

It is true, Christian believers are by nature in the same guilt *(in eadem culpa),* Rom. 3, 22. 23, as are all other men, so that, if they should compare themselves with those who are lost, they are "just like them and in no way any better" *(quam simillimi deprehensi),* Ps. 51, 5; John 3, 5. 6; Eph. 2, 3. Hence they have no reason whatever to boast of their goodness and to ascribe their faith and salvation to their own worthiness, 1 Cor. 4, 7, but must praise and glorify the indescribable mercy of God, who out of pure grace has endowed them with spiritual life *(Formula of Concord,* Thor. Decl., XI, 60).

Nevertheless Holy Scripture assures us that God most seriously offers His grace also to those who resist His Spirit, Acts 13, 46, and harden their hearts against His divine Word, Acts 7, 51, indeed, that with much long-suffering He endures the vessels of wrath, fitted to destruction by their own hardness of heart, Rom. 9, 22. 23, to the end that they, too, might be converted and saved, 2 Pet. 3, 9; Rom. 2, 4.

Thus Scripture everywhere extols the unspeakable mercy of God, which offers grace and salvation also to those who are lost, and leaves no room whatever for a doctrine of eternal reprobation.

With respect to the statement of St. Paul that "God endured with much long-suffering the vessels of wrath fitted to destruction," Rom. 9, 22, the *Formula of Concord* rightly says (Thor. Decl., XI, 80): "Here, then, the apostle clearly says that God *endured* with much long-suffering the vessels of wrath, but does not say that He *made* them vessels of wrath; for if this had been His will, He would not have required any great long-suffering for it. The fault, however, that they are fitted for destruction belongs to the devil and to men themselves and not to God."

God has indeed "afore prepared" (προητοίμασεν) unto glory the vessels of mercy, Rom. 9, 23, but not the vessels of wrath; for these, as the apostle plainly states, are "fitted to destruction" (κατηρτισμένα εἰς ἀπώλειαν), sc., by their own perverseness. According to Scripture, God earnestly desires the salvation of all men, John 1, 29; 3, 16; 2 Pet. 2, 1. "Hell was originally not built for men." If men enter into it, it is because of their own wicked rejection of divine grace (cp. Matt. 25, 34: "Come, ye blessed of My Father, inherit the kingdom *prepared for you* from the foundation of the world"; v. 41: "Depart from Me, ye cursed, into everlasting fire, *prepared for the devil and his angels*").

The *voluntas consequens,* according to which God judges and condemns all who do not believe the Gospel, Mark 16, 16; John 3, 16—18. 36, must therefore not be interpreted as an eternal decree of damnation, since according to His *voluntas antecedens* God desires the salvation of all sinners, 2 Pet. 3, 9; Matt. 18, 11; 1 Tim. 2, 4.

If the objection is raised that we must not speak of a *voluntas prima* and a *voluntas secunda* in God because there is neither a *prius* nor a *posterius* in Him, we answer that God is indeed the eternal, immutable Lord, in whom there is no change, or no *prius* or *posterius,* Mal. 3, 6; 1 Sam. 15, 29. However, since, in accommodation to our feeble understanding, God has revealed Himself to us as the loving Lord, who desires to save all men, John 3, 16. 17, and then again as the righteous Lord, who punishes eternally all who will not believe on Him, John 3, 18. 36, we must speak as Scripture does and predicate of Him both a will to save and a will to condemn. However, this will to condemn is not the "reverse side" of His gracious election unto life, but rather that just punishment *(iustitia vindicativa)* which He inflicts upon all who wickedly despise His *voluntas antecedens* and will not hear His Word, Rom. 10, 21.

As we must not argue from Scripture that "there is an eternal decree of damnation," so we must argue this error neither from *history.* That is indeed the mistake of Calvinism, which reasons: "The *result* is the interpretation of God's *purposes*" (cp. Calvin, *Inst.,* III, 24. 12). From the fact that not all men are saved or that not all nations enjoy the blessings of the Gospel, Calvinism infers that God does not desire to save them. But also this position is anti-Scriptural; for Scripture commands us not to draw conclusions from the unsearchable judgments of God, but to adore them with awe and reverence, Rom. 11, 33—36.

Of the unsearchable judgments of God the *Formula of Concord* says (Thor. Decl., XI, 57—63) : "Likewise, when we see that God gives His Word at one place, but not at another; removes it from one place and allows it to remain at another; also, that one is hardened, blinded, given over to a reprobate mind, while another, who is indeed in the same guilt *(qui in eadem culpa haeret),* is converted, etc., — in these and similar questions, Paul (Rom. 11, 22 ff.) fixes a certain limit to us how far we should go. namely, that in the one part we should recognize God's judgment [for He commands us to consider in those who perish the just judgment of God and the penalties of sins]. For they are well-deserved penalties of sins when God so punishes a land or nation for despising His Word that the punishment extends also to their posterity, as is to be seen in the Jews. . . . However, as regards these things in this disputation which would soar too high and beyond these limits, we should, with Paul, place the finger upon our lips and remember and say, Rom. 9, 20 : 'O man, who art thou that repliest against God?' "

Hence we must not conclude as the Calvinists do: "Since God does not save all men, He does not *desire* the salvation of all," and so try to explore the secret will of God; but we must rather adhere to the revealed will of God, made manifest in Scripture, which bears witness in many clear passages that God "will have all men to be saved and to come unto the knowledge of the truth," 1 Tim. 2, 4.

As proof for the "eternal reprobation of the damned" Calvinism cites also Rom. 9, 18: "Therefore hath He mercy on whom He will have mercy, and whom He will He hardeneth." But this passage does not teach an eternal election unto damnation, but merely reveals God in His supreme sovereignty, according to which He is not subject to human criticism.

That these words are not designed to deny universal grace is clear from St. Paul's express teaching of that doctrine in chap. 10, 21 and chap. 11, 32. In other words, the same God who has mercy on whom He will "stretched forth His hands all day unto a disobedient and gainsaying people" and "concluded them all in unbelief [that is, declared all men lost in unbelief] that He might have mercy upon all." Hence the passage (Rom. 9, 18) is not directed against the *gratia universalis,* but against the proud spirit of self-righteousness and work-righteousness in men, Rom. 9, 16.

The *Formula of Concord* rightly interprets the passage when it writes (Thor. Decl., XI, 61): "No injustice is done those who are punished and receive the wages of their sins; but in the rest, to whom God gives and preserves His Word, by which men are enlightened, converted, and preserved, God commends His pure [immense] grace and mercy, without their merit."

In conclusion we may say that just as we are not to solve the mystery of election by denying the *sola gratia* (synergism), so we must not solve it by denying the *gratia universalis* and ascribe to God, contrary to Scripture, an eternal decree of reprobation. Both "solutions" are equally rationalistic and in direct conflict with the Word of God.

7. WHY MANY REJECT THE SCRIPTURAL DOCTRINE OF ETERNAL ELECTION.

The Scriptural doctrine of eternal election is the final test of a believer's faith: "At the doctrine of the election of grace one writes his final examination in theology" *("An der Lehre von der Gnadenwahl wird das theologische Schlussexamen gemacht"), Christl. Dogmatik,* III, 568. The doctrine of eternal election as taught in Scripture allows not even a trace of Pelagianism or rationalism to stand. It rather demands unqualified acceptance of Scripture as the only source and norm of faith *(sola Scriptura),* unqualified trust in Christ's vicarious atonement as the sinner's only hope of salvation *(sola fide),* and unqualified recognition of the universality of the divine promises offered in the Gospel *(gratia universalis).*

In his excellent "Historical Introductions to the Symbolical Books" *(Concordia Triglotta,* p. 205) Dr. F. Bente writes: "According to the *Formula of Concord,* all Christians, theologians included, are bound to derive their entire doctrine from the Bible alone; matters of faith must be decided exclusively by clear passages of Holy Scripture; human reason ought not in any point to criticize, and lord it over, the infallible Word of God; reason must be subjected to the obedience of Christ and dare not hinder faith in believing the divine testimonies even when they seemingly contradict each other.

"We are not commanded to harmonize, says the *Formula,* but to believe, confess, defend, and faithfully to adhere to, the teachings of the Bible (1078, 52 ff.).

"In the doctrine of conversion and salvation (election) therefore Lutherans confess both the *sola gratia* and the *universalis gratia,* because they are convinced that both are clearly taught in the Bible and that to reject or modify either of them amounts to a criticism of the Word of God and hence of God Himself.

"Synergists differ from Lutherans, not in maintaining universal grace (which in reality they deny as to intention as well as extension, for they corrupt the Scriptural content of grace by making it dependent on man's conduct and thereby limit its extension to such only as comply with its conditions), but in denying the *sola gratia* and teaching that the will of man enters conversion as a factor alongside of grace.

"And Calvinists differ from Lutherans not in maintaining the *sola gratia, but in denying universal grace."*

But if the Christian believer, on the basis of Scripture, maintains both the *gratia universalis* and the *sola gratia,* then indeed the mystery remains: Why are some elected and others not? *(Cur alii, alii non? Cur alii prae aliis?)* This mystery the true Christian believer does not try to solve since it belongs to God's unsearchable judgments and His ways which are past finding out, Rom. 11, 33—36. But he keeps all his thoughts on the doctrines of eternal election, conversion, and salvation within the revealed teaching of Scripture: He who is saved is saved alone by grace; he who is lost perishes through His own unbelief, Hos. 13, 9. From any attempt to solve the mystery which is involved in the doctrine of eternal election he will abstain all the more, since God's Word tells him that he now knows in part, but that in heaven he shall know even as also he is known, 1 Cor. 13, 12.

In summary, it is clear why so many reject the Scriptural doctrine of eternal election, namely, for the simple reason that they wish to "harmonize the divine testimonies when they seemingly contradict each other" *(universalis gratia; sola gratia)*. Synergism harmonizes the divine testimonies by denying the *sola gratia;* Calvinism, by denying the *universalis gratia.* In both cases, as Dr. F. Bente says, "human reason criticizes, and lords it over, the infallible Word of God."

The real mystery in the doctrine of election exists because Holy Scripture does not explain why "some are struck by the Law and others are not struck, so that the former receive the proffered grace and the latter reject it" (Luther, St. L., XVIII, 1794 ff. 1965 f.). The *Formula of Concord* rightly says that "God has reserved this mystery for His wisdom and has revealed nothing to us concerning it in His Word" (Thor. Decl., XI, 54 f.). In place of this real mystery some Lutheran theologians have put the so-called "psychological mystery" *(das psychologische Geheimnis).* That is to say, "it is impossible for us to understand how a person can resist divine grace after God through His Word has put him into a position in which he can truly and really convert himself." Those who thus operate with a psychological mystery solve the real mystery in the doctrine of election in the old synergistic way; for not only do they assume a *status medius,* in which a still unconverted person can convert himself by means of divinely bestowed powers, but they also explain the question why one is converted and another is not by the synergistic formula: Conversion is due to the better conduct of the converted toward divine grace. For this reason we reject the "psychological mystery" as a synergistic notion and figment. The Scriptural doctrine of election is accepted in its truth and purity by those only who reject *in toto* every form of Pelagianism and rationalism.

In view of the endless confusion which rationalism has caused in the Christian Church by perverting the Scriptural doctrine of eternal election we conclude this article with the sincere prayer with which the *Formula of Concord* closes its treatise on predestination (Epit., XI, 23): "May Almighty God and the Father of our Lord Jesus grant the grace of His Holy Ghost that we all may be one in Him and constantly abide in this Christian unity, which is well-pleasing to Him! Amen."

THE DOCTRINE OF THE LAST THINGS.
(ESCHATOLOGY.)
(De Eschatologia.)

The Doctrine of the Last Things *(de novissimis)* is so called because it treats of that which is "the last," namely, that "with which the present world comes to an end" (Schmid). Of the last things Baier writes: "They are called the last things *(novissima)*, in Greek τὰ ἔσχατα, because some both are, and are called, *last* with respect to men as individuals and others with respect to men collectively and to the whole world. To the former class belong death and the state of the soul after death; to the latter, the resurrection of the dead and the corresponding change of the living, the final Judgment, and the conflagration of the world" (*Doctr. Theol.*, p. 625).

We shall discuss the subject of Eschatology under the following heads: 1) Temporal Death; 2) the Condition of the Soul between Death and the Resurrection *(status medius);* 3) the Second Advent of Christ; 4) the Resurrection of the Dead; 5) the Final Judgment; 6) the End of the World; 7) Eternal Damnation; and 8) Eternal Salvation.

1. TEMPORAL DEATH.
(De Morte Temporali.)

a. *What temporal death is.* Temporal, or bodily, death is not the total annihilation of man (Russellism; atheism), but the deprivation of natural life, occuring through the separation of soul and body (Baier). That temporal death is not the annihilation of the soul is clear from Matt. 10, 28; that it is not the annihilation of the body follows from John 5, 28. 29, where Christ tells us that the dead bodies, though turned to dust, are awaiting in their graves the day of resurrection (cp. also Dan. 12, 2). That death, properly speaking, is separation of the soul from the body is clearly taught in Luke 12, 20: "This night thy soul shall be required of thee"; and in Matt. 27, 50 (John 19, 30), where the death of our Lord on the cross is described as the "yielding up of the ghost," or as the "giving up of the ghost."

Quenstedt fittingly directs attention to the fact that the death of Christian believers is depicted in Scripture by "sweet names," such as "the gathering to their own people," Gen. 25, 8. 17; a "departure in peace," Luke 2, 29; "a turning away from the evil to come," Is. 57, 1; "a resting or sleeping," Matt. 9, 24; 1 Thess. 4, 13; etc. "Death has become the gateway of eternal life."

On the other hand, the death of the wicked is usually described in Scripture by names which in themselves suggest its bitterness and dreadfulness, such as "going to one's place," Acts 1, 25; "being slain by the Lord," Gen. 38, 7; etc.

b. *The cause of temporal death.* The cause of temporal death is not that man was originally created mortal or at least with a propensity to die, Gen. 2, 17, or that the matter of which the body consists is by its very nature perishable (Seneca: *Morieris, ista hominis natura, non poena est;* cp. also similar views of the Pelagians and Unitarians), but that man has fallen into sin, Gen. 2, 17; 3, 17 ff.; Rom. 5, 12; 6, 23. Luther: *"Der Tod kann die Suende nicht wegnehmen, weil er selbst verflucht und eben die ewige Strafe des Zornes Gottes ist."*

The view of some modern theologians (Kirn) that death existed already before sin, but became a punishment through sin, is unscriptural (ἄτερ γραφῆς). According to Holy Scripture, death did not exist until sin came into the world, Ps. 90, 7. 8. Death is therefore a direct punishment *(malum poenae),* which God inflicts upon guilty man by His vindictive justice *(iustitia vindicativa).*

Other causes of death which Scripture mentions must always be viewed in connection with man's fall and subsequent transgressions. Thus Satan is a cause of death inasmuch as he is a "murderer from the beginning," John 8, 44, while Adam is a cause of the death of all his descendants, Rom. 5, 12, because his guilt is imputed to all his children *(culpa hereditaria).*

All calamities, such as pestilences, storms, famines, floods, the sword, etc. (Rom. 8, 35. 36), are properly called "instrumental causes" *(Mittelursachen)* of death because they directly bring about the destruction of life; but they are instrumental causes of death only because sin, its principal and primary cause, has "entered into the world," Rom. 5, 12 ff. Hence we must not regard death as "nature's way of ridding itself of the unfit" (Modernists), but absolutely and solely as the "wages of sin," Rom. 6, 23. This truth the Christian believer must constantly keep in mind; for if he denies that death is a punishment of sin, he can neither understand properly nor estimate rightly Christ's atoning death on the cross. In fact, quite consistently those who have denied the guilt of sin as the sole cause of death (rationalists) have denied also the vicarious atonement *(satisfactio vicaria)* of Christ.

c. *The subjects of death.* Scripture teaches plainly that all descendants of Adam are subject to death (Rom. 5, 12: "Death passed upon all men for that all have sinned"); and this fact is corroborated by experience. Hence all attempts to find a cure for death are *a priori* futile. The only way in which sinful man may be freed from death is through faith in Christ, "who hath abolished death and hath brought life and immortality to light," 2 Tim. 1, 10; for while also the Christian believer is subject to temporal death, he does not "taste of death," John 8, 52; 11, 25. 26.

If the question is asked why also believers in Christ must die, Scripture replies, a) that they, too, are sinners according to the flesh (παλαιὸς ἄνθρωπος), so that also in their case death is the wages of sin, Rom. 6, 23; 7, 24; but b) that in their case death is not joined with the sense of divine wrath *(sensus irae divinae)* or the "sting of death," 1 Cor. 15, 55—57, so that to them death is no longer death in its proper sense, but a blessed sleep in Jesus, 1 Thess. 4, 13. 14; Luke 23, 43; Phil. 1, 23.

The *Apology* writes (Art. VI, 56): "Death itself serves this purpose, namely, to abolish this flesh of sin that we may rise absolutely new. Neither is there now in the death of the believer, since by faith he has overcome the terrors of death, that sting and sense of wrath of which Paul speaks, 1 Cor. 15, 56. This strength of sin, this sense of wrath, is truly a punishment as long as it is present; without this sense of wrath, death is not properly a punishment."

Instead of the sense of divine wrath *(sensus irae)* the Christian by faith rather experiences the sense of divine grace *(sensus gratiae),* so that, when death approaches him, he joyously commends his soul to His Redeemer and departs in peace, Luke 2, 29. 30; Acts 7, 59. (Cp. Luther, St. L., I, 1512.)

Moreover, the Christian believer knows by faith that he is free from the "second death," Rev. 20, 14, or eternal damnation, John 3, 16—18; 5, 24; 1 John 3, 14 (cp. Luther, St. L., I, 1514), so that temporal death is without terror for him, Rev. 14, 13.

Lastly, the Christian believer is also comforted by the "sweet names" *(epitheta ornantia)* which Holy Scripture ascribes to the death of God's saints. (Cp. Luther, St. L., XIII, 1328 ff.; VIII, 1230.) These sweet names *(mortis dulcia nomina)* are not empty titles, but true and blessed Gospel assurances of God's grace and love, which give ineffable consolation to the dying believer.

2. THE CONDITION OF THE SOUL BETWEEN DEATH AND THE RESURRECTION.

The number of Scripture-passages which describe the condition of the soul after death is comparatively small, since Holy Scripture principally directs the attention of Christian believers to the day of Judgment and the eternal salvation following it rather than to the blessedness which they enjoy immediately after death, 1 Cor. 1, 7; Phil. 3, 20. 21; Col. 3, 4; 1 Thess. 4, 13 ff.; 2 Tim. 4, 7. 8; Titus 2, 13. The Christian believer therefore patiently "waits" for the coming of our Lord Jesus Christ and rejoices in the glorious redemption which this day of salvation promises to him, Matt. 24, 44—46; Luke 21, 31. As Holy Scripture comforts the believer preeminently with the glory of Christ's second advent, so also it warns the unbeliever mainly by reminding him of the certainty of the final Judgment, 2 Thess. 1, 9. 10; Heb. 10, 27; 2 Pet. 2, 3—6; Jude 6. 7, rather than by direct references to his punishment after death, although such passages are not wholly lacking, Heb. 9, 27; Luke 16, 22. 23.

The godly should therefore always rejoice in Christ's second coming, Matt. 25, 34, while the ungodly must constantly dread His righteous judgment as the great and everlasting punishment which he shall not escape, Matt. 25, 41. 46.

Nevertheless Holy Scripture speaks also of the condition of the soul after death. It tells us that the souls of the ungodly are "spirits in prison," 1 Pet. 3, 19, and that they suffer excruciating and endless torments, Luke 16, 23—31, so that death leads them directly into everlasting agony and anguish, Ps. 106, 16—18.

On the other hand, Scripture assures us that the souls of the godly are in God's hand, Acts 7, 59. 60; Luke 23, 46, that they are with Christ in paradise, Phil. 1, 23; Luke 23, 43, and that they are supremely happy, Rev. 14, 13, in their new heavenly life, Ps. 16, 11; John 17, 24; Rom. 8, 18. In fact, they are so completely removed from all earthly trouble and sorrow that they are altogether ignorant of those who live upon earth, Is. 63, 16, and their needs no longer concern them, Is. 57, 1. 2.

Hence we conclude that the souls of the believers are in a condition of perfect blessedness and of perpetual enjoyment of God, though we cannot picture to ourselves in what manner this wonderful fruition of celestial bliss takes place. We therefore reject every kind of soul sleep (psychopannychism) which excludes the active enjoyment of God on the part of the departed believer, Phil. 1, 23; Luke 23, 43.

The statements of Scripture that "the dead sleep," 1 Cor. 15, 18, or that "the dead do not praise God," Ps. 6, 5, or that "they enter into rest," Heb. 4, 3, etc., do not prove the insensibility of the soul after death, but are figurative expressions, used in a sense which Scripture clearly explains.

To draw inferences with regard to the condition of the soul after death from the nature of the soul ("The soul is never inactive," etc.) is not permissible, since the conclusions so reached are most uncertain, and, above all, since Scripture is the only source and standard of faith, and its teaching must not be supplemented by human speculation.

A psychopannychy which includes a real enjoyment of heavenly bliss (Luther) must not be rejected as wrong since it does not contradict Scripture. Luther writes (St. L., I, 1758 ff.; II, 215 ff.): "It is divine truth that Abraham [after death] lives with God, serves Him, and rules with Him. But what kind of life that is, whether he sleeps or is awake, is a different question. How the soul rests we cannot know; but it is certain that it lives."

With respect to the habitation of the souls (paradise, prison, φυλακή) Gerhard writes: "Scripture, by a general appellation, speaks of a place, John 14, 2; Luke 16, 28; Acts 1, 25. Not that it is a corporeal and physical place, properly so called, but because it is a 'where' (ποῦ) into which souls, separated from their bodies, are brought together. Scripture enumerates only two such receptacles, or habitations, of the souls, one of which, prepared for the souls of the godly, is called by the most ordinary appellation *heaven,* and the other, intended for the souls of the wicked, is called *hell.*" (*Doctr. Theol.,* p. 632.)

The so-called purgatory *(purgatorium,* as also the *limbus infantium* and the *limbus patrum),* in which, according to papistic doctrine, the souls of believers must expiate the temporal punishments for their sins, is a figment of reason; for Scripture teaches that all believers through faith in Christ obtain (not purgatory, but) eternal life, John 5, 24; 3, 36. Moreover, it expressly teaches that not only the souls of saints, such as St. Paul and Stephen (Phil. 1, 23; Acts 7, 59), but also those of great sinners, converted in the last hour, such as the thief on the cross, entered with Christ into paradise, Luke 23, 43. (Cp. Luther on purgatory. St. L., II, 2067 ff.)

Among modern Protestant theologians Kahnis advocated the doctrine of purgatory. He writes: "In the idea of a purgatory there undoubtedly is some truth, namely, that many Christians still need a purging. Great is the number of Christians of whom it cannot be said that Christ is their life. But they are drawn to Him and confess that which they have known of Him with a sincerity, disinterestedness, and faithfulness in conduct which ought to put to shame many Christians who are stronger in words than in works." (Pieper, *Christl. Dogmatik,* III, 576.)

However, a Protestant purgatory has no more Scriptural foundation than has the papistic purgatory; for Christ promises to all who believe in Him eternal life, John 5, 24; 3, 36. In addition, Scripture teaches that only the blood of Christ cleanses from sin, 1 John 1, 7, and not man's work or suffering, Gal. 3, 10. Not even faith purges from sin inasmuch as it is a human work, Rom. 4, 3—5; it saves only because it is the receiving means (*medium* $\lambda\eta\pi\tau\iota\kappa\acute{o}\nu$), which lays hold of Christ's righteousness and thus regenerates the heart and frees the believer from the curse and dominion of sin, Rom. 6, 2. 14. All Protestant theologians who join Rome in teaching a purgatory *eo ipso* reject the *sola fide* and espouse the doctrine of work-righteousness.

From the many Scripture promises which are made to Christian believers it is clear that the soul of the dying Christian is entirely cleansed from all original and actual sin; for it is then in "paradise," the holy abode of God's perfected saints, Phil. 1, 23; Luke 23, 43. (Cp. Luther, St. L., X, 2119 ff.) Luther very aptly calls death the "last purgatory" of the Christians, meaning by this that the soul of the believer, after departing in Christ, is wholly free from sin.

With regard to purgatory, Hafenreffer writes: "Everything that is ascribed to the satisfactions either of purgatory or of the intercession of the saints is detracted from the merit of Christ, which alone cleanses us from sin." (*Doctr. Theol.,* p. 636.) The Lutheran Church thus rejects the doctrine of purgatory as conflicting with that of justification by faith alone.

Among modern Protestant theologians some (Schleiermacher) taught that the soul during the *status medius* (the time between death and the resurrection) must be endowed with a certain temporary body *(Zwischenleib),* since otherwise it could hardly exist (Macpherson: "The individual wears a body suitable to his condition during that period") But of such a temporary body Scripture knows nothing at all. The Christian believer may rest assured that God, who so wondrously created the soul for the body, is able to take care of it also while it is outside the body, 2 Cor. 5, 1—9.

The appearance of "Samuel" (1 Sam. 28) is best explained as a delusion of Satan (1 Sam. 28, 19: "Thou and thy sons shall be with me"). Those who hold that in this instance God really permitted Samuel to appear must regard his appearance as an exception to His fixed rule and must maintain, on the basis of Scripture, that Spiritism is a work and fraud of Satan, Deut. 18, 10—12.

With respect to the departed souls we may summarize the teachings of Scripture as follows: a) The departed souls do not return to earth, Luke 16, 27—31; the appearance of Moses and Elijah at the transfiguration of Christ, Matt. 17, 3, was not an exception to this rule, since these saints may be classified among the risen, Deut. 34, 6; 2 Kings 2, 11. b) The departed souls are ignorant of those living upon earth and of their affairs, Is. 63, 16. c) The adoration of the departed saints is not only unreasonable, but also idolatrous, Matt. 4, 10. d) Scripture emphatically denies the erroneous opinion of those rationalistic theologians who claim that even after death conversion is possible, Heb. 9, 27.

In 1 Pet. 3, 18. 19 St. Peter does not speak of the preaching of the Gospel, but rather of the proclamation of the divine judgment to those who during their life despised the saving Word of God. The ἐκήρυξεν ("He preached") denotes Law-preaching, and not Gospel-preaching, as the context shows.

3. THE SECOND ADVENT OF CHRIST.

Holy Scripture teaches most emphatically that in His appointed hour (Acts 1, 7; John 5, 28. 29) Christ, the God-man (Matt. 25, 31), will appear visibly (Acts 1, 9. 11) to all men at the same time (Matt. 24, 27. 30; 1 Thess. 5, 2) in divine glory, and surrounded by His assisting angels (Matt. 25, 31; 1 Thess. 4, 16; Matt. 13, 41. 42), to judge "all nations of the earth" (Matt. 25, 31), both the living and the dead, the latter after their resurrection (1 Cor. 15, 51; Dan. 12, 2; John 5, 28. 29), to cast the wicked into eternal hell-fire (Matt. 25, 46), and to lead His saints into eternal glory (Heb. 9, 28), so that the Church Militant *(ecclesia militans)* will in all eternity be the Church Triumphant *(ecclesia triumphans)*. (Cp. Luther, St. L., IX, 951 f.)

The Scriptural doctrine of Christ's glorious return must be emphasized both over against the blasphemies of the ungodly,

2 Pet. 3, 3. 4, and the forgetfulness of Christian believers, who because of the weakness of their flesh are prone to overlook their glorious hope, Mark 13, 23.

With respect to the exact time of Christ's second advent Holy Scripture teaches that this is both unknown, Matt. 24, 36; Mark 13, 32, and unknowable to men, 1 Thess. 5, 2. 3; Matt. 24, 44; Mark 13, 33—36. If in spite of Christ's warning even believing theologians (Bengel: 1836 is the day of the Lord's return) have tried to compute the time of His second advent, this proves how deeply sinful curiosity (Acts 1, 6) is embedded in the human heart.

However, while Christians should not try to compute the time of the Lord's return (against Russellism, Adventism, etc.), they should carefully observe the signs of the times, which God has appointed in order to arouse His saints to greater watchfulness and preparedness, Matt. 24, 32. 33; Luke 21, 29—31; 2 Thess. 2, 3 ff. Concerning the signs of the times Luther rightly says that "all creatures serve this day by means of signs" (St. L., XI, 59).

Among the signs of the times Holy Scripture names abnormal conditions a) in the realm of human activity and life (warfare, hatred against the Church, pestilences, famines, general distress, great wickedness, Matt. 24, 5—14. 37—39); b) in the realm of nature (earthquakes, floods, disturbances in the movements of the celestial bodies, Luke 21, 25. 26); c) in the realm of the Church (the rise of false teachers, apostasy from Christ, Antichrist, Luke 21, 8. 16. 17; 2 Thess. 2, 3. 4); etc. As sickness is a sign of the impending dissolution of the individual person (microcosm), so also the disturbances in the world (macrocosm) foretell its final destruction. (Cp. Luther, St. L., VII, 1480 ff.)

That these signs are not recognized as such by men is a proof of the amazing stupor *(mirabilis stupor)* which sin has wrought in man (Luther, St. L., I, 254 ff.). As Luther rightly says, man after the Fall lives in a veritable "Egyptian darkness" (St. L., I, 255).

Especially is the wanton persecution of Christ and His Gospel a most certain sign of the coming Judgment; for this sin of sins involves the basest ingratitude on the part of man. After Christ has redeemed the whole world by His holy suffering and death, all men should gladly worship Him and join and support His Church; but instead they persecute those who love and serve Christ, Matt. 24, 9; John 16, 2; Matt. 10, 17; Rom. 8, 36; Acts 14, 5. 6. 19; 16, 22 ff.

Despite this shameful ingratitude of men (Modernism; Anti-

_nrist), Christ most graciously preserves His Word upon earth and has it preached in all the world for a witness unto all nations, Matt. 24, 14. But this is at the same time an outstanding sign of the times (Matt. 24, 14: "Then shall the end come").

With respect to the signs which foreshadowed the destruction of Jerusalem and at the same time that of the world, Matt. 24, 2—14. 15—31. 32—51; 16, 27. 28, Dr. Stoeckhardt rightly remarks that the destruction of Jerusalem was "both a sign of the day of Judgment and the beginning of the final Judgment" (*Bibl. Gesch. d. N. T.,* p. 256). The "epitelesmatic" character of divine prophecy in general explains also this particular prediction; for in one undivided prophetic vision the Lord here views both the things that are near and those that are farther removed, that is, both the destruction of Jerusalem and that of the world.

With respect to the question whether the signs of the times have been fulfilled, Luther declares that "these signs have already largely *(das mehrere Teil)* come to pass, so that we cannot expect many others" (St. L., XI, 50f.). But to this we must add that intentionally the signs have been so arranged by God that no one can compute the exact day or hour of the Lord's second coming. Thus even during the apostolic period it could be said, *e. g.,* with regard to the sign given by Christ Matt. 24, 14, that the Christian faith was spoken of "throughout the whole world," Rom. 1, 8;. 10, 18; 1 Thess. 1, 8; Acts 19, 10; 1 Tim. 3, 16.

The purpose of the signs is not to lead Christian believers to determine the hour of the Lord's coming, but to incite them to perpetual watchfulness, Matt. 24, 42. There is a certain analogy between the end of the world and the death of the individual Christian; for while no one can know just when he will die, every one should always be prepared to meet God when in His appointed hour death should come to him, Amos 4, 12; 2 Cor. 5, 9.

The Lutheran Church, on the basis of Holy Scripture, rejects the doctrine of the MILLENNIUM as a figment of the human mind. The *Augsburg Confession* (Art. XVII) voices its disagreement with millennialism when it says: "They condemn also others, who are now spreading certain Jewish opinions, that before the resurrection of the dead the godly shall take possession of the kingdom of the world, the ungodly being everywhere suppressed."

The "Jewish opinion" (Acts 1, 6) appeared early in the Christian Church and was known as chiliasm (an earthly reign of Christ lasting a thousand years). It was taught and defended in many forms *(chiliasmus crassissimus, crassus, subtilis)*. While this classification is not quite accurate, it is helpful in distinguishing between the various types of chiliasm.

The crassest chiliasts *(crassissimi)* expect a period of great spiritual and temporal blessedness, during which the consequences of sin upon man and the world will be removed.

The cross chiliasts *(crassi)* expect the destruction of Antichrist and the general conversion of the Jews, so that during a thousand years the Christian Church will enjoy a period of great peace and prosperity. This type of chiliasm teaches a twofold visible return of Christ and a twofold resurrection of the dead and either includes or excludes the earthly reign of Christ in Jerusalem and the Holy Land.

It is a characteristic of the fanciful dream of chiliasm that its advocates never agree among themselves on particulars; the various theories are so contradictory that the whole subject becomes repulsive to the student of doctrinal aberrations because of its very complexity and inconsistency.

The subtle chiliasts *(subtiles)* reject the doctrine of the twofold coming and resurrection, but expect a period of unusual growth and prosperity for the Christian Church (Spener) before the world will be finally destroyed.

Millennialism (millenarianism) has no Scriptural foundation whatever. The passages which are usually quoted in its favor (Is. 2, 2—4; 11, 6—9; Zech. 9, 9. 10; Joel 3, 2 ff; Micah 4, 1—4; Rev. 20, 1—10) do not predict a millennial reign at all, but describe the spiritual glory of the Church of the New Testament, which is brought about through the coming of the Messiah and the preaching of the Gospel throughout the whole world, Luke 2, 13. 14; 1, 76—79; 1, 46—55.

Chiliasm is not only unscriptural, however, but also anti-Scriptural. It expressly contradicts Holy Scripture, which plainly teaches, a) that the time of the New Testament, and especially the last days before Christ's coming, shall be a period of great persecution and suffering for all who love the Lord Jesus Christ, John 16, 33; Matt. 24, 9—13. 21—27; Luke 21, 16. 17; and b) that Christ's kingdom is not earthly and external, but spiritual and internal, John 14, 27; 16, 33; Rom. 5, 1—5; Luke 17, 20. 21; Mark 1, 14. 15; Luke 10, 9—11; Rom. 14, 17—19. Moreover, by directing the Christian hope to a worldly reign of Christ, chiliasm misdirects and thus destroys the true Christian hope, which steadfastly

looks for that wonderful glory of heaven, Phil. 3, 20. 21; 1 Cor.
1, 6—8, into which the Church Militant shall be gathered at
Christ's second coming, Matt. 25, 34; 5, 3. 10—12.

To the objection of chiliasts that the small earthly Church of
Christ which we see now certainly does not represent the glorious
Church of our Lord we reply that our Savior deliberately foretells
and describes the small size (Luke 12, 32; Matt. 20, 16), the distress and tribulation (Acts 14, 22), and the apparent defeat (Matt.
24, 37. 38) of His Church on earth in order that His followers may
be kept from the deceitful snares of all chiliastic delusions, Matt.
24, 42—51.

Again, millennialism opposes other clearly established Scriptural truths; for it affirms a) a twofold visible coming of Christ,
contrary to the express teaching of Heb. 9, 28, and b) a twofold
resurrection, contrary to John 6, 40.

If chiliasts contend that millennialism is at least a beautiful
hope, which ought not to be weakened or destroyed in those who
hold it, we answer that nothing is good or beautiful that is opposed
to the teaching of Scripture. Eve, too, regarded the fruit of the
forbidden tree as beautiful, Gen. 3, 6; but the beautiful thought
of eating of the tree was a delusion of Satan, 1 Tim. 2, 14, which
resulted in her transgression and brought upon her and all her
descendants unspeakable woe.

Similarly many regard the thought of having a vicar of Christ
on earth to rule over the Church as very beautiful, 2 Thess. 2,
9—12; but the result is Antichrist, a servant of Satan, 2 Thess.
2, 3. 4, who misleads thousands into eternal damnation, 2 Thess.
2, 12, through his very external piety.

Chiliasm is Satan's most subtle way of inducing believers to
regard the crucified Christ as a stumbling-block and foolishness,
1 Cor. 1, 23; for their chiliastic dream is really the effect of their
inward dissatisfaction with the lowliness of Christ's Church
on earth.

To the objection that at least Rev. 20, 2 teaches a millennium,
we reply, a) that this passage does not teach a millennium at all,
since those "who lived and reigned with Christ a thousand years"
are clearly described as "the souls of them that were beheaded
for the witness of Jesus and for the Word of God," Rev. 20, 4,
so that the vision depicts not an earthly, but a heavenly scene;
b) that the whole passage, Rev. 20, 1—10, is so obscure, that it
cannot be a *sedes doctrinae* for chiliasm, especially since hardly

two interpreters will explain it alike; c) that the "little season" (μικρὸς χρόνος) together with the "thousand years" embraces the entire time of the New Testament (Luther), since immediately after this "little season" the last Judgment will follow, Rev. 20, 10; and d) that, since the Apocalypse is a prophetic book, "so full of obscure visions as well as allegorical and quasi-enigmatical forms of speech, extremely difficult to be understood, it must be expounded according to the analogy of faith or the clear and perspicuous Scripture passages" (Hollaz), which foretell the eschatological events in clear and unmistakable language.

As the millennium, so also the "GENERAL CONVERSION OF THE JEWS" is a figment of human reason. The champions of this error base their doctrine on Rom. 11, 26: "And so all Israel shall be saved." But that this passage does not teach a general conversion of all Jews is clear a) from the context, which shows that the apostle understands the expression *all Israel* (πᾶς Ἰσραήλ) in the sense of *"the elect of Israel"* (v. 28: "As touching the election, they are beloved");· and b) from the fact that in other passages he clearly states the fact that not all Jews, but only the elect will be saved (Rom. 11, 5: "There is a *remnant* according to the election of grace"; v. 7: "The election hath obtained it, and the rest were blinded").

St. Paul thus clearly distinguishes between spiritual Israel (Ἰσραὴλ κατὰ πνεῦμα), which shall be saved, and carnal Israel (Ἰσραὴλ κατὰ σάρκα), which shall be damned. Cp. Rom. 9, 6: "They are not all Israel which are of Israel"; v. 7: "Neither because they are the seed of Abraham, are they all children; but, In Isaac shall thy *seed* be called"; v. 8: "They which are *the children of the flesh,* these are *not the children of God;* but the children of the promise* are counted for the *seed"; v. 27: "Though the number of the children of Israel be as the sand of the sea, a *remnant* shall be saved"; v. 31: "Israel, which *followed after the law of righteousness,* hath not attained to the law of righteousness."

From this we conclude that the "all Israel that shall be saved" (Rom. 11, 26) is the spiritual Israel (the elect in Israel), just as the expression "fulness of the Gentiles" (Rom. 11, 25) denotes the elect of God among the Gentiles. The determination of time "until" (Rom. 11, 25: *"until [ἄχρι οὗ]* the fulness of the Gentiles be come in") stresses the truth that, as long as Gentiles shall be converted and saved, so long also shall the elect in Israel be brought in, that is, until the end of the world, Matt. 24, 14. The words "and so" (Rom. 11, 26: *καὶ οὕτως*) describe the manner in which "all Israel shall be saved," namely, by the divine calling of the elect in Israel through the Gospel, by which also the "fulness of the Gentiles shall come in," Rom. 10, 13—18.

In accord with this principle the apostles preached the Gospel to both Jews and Gentiles, Acts 13, 14—52, that during the same New Testament time of grace "all Israel" and "the fulness of the Gentiles" might come in, Rom. 10, 1—4. Just so the Church of Christ must preach the Gospel of salvation to every creature and make disciples of all nations till the end of time, Mark 16, 15. 16; Matt. 28, 20; for through the blessed proclamation of the Gospel the elect among both Jews and Gentiles will be saved, Acts 13, 43—49. (Cp. *Christl. Dogmatik,* III, 584 ff.)

The return of the Jews to Palestine, which is usually made a concomitant of the general conversion of the Jews, is based upon a bare literalism in interpreting Old Testament prophecies (Is. 11, 11. 12; Amos 9, 11—15; Ezek. 40—48; Zech. 6, 12; etc.), which is as unscriptural as it is ridiculous. (Cp. St. L., XIV, 53.) These passages of course foretell and describe the building of the New Testament Church in Old Testament phraseology.

4. THE RESURRECTION OF THE DEAD.
(De Resurrectione Mortuorum.)

While the doctrine of the resurrection of the dead is both doubted (1 Cor. 15, 35) and blasphemed (Acts 17, 32) by the ungodly, contrary to their own natural knowledge of God as the almighty Creator and King of the universe, who can do all things, Rom. 1, 19. 20, so that their unbelief is inexcusable, 1 Cor. 15, 35 f., it is to the believing Christian a source of supreme joy and sweet consolation, 1 Cor. 15, 20—22 (Third Article: "I believe in the resurrection of the dead").

The doctrine of the resurrection is taught not only in the New, but also in the Old Testament, Job 19, 25. 26; Is. 26, 19; Dan. 12, 2. The Sadducees, who denied the resurrection, were reproved by Christ as errorists, who "knew not the Scriptures," Matt. 22, 29. At the same time Christ pointed out to them the large number of passages in the Old Testament which attest the resurrection, when He said: "As touching the resurrection of the dead, have ye not read that which was spoken unto you by God, saying, I am the God of Abraham and the God of Isaac and the God of Jacob? God is not the God of the dead, but of the living,"

Matt. 22, 31. 32.   Hence, wherever in the Old Testament we read the gracious promise: "I am thy God," we have a passage teaching the resurrection of the dead, since "God is not the God of the dead, but of the living," Gen. 17, 7; 26, 24; 28, 13; Ezek. 37, 27; etc.

Luther therefore is fully justified in saying that in Gen. 3, 15 also the abolition of death and the resurrection are taught, since death is the wages of sin.   He writes (St. L., I, 240): "This passage embraces the redemption from the Law, sin, and death and points out a clear and sure hope of the resurrection and the renovation in a life after this.   For if the head of the serpent should be bruised, then also death must be abolished and annulled."

We therefore maintain that the Christian faith in the resurrection of the dead is as old as is the proclamation of the Gospel. It is a mistake on the part of modern theologians to claim that the doctrine of the resurrection was only gradually developed among the believers (Luthardt, *Dogmatik,* p. 412; Voigt: "The doctrine of the resurrection is found only in the later books of the Old Testament." *Biblical Dogmatics,* p. 239).

In opposition to this we hold that the doctrine of the resurrection is found not only in such passages as Dan. 12, 2; Ps. 17, 15; Hos. 13, 14; Is. 26, 19; Ezek. 37, 1—10; Job 19, 25—27, but also in all passages in which God reveals Himself as the God of His people, individually or collectively, Ex. 3, 6. 13; 4, 5, etc. Hofmann rightly says: "Nothing can be more erroneous than the opinion that the doctrine of the resurrection is a later idea, which resulted from human speculation. . . . There is no time in which faith can be conceived without this hope."

Since the doctrine of the resurrection belongs to the primary fundamental articles, without which the Christian faith cannot exist, 2 Tim. 2, 17. 18; 1 Tim. 1, 19. 20, Hofmann's statement that "faith cannot be conceived without this hope" is indeed Scriptural. The Old Testament believers would certainly have "made shipwreck concerning faith," 1 Tim. 1, 19, had they not believed in the resurrection.

It is nevertheless true that the full and complete revelation concerning the resurrection came with Christ and the fulness of His Gospel-preaching, John 5, 28. 29; 6, 39. 40; 1 Thess. 4, 16; 1 Cor. 15; etc.

According to Scripture the resurrection of the dead consists formally a) in the restoration of the same body which has perished by death, out of its atoms or particles that have been scattered and

THE DOCTRINE OF THE LAST THINGS (ESCHATOLOGY).

dispersed, Job 19, 25—27; 1 Cor. 15, 42—49; and b) in the reunion of the body with the soul, 1 Thess. 4, 14—17. The resurrection therefore lies beyond the comprehension of man; it is
a miracle of God's omnipotence, just as is creation, 2 Cor. 1, 9;
Rom. 4, 17.

Since the divine power, just as the divine essence, belongs to
the three Persons in the Godhead without division or multiplication
(una numero essentia, una numero potentia), Scripture ascribes
the resurrection sometimes to the Father and sometimes to the Son
in the same manner, John 5, 21, and to the latter not merely according to His divine, but also according to His human nature
(John 5, 22. 27: "because He is the Son of Man"). The divine-
human Redeemer of the world is also its divine Resurrector and
Judge (John 5, 28: "All that are in the graves shall hear His [the
Son of Man's] voice").

The fact that the *Verbum incarnatum* (λόγος ἔνσαρκος), or the
God-man, is the omnipotent Lord, who on the Last Day will bless
or condemn (Acts 17, 31: "by that Man"), is of great comfort to
all believers, John 11, 23—27; Rev. 1, 5. 6, while to all unbelievers
it is a cause of unspeakable terror, John 19, 37; Rev. 1, 7; 6, 16. 17.

That the denial of the communication of divine actions
(actiones) to the human nature is a most pernicious error (cp. the
Calvinistic denial of the *genus maiestaticum*) is proved convincingly by the very passages of Scripture which describe the resurrection and the final Judgment as the work of the Son of Man.

With respect to the question, Who will be raised from the dead?
(subiectum quod resurrectionis), Scripture answers very clearly
that all men will rise again, both believers, 1 Cor. 15, 20—22;
1 Thess. 4, 13—18, and unbelievers, John 5, 28; Acts 24, 15.
Unitarians and other antichristian sects have invariably denied
the resurrection of the wicked (Socinians, Adventists, Russellites, etc.); but Scripture asserts this fact in unmistakable terms.
While Christ's exhortation to rise spiritually through faith in His
divine Gospel promises, Matt. 11, 28—30, can be resisted, Matt.
23, 37, since He now works through means *(potentia ordinata)*,
His command on the day of Judgment to rise bodily from the grave
cannot be resisted, Matt. 25, 31. 32, since He will then exert His
divine power without means *(potentia absoluta, efficacia irresistibilis, in nuda maiestate, ἐν τῇ δόξῃ αὐτοῦ)*.

If the question is asked, Just what of man will rise from the
dead? *(subiectum quo resurrectionis)*, Scripture designates "the

entire man that previously died" (Quenstedt; Dan. 12, 2; John 5, 28. 29), in particular the body, the same in number and essence which was born in this life and which perished through death, Job 19, 25—27; Is. 26, 19; Rom. 8, 11; 1 Cor. 15, 53; 2 Cor. 5, 4; Phil. 3, 21.

The body, of course, will be united with the soul, as the very concept of resurrection implies; for as death is the separation of the body and soul, so the resurrection is the reunion of the body with the soul. *Vox ἀναστάσεως importat iteratam stationem eius, quod ante steterat et ceciderat.* Hence all who deny the numerical identity of the dead and the raised body deny *eo ipso* also the resurrection. Neither the resurrection nor the "change" (1 Cor. 15, 51. 52: "We shall all be changed in a moment, in the twinkling of an eye") of those who will live when the day of Judgment breaks will destroy the identity of the body. All those who doubt or deny the possibility of the resurrection our sovereign Lord reproves very severely: "Ye do err, not knowing . . . the power of God," Matt. 22, 29.

However, while the same body will rise from the grave, it will have new qualities. The resurrected bodies of the believers will be spiritual (σώματα πνευματικά), 1 Cor. 15, 51. 52, that is, suited to the spiritual, heavenly life with God in glory. Holy Scripture describes the spiritual bodies of God's saints as incorruptible, glorious, and powerful, 1 Cor. 15, 42—45; as "fashioned like unto His [Christ's] glorious body," Phil. 3, 21; and lastly as "like unto the angels of God in heaven," Luke 20, 36; Matt. 22, 30. This similarity, however, must not be extended to the bodilessness and sexlessness of the angels; for while the human body will not perform its former earthly functions in heaven (cp. the error of the Mormons), it will nevertheless be essentially the same body that lived upon earth, 1 Cor. 15, 47—49.

Luther thus says (St. L., VIII, 1222): "The body remains according to its nature, but not the same use of the body [remains]." (Cp. also IX, 1242 f.) Luther correctly describes the "natural body" (σῶμα ψυχικόν), 1 Cor. 15, 44, as "the whole man as he lives with his five senses in this world and sustains himself by eating, drinking, maintaining house and home, wife and children," etc., but the "spiritual body" (σῶμα πνευματικόν) as the glorified body, fitted for heavenly bliss. Of the saints of Christ Holy Scripture tells us in particular that "the righteous shall shine forth as the sun in the kingdom of their Father," Matt. 13, 43.

That the bodies will rise in the same stature in which they were in death (children, youth, men, old men, etc.) is quite probable, since in the Book of Revelation we read: "And I saw the dead, small and great, stand before God," Rev. 20, 12.

It goes without saying that the bodies of the righteous there will have no physical defects nor any traces of age or suffering, since all these are the consequences of sin. Chemnitz is correct when he says (*De Duabis Naturis,* p. 175): "The bodies are heavenly, not with respect to substance, but with respect to qualities, because they will shine with heavenly light and glory, will no longer be subject to earthly infirmities, but will be distinguished by their heavenly luster and no longer be disfigured, corrupt, imperfect, maimed, and unsightly, but most beautiful, pleasing to the sight, perfect, handsome, and complete in members, etc. An illustration of these qualities is presented to us in the body of Christ, as raised from the dead and placed at the right hand of God, to which our body is to be made like." (*Doctr. Theol.,* p. 642 f.)

Since the ungodly remain in their sin and under the divine curse, John 3, 18. 36, their bodies will come forth from the graves "unto shame and everlasting contempt," Dan. 12, 2, so that all the defects and consequences of sin will be the more visible in their bodies, raised to everlasting disgrace.

Chemnitz writes of this: "Although the bodies of the wicked and the damned will be incorruptible and immortal, yet they will not be impassible, but will be subject to eternal tortures and will be adorned by no honor, no glory, no power, no spiritual excellence, but will be marked by perpetual foulness and ignominy, destined to eternal disgrace, and oppressed by infernal darkness. They are vessels made unto dishonor and disgrace, Rom. 9, 21; 2 Tim. 2, 20." (*Doctr. Theol.,* p. 643.)

While the righteous shall rise from the dead by virtue of the merit of Christ, 1 Cor. 15, 20—22, the godless will rise by the divine power communicated to Christ's human nature through the personal union and exaltation to the right hand of God, by which He sustains, rules, and governs all things in heaven and earth in His general Kingdom of Power *(regnum potentiae),* John 5, 25—29. As Gerhard well remarks, the resurrection of the godless pertains to Christ's functions as Judge and not to His functions as Mediator and Savior (*Doctr. Theol.,* p. 643).

The view of some modern theologians (Kahnis, Nitzsch, Martensen, etc.) that a germ of the resurrection body is implanted in the believers in this life, which either develops into, or serves as the nucleus of, the glorified body, is unscriptural. Holy Scripture does not teach such an *Auferstehungsleib,* nor does it say that it is implanted in the believer through the use of the Lord's Supper.

5. THE FINAL JUDGMENT.
(De Iudicio Extremo.)

Immediately upon the second advent of Christ and the resurrection of the dead there will follow the final Judgment (Matt. 25, 31. 32: "When the Son of Man shall come in His glory, . . . *then* shall He sit upon the throne of His glory, and before Him shall be gathered all nations"). This immediate connection of the second coming of Christ with the general resurrection and the final Judgment excludes every possibility of a millennium; for when Scripture speaks of the last things *ex professo (sedes doctrinae),* it leaves no room for a chiliastic earthly kingdom of Christ.

Those who will be judged are all men without exception, the pious as well as the impious, 2 Cor. 5, 10; Rom. 14, 10, the living as well as the dead, Acts 10, 42, as also the evil angels, 2 Pet. 2, 4; Jude 6. The basis of Christ's judgment will be His revealed truth, the Word of God, as Scripture clearly attests, Rom. 2, 16; John 12, 48; Rev. 20, 12. The norm of judgment *(norma iudicii)* will be the works of men, 2 Cor. 5, 10; Matt. 25, 35—45. But the righteous will be judged only according to their good works, Matt. 25, 34—40; Rev. 12, 11, since their evil works, or sins, have been cast into the depths of the sea, Micah 7, 19, or forgiven.

When, on the one hand, Holy Scripture declares that all men will be judged (2 Cor. 5, 10; Rom. 14, 10: "we," that is, believers), and, on the other, that the believer in Christ will not come into condemnation (John 5, 24: εἰς κρίσιν οὐκ ἔρχεται), this seeming contradiction is the old contradiction between the Law and the Gospel. According to the Law all men must appear before the judgment-seat of Christ. According to the Gospel the believers shall not come into condemnation. The appearance of the believers before God's judgment-seat will therefore not have the nature of a condemnatory judgment since their sins are forgiven through faith in Christ, Matt. 25, 34.

Gerhard rightly remarks that also the eschatological teachings of Christ are both Law and Gospel and that also in this case the Law admonishes and warns all Christians so far as they are flesh,

2 Cor. 5, 10; Rom. 14, 10, while the Gospel comforts them in their fears and doubts, Luke 21, 28. Luther declares (St. L., VII, 1794 f.): "The Judgment pertains to the believers as little as it does to the holy angels. All believers enter out of this life into the kingdom of heaven without judgment and are even the judges of others." This statement is true; for Christ expressly declares that the righteous will be separated from the unrighteous before the Judgment begins, Matt. 25, 32. 33.

According to Scripture the Judgment is not a long-drawn-out process *(iudicium discussionis),* but a momentary event *(actio momentanea),* Matt. 24, 27; Luke 17, 24. It takes place ἐν ἀτόμῳ, in an instant, ἐν ῥιπῇ ὀφθαλμοῦ, in the twinkling of an eye, 1 Cor. 15, 51. 52.

That the righteous shall judge the world with Christ is a clear doctrine of Scripture, 1 Cor. 6, 2—4. They will judge the world and the evil angels, inasmuch as they cooperate in Christ's decisions and support His verdict *(assessores).* This great dignity, which Christ confers upon them out of pure grace, should prompt them to judge rightly between their brethren already in this life, 1 Cor. 6, 5.

6. THE END OF THE WORLD.
(De Consummatione Mundi.)

With regard to heaven and earth, or the world which God created in the beginning, Gen. 1, 1, Holy Scripture teaches in unmistakable terms that they shall "pass away" (Luke 21, 33: παρελεύσονται; Heb. 1, 10—12: ἀπολοῦνται, "they shall perish"; ἀλλαγήσονται, "they shall be changed"; Ps. 102, 26—28: וְיַחֲלֹפוּ, יֹאבֵדוּ).

The meaning of the words *pass away, perish, be changed,* etc., in these passages is clear from the contrast in which the perishable "works of God's hands" stand to Him, the eternal, imperishable Creator; for while He remains, they perish; while He continues the same and His years do not fail, they "wax old as a garment," "are folded up," and are "changed." In the same contrast "heaven and earth" stand (Luke 21, 33) to the "words of Christ"; for while Christ's words do in no wise pass away, heaven and earth will pass away.

In 1 Cor. 7, 31 St. Paul writes: "The fashion of this world passeth away (παράγει τὸ σχῆμα τοῦ κόσμου τούτου). The "fashion of this world" is its present form, or the "present circumstances or conditions of all earthly things." Similarly St. John writes:

"The world is passing away" (ὁ κόσμος παράγεται), 1 John 2, 17.
On the basis of these Scripture-passages Christian theology
teaches that the world in its present form will be entirely destroyed
(2 Pet. 3, 10: "The heavens shall pass away with a great noise, and
the elements shall melt with fervent heat, the earth also and the
works that are therein shall be burned up").

However, our dogmaticians are divided with respect to the
manner in which this shall occur. While most Lutheran divines
(Gerhard, Quenstedt, Calov, etc.) teach a total destruction
(annihilation) of the world *quoad substantiam,* others (Luther,
Brenz, etc.) affirm that only the form of this world as it appears
now will pass away; in other words, that the world will be destroyed
only as it appears now. This teaching is based also on Rom. 8, 21,
where the apostle writes: "The creature itself also shall be delivered from the bondage of corruption into the glorious liberty of
the children of God."

Luther thus writes (St. L., XII, 729 f.): "The sun is waiting
for another embellishment, which it shall have, together with the
earth and all other creatures; namely, they shall be cleansed from
every abuse of Satan and the world."

Quenstedt rejects this doctrine and writes: "The form of this
consummation consists not in the mere change, alteration, or renewing of qualities, but in the total abolition and reduction of the
world's substance itself to nothing." (*Doctr. Theol.,* p. 656.) This
doctrine he bases on such passages as Ps. 102, 26; 2 Pet. 3, 10—13;
Rev. 20, 11; Is. 34, 4; Luke 21, 33; Job 14, 12. He states, however, that this belief must not be defended as an article of faith,
though "it corresponds more to the Scripture-passages which describe the end of the world." Nevertheless those who regard the
destruction of the world as a change or renewal "should not be
accused of heresy." (Cp. *Christl. Dogmatik,* III, 609 f.)

In view of the fact that the matter cannot be fully decided on
the basis of clear Scripture-passages, other dogmaticians (Heerbrand, Hutter, Balthasar Meisner) suggest that the theologian also
at this point place his hand upon his mouth and refrain from any
definite teaching. Yet it may be added that even those dogmaticians who regard the destruction of the world as a renovation
of all things teach that *in its present form* the world will indeed
pass away. Cp. 1 Cor. 15, 24: "Then cometh the *end*" (τέλος).
So also Luther teaches (St. L., VIII, 1222): "In short, all that
shall cease which belongs to the substance of these temporal things,

or to the perishable life and works." It is therefore an open question whether the world will pass away *quoad substantiam,* by annihilation, or only *secundum accidentia,* according to its form and external appearance, by transformation.

It is not advisable to take the passages speaking of a new heaven and a new earth (Is. 65, 17; 66, 22; 2 Pet. 3, 13; Rev. 21, 1) in a literal sense, since the "new heaven and the new earth" are "symbols of the heavenly mansions and eternal life." Buechner *(Handkonkordanz)* remarks concerning these passages: "Just as this earth now offers man a comfortable home, so the children of God receive the most comfortable homes, full of all manner of blessedness, in heaven." (John 14, 1—4.)

7. ETERNAL DAMNATION.
(De Damnatione Aeterna.)

At the last Judgment a complete and eternal separation takes place between the ungodly and the godly. Matt. 25, 46: "These shall go away into *everlasting punishment,* but the righteous into *life eternal.*"

The fact that there will be an *everlasting* punishment may be deduced to some extent also from the natural knowledge which man has of divine things, Rom. 1, 18—21. The knowledge of God's *judgment* (δικαίωμα) is a part of the divine Law which God has written in the human heart, Rom. 1, 32. On the basis of the Law, conscience condemns the sinful acts of man as transgressions, for which he is held accountable to God, Rom. 2, 15; 1, 20. 32. Hence also among the heathen we find a certain doctrine of an eternal retribution, though this, of course, is distorted by many fanciful speculations. (Cf. *Christl. Dogmatik,* III, 611 f.)

Holy Scripture teaches the doctrine of eternal damnation so clearly and definitely that only those can rightly deny it who reject the divine authority of God's Word (cf. the doctrine of restitution, ἀποκατάστασις τῶν πάντων, παλιγγενεσία, *restitutio omnium*). If any one presumes to reject the everlasting punishment (εἰς κόλασιν αἰώνιον), he must reject also the everlasting life (εἰς ζωὴν αἰώνιον), since both are placed side by side, indeed, in contrast to each other, Matt. 25, 46; John 3, 36.

While it is true that the term *eternity* is sometimes used in Scripture in the weakened sense of "long duration" (עַד־עוֹלָם, Ex. 12, 14. 24; 21, 6, etc.), it is employed in its strict sense *(sine fine)* in all those passages where it describes either the blessedness of God's saints in heaven or the misery of the damned in hell, 2 Thess. 1, 9; Matt. 18, 8; Mark 3, 29.

In addition, the endless duration of the agonies of the damned is clearly described in other unmistakable terms (Is. 66, 24; Mark 9, 48: "where their worm dieth not and the fire is not quenched"; Rev. 14, 11: "The smoke of their torment ascendeth up forever and ever; and they have no rest day nor night"; Rev. 20, 10: "And shall be tormented day and night forever and ever").

The *Augsburg Confession* therefore justly condemns all who deny the eternal punishment of Satan and his followers when it writes (Art. XVII): "They condemn the Anabaptists, who think that there will be an end to the punishments of condemned men and devils." Also the *Apology* declares (Art. XVII, *Triglot*, p. 335): "At the consummation of the world Christ shall appear and shall raise up all the dead and shall give to the godly eternal life and eternal joys, but shall condemn the ungodly to be punished with the devil without end *(sine fine)."*

If the objection is raised that the very idea of an eternal punishment is so dreadful that it cannot be true, we reply that it is not for finite man, but for the infinite God to determine the punishment of those who have rebelled against Him, Jude 6—8.

The argument that the idea of an eternal punishment is irreconcilable with divine love or with divine justice or with the unity of the divine "world-plan" (the final conversion of the penitent in hell and the annihilation of the impenitent) is based upon human speculation and not upon God's Word, so that it is worthless, since God cannot be judged by our feeble sense, 1 Tim. 6, 16; Rom. 11, 33—36.

While the terms שְׁאוֹל and ᾅδης may denote either the state of death or the grave, Ps. 16, 10; Acts 2, 27. 31, they properly signify "the place (ποῦ) in which the wicked suffer and in all eternity sustain the most miserable condition and ineffable tortures" (Gerhard). (Cp. Deut. 32, 22; Ps. 49, 14; Prov. 15, 24; Matt. 11, 23; Luke 10, 15; 16, 23; etc.)

Against the Russellites, who claim that neither שְׁאוֹל nor ᾅδης can mean hell in the sense of "the place of the damned," we reply that we do not depend on these terms alone to prove the existence of hell, since the doctrine of an eternal punishment is otherwise clearly taught in Scripture (cp. γέεννα, Matt. 5, 22; Mark 9, 43. 44; Luke 12, 5).

The valley of Hinnom (Gehinnom) near Jerusalem, with its

ceaselessly burning fires to consume the city offal, was surely a fitting symbol of the eternal hell-fire, "where their worm dieth not and their fire is not quenched." It is certainly most impressive that our beloved Savior, who is Love (1 John 4, 8), Himself taught the eternal punishment of the damned so persistently and emphatically, Matt. 5, 29. 30; 10, 28; 11, 23; Luke 16, 23. The eternal punishment of the damned is proved also by Christ's descent into hell (τοῖς ἐν φυλακῇ πνεύμασιν ... ἀπειθήσασιν), 1 Pet. 3, 18—20.

Upon the basis of clear Scripture-passages we teach that the form (forma), or essence, of the eternal damnation consists in everlasting banishment from divine grace and communion, or in the everlasting separation of the damned from God's love and mercy, Matt. 25, 41; 8, 12; 2 Thess. 1, 7—9. Originally man was created for communion with God, and in this alone he finds supreme happiness, John 17, 20—23; Ps. 17, 15; Matt. 11, 28f. Hence separation from God, the Supreme Good (summum bonum) and the only Source of every good and perfect gift, Jas. 1, 17, in itself means suffering the greatest bodily and spiritual anguish.

Holy Scripture, moreover, very carefully describes the unspeakable sufferings of the damned as "tribulation and anguish" (Rom. 2, 9), "being in torments" (Luke 16, 23), "being tormented in this flame" (Luke 16, 24), "being cast into unquenchable fire, where the worm dieth not and the fire is not quenched" (Mark 9, 43. 44), "weeping and gnashing of teeth" (Matt. 8, 12), "wailing and gnashing of teeth" (Matt. 13, 50), etc. In short, Scripture employs the strongest terms to show that the sufferings of the damned in soul and body are the greatest conceivable. In fact, they surpass our feeble understanding, since they are both continuous and everlasting, the fire burning endlessly and yet not consuming, Mark 3, 29.

While the suffering of the body in hell-fire will be extreme, the soul will be perpetually tortured with the sense of God's wrath (sensus irae) and His eternal condemnation, Gal. 3, 10, as also by the terrors of a fully awakened conscience (terrores conscientiae), Luke 16, 27. 28. Hollaz adds the pertinent remark that "the tortures of hell will befall the souls of the damned as soon as they have departed from the body," i. e., in death, Luke 16, 23.

To describe the torments of the damned more accurately, our dogmaticians divide them into privative and positive sufferings. The privative sufferings include a) forfeiture of the beatific sight of God, Matt. 25, 41; b) separation from the communion of the blessed, Luke 16, 26; c) exclusion from heavenly light, rest, and happiness, Matt. 8, 12; d) entire denial of pity, divine and human, Luke 16, 25. 26; and e) complete lack of everything that might comfort them, Rev. 6, 16. 17.

The *positive sufferings* are both internal and external. The *internal* are the most inexplicable pains and tortures of the soul, Mark 9, 44, and the *external,* their association with devils, Matt. 25, 41, their everlasting confinement in a place of unspeakable sorrow, Matt. 25, 30; 1 Pet. 3, 18—20, and their ceaseless torments in fire that burns, but does not consume, Luke 16, 23. 24; Rev. 14, 10. 11; 20, 10. 15.

Whether the fire of hell is material (real fire) or immaterial (unspeakable torment) does not matter, for even in its figurative meaning (Gerhard, Quenstedt) the term denotes indescribable anguish and agony, Is. 66, 24. Our dogmaticians rightly warn all curious minds that it is much more profitable to seek to escape the agony of hell than to argue concerning what the fire of hell may be (Gerhard).

Dr. Pieper aptly remarks that in hell there will be no atheists, since their torment in endless punishment will convince them of the existence of a righteous and omnipotent Judge, whose sovereignty must be recognized, Luke 16, 27. 28.

The question whether the damned in hell will continue in sin may be affirmed in the sense that their entire moral condition of reprobation (lack of faith, hope, and inward obedience) is a ceaseless state of transgression. To this we may add that the fire of hell is not cleansing (hell is no purgatory), but punitive, so that the damned will not be morally improved by it. Hence, if they do acknowledge God's majesty, they will do so only under coercion in endless agony.

That the damned will actually blaspheme God is hardly probable, Luke 16, 27. 28. The passage Rev. 16, 11 no doubt refers to men who blaspheme God on account of the tribulations of this present life.

That the punishments of hell differ *in degree,* according to the quality and measure of sin, Scripture teaches very plainly, Matt. 11, 24; Luke 12, 47; Matt. 23, 15. The sin that will be punished most severely is that of malicious opposition to the Gospel of Christ, Matt. 11, 16—24.

While on the basis of clear Scripture-passages we speak of hell as a place, Luke 16, 28; 1 Pet. 3, 19, this must not be understood in a physical sense. Nor are we to determine where this place is, since Scripture does not give us any information on this matter. Hell may be said to be where God reveals to the damned His eternal punitive justice by banishing them from His gracious countenance (Pieper). Quenstedt quotes Chrysostom on this point, who says: "Let us not seek where it is, but how we may escape it."

Hollaz concludes the whole matter with the fitting remark: "It is certain that the infernal prison is a real locality, Luke 16, 28; 1 Pet. 3, 19, separated from the abode of the blessed, Rev. 22, 15; Luke 16, 23. It is also probable that it is outside this habitable world, 2 Pet. 3, 10; Matt. 8, 12; but *where* this place definitely is, is unknown to men during the present life." (*Doctr. Theol.*, p. 658.)

With respect to the *cause* of eternal damnation it is clear that, while every sin (both original, Eph. 2, 3, and actual, Ezek. 18, 20) is by its very nature *(natura sua, ut sic, meritorie)* damnable, 1 Cor. 5, 11; Rev. 21, 8; Gal. 3, 10, it is, in the final analysis, the sin of unbelief that actually condemns, John 3, 16—18. 36; Mark 16, 16. Through His vicarious atonement *(satisfactio vicaria)* Christ has secured perfect reconciliation for all men with God, so that in Him every sinner in this world is absolved from all transgressions, 2 Cor. 5, 19—21 (objective justification). Hence a sinner is punished eternally only if he refuses to accept God's gracious forgiveness by faith in Christ. This is an offense so great that it is rightly punished with everlasting damnation in hell.

However, if a sinner refuses to accept God's gracious pardon in Christ Jesus, then both his original sin and his actual sins will also condemn him, since he can never atone for them, and so they are forever charged against him. It is for this reason that Scripture, on the one hand, ascribes eternal damnation to the sin of unbelief, John 3, 18, and, on the other, also to all other sins, Eph. 5, 6; Gal. 5, 19—21; 1 Cor. 6, 9. 10; Rev. 22, 15.

If we bear in mind the explanation just given, we shall neither minimize the vicarious atonement of Christ (by teaching work-righteousness) nor the condemnable character of human transgression (Rom. 6, 1: "Shall we continue in sin that grace may abound?"), but we shall trust the more in Christ Jesus, our divine Savior, and in the power of faith flee and combat sin, Rom. 6, 2, 11—15.

The purpose of Holy Scripture in revealing to us the doctrine of eternal damnation is to warn us against both unbelief (Mark

16, 16) and carnal security (Matt. 26, 41; 1 Cor. 10, 12) and so to move us to seek Christ's gracious salvation, offered to all men in the means of grace. The doctrine of eternal damnation is the severest kind of Law-preaching, and its object is repentance, Matt. 3, 7—12.

The warning, implied in the doctrine of everlasting punishment, is, however, meant not only for unbelievers, but also for believers inasmuch as they still are flesh (Matt. 8, 11. 12, addressed to "the children of the Kingdom"; 26, 24, addressed to Judas; 24, 42—51, addressed to the disciples).

> *Mors tua, iudicium postremum, gloria coeli,*
> *Et dolor inferni sunt meditanda tibi.*

While the doctrine of hell will never convert a soul, since the Law only "worketh wrath," Rom. 4, 15, it is nevertheless "our schoolmaster to bring us unto Christ that we might be justified by faith," Gal. 3, 24. Hence all preachers who deny the eternal punishment of the wicked are not "merciful theologians" *(misericordes theologi),* but the most cruel of all false prophets, who, instead of warning the sinner against his terrible doom, Ezek. 3, 17—19, do all in their power "to drown men in destruction and perdition," 1 Tim. 6, 3—5. Christ and His holy apostles taught the doctrine of eternal retribution with great clearness and emphasis, Mark 9, 43 ff.; 2 Thess. 2, 9, and their example every Christian preacher must follow as a faithful minister of Christ and a loyal steward of God's mysteries, 1 Cor. 4, 1. 2.

The doctrine of eternal damnation serves also to illustrate God's righteous judgment over all transgressors, Rom. 2, 5. 6; 3, 4. But since God earnestly desires that all men be saved *(voluntas antecedens),* John 3, 16, it is only by His *voluntas consequens,* John 3, 18. 36, that He exhibits and glorifies His righteous wrath and punishment.

The Calvinistic doctrine of a reprobation to hell "from eternity" is unscriptural. God never intended man for hell, but only for heaven, 1 Tim. 2, 4—6.

The doctrine of eternal damnation is denied by the *Restorationists,* who teach that the future punishment is not retributive, but remedial and will result in the salvation of all men and, as some hold, of the evil angels. (Restitution of all things; ἀποκατάστασις; second probation). Likewise it is denied by the *Annihilationists,* who teach that the wicked will be completely destroyed either at the Judgment or later. Both errors are opposed to the clear statements of Scripture.

8. ETERNAL SALVATION.
(De Beatitudine Aeterna.)

a. *The fact of eternal salvation.* That there is an everlasting life in glory and bliss for all true believers in Christ Jesus is the culmination of all Gospel revelation in Holy Scripture, Rom. 5, 1. 2; Eph. 2, 4—6. The explanation of the Second Article of the Creed thus says: "I believe that Jesus Christ has redeemed me . . . that I may be His own and live under Him in His kingdom and serve Him in everlasting righteousness, innocence, and blessedness, even as He is risen from the dead, lives, and reigns to all eternity." So also the *Formula of Concord* (Thor. Decl., XI, 14—22): "God in His purpose and counsel [of grace] ordained that finally He will eternally save and glorify in life eternal those whom He has elected, called, and justified."

The blessed doctrine of life eternal through faith in Christ cannot be learned from reason since it belongs to "the wisdom of God in a mystery, even the hidden wisdom, which God ordained before the world unto our glory," 1 Cor. 2, 7—9.

The Christian hope of eternal life (John 17, 3) must therefore not be confounded with the pagan doctrine of the immortality of the soul or of its continued existence after death, which even human reason may excogitate. Concerning the arguments for the immortality of the soul we may note the following: a) "Since the soul is immaterial and simple, it is indissoluble" (Plato, Leibniz; *the metaphysical proof*); b) "The rich capacities of the soul cannot be satisfactorily developed in this life; its destiny must therefore be extended to a future life" (Cicero, Lotze; *teleological proof*); c) "Man strives after virtue as well as after happiness; but this life affords no satisfaction with regard to either" (Kant; *argumentum ethonomicum*); d) "Love for country is inspired only by the promise of life beyond death" (J. G. Fichte; *argumentum iuridicum*); e) "All men by nature believe in the immortality of the soul" (Homer, Vergil, Cicero; *argumentum e consensu gentium;* cp. *Doctr. Theol.,* p. 631 f.).

However, all the "heavens" of the heathen (unbelievers) are man-made and are just as much a caricature of the heaven of Scripture as every man-made savior is a caricature of the divine Savior. Though the heathen have always speculated on the immortality of the soul, St. Paul bears witness that despite their eschatological speculations they are "without God," "having no hope . . . in the world," Eph. 2, 12. Karl Hase rightly states that "in the hovel of the poorest peasant there is a stronger faith in an eternal life than in the lecture halls of the greatest philosophers." (Cf. *Christl. Dogmatik,* III, 619.)

Only he can in reality have the hope of eternal life who truly believes in Christ Jesus, God's only-begotten Son, and in His vicarious death for the sins of the world, John 3, 16; 11, 23—27. Even the "sweetest thoughts" on the future life of the soul are dreadful without faith in Christ, since they can never silence the accusing and condemning voice of conscience, Rom. 2, 15. 16.

b. *What eternal life is (forma beatitudinis aeternae).* According to Holy Scripture the life eternal which Christ will graciously bestow upon His followers consists in the perpetual beatific vision of God, Job 19, 25—27; Acts 7, 55; Matt. 5, 8; 2 Cor. 5, 1—6; 1 Cor. 13, 12; 1 John 3, 2. In this life Christian believers see God only through faith by means of His Word, and, as it were, in an image, 1 Cor. 13, 12 *(cognitio Dei abstractiva);* but in heaven they will behold Him without an image or veil, face to face *(cognitio Dei intuitiva).*

This beholding of God is beatific, that is, it is joined with supreme bliss, Ps. 17, 15, so that the blessed will never desire any other happiness than that of seeing God, the Supreme Good and Source of all perfect enjoyment. From this it follows that they can never fall away from Him, but they are confirmed in their heavenly glory (Rev. 14, 13; John 10, 27—29; Ps. 16, 11; John 17, 24; Rev. 7, 9—17). There will be no spiritual foe to interfere with their bliss (Rev. 20, 10).

Quenstedt describes the everlasting happiness of the blessed as follows: "The form [of eternal life] consists, generally speaking, in the ineffable, most full, and never-ending reception of incomprehensible blessings. The blessings of eternal life are either privative or positive.

"The *privative blessings* are the absence of sin and of all causes of sin, namely, the flesh inciting, the devil suggesting, the world seducing, and of the punishments of sin, such as various calamities, Is. 25, 8; 49, 10; Rev. 21, 4; temporal death, Hos. 13, 14; 1 Cor. 15, 26. 55—57; Rev. 2, 7, and eternal damnation, Rev. 2, 11; 20, 14. Here also belongs immunity from the affections and actions of the animal body as such, as, for example, hunger, thirst, eating, drinking, the use of marriage, etc., Rev. 7, 16. 17; Matt. 22, 30.

"Some of the *positive blessings* of life eternal are *internal,* while others are *external.* The *internal positive blessings,* among which the beatific and immediate sight of God is preeminent, belong to the entire composite being and affect both body and soul of the blessed. The internal blessings of either part of the composite being belong either to the soul or to the body. Those of the soul are: a) the perfect enlightenment of the intellect, 1 Cor. 13, 9—12; b) complete rectitude of the will as well as the appetite, Ps. 17, 15; Eph. 5, 27; c) the highest security concerning the perpetual duration of this blessedness, John 16, 22. Those of the body are: a) spirituality, 1 Cor. 15, 44. 47; Phil. 3, 21; b) invisibility, 1 Cor. 15, 44; c) impalpability, 1 Cor. 15, 44. 48; d) illocality (*ibid.*); e) subtility (*ibid.*); f) agility, 1 Thess. 4, 17; g) impassibility, Rev. 7, 16; 21, 4; h) immortality and incorruptibility, 1 Cor. 15, 42—48. 53; 2 Cor. 5, 4; i) strength and soundness, 1 Cor. 15, 43; j) brilliancy, Dan. 12, 3; Matt. 13, 43; 1 Cor. 15, 41. 43; k) beauty, 1 Cor. 15, 43; Phil. 3, 21.

"The *external positive blessings* are those which the blessed experience deeply outside of themselves. Of these two are chief: a) the most delightful communion with God, Luke 23, 43; John 12, 26; 14, 3; 17, 24; 2 Cor. 5, 8; Phil. 1, 23; 1 Thess. 4, 17; Rev. 21, 3, with the angels, Heb. 12, 22, and with all the blessed, Matt. 8, 11; Luke 13, 29; Heb. 12, 23, consisting in the mutual presence, the most agreeable conversations, and the rendering of mutual honor, joined with mutual love; and b) a most beautiful and magnificent abode." (*Doctr. Theol.*, p. 661f.)

With respect to the beatific vision, Scripture teaches that this is accomplished not merely by means of mental contemplation (*visio mentalis*), but by the actual sight of the eyes (*visio corporalis*), 1 Cor. 9, 12; Job 19, 25—27; 1 John 3, 2. Those who doubt the possibility of the beatific vision may just as well doubt the possibility of all of heaven, since the entire doctrine of eternal life transcends our feeble understanding. That the blessed in heaven will recognize not only God, but one another is plainly taught in Scripture, Matt. 17, 3. 4; Rev. 7, 13. 14. Hafenreffer writes: "Because the perfect image of God in which we had been created will be fully restored, we shall be endowed also with perfect wisdom and knowledge. Hence, if Adam before the Fall immediately recognized his rib in Eve, much more in the life to come, when all these gifts will be far more perfect, shall we recognize one another, Luke 16, 23; Matt. 17, 1 ff." (*Doctr. Theol.*, p. 662.)

Whether the blessed will recognize the damned in hell is not certain, though it is quite probable, Luke 16, 23ff. Dr. Pieper wisely suggests that it is best to leave this question unanswered. That such recognition, if it should occur, does not disturb the happiness of the saints, Hutter explains as follows: "The will of the blessed will in all things concur with that of God. Such carnal affections as are signs of our weakness in this life will entirely cease in the life to come, when our love will extend to those who are beloved of God and whom He has made heirs of everlasting life. But in the damned they will supremely admire and eternally praise the exalted justice of God." (*Doctr. Theol.*, p. 662.)

c. *How Scripture describes life eternal.* Gerhard rightly suggests that what eternal life is can be known from the revelation of the Word only in a general and obscure manner (αἰνιγματικῶς). As a matter of fact, while Holy Scripture speaks of eternal life in many places, it does not supply us with many details regarding its exalted nature. This method of teaching the Holy Spirit has chosen designedly; for in this life we have no adequate conception of the nature of things that lie beyond space and time.

Nevertheless the description of eternal life which God's Word provides is sufficient to give us a foretaste of the coming glory, Rom. 8, 18, and to make us long for heaven, Phil. 1, 23. Negatively Scripture describes the blessedness of God's saints in heaven as complete freedom from all the ills of this life, 2 Tim. 4, 18; Rev. 7, 16. 17; 21, 4; positively, as supreme and perfect bliss, 1 Pet. 1, 8. 9; Ps. 16, 11; John 17, 24. Moreover, Scripture depicts the perfect joy of eternal life by means of symbols that give us a foretaste of heaven's perfect glory (Matt. 25, 10; Rev. 19, 9: marriage; Luke 13, 29; Matt. 8, 11: a feast of joy; Luke 22, 30: sitting upon thrones). That these pictures must not be explained in a physical or earthly sense Scripture expressly shows, Luke 22, 24—30; Matt. 22, 30.

However, not only the soul, but also the body will share in the eternal bliss of heaven, 1 Cor. 15, 44; for it shall be like the glorified body of Christ, Phil. 3, 21, and shall shine as the sun, Matt. 13, 43, being free from all consequences of sin, 1 Cor. 15, 42. 43.

The language which will be used in heaven is not earthly, but heavenly, so that it cannot be known upon earth (2 Cor. 12, 4: "unspeakable words, which it is not lawful for a man to utter").

While there are no degrees of bliss, since all the saints of Christ shall see God and so will be completely blessed, Scripture teaches that there are degrees of glory (δόξα, *gloria*), commensurate with the faithfulness and sufferings of Christian believers in this life, 2 Cor. 9, 6; 1 Cor. 15, 41. 42; Dan. 12, 3. (*Omnibus una salus sanctis, sed gloria dispar;* cp. Luther, St. L., VIII,

1223 f.) These differences in glory will of course not arouse envy, since jealousy is sin, Gal. 5, 20. 21, and sin will be completely abolished in heaven, Ps. 17, 15; 16, 11.

Heaven indeed must be conceived of as a certain place (πού), where the blessed will see God and perfectly enjoy supreme glory, Matt. 5, 12; 6, 20; 1 Pet. 1, 4; Mark 16, 19; yet we must not understand this "certain πού" in a physical sense. As the πού *damnatorum* is everywhere where God reveals His eternal punitive justice, so the πού *beatorum* is everywhere where God reveals His eternal grace and love in unveiled glory. Thus the angels are always in heaven, even when they minister to the saints on earth, Matt. 18, 10; Luke 1, 19.

d. *The saints in heaven.* Scripture describes as the saints of God who shall inherit eternal life all those who believe in Christ, John 3, 16—18. 36. For this reason it is wrong to ascribe eternal life also to non-believers on the basis of their *iustitia naturalis et civilis* (Zwingli, Hofmann; cp. Luther, St. L., XX, 1766f., against Zwingli, who expressed the hope to find such heathen as Hercules, Theseus, Socrates, etc., in heaven). Christ expressly commanded His disciples to preach the Gospel to every creature, adding the warning that whosoever believeth not shall be damned, Mark 16, 15. 16; Luke 24, 47; cp. also Acts 26, 18.

That only true believers shall be eternally saved appears also from all passages in Scripture, a) in which Christian ministers are commanded to be faithful and diligent in their sacred office in order that not a soul may be lost through unbelief, Ezek. 3, 18. 19; 2 Tim. 4, 1. 2; 2, 23—26; 1 Tim. 4, 15. 16; b) in which all Christians are exhorted to instruct, reprove, and warn their erring brethren lest they lose their soul's salvation through apostasy, Matt. 18, 15—17; 1 Cor. 5; and c) in which all Christians are admonished to lead a holy life lest they become guilty of any one's damnation through the offense of denying the Christian faith and profession, Matt. 18, 6. 7.

e. *The purpose of the doctrine of eternal salvation.* As the doctrine of eternal damnation serves to warn men against unbelief and carnal security, so the doctrine of eternal life serves to incite the believers to greater faith and to sustain them in their faithful following of Christ, Matt. 10, 22; 24, 13; Mark 13, 13. A truly Christian life is impossible without constant consideration of the sure hope of eternal life, Phil. 3, 12—14; 1, 23. 24; Matt. 6, 19—21. (Cp. Luther, St. L., IX, 930 ff.)

In this life Christian believers do not receive that recognition which they deserve as children of God, 1 John 3, 2, just as little as their Savior was appreciated during His sojourn on earth, Is. 53, 1—3; John 1, 10. 11. Moreover, as they are hated and troubled by "all men," Matt. 10, 22. 25; 24, 9, they must endure much tribulation in general before they can enter into God's Kingdom of Glory, Acts 14, 22. Hence they should constantly direct their attention to their sure inheritance in heaven in order that they may overcome all evil and gain the eternal victory, Matt. 5, 12; 2 Cor. 4, 16—18. All manner of tribulation is the earthly lot especially of the Christian ministers, 2 Tim. 2, 9; 2 Cor. 4, 7—11, since the world detests the Gospel of Christ, 1 Cor. 1, 23, and will abominate it till the end of time, 2 Tim. 4, 10.

But in all their tribulation Christian believers will overcome and gain the victory, Rom. 8, 35—39, if after the example of the apostle, 2 Tim. 1, 12, they continue in faith and hold fast their Spirit-sealed hope of eternal glory, John 16, 33; 1 John 5, 4. 5; Rev. 2, 7—11; 12, 11. (Cp. Luther, St. L., II, 1237.)

Of the practical use of the doctrine of eternal life, Gerhard writes very beautifully: "The doctrine concerning the heaven of the blessed and eternal life is set forth in Holy Scripture not that we may idly dispute as theorists concerning the locality of heaven, the beatific vision, the properties of the glorified bodies, but that, as practical men, considering the promised joys of eternal life every day, aye, every hour, aye, every moment, we may keep closely to the way leading thither and carefully avoid all that may cause delay or recall us from entrance into life eternal.

"In 2 Cor. 4, 18 the godly are well described by the apostle as looking not at the things which are seen ($\tau \grave{a} \ \beta \lambda \varepsilon \pi \acute{o} \mu \varepsilon \nu a$), but at the things which are not seen ($\tau \grave{a} \ \mu \grave{\eta} \ \beta \lambda \varepsilon \pi \acute{o} \mu \varepsilon \nu a$). One of the ancients who was asked what books he used in his daily studies answered that he studied every day a book with three pages, one red, one black, one white; that on the red page he read of our Lord's Passion, on the black, of the torments of the lost, and on the white, of the joys of the glorified, and that from this study he derived more profit than if he would ponder all the works of the philosophers." (*Doctr. Theol.*, p. 663.)

"Christus gubernet mentes nostras ad veram pietatem,
Et restituat ecclesiae piam et perpetuam concordiam! Amen."

SOLI DEO GLORIA!

TOPICAL INDEX.

A debito ad posse non valet consequentia, 355.

A praecepto ad posse non valet consequentia, 239. 401.

Abelard denied vicarious atonement, 14.

Absolution a sacrament, 448; Gospel is —, 458; doctrine of — taught in Scripture, 460; the — of the papistic Church, 460; the Scriptural doctrine of — against errorists, 462; Dr. Spaeth on power of — given to disciples, 462; objections to —, 463; Baptism and Lord's Supper are forms of —, 464; — not to be pronounced conditionally, 464; questions asked in —, 465.

Academic freedom, 76; true freedom, 77; points to be regarded in connection with —, 77; disastrous consequences of —, 78.

Actio praevia, 191.

Acts, divine, of generation and spiration, 155; internal and external, 156.

Acts 2, 24, explanation of, 297.

Acts 13, 48, explanation of, 606.

Acts 19, 1—6, explanation of, 504.

Actual sins, definition of, 224.

Actus personales, 155.

Adhortationes, legales, evangelicae, 239.

Adiaphora, 212. 561. 578.

Administrants of Baptism, 499.

Admonitiones, legales, evangelicae, 355.

Adoptionists, 150.

Advent, the, of our Lord, 434; second — of Christ, 619; signs that precede the —, 620; destruction of Jerusalem sign and beginning of final Judgment, 621; Lutheran Church rejects millennium, 621.

Agnosticism, 168.

Agraphos, vox, 31.

Aliquid discrimen in homine, 81.

Alloiosis, 274; Zwingli's — applied to absolution, 461.

Allos. The Father is another, *allos,* than the Son, 151.

Amyraldists, 249.

Analogia fidei, 139.

Analytic method, 84. 85.

Angelus increatus, 196.

Angels, doctrine of, 196; name of, 196; nature of, 197; knowledge of, 197; attributes of, 198; — and miracles, 198; marriage of — to man, 198; number and ranks of, 199; good and evil —, 199; originally — positively good, 199; their confirmation in that which is good, 200; their election, 200; service of good angels, 201; their beatific vision of, and love for, God, 201; whom they serve, 201; we should esteem, but not worship —, 202.

Angels, evil, enemies of God, 198; their miracles, 198; — not predestinated to damnation, 200; why they fell away, 200. 202; their state of misery, 200; why not restored to divine favor, 200; their punishment, 202; how they injure men, 202; — hate the Church, 203; their damnation, 204; purpose of Scripture in revealing the doctrine of evil angels, 204.

Annihilationists, 638.

Anselm of Canterbury; his religious philosophy, 13; denied active obedience of Christ, 14.

Antichrist, 305. 380. 422. 550. 561. 580; the Scriptural doctrine of Antichrist, 580; the twofold use of the term, 580; characteristics of —, 581.

Antichrists, 78.

Antigraphos, vox, 31.

Antilegomena, 110. 117. 130. 131.

Antinomianism, 396. 470. 472.

Apocrypha, 130.

Apokalypsis, 31.

Apokatastasis, 638.

Apollinaris, 258.

Apologetics, its function, 71.

Apology. On works, 15; on divisions, 36; on *sola fide,* 50; on free will, 237; on retaining the Gospel, 246; on Christ's atonement, 309; on faith, 310; on Trinity, 148; on wrong definition of sin by papists, 211; on *opinio legis,* 344; on Romanistic errors regarding repentance, 366; on meaning of justification, 375.

378; on justification by works,
379; on doing good works, 407.
410; on reward of grace, 416;
on praise of good works, 416;
on Sacraments, 444; on absolution, 459; on purpose of Lord's
Supper, 508; on members of
Church, 542. 543; on divine institution of public ministry, 567;
against the claim that priests
must be obeyed in all things,
578; on purpose of death, 615;
on eternal punishment of the
wicked, 634.
Apostolic Succession, 568. 573. 576.
Apotelcsmata, what is meant by,
285.
Appetition of man corrupt, 221.
Appetitus sensitivus, 205. 221.
Apprehensio, simplex, 140; — *spiri-
tualis*, 141.
Appropriation, 153. 157.
A priori. Scripture to be accepted
as true —, 13.
Aquinas, Thomas, on the meaning
and function of theology, 30.
Archetypal theology, 39.
Argumentum in circulo, 122.
Arianism, 150. 153. 258.
Arminians, 22. 50. 245.
Articles of faith, what they are, 59;
mixed, pure —, 60. 146.
Articuli antecedentes, consequentes,
79. 372.
Articulus fundamentalissimus, 48.
*Articulus stantis et cadentis eccle-
siae*, 255.
Ascension of Christ, 299.
Aseity, divine, 165.
Assurance, positive, 72; self-assur-
ance condemned, 73; how — may
be attained, 73.
Astronomical systems, 183.
Athanasius on equality of divine
Persons, 152; — on *genus apotelesmaticum*, 285.
Atheism, 144. 168. 191. 193. 214.
Atonement, theories of —, 27; doctrine of vicarious — a fundamental article, 50; vicarious —
of Christ, 309; errors on vicarious —, 311; modern — theories, 312.
Attributes, divine, and God's essence,
161; how ascribed to God and
creatures, 162; division of, 162;
modern divisions of, 163; negative —, 163; positive —, 167;
— communicated to Christ's human nature, 282.
Augsburg Confession. On Trinity,
148; on God, 148; on term

person, 150; on hexaemeron, 180;
on cause of sin, 214; on propagation of original corruption,
218; on effects of Fall, 220; on
original sin, 221; on justifying
faith, 248; on the office of
Christ, 302; on repentance, 365;
on justification, 370; on source
of good works, 403; on amissibility of faith, 436; on means of
grace, 441; on purpose of Sacraments, 445; on absolution, 460;
on essence of Lord's Supper, 510;
on what the Church properly is,
542; the State an ordinance of
God, 552; on necessity of call,
570.
Aureolus, Peter, 162.
Authority of the Bible, 120; proofs
for —, 123; if the Church rejects —, 127; — of Old Testament, 130; — of New Testament,
130.
Autopistos (authoritative), Scripture is, 121.
"Awakened," right and wrong use
of the term, 363.
Axioms, rationalistic, 20.

Baier. On non-fundamental doctrines, 57; on open questions,
59; on perspicuity of Bible, 138;
our attitude to angels, 202; on
Christ's state of humiliation,
287; on efficacy of Bible, 134;
on transitive and intransitive
conversion, 353; on justification,
367; definition of Church, 542.
Ban, 556; lying —, 578.
Baptism, doctrine of, 486; a secondary fundamental article, 52;
purpose of, 444; divine institution of —, 486; application of
water in —, 487; what makes
— a Sacrament, 488; man-made
baptisms, 489; — in the name
of Christ, 489; the formula of
—, 490; — baptismal acts of
anti-Trinitarian sects, 490; —
a means of grace, 491; distinction between — and the Gospel,
492; the papistic doctrine *ex
opere operato* in —, 492; Calvinists deny the efficacy of —,
494; — a means of regeneration
in adults, 495; *materia coelestis*
in —, 495; the use of —, 496;
whom the Church should baptize,
497; — of infants, 497; — for
the dead, 498; administrants of
—, 499; necessity of —, 499;
— not absolutely necessary, 500;

customs of —, 500. 501; — works faith, 502; — does not work *ex opere operato*, 502; to whom questions are to be put at —, 503; when faith is engendered in —, 503; — of John the Baptist, 504; — *sacramentum initiationis*, 507.

Baptismus fluminis et flaminis, 505.

Believers only are members of the Church, 542; — are instrumental means of the Church, 551; Christian — in state offices, 553; all — should profess divine truth, 565; Scripture distinguishes between — and pastors, 567; — must organize local churches, 567; — must watch over the doctrine, 567; — have the right to call, 571; all — should regard themselves as elect, 591. 594; — are sure of their election only if they cling to Christ, 595; — cannot be sure of their election if they account for the salvation of some by a different conduct in men, 596; — are warned in Scripture because of their flesh, 597; as new creatures — must forget warnings and threatenings of Law, 598; references to temporary — are warnings of Law, 598.

Bente, Dr., on eventual victory of synergism, 346; on *sola gratia*, 361; on Antinomianism, 472; on Calvin's doctrine of Lord's Supper, 514; on doctrine of election and salvation, 611.

Beza, against Calvin's explanation of words of institution, 516.

Bible; cf. *Authority of the Bible.*

Bible translations, necessity of —, 129; their relation to the original, 132; Luther's advice on use of their texts, 132.

Biblicism, 40. 114.

Brenz on why eating of forbidden fruit brought death, 223.

Buchstabendienst, 95.

Burial of Christ, 295.

Caesaropapism, 561.

Calixtus on inspiration, 104. 108.

Call, immediate and mediate, 570. 571; the divinity of the mediate —, 571; through the — congregations *confer* the ministry, 577.

Calov. Tradition not source of faith, 16; on inerrancy of Scripture, 105; on canonical authority of Scripture, 125; on eternal divine essence and attributes, 161; on creation, 179; on the efficient cause of creation, 180; on state of integrity, 205.

Calvin. Taught Zwinglian doctrine of Lord's Supper, 513; accommodation to Lutheran terminology, 514; his explanation of the words of institution, 514. 515; rationalistic argumentation with regard to real presence, 517; taught that the visible sign does not impart grace, 535. Cp. *Calvinistic Theology.*

Calvinistic theology, 20; denial of *gratia universalis*, 22. 81; — errs with regard to sin against Holy Ghost, 233; teaches God is cause why some are lost, 249; divine grace cannot be resisted, 249; limits divine grace to elect, 250; explores hidden will of God, 254; denies communion of natures, 269. 270; denies *genus maiestaticum*, 276; its "either — or" in regard to this genus, 283; errs with respect to Christ's descent into hell, 297; its view of heaven, 300; teaches that *peccata enormia* of Christians do not destroy faith, 231; teaches that heaven is created space, 300; denies amissibility of faith, 436; does not comfort alarmed sinners, 437; ascribes ability to persevere in faith to man, 437; its error regarding means of grace, 442. 445. 446; makes efficacy of Sacraments depend on faith, 446; denies necessity of Sacraments, 446; has no means of grace for non-elect, 449; nor for elect, 450; bases certainty of salvation on inward illumination, 450; its error regarding immediate operation of Holy Ghost, 20. 451. 458; destroys doctrine of saving grace and faith, 451; its close connection with Romanism, 452; rejects absolution, 459; makes prayer means of grace, 468; mingles Law and Gospel, 484; denies efficacy of Baptism, 493; discountenances baptism by laymen, 499; perverts doctrine of Lord's Supper, 509; teaches spiritual eating and drinking, 511; agrees with regard to doctrine of Lord's Supper, 513; its error respecting Lord's Supper refuted, 516; accuses Lutheranism of having given up literal sense of words of institution, 521; teaches only a local presence of Christ's body, 522; faith makes eating and drinking a sacrament, 529; charges Lutheranism with teaching that the word of man produces real presence, 529; has no Lord's Supper, but Baptism, 532; should not speak of Lord's Supper as a seal of divine grace, 536; teaches absolute election, 593; limits *gratia universalis*, 596; teaches that is the interpretation of God's purposes, 609; teaches eternal reprobation to damnation, 638.

Canon, Biblical, how fixed, 131.

Capernaitic eating of Lord's body, 511.

Castigationes paternae, 216. Cp. *Chastisements*.

Causae formaliter causantes non sunt in Deo, 170.

Causes, no three, of conversion, 345.

Causae secundae, 173. 190.

Causae virtualiter causantes sunt in Deo, 171.

Causative authority, 122.

Celestial bodies, 183.

Certainty of salvation impossible if Law and Gospel are mingled, 481.

Chalcedon, Council of, 265.

Character, historical, of Christianity, 43.

Chastisements, fatherly, 216. 390. 425.

Chemnitz. On fixing Biblical canon, 131; on saving knowledge of God, 146; on God, the Creator, 187; on divine grace, 246; on necessity of Christ's death, 248; on *genus apotelesmaticum*, 284; on redemption, 286; on article of justification, 373; on right of the Church to call, 573; on faith following election, 599; on the resurrection body, 629.

Chiliasm, 318. 622. Cp. *Millennium*.

Christ, doctrine of the person of, a fundamental article, 49; divine providence ascribed to —, 190; doctrine of —, 255; — would not have become man had man not fallen, 255; person of —, 256; deity of —, 256; — called God in the predicate, 257; Subordinationists teach — is God in secondary sense, 257; humanity of —, 258; the sinlessness of —, 259; — free from original sin, 260; immortality of —, 260;

external appearance of —, 261; impersonality of —, 261; modern rationalists teach that the human and divine natures of — gradually coalesced, 262; personal union in —, 263; communion of natures in —, 268; communication of attributes, 272; the death of —, 286; states of —, 287; — did not always use majesty communicated to human nature, 288; erroneous views regarding His humiliation, 289; — worked *in, with*, and *through* His human nature, 292; His conception and nativity, 292; circumcision, education, and life, 293; suffering and death, 294; burial, 295; exaltation, 295; resurrection, 298; ascension, 299; session, 300; His office, 301; — not a new Lawgiver, 304; — the Prophet of the Old Testament Church, 305; — shed His own blood, 306; His priestly intercession, 313; kingly office, 314; threefold kingdom, 315; membership in — result of justification, 383; glorified body of — not *materia coelestis* of Sacrament of Altar, 527; His institution makes the Lord's Supper a Sacrament, 529.

Christening of *res inanimatae*, 498.

Christian Church has only one teacher, 77; repudiates Unitarianism, 91; not to make doctrines, 94.

Christian consciousness, 23. 35. 40. 41. 82.

Christianity is God-made religion; all other religions are man-made, 28.

Christian religion the absolute religion, 25; when it was given, 28; — not merely "the highest religion," 28; — and Christian theology, 29; religious and theological knowledge fundamentally the same, 30; historical character of —, 43.

Christian theology and Christian religion, 29; etymological meaning of —, 30; what — comprises, 31; purpose of —, 64; means by which this purpose is accomplished, 66; — is a system, 79; methodology of —, 86.

Christian theologian; his work, 83.

"*Christum treiben*," 117.

Chrysostom on Lord's Supper, 529.

Church, the universal, 541; defini-

tion of —, 541; papistic definition of —, 542. 545; errors regarding the —, 543; doctrine
of — rests on justification by
faith, 544; the properties of the
—, 547; the glory of the —,
549; Christ did not build the —
on Peter, 550; how the — is
founded and preserved, 551; local
churches, 553; definition of term,
553; — divinely instituted, 555;
orthodox and heterodox churches,
556; heterodox churches and
true discipleship, 558; no fellowship with heterodox churches,
559; right use of the doctrine of
the —, 560; the representative
—, 561. Cp. *Ecclesia.*
Civic righteousness no aid to conversion, 358.
Clauso utero, 293.
Close communion, 537.
Coadamites, 185.
Commandment, the new, 304.
Commission, sins of, 230.
Communicants. Who may be admitted to Lord's Supper as —,
538; — should examine themselves, 539; unworthy — should
not be admitted to Lord's Table,
539.
Communion of natures in Christ,
268; — is real, 269; — not
mere contiguity, 269; no mingling of natures, 270; — inseparable, 270.
Comparative religion, 10.
Concomitance, 511. 520.
Concrete of Christ's divine nature,
of human nature, and of both
natures, 274.
Concurrence, divine, in good and evil
actions, 191. 214.
Concursus in divine providence, 189.
Condescendit nobis Deus, etc., 162.
Confession, public and private,
should be retained, 539.
Confessions are secondary norms,
129; *quia,* not *quatenus* sub-
scriptions, 129; necessity of —,
129; — of the Church, 129.
Confirmation not a "confirmation"
of Baptism, 496; why we retain
—, 496.
Conscience, 213; sins against —,
229.
Consecration, act of, in Lord's Supper to be retained, 530; Calvin
denied necessity of —, 530.
Consensus ecclesiae, 94; — *patrum,*
95.

Consequences of denying inspiration,
119; — of sin, 215.
Consequentiae legitimae, 128.
Conservatio, 189.
Constitution of Missouri Synod, 561.
Consubstantialis, 153.
Consubstantiation, 528.
*Contemptus sacramenti damnat, non
privatio,* 500. 540.
Contradictions, alleged, in Scripture, 111.
Contradictory wills in God, 171.
Contrition and faith, 349. 350; papistic doctrine of contrition, 365.
366.
Conversio prima, 353; — *secunda,*
354; — *reiterata,* 354.
Conversion, the doctrine of, 336;
definition of, 336; — not a mere
change of mind or moral improvement, 337; special points
to consider in connection with
—, 338; starting-point and terminus of —, 340; efficient cause
of —, 342; — the work of God
alone, 343; cooperation after —,
344; means of —, 346; internal
motions in —, 349; — is instantaneous, 350; successive —, 351;
grace of — is resistible, 352;
transitive and intransitive —,
352; continued —, 353; reiterated —, 354; objections against
monergism in —, 355; synonyms
of —, 362.
Cooperation begins after conversion,
344.
1 Cor. 11, 25, explanation of, 533.
1 Cor. 15, 29, explanation of, 498.
2 Cor. 5, 18—21, explanation of, 310.
Corpus Christi festival, 511.
Corruption, state of, 210; original
— propagated to all men, 218;
known to man by nature, 218;
must be learned from Scripture,
218; false views on spread of —,
218; — and the will of man, 219.
Cost of our redemption, 247.
Council of Trent. On the interpretation of Scripture, 19; good
works necessary for justification,
26; mingles grace and gifts of
grace, 244; anathematizes Lutheran definition of justifying
grace, 244; curses Scriptural
doctrine of justification by faith,
368; teaches necessity of good
works for salvation, 392; perverts and condemns the Gospel,
421. Cp. Roman Catholic Church.
Creatio continuata, 190.

Creation, doctrine of, 179; order of —, 179; hexaemeron, 180; six days of —, 181; mediate —, 181; man's —, 184; definition of —, 185; — a free act of God, 186; — of angels, 186; facts of — known by Moses, 186; — an external act of God, 187; — by Father through Son and Holy Ghost, 187; end of —, 188.

Creationism, 58.

Creedless religion championed by Modernists, 60.

Cremer defends divine institution of Lord's Supper, 506.

Creeds, opposition of Modernism to, 60; Catholic —, 61; Christian — do not develop doctrine, 75.

Crimen laesae maiestatis, 82.

Cross is a concio legis realis, 348; the — of Christians, 424; what the — implies, 424; connection between Christianity and —, 425; how Christians regard their —, 426; benefits of cross-bearing, 427; strength to bear —, 427.

Crux theologorum, 58. 81.

Crying sins, 232.

Culpa, all men by nature are in eadem —, 607. 609.

Cur alii, alii non? 58. 81. 251. 359. 440. 611.

Cur alii prae aliis? 58. 81. 359. 592. 596. 611.

Cur non omnes? 58. Cp. Cur alii prae aliis?

Cyprian on 1 John 5, 7, 159.

Cryptist-kenotist Controversy, 290.

Damnation, eternal, of evil angels, 204; doctrine of eternal —, 633; punishment of the damned, 634. 635; causes of —, 637; purpose of the doctrine of —, 638.

Death, cause of, 207; its threefold aspects, 215. 223; temporal —, 613; what — is, 613; the sweet names of —, 613. 615; names applied to death of unbelievers, 614; causes of —, 614; subjects of —, 615; second —, 615; condition of soul between — and resurrection, 616; doctrine of Scripture with regard to departed souls, 619.

Decalog contains ceremonial features, 213.

Declaratory theory, 27.

Decrees, doctrine of, 176; — of creation, 176; — of redemption, 176; — of predestination, 177.

Deity of Christ, proofs for, 256.

Descent of Christ into hell, 296; its denial, 297.

Desertio Christi, 294.

Deszendenztheorie, 180.

Deus assumpsit naturam humanam, non hominem, 262.

Deus impleat vos odio Papae, 584.

Deus non dat interna nisi per externa, 349.

Dichotomy, 184.

Dicta probantia, 93.

Dieckhoff's synergism, 353.

Diesseitigkeitstheologie, 60.

Dii nuncupativi, 160.

Disciplines, four theological, 63.

Divisions in Church, 17; — not willed by God, 18; their causes, 18. 36; Romanistic —, 19; Reformed —, 20; — due to "scientific theology," 23.

Docetae, 50. 256.

Doctrina divina, 38.

Doctrinal development, 60. 74; why — must be condemned, 74; creeds no —, 75; — impossible, 76; Luther accused of —, 83.

Doctrines, confusion of, 3; fundamental and non-fundamental —, 47; which is the most fundamental of all —, 48; primary fundamental —, 48; secondary fundamental —, 52; what must be remembered as to —, 54; indifference toward —, 55; non-fundamental —, 56; no new — given to the Church, 96.

Dogma of the Church, what it is, 61.

Dogmas, Church and, 60; what a dogma is, 61; — and theological disciplines, 63.

Dominant sins, 231.

Dominion, man's, over creatures, 208.

Donatio fidei is conversion, 341.

Donatio virium spiritualium est conversio, 344.

Donum supernaturale, — superadditum, 206; — concreatum, 206.

Dorner, 290.

Dort, Synod of, 249.

Doubts regarding salvation; when they arise, 439.

Dualism, Christian, 164.

Ecclesia est invisibilis, 547; una, 548; sancta, 548; catholica, 549; apostolica, 549; — est mater fidelium, 552; ecclesiae particulares, 553; ecclesiae purae, corruptae, 557; — repraesentativa, 561.

Ecclesia primitiva, 130; how — fixed the canon, 131.

Ectypal theology, 39.
Efficacia resistibilis, 134.
Efficacious grace, 96.
Efficaciousness of divine grace denied, 250.
Efficacy of Bible, 133; — denied by Unitarians and Pelagians, 133; divine power of Word resistible, 134; efficacy *extra usum*, 136; the Spirit's activity through the Word not to be judged from feeling, 136; efficacy of Law and Gospel, 136.
Eggraphos, vox, 31.
Einheitliches Ganzes, ein, constructed on the basis of "Christian consciousness," etc., 82.
Eisegesis, 139.
Election, doctrine of, 177. 585; definition of decree of predestination, 178. 585; — did not take place *intuitu fidei*, 587; — embraces the whole order of salvation, 588; — not a mere predestination of *means* of salvation, 588; — is *Personenwahl, Einzelwahl*, 589; how believers are to consider their —, 589; — a doctrine of joy and comfort, 590; — used as a warning, 590; the right view of one's —, 591; in studying the doctrine of —, we must not ask questions to satisfy reason, 592; there is no absolute —, 593; we must not consider our — in a bare manner, 593; *Formula of Concord* does not teach — in a wider sense, 593. 594; the objects of —, 593; — extends only over those who are saved, 594; — is not the decree that those shall be saved who believe, 594; — is not the *ordinatio mediorum*, 594; the object of — is not simply the Church, 594; there is no — *ex praevisa fide finali*, 595; believers are sure of their — only if they cling to Christ, 595; the certainty of — is a certainty of faith, 597; the relation of faith to —, 598; faith the effect of —, 599; the purpose of the doctrine of —, 602; — inculcates the *sola gratia*, 603; — is a warning against self-righteousness, 603; how — comforts the believer, 604; there is no — to damnation, 606; why men reject the Scriptural doctrine of —, 610.
Elipandus of Toledo, 267.
Empyrean, 181.

Enthusiasm, separates power from the Word, 134; rejects *principium cognoscendi*, 138; Papacy is sheer enthusiasm, 96; — rejects means of grace, 453; its arguments against the means of grace, 454.
Enthusiasts claim private revelations, 95. 96. 97.
Erasmus, 22. 602.
Erkenntnis-theoretische Frage, 72.
Erlebnis, das christliche, 2.
Errare in Deum non cadit, 69.
Erring, Christian, unchristian, 55.
Erring key of papistic Church, 460; there is no —, 463.
Erscheinungen, Gleichartigkeit der theologischen, 10.
Eschatology, the doctrine of, 615; temporal death, 613; condition of the soul between death and the resurrection, 616; second advent of Christ, 619; resurrection of the dead, 625; final Judgment, 630; the end of the world, 631; eternal damnation, 633; eternal salvation, 639.
Essence, meaning of divine, 152. 154.
Eternity, divine, 165.
Eucharistic Congress, 511.
Eutychianism, 264. 267. 270.
Eve, how created, 185; subordinate to Adam, 185; how her soul was created, 186.
Evil thoughts and desires are actual sins, 225.
Evolution, 144. 180. 181. 206. 210.
Ex opere operato, 446. Cf. *Roman Catholic Church*.
Exaltation, Christ's, 295; stages of Christ's —, 296.
Excommunication, 556. 578.
Exegete, function of Christian, 139.
Experience, Christian, 2. 40. 41.
Experimentalism, modern, rejects means of grace, 454.
Experimentalists, 371.
Ex sensu, 136.
Ex nolentibus volentes facit, 358.
Extra ecclesiam nulla salus, 549.
Extra illud Calvinisticum, 280.

Faith, sources of, 14. 30. 69. 82. 91. 97. 114; how — justifies, 244. 255; doctrine of saving —, 321; nature of —, 322; synonyms of —, 325; why — justifies, 326; — a passive act or instrument, 327; true —, living —, 329; — and assurance of salvation, 329; whether the believer can be sure of possessing saving —, 329; —

of infants, 332; use of the term
— in Scripture, 333; the terminology of the Church regarding
—, 334; kindling of — the essential feature of conversion, 341;
righteousness of — and righteousness of life, 385; amissibility
of —, 436; relation of — to
means of grace, 446; — must
not be based on —, 456; — of
infants, 498. 502; the — of man
does not make Lord's Supper a
Sacrament, 529; the specific object of the communicant's —,
535.

Faith-consciousness, 2.

Fall of man, 210. 223.

Fatalism, 194.

Father, term, used essentially, personally, 157.

Felix of Urgel, 267.

Fidei ratio, 20.

Fides humana, divina, 70; Luther
on — *divina*, 70. 120; where —
divina is found, 124; — *heroica*,
174; *patitur sibi benefieri*, 327;
— *infantium fides actualis est*,
333; — *caritate formata*, 393.

Filioque, 156.

Finis theologiae, 65.

Finis cuius Scripturae, 129.

Finitum non est capax infiniti, 517.

Fire of hell, material or immaterial,
636.

Firmament, 182.

Flacianism, 221.

Flesh, 15.

Foreign sins whose guilt we share,
234.

Foreknowledge, divine, and human
responsibility, 168; divine —
and origin of evil, 169.

Formula of Concord on Law, 44; on
Gospel, 44; on mystery of election, 178; on original sin, 217;
on how original sin can be
known, 218; on effects of hereditary corruption, 219. 220. 222;
why original sin is nature-sin,
224; on man's will in spiritual
things, 237. 238; on conversion,
against Eutychianism and Nestorianism, 271. 277; on Christ's
vicarious atonement, 309; on
faith, 310. 327; on concealment
of Christ's majesty, 291; on
comfort of Christ's session, 301;
on synergism, 342; on the unregenerate, 344; on monergism,
344. 345; on means of conversion, 346; on Law and Gospel,
348; on enthusiasts, 348; on

new motions in conversion, 349;
on change in conversion, 356; on
externally hearing God's Word,
359; on mystery in election and
conversion, 360; on resuscitation, 363; on *sola fide*, 369; on
justifying faith, 372; on presence of works in justification,
377; on order between justification and sanctification, 385; on
efficient cause of sanctification,
386; on means of sanctification,
389; on necessity of good works,
391; teaches good works not
necessary for salvation, 392; rejects Majorism, 393; on error of
Amsdorf, 394; on necessity of
sanctification and good works,
395; on struggle of flesh against
spirit, 398; on perfectionism,
398; on mingling imputed righteousness and incipient righteousness, 402; on source of good
works, 406; why good works are
pleasing to God, 408; unsearchable judgments of God not to be
explored, 440; on means of
grace, 441; its definition of Law,
470; its definition of Gospel,
471; its explanation of the use
of the term *Gospel*, 471; features common to —, 471; on
distinction between Law and
Gospel, 482; on essence of Lord's
Supper, 510; on Sacramentarians, 513; on what makes the
Lord's Supper a Sacrament, 528;
on what makes a Sacrament,
529; on necessity of the consecration in the Lord's Supper,
530; on Mass of Romanists,
531; on the necessity of the entire action of the Lord's Supper,
532; on meaning of words of institution, 534; on election, 587;
election is a cause of salvation,
587; election embraces the way
of salvation, 588; believers
should not speculate on God's
secret foreknowledge, 589; we
are elected in Christ, 591; we
must not sound the abyss of
God's hidden predestination, 592;
we must concern ourselves with
God's revealed will, 592; on the
mystery in doctrine of election,
595; on considering our election,
595; on *sola gratia* in election,
596. 603; effect of election, 599;
election a cause of our salvation,
599; warning not to reject the
means of grace, 603; the com-

fort of election, 605; mystery in election, 609; God not unjust when condemning unbelievers, 610; on eternal salvation, 639.

"Fortunate inconsistency," 55.

Freedom, academic, 76; — from coercion, 193.

Free position of Luther on inspiration, as to, 116.

Free will, doctrine of the freedom of the will, 236; no — in spiritual matters, 237. 238; arguments for —, 239.

Freedom of will, 236; arguments for —, 239.

Fruit, forbidden; why the eating thereof was fatal, 223.

Fundamental articles, 47; secondary —, 52.

Fundamentalism, doctrines of, 457; denies necessity of means of grace, 457.

Fundamentalists, 78.

Generatio aequivoca, 180.

Gen. 1 and 2, 186; Gen. 3, 15, explanation of, 626.

Genus idiomaticum, 273; — *maiestaticum*, 275; no fourth —, 277; — *apotelesmaticum*, 284.

Gerhard. On the source of faith, 128; divine perfection, 137; Trinity in Old Testament, 159; obscure and clear passages of Scripture, 139; clearness of Scripture, 141; ascription of creation to Father, Son, and Holy Ghost, 152; divine attributes, 161; anthropomorphism, 164; no mutability in God, 164; divine presence, 166; divine goodness, 174; Providence, 189; why evil angels were not restored, 200; why original corruption is propagated, 218; free will, 237; suffering and death of Christ, 286; Christ the Priest, 308; divine appointment of ministry, 564; divinity of the mediate call, 571; habitation of soul after death, 617.

Gibbons, Cardinal, 421.

Glaubensbewusstsein, christliches, 2.

Gnosticism, 215. 258.

God, doctrine of, 143; Holy Trinity, 147; definition of —, 158; Holy Trinity revealed in Old Testament, 158; essence and attributes of —, 160; — not moved by anything outside Himself, 170; — not the cause of sin, 193. 214; sins against —, 230;

— can be resisted in the realm of grace, 249; term — not a generic term, 257.

God's power, when it can be resisted and when not, 134.

God's Word, doctrine of, a fundamental article, 51; the perversion of — a scandal, 54. 82.

Good intention does not make a Sacrament, 530.

Good works and faith, 385; — and sanctification, 385; necessity of —, 390; — are necessary, 391; but not effects of coercion, 391; — not necessary for salvation, 392; — tokens of faith, 393; — not injurious to salvation, 394; why — should be done, 396; — are not free, 396; doctrine of —, 403; norm of —, 405; — done only by believers, 407; — of believers not perfect, 407; why — of believers are pleasing to God, 408; — of heathen, 408; Christian's growth in —, 417; perversion of doctrine of —, 420; why the — of Romanists must be condemned, 420. 421.

Goodness, divine, 174; objections to —, 175.

Gordon, A. J., on perfectionism, 401.

Gospel defined by the *Formula of Concord*, 44; doctrine of — a fundamental article, 44; the — as absolution, 442. 443; error of modern theologians on this matter, 443; supernatural power of —, 443; definition of —, 471; peculiar use of the term —, 471; — imperatives, 474; the — does not reprove sin, 476; modern rationalists change — into a law, 482.

Gospels, Mark's and Luke's, 131.

Governmental theory, 27.

Grace, efficacious, acts immediately (Hodge), 96.

Grace of God, doctrine of, 242; necessity of —, 242; definition of —, 243; attributes of justifying —, 246; terminology, 251; saving — is *Dei favor*, 370.

Graebner, A. L., defines subjective and objective theology, 33; defines decree of predestination, 178.

Grape juice in celebration of Lord's Supper, 525.

Gratia infusa, 26. 245. 370. 376.

Gratia particularis, 21. 81.

Gratia universalis, 21. 81. 251.

Grievous sins, 230.

Gubernatio divina, 110. 189.

Guilt of Adam imputed to descendants, 217.

Habitude, theological, 33; **acquisition of —**, 86.

Habitus spiritualis, 33; — *practicus*, 64; — *exhibitivus*, — *demonstrativus*, 71; how — *practicus* is acquired, 86.

Hades, 634.

Hafenreffer on purgatory, 618.

Harmful things, 184.

Harnack. God gracious without Christ's death, 247.

Hastings's *Encyclopedia* on inspiration, 118.

Hay, straw, and stubble, 117.

Heathen's, the, being without Gospel does not disprove universal grace, 251.

"Heaven and earth" Scriptural designation of universe, 181.

Heaven to which Christ ascended, 299; purpose of —, 300; degrees of glory in —, 642; language of —, 642; — a place, 643; saints in —, 643; purpose of doctrine of —, 643.

Heb. 6, 4—6; 10, 26. 27, explanations of, 234.

Heerbrand: "Faith is no condition," 253.

Heilanstalt, Church not a, 543.

Hell, 636; degrees of punishment in —, 636; where — is, 637.

Heroic faith, 174.

Heterodox churches, 556. 558.

Hexaemeron, 180.

Hilary, 181.

Hiley on inspiration, 102.

"Historical character" of the Christian religion, 43.

Historical investigation, 97.

Hodge, Charles; *Systematic Theology*, 20. 22; his view on inspiration, 108; efficacious grace acts immediately, 135; — teaches that result is the interpretation of God's purposes, 249; on Christ's death, 286; on the blessing of the cup, 530.

Hoefling, 567. 568.

Hofmann, father of subjective theology, 3. 594; on image of God, 207; on doctrine of resurrection in Old Testament, 626.

Holiness, divine, 172.

Hollaz. Defines religion, 4. 9; private revelation not source of faith, 16; on fundamental articles, 52; secondary fundamental articles, 54; non-fundamental articles, 56; articles of faith, 59; inspiration, 104; *impulsus divinus*, 106; authority of Scripture, 122. 125; ministerial use of reason, 127; efficacy of divine Word, 135; three persons in God, 157; divine unity, 163; creation, 179; God, the Creator, 187; concurrence, 191; permissive providence, 192; knowledge of evil angels, 200; original sin, 217; cause of original sin, 223; definition of actual sin, 224; consequent will, 253; communication of attributes, 272; *genus idiomaticum*, 273; Christ's descent, 296; ascension, 300; faith, 327; conversion, 337. 348; justification, 367; imperfection of sanctification, 397; definition of good works, 403; on words of institution, 512. 515; where hell is, 637.

Holtzmann denies institution of Baptism, 486.

Holy Ghost, sin against, 232; reiterated conversion impossible if the sin against the — is committed, 354; operates through Word, 443.

"Holy Mother Church," 19.

Holy writers, relation of, to Holy Ghost, 106; their study and research, 110.

Hominis voluntas in conversione non est otiosa, etc., 352.

Homo certus est passive, etc., 72.

Homo in conversione passive sese habet, 344.

Hom 'ogumena, 110. 117. 130. 131.

Homo peccator, 65.

Hope of eternal life, 434; — a characteristic of believers, 434; its effect on Christian life, 434; the Christian's imperfection regarding the —, 435; Luther on the —, 435.

Horribile decretum, 607.

Huber, Samuel, 593.

Human race, unity of, 185.

Human nature of Christ, 258; peculiarities of, 259; divine attributes ascribed to the —, 278; — was not an *instrumentum passivum*, 279. 284; the modes of presence of the —, 281; adoration of the —, 281; Christ did not always use attributes communicated to His human nature,

288; Christ worked in, with, and through His human nature, 292.

Humanity of Christ, proofs for, 258.

Humboldt, Alexander von, 185.

Humiliation of Christ, state of, 287; erroneous views regarding the —, 289; stages of —, 292.

Hunnius, 599. 601.

Hutter. On actual sin, 224; meaning of term *free will*, 236; on the divine institution of the ministry, 564.

Hylozoism, 144.

Hypocrites are outside the Church, 542; not truly members of local churches, 554.

Ich, das wiedergeborne, 2.

Idiomata, meaning of, 272.

Illumination; what it is, 364.

Image of God, 205; definition of —, 205; — and man's nature, 206; — lost through Fall, 207; — in a wider sense, 207; seat of —, 207; results of —, 208; — and woman, 209; end of —, 209.

Immaculate conception, 218.

Immensity, divine, 165.

Immortality, absolute and relative, 208.

Immutability, 164.

Impanation, 528.

Impulsus scribendi, 105. 110; Hollaz on —, 106; Quenstedt on —, 106; denied by Catholics, 106.

"In, with, and under," 521.

Inaccuracies in Holy Scripture, Calvin on, 107.

In corde meo iste unus regnat articulus, sc. fides Christi, etc., 320.

Index Generalis of Jesuits, 422.

Indwelling of Holy Ghost, 381.

Inerrancy of Holy Scripture, denial of, 23.

Infants. Why — should be baptized, 497; — can believe, 498. 502; baptism of — in the early Church, 498; — who die without baptism, 498; faith of —, 502.

Infinity, divine, 164.

Infirmity, sins of, 229.

Infralapsarians, 248.

Infused grace, 26.

Inspiration, denial of —, 23; plenary —, 82. 104; proof for —, 99; doctrine of —, 101; verbal —, 101; Hiley on —, 102; *suggestio verborum*, 102; *suggestio realis*, 103; manner of —, 103; Hollaz on —, 104; involves an

a-priori certainty, 105; — includes the divine impulse to write, 105; objections to —, 107; — denied by special passages, 113; alleged evil consequences of —, 114; confessional Lutheranism on —, 115; *eine kuenstliche Theorie*, 116. 119; cause and consequences of denying —, 118.

Institution, Christ's, of the Holy Supper makes it a Sacrament, 529; meaning of words of —, 534.

Instrumentum *aërgon*, 284.

Integrity, of New Testament, 132; of man, 205; state of —, why blessed, 207.

Intellectualism, 40.

Intelligence, divine, 170.

Intercession of Christ, 313; — of Holy Spirit, 314.

Intuitu fidei, 595. 599; doctrine of — unscriptural, 601; can be understood only in a synergistic sense, 602; not all who taught the — were synergists, 602.

Involuntary sins, 229.

Irresistible grace, 249.

Israel, all, to be saved; how to be understood, 624.

Iustitia civilis, — *spiritualis*, 239. 358. 409; — *legalis, evangelica,* 172.

Jehovah, *nomen Dei essentiale*, 160; pronunciation of —, 160.

Jenseitstheologie, 60.

Jews, general conversion of, 624; return of — to Palestine, 625.

1 John 1, 8—10, explanation of, 399.

Judas not coerced to sin, 193.

Judgment, final, 630; the — of believers and unbelievers, 630. 631; the — not a long-drawn-out process, 631; how believers will judge with Christ, 631.

Justice, divine, 172.

Justification by faith, doctrine of, 367; objective, subjective —, 367; *sola fide*, 369; what is meant by —, 370; what — presupposes, 371; the doctrine of — the central doctrine of the Christian religion, 371; terminology to guard correct doctrine of —, 373; — a forensic act, 374; — does not require presence of good works, 376; — has no degrees, 377; — is forgiveness of sins, 378; — on basis of works, 379; effects of —, 380;

— source of sanctification, 385;
insistence on — does not lead to
neglect of sanctification, 413;
— regarded as too "juridical" or
not sufficiently "ethical," 423.

Justification by grace, denial of —,
23. 27; Luther on —, 48; cannot be taught if Law and Gospel
are mingled, 481.

Justifying grace, not absolute, 246;
— is grace in Christ, 246;
— does not exclude divine justice, 246; — is universal, 248;
— is serious and efficacious, 250.

Kaftan, Theo., on inspiration, 118;
on authority of Bible, 118.
Kahnis on purgatory, 618.
Kant's religious philosophy, 12.
Keckermann rejected Zwingli's explanation of words of institution, 515; claimed that the
words of institution in their entirety must be explained figuratively, 517.
Kirn. Death existed before sin, 614.
Kliefoth, 568.
Kenoticism, 268. 277. 289.
Kenoticists, 289.
Kingdom, Christ's threefold, 315.
Knowledge of God, natural, 143;
— is true, 145; its value, 145;
its limitations, 146; Christian
—, 146. 168.
Koine, 113.
Krauth on words of institution, 514.
515.
Kretzmann, P. E., on elemental
light, 182; on work of third
creation day, 182.

Lacunae, 80.
Last things, doctrine of the, 613.
Cp. *Eschatology*.
Latermann, synergism of, 241. 351.
353. 357. 360.
Law, divine, and sin, 211; — defined by *Formula of Concord*,
212; Moral —, 212. 213; Ceremonial —, 212; Church has no
right to make laws, 212; how
the — can be known, 213; definition of the —, 470; — is
God's Word, 471; promises of
the —, 474; the — a ministration of condemnation, 475; the
goal of the —, 475; the — reproves sin and unbelief, 476;
uses of the —, 478. 479. 480;
how the — is a schoolmaster to
Christ, 478.
Law and Gospel are opposites, 44;

doctrine of —, 44; defined by
Formula of Concord, 44; distinction between —, 46. 136; uses
of Law, 390; — are contradictions, 45; mingling of — causes
doubts regarding salvation, 439;
the doctrine of —, 470; definition of —, 470; — considered
as opposites, 473; promises of
—, 474; — only different aspects
of God in relation to the sinner,
477; close connection between
—, 477; the art of distinguishing between —, 480; by whom
the proper distinction between
— is denied, 484; modern theologians affirm higher unity between —, 484; how — are
mingled in a subtle manner, 485.
Law of affinity and consanguinity,
214.
Law of propagation, 183; laws of
nature, 191.
"Legalistic character" of Baptism,
486.
Lehrfortbildung, 60. 74; Luther
not guilty of —, 83.
Lehrverwirrung, 3.
Leo the Great on *genus apotelesmá-
ticum*, 285.
Levicula, 112.
Levirate Law, 214.
Lex necat peccatorem, non peccatum,
etc., 47.
Lex praescribit, evangelium inscribit,
136.
Libertas a coactione, 193.
Liberty, Christian, when it must be
yielded and when not, 226; —
effect of justification, 382.
Life, divine, 167.
Light of first creation day, 182.
Local churches, rights and duties of,
562; their right to call and or-
dain, 572; objections to their
right to call and ordain, 572;
— should watch over the min-
istry, 577.
Local extension of Christ's human
nature, 270.
Locutio exhibitiva, 513. 522.
Lodges, 431; lodge-members not to
be admitted to Lord's Supper,
538; lodgery a pagan cult, 538.
Loehe, 568. 574.
Logic, right use of, 127; wrong use
of —, 128.
Logos, the preexistent, the true
Teacher in the Old Testament,
305.
Lord's Supper, doctrine of, a secondary fundamental article, 52;

— a means of grace, 444; what the — offers and gives, 444; institution of the —, 506; — *sacramentum confirmationis,* 507; names of —, 507. 536; relation of — to other means of grace, 507; — a *medium iustificationis,* 507; special characteristic of —, 508; "physical operation" of —, 509; doctrine of —, 509; Reformed doctrine of —, 509; Lutheran doctrine and the words of institution in the —, 520; different accounts of words of institution, 523; material elements in —, 524; distribution of elements necessary, 525; what makes the — a Sacrament, 528; purpose of the —, 533; blessings of —, 536; who may be admitted to —, 537; lodge members should not be admitted to —, 538; the necessity of the —, 540.

Luke 22, 20, explanation of, 533.

Los-von-der-Schrift-Bewegung, 2.

Luthardt, 594.

Luther. His attitude towards Bible, 3. 42; on making a theologian, 34; theologians, 38; distinguishing between Law and Gospel, 47; justification, 48; Christian erring, 55; means by which Christians are ruled, 67; *fides divina,* 70; positive assurance, 72; creeds, 75; retaining Word of God, 75; effects of small errors, 80; accused of doctrinal development, 84; *oratio, meditatio, tentatio,* 86; Papacy is enthusiasm, 96; Scripture, 98; inspiration, 98. 105; 1 Cor. 7, 10, 114; his alleged "free attitude" toward the Bible, 116; "hay, straw, and stubble," 116; on *Homologumena* and *Antilegomena,* 117; *"in acie minus valet,"* 117; "strawy epistle," 117; "urge Christ," 117; right to judge doctrine, 125; methodological advice to ministers, 132; efficacy of Bible, 133; effecting anything through Word, 135; clearness of Scripture, 138. 139; God, the Creator, 188; Gen. 9, 6 and Jas. 3, 9, 207; woman, 209; satanic obedience of Pope, 212; chastisements, 216; costs paid by Christ, 247; Christ's supernatural conception, 293; conversion, 337; against Erasmus, 346. 361; efficacy of Word, 347. 349; God's drawing in conversion, 356; regeneration,

363; *sola fide,* 372; faith, 386; growth in sanctification, 389; norm of good works, 404. 406; works of Alexander the Great, 409; inability of unregenerate man to do good works, 411; Christian ministry, 413; an evangelical pastor to urge growth in sanctification, 414; tithing, 414; on passages promising reward, 417; value of good works, 418; works done outside faith, 421; cross of believers, 425; Christian prayer, 429; prayer of the unregenerate, 431; efficacy of true prayer, 432; Lord's Prayer, 433; forms of prayer, 433; hope of eternal life, 434; the Gospel as absolution, 442; having faith and relying on faith, 456; absolution, 459; means of grace in Old Testament, 466; Antinomianism, 472; goal of Law and Gospel, 475; close connection between Law and Gospel, 477; need of the Holy Ghost in distinguishing between Law and Gospel, 481; distinction between Law and Gospel, 485; effects of Baptism, 495; infant baptism, 502; faith of infants, 502; purpose of Lord's Supper, 508; Lord's Supper, 510; transubstantiation, 511; private masses, 531; the purpose of the Lord's Supper, 533; close communion, 537; on those who despise Holy Communion, 541; error producing error, 560; spiritual priesthood of all believers, 566; necessity of means of grace by which the Holy Spirit operates, 570; all Christians are Peters, 573; ordination, 575; Paul was a *servus,* 577; equality of Christian pastors, 579; the public ministry the supreme office, 580; condition of soul after death, 617; the resurrection body, 628; judgment of believers, 631; destruction of world in its present form, 632.

Lutheran Church not a sect, 24; what the term — means, 24; — defines justifying grace Scripturally, 245; — not the *una sancta,* but the true orthodox Church, 558.

Macpherson on *Zwischenleib,* 618.

Majorism, 392. 393.

Man, doctrine of, 205; created in

God's image, 205; created in image of Triune God, 205; man's nature and divine image, 206; end of the divine image in man, 209; man's state of corruption, 210; "old —," "new —," 388.

Mandatum divinum, 106.

Manducatio generalis, indignorum, 530.

Manicheism, 221.

Mary, the Virgin, no immaculate conception of, 218. 222; *semper virgo*, 293.

Mass, papistic, 313; sacrifice of —, 511; — no Sacrament, 531; Council of Trent on —, 536.

Mater ecclesia sancta, 19.

Materia coelestis, 508. 524. 526; *materia terrena*, 525; what the *materia coelestis* is not, 526.

Materia est principium passivum, 184.

Material substance, sin no, 221.

Materialism, 144.

Matt. 16, 18, explanation of, 550.

Matt. 20, 1—16; 22, 1—14, explanation of, 604.

Matt. 25, 46, explanation of, 633.

Means by which Christian theology accomplishes its purpose, 66; — prescribed by God must be used, 194.

Means of grace, doctrine of, 441; their twofold power, 441; perversion of doctrine of —, 442; how Calvinism regards the —, 442; how synergism corrupts the —, 442; the Gospel a —, 443; Baptism a —, 444; Lord's Supper a —, 444; why God ordained many —, 447; erroneous doctrines regarding the —, 448; the importance of the doctrine of the —, 455. 457; — in form of absolution, 458; — in Old Testament, 465; — and prayer, 467.

Media dativa, effectiva, 319.

Media dotika, 252.

Meditatio. Meditation in theology, 86.

Medium cognoscendi, 68.

Medium iustificationis, 536.

Medium leptikon, 252.

Medius, status, 612.

Meisner on purpose of theology, 65.

Melanchthon introduced synergism, 22. 241; three causes of conversion, 345; his synergistic conclusion, 360; will of man assents, 360; his synergism, 596.

Memorial feast, 536.

Meritum de congruo, de condigno, 420.

Metabasis eis allo genos, 91.

Methods, theological, 84; synthetic and analytic —, 84; by whom these are used, 85.

Millenarians, 318.

Millennium, the doctrine of, unscriptural, 621. 622. 623.

Ministers, Christian, stewards of Christ, 537.

Ministry, public, definition of, 563; — divinely appointed, 564; in what sense the — is public, 574; the — and the spiritual priesthood of all believers, 564; proofs that the — is a divine ordinance, 566; the necessity of the —, 569; the call into the —, 570; how the — is despised, 570; Christian — not a special spiritual estate, 576; the power of the —, 578; the relation of Christian ministers to one another, 579; the — is the supreme office in the Church, 580.

Mirabilia seu mira, 198.

Miracles, explanation of 174; performed by angels, 198.

Miraculous conception, 259. 260.

Missing links in theological system, 81.

Modernism the result of the application of philosophy to theology, 14; — rejects Holy Scripture altogether, 27; — the result of indifferentism, 56; — shows the disastrous consequences of academic freedom, 78; — regards human reason as the source of faith, 91; — a direct outgrowth of the crass rationalism of the 18th and 19th centuries, 108; — denies the necessity of Christ's vicarious atonement, 163; — rejects Scripture as the only source of truth, 170.

Modernistic theologian, viewpoint of, 1. 173.

Modern rationalistic theology, 23. 40. 43. 73. 78. 79. 82. 93.

Modus subsistendi, 152; — *operandi*, 152; — *loquendi*, 164. 167.

Moles coeli et terrae, 179. 180.

Monarchianism, 150.

Monergism of divine grace, to, we owe our preservation, 437. 438.

Monothelitism, 258.

"Monsters"; whom Luther branded thus, 3.

Monstrum incertitudinis, 26. 381.

Moral Example Theory, 27.

Moral Law not the Decalog, 213;
— norm of good works, but not
their source, 406.

Mortal sins, 231; seven — of papists, 231.

Mosaic creation report alone authentic, 181.

Mueller, Max, on religion, 5; on the
difference between the Christian
religion and other so-called religions, 22.

Muenchmeyer, 568. 574.

Mutatio nulla cadit in Deum, 164.

Mystery in doctrine of election, 612;
the psychological —, 612.

Nature and concept of theology, 1.

Nazianzen, Gregory of, 32.

Necessitas immutabilitatis, 193.

Nestorianism, 264. 267. 270. 271.
272.

New Testament. Its essential difference from the Old, 29; as canonical as the Old, 100; historical
testimony of —, 130; integrity
of —, 132.

*Nihil habet rationem sacramenti
extra usum a Christo institutum*,
526.

Nitzsch-Stephan on the source of
faith, 40.

Non-fundamental articles, 56.

Norma normans, norma normata,
95. 129.

Norma discretionis, 129; — *remissiva*, 137.

Norms other than Scripture, 135.

Nosse cum affectu et effectu, 169.
600.

Notations, personal, 156.

Notitia innata, 145; — *acquisita*,
145.

Obduration, doctrine of, 227; causes
of, 227. 607.

Obedience, active and passive, 25.
306. 307.

Objectivity of the Lutheran Church,
456.

Obsession, spiritual and physical,
203.

Offenbarungsurkunde, 108.

Offense, doctrine of, 226; — given
and taken, 227.

Office of Christ, 301; threefold —,
302; prophetic —, 303; execution of — in state of exaltation,
304; sacerdotal —, 305; kingly
—, 314; errors regarding kingly
—, 317.

Old Testament. Its essential difference from the New, 29; —

quoted as God's Word in the
New, 99.

Omission, sins of, why sins, 224,
230.

Omnipraesentia intima, extima, 291.

Omnipresence, divine, 165.

Open questions, or theological problems, 58.

Opera ad extra, 156. 176; — *ad
intra*, 156. 176.

Opinio legis, 9. 15. 97.

Optimism of Leibniz, 187.

Oratio, 86.

Ordination, 574; absolute —, 574.

Ordo salutis, relation of the various
articles in the, 320, 362.

Original sin, doctrine of, 216; definition of —, 216; why so called,
216; — a positive evil, 221;
negative and positive side of —,
221; — not a *substantia*, 221;
— an *accidens;* however, not a
spot or stain, but total corruption, 222; universality of —,
222; cause of —, 223; effects of
—, 223; — source of all actual
sins, 224; — a nature-sin, 224;
reference to — in Baptism, 501.

*Panis extra usum a Christo insti-
tutum non est corpus Christi*,
525.

Pantheism, 144. 164. 173. 186. 191.
192. 210. 214.

Papists teach that man was originally indifferent, 206; — deny
communion of natures in Christ,
269. Cp. *Roman Catholic Church*.

Pardonable sins, 232.

Parsimonius, 297.

Participation in sins of others, 235.

Particulae exclusivae, 392.

Particularism, 249. 251.

Passages allegedly contradicting inspiration, 113.

Patripassians, 150.

Peccata enormia do not destroy
faith (Calvinists), 231.

Pelagians say foreign guilt cannot
be imputed, 217; — deny hereditary corruption, 221. 241.

Perfection of Scripture, 137.

Perfectionism, 398. 399. 400. 401.

Perichoresis, 157.

Personal acts of God, 156; — notations, 156; — properties, 156;
— sins, 234.

Personal propositions are real (doctrine of Christ), 271.

Personal sins, 234.

Personal union in Christ, 263; —

unique, 264; erroneous views regarding the —, 265.

Persons, divine; meaning of the term, 154.

Perspicuitas rerum, verborum, 140.

Perspicuity of Scripture, 138; in what respect Scripture is perspicuous, 139; with what — must not be identified, 140; to whom Scripture is not perspicuous, 141; objections to —, 141; —denied by papists and enthusiasts, 142.

Pessimism, 144.

Pestilentissima pestis, 375.

Peter; why he fell from grace, 438.

1 Pet. 3, 18—20, explanation of, 296.

1 Pet. 4, 6, explanation of, 297.

2 Pet. 1, 10, explanation of, 604.

Petros, petra, 550. 551. 573.

Pfeffinger, 596.

Pfeiffer on positive theology, 38.

Pheromenoi, 103. 105.

Philippi on image of God, 207. 600. 601.

Photinians, 150.

Physical operation of Baptism, 509.

Pietists; how they direct alarmed sinners, 455; — reject absolution, 459. 461; — make prayer a means of grace, 468.

Piscator on copula *is,* 515.

Poenitentia continuata, 353; *poenitentia quotidiana,* 401. Cp. *Repentance.*

Polemics of Christ and His apostles, 36.

Polytheism, definition of, 144. 166.

Pope the Antichrist, because he anathematizes Scriptural doctrine of *sola fide,* 380.

Portenta; whom Luther calls thus, 3.

Positive theology, 38.

Positivism, 144.

Potestas ministerialis, ordinis, clavium, iurisdictionis, 578; beyond the *potestas clavium* ministers have no authority, 579.

Potestas clavium, 383.

Power, divine, 173.

Praedestinatio non est absoluta, sed ordinata, 594.

Praesentia divina, localis, 21. 166; — *illocalis,* — *repletiva,* 166.

Prayer and theology, 86; the Christian life and —, 428; what — presupposes, 429; heathen prayers, 430; prayers of lodges, 431, what — works, 431; what — asks for, 432; conditional —, 433; unconditional —, 433; heroic —, 433; Lord's —, 433;

prayers to departed saints, 433; to angels, 433; to Son of Man, 433; extemporaneous —, 433; forms of —, 433; — not a means of grace, 467; why Calvinists make — a means of grace, 468.

Preadamites, 185.

Predestination, decree of, 177; second form of, 601. Cf. *Election.*

Predigtamt, Pfarramt, 563. 567.

Prepositions *anti, hyper,* meaning of, 307.

Presbyterian Confession of Faith on powers of church conventions, 562.

Presbyters, 579.

Presence, three modes of Christ's, 522.

Preservation, the doctrine of —, 436; two vital facts regarding —, 436; Calvinistic errors regarding —, 436; synergistic error regarding —, 437.

Priesthood, the power of the, does not make the eating and drinking a Sacrament, 529.

Principium cognoscendi, 14. 30. 69. 82. 91. 97. 114; substitutes for —, 91.

Problems, theological, 58.

Proegno (foreknew), 600.

Properties, personal, 156.

Progress in theology, 60. 74; Luther not guilty of —, 83.

Prolegomena, 1.

Proofs for authority of Scripture, 123; — for God's existence, 145.

Properties of Holy Scripture, 120.

Protevangelium, 90. 210.

Providence, divine, 189; definition of —, 189; objects of —, 190; objections to —, 190; — and secondary causes, 190; divine concurrence in good and evil actions, 191; permissive —, 192; — and free will, 193.

Psychological phenomena, 11.

Psychology, religious, 10—12.

Psychopannychism, 616. 617.

Purgatory, 617.

Quakers deny institution of Baptism, 486; reject Lord's Supper, 506.

Quenstedt on the term *religion,* 10: Scripture the only source of faith, 16; consent of Church not source of faith, 16. 62; how holy penmen wrote, 103; *impulsus scribendi,* 106; *fides divina,* 121; arguments of reason, 123; efficacy of Bible, 133; resistibility of efficacy, 134; obscure passages, 139; natural knowledge of God, 146; empyrean, 182; permissive providence, 192; state of corruption, 210; original sin, 217; communion of natures, 270; imperfection of sanctification, 396; norm of good works, 404; why works please God, 408; efficacy of divine Word, 444; necessity of entire action of Lord's Supper, 532; eternal salvation, 640.

Quoad materiale, — formale, 192. 409.

Quod non est biblicum, etc., 38.

Quod ubique, etc., 95.

Quot humanae naturae, tot personae humanae, 262.

Quotations, inaccurate, in Scripture, 112.

Quot personae, tot essentiae, not true of God, 154.

Rationalism. Rationalistic axiom of Reformed, 20; unified system of —, 82.

Rationalistic theology seeks to construct unified system, 82; — imperfect and incomplete, 84; — relies on "Christian experience," etc., 96; denies incarnation of Christ, 262.

Real presence, 21. 167. 516; on what — rests, 522. 527; Luther said to have emphasized the — too much, 534.

Reason, human, not source of faith, 16; its two functions, 80. 92. 127; its *usus instrumentalis, usus magisterialis*, 80. 92; — when opposed to Scripture, 91; — has been substituted for Scripture, 91; enlightened — not a source of faith, 93; ministerial use of —, 127.

Reatus culpae, poenae, 215.

Reconciliation, objective and subjective, 310.

Reformed theology, 20. Cp. *Calvinistic theology*.

Regenerate heart, 42.

Regeneration; what it is, 363.

Relation of Holy Ghost to writers, doctrine of, 106.

Religion, definition of, 4. 7; heathen —, 4; synonyms of —, 4; number of religions, 6; comparative —, 10; philosophy of —, 12; sources of —, 14; — of faith, 15; — in Old Testament, 17; — of flesh, 20.

Religionsgeschichte, 10. 12.

Religionsmengerei, 559.

Renovation a synonym of sanctification, 385; — imperfect in this life, 400.

Renunciation in Baptism, 502.

Repentance comprises contrition and faith, 347; doctrine of —, 365; daily — a return to Baptism, 496; — of apostates a return to Baptism, 496.

Repristinationst eologen, 74.

Resistance against grace, natural and wilful, 62.

Restitution of all things, 633.

Restorationists, 638.

Resurrection, doctrine of, a fundamental article, 51; — of Christ, 298; God raised up Christ, 298; Christ rose, 298; Christ's resurrection body, 298; — of the dead, 625; — taught in Old Testament, 625; in what — consists, 626; to whom Scripture ascribes the —, 627.

Reusch on theological problems, 59.

Rev. 16, 11, explanation of, 636.

Rev. 20, explanation of, 623.

Revelations, fixed, 16; private — not source of faith, 16. 95. 137.

Reward of grace, 416.

Righteousness of faith and righteousness of life, 385. 402.

Ritschl, 23; rejects the Gospel of Christ, 82; God gracious without Christ's redemption, 247.

Roman Catholic Church accepts tradition as source of faith, 1; anathematizes justification by faith, 19; its chief error, 26; teaches justification by works and paganizes Christianity, 26; perverts the ancient creeds by antichristian errors, 61; stigmatizes Luther as a heretic, 88; its theology is sheer enthusiasm, 96; denies *impulsus scribendi*, 106; accuses Lutherans of arguing in a circle, 122; accepts apocrypha, 130; makes the Vulgate the only authoritative text, 132; rejects perspicuity of Scripture, 138. 142; teaches that man was originally in a state of moral indifference, 206; image of God a superadded gift, 206; wrong definition of sin, 211; fills the world with satanic obedience, 212; immaculate conception of Mary, 218; minimizes original sin, denying total corruption of fallen man, 218; its antichristian character proved by Mariolatry, 222; wrong definition of actual sins, 231; free will in spiritual matters, 241; mingles grace and gift of grace, 244; anathematizes justifying grace as *gratuitus favor Dei*, 244; denies communion of natures in Christ, 268; teaches that finite is incapable of infinite, 275; denies *genus maiestaticum*, 276; denies adoration to human nature of Christ, 281; teaches Christ was a new Lawgiver, 304; teaches workrighteousness, 312; teaches the abomination of the Mass, 313; denies communication of attributes, 317; substitutes for God's Word commandments of men, 318; is the Church of Antichrist, 318; teaches faith is assent, not trust in Gospel, 322; anathematizes faith as trust in Christ, 323. 324; teaches faith is *otiosus habitus*, 323; faith saves because it is a good work or the source of good works, 327; denies that a believer may be sure of salvation, 330; teaches conversion is a meritorious work, 338; sinner begins conversion, and God completes it, 342; erroneous definition of repentance, 365; its false doctrine of contrition makes true contrition impossible, 366; is the greatest enemy of the Christian Church because it denies *sola fide*, 368; its false doctrine of justification, 370; anathematizes *sola fide*, 370; teaches justification by works, 379; makes sanctification the basis of justification, 385; teaches good works are necessary for salvation, 392; teaches faith saves because it works by love, 393; teaches perfectionism, 398; false standards of good works, 405; regards works of heathen as good, 409; a perfecter of good works, 420; false doctrine of penitence, 422; vicious teaching of doing evil for a good purpose, 422; error regarding the Sacraments, working *ex opere operato*, 446; error on purpose of Christ's death, 448; error regarding the means of grace, 449; "doctrine of penance," 449; error regarding the "erring key," 460; denies certainty of salvation, 460; mingles Law and Gospel, 484; teaches

Baptism works *ex opere operato*, 492; anathematizes doctrine that we receive forgiveness in Baptism by faith, 492; teaches absolute necessity of baptism, 500; perverts doctrine of Lord's Supper, 509; denies that in Lord's Supper forgiveness of sins is offered, 535; false doctrine of the Church, 543. 544; repudiation of all pastors not ordained by bishops, 575; the "sacrament" of ordination confers *ex opere operato* an indelible character, 575; also the power to transubstantiate bread and wine, 575; teaches purgatory, 617.

Romanism is sheer enthusiasm, 96. Cp. *Roman Catholic Church.*

Rom. 8, 29, explanation of, 599; 9, 18, do., 610; 9, 22, do., 608; 11, 26, do., 624; 11, 25, do., 625.

Russellism, 163. 634.

Sabellians, 150.

Sacramental union, 510; what it is not, 519; the Calvinists do not teach —, 527; Lutheran doctrine of the —, 527; when it occurs, 532.

Sacramentalis unio non fit nisi in distributione, 525.

Sacraments are *Verbum visibile*, 53; their essence and purpose, 53; doctrine of —, 53; effective means of grace, 347; — the visible Word, 444; — means of grace, 444; the pardon they offer, 445; — of the papistic Church, 447; the Sacrament of Baptism, 488; doctrine of the Lord's Supper, 506.

Salvation Army denies institution of Baptism, 486; rejects the Lord's Supper, 506.

Salvation, eternal, doctrine of, 639; in what it consists, 640; the glory of, 642; the purpose of the doctrine of —, 643; the practical use of the doctrine of —, 644.

1 Sam. 28, 19, explanation of, 619.

Sanctification effect of justification, 382; doctrine of —, 384; — in wider and in narrower sense, 384; — and good works, 385; — not an idle state, 385; efficient cause of —, 386; inner motions of —, 387; means of —, 389; necessity of —, 390; imperfection of —, 396; article of — is kept pure only if article of justification is kept pure, 402; — and the Christian life, 424.

Schismatics, 560.

Semper virgo, 293.

Schleiermacher, 23. 73. 82. 93; on *Zwischenleib*, 618.

Schriftganze, das, 83.

Schriftprinzip, 91. 127. 137.

Science and theology, 67; in what sense theology is not a science, 67; in what sense it is, 69; preferable not to define Christian theology primarily as a science, 70.

Scientia naturalis, libera, media; scientia de futuro conditionata, 168.

Scintillula fidei, 341. 350.

Scotus, Duns, 162.

Scriptura locuta, etc., 2.

Scriptura Sacra est Deus incarnatus, 92; — *non est muta*, etc., 126; *finis cui — sunt omnes homines*, 128; *finis cuius —*, 129; *versiones — non solum utiles*, etc., 129; — *Scripturam interpretatur*, 139.

Scriptura Scripturam interpretatur, 139.

Scripture, Holy, only source and norm of Christian faith and life, 2. 16. 17. 61. 90; — rejected to-day, 40; *lacunae* (omissions) in —, 80; — infallible, 83; doctrine of —, 90; substitutes for —, 91; — is *Deus incarnatus*, 92; general scope of —, 93; attitude of Romanists toward —, 96; of Calvinists, 96; of rationalistic theology, 96; — the Word of God, 98; proof for this, 99; — *causa principalis*, 103; the holy writers were *causae instrumentales* of —, 103; diversity of style in —, 107; objections to its inspiration, 108; *Offenbarungsurkunde*, 108; variant readings in —, 109; contradictions in —, 111; inaccurate quotations in —, 112; trivial matters in —, 112; properties of —, 120; canonical authority of —, 125; use of —, 125; — "a dumb book" (papists), 126; — a book for all men, 128; *finis cuius* of —, 129; translations of —, 129; — the absolute norm, 129; efficacy of —, 133; perfection or sufficiency of —, 137; how — sets forth doctrines, 138; perspicuity of —, 138; — and as-

tronomical systems, 183; — the only norm of faith, 561.

Second board of Romanism, 422. 493. 496.

Second form of predestination, 601.

Secret sins, 234.

Sedes doctrinae, 83. 93. 126. 139.

Selbstbewusstsein, das fromme, 2.

Self-assurance, 73.

Semi-Pelagians, 50. 241.

Seneca, 614.

Sensus gratiae, 245.

Separatists, 560.

Servitude of letter, 77.

Session, Christ's, 300; definition of Christ's —, 301; comfort of Christ's —, 301.

Shedd, William, 108. 606.

Sheol, 634.

Si homo non periisset, etc., 255.

Simplicitas divina, 163.

Sin, doctrine of, and its consequences a fundamental article, 48; doctrine of —, 210; definition of —, 210; — and divine Law, 211; causes of —, 214; *subiectum quod* of —, 215; *subiectum quo* of —, 215; consequences of —, 215; effects of — denied, 215; original sin, 216; definition of actual sin, 224; — of commission and omission, 224; what belongs to —, 225; causes of actual —, 225; God not the cause of —, 226; classification of —, 228; — against Holy Ghost, 233.

Sitting at right hand of God, what this — does not mean, 281.

Skandalon, 54. 558.

Smalcald Articles on hereditary sin, 218; losing faith, 354; justifying faith, 372; means of grace, 441; absolution, 459; purpose of Lord's Supper, 508; power of churches, 563; right of local churches to call, 572. 574; the Pope the Antichrist, 583; doctrine concerning Antichrist not fundamental, 584.

Socrates, 12.

Sola fide, the doctrine of, 369; what is meant by —, 370. 376; Pope the Antichrist for anathematizing —, 380.

Sola fides membra ecclesiae constituit, 541.

Sola gratia, 22. 81. 82. 85. 251; the doctrine of election inculcates the —, 602.

Sola Scriptura, 85.

Solus Deus convertit hominem, 346.

Son of God did not assume a human person, 262.
Son of Man; what this term denotes, 262.
Sophismata, 174.
Soteriology, doctrine of, **319.**
Soul, proof for immortality of, 639; Christian hope of salvation not identical with pagan doctrine of immortality of —, 639.
Sources of faith, true, 18. 82; false —, 82.
Spaeth, Dr. A., on John 20, 19—24, 462.
Spark, a mere, of faith means complete conversion, 341. 350.
Sponsors, the use of, in baptism, 501.
State not a maid of the Church, 552; forms of — government, 552; — and Church must be separate, 553.
State of grace, 381.
States of Christ, doctrine of the, 287; state of humiliation, 287.
Status medius, no, 351. 363.
Stoicism, 168.
"Strawy epistle" (of James), 117.
Stroebel, 568.
Strong. On creation, 185; on modern prophecy, 304.
Struggle of spirit against flesh, 388.
Style, diversity in, of Holy Scripture, 107. 109.
Sub specie aeternitatis, 434.
Subordinationists, 151. 155.
Suggestio verborum, 102; — *realis*, 103; — *literalis*, 105.
"Supper," the, of the Calvinists and the papists outside the institution of Christ, 531; judgment of Lutheran theologians regarding it, 531.
Supralapsarians, 248.
Suspension from the Lord's Table, 539.
Syncretism, 559.
Synergism, 22. 50. 81. 241. 250. 254; pernicious character of —, 360; from what source — derives its doctrines, 361; subtle —, 362; its corruption of the means of grace, 442. 452; denies certainty of salvation, 483; mingles Law and Gospel, 484; limits the *gratia universalis*, 596.
Synods have only advisory power, 561; — are not superchurches, 562.
Synthetic method, 84.
Systems, theological, 79; in what sense Christian theology is a system, 79; why it nevertheless should not be called a system, 80.

Temptation, doctrine of, 228.
Tentatio necessary to acquire the theological habitude, 87.
Terministic Controversy, 354.
Terminus peremptorius, 355.
Terminus vitae, 194.
Terrores conscientiae not meritorious, 349.
Testimonium Spiritus Sancti, 121. 124. 332. 379. 393. 426.
Theologesantes, 31.
Theologia debet esse grammatica, 92.
Theologia irregenitorum, 33.
Theological problems, 58.
Theologos, 32. 86.
Theology, scientific, 13. 23. 40; rationalistic —, 23; what Christian — is, 29; the term —, 30; subjective or concrete —, 32; objective or abstract —, 32. 33; — considered as a habitude, 33; — considered as doctrine, 37; archetypal —, ectypal —, 39; divisions of —, 43; purpose of Christian —, 64; — and science, 67; in what sense — is a science, 69; why — should not be called a science, 70; — and positive assurance, 72; theological systems, 79; *theologia est habitus practicus*, 86; *theologia debet esse grammatica*, 92.
Theopassianism, theopaschitism, 275.
Theopneustos, 101. 102.
Theorie, kuenstliche, 119.
Theories of atonement, 27. 312.
Thomasius, 594.
Tithing, 414.
Tohuvabohu, 182.
Tradition not source of faith, 16.
Traducianism, 58.
Transmutationshypothese, 180.
Transubstantiation, 509. 511. 520.
Tribulation and affliction, God the cause of, 226.
Trichotomy, 184.
Trinity, Holy, 147; doctrine of — incomprehensible to reason, 149; doctrine of — in controversy, 150; terminology of doctrine of —, 153; Luther on —, 155; — revealed in Old Testament, 158.
Tritheites, 151. 155.
Trivial matters in Scripture, 112. 113.

Ubiquity, 280. 518.
Unbelief the work of Satan, 203.
"Unfortunate consistency," 55. 560.

Unio nominalis, — *naturalis,* 265; — *accidentalis,* — *sustentativa,* — *habitualis,* 266; — *essentialis,* — *per adoptionem,* 267; — *mystica,* 320. 381.

Unionism, 559; arguments against, 559.

Unity, Christian, the work of divine grace, 24; divine —, 163; — of human race, 185.

Universal grace denied by Calvinists, 248; — must be maintained though heathen die without Gospel, 251; — must be maintained even when God hardens those who harden themselves, 250.

Universalism, 163. 200.

Unsearchable judgments of God, 254; must not be explored, 254.

Unworthy guests receive body and blood of Christ, 530.

Usus loquendi, 4; — *magisterialis,* — *ministerialis* of reason, 80. 92. 127.

Variant readings, 109.

Venial sins, 231.

Veracity, divine, 173.

Verbum internum, 135; *verbum externum,* 135. 570.

Versiones Scripturae Sacrae, 129.

Verstockung eine Folge der Selbstverstockung, 607.

Vicarious atonement, 50.

Viewpoint, theological, 1; — of various divisions, 1; Christian —, 2; the only correct —, 2.

Vilmar, 568. 574. 594.

Vincentius of Lerinum, 95.

Vis dativa, effectiva, 346.

Vision, the beatific, 641.

Vivification (resuscitation), what it is, 363.

Vocatio immediata, — *mediata,* 570.

Vocatio seria, 607.

Vocation; what it is, 364.

Voluntary sins, 228.

Voluntas gratiae, 252; — *ordinata,* 252; — *antecedens* and *consequens,* 253. 607. 608. 609. 638; — *divina,* — *prima,* — *secunda,* why we speak of —, 608.

Wafers used in Lord's Supper, 525.

Walther, Dr., on institution of public ministry, 567; on the necessity of the pastoral office, 569; the public ministry not a spiritual estate, 577; salvation of elect through faith, 599.

Warfield, Benjamin, 108.

Warnings of Scripture against defection, 439.

Will, human, and God's foreknowledge, 168; divine —, 170; antecedent, consequent divine —, 171. 253; resistible, irresistible divine —, 171; absolute, ordinate divine —, 171. 252; gracious, conditional divine —, 171. 252; revealed, hidden divine —, 172. 254; human — free from coercion, 193; corrupt — of man, 220; doctrine of the freedom of the —. 236; Hutter on —, 236; not two wills in God, 253; — of God only norm of Christian prayer, 433.

Wine, use of, in the Lord's Supper, 525.

Wirklichkeitsmenschen, 118.

Wirklichkeitssinn, 3.

Wisdom, divine, 170.

Wittenberg Concordia, 531.

Woman created in God's image, 209; — subject to man, 209.

Words of institution, what they say, 512. 533; how Calvinists misinterpret them, 514; the Calvinistic argument against the — from John 6, 518.

Works, good, 51. 65; *Apology* on —, 15; endless multiplication of —, 18; outward — done by unregenerate and rewarded in this life, 337; why — must be excluded from justification, 370; papistic doctrine of —, 370; — of heathen, 408.

World, the end of the, 631.

Zorneswahl, there is no, 606.

Zweinaturenlehre, 262.

Zwingli. The Holy Spirit requires no leader or vehicle, 135. 245; on words of institution, 514. 515; the Eucharist a *commemoratio,* 531; denied that Lord's Supper offers forgiveness of sins, 535. 537.